CCEA A2
PURE MATHEMATICS
2nd Edition

COLOURPOINT EDUCATIONAL

© Luke Robinson and
Colourpoint Creative Ltd 2020

Second Edition, 2020
Reprinted 2021, 2022

Print ISBN: 978-1-78073-266-4
eBook ISBN: 978-1-78073-299-2

Layout and design: April Sky Design
Printed by: GPS Colour Graphics Ltd, Belfast

All rights reserved. No part of this publication may be reproduced, stored in a retrieval system or transmitted in any form or by any means, electronic, mechanical, photocopying, scanning, recording or otherwise, without the prior written permission of the copyright owners and publisher of this book.

Copyright has been acknowledged to the best of our ability. If there are any inadvertent errors or omissions, we shall be happy to correct them in any future editions.

The Author
Luke Robinson took a mathematics degree, followed by an MSc and PhD in meteorology. He taught at Northwood College in London before becoming a freelance mathematics tutor and writer. He now lives in County Down with his wife and son.

Colourpoint Educational
An imprint of Colourpoint Creative Ltd
Colourpoint House
Jubilee Business Park
21 Jubilee Road
Newtownards
County Down
Northern Ireland
BT23 4YH

Tel: 028 9182 6339
E-mail: sales@colourpoint.co.uk
Web site: www.colourpointeducational.com

Note: This book has been written to meet the A2 Mathematics specification from CCEA. While the authors and Colourpoint Creative Limited have taken all reasonable care in the preparation of this book, it is the responsibility of each candidate to satisfy themselves that they have covered all necessary material before sitting an examination or attempting coursework based on the CCEA specification. The publishers will therefore accept no legal responsibility or liability for any errors or omissions from this book or the consequences thereof.

Contents

Introduction 4
1 Algebra and Graphs 6
2 Functions 24
3 Radian Measure 43
4 Coordinate Geometry 53
5 Sequences and Series 61
6 Binomial Expansion 83
7 Trigonometric Functions 92
8 Trigonometric Identities and Equations 106
9 Differentiation 128
10 Further Differentiation 142
11 Integration 151
12 Differential Equations 179
13 Numerical Methods 186
14 Problem Solving 203

Answers 208

Introduction

Changes to the Specification

This book covers the revised specification for Unit A2 1: Pure Mathematics for CCEA, which was available for teaching from September 2018 onwards.

The following changes from the previous specification are worth paying particular attention to.

Problem solving

The new specification has a greater emphasis on **problem solving** and the final chapter of this book (Chapter 14: Problem Solving) has been included to address this. This chapter includes material explaining what a problem solving task will look like, as well as examples and an exercise of practice questions.

Problem solving questions may require techniques from any of the preceding chapters, and often more than one. They may also require understanding of the mathematics taught at GCSE level.

Questions in context

In addition, there are questions involving **trigonometric functions** and **differential equations** that are set in a real-world context. In these questions, the answers given should be expressed in terms of the context of the question.

Proofs

Fewer proofs are required at A2 Level in the new specification. The complete list of proofs required for A2 Pure Mathematics is as follows.

Chapter 4: Sequences and Series

- The sum of the first n natural numbers:
$S_n = \dfrac{n}{2}(1 + n)$

- The sum of the first n terms of an arithmetic series:
$S_n = \dfrac{n}{2}[2a + (n-1)d]$

- The sum of the first n terms of a geometric series:
$S_n = \dfrac{a(1 - r^n)}{1 - r}$

Chapter 8: Trigonometric Identities and Equations

- Derivation of the three double angle formulae:
$\cos 2A = \cos^2 A - \sin^2 A$
$\sin 2A = 2 \sin A \cos A$
$\tan 2A = \dfrac{2 \tan A}{1 - \tan^2 A}$

Modelling

The new specification also has a greater emphasis on **modelling**. Modelling questions will be set in relation to **functions**, **parametric equations** and **sequences and series**.

What does a modelling question look like?

A modelling question typically involves several of the following features, but not necessarily all of them:

- There may be a requirement to make simplifications. The question will ask what simplifications or assumptions have been made.
- The candidate may be required to discuss the limitations of the model used.
- There may also be a requirement to refine or adapt the model or to consider different models.

The Modelling Cycle

The **Modelling Cycle** is outlined in the diagram on the next page. From the wording of the problem, the student should devise a way to model the situation. Simplifications and assumptions may be required.

The model should be applied to obtain a solution and this solution is interpreted and evaluated. At this point, it may become clear that certain assumptions were inappropriate, wrong, or not needed. It may be the case that different assumptions are required. In this way the model can be refined, and this modified version of the model is applied to the problem.

The final report should detail results, conclusions, any assumptions made and any limitations of the model being used. In A2 Level Mathematics, the report will comprise the solution to the problem.

INTRODUCTION

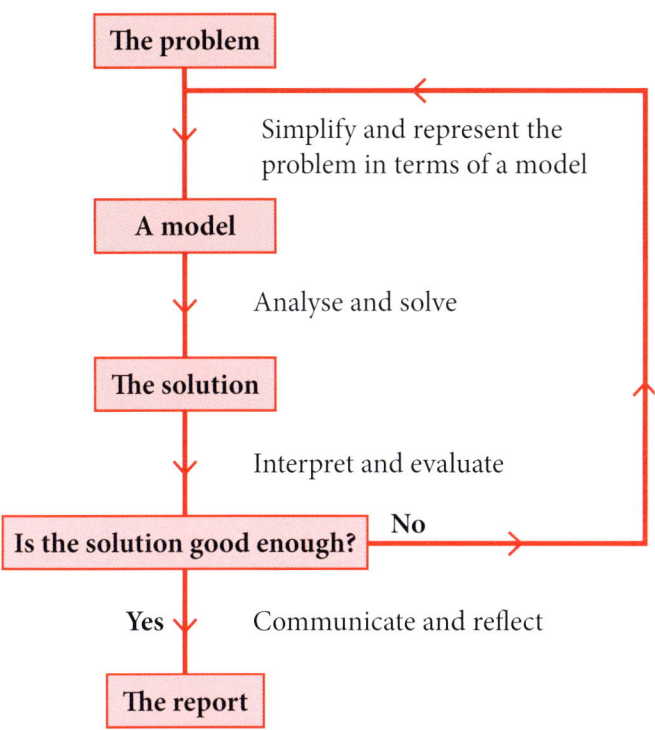

The Modelling Cycle

Chapter 1
Algebra and Graphs

1.1 Introduction

In AS Mathematics you learnt various techniques involved in algebraic manipulation: division by an algebraic fraction, cancelling algebraic terms, putting an algebraic expression over a common denominator and performing algebraic division. You also learnt about the transformations of graphs.

In this chapter, we extend this work. You will learn how to combine two or more transformations of graphs, learn some more advanced methods of algebraic manipulation and some new concepts, such as the modulus function.

Key words

- **Function**: An equation to obtain an output value, e.g. $f(x)$, from an input, for example x.
- **Rational expression**: Any algebraic expression that can be written as a fraction $\dfrac{P(x)}{Q(x)}$, for example $\dfrac{2x+1}{x^2}$.
- **Rational function**: Any function that can be written in the form $f(x) = \dfrac{P(x)}{Q(x)}$.
- **Polynomial**: A function of x, whose terms are ax^n for any values of a and a whole number n, for example $4x^2 + 2x + 1$. (The last term has $a = 1$ and $n = 0$).
- **Order**: The order of a polynomial is its highest index. For example, $4x^2 + 2x + 1$ has order 2.
- **Algebraic long division** or **polynomial long division**: A technique for dividing one polynomial by another, similar to numerical long division.
- **Proper fraction**: A fraction whose numerator is smaller than its denominator. In rational functions, a proper fraction is a function whose numerator has a smaller order than the denominator.
- **Partial fractions**: Obtained when splitting a fraction into a sum of fractions; the opposite of finding a common denominator.
- **Modulus**: The size or magnitude of a number. It is always positive.
- **Transformation**: Acting on a function in a particular way to obtain a second function, usually considering the graphs of both functions

Before you start

You should know:

- How to add and multiply fractions.
- How to sketch graphs of functions.
- How to perform transformations on the graphs of functions.
- How to factorise quadratic functions.

Worked Examples

1. Find:

   (a) $\dfrac{2}{5} \times \dfrac{3}{4}$ (b) $\dfrac{2}{5} + \dfrac{3}{4}$

   (a) When multiplying fractions, we multiply the numerators and multiply the denominators:
   $$\frac{2}{5} \times \frac{3}{4} = \frac{6}{20}$$
   $$= \frac{3}{10}$$

   (b) When adding fractions, we must find a common denominator. In this case, the smallest possible denominator is 20:
   $$\frac{2}{5} + \frac{3}{4} = \frac{8}{20} + \frac{15}{20}$$
   $$= \frac{23}{20}$$

2. Sketch the graph of $y = f(x)$ where $f(x) = x(x + 2)$.

   Solving $f(x) = 0$ we can see that the curve intersects the x-axis at $x = 0$ and $x = -2$.

   A positive coefficient of x^2 tells us that this quadratic curve has a minimum point.

Completing the square:
$f(x) = x^2 + 2x$
$f(x) = (x+1)^2 - 1$

This shows that the minimum point lies at $(-1, -1)$.
So we can sketch the graph:

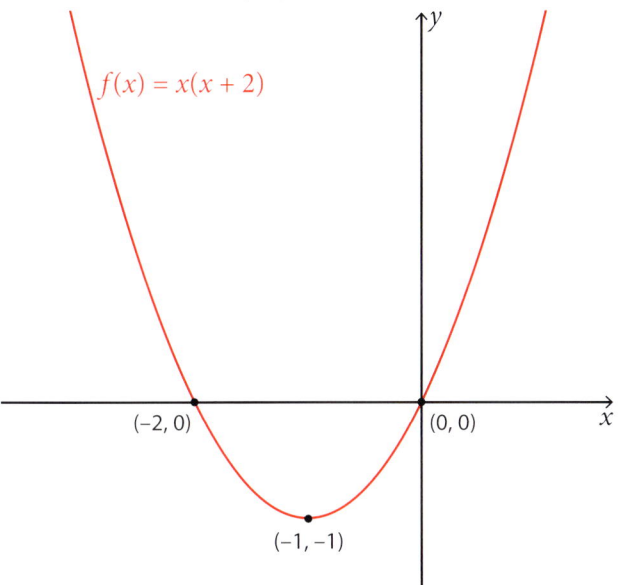

3. $f(x) = \dfrac{1}{x}$

The function $g(x)$ is a translation of $f(x)$ by 1 unit in the negative x-direction.
The function $h(x)$ is a translation of $f(x)$ by 2 units in the negative y-direction.
(a) Write down the equation of the function $g(x)$ and sketch the graph of $y = g(x)$.
(b) Write down the equation of the function $h(x)$ and sketch the graph of $y = h(x)$.

(a) For $g(x)$: wherever x appears, substitute with $x + 1$. Therefore:
$g(x) = \dfrac{1}{x+1}$

We know that $f(x) = \dfrac{1}{x}$ has asymptotes at $x = 0$ and $y = 0$. $g(x)$ is a translation by 1 unit in the negative x-direction. So it has a vertical asymptote at $x = -1$. Its horizontal asymptote remains at $y = 0$.

$y = g(x)$ crosses the y-axis when $x = 0$. So:
$y = \dfrac{1}{0+1} = 1$

So we can sketch the graph of $y = g(x)$:

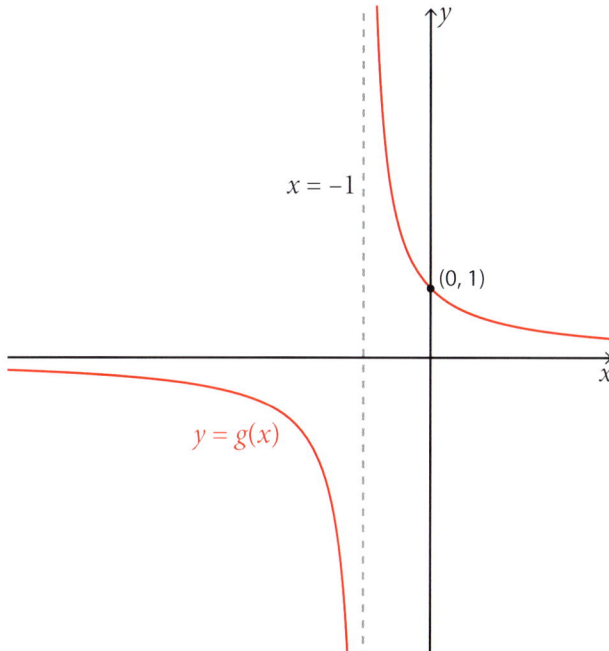

(b) For $h(x)$: subtract 2 to perform the translation in the y-direction. Therefore:
$h(x) = \dfrac{1}{x} - 2$

We know that $f(x) = \dfrac{1}{x}$ has asymptotes at $x = 0$ and $y = 0$. $h(x)$ is a translation by 2 units in the negative y-direction. It has a horizontal asymptote at $y = -2$. Its vertical asymptote remains at $x = 0$.

$y = h(x)$ crosses the x-axis when $y = 0$. So:
$0 = \dfrac{1}{x} - 2 \Rightarrow x = \dfrac{1}{2}$

So we can sketch the graph of $y = h(x)$:

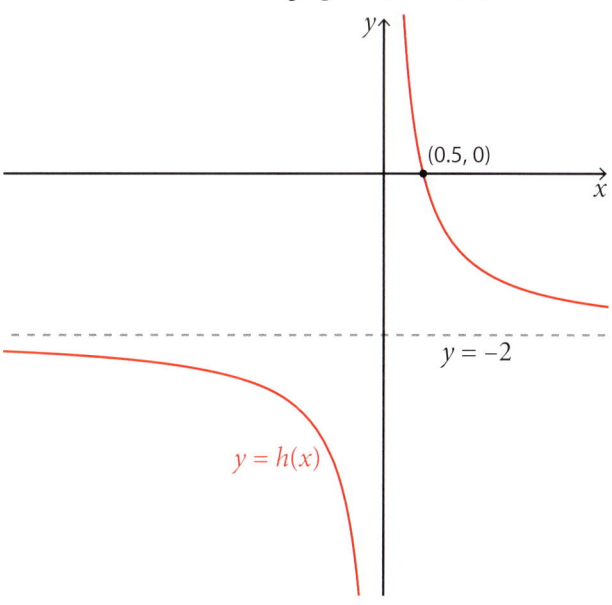

4. Factorise:
   (a) $x^2 - 3x - 28$ (b) $7x^2 + 20x - 3$

   (a) Find two numbers whose sum is −3 and product is −28. The required numbers are −7 and 4. So:
   $$x^2 - 3x - 28 = (x - 7)(x + 4)$$

   (b) Find two numbers whose sum is 20 and product is $-3 \times 7 = -21$. The required numbers are 21 and −1. So split the middle term:
   $$7x^2 + 20x - 3 = 7x^2 + 21x - x - 3$$
   $$= 7x(x + 3) - 1(x + 3)$$
   $$= (7x - 1)(x + 3)$$

What you will learn
In this chapter you will learn how to:
- Simplify rational expressions.
- Perform more complicated algebraic division.
- Use partial fractions to separate algebraic fractions.
- Use the modulus function.
- Use combinations of transformations to transform the graphs of functions.

In the real world...
Partial fractions are used to split a complicated fraction into the sum of simpler fractions. They are often used in a branch of mathematics called Laplace Transforms, which are often used in engineering.

If a set of equations is defined in terms of time, a Laplace Transform can be applied to obtain a different, simpler set of equations defined in terms of the Laplace operator s. After solving these new equations, the inverse Laplace Transform can be applied to find the solution in terms of t.

The Laplace Transform, often using partial fractions, is widely used in the design and analysis of electronic circuit boards.

Exercise 1A (Revision)

1. Evaluate the following.
   (a) $\dfrac{15}{4} \times \dfrac{3}{4}$ (b) $\dfrac{15}{4} + \dfrac{3}{4}$
   (c) $\dfrac{6}{7} + \dfrac{7}{8}$ (d) $\dfrac{6}{7} \times \dfrac{7}{8}$

2. Factorise the following.
   (a) $x^2 + 5x + 4$ (b) $x^2 - 2x + 1$
   (c) $2x^2 + 5x + 2$ (d) $4x^2 + 3x - 1$
   (e) $7x^2 - 4x - 3$

Exercise 1A...

3. Sketch the graphs of these curves.
   (a) $f(x) = x^2 + 3x + 2$
   (b) $f(x) = (x - 2)^3$
   (c) $f(x) = \dfrac{1}{x - 1}$

4. Write down the equations of the curves obtained from the following transformations.
   (a) $f(x) = x^2$ translated by 3 units in the positive y-direction.
   (b) $f(x) = x^3$ translated by 2 units in the negative x-direction.
   (c) $f(x) = \dfrac{1}{2x}$ reflected in the x-axis.
   (d) $f(x) = 2 + x$ reflected in the y-axis.
   (e) $f(x) = x^2 + 2x + 1$ stretched by a scale factor 2 in the y-direction.

1.2 Simplifying Rational Expressions

In AS Mathematics you learnt how to manipulate algebraic expressions in various ways, including factorising quadratics, using the difference of two squares and cancelling.

In this section we will learn more about combining algebraic fractions, or **rational expressions**.

> A rational expression is an algebraic expression that can be written as a fraction. Examples of rational expressions are:
> $$\dfrac{x}{x^2 + 1} \qquad \dfrac{1}{x} \qquad \dfrac{x^2 + 3x + 1}{4x}$$

When you are adding or subtracting numerical fractions, you must find a common denominator. The same is true when adding or subtracting rational functions. In both cases, you should always try to find the **lowest common denominator**.

You can always find **a** common denominator by multiplying the two denominators. However, this is not always the **lowest** common denominator.

When adding $\dfrac{9}{10}$ and $\dfrac{7}{8}$, for example, the lowest common denominator is 40, not 80.

1: ALGEBRA AND GRAPHS

Worked Example

5. Express as a single fraction:
$$\frac{x+2}{(x+1)(x-3)} + \frac{x-2}{(x+1)(x+6)}$$

Firstly find the lowest common denominator. Since $(x+1)$ is a factor of both denominators, it is included only once. The lowest common denominator is:
$(x+1)(x-3)(x+6)$

To use the common denominator, multiply the top and bottom of each fraction by an appropriate factor.
So the first fraction is multiplied by $\frac{(x+6)}{(x+6)}$, the second by $\frac{(x-3)}{(x-3)}$. So:

$$\frac{x+2}{(x+1)(x-3)} + \frac{x-2}{(x+1)(x+6)}$$

$$= \frac{(x+2)(x+6)}{(x+1)(x-3)(x+6)} + \frac{(x-2)(x-3)}{(x+1)(x-3)(x+6)}$$

$$= \frac{(x^2+8x+12)+(x^2-5x+6)}{(x+1)(x-3)(x+6)}$$

$$= \frac{2x^2+3x+18}{(x+1)(x-3)(x+6)}$$

Multiplying rational functions is easier than adding and subtracting. Multiply together the numerators and multiply together the denominators, just as you would with numerical fractions. You may cancel factors appearing in both numerator and denominator before or after you multiply.

Worked Example

6. Simplify: $\frac{x^2+5x-50}{x-5} \times \frac{2}{x+10}$

Factorise the quadratic:
$$\frac{x^2+5x-50}{x-5} \times \frac{2}{x+10} = \frac{(x+10)(x-5)}{x-5} \times \frac{2}{x+10}$$

You can then cancel the factor of $(x-5)$ and the factor of $(x+10)$ leaving the answer
$= 2$

To divide two rational functions, find the reciprocal of the second function and multiply. Again, this approach is identical to that used with numerical fractions.

Worked Example

7. Simplify: $\frac{(x^2+4x-45)}{(x^2-25)} \div \frac{x+9}{3}$.

Find the reciprocal of the second fraction and multiply:
$$\frac{(x^2+4x-45)}{(x^2-25)} \div \frac{x+9}{3} = \frac{(x^2+4x-45)}{(x^2-25)} \times \frac{3}{x+9}$$

Factorise the two quadratics:
$$= \frac{(x-5)(x+9)}{(x-5)(x+5)} \times \frac{3}{x+9}$$

Cancel factors:
$$= \frac{3}{x+5}$$

> **Note:** You must find the reciprocal of the second fraction before you attempt any cancellation of terms.

Exercise 1B

1. Simplify:
   (a) $\frac{a}{a^2b}$
   (b) $\frac{6m}{5n} \times 15mn$
   (c) $\frac{abc}{c^2} \times \frac{abd}{c^2}$
   (d) $\frac{abc}{c^2} \div \frac{abd}{c^2}$
   (e) $\frac{2c^{10}d^9}{cd}$
   (f) $\frac{5p^8(q+4)}{p^9(q+4)}$
   (g) $\frac{x^2+5x-84}{x-7}$
   (h) $\frac{x^2+5x-150}{x^2-100}$

2. Express each expression as a single fraction.
   (a) $\frac{x+11}{x-8} - \frac{x}{6}$
   (b) $\frac{x}{x-8} + \frac{3}{x+13}$
   (c) $\frac{x}{x-6} + \frac{4}{x+10}$
   (d) $\frac{x+12}{x-6} - \frac{x}{4}$
   (e) $\frac{x}{x^2-9} - \frac{9}{x+3}$
   (f) $\frac{x}{x^2-144} - \frac{5}{x+12}$

3. Simplify:
   (a) $\frac{x^2+5x-150}{x-10} \times \frac{2}{x+15}$
   (b) $\frac{x^2+5x-150}{x^2-100} \div \frac{x+15}{5}$
   (c) $\frac{x^2+3x-108}{x-9} \times \frac{1}{x+12}$
   (d) $\frac{x^2+6x-135}{x^2-81} \div \frac{x+15}{4}$

Exercise 1B...

4. Express $\dfrac{7(x-4)(x+2)}{(x-24)(x+4)} - \dfrac{5(x+2)}{x-24}$

   as a single fraction in its simplest form.

5. Write the following as single fractions, factorising where possible.

   (a) $\dfrac{a}{b} + \dfrac{b}{c}$ \quad (b) $\dfrac{p}{q} - \dfrac{q}{p}$

   (c) $1 - \dfrac{1}{x+1}$ \quad (d) $2g - \dfrac{2}{g^2}$

   (e) $\dfrac{1}{b-1} - \dfrac{1}{b+1}$ \quad (f) $\dfrac{2}{x^2+3x+2} + \dfrac{1}{x+2}$

   (g) $\dfrac{1}{p} + \dfrac{2}{p^2+2p}$

   (h) $\dfrac{1}{x^2+9x+20} - \dfrac{1}{x^2+7x+12}$

   (i) $\dfrac{4}{l} + \dfrac{4}{5}$ \quad (j) $\dfrac{6-xy}{x} + \dfrac{6-x}{xy}$

   (k) $\dfrac{2}{s(s+4)} + \dfrac{3}{s^2-16}$

6. Simplify:

   (a) $\dfrac{a}{2} \div \dfrac{2}{a}$ \quad (b) $\dfrac{1+\frac{1}{b}}{c+\frac{1}{2}}$

   (c) $\left(d - \dfrac{1}{d}\right) \div \dfrac{d^2}{3}$ \quad (d) $\dfrac{e^2}{e-1} \div \dfrac{1}{e^2+e-2}$

1.3 Algebraic Division

Division by linear expressions

In AS Mathematics, you learnt how to perform **algebraic long division**, sometimes known as **polynomial long division**. This process is very similar to numerical long division.

At AS Level, you were only asked to divide by linear factors, such as $(x+1)$ or $(2x-5)$. In this section you will also divide by quadratic factors.

Polynomial long division has a lot in common with numerical long division. Here are some rules to follow, to help you organise your work:

- You can use polynomial long division if the degree of the divisor is less than or equal to the degree of the dividend. In the Example 8 below, the divisor has degree 1; the dividend has degree 3.

- Sometimes the dividend will not have a term in (for example) x^2. If any terms are missing from the dividend, fill them in with zero terms, as will be shown in Example 9.

Worked Example (Revision)

8. Work out: $\dfrac{x^3 + 3x^2 - 10x - 24}{x+4}$.

Because this is a division, we set it out like this:

$$\text{Quotient} \searrow$$
$$x+4 \,\overline{)\, x^3 + 3x^2 - 10x - 24}$$
$$\text{Divisor} \nearrow \qquad\qquad \text{Dividend} \nwarrow$$

In the **divisor** $(x+4)$, the **lead term** is x. What must we multiply x by to get x^3? The answer is x^2. This becomes the first term in the quotient:

$$\begin{array}{r} x^2 \\ x+4 \,\overline{)\, x^3 + 3x^2 - 10x - 24} \end{array}$$

Now, multiply the divisor by this part of the answer, write the result on the next line down and subtract:

$$\begin{array}{r} x^2 \\ x+4 \,\overline{)\, x^3 + 3x^2 - 10x - 24} \\ \underline{x^3 + 4x^2 } \\ -x^2 \end{array}$$

At this point, we must bring down the term in the next column, $-10x$:

$$\begin{array}{r} x^2 \\ x+4 \,\overline{)\, x^3 + 3x^2 - 10x - 24} \\ \underline{x^3 + 4x^2 } \\ -x^2 - 10x \end{array}$$

Repeat the operation: what must we multiply the lead term x by, in order to get $-x^2$?

The answer is $-x$, so this becomes the second term in the quotient. Then multiply the divisor by the $-x$, write the result in the next line down, subtract and bring down the next term, -24:

$$\begin{array}{r} x^2 - x \\ x+4 \,\overline{)\, x^3 + 3x^2 - 10x - 24} \\ \underline{x^3 + 4x^2 } \\ -x^2 - 10x \\ \underline{-x^2 - 4x } \\ -6x - 24 \end{array}$$

We perform the division for a third time: the lead term x goes into $-6x$ a total of -6 times.

So -6 is the third term of the quotient. Again, multiply the divisor by this and write the result, $-6x - 24$, in the next line down. Performing the subtraction again gives 0:

1: ALGEBRA AND GRAPHS

$$\begin{array}{r}x^2 - x - 6\\x+4\overline{\smash{)}x^3 + 3x^2 - 10x - 24}\\\underline{x^3 + 4x^2}\\-x^2 - 10x\\\underline{-x^2 - 4x}\\-6x - 24\\\underline{-6x - 24}\\0\end{array}$$

The zero indicates that there is no remainder. So from this we can write down:
$$\frac{x^3 + 3x^2 - 10x - 24}{x+4} = x^2 - x - 6$$

Because there is no remainder, we know that $(x+4)$ is a factor of $x^3 + 3x^2 - 10x - 24$.

Division by quadratic expressions

You can use the same technique to divide polynomials by quadratic expressions.

Worked Example

9. Divide $5x^3 + x^2 + 1$ by $x^2 - 2x + 1$.

Remember to include $0x$, since the dividend does not have a term in x:

$$\begin{array}{r}5x + 11\\x^2 - 2x + 1\overline{\smash{)}5x^3 + x^2 + 0x + 1}\\\underline{5x^3 - 10x^2 + 5x}\\11x^2 - 5x + 1\\\underline{11x^2 - 22x + 11}\\17x - 10\end{array}$$

Therefore:
$$\frac{5x^3 + x^2 + 1}{x^2 - 2x + 1} = 5x + 11 + \frac{17x - 10}{x^2 - 2x + 1}$$

Exercise 1C

1. Use long division to find the following.
(a) $(3x^2 - 7x + 4) \div (3x - 4)$
(b) $(-9x^2 - 3x + 2) \div (3x + 2)$
(c) $(-7x^2 + 6x + 1) \div (x - 1)$
(d) $(4x^2 + 5x - 9) \div (-6x + 6)$
(e) $(8x^2 - x - 9) \div (4x + 4)$
(f) $(-2x^2 - 8x - 6) \div (x + 1)$
(g) $(4x^3 - 6x^2 - 4x) \div (4x - 8)$
(h) $(x^3 + 4x^2 - 2x - 8) \div (2x + 8)$
(i) $(-7x^3 - 4x^2 - 2x - 5) \div (-x - 1)$
(j) $(-3x^3 + 2x^2 + x) \div (x - 1)$
(k) $(x^3 - 1) \div (x - 1)$

Exercise 1C...

2. Use long division to rewrite these expressions with a remainder.
(a) $(4x^2 + 4x + 9) \div (2x - 2)$
(b) $(-7x^2 + 6x + 2) \div (-x + 5)$
(c) $(-9x^2 + 2x + 9) \div (-x + 3)$
(d) $(-6x^2 - 8x + 8) \div (6x + 2)$
(e) $(2x^2 - x + 6) \div (-x + 4)$
(f) $(-2x^2 + 5x + 9) \div (-2x + 1)$
(g) $(-8x^3 - 6x - 6) \div (6x + 9)$
(h) $(x^3 - 4x^2 + 9x - 4) \div (3 - x)$
(i) $(6x^3 - 9x^2 + 9x + 3) \div (6 - 3x)$
(j) $(-2x^3 - 7x^2 + 7x - 6) \div (-2x - 9)$

3. Use long division to rewrite these expressions.
(a) $(2x^3 - 2x^2 - 2x - 4) \div (2x^2 + 2x + 2)$
(b) $(3x^3 - x^2 - x - 1) \div (3x^2 + 2x + 1)$
(c) $(x^3 + 2x^2 - x - 2) \div (x^2 + 3x + 2)$
(d) $(3x^3 + x^2 + 4x - 4) \div (x^2 + x + 2)$
(e) $(x^3 + 3x^2 + 3x + 1) \div (x^2 + 2x + 1)$
(f) $(2x^3 - 2) \div (x^2 + x + 1)$
(g) $(x^3 + 2x^2 - 2x - 1) \div (x^2 + 3x + 1)$
(h) $(2x^3 + 3x - 4) \div (x^2 + 2x + 3)$
(i) $(x^4 - 1) \div (x^2 - 1)$
(j) $(x^4 + 4x^3 + 4x^2) \div (x^2 + 2x)$
(k) $(x^4 - x^3 - x^2 + x) \div (x^2 + x)$

4. Given one factor for each of the following expressions, use long division to factorise the expression fully.
(a) $x^2 + 2x - 3$ with factor $x - 1$
(b) $x^2 + 3x + 2$ with factor $x + 1$
(c) $x^3 - 5x^2 + 8x - 4$ with factor $x - 1$
(d) $(3x^3 - 2x^2 - x)$ with factor $x - 1$
(e) $-9x^3 + 7x^2 + x + 1$ with factor $x - 1$
(f) $7x^3 - 8x^2 - 6x + 1$ with factor $7x - 1$
(g) $-3x^3 - 8x^2 - 6x - 4$ with factor $x + 2$
(h) $-2x^3 - 3x^2 - 2x + 7$ with factor $-x + 1$
(i) $x^3 - 64$ with factor $x - 4$
(j) $x^4 + x^3 - 2x^2 - 4x - 8$ with factor $x^2 - 4$

5. Use long division to rewrite these expressions with a remainder.
(a) $(x^3 + x^2 + x - 1) \div (x^2 + 2x + 1)$
(b) $(x^3 - 4x^2 - x) \div (x^2 + 3x + 3)$
(c) $(x^3 + 2x^2 - 4x - 1) \div (x^2 + x + 3)$
(d) $(2x^3 + 2x^2 - 2x + 1) \div (2x^2 + 2x + 3)$
(e) $(3x^3 + 3x^2 + 2x + 3) \div (x^2 + 3x + 1)$

11

Exercise 1C...

6. Use long division to rewrite these expressions with a remainder.
   (a) $(-4x^4 - 3x^3 + 4x^2 - 7) \div (-x - 1)$
   (b) $(-2x^3 + 3x^2 + 5x + 6) \div (2x + 3)$
   (c) $(-2x^4 + 5x^3 - 6x^2 - 5x + 6) \div (-x - 2)$
   (d) $(-9x^4 - 6x^3 - 5x^2 - 7x + 1) \div (x + 1)$
   (e) $(-2x^4 - x^3 + 7x^2 - 7x + 2) \div (-2x + 1)$
   (f) $(-4x^4 - 8x^3 - 5x^2 + 6x + 7) \div (x + 1)$
   (g) $(2x^4 - 2x^3 - 4x^2 + 9x - 6) \div (-2x^2 + 2x - 4)$
   (h) $(-6x^4 - 5x^3 + 8x^2 - 8x + 6) \div (-x^2 + x + 2)$
   (i) $(-3x^4 - x^3 + 9x^2 + x - 8) \div (x^2 - 3)$
   (j) $(-2x^4 - x^3 + 7x^2 - 4x - 8) \div (x^2 + 2x - 1)$

1.4 Partial Fractions

Linear factors

If a rational function is a proper fraction of the form:

$$\frac{f(x)}{(ax+b)(cx+d)(ex+f)}$$

it can be rewritten:

$$\boxed{\frac{f(x)}{(ax+b)(cx+d)(ex+f)} = \frac{A}{ax+b} + \frac{B}{cx+d} + \frac{C}{ex+f}}$$

The fractions on the right-hand side are known as **partial fractions**. The process of separating such a function into its partial fractions is the reverse of adding or subtracting algebraic fractions by finding a common denominator.

Two techniques are commonly used to find the values of A, B and C. Example 10 below demonstrates the technique of comparing coefficients.

Worked Example

10. Express $\dfrac{7x-1}{(x-1)(2x+1)}$ in partial fractions.

    In this case the denominator contains two factors, so there will be two partial fractions.

    $$\frac{7x-1}{(x-1)(2x+1)} \equiv \frac{A}{x-1} + \frac{B}{2x+1}$$

    Note: The sign $\equiv$ indicates this is an **identity**. It is always true, not just for certain values of x.

Multiply both sides by $(x-1)(2x+1)$:
$7x - 1 \equiv A(2x+1) + B(x-1)$

Comparing coefficients of x:
$\quad 7 = 2A + B \quad$ (1)

Comparing constant terms:
$\quad -1 = A - B \quad$ (2)

We now have two simultaneous equations in A and B. Add equations (1) and (2):
$\quad 6 = 3A \Rightarrow A = 2$

Using (1), $B = 3$

$\therefore \dfrac{7x-1}{(x-1)(2x+1)} \equiv \dfrac{2}{x-1} + \dfrac{3}{2x+1}$

Check your answer by adding the two fractions on the right-hand side.

The second technique for finding partial fractions is substitution.

Worked Example

11. Express $\dfrac{11x-6}{(4x+3)(5x-1)}$ in partial fractions.

    $$\frac{11x-6}{(4x+3)(5x-1)} \equiv \frac{A}{(4x+3)} + \frac{B}{(5x-1)}$$

    $11x - 6 \equiv A(5x-1) + B(4x+3) \quad (1)$

    Because equation (1) is an identity, it remains true for any value of x.

    Substitute $x = \dfrac{1}{5}$ into (1):

    $$11\left(\frac{1}{5}\right) - 6 = A(0) + B\left(\frac{4}{5} + 3\right)$$

    $$-\frac{19}{5} = \frac{19B}{5}$$

    $$B = -1$$

    Substitute $x = -\dfrac{3}{4}$ into (1):

    $$11\left(-\frac{3}{4}\right) - 6 = A\left(5\left(-\frac{3}{4}\right) - 1\right) + B(0)$$

    $$-\frac{57}{4} = A\left(-\frac{19}{4}\right)$$

    $$A = 3$$

    $\therefore \dfrac{11x-6}{(4x+3)(5x-1)} \equiv \dfrac{3}{(4x+3)} - \dfrac{1}{(5x-1)}$

Sometimes you may use a combination of these two techniques.

The previous examples involve only linear factors. In these cases, it is possible to use another technique called the **cover-up rule**.

Worked Example

12. Express $\dfrac{10x^2 + 24x + 2}{(x-2)(2x-1)(3x+4)}$ in partial fractions.

$$\frac{10x^2 + 24x + 2}{(x-2)(2x-1)(3x+4)} \equiv \frac{A}{x-2} + \frac{B}{2x-1} + \frac{C}{3x+4}$$

Since all the factors in the denominator are linear, we can obtain the coefficients using the cover-up rule.

Taking the original expression, use your finger to cover up each factor in the denominator in turn. When covering up a factor $(x-a)$, substitute $x = a$ into the rest of the expression.

To find A: cover up $(x-2)$ and substitute $x = 2$:

$$A = \frac{10(2)^2 + 24(2) + 2}{(2(2)-1)(3(2)+4)}$$

$$= \frac{90}{30} = 3$$

When covering up a factor $(bx - c)$, substitute $x = \dfrac{c}{b}$ into the rest of the expression.

To find B: cover up $(2x-1)$ and substitute $x = \dfrac{1}{2}$:

$$B = \frac{10\left(\frac{1}{2}\right)^2 + 24\left(\frac{1}{2}\right) + 2}{\left(\frac{1}{2}-2\right)\left(3\left(\frac{1}{2}\right)+4\right)}$$

$$= \frac{\left(\frac{33}{2}\right)}{\left(-\frac{3}{2}\right)\left(\frac{11}{2}\right)} = -2$$

To find C: cover up $(3x+4)$ and substitute $x = -\dfrac{4}{3}$:

$$C = \frac{10\left(-\frac{4}{3}\right)^2 + 24\left(-\frac{4}{3}\right) + 2}{\left(-\frac{4}{3}-2\right)\left(2\left(-\frac{4}{3}\right)-1\right)}$$

$$= \frac{-\frac{110}{9}}{\left(-\frac{10}{3}\right)\left(-\frac{11}{3}\right)}$$

$$= -1$$

$\therefore \dfrac{10x^2 + 24x + 2}{(x-2)(2x-1)(3x+4)} \equiv \dfrac{3}{x-2} - \dfrac{2}{2x-1} - \dfrac{1}{3x+4}$

Exercise 1D

1. Use the method of equating coefficients to express the following in partial fractions.

   (a) $\dfrac{4x+2}{(2x-2)(x+2)}$ (b) $\dfrac{1}{(x+1)(x+2)}$

   (c) $\dfrac{7x+5}{(2x-5)(x+2)}$ (d) $\dfrac{5(x+2)}{(x+1)(x+6)}$

   (e) $\dfrac{2-x}{(1+2x)(3+x)}$ (f) $\dfrac{3}{(x+1)(x+2)}$

   (g) $\dfrac{2x+3}{(x-1)(x-2)}$ (h) $\dfrac{6x-30}{x(x+3)}$

   (i) $\dfrac{x}{x^2-7x+12}$ (j) $\dfrac{3x+5}{2x^2-5x-3}$

2. Use the method of substitution to express the following in partial fractions.

   (a) $\dfrac{3x}{(x-1)(x+2)}$ (b) $\dfrac{2x-1}{(x-3)(x+2)}$

   (c) $\dfrac{2x+5}{(x-2)(x+1)}$ (d) $\dfrac{3}{(x-1)(2x-1)}$

   (e) $\dfrac{1}{(x-2)(x+4)}$ (f) $\dfrac{5x-1}{(x+1)(x-2)}$

   (g) $\dfrac{7x+25}{(x+4)(x+3)}$ (h) $\dfrac{3}{(x-3)(2x+1)}$

   (i) $\dfrac{3x+1}{x(x-2)}$ (j) $\dfrac{1}{x^2+2x-3}$

3. Express these rational functions in terms of their partial fractions. Use your preferred method, or a combination.

   (a) $\dfrac{2x-4}{x(x-1)(x-3)}$

   (b) $\dfrac{x^2+1}{(2x+1)(x-1)(x-3)}$

   (c) $\dfrac{2x+1}{(x+1)(x-2)(x-3)}$

Repeated linear factors

If one of the linear factors in the denominator is repeated, then a special method is required to generate partial fractions. In general:

$$\frac{f(x)}{(ax+b)(cx+d)^2} = \frac{A}{ax+b} + \frac{B}{cx+d} + \frac{C}{(cx+d)^2}$$

Worked Examples

13. Express $\dfrac{x+5}{(x+3)^2}$ in terms of its partial fractions.

The repeated linear factor here is $(x+3)$.
$$\dfrac{x+5}{(x+3)^2} \equiv \dfrac{A}{x+3} + \dfrac{B}{(x+3)^2}$$
$$x + 5 = A(x+3) + B$$

Equate coefficients of x:
$$1 = A$$

Equate constant terms:
$$5 = 3A + B$$
$$\therefore B = 2$$

$$\therefore \dfrac{x+5}{(x+3)^2} = \dfrac{1}{x+3} + \dfrac{2}{(x+3)^2}$$

14. Express $\dfrac{5x^2 + 2x - 27}{(x+1)^2(x-5)}$ as a sum of its partial fractions.

The denominator contains the repeated factor $(x+1)$.
$$\dfrac{5x^2 + 2x - 27}{(x+1)^2(x-5)} \equiv \dfrac{A}{x+1} + \dfrac{B}{(x+1)^2} + \dfrac{C}{x-5}$$
$$5x^2 + 2x - 27 = A(x+1)(x-5) + B(x-5) + C(x+1)^2$$

Substitute $x = -1$: $\quad -24 = -6B \Rightarrow B = 4$
Substitute $x = 5$: $\quad 108 = 36C \Rightarrow C = 3$
Compare coefficients of x^2: $\quad 5 = A + C$
$$\therefore A = 2$$

$$\dfrac{5x^2 + 2x - 27}{(x+1)^2(x-5)} \equiv \dfrac{2}{x+1} + \dfrac{4}{(x+1)^2} + \dfrac{3}{x-5}$$

Improper fractions

You may be required to use partial fractions for **improper fractions**. An improper fraction is a rational function in which the **order** of the numerator is greater than or equal to the order of the denominator.

The order is the highest power of x.

For example, in Example 14, we considered:
$$\dfrac{5x^2 + 2x - 27}{(x+1)^2(x-5)}$$

This is a proper fraction. The order of the numerator is 2 and the order of the denominator is 3 (we would get a term in x^3 if we expanded the brackets).

Now consider:
$$\dfrac{5x^2 + 2x - 27}{(x+1)(x-5)}$$

This is an improper fraction. The orders of the numerator and denominator are both 2.

For improper fractions, we must use long division to rewrite the rational function.

Worked Example

15. Use partial fractions to rewrite the following:
$$\dfrac{2x^2 - 2x - 1}{(x-1)(x-2)}$$

$$\dfrac{2x^2 - 2x - 1}{(x-1)(x-2)} = \dfrac{2x^2 - 2x - 1}{x^2 - 3x + 2}$$

Using long division:

$$\begin{array}{r} 2 \\ x^2 - 3x + 2 \overline{)\, 2x^2 - 2x - 1} \\ \underline{2x^2 - 6x + 4} \\ 4x - 5 \end{array}$$

$$\therefore \dfrac{2x^2 - 2x - 1}{(x-1)(x-2)} = 2 + \dfrac{4x - 5}{x^2 - 3x + 2}$$

Rewrite the right-hand side:
$$\dfrac{2x^2 - 2x - 1}{(x-1)(x-2)} = 2 + \dfrac{4x - 5}{(x-1)(x-2)}$$

Now let:
$$\dfrac{4x - 5}{(x-1)(x-2)} = \dfrac{A}{x-1} + \dfrac{B}{x-2}$$
$$4x - 5 = A(x-2) + B(x-1)$$

Let $x = 1$: $\quad -1 = -A \Rightarrow A = 1$
Let $x = 2$: $\quad 3 = B$

$$\therefore \dfrac{2x^2 - 2x - 1}{(x-1)(x-2)} = 2 + \dfrac{1}{x-1} + \dfrac{3}{x-2}$$

If the order of the numerator is equal to the order of the denominator, you will obtain an additional constant term, as in Example 15 above.

In Example 16 the order of the numerator is one more than the order of the denominator. In this case, there will be two additional terms, $ax + b$.

1: ALGEBRA AND GRAPHS

Worked Example

16. Rewrite using partial fractions: $\dfrac{x^3 - 3x^2 - 3x - 1}{x^2 - 5x + 4}$

The order of the numerator, 3, is greater than or equal to the order of the denominator, 2, so we use long division:

$$\begin{array}{r}
x + 2 \\
x^2 - 5x + 4 \overline{\smash{)}\, x^3 - 3x^2 - 3x - 1}\\
\underline{x^3 - 5x^2 + 4x }\\
2x^2 - 7x - 1\\
\underline{2x^2 - 10x + 8}\\
3x - 9
\end{array}$$

$\therefore \dfrac{x^3 - 3x^2 - 3x - 1}{x^2 - 5x + 4} = x + 2 + \dfrac{3x - 9}{x^2 - 5x + 4}$

Consider the fraction part. Factorise the denominator.

$\dfrac{3x - 9}{x^2 - 5x + 4} = \dfrac{3x - 9}{(x - 4)(x - 1)}$

Then express as partial fractions:

$\dfrac{3x - 9}{(x - 4)(x - 1)} = \dfrac{A}{x - 4} + \dfrac{B}{x - 1}$

$3x - 9 = A(x - 1) + B(x - 4)$

Let $x = 1$: $-6 = -3B \Rightarrow B = 2$
Let $x = 4$: $3 = 3A \Rightarrow A = 1$

$\therefore \dfrac{x^3 - 3x^2 - 3x - 1}{x^2 - 5x + 4} = x + 2 + \dfrac{1}{x - 4} + \dfrac{2}{x - 1}$

Exercise 1E

1. Express the following in terms of their partial fractions.

   (a) $\dfrac{x + 2}{(x + 1)^2}$ (b) $\dfrac{2x + 3}{x^2}$

   (c) $\dfrac{2x - 5}{(x - 3)^2}$ (d) $\dfrac{3x - 2}{(2x - 1)^2}$

   (e) $\dfrac{15 - 7x}{(x - 1)^2}$ (f) $\dfrac{3 - x}{x^2 - 2x + 1}$

   (g) $\dfrac{3x + 14}{x^2 + 8x + 16}$ (h) $\dfrac{5x + 18}{(x + 4)^2}$

2. Express the following in terms of their partial fractions.

   (a) $\dfrac{1}{(x + 2)(x + 1)^2}$ (b) $\dfrac{1}{(x - 3)(x + 1)^2}$

   (c) $\dfrac{x - 2}{(x + 1)(x - 1)^2}$ (d) $\dfrac{3x + 1}{(x - 1)^2(x + 2)}$

Exercise 1E...

   (e) $\dfrac{x^2 + 1}{(x - 1)^2(x + 1)}$ (f) $\dfrac{2x^2 - x + 1}{(x + 1)(x - 1)^2}$

   (g) $\dfrac{5x^2 + 23x + 24}{(x + 2)^2(2x + 3)}$ (h) $\dfrac{6x^2 - 30x + 25}{(x + 7)(3x - 2)^2}$

3. Use long division and partial fractions to rewrite the following improper fractions.

   (a) $\dfrac{2x^2 - 7}{x(x - 2)}$ (b) $\dfrac{x^3 + 1}{x^2 - 4}$

   (c) $\dfrac{2x^4 + 3x^2 + 1}{x^2 + 3x + 2}$ (d) $\dfrac{3x^3 - 2x^2 - 19x - 7}{x^2 - x - 6}$

   (e) $\dfrac{x^3 + 2x^2 + 1}{(x - 1)(x + 2)}$

1.5 The Modulus Function

The **modulus** of a number is its **magnitude** or size. The modulus of a number is always positive. You may also hear the term **absolute value**.

We use the notation $|x|$ to denote the modulus of x.

> Many calculators have an ABS button for modulus.

Worked Examples

17. Find $|x|$ for the following.
   (a) $x = 2$ (b) $x = -3$

   (a) If $x = 2, |x| = 2$
   (b) If $x = -3, |x| = 3$

18. Find y where:
   (a) $y = |3x + 2|$ and $x = 1$
   (b) $y = |3x + 2|$ and $x = -1$

   (a) $y = |3(1) + 2|$
   $= |5|$
   $= 5$

   (b) $y = |3(-1) + 2|$
   $= |-1|$
   $= 1$

The graph of the modulus function

Because the value of $|x|$ is always positive, the graph of $y = |x|$ lies above the x-axis for all values of x:

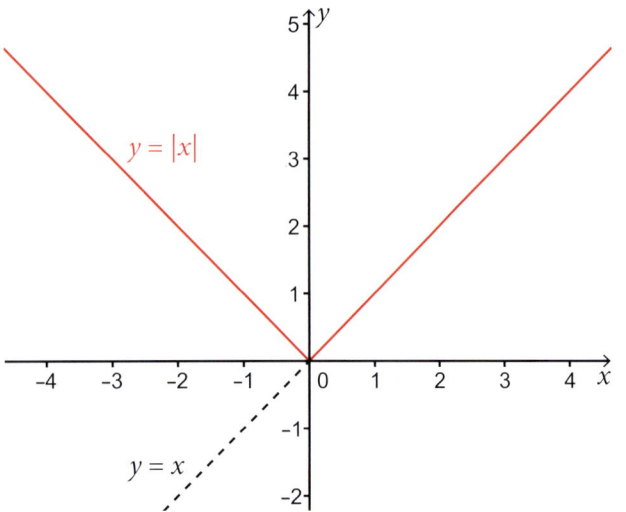

You may be asked to sketch the graph of other modulus functions.

Functions of the type $y = |f(x)|$

As in the graph of $y = |x|$ above, the graph of $y = |f(x)|$ will always remain above the x-axis. Any section of the curve below the x-axis in the graph of $y = f(x)$ will be reflected above it.

Worked Example

19. Sketch the graph of the function $y = |2x + 1|$

The function is of the form $y = |f(x)|$, so the graph will remain above the x-axis.

Consider the graph of the straight line $f(x) = 2x + 1$. It is a straight line with gradient 2, crossing the y-axis at $(0, 1)$ and the x-axis at $(-½, 0)$.

So, in the graph of $y = |f(x)|$, the section of the line below the x-axis is reflected above it:

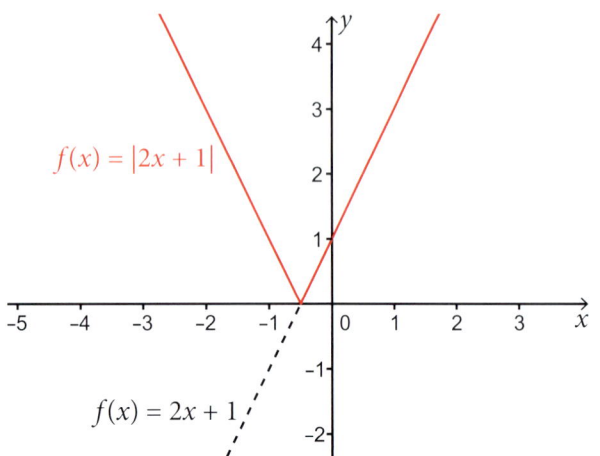

Functions of the type $y = f(|x|)$

For any value $x = a$, the value of $|a|$ is always equal to $|-a|$. Hence, the value of $f(|a|)$ is always equal to the value of $f(|-a|)$. Hence any graph of the form $y = f(|x|)$ is symmetrical about the y-axis. The part of the graph to the left of the y-axis is always a reflection of the part to the right.

Worked Example

20. Sketch the graph of the function $y = (|x| - 1)^2$

This is of the form $y = f(|x|)$. The curve is symmetrical about the y-axis.

Consider the function $f(x) = (x - 1)^2$. This is a translation by one unit in the positive x-direction of the curve $y = x^2$.

So, in the graph of $y = f(|x|)$, the curve to the left of the y-axis is a reflection of the part of the curve to the right:

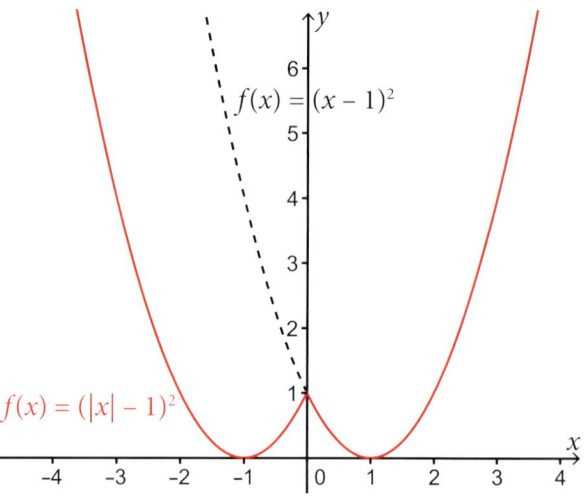

Exercise 1F

1. Determine whether each of the following is of the form $y = f(|x|)$ or $y = |f(x)|$. Sketch the graph in each case, marking clearly where each graph meets the coordinate axes.
   - (a) $y = |3x|$
   - (b) $y = |3x + 1|$
   - (c) $y = 3|x| + 1$
   - (d) $y = -3|x|$
   - (e) $y = |1 - 3x|$
   - (f) $y = |x^2 - 2x - 3|$
   - (g) $y = |x|^2 - 2|x| - 3$
   - (h) $y = \left|\dfrac{1}{x}\right|$
   - (i) $y = \dfrac{1}{|x|}$
   - (j) $y = 2^{|x|}$
   - (k) $y = |2^x|$
   - (l) $y = |2^x + 1|$

Exercise 1F...

2. Given $f(x) = x^2 - 3x - 4$, sketch, on separate diagrams, the graphs of:
   (a) $y = f(x)$
   (b) $y = |f(x)|$
   (c) $y = f(|x|)$

3. Sketch the following curves for $-180° \leq x \leq 180°$.
   (a) $y = \cos x$
   (b) $y = |\cos x|$
   (c) $y = \cos|x|$
   (d) $y = \cos 2x$
   (e) $y = |\cos 2x|$
   (f) $y = \cos |2x|$

4. Sketch the graphs of the following functions.
   (a) $f(x) = e^{|x|}$
   (b) $f(x) = |e^x|$
   (c) $f(x) = |e^{x+1}|$
   (d) $f(x) = |e^x + 1|$
   (e) $f(x) = |e^x| + 1$
   (f) $f(x) = e^{|x|} + 1$
   (g) $f(x) = \ln|x|$
   (h) $f(x) = |\ln x|$
   (i) $f(x) = |\ln(x+1)|$
   (j) $f(x) = |\ln(x)| + 1|$
   (k) $f(x) = |\ln(x)| + 1$
   (l) $f(x) = \ln|x| + 1$

1.6 Equations and Inequalities Involving the Modulus Function

You will be asked to solve equations and inequalities involving the modulus function.

Two methods are available:
- **Method 1** is to separate the equation into two. This is best done with the help of a sketch.
- **Method 2** involves squaring both sides of the equation or inequality.

Note: Method 2 works well when the equation or inequality involves the modulus function. Extreme caution should be exercised when squaring both sides of any other equation, since this process can introduce spurious answers.

Worked Examples

21. Find solutions to the equation: $|x - 3| = 1$

Method 1: Sketch the graphs of $y = |x - 3|$ and $y = 1$. We must find the intersection points. The graph of $y = |x - 3|$ is of the form $y = |f(x)|$. The section of the graph of $y = x - 3$ below the x-axis is reflected above it. So we can sketch:

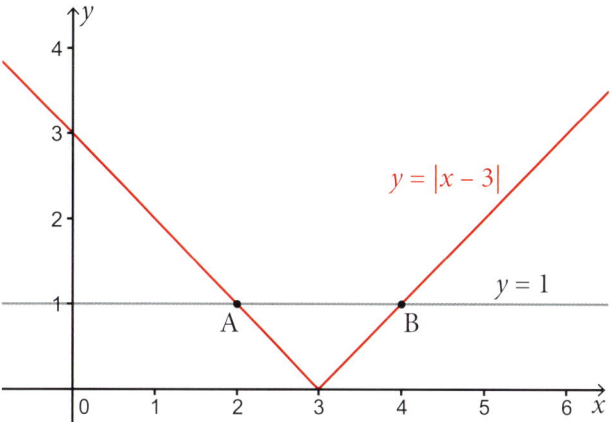

The right-hand branch of $y = |x - 3|$ has equation $y = x - 3$. The left-hand branch has equation $y = -(x - 3)$.

Therefore to find point B we must solve:
$$x - 3 = 1$$
$$x = 4$$

To find point A solve:
$$-(x - 3) = 1$$
$$x - 3 = -1$$
$$x = 2$$

Method 2: Squaring both sides.

When squaring a modulus equation, we can drop the modulus signs. So:
$$(x - 3)^2 = 1^2$$
$$x^2 - 6x + 9 = 1$$
$$x^2 - 6x + 8 = 0$$
$$(x - 2)(x - 4) = 0$$
$$x = 2 \text{ or } x = 4$$

22. Solve: $|2x - 5| < 3$.

Method 1: Graphically

We are interested in the region of the graph where $y = |2x - 5|$ lies below $y = 3$. So we sketch:

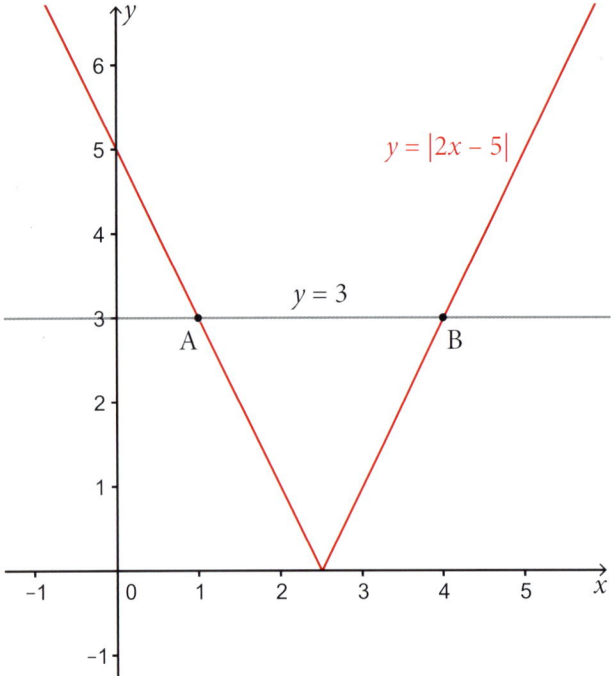

To find the coordinates of points A and B, solve:

To find point B: $(2x - 5) = 3$
$x = 4$

To find point A: $-(2x - 5) = 3$
$x = 1$

The graph shows that the inequality is satisfied for a range of values of x lying between these two intersection points.

Therefore, $1 < x < 4$

Note: If the question had been to solve $|2x - 5| \leq 3$, the solution would be $1 \leq x \leq 4$. Graphically, the points A and B in the diagram above would be included, as well as the region of the graph between them.

Method 2: Squaring both sides.

When squaring a modulus equation, we can drop the modulus signs:
$(2x - 5)^2 < 9$
$4x^2 - 20x + 25 < 9$
$4x^2 - 20x + 16 < 0$
$x^2 - 5x - 4 < 0$
$(x - 1)(x - 4) < 0$

A sketch of the graph of $y = (x - 1)(x - 4)$ shows that it lies below the x-axis between $x = 1$ and $x = 4$.

So: $1 < x < 4$

23. Solve: $|8x - 2| < -4$

There are no solutions. The function on the left-hand side is always positive, so it cannot be less than -4.

Graphically, the graph of $y = |8x - 2|$ lies above the x-axis. It never goes below the line $y = -4$.

Exercise 1G

1. Use the graph shown to solve the following.
   (a) $|2x - 1| = 3$
   (b) $|2x - 1| < 3$

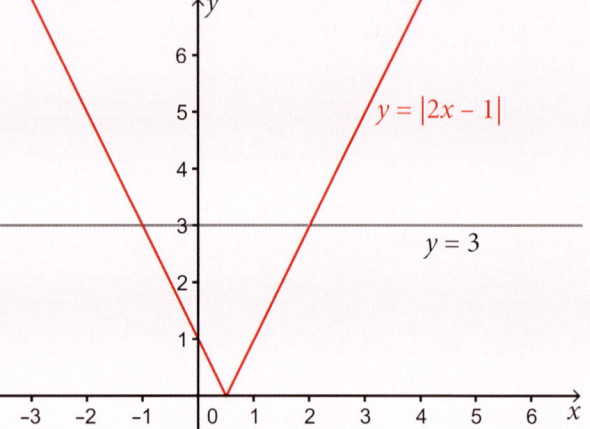

2. Solve the following equations.
   (a) $|2x - 7| = 5$ (b) $|x + 1| = -9$
   (c) $|-5x - 4| = 8$ (d) $|3x + 6| = 3$
   (e) $|2x - 7| = -7$ (f) $|4x + 5| = 8$
   (g) $|-8x + 8| = 8$

3. Solve the following inequalities.
   (a) $|5x - 2| \leq 3$ (b) $|-2x + 6| < -2$
   (c) $|-4x + 3| < 6$ (d) $|x + 6| \leq 7$
   (e) $|2x + 5| < 7$

4. $f(x) = 4 - \dfrac{x}{2}$
   (a) Sketch the graph of $y = f(x)$ for $-12 \leq x \leq 12$.
   (b) Sketch the graph of $y = |f(x)|$ for $-12 \leq x \leq 12$.
   (c) Sketch the graph of $y = f(|x|)$ for $-12 \leq x \leq 12$.
   (d) Using your sketch from part (b), solve the equation: $\left|4 - \dfrac{x}{2}\right| = 2$

1: ALGEBRA AND GRAPHS

1.7 Combining Transformations of Graphs

You learnt about transformations of graphs in AS Mathematics.

The graph of $y = f(x)$ is transformed according to the following rules:

- $y = f(x) - a$ Translation by a units in the negative y-direction.
- $y = f(x - a)$ Translation by a units in the positive x-direction.
- $y = af(x)$ Stretch in y-direction, scale factor a.
- $y = f(ax)$ Stretch in x-direction, scale factor $\frac{1}{a}$.
- $y = f(-x)$ Reflection in the y-axis.
- $y = -f(x)$ Reflection in the x-axis.

In this section you will learn how to combine these transformations.

Be careful to apply transformations in the correct order to get the correct results. When one transformation is in the x-direction and one in the y-direction, the order in which they are applied does not matter.

The following example demonstrates two transformations, both in the y-direction. In this case apply transformations in BIDMAS order: the multiplication comes before the subtraction.

You may be asked to mark the **image** of a point on the curve, i.e. the position of the point after the transformation has been applied.

Worked Example

24. The graph of $y = f(x)$ is shown below, where $f(x) = |x|$. Point A$(-1, 1)$ lies on the curve.

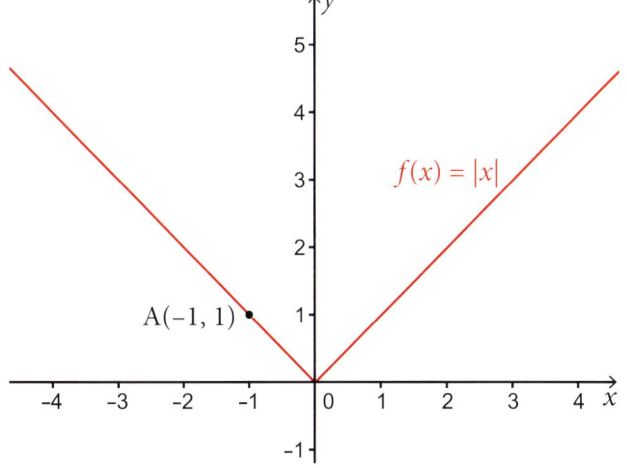

(a) By considering two transformations of the graph shown, sketch the graph of: $y = 3f(x) - 4$. Show clearly the image of point A.

(b) State the equation of the transformed curve.

Since there are two transformations, we will consider two steps.

First consider $y = 3f(x)$. This is a stretch by a scale factor of 3 in the y-direction. The graph is shown below. This curve has the equation $y = 3|x|$.

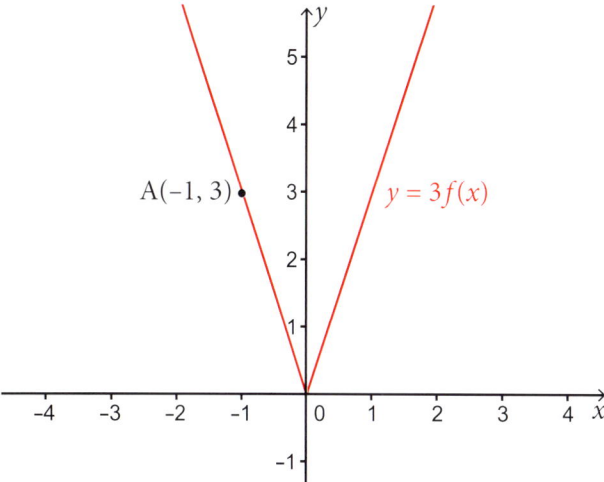

Secondly consider $y = 3f(x) - 4$, i.e perform a translation by 4 units in the negative y-direction. The graph is shown below. This curve has the equation $y = 3|x| - 4$.

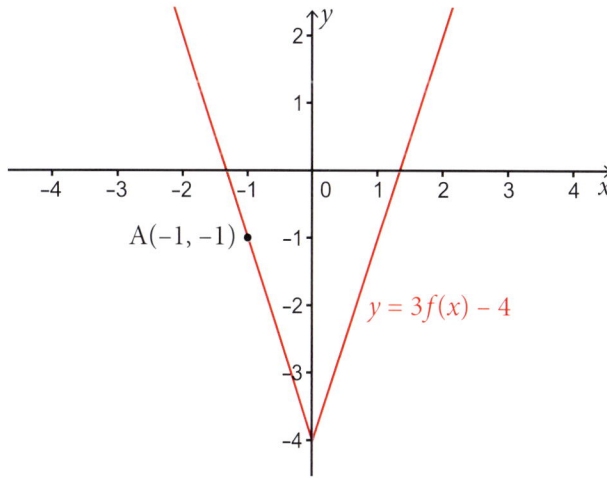

Sometimes you may not be given the equation of the curve.

Worked Example

25. The graph of $y = f(x)$ is shown below. It has a stationary point at the origin. Sketch the graph of $y = f(x - 4) + 2$ on the same diagram and state the coordinates of the stationary point.

There are two translations here: in the positive x-direction by 4 units; then in the positive y-direction by 2 units. We could also say the curve is being translated by the vector $\begin{pmatrix} 4 \\ 2 \end{pmatrix}$. So we can sketch:

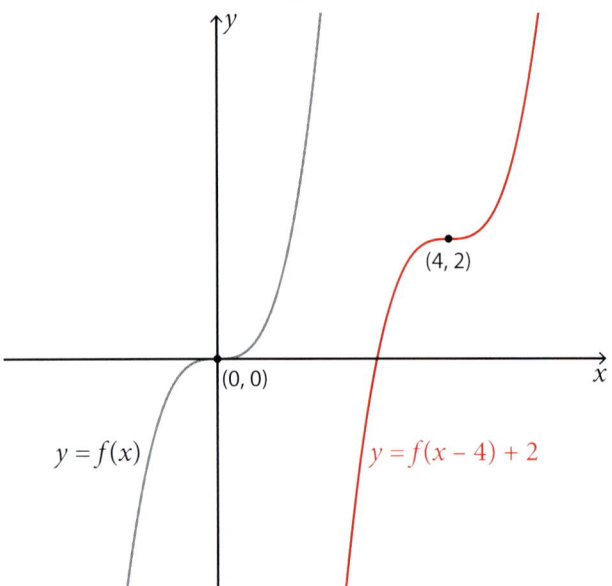

The stationary point of the new function is at the point (4, 2).

In the following example, part (c) demonstrates two transformations both in the x-direction. In this case apply transformations in **reverse** BIDMAS order: the subtraction comes before the multiplication.

Worked Examples

26. The diagram shows a part of the graph of $y = f(x)$. It crosses the y-axis at A(0, 5) and it has a minimum turning point at B(3, −4).

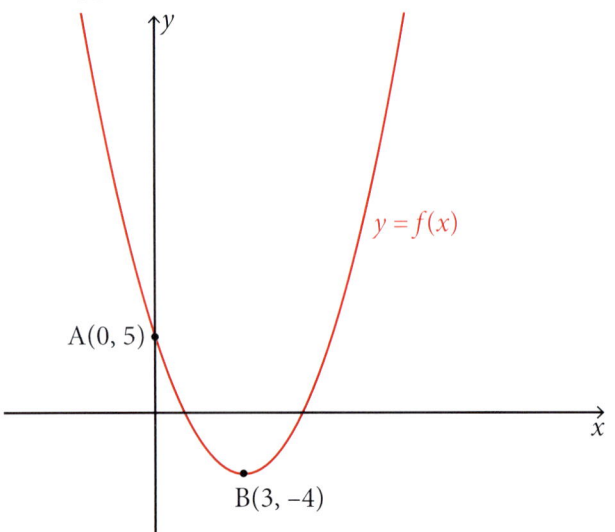

Sketch the following curves, marking the images of points A and B:

(a) $y = \dfrac{1}{2} f(x)$ (b) $y = 1 - \dfrac{1}{2} f(x)$

(c) $y = f(2x - 4)$

(a) $y = \dfrac{1}{2} f(x)$ is a stretch, scale factor ½ in the y-direction. The y-coordinates of all 2 points on the curve are halved. So we sketch:

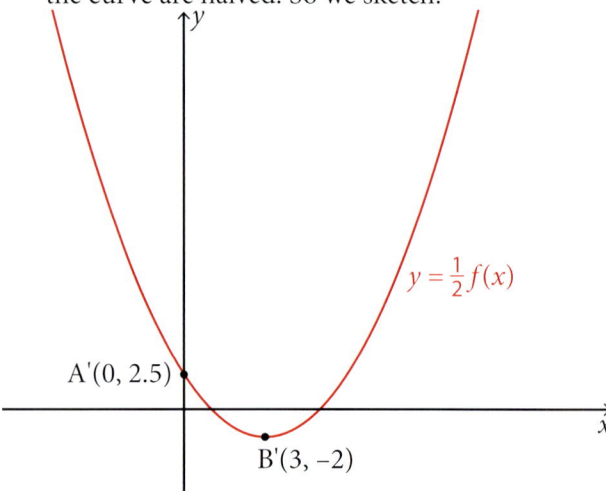

(b) $y = 1 - \dfrac{1}{2} f(x)$ is a reflection of part (a) in the x-axis, followed by a translation by 1 unit in the positive y-direction. So we sketch:

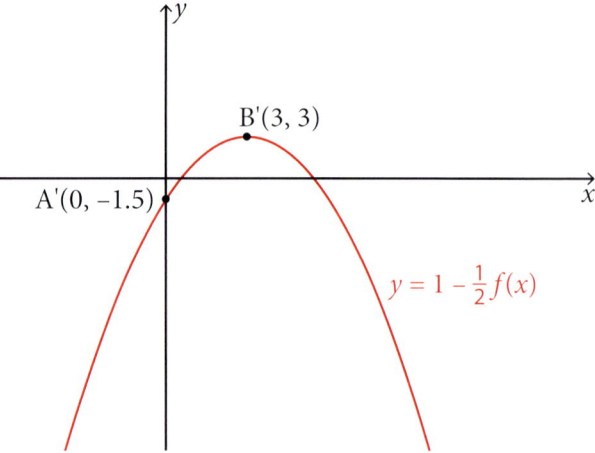

(c) $y = f(2x - 4)$ is an example of two transformations both in the x-direction. Perform the translation first, 4 units to the right. Then perform the stretch, by a scale factor of ½ in the x-direction. So we sketch:

1: ALGEBRA AND GRAPHS

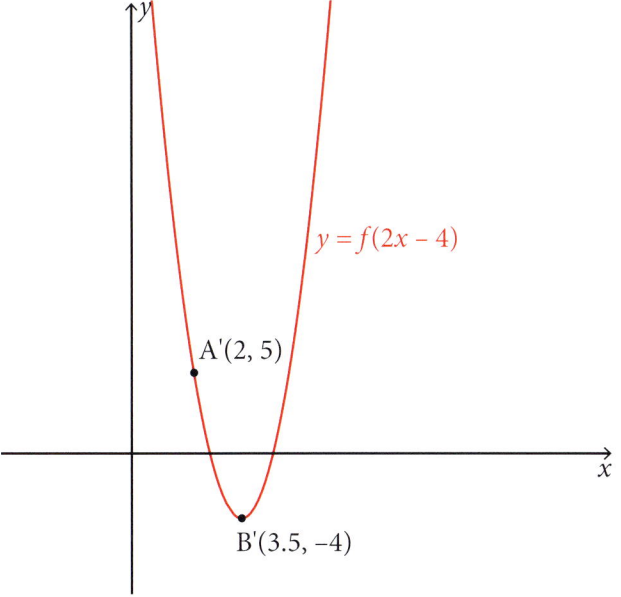

27. The trigonometric graph $y = f(x)$ is defined for $0 \leq x \leq 360°$ as shown below. The point A on the curve has coordinates (90, 1).

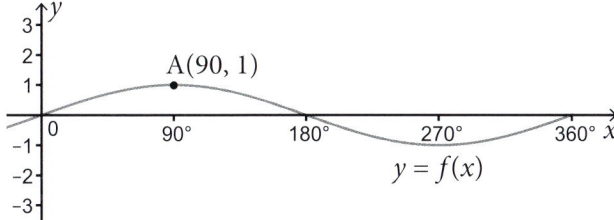

(a) Sketch the graph of $y = 3f(2x)$ on the same diagram. Mark the image of point A, labelling it as A' and giving its coordinates.
(b) State the period of the curve $y = f(x)$ and the period of $y = 3f(2x)$.

(a) When compared with $y = f(x)$, this is a stretch, scale factor ½, in the x-direction, followed by a stretch, scale factor 3, in the y-direction. So we sketch:

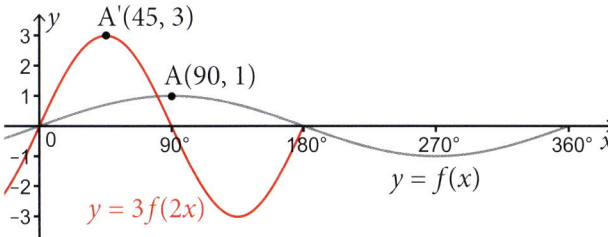

(b) The period of $y = f(x)$ is 360°. The period of $y = 3f(2x)$ is 180°.

The following two examples demonstrate how you can use your knowledge of transformations to the equation of a curve, without drawing a sketch.

Worked Examples

28. $f(x) = x^2 + 1$
    What is the equation of the function $h(x)$ obtained after the following two transformations have acted on the graph of $y = f(x)$?
    1. A translation by $\begin{pmatrix} 1 \\ 5 \end{pmatrix}$.
    2. A reflection in the x-axis.

    1. The x is replaced by $x - 1$ to perform the translation in the x-direction. Then 5 is added to perform the translation in the y-direction. We will call this new function $g(x)$.
       Therefore, translating $y = f(x)$ by $\begin{pmatrix} 1 \\ 5 \end{pmatrix}$ gives the function $g(x) = (x - 1)^2 + 6$
    2. Reflection in the x-axis is performed by making the function negative. Therefore:
       $h(x) = -(x - 1)^2 - 6$
       $= -x^2 + 2x - 7$

29. Which two transformations are required to transform the graph of $f(x) = x^2$ into the graph of $h(x) = \left(\dfrac{x}{2}\right)^2 + 3$?

    $f(x) = x^2$ can be transformed into $g(x) = \left(\dfrac{x}{2}\right)^2$ by a stretch, scale factor 2, in the x-direction.
    $g(x) = \left(\dfrac{x}{2}\right)^2$ can be transformed into $h(x) = \left(\dfrac{x}{2}\right)^2 + 3$ by a translation by vector $\begin{pmatrix} 0 \\ 3 \end{pmatrix}$.
    So the two transformations are:
    1. Stretch, scale factor 2, in the x-direction.
    2. Translation by vector $\begin{pmatrix} 0 \\ 3 \end{pmatrix}$.

Exercise 1H

1. $f(x) = |x|$. The point A(1, 1) lies on the graph of $y = f(x)$ as shown below.

   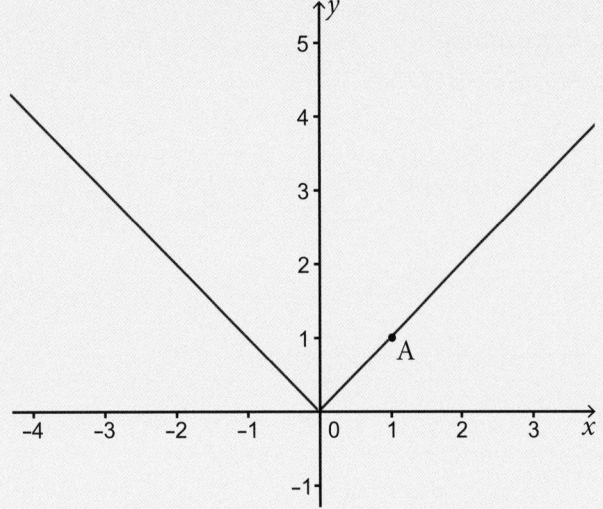

   Write down the equation of the function given by the following transformations. In each case, sketch the graph. Mark carefully the image of the point A and label it A'.
   (a) $y = f(x) - 2$ (b) $y = 2f(x)$
   (c) $y = 2f(x) - 2$ (d) $y = f(2x)$
   (e) $y = f(2x) - 2$ (f) $y = 2f(2x)$
   (g) $y = 2f(2x) - 2$

2. In each case, what is the equation of the function obtained after applying the transformations given?
   (a) $f(x) = x^2$, Reflection in the x-axis.
   (b) $f(x) = 4x^2$, Stretch factor 2 in y-direction.
   (c) $f(x) = 4x^2$, Reflection in the y-axis.
   (d) $f(x) = (x - 1)^2$, Translation by vector $\binom{2}{1}$.
   (e) $f(x) = (x + 1)^2$, Reflection in the x-axis; reflection in the y-axis.
   (f) $f(x) = x^2 - 2x + 3$, Reflection in the x-axis; translation by $\binom{0}{1}$.
   (g) $f(x) = -x^2$, Reflection in the x-axis; Reflection in the y-axis.
   (h) $f(x) = (x - 1)^2 - 1$, Reflection in the x-axis; translation by $\binom{-1}{-1}$.

3. What single transformation has been applied to the function $f(x)$ to obtain the function $g(x)$?
   (a) $f(x) = x^2$; $g(x) = 2x^2$
   (b) $f(x) = x + 1$; $g(x) = x - 1$
   (c) $f(x) = x^2 + 3$; $g(x) = (x + 3)^2$

Exercise 1H...

   (d) $f(x) = \cos x$; $g(x) = \cos 2x$
   (e) $f(x) = \tan x$; $g(x) = \tan(x + 45°)$
   (f) $f(x) = 2^x$; $g(x) = 2^{2x}$
   (g) $f(x) = 5x$; $g(x) = 2x$
   (h) $f(x) = (x - 1)(x + 1)$; $g(x) = x^2$
   (i) $f(x) = abx^2$; $g(x) = ax^2$
   (j) $f(x) = p^2qx^3$; $g(x) = pq^2x^3$
   (k) $f(x) = \sin(2x)$; $g(x) = \sin(-2x)$

4. Which two transformations have been applied to the function $f(x)$ to obtain the function $g(x)$?
   (a) $f(x) = x^2$; $g(x) = 2x^2 + 1$
   (b) $f(x) = x + 1$; $g(x) = -2(x + 1)$
   (c) $f(x) = x^2 + 3$; $g(x) = -(x + 3)^2$
   (d) $f(x) = \sin x$; $g(x) = -2 \sin x$
   (e) $f(x) = 2^x$; $g(x) = 1 - 2^x$
   (f) $f(x) = (x - 1)^3$; $g(x) = x^3 + 1$
   (g) $f(x) = 2^{-x}$; $g(x) = -2^x$
   (h) $f(x) = (2x - 3)(2x + 3)$; $g(x) = 2x^2$
   (i) $f(x) = a + bx^2$; $g(x) = b + ax^2$
   (j) $f(x) = p^2x^3$; $g(x) = p(x + 1)^3$
   (k) $f(x) = \sin(2x)\cos(2x)$; $g(x) = -\sin(3x)\cos(3x)$

5. Apply the following transformations to obtain a new function $g(x)$.
   (a) $f(x) = \sqrt{x}$; stretch factor 2 in y-direction.
   (b) $f(x) = \sqrt{x}$; stretch factor ½ in x-direction; reflection in the x-axis.
   (c) $f(x) = x^{-\frac{1}{2}}$; stretch factor 3 in x-direction.
   (d) $f(x) = x^{-\frac{1}{2}}$; stretch factor 2 in y-direction; reflection in the x-axis.
   (e) $f(x) = \sin x$; translation by $\binom{60°}{2}$.
   (f) $f(x) = \cos 2x$; stretch factor 2 in x-direction.
   (g) $f(x) = \tan 3x$; stretch factor ⅓ in y-direction; reflection in the y-axis.
   (h) $f(x) = \cos x \sin x$; stretch factor 2 in y-direction; translation by $\binom{45°}{-2}$.
   (i) $f(x) = |x|$; translation by $\binom{6}{-1}$.
   (j) $f(x) = |2x|$; translation by $\binom{1}{0}$; reflection in the y-axis.

1: ALGEBRA AND GRAPHS

Exercise 1H...

6. The diagram below shows a part of the graph of $y = f(x)$, with the points A and B marked, where the curve crosses the x-axis.

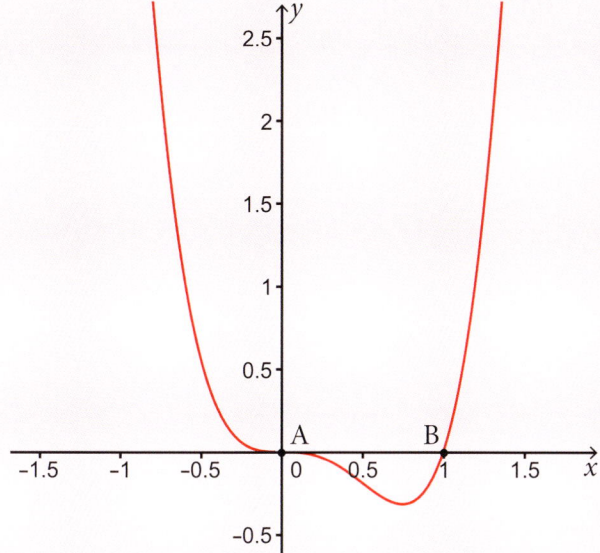

On separate diagrams, sketch the following curves. Mark the points A' and B' carefully, the images of points A and B. State also which transformation, or transformations, have taken place.
   (a) $y = f(2x)$ (b) $y = 2f(x)$
   (c) $y = f(x) + 1$ (d) $y = f(x - 1)$
   (e) $y = f(x - 1) - 1$ (f) $y = -f(x)$
   (g) $y = 1 - f(x)$

7. Sketch the following pairs of curves for $0° \leq x \leq 360°$ on the same diagram.
   (a) $y = f(x)$ and $y = -f(x + 30°)$ where $f(x) = \sin x$
   (b) $y = f(x)$ and $y = 2f(x - 60°)$ where $f(x) = \cos x$
   (c) $y = f(x)$ and $y = 2f(-x)$ where $f(x) = \tan x$

8. Sketch the graph of the function $f(x) = -\dfrac{5}{x}$.
   On the same diagram, sketch the curve $g(x) = f(x + 2) + 5$
   Mark the asymptotes clearly.

9. $f(x) = (x - 1)^2 + 3$
   Which transformation or transformations take place to obtain the function $g(x) = x^2$?

Exercise 1H...

10. $f(x) = -x(x - 2)$
    (a) What is the equation of the function $g(x)$, if $g(x) = f(x + 1) - 1$?
    (b) Describe the transformation that has taken place.

1.8 Summary

Simplification of algebraic expressions can be performed using a variety of techniques, including **factorising** and **cancelling** terms. Dividing by an algebraic fraction is equivalent to multiplying by the **reciprocal** of the fraction.

Algebraic long division can be used to simplify an **algebraic fraction** in which the numerator and denominator are both **polynomials**. This technique can be used to divide by linear and quadratic expressions. Sometimes there will be a remainder. This technique works only for **improper fractions**.

Writing an **algebraic fraction** in terms of its **partial fractions** is the process of splitting a fraction, or the opposite of finding a common denominator. It can be used when the denominator is a product of linear factors, including repeated linear factors. To find partial fractions for an improper fraction, first use long division.

The **modulus function** always gives a positive value. Hence, a graph of a function of the form $y = |f(x)|$ will never go below the x-axis. The graph of a function of the form $y = f(|x|)$ is always symmetrical about the y-axis.

To solve equations and inequalities involving the modulus function, it is often a good idea to draw a graph of the function and consider two separate equations: one for each branch of the curve. You can also solve equations involving the modulus function by squaring both sides.

Transformations of functions (translations, reflections and stretches) can be combined. It is important to perform the transformations in the correct order.

Chapter 2
Functions

2.1 Introduction

In AS Mathematics you learnt about transformations of functions (stretches, translations and reflections). In this chapter you will learn how to combine these transformations. You will also learn some techniques for the manipulation of functions, including combining functions algebraically and finding inverse functions.

Key words
- **Domain**: The set of x-values a function can take.
- **Range**: The set of y-values that can result from a function.
- **Composite function**: A function formed by combining two or more functions.
- **Inverse function**: A function that does the reverse of the original function.

Before you start
You should know:
- How to change the subject of an equation or formula.
- How to sketch the graph of a function.
- How to perform transformations on the graph of a function.

Worked Examples

1. Re-arrange this equation to make m the subject:

$$n = \sqrt{\frac{3m+2}{5} - 1} + 1$$

$$n - 1 = \sqrt{\frac{3m+2}{5} - 1}$$

$$(n-1)^2 = \frac{3m+2}{5} - 1$$

$$(n-1)^2 + 1 = \frac{3m+2}{5}$$

$$5[(n-1)^2 + 1] = 3m + 2$$

$$5[(n-1)^2 + 1] - 2 = 3m$$

$$m = \frac{5[(n-1)^2 + 1] - 2}{3}$$

2. Factorise the following quadratic expressions:
   (a) $x^2 - 9x + 8$ (b) $3x^2 + 5x - 2$

   (a) Look for two numbers that have a product of 8 and a sum of -9. These two numbers are -8 and -1. So: $x^2 - 9x + 8 = (x-8)(x-1)$
   (b) Factorising the expression $3x^2 + 5x - 2$ can be done by inspection. We need to multiply $3x$ and x to give $3x^2$. We will also need to multiply -2 and 1 or 2 and -1 to give -2. Inspection shows that:
   $3x^2 + 5x - 2 = (3x - 1)(x + 2)$

3. (a) Sketch the graph of $y = f(x)$ where $f(x) = \frac{1}{x+2}$. Mark on your sketch the point A, where the curve crosses the y-axis.
   (b) Sketch the curve $y = g(x)$ where $g(x) = f(x) + 2$. Mark clearly the image of point A.

   (a) When $x = 0$, $y = \frac{1}{2}$. So the point A has coordinates $(0, \frac{1}{2})$.

   x cannot take the value -2, so the line $x = -2$ is a vertical asymptote.

   As $x \to \infty, y \to 0$. As $x \to -\infty, y \to 0$. Therefore $y = 0$ is a horizontal asymptote.

   So we can sketch:

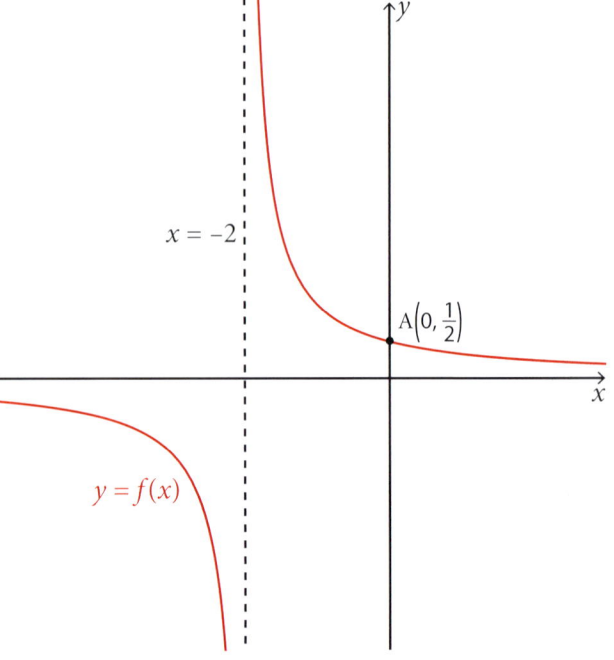

(b) This is a translation of the curve $y = f(x)$ by 2 units in the positive y-direction.

This curve has asymptotes at $x = -2$ and $y = 2$.

So we can sketch:

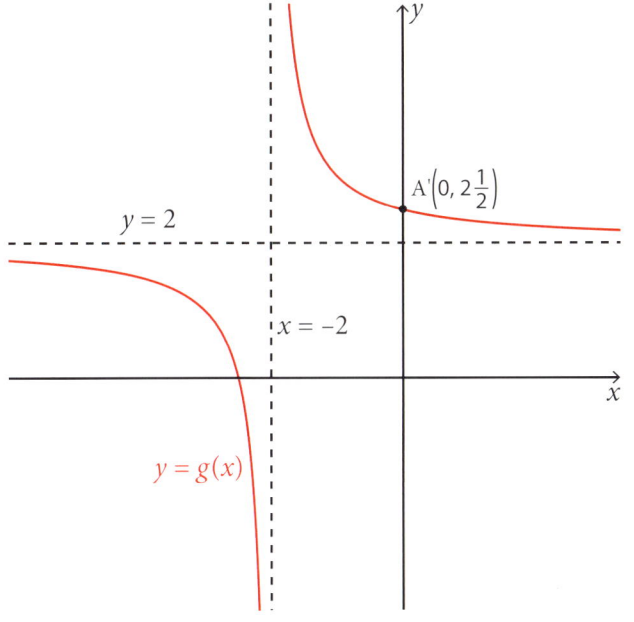

What you will learn

In this chapter you will learn:

- How to combine transformations.
- A formal definition of a function.
- About **inverse functions**.
- About the **domain** and **range**.
- How to create **composite functions**.

In the real world…

In computer science, a function is often a part of a computer program, a tiny program in itself. For example, a function that adds 2 to a number might be called *Add2*. Another function to square a number might be called *Square*.

In mathematics, **function composition** combines simple functions to build more complicated ones called **composite functions**. The output from one function is passed on as the input for the next. The output from the final function is the value of the composite function.

In the same way, all programming languages allow functions to be built up from smaller, simpler functions, and this is a technique widely used in computer programming. This technique of writing functions that perform small, simple operations is considered good practice in computer programming. Computer programmers call it **factoring**. Factoring means a computer program is easier to maintain and allows programming code to be reused.

The code for huge systems – such as Facebook™ – which use millions of lines of code, often comprises hundreds or thousands of smaller functions and subroutines.

Exercise 2A (Revision)

1. Re-arrange the following to make the variable on the right-hand side the subject.
   (a) $n = \dfrac{2m + 1}{3}$
   (b) $p = \sqrt{q^2 + 1}$
   (c) $s = (t^3 - 1)$
   (d) $y = \dfrac{x}{1 - x}$

2. Sketch the graphs of $y = f(x)$, where:
   (a) $f(x) = x^2 + 1$
   (b) $f(x) = \cos(2x)$ for $-90° \leq x \leq 180°$
   (c) $f(x) = \dfrac{1}{x - 2}$
   (d) $f(x) = 1 - x^3$

3. On the same graph, sketch:
   (a) $y = f(x)$ where $f(x) = x^2$; and $y = f(x) - 2$
   (b) $y = f(x)$ where $f(x) = \cos x$; and $y = f(x - 90°)$ for $0° \leq x \leq 360°$
   (c) $y = f(x)$ where $f(x) = \dfrac{1}{x}$; and $y = -f(x)$
   (d) $y = f(x)$ where $f(x) = x^3$; and $y = 2f(x)$

2.2 The Definition of a Function

Mappings

A mapping transforms one set of values onto another.

Worked Example

4. Consider the set of x-values X{1, 2, 3, 4}. Find the set of y-values Y obtained under the mapping $y = 3x - 2$.

   You can use a table of values to help calculate the values of y:

x	1	2	3	4
y	1	4	7	10

   So the set of y-values Y is {1, 4, 7, 10}.

   This relationship can be shown using a mapping diagram:

   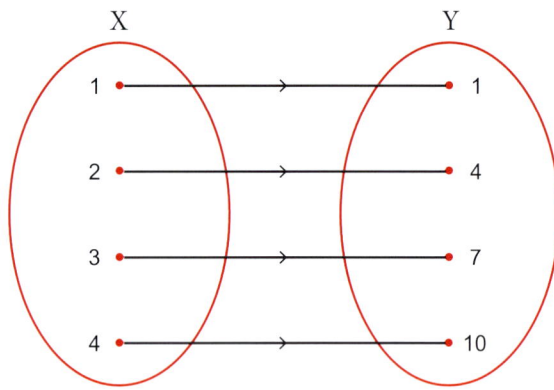

   It can also be shown on a graph:

   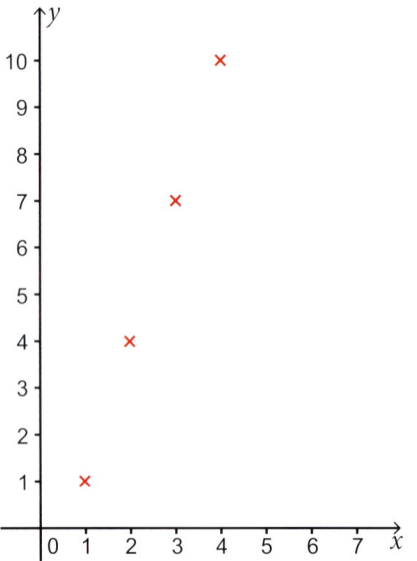

Note: You should not draw a straight line through these four points. The mapping is only defined for these particular pairs of x and y values, not anything in between or beyond.

Domain and range

In the previous example, the mapping maps the set of values X{1, 2, 3, 4} onto the set of values Y{1, 4, 7, 10}.

The set of values of x is called the **domain** of the mapping.

The set of values of y is called the **range** of the mapping.

You may also hear the terms **independent variable** and **dependent variable**. Because the values of y depend on the values of x, x is known as the independent variable while y is called the dependent variable.

Types of mapping

There are four types of mapping:

One-to-one mappings

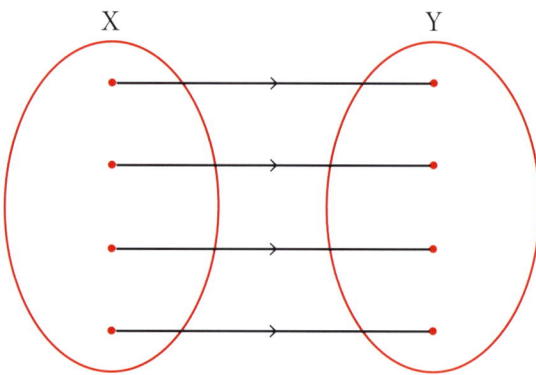

An example of a one-to-one mapping is a straight line. Every value in the domain maps onto exactly one value in the range:

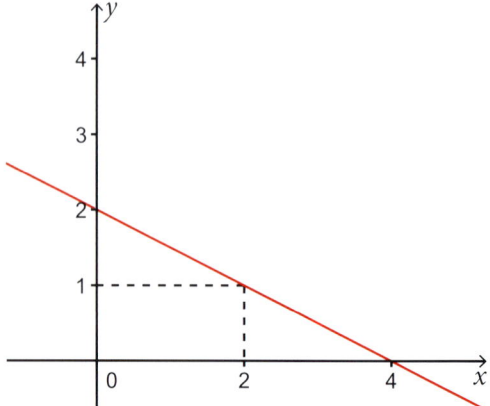

One-to-many mappings

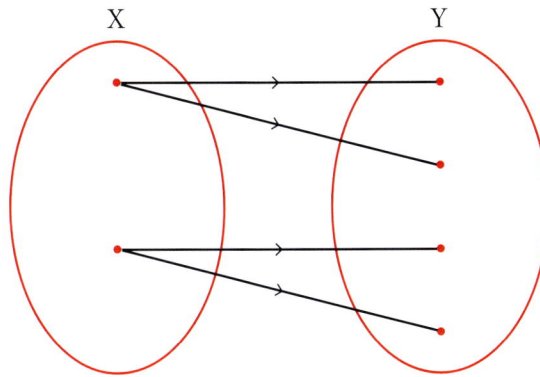

An example of a one-to-many mapping is the square root. A single value in the domain maps onto two values in the range:

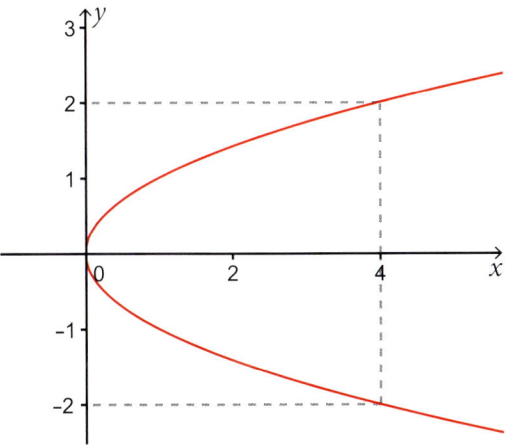

Many-to-one mappings

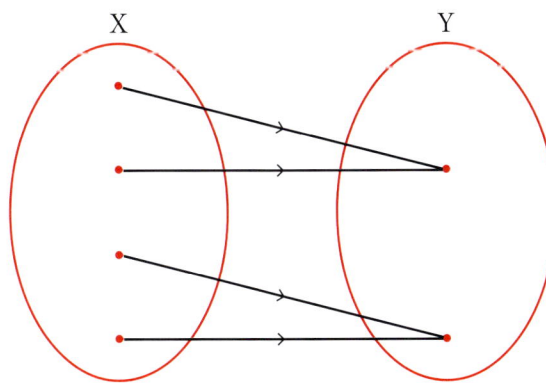

An example of a many-to-one mapping is a quadratic. Two values in the domain map onto the same value in the range:

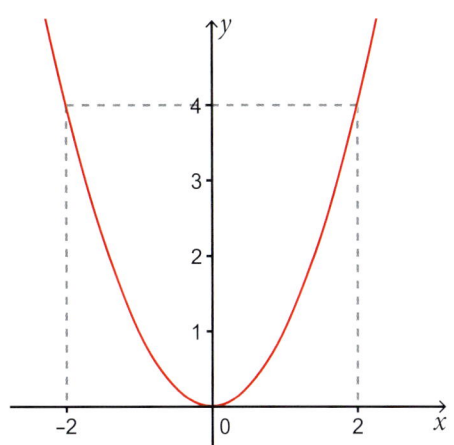

Many-to-many mappings

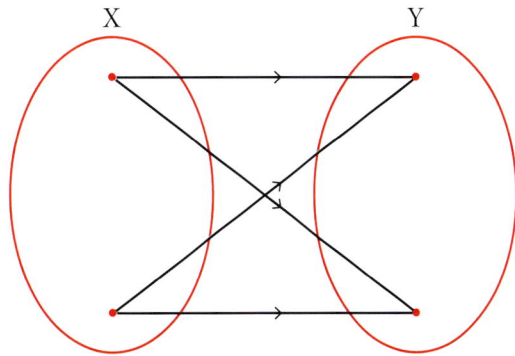

An example of a many-to-one mapping is a circle. Each value in the domain maps to more than one value in the range. Each value in the range is given by more than one value in the domain:

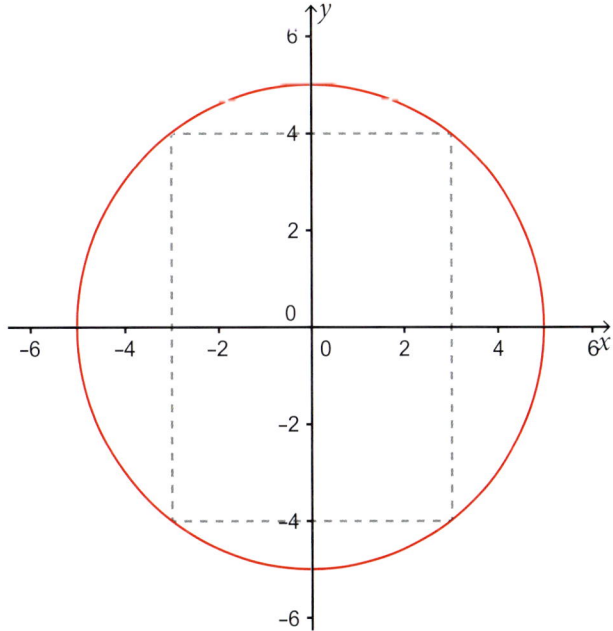

PURE MATHEMATICS FOR CCEA A2

Functions

Of the four types of mapping, only two are functions: **one-to-one** and **many-to-one**. In other words:

> For each value in the domain, there must be **a single value in the range**. A function does not give more than one answer.

Worked Example

5. Determine whether each of the following mappings is a function.
   (a) $y = x + 2$
   (b) $y = \begin{cases} x + 2 \text{ for } x < 2 \\ x + 3 \text{ for } x \geq 2 \end{cases}$
   (c) $y = \begin{cases} x + 2 \text{ for } x \leq 2 \\ x + 3 \text{ for } x \geq 2 \end{cases}$

(a) $y = x + 2$ is a straight line. Each value in the domain maps onto exactly one value in the range. This is a function.

(b) $y = \begin{cases} x + 2 \text{ for } x < 2 \\ x + 3 \text{ for } x \geq 2 \end{cases}$

This is known as a piece-wise mapping because it is defined in two pieces, as shown below:

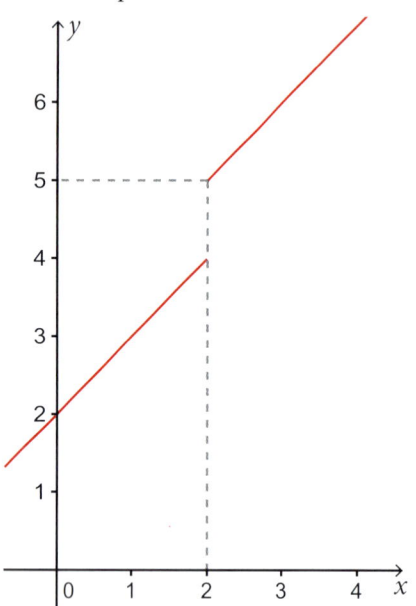

Each value in the range maps onto exactly one value in the range. This is a function.

(c) $y = \begin{cases} x + 2 \text{ for } x \leq 2 \\ x + 3 \text{ for } x \geq 2 \end{cases}$

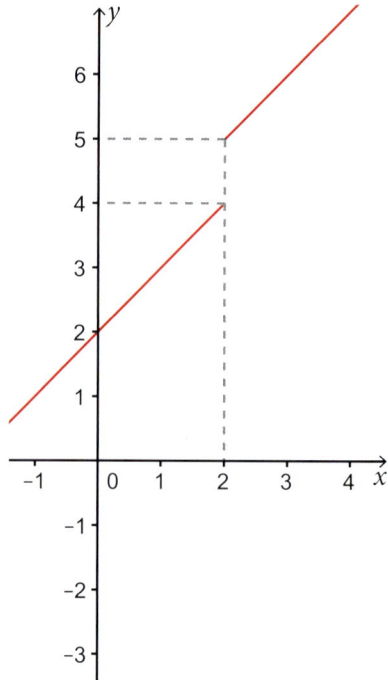

In this piece-wise mapping, more than one value of y is given when $x = 2$, as shown above. Therefore, this is not a function.

You may be asked to find the range of a function, given its domain. You will come across the following notation:

$f(x)$	the definition of function f, e.g. $f(x) = x^2 + 1$
$f : x \to$	this is the alternative notation for a function definition, e.g. $f : x \to x^2 + 1$
$\in$	is a member of
$\mathbb{R}$	the set of real numbers

Domains and ranges may be expressed as a set of values, e.g. {0, 1, 2, 3}, or as an inequality, e.g. $-2 \leq x < 2$.

The **identity function** is a function that maps every element to itself, i.e. $f(x) = x$.

Worked Example

6. Find the range for the following functions.
   (a) $f(x) = -2x + 3, x \in \{-1, 0, 1, 2, 3\}$
   (b) $f(x) = x - 1, x \in \mathbb{R}, x \geq 0$
   (c) $f(x) = x^2 + 1, x \in \mathbb{R}$

(a) $f(x) = -2x + 3, x \in \{-1, 0, 1, 2, 3\}$
The domain of this function is the set of integer values −1, 0, 1, 2, 3. It can be shown on a graph:

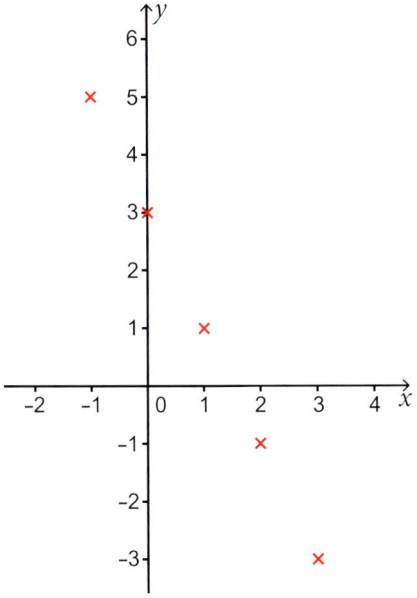

The range of the function is:
$f(x) \in \{-3, -1, 1, 3, 5\}$.

Note: You should not draw a straight line through the points on this graph, since the function is only defined at these five points. This type of function is known as a **discrete** function. The opposite of a discrete function is a **continuous** function. A continuous function is defined for all values within an interval. A straight line could be drawn for a continuous function.

(b) $f(x) = x - 1, x \in \mathbb{R}, x \geq 0$
This function is a straight line, but only for positive values of x.

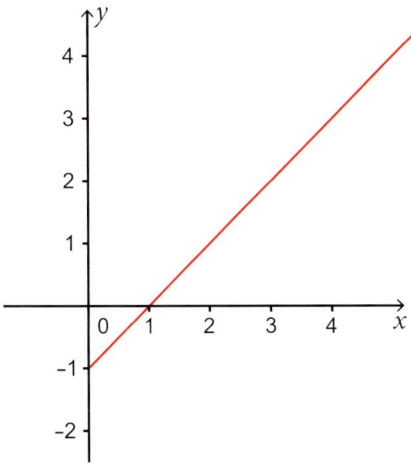

The graph shows that y can take any values greater than or equal to –1.

Therefore, the range is $f(x) \in \mathbb{R}, f(x) \geq -1$.

(c) $f(x) = x^2 + 1, x \in \mathbb{R}$
x can take any real value. However, the graph shows that the values of y are restricted:

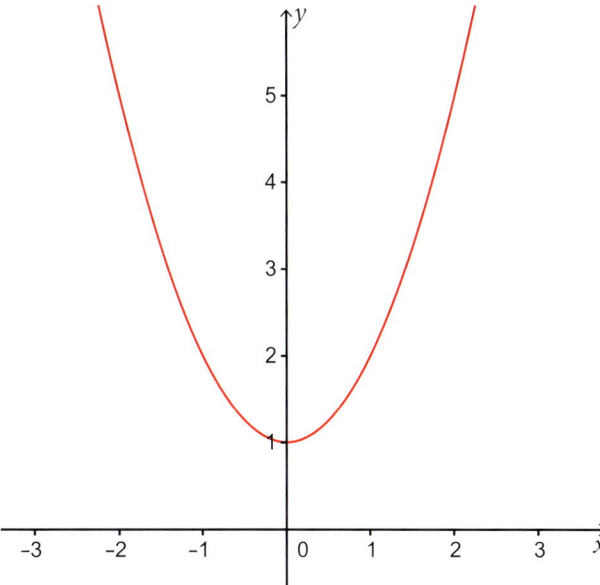

The range of the function is $f(x) \in \mathbb{R}, f(x) \geq 1$.

Reciprocal functions always have a restricted domain.

Worked Example

7. The function $h(x) = \dfrac{5}{x + 3}$ has domain $x \in \mathbb{R}, x \neq k$. Find the value of k.

$h(x) = \dfrac{5}{x + 3}$

The denominator of the fraction cannot be zero. Therefore $k = -3$.

So the function definition is:
$h(x) = \dfrac{5}{x + 3}, x \in \mathbb{R}, x \neq -3$

Sometimes the domain of a function may be restricted further. A restricted domain often leads to a restricted range.

Worked Examples

8. Find the range of the function $f(x) = \dfrac{1}{x}$ when the domain is:
   (a) $x \in \mathbb{R}, x \neq 0$
   (b) $x \in \mathbb{R}, x > 0$
   (c) $x \in \mathbb{R}, 1 \leq x < 5$

Note: You learnt about sketching reciprocal curves in AS Mathematics.

(a) When the domain is $x \in \mathbb{R}, x \neq 0$, we sketch:

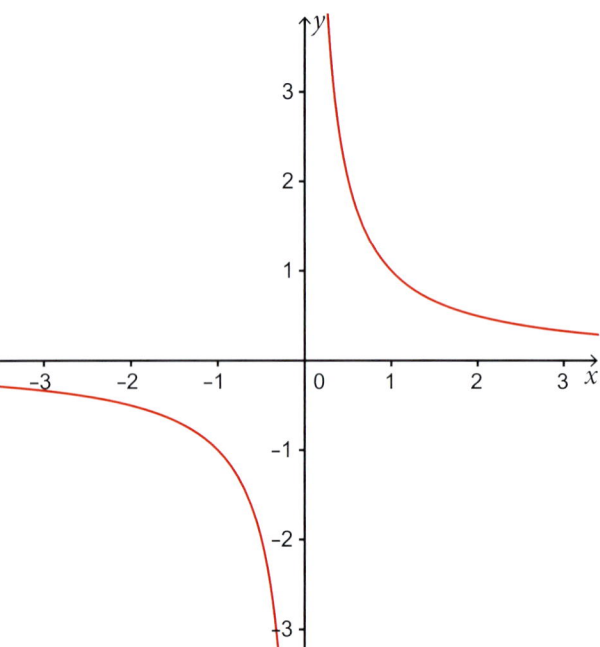

The sketch shows that y can take any value except for 0, where there is a horizontal asymptote. Therefore, the range is: $f(x) \in \mathbb{R}, f(x) \neq 0$.

(b) When the domain is $x \in \mathbb{R}, x > 0$, we are interested in the part of the curve where x is positive. We sketch:

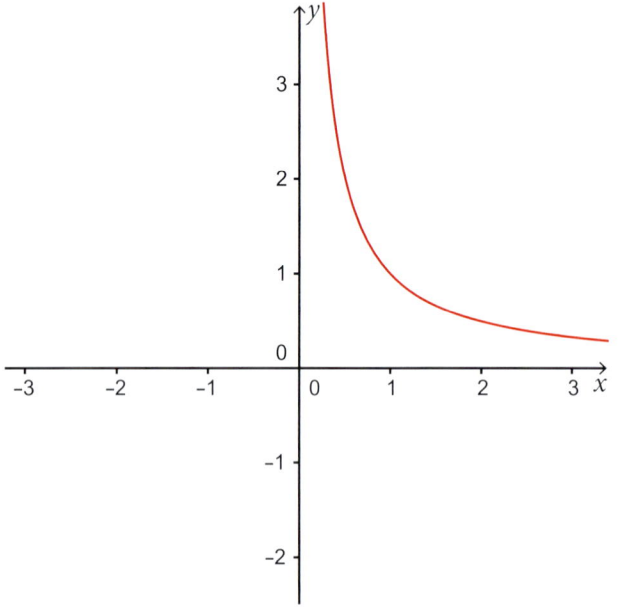

The sketch shows that y can take any positive value. Therefore, the range is: $f(x) \in \mathbb{R}, f(x) > 0$.

(c) When the domain is $x \in \mathbb{R}, 1 \leq x < 5$ we are interested in only a small section of the curve:

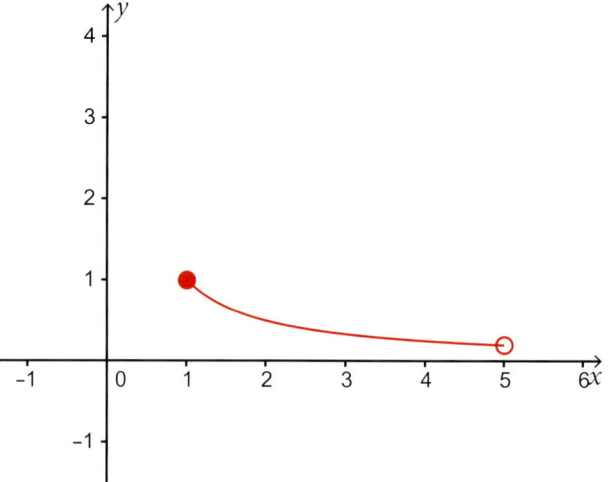

When $x = 1, y = 1$.
When $x = 5, y = \frac{1}{5}$.

The closed circle at $(1, 1)$ shows that the point $(1, 1)$ **is** included in the set of points.

The open circle at $(5, \frac{1}{5})$ shows that the point $(5, \frac{1}{5})$ **is not** included in the set of points.

Therefore, the range is: $f(x) \in \mathbb{R}, \dfrac{1}{5} < f(x) \leq 1$.

9. (a) Find the range of the function $f(x) = x^2 - 2x + 4, x \in \mathbb{R}, -1 < x \leq 4$
   (b) Find the value of p if $f(p) = 7$.

(a) The easiest way to sketch a quadratic curve is by completing the square:
$$f(x) = x^2 - 2x + 4$$
$$= (x-1)^2 - 1 + 4$$
$$= (x-1)^2 + 3$$

This shows that the curve has its stationary point at $(1, 3)$.

The positive coefficient of x^2 tells us that the curve has a minimum point.

The domain is $-1 < x \leq 4$.

When $x = -1, f(x) = 7$. The point $(-1, 7)$ is not included in the set of points.

When $x = 4, f(x) = 12$. The point $(4, 12)$ is included in the set of points.

So we can sketch:

2: FUNCTIONS

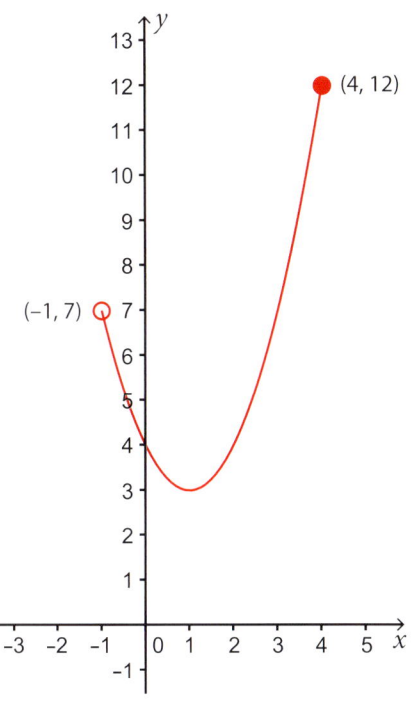

The sketch shows that the range is $3 \leq f(x) \leq 12$.

(b) To find the value of p if $f(p) = 7$ we must find a value of x that makes the value of the function 7:
$$x^2 - 2x + 4 = 7$$
$$x^2 - 2x - 3 = 0$$
$$(x-3)(x+1) = 0$$
$$x = 3 \text{ or } x = -1$$

However, we know that $x = -1$ is not in the domain. Hence $p = 3$.

10. Find the domain of the function $f(x)$, given its range: $f(x) = 3x$, Range: $f(x) > 2$

A sketch of the function $f(x) = 3x$ is shown below:

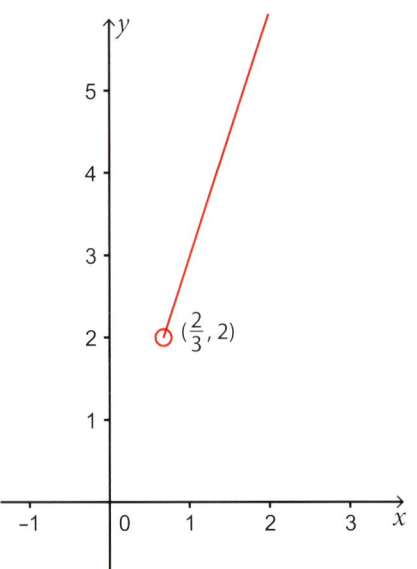

From the sketch, the domain is $x > \dfrac{2}{3}$.

11. (a) Find the domain of the function $f(x)$, given its range. $f(x) = x^2 - 1$, Range: $f(x) \geq -1$
There may be more than one possible answer.
(b) The function $f(x) = x^2 - 1, x \geq b$ has the range: $f(x) \geq -1$. Find the value of b that would make $f(x)$ a one-to-one function.

(a) $f(x) = x^2 - 1$
One possible sketch of the function is:

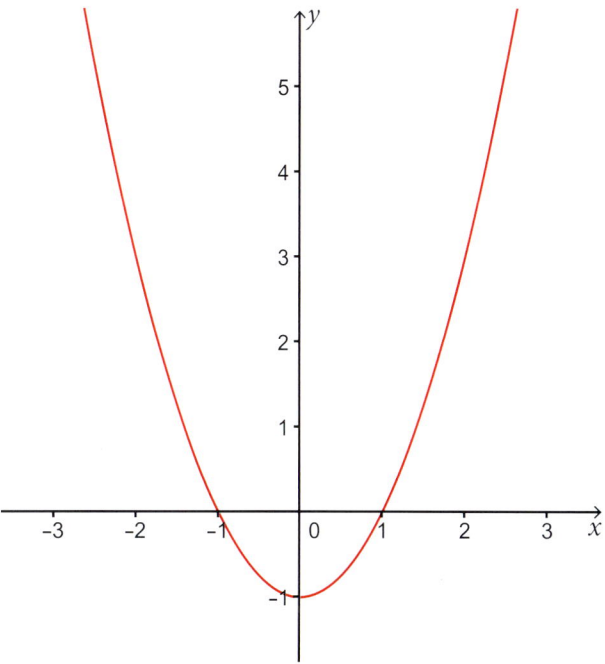

The domain giving rise to this sketch is $x \in \mathbb{R}$.

(b) A sketch of $f(x) = x^2 - 1, x \geq 0$ is:

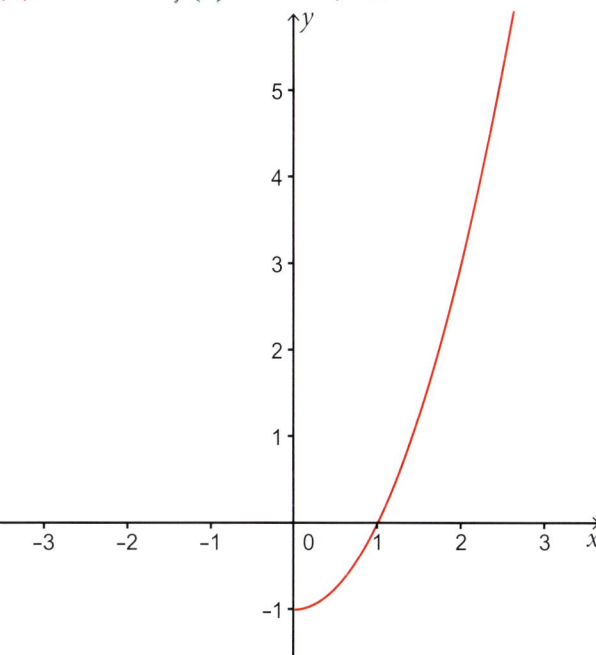

This is a one-to-one function and has the required range $f(x) \geq -1$.

The answer is $b = 0$. If b were smaller, f would not be a one-to-one function. If b were larger, f would not have the required range.

Exercise 2B

1. Sketch the following functions.
   (a) $f(x) = 2 - x, x \in \mathbb{R}, x \geq 0$
   (b) $f(x) = \dfrac{x}{2} + 1, x \in \mathbb{R}$
   (c) $f(x) = 2x + 1, x \in \mathbb{R}, x \geq 0$
   (d) $f(x) = x^2 - 3, x \in \mathbb{R}, -2 \leq x \leq 2$
   (e) $f(x) = \dfrac{1}{x} + 1, x \in \mathbb{R}, x \geq 1$
   (f) $f(x) = x^2 - 4x + 5, x \in \mathbb{R}, x < 3$
   (g) $f(x) = \dfrac{1}{x^2}, x \in \mathbb{R}, -3 < x < 3, x \neq 0$
   (h) $f(x) = \begin{cases} 1 + x \text{ for } 0 \leq x < 1 \\ 1 + x^2 \text{ for } x \geq 1 \end{cases}$

2. By drawing a sketch or otherwise, state whether each mapping is (i) one-to-one, one-to-many, many-to-one or many-to-many (ii) a function.
   (a) $y = -x - 3$
   (b) $y = \pm 3\sqrt{x}$
   (c) $y^2 + (x - 4)^2 = 3$
   (d) $y = x, x \leq 10$
   (e) $y = \dfrac{2}{x}, x \neq 0$
   (f) $y = (x - 1)^2, 0 \leq x < 2$
   (g) $y = (x - 1)^2, 1 \leq x < 3$
   (h) $y = |x|$
   (i) $y = \begin{cases} 3 - x \text{ for } x \leq 2 \\ 0 \text{ for } x \geq 2 \end{cases}$
   (j) $y = \begin{cases} 2 - x \text{ for } x \leq 2 \\ 0 \text{ for } x \geq 2 \end{cases}$

3. By drawing a mapping diagram or sketching the graph, find the range of the following functions. State whether each function is one-to-one or many-to-one.
   (a) $f(x) = 3x - 5, x \in \{0, 1, 2, 3\}$
   (b) $f(x) = -x^2 + 2, x \in \mathbb{R}$
   (c) $f(x) = 2 - \dfrac{1}{x^2}, x \in \mathbb{R}, -2 < x < 2$
   (d) $f(x) = |x| + 1, x \in \mathbb{R}$
   (e) $f(x) = |2x|, -2 < x < 2$
   (f) $f(x) = 1 - x^3, x \in \mathbb{R}, 0 \leq x \leq 2$

Exercise 2B...

   (g) $f(x) = (x - 1)^3, x \in \mathbb{R}, 0 \leq x \leq 2$
   (h) $f(x) = +\sqrt{x + 1}, x \in \{0, 3, 8, 15, 24\}$
   (i) $f(x) = \dfrac{1}{x + 1}, x \in \mathbb{R}, x > -1$

4. Find the domain of the following functions, given the range.
   (a) $f(x) = 1 - x, f(x) < 2$
   (b) $f(x) = 3x^2 + 1, f(x) \geq 1$
   (c) $f(x) = 3x^2 + 1, f(x) \geq 13$
   (d) $f(x) = \sqrt{x + 1}, 0 \leq f(x) \leq 2$
   (e) $f(x) = \dfrac{2}{x + 2}, 0 < f(x) \leq 1$
   (f) $f(x) = \dfrac{2 + x}{2 - x}, 0 < f(x) \leq 1$

5. Find the value of k, given that:
   $f(x) = 1 + x^3$ and $f(k) = 9$

6. Find the two possible values of p given that:
   $f(x) = 1 + x^2$ and $f(p + 1) = 5$

7. The function f is defined such that $f(x) = mx + c$, where m and c are constants. Given that $f(3) = 14$ and $f(-2) = -6$, find the constants m and c.

8. The function g is defined such that $g(x) = ax^2 + bx + c$, where a, b and c are constants. Given that $g(0) = 4, g(1) = 5$ and $g(-1) = 7$, find the constants a, b and c.

9. The function f has domain $\mathbb{R}$.
   $f(x) = x^2 - 3ax, x \geq 0$
   where a is a positive constant.
   (a) Sketch the curve with equation $y = f(x)$, showing the coordinates of all the points at which the curve meets the axes.
   (b) Find, in terms of a, the value of $f(5a)$.
   (c) Given that $a = 3$, use algebra to find the value of x for which $f(x) = 36$.

10. The function f is defined such that:
    $f(x) = x^2 + 6x + 2, x \geq b$
    Find the smallest possible value of b that would make $f(x)$ a one-to-one function.

2.3 Composite Functions

A composite function is formed by combining two or more functions. The output of one function becomes the input for another.

Notation

$fg(x)$ means $f(g(x))$. In other words, the output from $g(x)$ is used as input, or x value, for the function $f(x)$.

$f^2(x)$ means $f(f(x))$.

You may come across the terms "inner" and "outer" functions. In $fg(x)$, $g(x)$ is the inner function and $f(x)$ is the outer function.

Worked Example

12. $f(x) = 3x + 1$ and $g(x) = 2x^2$. Find:
    (a) $fg(x)$ (b) $gf(x)$ (c) $f^2(x)$ (d) $g^2(x)$

    (a) $fg(x)$ means that the output from $g(x)$ is used as input for $f(x)$.
    The output from $g(x)$ is $2x^2$. So:
    $fg(x) = 3(2x^2) + 1$
    $= 6x^2 + 1$

    (b) $gf(x)$ means that the output from $f(x)$ is used as input for $g(x)$.
    The output from $f(x)$ is $3x + 1$. So:
    $gf(x) = 2(3x + 1)^2$

    (c) $f^2(x)$. Use the output from $f(x)$ as input to $f(x)$.
    $f(x) = 3x + 1$
    $f^2(x) = 3(3x + 1) + 1$
    $= 9x + 3 + 1$
    $= 9x + 4$

    (d) $g(x) = 2x^2$
    $g^2(x) = 2(2x^2)^2$
    $= 2(4x^4)$
    $= 8x^4$

You may be asked to find the value of a composite function for a particular value of x. There are two ways to do this.

Worked Example

13. Given $f(x) = 2x - 5$ and $g(x) = x^2 - 14$ evaluate $fg(4)$.

    Method 1: First find the composite function $fg(x)$.
    $fg(x) = 2(x^2 - 14) - 5$
    $= 2x^2 - 33$

    Therefore:
    $fg(4) = 2(4)^2 - 33 = -1$

    Method 2: First find the value of $g(4)$.
    $g(4) = (4)^2 - 14 = 2$
    Therefore:
    $fg(4) = f(2)$
    $= 2(2) - 5 = -1$

To find the domain of a composite function, follow these steps:

- Use the domain of the inner function.
- Add in any restrictions due to fractions in the composite function, square roots, etc.

Worked Example

14. $f(x) = \dfrac{1}{x}, x \in \mathbb{R}, x \neq 0$
    $g(x) = 3 + x, x \in \mathbb{R}$
    $h(x) = \sqrt{x}, x \in \mathbb{R}, x \geq 0$

    (a) Find the composite function $fg(x)$ and state its domain.
    (b) Find the composite function $gf(x)$ and state its domain.
    (c) Find the composite function $hg(x)$ and state its domain.

    (a) $fg(x) = \dfrac{1}{3 + x}$
    The domain is the domain of the inner function $g(x): x \in \mathbb{R}$. Also, there is a restriction because of the fraction in the composite function: $x \neq -3$.
    $\therefore fg(x) = \dfrac{1}{3 + x}, x \in \mathbb{R}, x \neq -3$

    (b) $gf(x) = 3 + \dfrac{1}{x}$
    The domain is the domain of the inner function $f(x): x \in \mathbb{R}, x \neq 0$. No other restrictions are needed.
    $\therefore gf(x) = 3 + \dfrac{1}{x}, x \in \mathbb{R}, x \neq 0$

    (c) $hg(x) = \sqrt{3 + x}$
    The domain is the domain of the inner function $g(x): x \in \mathbb{R}$. Also, there is a restriction because of the square root in the composite function: $x \geq -3$ (because we cannot take the square root of a negative number).
    $\therefore hg(x) = \sqrt{3 + x}, x \in \mathbb{R}, x \geq -3$

PURE MATHEMATICS FOR CCEA A2

> In general, $fg(x) \neq gf(x)$

But you may be asked to find particular values of x for which two composite functions are equal.

Worked Example

15. $f(x) = \dfrac{1}{x}, x \in \mathbb{R}, x \neq 0$

$g(x) = 3 + x, x \in \mathbb{R}$

Find the two values of x for which $fg(x) = gf(x)$.

$$fg(x) = \dfrac{1}{3+x}$$

$$gf(x) = 3 + \dfrac{1}{x} = \dfrac{3x+1}{x}$$

$$fg(x) = gf(x)$$

$$\dfrac{1}{3+x} = \dfrac{3x+1}{x}$$

$$(3x+1)(x+3) = x$$

$$3x^2 + 10x + 3 = x$$

$$3x^2 + 9x + 3 = 0$$

$$x^2 + 3x + 1 = 0$$

$$x = \dfrac{-3 \pm \sqrt{3^2 - 4(1)(1)}}{2}$$

$$x = \dfrac{-3 \pm \sqrt{5}}{2}$$

When evaluating a composite function for a particular value of x, the value of the inner function must be within the domain of the outer function. If this is not true, the value of the composite function is not defined.

Worked Example

16. $g(x) = +\sqrt{x}, x \in \mathbb{R}, x > 0$

$h(x) = -x, x \in \mathbb{R}$

Find:
(a) $hg(4)$ (b) $gh(4)$

(a) $g(4) = +\sqrt{4} = 2$
    $\therefore hg(4) = h(2) = -2$

(b) $h(4) = -4$
    $gh(4)$ is undefined because the domain of g is $x > 0$.

You may be asked to find two functions that, when composited, give a given function.

Worked Example

17. $f(x) = \dfrac{x-1}{x+2}, x \in \mathbb{R}, x \neq -2$

(a) Write $f(x)$ in the form $a - \dfrac{b}{x+2}$

(b) Hence or otherwise, find two functions $p(x)$ and $q(x)$ such that $pq(x) = f(x)$. Neither $p(x)$ nor $q(x)$ are the identity function.

(a) $f(x) = \dfrac{x-1}{x+2}$

$$= \dfrac{x+2-3}{x+2}$$

$$= \dfrac{x+2}{x+2} - \dfrac{3}{x+2}$$

$$f(x) = 1 - \dfrac{3}{x+2}$$

$\therefore a = 1, b = 3$

Alternatively, this form for $f(x)$ could be found using long division.

(b) The word "hence" suggests that we can use our answer to part (a). We have shown that:

$$f(x) = 1 - \dfrac{3}{x+2}$$

We can choose $q(x) = \dfrac{3}{x+2}$ and $p(x) = 1 - x$.

Checking:

$$pq(x) = 1 - \dfrac{3}{x+2}$$

$$= f(x)$$

> **Note:** There are other solutions, but this is the simplest. If we were allowed to use the identity function, the simplest solution would be:
>
> $p(x) = 1 - \dfrac{3}{x+2}$
>
> $q(x) = x$ (the identity function)

Exercise 2C

1. Given:
   $f(x) = x^2, x \in \mathbb{R}$
   $g(x) = x^3 + 5, x \in \mathbb{R}$
   $h(x) = 3x - 15, x \in \mathbb{R}, x > 0$
   find:
   (a) $fg(-2)$
   (b) $gf(-2)$
   (c) $gh(9)$
   (d) $h^2(6)$
   (e) Explain why it is not possible to find $h^2(5)$.

Exercise 2C...

2. The functions f, g, h are defined as follows:
   $f: y \to y^2 + 5, y \in \mathbb{R}$
   $g: y \to 4 - 4y, y \in \mathbb{R}$
   $h: y \to 2y - 10, y \in \mathbb{R}, y > 10$
   Find:
   (a) $fg(3)$ (b) $gf(3)$
   (c) $gh(5)$ (d) $h^2(13)$

3. Given:
   $f: y \to 6y + 6, y \in \mathbb{R}$
   $g: y \to \dfrac{7}{y+1}, y \in \mathbb{R}, y \neq -1$
   find:
   (a) $fg(1)$ (b) $gf(1)$
   (c) $f^2(1)$ (d) $g^2(9)$

4. $f(x) = e^x, x \in \mathbb{R}$; $g(x) = \ln(2x), x \in \mathbb{R}, x > 0$
   Show that $fg(x) = gf(x)$ when $x = \ln 2$.

5. The functions f and g are defined by:
   $f(x) = 3x + \ln 4, x \in \mathbb{R}$
   $g(x) = e^{2x}, x \in \mathbb{R}$
   (a) Prove that the composite function $gf(x)$ is:
   $gf(x) = 16e^{6x}, x \in \mathbb{R}$
   (b) Write down the range of the function $gf(x)$.

6. $f(x) = \dfrac{k}{x}, x \in \mathbb{R}, x \neq 0$
   $g(x) = k + x, x \in \mathbb{R}; k > 0$
   (a) Find the composite functions $fg(x)$ and $gf(x)$ and state their domains.
   (b) Show that $fg(x) = gf(x)$ when $x^2 + kx + k = 0$.
   (c) Show that this equation has exactly one solution if $k = 4$, and find the value of x that gives this solution.
   (d) Find the two solutions that exist when $k = 5$, giving your answers in surd form.

7. The functions f and g are defined by:
   $f: x \to x^2 - 4x + 8, x \in \mathbb{R}, 0 \leq x \leq 5$
   $g: x \to \lambda x^2 + 4, x \in \mathbb{R}$, where λ is a constant.
   (a) Find the range of f.
   (b) Given that $gf(2) = 20$, find the value of λ.

8. The function f is given by:
   $f: x \to \dfrac{4}{(x-4)(x+4)}, x \in \mathbb{R}, x > 4$
   The function g is given by:
   $g: x \to \dfrac{4}{x}, x \in \mathbb{R}, x > 0$
   Solve: $gf(x) = 84$

Exercise 2C...

9. The function f is defined such that:
   $f(x) = \dfrac{6+x}{6-x}, x \in \mathbb{R}, x \neq 6$
   (a) Write $f(x)$ in the form $a + \dfrac{b}{6-x}$
   (b) Find functions $p(x)$ and $q(x)$ such that $pq(x) = f(x)$. Neither $p(x)$ nor $q(x)$ are the identity function.

2.4 Inverse Functions and Their Graphs

An **inverse function** does the opposite of the function. For example, the square root function is the inverse of the square function.

We use the notation $f^{-1}(x)$ to denote the inverse function.

So if $f(x) = 2x$ then $f^{-1}(x) = \dfrac{x}{2}$.

Note:
- Only one-to-one functions have inverse functions. The inverse of a many-to-one function is a one-to-many mapping.
- Do not confuse the inverse function $f^{-1}(x)$ with a reciprocal. You have seen in AS Mathematics that a power of –1 denotes a reciprocal; for example $3^{-1} = \frac{1}{3}$. In function notation, $f^{-1}(x)$ denotes an inverse, not a reciprocal.
- Do not get $f^{-1}(x)$ confused with $f'(x)$, which is the gradient function!

To find the inverse function, follow these steps:
- Write the equation of the function as $y = f(x)$
- Re-arrange to make x the subject.
- On the left-hand side, swap x for $f^{-1}(x)$
- On the right-hand side, swap y for x.

Worked Example

18. $f(x) = \dfrac{1}{1+x}$
    Find $f^{-1}(x)$

Write the equation of the function as $y = f(x)$:
$$y = \dfrac{1}{1+x}$$

Re-arrange to make x the subject.

$y(1 + x) = 1$

$1 + x = \dfrac{1}{y}$

$x = \dfrac{1}{y} - 1$

On the left-hand side, swap x for $f^{-1}(x)$, and on the right-hand side, swap y for x:

$f^{-1}(x) = \dfrac{1}{x} - 1$

$f^{-1}(x) = \dfrac{1 - x}{x}$

Note:
- The domain of a function is the range of its inverse.
- The range of a function is the domain of its inverse.

You may be asked to find the domain and range of an inverse function. These are straightforward if you know the domain and range of the original function.

Worked Example

19. (a) Sketch the function $f(x) = x^2 - 3, x \geq 0$
(b) Hence state the domain and range of $f(x)$.
(c) Find the inverse function $f^{-1}(x)$ and state its domain and range.

(a) Sketch of the function:

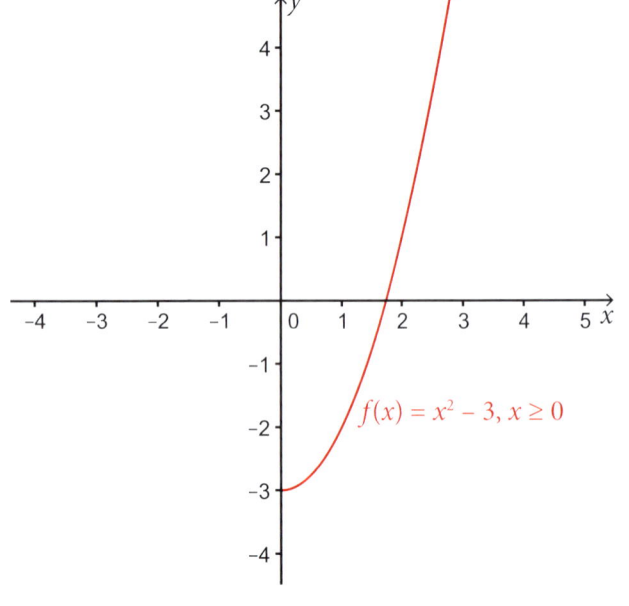

(b) The domain was given in the question: $x \geq 0$
Range: $f(x) \geq -3$

(c) $y = x^2 - 3$
$x^2 = y + 3$
$x = \sqrt{y + 3}$

So inverse function: $f^{-1}(x) = \sqrt{x + 3}$

The domain of $f^{-1}(x)$ is the range of $f(x)$.
The range of $f^{-1}(x)$ is the domain of $f(x)$. So:

Domain: $x \geq -3$
Range: $f^{-1}(x) \geq 0$

Note: If you are asked for a domain, your answer will always have x on the left-hand side.

If you are asked for a range, your answer will always have the name of the function on the left-hand side.

Graphically, the inverse function $f^{-1}(x)$ is a reflection of $f(x)$ in the line $y = x$. You can use this to sketch inverse functions.

Worked Examples

20. (a) Sketch the curve $y = f(x)$ where $f(x) = e^{-2x}$
(b) State the domain and range of $f(x)$.
(c) Find the inverse function $f^{-1}(x)$ and state its domain and range.
(d) Sketch $y = f^{-1}(x)$

(a) The graph of $y = e^{-2x}$ can be obtained by applying two transformations to the graph of $y = e^x$: stretch factor ½ in the x-direction, followed by reflection in the y-axis. So we sketch:

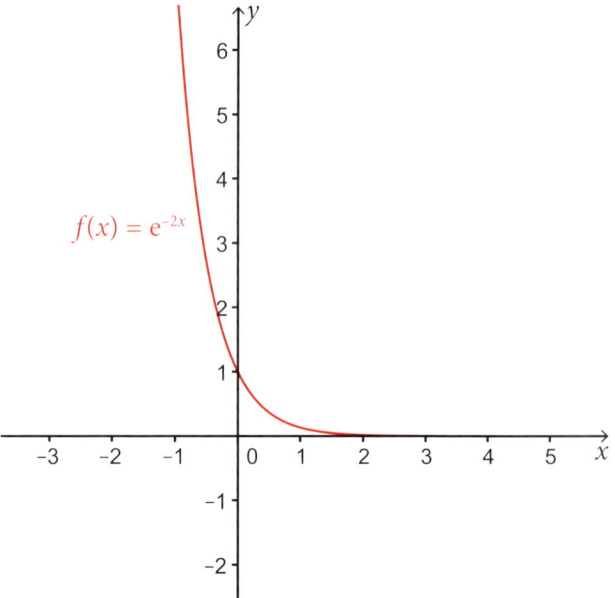

(b) By inspecting the graph:
Domain: $x \in \mathbb{R}$
Range: $f(x) > 0$

(c) $\qquad y = e^{-2x}$

Take logs of both sides:
$$\ln y = -2x$$
$$x = -\frac{1}{2}\ln y$$

So the inverse function is:
$$f^{-1}(x) = -\frac{1}{2}\ln x$$

From the domain and range of $f(x)$, we obtain:
Domain: $x > 0$
Range: $f^{-1}(x) \in \mathbb{R}$

(d) So we can sketch:

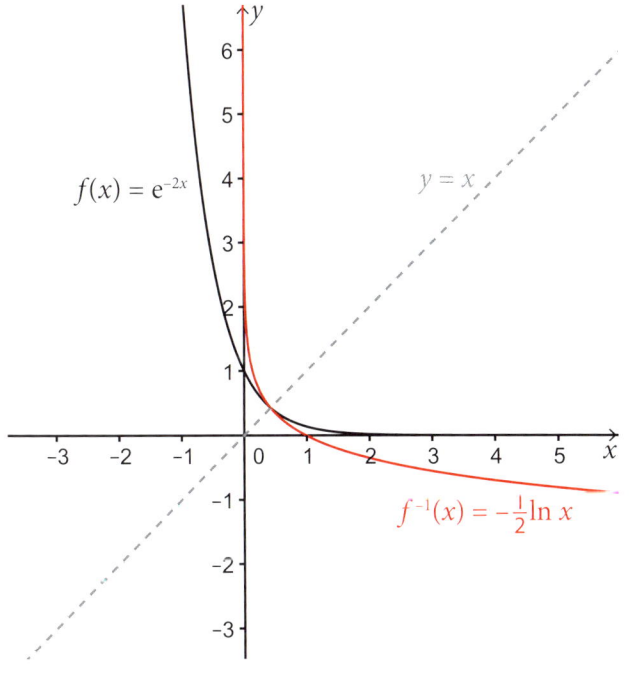

21. Find the inverse of the function $f(x) = e^{2x} + 1$

$$y = e^{2x} + 1$$
$$e^{2x} = y - 1$$

Take logs (base e) of both sides:
$$2x = \ln(y - 1)$$
$$x = \frac{1}{2}\ln(y - 1)$$

So the inverse function is:
$$f^{-1}(x) = \frac{1}{2}\ln(x - 1)$$

The composite functions $ff^{-1}(x)$ and $f^{-1}f(x)$ are both equal to x.

Worked Example

22. $f(x) = \dfrac{1}{1+x}, x \neq -1$

(a) Find $f^{-1}(x)$.
(b) Show that $ff^{-1}(x) = x$.
(c) Show that $f^{-1}f(x) = x$.

(a) $\qquad f(x) = \dfrac{1}{1+x}, x \neq -1$
$$y = \frac{1}{1+x}$$
$$1 + x = \frac{1}{y}$$
$$x = \frac{1}{y} - 1$$
$$\therefore f^{-1}(x) = \frac{1}{x} - 1$$

(b) To find $ff^{-1}(x)$, the output from $f^{-1}(x)$ is used as input to $f(x)$:
$$ff^{-1}(x) = \frac{1}{1 + \left(\frac{1}{x} - 1\right)}$$
$$= \frac{1}{\frac{1}{x}}$$
$$= x$$

(c) To find $f^{-1}f(x)$, the output from $f(x)$ is used as input to $f^{-1}(x)$:
$$f^{-1}f(x) = \frac{1}{\left(\frac{1}{1+x}\right)} - 1$$
$$= (1 + x) - 1$$
$$= x$$

If a function and its inverse are the same, the function is described as a **self-inverse**.

Worked Example

23. The function $f(x)$ is defined such that:
$$f(x) = \frac{1}{x-1} + 1, x \in \mathbb{R}, x \neq 1$$

Show that $f(x)$ is a self-inverse.

$$y = \frac{1}{x-1} + 1$$
$$y - 1 = \frac{1}{x-1}$$
$$x - 1 = \frac{1}{y-1}$$
$$x = \frac{1}{y-1} + 1$$
$$f^{-1}(x) = \frac{1}{x-1} + 1$$
$$f(x) = f^{-1}(x)$$

Therefore the function is a self-inverse.

Note: A function that is a self-inverse is symmetrical in the line $y = x$.
For example, $f(x) = \frac{1}{x}$:

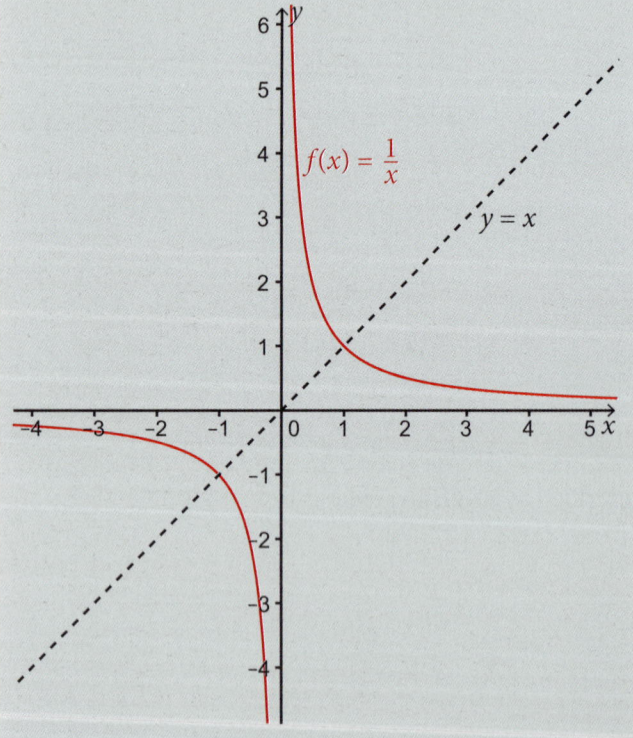

$f(x) = \frac{1}{x}$ is a self-inverse.
It is symmetrical in the line $y = x$.

Exercise 2D

1. The function f is given by
$$f: x \to \frac{x+2}{x}, x \in \mathbb{R}, x \neq 0$$
   (a) Find $f^{-1}(x)$.
   (b) Find the values of x that satisfy $f(x) = f^{-1}(x)$.

2. Given:
$$f: x \to x^2 - 2, \ x \geq 0$$
$$g: x \to \sqrt{28 - 7x}, \ x \leq 4$$
$$h: x \to 2x + 8, \ x \in \mathbb{R}$$
find the following inverse functions, and state the domain of each:
   (a) $f^{-1}(x)$ (b) $g^{-1}(x)$ (c) $h^{-1}(x)$

3. Given:
$$f: y \to y^2 + 4, \ y \geq 0$$
$$g: y \to 5 - 7y, \ y \in \mathbb{R}$$
$$h: y \to -2y - 9, \ y \in \mathbb{R}$$
find:
   (a) $f^{-1}(y)$ (b) $g^{-1}(y)$ (c) $h^{-1}(y)$

4. The function f is defined such that:
$$f(x) = e^{x-10} - 9, x \in \mathbb{R}$$
Find the inverse function $f^{-1}(x)$ and state its domain.

5. The function f is given by:
$$f: x \to 7 + \frac{7}{x+8}, x \in \mathbb{R}, x \neq -8$$
   (a) Express $7 + \frac{7}{x+8}$ as a single fraction.
   (b) Find an expression for $f^{-1}(x)$.
   (c) Write down the domain of $f^{-1}(x)$.

6. The function f is given by:
$$f: x \to \frac{4}{x-3}, x > 3$$
   (a) Find $f^{-1}(x)$.
   The function g is defined by:
$$g: x \to x^2 + 7, x \in \mathbb{R}.$$
   (b) Solve $fg(x) = \frac{1}{5}$.

7. The functions f and g are defined such that:
$$f: x \to \ln(6x - 5), x \in \mathbb{R}, x > \frac{5}{6}$$
$$g: x \to \frac{4}{x-4}, x \in \mathbb{R}, x \neq 4$$
   (a) Find the exact value of $fg(5)$.
   (b) Find the inverse function $f^{-1}(x)$, stating its domain.

Exercise 2D...

8. Two functions f and g are defined as:
   $f(x) = 7x + 6, x \in \mathbb{R}$
   $g(x) = \dfrac{6}{x+5}, x \in \mathbb{R}, x \neq -5$
   Find, stating the domains:
   (a) $fg(x)$ (b) $gf(x)$ (c) $f^{-1}(x)$
   (d) $g^{-1}(x)$ (e) $(fg)^{-1}(x)$ (f) $(gf)^{-1}(x)$

9. $f(x) = 2 - \dfrac{2}{x-2},\quad x \in \mathbb{R}, x \neq 2$
   (a) Find $f^{-1}(x)$ and hence show that $f(x)$ is a self-inverse.
   (b) Sketch the graph of $y = f(x)$, showing that it is symmetrical in the line $y = x$.

10. The two functions $f(x)$ and $g(x)$ are defined such that:
    $f(x) = 3 + e^{2x}, x \in \mathbb{R}$
    $g(x) = \dfrac{1}{2}\ln(x-3), x \in \mathbb{R}, x > 3$
    (a) Find $fg(x)$.
    (b) Find $gf(x)$.
    (c) What can you conclude about the two functions?

11. Find the inverse function for each of the following functions.
    (a) $f(x) = \ln(2x)$
    (b) $f(x) = 6\ln x$
    (c) $f(x) = \ln 2x + \ln(2x)^2$
    (d) $f(x) - \dfrac{1}{2}e^x$
    (e) $f(x) = e^{2x}$
    (f) $f(x) = 1 + e^{x+1}$
    (g) $f(x) = 1 - \ln x$
    (h) $f(x) = (e^x)^2$
    (i) $f(x) = ae^{bx}$
    (j) $f(x) = -2 + \ln(3x+1)$

2.5 Functions in Modelling

You will be asked to use functions to model real-life situations. In doing this, you will consider the limitations of the model and possible refinements of the model to improve it.

Worked Examples

24. The height $h(t)$ of a tree is modelled as a function of its age according to the function: $h(t) = 5\log t$ where t is the age of the tree in years.
    (a) Using this model, estimate the height of the tree when it is 10 years old.
    (b) The number of leaves on the tree is modelled as being dependent on the square of its height, according to the function: $n(h) = 100h^2$
        Using your answer from part (a), estimate the number of leaves when the tree is 10 years old.
    (c) Find the composite function $nh(t)$.
    (d) Hence estimate the number of leaves on the tree when it is 40 years old.
    (e) State one limitation in the modelling of the height of the tree and suggest one possible refinement of the model.

    (a) $h(10) = 5\log 10$
    $\qquad = 5$ m

    (b) $n(5) = 100h^2$
    $\qquad = 100 \times 5^2$
    $\qquad = 2500$

    (c) $nh(t) = 100 \times (5\log t)^2$
    $\qquad = 2500(\log t)^2$

    (d) $nh(40) = 100 \times (5\log 40)^2$
    $\qquad = 2500(\log 40)^2$
    $\qquad = 6416$
    $\qquad = 6420$ (3 s.f.)

    (e) $h(t)$ is undefined when $t = 0$. The model could be refined by using:
    $h(t) = 5\log(t+1)$

    This, however, wouldn't give a realistic result when $t = 0$. If the tree is 1 m tall at time $t = 0$, it may be more realistic to use a function such as:
    $h(t) = 5\log(t+1) + 1$

    Otherwise, non-logarithmic models may be considered.

25. David works 40 hours a week as an estate agent. He receives a £450 weekly salary, plus 3% commission on sales over £5000. David makes sales worth £x this week. Assume that he gets commission (i.e. $x > 5000$). Given the functions:
    $f(x) = 0.03x$
    $g(x) = x - 5000$
    which of $fg(x)$ and $gf(x)$ represents David's commission?

    Consider $fg(x) = 0.03(x - 5000)$

    This would represent taking David's sales x, subtracting the £5000 that didn't get the commission, and then multiplying by 3%.

Consider $gf(x) = 0.03x - 5000$.

This would represent taking David's sales x, multiplying by 3%, and then subtracting £5000 from the result. This does things in the wrong order. (It could result in a negative number.)

$fg(x)$ does what we require and so it represents David's commission.

Exercise 2E

1. In a medical journal it is suggested that the height of an average child can be modelled using the function:

   $$h(t) = 40 \ln\left(\frac{t}{100} + 4\right)$$

   where t is the age of the child in days and $h(t)$ is in cm.

   (a) Use the model to predict the height of a child on their 4th birthday.
   (b) Using the model, at what age would you expect a child to reach 150 cm? Give your answer in years and months, to the nearest month.
   (c) Discuss any limitations of this model.
   (d) Do you think this model could be used to predict the height of a person throughout their life? Explain your answer.

2. There are s sick people in Pleasantown. s is not a constant: it tends to be higher in the winter time, or when there is an outbreak of a virus, etc. The town's health centre is a very busy place. The waiting time $w(s)$ for an appointment tends to increase when s increases. But if $w(s)$ is very high, some sick people are put off by the long wait and decide not to make an appointment with the doctor. The five graphs below show possible relationships between s and $w(s)$.

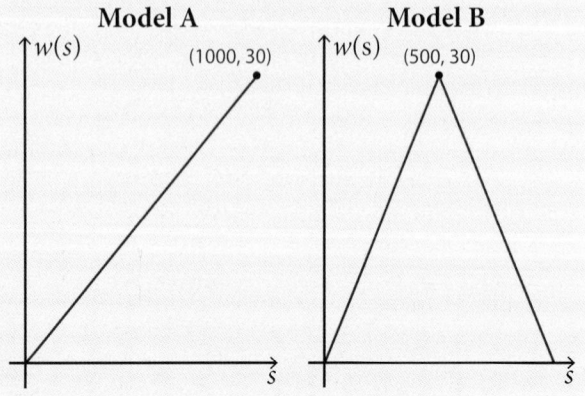

Exercise 2E...

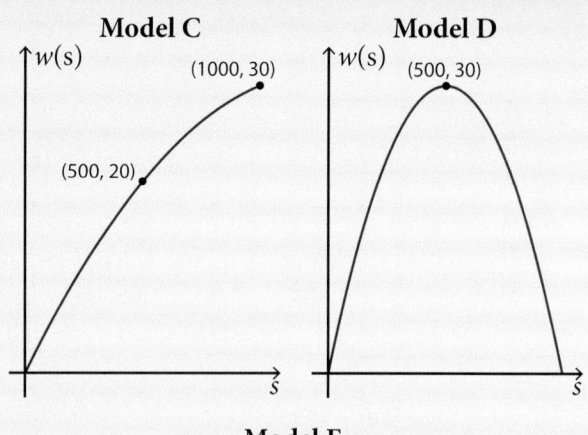

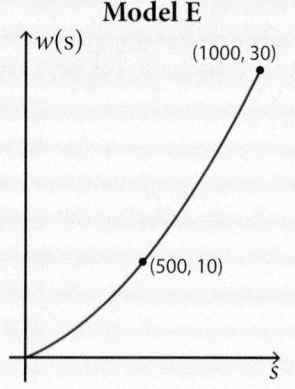

(a) Why are Models B and D unrealistic for values of s up to 1000?
(b) Explain how Model C is more realistic than models A and E for values of s up to 1000.
(c) Show that an equation of the quadratic curve used in Model C is:

$$w(s) = -\frac{s^2}{50000} + \frac{s}{20}$$

(d) Use the equation in part (c) to estimate the waiting time in days if there are 900 sick people in Pleasantown.
(e) The health centre finds that Model C works well when $s < 1000$. Explain why it stops being realistic if s rises above 1250.
(f) The practice aims to have average waiting times no longer than 4.8 days. Using Model C, predict how many sick people there would have to be in the town to achieve this.

3. A cargo ship carries containers full of sports balls to the UK. The balls vary in size from small (e.g. tennis balls) to large (e.g. basketballs). Each container holds only one type of ball. The number of balls it holds depends on the radius of the balls.

Exercise 2E...

It can be modelled using the function:
$n(r) = 20r^{-3}$
where r is the radius of the balls in metres.
(a) Use this model to estimate the number of footballs, with a diameter of 22 cm, that would fit in one container. Give your answer to 3 significant figures.
(b) A sports company in the UK orders one container full of balls. The total cost of the shipment depends on the number of balls and is modelled by the function:
$c(n) = 1000 \ln(n + 1)$
Find the composite function $cn(r)$.
(c) Use your answer to part (b) to find the total cost of the delivery if the balls are:
  (i) Footballs with diameter 22 cm.
  (ii) Tennis balls with diameter 6.8 cm.

4. A farmer grows wheat in a field. The average height of the crop in centimetres is modelled by the function:
$h(t) = 10 \log(t)$
where t is the number of days after the seeds were sown.
(a) Use the model to predict the height of the wheat 8 weeks after sowing the crop.
(b) The farmer wishes to harvest the wheat when it reaches a height of 22.5 cm. If the seeds were sown on 1st March, use the model to find a date for harvesting.
(c) What other considerations would the farmer make when deciding on a date for harvesting?
(d) State one limitation of this model and one possible refinement.

5. A computer model calculates the probability of flooding in a coastal area. The model considers the rise and fall of the tide and the effects of atmospheric pressure. Low pressure is associated with storms. The sea is known to experience a "storm surge" in these conditions, which makes flooding more likely.
The function $h(t)$, given below, models the height of the tide, where t is the time after midnight in hours:
$h(t) = 0.3(\sin(30t) + 1)$
(a) Sketch a graph of $h(t)$ (on the y-axis) against t (on the x-axis).

Exercise 2E...

(b) $w(p)$ is a function that depends on the air pressure p measured in millibars. It is a piece-wise function modelled as:

$$w(p) = \begin{cases} 0.4 & \text{for } p < 960 \\ \dfrac{1000 - p}{100} & \text{for } 960 \leq p \leq 1000 \\ 0 & \text{for } p > 1000 \end{cases}$$

Sketch a graph of $w(p)$ (on the y-axis) against p (on the x-axis).
(c) The probability of flooding is given by the following formula:
$P = h(t) + w(p)$
Calculate the probability of flooding at 3 a.m. if the air pressure falls to 970 millibars.
(d) Discuss any limitations in this model.

6. Roisin makes a purchase at a local hardware store. For a small fee, she arranges to have the item delivered. She pays for the purchase, plus the VAT, plus the delivery fee. VAT is charged at 20% and the delivery fee is £15.
(a) Write a function $t(x)$ for the total, after taxes, on the purchase amount x (ignoring the delivery fee).
(b) Write another function $f(x)$ for the total, including the delivery fee, on the purchase amount x (ignoring the VAT).
(c) Find the composite functions $ft(x)$ and $tf(x)$ and interpret them. Which of these composite functions would result in a lower cost to Roisin?
(d) Suppose taxes, by law, are not to be charged on delivery fees. Which of the composite functions $ft(x)$ and $tf(x)$ should be used?

7. A circle starts as a dot and expands outwards with its radius increasing at a constant rate. After 4 seconds, the circle's radius is 12 cm.
(a) Find a function $r(t)$ that represents the radius in terms of t.
(b) The formula for the area of a circle is $A = \pi r^2$. Since A is a function of r, this can be written: $A(r) = \pi r^2$. By finding a composite function, express the area A of the circle as a function of the time t seconds.

2.6 Summary

A mapping transforms one set of values onto another.

A mapping can be either: **one-to-one**, **many-to-one**, **one-to-many** or **many-to-many**.

Of the four types of mapping, only two are functions: **one-to-one** and **many-to-one**.

> A function does not give more than one answer.

The **domain** is the set of x values that a function can take.

The **range** is the set of possible y values the function can give.

Sometimes a function has a restricted domain, which may lead to a restricted range.

A **compound** or **composite function** is formed by combining two or more functions. The output of one function becomes the input for another.

$fg(x)$ means $f(g(x))$. In other words, the output from $g(x)$ is used as input, or x value, for the function $f(x)$.

An **inverse function**, denoted $f^{-1}(x)$, does the reverse of the function $f(x)$. You must learn how to find the inverse function.

The domain of a function is the range of its inverse.

The range of a function is the domain of its inverse.

Graphically, the inverse function $f^{-1}(x)$ is a reflection of $f(x)$ in the line $y = x$.

The composite functions $ff^{-1}(x)$ and $f^{-1}f(x)$ are both equal to x.

If a function and its inverse are the same, the function is described as a **self-inverse**.

Functions can be used to model real-life situations. You will be asked to consider limitations of these models and possible refinements.

Chapter 3
Radian Measure

3.1 Introduction

Until now, you have measured angles in degrees. In this chapter and your further work, you will increasingly use a different unit of measure for angles: **radians**.

Key words
- **Radian**: A unit of measurement for angles.
- **Arc**: A part of the circumference of a circle.
- **Sector**: The area enclosed by an arc and two radii of a circle.

Before you start
You should know:
- The sine rule.
- The cosine rule.
- The formula for the area of a triangle $A = \frac{1}{2} ab \sin C$.
- How to use the CAST diagram for angles measured in degrees.

Worked Example
1. A triangle has the following side lengths:
   $a = 10$ cm, $b = 7$ cm, $c = 6$ cm
   (a) Solve the triangle.
   (b) Find the area of the triangle.

   (a) Draw a sketch of the triangle. Remember that angle A lies opposite side a, etc.

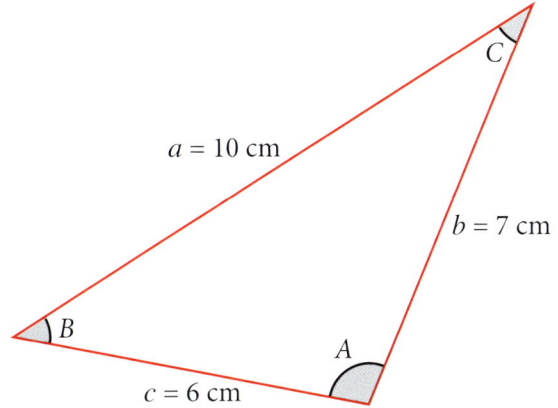

When solving a triangle we must find all unknown sides and angles. We have three side lengths. Use the cosine rule to find one of the angles:

$$a^2 = b^2 + c^2 - 2bc \cos A$$

$$\Rightarrow \cos A = \frac{b^2 + c^2 - a^2}{2bc}$$

$$\cos A = \frac{7^2 + 6^2 - 10^2}{2 \times 7 \times 6} = -\frac{15}{84}$$

$$A = \cos^{-1}\left(-\frac{15}{84}\right) = 100.29°$$

$$= 100° \text{ (3 s.f.)}$$

The sine rule is the simplest way to find the two remaining angles:

$$\frac{\sin A}{a} = \frac{\sin B}{b} = \frac{\sin C}{c}$$

$$\Rightarrow B = \sin^{-1}\left(\frac{b \sin A}{a}\right)$$

$$= \sin^{-1}\left(\frac{7 \sin 100.29}{10}\right)$$

$$= 43.5° \text{ (3 s.f.)}$$

$$C = \sin^{-1}\left(\frac{c \sin A}{a}\right)$$

$$= \sin^{-1}\left(\frac{6 \sin 100.29}{10}\right)$$

$$= 36.2° \text{ (3 s.f.)}$$

(b) Area $= \frac{1}{2} bc \sin A$

Remember, when using this formula, that angle A must lie between the sides b and c.

Area $= \frac{1}{2} \times 7 \times 6 \times \sin 100.29$

$= 20.7$ cm^2

In AS Mathematics you learnt how to use the CAST diagram.

You can use the diagram to find trigonometric ratios for angles with the same **related acute angle**, the acute angle between an angle and the horizontal line.

Worked Example

2. **(a)** Find θ using a calculator if $\tan \theta = \sqrt{3}$.
   (b) Plot θ on a CAST diagram.
   (c) Using your CAST diagram, find $\tan 120°$ and $\tan 240°$, giving your answers as simplified surds.

(a) $\theta = \tan^{-1} \sqrt{3} = 60°$

(b) The CAST diagram below shows the angle $\theta = 60°$. It also shows $120°$ and $240°$.

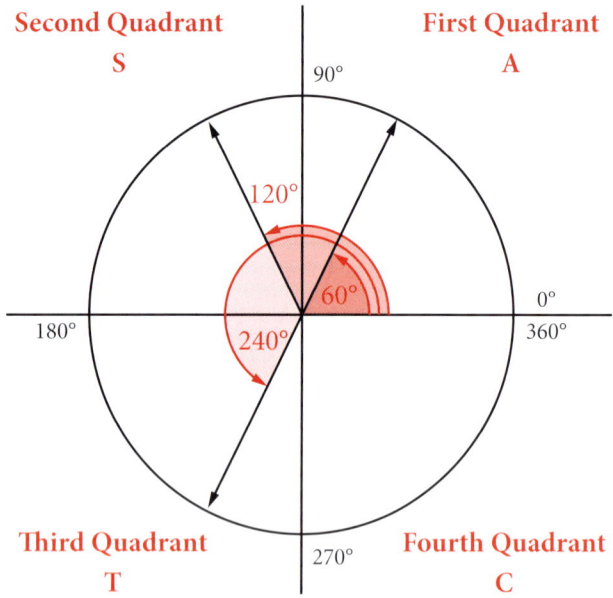

(c) For both $120°$ and $240°$ the related acute angle is $60°$. The angle $120°$ lies in the second quadrant, where tan is negative. The angle $240°$ lies in the third quadrant, where tan is positive.

$\tan 60° = \sqrt{3}$

Therefore:
$\tan 120° = -\sqrt{3}$
$\tan 240° = \sqrt{3}$

Check these results on your calculator.

What you will learn
In this chapter you will learn:

- About radian measure.
- About conversion between radians and degrees.
- How to use the CAST diagram with angles measured in radians.
- How to calculate some properties of a circle, such as arc length and the area of a sector.

In the real world...
Where are you?

In the past it was possible to keep this information private. Today, if you carry a mobile phone, it is always possible for somebody to work out where you are. The method used is called **triangulation**. It relies on the fact that you are usually within range of three or more mobile phone masts.

The strength of the signal measured by each of these masts is used in conjunction with trigonometry to pinpoint the phone's exact location. This technique has been used to catch some criminals, by proving they were in a particular place at a certain time.

It is also used by some parents. A mobile phone app can track the location of their children, to make sure they are not in any danger.

Finally, some insurance companies use the information. If you are involved in a car crash, the insurance company would like to know whether you were using your mobile phone at the time. Triangulation, combined with information about the data being sent and received by your phone, will tell them whether you were being careless at the wheel!

Exercise 3A (Revision)

1. Solve the following triangle, giving all your answers to 1 decimal place:
   $b = 5$ mm, $c = 3$ mm, $A = 149°$

2. Calculate the area of the following triangle to 3 significant figures:
   $b = 9$ cm, $c = 16$ cm, $A = 37°$

3. **(a)** Mark the angles $30°$, $150°$, $210°$ and $330°$ on the same CAST diagram.
   (b) Find $\cos 30°$ using a calculator.
   (c) Using your diagram, write down the values of $\cos 150°$, $\cos 210°$ and $\cos 330°$.

3.2 Converting Between Degrees and Radians

Some key results
Try to remember the key results in the following table. Knowing these results without having to use a calculator will help you to convert quickly between degrees and radians.

3: RADIAN MEASURE

Degrees	0°	30°	45°	60°	90°	180°	360°
Radians	0	$\frac{\pi}{6}$	$\frac{\pi}{4}$	$\frac{\pi}{3}$	$\frac{\pi}{2}$	π	2π

There are 2π radians in a circle (roughly 6.28 radians).
The angles in a triangle add up to π radians (roughly 3.14 radians).

The following facts are useful to remember when converting between units:

$$1 \text{ radian} = \left(\frac{180}{\pi}\right)^{\circ}$$
$$1° = \frac{\pi}{180} \text{ radians}$$

As an approximation, you may find it helpful to remember:

One radian is roughly 57°.

Units
When writing down the units for an angle measured in radians, you may use any of the following styles: π radians, π rads or π^c. Alternatively, you may omit the units, since an angle measured in radians is considered a number. The style often used in the remainder of this book is to omit the units.

Calculator tip
Learn how to put your calculator into RADIANS mode and back into DEGREES mode. These will usually be options under SETUP.

You will need to be in the correct mode whenever you use one of the trigonometric functions on the calculator.

Worked Examples
3. Without using a calculator, convert:
   (a) 4π radians to degrees
   (b) 15° to radians
   (c) 540° to radians

(a) 2π radians = 360°
     so 4π radians = 720°
(b) $30° = \frac{\pi}{6}$ radians
     so $15° = \frac{\pi}{12}$ radians
(c) $180° = \pi$ radians
     and $360° = 2\pi$ radians
     so $540° = 3\pi$ radians

4. Using a calculator, convert:
   (a) 20° to radians
   (b) 135° to radians
   (c) $\frac{5\pi}{4}$ to degrees
   (d) -5π to degrees

To convert from degrees to radians, multiply by $\frac{\pi}{180}$.
(a) $20 \times \frac{\pi}{180} = \frac{\pi}{9}$
(b) $135 \times \frac{\pi}{180} = \frac{3\pi}{4}$

To convert from radians to degrees, multiply by $\frac{180}{\pi}$.
(c) $\frac{5\pi}{4} \times \frac{180}{\pi} = 225°$
(d) $-5\pi \times \frac{180}{\pi} = 900°$

Exercise 3B

1. Using radians mode on your calculator, find:
   (a) $\cos\left(\frac{3\pi}{2}\right)$
   (b) $\sin\left(\frac{5\pi}{4}\right)$
   (c) $\tan\left(-\frac{\pi}{4}\right)$

2. Convert the following angles from degrees to radians, leaving your answer in exact form.
   (a) 30°
   (b) 45°
   (c) 60°
   (d) −60°
   (e) −90°
   (f) −360°
   (g) 540°
   (h) 3600°

3. Convert the following angles from radians to degrees.
   (a) $\frac{2\pi}{3}$
   (b) $\frac{4\pi}{3}$
   (c) $\frac{\pi}{18}$
   (d) $\frac{\pi}{180}$
   (e) $-\frac{\pi}{30}$
   (f) $\frac{5\pi}{2}$
   (g) $\frac{3\pi}{20}$
   (h) 0
   (i) $\frac{4\pi}{9}$

4. Find the following angles in radians, giving your answers to 3 significant figures.
   (a) 33°
   (b) 28°
   (c) 182°
   (d) 329°
   (e) 179°
   (f) 68°
   (g) 595°
   (h) −89°
   (i) −235°

5. Find the following angles in degrees, giving exact answers.
   (a) 4π
   (b) 9π
   (c) $\frac{9\pi}{2}$
   (d) $\frac{\pi}{6}$
   (e) $\frac{5\pi}{6}$
   (f) $-\frac{\pi}{4}$
   (g) 1
   (h) −2.5

3.3 Using Radians with the Area of a Triangle, the Sine Rule and the Cosine Rule

You will be asked to solve triangles using angles measured in radians. To do this, use the sine rule and cosine rule formulae with your calculator in radians mode.

Worked Example

5. Solve the triangle from Worked Example 1, giving all angles in radians.

Set the calculator to radians mode.

$$\cos A = \frac{7^2 + 6^2 - 10^2}{2 \times 7 \times 6} = -\frac{15}{84}$$

$$A = \cos^{-1}\left(-\frac{15}{84}\right) = 1.7503$$

$$= 1.75 \text{ radians (3 s.f.)}$$

$$B = \sin^{-1}\left(\frac{7 \sin 1.7503}{10}\right)$$

$$= 0.760 \text{ radians (3 s.f.)}$$

$$C = \sin^{-1}\left(\frac{6 \sin 1.7503}{10}\right)$$

$$= 0.632 \text{ radians (3 s.f.)}$$

Exercise 3C

1. Find the side length b in the triangle ABC with angles $A = 1.5$ radians and $B = 0.9$ radians. One side a has length 5 cm.

2. Find the angle C in the triangle ABC, if angle $A = 1.4$ radians and two of the sides have lengths $a = 17$ cm and $c = 5$ cm. Give your answer in radians to 3 significant figures.

3. Find the length of the side a in the following triangle to 3 significant figures:
   $b = 8$ m, $c = 8$ m, $A = \frac{2\pi}{3}$ radians

4. Find the size of angle B in this triangle, to one decimal place:
   $a = 10$ cm, $b = 11$ cm, $c = 12$ cm

Exercise 3C...

5. Solve the following triangle. Give angles in radians and give all your answers to 3 significant figures:
   $a = 15$ cm, $b = 2$ cm, $A = 2$ radians

6. Calculate the area of the following triangle to 3 significant figures:
   $d = 7$ cm, $e = 12$ cm, $E = \frac{\pi}{3}$

7. Find the length of the side b to 3 significant figures in the triangle ABC, where $a = 16$ cm, the area is 43 cm² and angle $C = 1$ radian.

8. Find the acute angle C in the triangle ABC, where $a = 5$ cm, $b = 20$ cm and the area is 29 cm². Give your answer in radians to 3 significant figures.

3.4 The CAST Diagram With Radians

You can use the CAST diagram with angles measured in radians. The circle will usually be labelled either from 0 to 2π or from $-\pi$ to π.

Worked Examples

6. (a) Given $\tan \theta = \frac{\sqrt{3}}{3}$, where θ is an acute angle in radians, find θ on your calculator.

   (b) Use a CAST diagram to find:

   (i) $\tan\left(-\frac{\pi}{6}\right)$ (ii) $\tan\left(\frac{5\pi}{6}\right)$

(a) $\theta = \tan^{-1}\left(\frac{\sqrt{3}}{3}\right)$

$\theta = \frac{\pi}{6}$ (from the calculator)

(b) The CAST diagram is shown on the following page.

Note that the related acute angle for both $\frac{5\pi}{6}$ and $-\frac{\pi}{6}$ is $\frac{\pi}{6}$.

This means we can work out the sine, cosine and tangent of these angles using the sine, cosine and tangent of $\frac{\pi}{6}$.

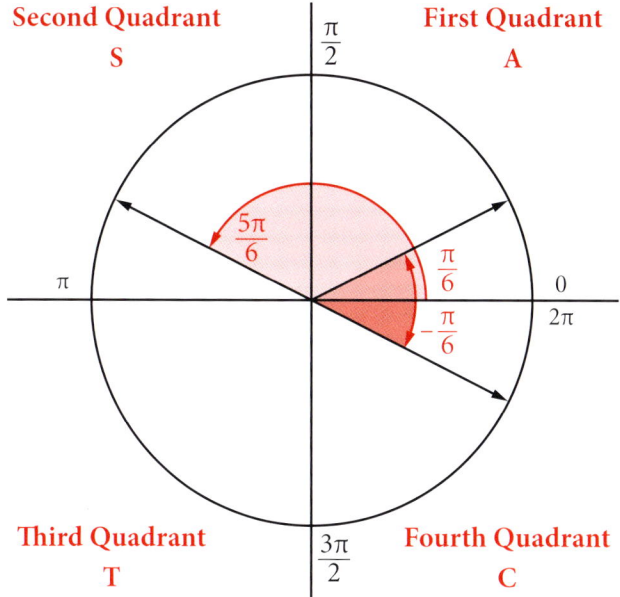
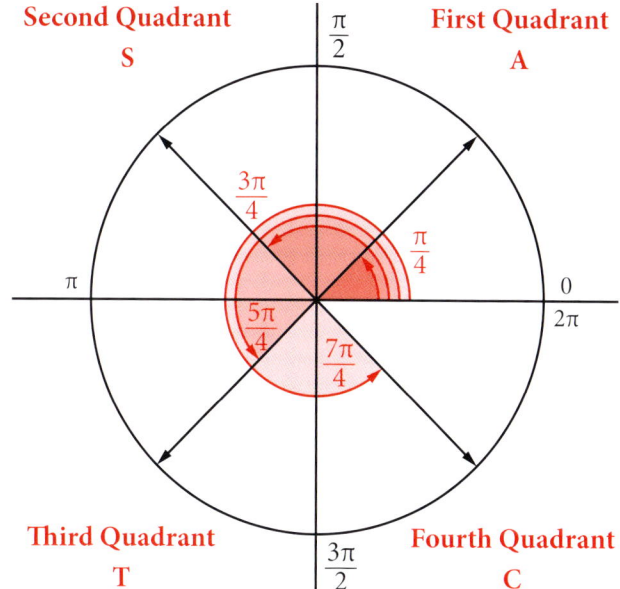

We are told that: $\tan\left(\dfrac{\pi}{6}\right) = \dfrac{\sqrt{3}}{3}$

(i) $-\dfrac{\pi}{6}$ lies in the fourth quadrant, so the tan function is negative. Therefore:

$$\tan\left(-\dfrac{\pi}{6}\right) = -\dfrac{\sqrt{3}}{3}$$

(ii) $\dfrac{5\pi}{6}$ lies in the second quadrant, so the tan function is negative.

$$\tan\left(\dfrac{5\pi}{6}\right) = -\dfrac{\sqrt{3}}{3}$$

Check these results on your calculator.

7. Given $\sin\left(\dfrac{\pi}{4}\right) = \dfrac{\sqrt{2}}{2}$ and $\cos\left(\dfrac{\pi}{4}\right) = \dfrac{\sqrt{2}}{2}$, use a CAST diagram to find the following:

(a) $\sin\left(\dfrac{3\pi}{4}\right)$ and $\cos\left(\dfrac{3\pi}{4}\right)$

(b) $\sin\left(\dfrac{5\pi}{4}\right)$ and $\cos\left(\dfrac{5\pi}{4}\right)$

(c) $\sin\left(\dfrac{7\pi}{4}\right)$ and $\cos\left(\dfrac{7\pi}{4}\right)$

The CAST diagram is as follows:

For $\dfrac{3\pi}{4}, \dfrac{5\pi}{4}$ and $\dfrac{7\pi}{4}$ the related acute angle is $\dfrac{\pi}{4}$.

We have been told that:

$$\sin\left(\dfrac{\pi}{4}\right) = \dfrac{\sqrt{2}}{2} \text{ and } \cos\left(\dfrac{\pi}{4}\right) = \dfrac{\sqrt{2}}{2}$$

(a) $\dfrac{3\pi}{4}$ is in the second quadrant, where only sine is positive. Therefore:

$$\sin\left(\dfrac{3\pi}{4}\right) = \dfrac{\sqrt{2}}{2} \text{ and } \cos\left(\dfrac{3\pi}{4}\right) = -\dfrac{\sqrt{2}}{2}$$

(b) $\dfrac{5\pi}{4}$ is in the third quadrant, where only tan is positive. Therefore:

$$\sin\left(\dfrac{5\pi}{4}\right) = -\dfrac{\sqrt{2}}{2} \text{ and } \cos\left(\dfrac{5\pi}{4}\right) = -\dfrac{\sqrt{2}}{2}$$

(c) $\dfrac{7\pi}{4}$ is in the fourth quadrant, where only cosine is positive. Therefore:

$$\sin\left(\dfrac{7\pi}{4}\right) = -\dfrac{\sqrt{2}}{2} \text{ and } \cos\left(\dfrac{7\pi}{4}\right) = \dfrac{\sqrt{2}}{2}$$

Exercise 3D

1. Sketch the following angles in radians on the same CAST diagram, showing clearly which quadrant they are in.

(a) $\dfrac{\pi}{4}$ (b) $\dfrac{\pi}{3}$ (c) $\dfrac{3\pi}{4}$

(d) $\dfrac{5\pi}{4}$ (e) $\dfrac{11\pi}{8}$ (f) $\dfrac{7\pi}{4}$

Exercise 3D...

2. Given $\sin \theta = \dfrac{\sqrt{3}}{2}$, where θ is an acute angle in radians,
   (a) find θ on your calculator.
   Use a CAST diagram to find:
   (b) $\sin\left(\dfrac{2\pi}{3}\right)$
   (c) $\sin\left(-\dfrac{\pi}{3}\right)$

3. Using a CAST diagram, copy and complete the following table.

θ	$-\dfrac{\pi}{12}$	$\dfrac{\pi}{12}$	$\dfrac{11\pi}{12}$	$\dfrac{13\pi}{12}$	$\dfrac{23\pi}{12}$
$\sin\theta$	$\dfrac{\sqrt{2}-\sqrt{6}}{4}$	$\dfrac{\sqrt{6}-\sqrt{2}}{4}$			
$\cos\theta$		$\dfrac{\sqrt{6}+\sqrt{2}}{4}$			
$\tan\theta$		$2-\sqrt{3}$			

3.5 Arc Length and Sector Area

Length of an arc of a circle

There is an important relationship between the length of an arc of a circle and the angle **subtended** by that arc at the circle's centre.

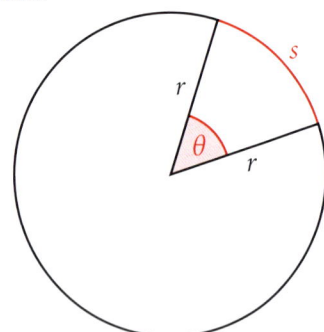

If s is the length of an arc, r is the radius and θ is the angle **measured in radians**, then:

$$s = r\theta$$

Proof of the arc length formula

Note: At the time of writing, the CCEA specification does not require you to know this proof. However, you should remember the formula.

Work out the fraction of the circle occupied by the arc and the angle:

Arc: $\dfrac{s}{2\pi r}$

Angle: $\dfrac{\theta}{360°}$ or $\dfrac{\theta}{2\pi}$ in radians

These fractions must be equal.

Therefore: $\dfrac{s}{2\pi r} = \dfrac{\theta}{2\pi}$

or $s = r\theta$

Worked Examples

8. An arc subtends an angle of 30° at the centre of a circle of radius 15 cm. Calculate the length of the arc to 3 significant figures.

Draw a sketch:

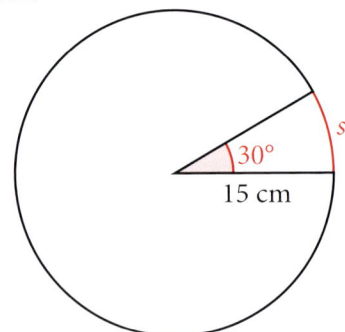

The angle must be converted to radians.

So: $30° = \dfrac{\pi}{6}$ radians

Then: $s = r\theta$

$s = 15 \times \dfrac{\pi}{6}$

$= 7.85$ cm (3 s.f.)

9. Calculate the perimeter of this image used in a computer game. It is based on a circle of radius 5 cm. The angle subtended by the missing region is 50°.

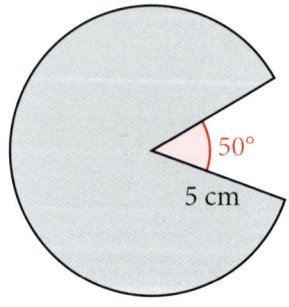

Angle subtended by major arc is:
360 − 50 = 310°
= 5.4105 radians

Arc length:
$$s = r\theta$$
$$= 5 \times 5.41...$$
$$= 27.0526 \text{ cm}$$

The entire perimeter comprises the major arc and two radii. So:
Perimeter = 27.0526 + 5 + 5
= 37.1 cm (3 s.f.)

Area of a sector

There is also a formula for the area of a sector of a circle.

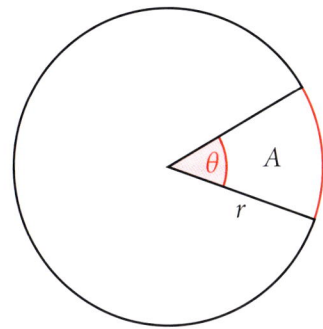

If A is the area of a sector, r is the radius and θ is the angle **measured in radians**, then:

$$A = \frac{1}{2}r^2\theta$$

Proof of the sector area formula

Note: At the time of writing, the CCEA specification does not require you to know this proof. However, you should remember the formula.

Work out the fraction of the circle occupied by the sector:

$$\frac{\theta}{360°} \text{ or } \frac{\theta}{2\pi} \text{ in radians}$$

Area of whole circle: πr^2

Therefore area of sector: $A = \pi r^2 \times \frac{\theta}{2\pi}$

or $A = \frac{1}{2}r^2\theta$

Worked Example

10. A circle has radius 10 cm. Find the exact area of a minor sector of this circle subtending an angle of 60°.

Calculate θ in radians:

$$\theta = 60 \times \frac{\pi}{180} = \frac{\pi}{3}$$

Then:
$$A = \frac{1}{2}r^2\theta$$
$$A = \frac{1}{2} \times 10^2 \times \left(\frac{\pi}{3}\right)$$
$$= \frac{50\pi}{3}$$

Exercise 3E

1. Find the lengths of the arcs of each circle, giving your answers to 3 significant figures.
   (a) Radius 1 cm, angle π radians
   (b) Radius 2 m, angle $\frac{3\pi}{2}$ radians
   (c) Radius 4 cm, angle 60°
   (d) Radius 100 m, angle 120°
   (e) Radius 5 mm, angle 90°

2. Find the areas of the following circle sectors, correct to 3 significant figures. Be careful to convert from degrees to radians if necessary.
   (a) Radius 4 cm, angle subtended 60°
   (b) Radius 10 cm, angle subtended $\frac{\pi}{2}$
   (c) Radius 1 cm, angle subtended $\frac{\pi}{4}$
   (d) Radius 0.2 m, angle subtended 24°
   (e) Radius 9 km, angle subtended 30°

3. The diagram shows a sector of a circle. The arc length is 3 cm and the circle's radius is 8 cm. Find the angle θ in radians.

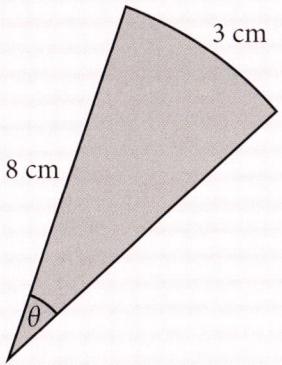

4. The area of a sector of a circle is 12 m² and the angle subtended by this sector at the centre is 45°. Find the radius of the circle.

5. Find the perimeter of the sector of a circle if the radius of the circle is 20 m and the angle subtended by the sector at the centre of the circle is 20°.

3.6 Problems in Context

You may be asked to solve problems involving radian measure in a real-life context. There may be little guidance in the wording of the question about which approach to take. You may need a combination of the techniques you have learnt in this chapter.

Worked Example

11. A public garden, shown in the diagram, is designed as a sector of a circle. A part of the garden with area 30 m² is to be planted with roses. This area is a **segment** of the circle and is bounded by the circumference of the circle and the chord AB. The angle at the centre of the circle is $\frac{4\pi}{9}$ radians.

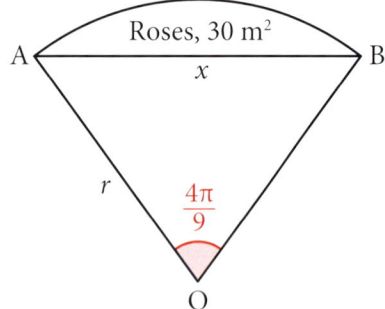

(a) Find the radius r of the circle.
(b) Using the cosine rule find x, the length of the chord AB.
(c) The gardener must put a border around the perimeter of the rose bed. What length of border is required?

(a) The area of the segment is the difference between the area of the sector and the area of the triangle OAB. The area of the sector is $\frac{1}{2}r^2\theta$ and the area of the triangle is $\frac{1}{2}r^2 \sin \theta$.

$$\therefore \frac{1}{2}r^2\left(\frac{4\pi}{9}\right) - \frac{1}{2}r^2 \sin\left(\frac{4\pi}{9}\right) = 30$$

$$\frac{1}{2}r^2\left(\frac{4\pi}{9} - \sin\left(\frac{4\pi}{9}\right)\right) = 30$$

$$\frac{1}{2}r^2\left(\frac{4\pi}{9} - 0.984\ldots\right) = 30$$

$$0.2057r^2 = 30$$

$$r^2 = \frac{30}{0.2057\ldots}$$

$$r^2 = 145.82\ldots$$

$$r = \sqrt{145.82\ldots}$$

$$= 12.0757\ldots$$

$$= 12.1 \text{ m (3 s.f.)}$$

(b) Using the cosine rule:

$$a^2 = b^2 + c^2 - 2bc \cos A$$

$$x^2 = r^2 + r^2 - 2r^2 \cos\left(\frac{4\pi}{9}\right)$$

$$x^2 = 12.0757^2 + 12.0757^2 - 2 \times 12.0757^2 \cos\left(\frac{4\pi}{9}\right)$$

$$x^2 = 241.003\ldots$$

$$x = 15.524\ldots \text{ m}$$

$$x = 15.5 \text{ m (3 s.f.)}$$

(c) To find the arc length AB:

$$s = r\theta$$

$$s = 12.0757\ldots \times \frac{4\pi}{9}$$

$$= 16.861$$

Total perimeter

$$= 2 \times 12.0757\ldots + 16.861$$

$$= 41.012\ldots = 41.0 \text{ m (3 s.f.)}$$

Exercise 3F

1. The solid lines on the diagram are the outline of a Christmas decoration ABC. AB and AC are straight lines, with AB = AC = 9 mm. The curve BC is an arc of a circle, centre O, where OB = OC = 9 mm and O is in the same plane as ABC. The angle BAC is 0.5 radians.

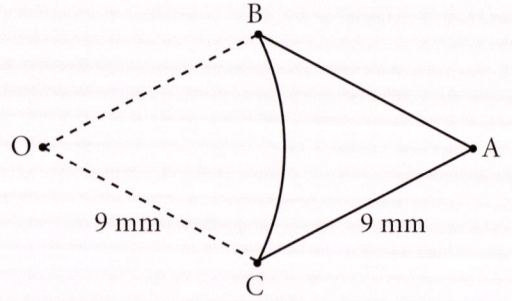

Giving your answers to 3 significant figures:
(a) Find the perimeter of the decoration.
(b) Find the area of the decoration.

Exercise 3F...

2. The diagram shows some of the markings on a sports field. *OAB* is a sector of a circle radius 6 m. The chord *AB* is 4 m long.

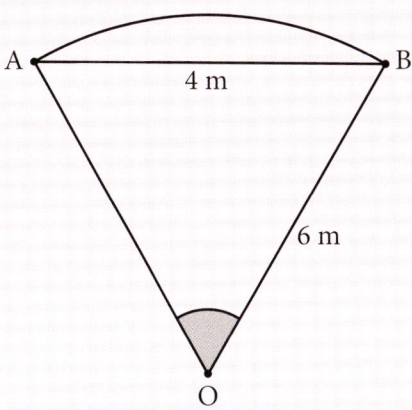

(a) Using the cosine rule, show that $\cos AOB = \frac{7}{9}$.
(b) Hence find the angle *AOB* in radians, giving your answer to 3 decimal places.
(c) Calculate the area of the sector *AOB* to 3 significant figures.
(d) Hence calculate the area of the segment bounded by the chord *AB* and the arc *AB*.

3. The diagram shows the outline of a company logo. It is in the shape of a sector *ABC* of a circle with centre *A* and radius *AB*. The triangle *ABC* is equilateral and has perpendicular height $h = 3$ cm.

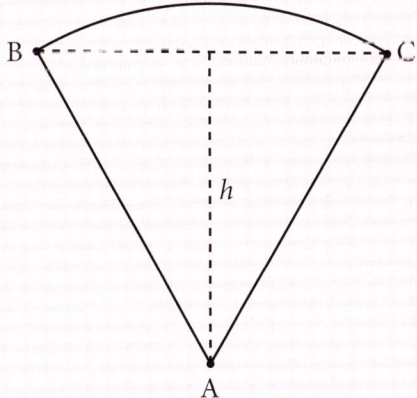

(a) Find, in surd form, the length of *AB*.
(b) Find, in terms of π, the area of the logo.
(c) Prove that the perimeter of the logo is:
$\frac{2\sqrt{3}}{3}(\pi + 6)$ cm

Exercise 3F...

4. A man takes three bites out of a triangular slice of pizza, as shown in the diagram. Each of the man's bites has radius 2 cm.

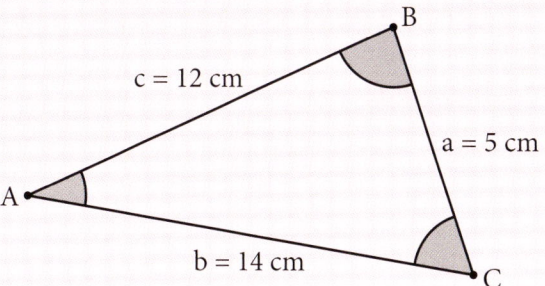

If the lengths of the sides of the triangle were 5, 12 and 14 cm, before the bites were taken, what area of pizza is left?

5. The diagram shows an earring, made of a sector of a circle ABC, with a circle P removed. Circle P just touches the radii AB and AC and the arc BC. AB and AC both measure 12 cm. Angle BAC is $\frac{\pi}{3}$ radians.

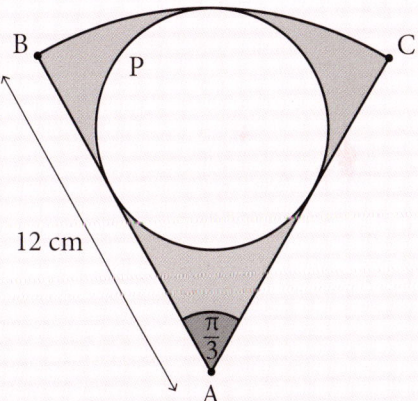

(a) Find the exact area of sector ABC.
(b) Find the radius of circle P.
(c) Find, in cm², the area of metal required to make the earring.

3.7 Summary

Radians are used widely to measure angles in A2 Mathematics, but you will still work in degrees as well.

To convert between degrees and radians, use:
π radians = $180°$

Always use radians when calculating:

- the **length of an arc** using: $s = r\theta$
- the **area of a sector** using: $A = \frac{1}{2}r^2\theta$

The CAST diagram can be used with angles measured in radians.

Questions involving radian measure may be asked in a real-life context. In these questions you should give your answers in the context of the question.

Chapter 4
Coordinate Geometry

4.1 Introduction

Key words
- **Cartesian equation**: An equation linking x and y.
- **Parameter**: A variable that is used to define x and y in a set of equations.
- **Parametric equations**: A set of equations that do not link x and y directly. Instead, x and y are both defined in terms of a parameter.

Before you start
You should know:
- How to substitute values into expressions.
- How to solve simultaneous equations.

Worked Examples

1. $x = \dfrac{t^2}{2000} - 1$ and $y = \dfrac{t - 100}{5}$

   Find the values of x and y if $t = 50$.

   $x = \dfrac{(50)^2}{2000} - 1$

   $= \dfrac{2500}{2000} - 1$

   $= \dfrac{1}{4}$

   $y = \dfrac{50 - 100}{5}$

   $= -\dfrac{50}{5}$

   $= -10$

2. Solve the simultaneous equations:

   $x - 3y = 11 \quad (1)$
   $2x + y = 1 \quad (2)$

   $2 \times (1)$:
   $\quad 2x - 6y = 22 \quad (3)$

   $(2) - (3)$:
   $\quad\quad 7y = -21$
   $\quad \Rightarrow y = -3$

Substitute into (1):
$x - 3(-3) = 11$
$x + 9 = 11$
$x = 2$

What you will learn
In this chapter you will learn how to:
- Understand equations defined by a parameter.
- Convert equations from parametric to Cartesian form.

In the real world...
When an object flies through the air, its position in the horizontal and vertical (x and y respectively) is given by the following equations:

$x = ut \cos \theta$

$y = ut \sin \theta - \tfrac{1}{2}gt^2$

where θ is the angle at which the object is projected into the air. The variable t, which is the time in this case, is the parameter linking both equations.

The study of objects flying through the air is called projectiles. It is a field of mathematics used extensively in sports science and the defence industry – for obvious reasons!

Exercise 4A (Revision)

1. In each case, substitute the value into the expression or equation given.

   (a) $x = 3a^2 + \dfrac{1}{a}$ where $a = 2$

   (b) $y = 12 + st^2$ where $s = 3$; $t = -2$

   (c) $z = \dfrac{1}{x^3}$ where $x = \dfrac{1}{2}$

2. Substitute $p = 3(x + 1)$ and $q = \dfrac{1}{2x}$ into these expressions to find y in terms of x in its simplest form.

   (a) $y = p\left(q - \dfrac{1}{6x}\right)$

Exercise 4A...

(b) $y = \dfrac{3}{2pqx}$

(c) $y = q(p-3)$

3. Solve the following pairs of simultaneous equations.
   (a) $x + 3y = 2$
   $\dfrac{x}{2y} = -2$
   (b) $a + b = 4$
   $a - b = -4$
   (c) $x^2 + 3y^2 = 175$
   $x - 3y = -5$

4.2 Parametric Equations of Curves

Until now, you have dealt with **Cartesian equations**, which link x and y directly, for example $y = x^2 + 3x + 1$.

Sometimes the relationship between x and y is more complicated: it involves a third variable, known as a **parameter**. An example of a set of **parametric equations** would be:

$x = 2t$
$y = 3t^2$

In this case, you could eliminate t to find the Cartesian equation. You will often be asked to find the Cartesian equation, but you should be aware that this is not always possible.

In general, a Cartesian equation is of the form:
$y = f(x)$

Parametric equations take the form:
$y = f(t)$
$x = f(t)$

Worked Example

3. The curve C is defined by the parametric equations:
   $x = 2t$
   $y = t^2$
   (a) Find the coordinates of any points where the curve crosses the coordinate axes.
   (b) Calculate values of x and y for integer values of t from -3 to 3.
   (c) Using the table of values, sketch the curve C.

(a) When $x = 0, t = 0$ and $y = 0$.
When $y = 0, t = 0$ and $x = 0$.
Hence $(0, 0)$ is the only point of intersection with the coordinate axes.

(b) The values of x and y calculated are shown in the table below.

t	-3	-2	-1	0	1	2	3
x	-6	-4	-2	0	2	4	6
y	9	4	1	0	1	4	9

(c)

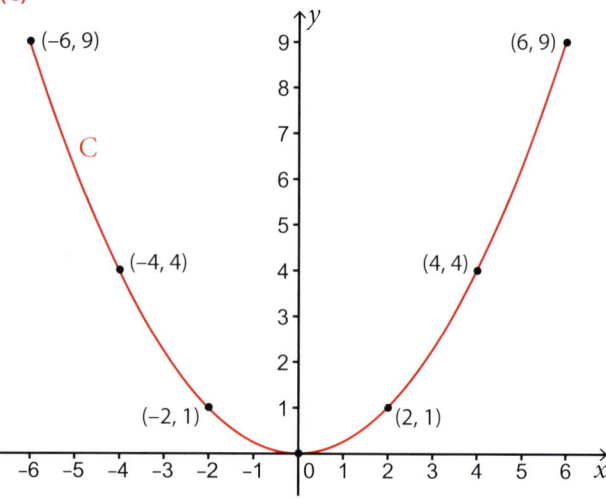

The parameter can be any variable, for example t, θ or s.

Worked Example

4. The curve C is defined by the parametric equations:
   $x = \cos 2\theta, \quad y = \sin\theta \quad -\dfrac{\pi}{2} \le \theta \le \dfrac{\pi}{2}.$
   (a) Find the coordinates of the three points of intersection with the coordinate axes.
   (b) What are the two possible y-coordinates when $x = -1$?
   (c) Using values of θ between $-\dfrac{\pi}{2}$ and $\dfrac{\pi}{2}$, sketch the curve.

(a) When $y = 0, \sin\theta = 0 \Rightarrow \theta = 0$

When $\theta = 0, x = \cos(0) = 1$
So the curve crosses the x-axis at $(1, 0)$.

When $x = 0, \cos 2\theta = 0$
$\Rightarrow 2\theta = -\dfrac{\pi}{2}$ or $2\theta = \dfrac{\pi}{2}$
$\Rightarrow \theta = -\dfrac{\pi}{4}$ or $\theta = \dfrac{\pi}{4}$

When $\theta = -\dfrac{\pi}{4}, y = \sin\left(-\dfrac{\pi}{4}\right) = -\dfrac{\sqrt{2}}{2} \approx -0.707$

When $\theta = \dfrac{\pi}{4}, y = \sin\left(\dfrac{\pi}{4}\right) = \dfrac{\sqrt{2}}{2} \approx 0.707$

So the curve crosses the y-axis at $(0, 0.707)$ and $(0, -0.707)$.

(b) When $x = -1$, $\cos 2\theta = -1$
  $\Rightarrow 2\theta = -\pi$ or $2\theta = \pi$
  $\Rightarrow \theta = -\frac{\pi}{2}$ or $\theta = \frac{\pi}{2}$

  When $\theta = -\frac{\pi}{2}, y = \sin\left(-\frac{\pi}{2}\right) = -1$

  When $\theta = \frac{\pi}{2}, y = \sin\left(\frac{\pi}{2}\right) = 1$

  So the curve passes through the points $(-1, 1)$ and $(-1, -1)$.

(c) Using the information from parts (a) and (b) above, we can construct a table of values and then sketch the graph.

θ	$-\frac{\pi}{2}$	$-\frac{\pi}{4}$	0	$\frac{\pi}{4}$	$\frac{\pi}{2}$
x	-1	0	1	0	-1
y	-1	-0.707	0	0.707	1

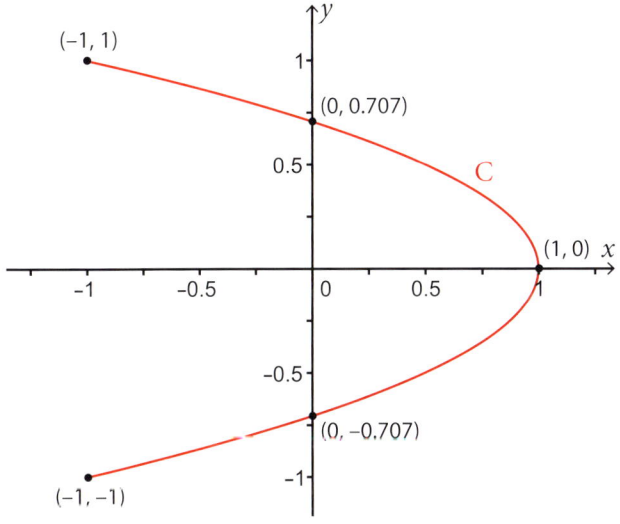

Exercise 4B

1. Find the coordinates of the points where the following parametric curves intersect the coordinate axes.
   (a) $x = 4t$, $y = t^2 + 1$, $0 \leq t \leq 5$
   (b) $x = t^2$, $y = t - 1$, $-5 \leq t \leq 5$
   (c) $x = t^3$, $y = t - 2$, $-5 \leq t \leq 5$
   (d) $x = \frac{t}{2} - 1$, $y = 2t + 1$, $-5 \leq t \leq 5$
   (e) $x = t^4$, $y = 2t^3$, $-5 \leq t \leq 5$
   (f) $x = \sin\theta$, $y = 2\theta^2$, $0 \leq \theta \leq \pi$
   (g) $x = \theta$, $y = 2\cos\theta$, $0 \leq \theta \leq \pi$
   (h) $x = \cos\theta$, $y = 2\sin 2\theta$, $-\pi \leq \theta \leq \pi$
   (i) $x = \cos\theta$, $y = \sin 3\theta$, $-\pi \leq \theta \leq \pi$
   (j) $x = \sqrt{\theta}$, $y = \sin\theta$, $-\pi \leq \theta \leq \pi$

Exercise 4B...

   (k) $x = t^3 - 1$, $y = 2t$, $-5 \leq t \leq 5$
   (l) $x = \cos\theta$, $y = 2\sin\theta + 1$, $-\pi \leq \theta \leq \pi$

2. The parametric equations for a circle of radius 1 are: $x = \cos\theta$, $y = \sin\theta$ for $0 \leq \theta < 2\pi$. The diagram shows this circle and various points on its circumference.

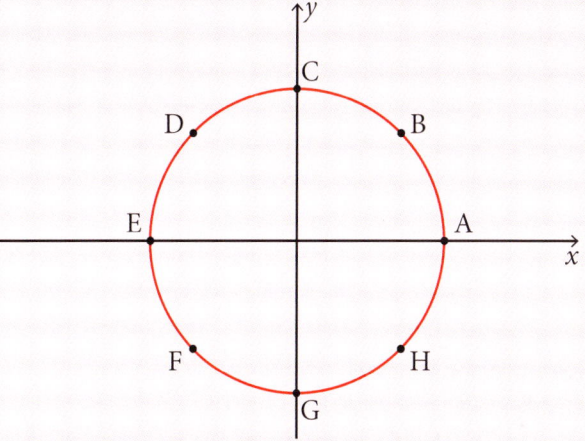

Copy and complete the table below.

	A	B	C	D	E	F	G	H
θ	0		$\frac{\pi}{2}$					
x		$\frac{\sqrt{2}}{2}$			-1			
y		$\frac{\sqrt{2}}{2}$					0	

3. The diagram shows a part of the curve C given by the parametric equations: $x = \tan t$, $y = 2\sin t - 1$ where $0 \leq t \leq \pi$.

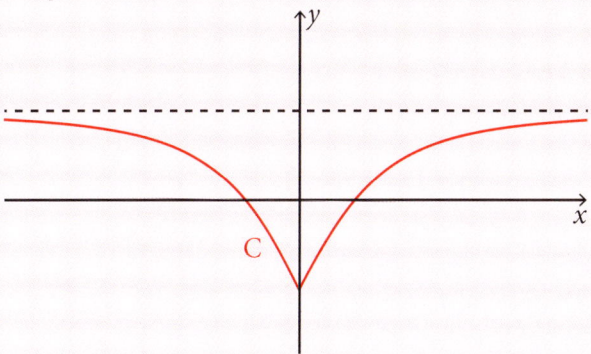

   (a) Calculate the coordinates of the point where C intersects the y-axis.
   (b) Calculate the coordinates of the points where C intersects the x-axis.
   (c) By considering the maximum possible value of y, write down the equation of the asymptote shown.

Exercise 4B...

4. The diagram shows a sketch of the curve C with parametric equations:
$x = 12\cos t$, $y = 6\sin 2t$, $0 \leq t \leq \dfrac{\pi}{2}$

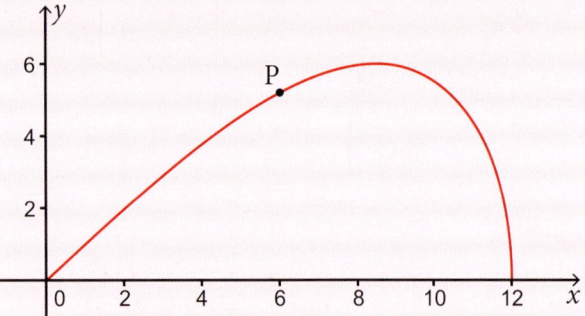

The point P lies on C and has x-coordinate 6.
(a) Find the value of t at the point P.
(b) Find the y-coordinate of the point P.

5. The diagram shows the curve C given by:
$x = \dfrac{1}{2-t}$, $y = \dfrac{3-2t}{2-t^2}$
and three points, O, A and B, on the curve. Point O is at the origin, point A lies on the x-axis and point B has y-coordinate 1.

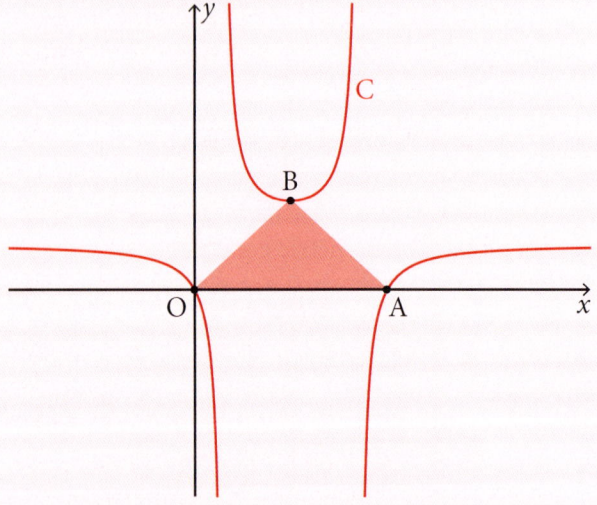

(a) Work out the x-coordinate of A.
(b) Work out the x-coordinate of B.
(c) Work out the area of the triangle ABO.

6. The diagram that follows shows the curve with parametric equations: $x = at^2 - 3$, $y = 4at$ where a is a non-zero constant.

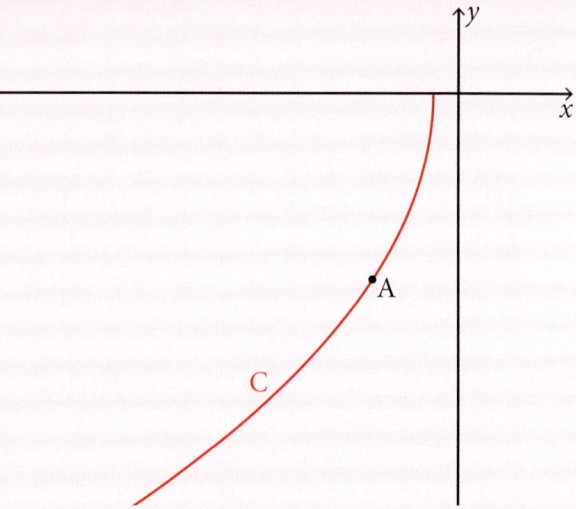

The point A lies on C and has coordinates $(-8, -20)$.
(a) Calculate the value of t at point A.
(b) Calculate the value of a.
(c) Work out the coordinates of the point where C meets the x-axis.

7. A straight line has parametric equations: $x = a + bt$, $y = a^2 t + 2b$. The line crosses the y-axis at the point $(0, 36)$ when $t = 2$. Find the two possible values of a and the corresponding values of b.

8. The curve C is given by the parametric equations: $x = \theta \sin \theta$, $y = \theta \cos \theta$.
(a) Copy and complete the following table of values, using increments of $\dfrac{\pi}{4}$ for θ. Give your x and y values to 2 decimal places.

	P1	P2	P3	P4	P5	P6	P7	P8	P9	P10
θ	0	$\dfrac{\pi}{4}$	$\dfrac{\pi}{2}$	$\dfrac{3\pi}{4}$	π					$\dfrac{9\pi}{4}$
x										
y										

(b) Sketch the curve C, marking each point from P1 to P10.

4.3 Conversion Between Parametric and Cartesian Forms

As stated in the previous section, it is often possible to eliminate the parameter from a set of parametric equations to obtain the Cartesian equation.

Worked Example

5. Find the Cartesian equations of the following curves:
(a) $x = 1 - t, y = 3t^2$
(b) $x = -\sin\theta, y = \cos\theta$

(a) $x = 1 - t \Rightarrow t = 1 - x$

Substitute into $y = 3t^2$:
$y = 3(1-x)^2$

Expanding brackets:
$y = 3x^2 - 6x + 3$

(b) $x = -\sin\theta \Rightarrow x^2 = \sin^2\theta$
$y = \cos\theta \Rightarrow y^2 = \cos^2\theta$
$\sin^2\theta + \cos^2\theta \equiv 1$
$\therefore x^2 + y^2 = 1$
This is the equation of a circle, with centre $(0, 0)$ and radius 1.

> **Note:** You will often use trigonometric identities, as above, when converting between Cartesian and parametric forms.

You may be given a Cartesian equation and asked to find parametric equations. There is often more than one answer, so you may be given one of the parametric equations.

Worked Example

6. Find parametric equations for the curve $y = x\sqrt{4 - x^2}$ where $x = 2\sin\theta$.

$y = x\sqrt{4 - x^2}$
$= 2\sin\theta\sqrt{4 - 4\sin^2\theta}$
$= 2\sin\theta\sqrt{4(1 - \sin^2\theta)}$
$= 2\sin\theta\sqrt{4\cos^2\theta}$
$= 2\sin\theta \times 2\cos\theta$
$= 4\sin\theta\cos\theta$

> **Note:** In Chapter 8 you will learn that this can be written $y = 2\sin 2\theta$.

Exercise 4C

1. In each case, eliminate the parameter to obtain a Cartesian equation.
(a) $x = 2 + t,\quad y = 4 - 2t$
(b) $x = \dfrac{1}{t},\quad y = 4t^2$
(c) $x = 5t + 1,\quad y = 100t^2 - 2$
(d) $x = 2t^2,\quad y = \dfrac{t^3}{2}$
(e) $x = \dfrac{t^2}{2},\quad y = \dfrac{3}{t}$
(f) $x = \dfrac{t+1}{t-1},\quad y = 3t^2$
(g) $x = \cos\theta,\quad y = 1 - \sin\theta$
(h) $x = 4\cos\left(\theta - \dfrac{\pi}{4}\right), y = 2\sqrt{\sin\left(\theta - \dfrac{\pi}{4}\right)}$
(i) $x = \sin 2\theta,\quad y = 3\cos 2\theta$

2. A quadratic curve is defined by the parametric equations: $y = 3t^2, x = 4t$. Find a Cartesian equation for the curve.

3. A circle has the parametric equations:
$x = -4 + 5\sin\theta, y = 3 + 5\cos\theta$.
(a) Eliminate θ to obtain the Cartesian equation.
(b) Write down the coordinates of the centre of this circle, and its radius.

4. An ellipse is given by the parametric equations:
$x = 2 - 2\sin t, y = 4 - 4\cos t$.
(a) Eliminate t to obtain a Cartesian equation.
(b) Hence find where the curve touches the x-axis.
(c) Where does the curve touch the y-axis?

5. A curve is defined by the Cartesian equation:
$y = \sqrt{\dfrac{7-x}{2}}$

Using $x = 5 - 2\sin\theta$, find a pair of parametric equations for the curve.

6. The curve C is given by the parametric equations: $x = 2a\sin t, y = 1 + a\cos t$. C crosses the x-axis at the point $(2\sqrt{3}, 0)$. Find the two possible values of a.

7. The curve C has parametric equations:
$x = \sin^2 t, y = \cos t$.
(a) Eliminate t to obtain a Cartesian equation for C.

Exercise 4C...

(b) Explain why the value of x cannot be greater than 1, firstly using the parametric equations, then using the Cartesian equation.

8. (a) Given $x = \dfrac{1}{t^3 - 1}$ find expressions for x^3 and x^2.
   (b) Given also $y = \dfrac{t}{t^3 - 1}$, find an expression for y^3.
   (c) Show that $y^3 = x^3 + x^2$ is a Cartesian equivalent to the parametric equations:
   $$x = \dfrac{1}{t^3 - 1}, \; y = \dfrac{t}{t^3 - 1}$$

9. The curve f is shown in the diagram below.

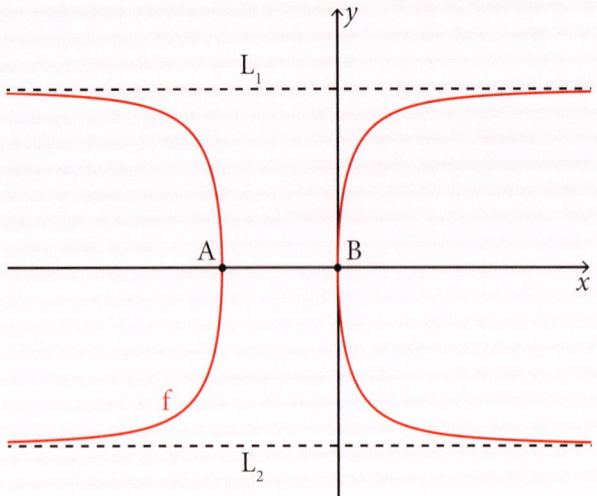

(a) The Cartesian equation of f is:
$$\left(\dfrac{3}{x+3}\right)^2 + \left(\dfrac{y}{3}\right)^2 = 1$$
Given that $y = 3\cos t$, find the second parametric equation.
(b) Given also that $0 \leq t \leq 2\pi$, find the two values of t at the points A and B, where the curve crosses the x-axis.
(c) The coordinates of B are $(0, 0)$. Find the coordinates of A.
(d) What are the maximum and minimum possible values of y? Hence write down the equations of the asymptotes L_1 and L_2.

10. The Cartesian equation of a straight line L is: $2x + y = 2$. L can be represented using parametric equations in various ways.
    (a) If $x = \sin^2 \theta$, find y in terms of θ.
    (b) If $y = \dfrac{4}{t+1}$, find x in terms of t.

11. The equation of a curve is $x - y = 2xy$. Given $y = tx$, substitute this into the equation of the curve to obtain the two parametric equations $x = f(t)$ and $y = g(t)$.

4.4 Parametric Equations in Modelling

Parametric equations can be used to model real-life situations. They are commonly used in relation to the trajectory of a projectile. In these cases, the parameter t represents time; x and y are the horizontal and vertical position of the projectile respectively.

You may be asked to consider such a model and you will apply all of the techniques discussed above. You may also have to discuss limitations of the model and possible refinements to it.

Worked Example

7. A ball is thrown from the window of a house as shown in the diagram.

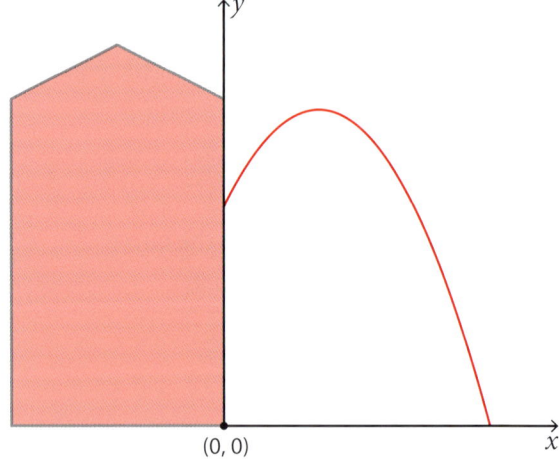

The ball's horizontal position and vertical position are modelled respectively by the formulae:
$$x = 3t \quad (1)$$
$$y = 4 + 6t - \dfrac{1}{2}gt^2 \quad (2)$$

where t is the time in seconds and g is the acceleration due to gravity. In this model it is assumed that $g = 10 \text{ ms}^{-2}$. At the time the ball is thrown $t = 0$ and $x = 0$.

(a) From what height above the ground was the ball thrown?
(b) Eliminate t to form a Cartesian equation.
(c) Hence find how far the ball lands from the base of

the house.
(d) How long does it take for the ball to reach the ground?
(e) What assumptions have been made in this model?

(a) $y = 4 + 6t - \frac{1}{2}gt^2$

Since $g = 10$:
$y = 4 + 6t - 5t^2$

When $t = 0, y = 4$.
So the ball is thrown from a height of 4 m.

(b) From equation (1):
$t = \frac{x}{3}$
Substitute for t in (2):
$y = 4 + 6\left(\frac{x}{3}\right) - 5\left(\frac{x}{3}\right)^2$
$y = 4 + 2x - \frac{5}{9}x^2$

(c) When $y = 0$:
$0 = 4 + 2x - \frac{5}{9}x^2$
$\frac{5}{9}x^2 - 2x - 4 = 0$
$5x^2 - 18x - 36 = 0$
$x = \frac{18 \pm \sqrt{18^2 - 4(5)(-36)}}{2(5)}$
$x = 5.03$ m or $x = -1.43$ m (ignore)
So $x = 5.03$ m

(d) From equation (1):
$t = \frac{x}{3}$
$t = \frac{5.03...}{3}$
$t = 1.68$ s (3 s.f.)

(e) Assumptions made: $g = 10$ ms^{-2}; air resistance is negligible.

Exercise 4D

1. The horizontal and vertical positions, x and y, of a baseball after being struck, are given by:
$x = ut\cos\theta - wt$
$y = ut\sin\theta - \frac{1}{2}gt^2 + h$

where t is the time in seconds after the ball is

Exercise 4D...

struck, u is the ball's initial velocity in ms^{-1}, θ is the ball's angle of projection, w is the wind speed against the batter, g is the acceleration due to gravity and h is the height at which the ball is struck.
The baseball is hit when it is 1 m above the ground and leaves the bat with initial velocity u of 50 ms^{-1} and at an angle of elevation θ of 30°. A 3 ms^{-1} wind is blowing in the horizontal direction against the batter. You may assume $g = 10$ ms^{-2} for this question.
The boundary fence is 120 m from the batsman.
(a) Calculate the time at which the ball reaches the boundary.
(b) Given that the boundary fence is 10 m high, determine whether the ball clears the fence.

2. The entrance of a tunnel is modelled using the parametric equations:
$x = \cos t, y = 2\sqrt{\sin t}$ for $0 \le t \le \pi$.
(a) Find the coordinates of the points where this curve crosses the coordinate axes.
(b) Sketch the curve.

3. To film a scene for an action movie, a remote-controlled car is driven off a 50 m high cliff with a horizontal speed of 5 ms^{-1}.

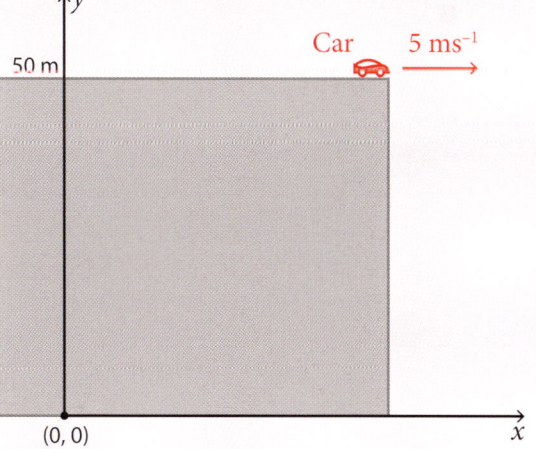

The car's horizontal and vertical distance from the cliff edge are modelled respectively by the parametric equations: $x = 5t + 10$, $y = 50 - 5t^2$.
(a) At time $t = 0$ the car is moving at 5 ms^{-1} and is on the edge of the cliff. How long does the car take to hit the ground?

Exercise 4D...

(b) How far from the cliff is the car when it hits the ground?
(c) Find an equation linking x and y.
(d) What factors might affect the accuracy of the equations used in this model?

4.5 Summary

In a set of parametric equations, x and y are not linked directly. Instead they are both defined in terms of a parameter.

To draw a sketch of a curve defined by parametric equations, construct a table of values. Instead of having only two rows for x and y, this table will have an extra row for the parameter (often t).

It may be possible to eliminate the parameter to obtain the Cartesian equation.

Given a Cartesian equation, you can find an equivalent set of parametric equations. There may be more than one way to do this.

Parametric equations can be used to model real-life situations, especially involving projectiles.

Chapter 5
Sequences and Series

5.1 Introduction

Key words

- **Sequence**: A list of numbers, generated by some rule. Another word for a sequence is a **progression**.
- **Series**: The summation of a sequence of numbers.
- **Term**: One of the numbers in a sequence or series.
- **Recurrence formula** or **recurrence relationship** or **recursion relationship**: A formula for a sequence, in which each term is defined as some function of the previous terms.
- **Oscillate**: A sequence oscillates if its terms alternately go up and down.
- **Converge**: A sequence converges if the terms get closer and closer to a particular value. A series converges if there is a non-infinite value for the sum.
- **Diverge**: A sequence or series diverges if it doesn't converge.
- **Arithmetic series**: A series in which the **difference** between consecutive terms is constant.
- **Geometric Series**: A series in which the **ratio** of consecutive terms is constant.

Before you start

You should know how to:

- Solve linear equations.
- Solve quadratic equations.
- Solve simultaneous equations in 2 and 3 variables.
- Find the nth term of a sequence.

Worked Examples

1. Solve the following equation to find x:
$4x - 1 = 3(2x - 2)$

    Expand brackets:
    $4x - 1 = 6x - 6$

    Re-arrange:
    $2x = 5$
    $x = \dfrac{5}{2}$

2. Solve the following equation to find x:
$x^2 - 4x - 21 = 0$

    Two numbers whose sum is -4 and product is -21 are 3 and -7. So:
    $(x - 7)(x + 3) = 0$

    Either $x - 7 = 0$ or $x + 3 = 0$

    Therefore $x = 7$ or $x = -3$

3. Solve the following simultaneous equations for a and b:
$2a - 3b = -17$ (1)
$3a - 2b = -8$ (2)

    Multiply (1) by 3:
    $6a - 9b = -51$ (3)

    Multiply (2) by 2:
    $6a - 4b = -16$ (4)

    Subtract (3) from (4):
    $5b = 35$
    $b = 7$

    Substitute into (1):
    $2a - 3(7) = -17$
    $2a = 4$
    $a = 2$

    Now check these values by substituting them into equation (2):
    $3(2) - 2(7) = 6 - 14 = -8$, which is correct.

4. Find the nth term of the following sequence:
2, 6, 10, 14, …   (1)

    The **common difference** is 4. This means that the nth term contains $4n$.

    The sequence whose n^{th} term is $4n$ is:
    4, 8, 12, 16, …

    To get the nth term of (1), therefore, we adjust by subtracting 2:
    $4n - 2$

    Check this formula:
    When $n = 1$, the formula gives $4(1) - 2 = 2$
    When $n = 2$, the formula gives $4(2) - 2 = 6$
    When $n = 3$, the formula gives $4(3) - 2 = 10$

    The formula $4n - 2$ is giving the correct results.

PURE MATHEMATICS FOR CCEA A2

What you will learn

In this chapter you will learn how to:

- Use recurrence relations to form sequences.
- Recognise an arithmetic progression; use the formulae for the general term and the sum.
- Recognise a geometric progression; use the formulae for the general term and the sum.
- Understand sigma notation.

In the real world...

Mathematical sequences crop up in surprising places, particularly in nature.

The nautilus is a shellfish and one of the oldest known animals on Earth. It has been in existence for half a billion years.

One of the reasons for the survival of this species over such a long time is the ingenious design of the creature's shell. The shell grows in a spiral shape and is divided into chambers, with the fish living in the newest, largest chamber. All the older chambers are used for buoyancy. The nautilus can raise or lower itself in the water by adjusting the amount of air in these chambers, and this technique enables it to reach waters where the temperature is suitable and there is sufficient food.

Each time the nautilus grows a new chamber, the new one is larger than the one before. When the size of each chamber is compared with the last, a remarkably consistent mathematical sequence is formed: a geometric progression.

Exercise 5A (Revision)

1. Solve the following linear equations.
   (a) $2x - 3 = 1$
   (b) $6(w + 1) = -18$
   (c) $z = 4(2z + 3)$
   (d) $2(y - 1) = 3(2y + 1)$
   (e) $\dfrac{1}{v + 2} = \dfrac{3}{4v + 5}$

2. Solve the following quadratic equations.
   (a) $x^2 + 6x - 7 = 0$
   (b) $(x + 10)(x - 8) = 0$
   (c) $x^2 - 6x = -8$
   (d) $x^2 = 2x - 1$
   (e) $(1 - x)^2 = 3x + 1$

Exercise 5A...

3. Solve the following sets of simultaneous equations.
   (a) $-5x + 5y = -25$
       $5x - 2y = 40$
   (b) $6x - 4y = 64$
       $-4x - 2y = -38$
   (c) $x - 10y = 71$
       $x - 8y = 55$
   (d) $-9x + 4y = 14$
       $-6x + 9y = 3$
   (e) $-2x + y = 3$
       $8x - 10y = 30$
   (f) $-4x - 7y - 3z = 19$
       $-6x - 2y + z = -8$
       $-2x - 2y + 7z = -12$

4. Find the nth term of the following sequences.
   (a) $1, 4, 7, 10, \ldots$
   (b) $5, 7, 9, 11, \ldots$
   (c) $-3, 1, 5, 9, \ldots$
   (d) $-5, -15, -25, -35, \ldots$
   (e) $17, -3, -23, -43, \ldots$

5.2 Definitions

A **sequence** is a list of numbers that follows some rule. Each number in the list is called a **term**.

A **series** is the summation of all the terms in a sequence.

For example, a sequence could be:

$1, \dfrac{1}{2}, \dfrac{1}{4}, \dfrac{1}{8}, \ldots$

The corresponding series would be:

$1 + \dfrac{1}{2} + \dfrac{1}{4} + \dfrac{1}{8} + \ldots$

Sequences and series do not have to be infinite. For example, a sequence with only 5 terms is:

$17, 15, 13, 11, 9$

5.3 Sequences Given By a Formula

You have already revised finding the nth term for a sequence. We often denote this as u_n.

Sometimes you will be given the formula and asked to find particular terms.

5: SEQUENCES AND SERIES

Worked Examples

5. Find the second, third and fourth terms, u_2, u_3 and u_4, for the sequence: $u_n = -4n + 6$.

   When $n = 2$, the formula gives:
   $u_2 = -4(2) + 6$
   $ = -2$

   When $n = 3$:
   $u_3 = -4(3) + 6$
   $ = -6$

   When $n = 4$:
   $u_4 = -4(4) + 6$
   $ = -10$

6. Find u_2 and u_8 where: $u_n = -(n+2)^2$

   $u_2 = -(2+2)^2$
   $ = -16$
   $u_8 = -(8+2)^2$
   $ = -100$

Sometimes you must find which term of the sequence gives a particular value.

Worked Example

7. The nth term of a sequence is given by the formula: $u_n = (n-1)(n-5)$. Which terms of the sequence give the result $u_n = -3$?

   $(n-1)(n-5) = -3$

   Expand brackets:
   $n^2 - 6n + 5 = -3$

   Re-arrange:
   $n^2 - 6n + 8 = 0$

   Factorise:
   $(n-2)(n-4) = 0$
   $ n = 2$ or $n = 4$

   Check the answers:
   When $n = 2$, $u_n = (2-1)(2-5) = (1)(-3) = -3$
   When $n = 4$, $u_n = (4-1)(4-5) = (3)(-1) = -3$
   The second and fourth terms of the sequence are both -3.

Sometimes n may take an algebraic value.

Worked Example

8. A sequence is defined by the formula: $u_n = n^2$
   Find the term in the sequence when $n = 3k + 1$

   $u_{3k+1} = (3k+1)^2$
   $\phantom{u_{3k+1}} = 9k^2 + 6k + 1$

You may be asked to find specific constants in the formula for a sequence. Where more than one constant is required, this involves solving simultaneous equations.

Worked Example

9. The terms of a sequence are given by the formula: $u_n = 2pn + qn^2$ where p and q are constants. Find p and q, given that $u_3 = 48$ and $u_4 = 72$.

   Given that $u_3 = 48$, therefore:
   $2p(3) + q(3)^2 = 48$
   $6p + 9q = 48$

   Divide by 3:
   $2p + 3q = 16$ \quad (1)

   Given that $u_4 = 72$, therefore:
   $2p(4) + q(4)^2 = 72$
   $8p + 16q = 72$

   Divide by 8:
   $p + 2q = 9$
   $p = 9 - 2q$ \quad (2)

   Substitute (2) into (1):
   $2(9 - 2q) + 3q = 16$
   $18 - q = 16$
   $q = 2$

   Substitute into (2):
   $p = 9 - 2(2) = 5$

   So $p = 5, q = 2$.

Some sequences **oscillate**. An oscillating sequence is one whose terms alternately go up and down.

Worked Example

10. A sequence is defined by the formula: $u_n = 2(-1)^n$
    Find the first 4 terms.

    When $n = 1$, $u_n = 2(-1)^1 = -2$

    When $n = 2$, $u_n = 2(-1)^2 = 2$

    When $n = 3$, $u_n = 2(-1)^3 = -2$

    When $n = 4$, $u_n = 2(-1)^4 = 2$

Exercise 5B

1. Find the first 4 terms of each sequence.
   (a) $u_n = 2n - 3$
   (b) $u_n = 10 - 3n^2$
   (c) $u_n = (n - 2)^2$
   (d) $u_n = n^2 + 3n - 6$
   (e) $u_n = (n - 3)(n + 2)$
   (f) $u_n = n^3 + 1$
   (g) $u_n = (1 - n^2)(1 - n)$
   (h) $u_n = 2pn^2 + qn$ where $p = 2, q = 3$
   (i) $u_n = (-1)^n (1 + n)$
   (j) $u_n = \dfrac{2 + 3n}{3 + 2n}$

2. Find which term of the sequence gives the following values.
   (a) $u_n = 4n + 1$, $u_n = 45$
   (b) $u_n = 9 - 3n^2$, $u_n = -39$
   (c) $u_n = (2n + 1)^2$, $u_n = 49$
   (d) $u_n = n^2 - 3n + 3$, $u_n = 13$
   (e) $u_n = (n - 1)(n + 4)$, $u_n = 50$
   (f) $u_n = 8 - n^3$, $u_n = 0$
   (g) $u_n = (n^2 + 1)(n - 3)$, $u_n = 0$
   (h) $u_n = (p + q)n + pqn^2$
      where $p = 1$, $q = 2$, $u_n = 14$
   (i) $u_n = n(-1)^n$, $u_n = 10$
   (j) $u_n = \dfrac{1 + 2n}{3 + 4n}$, $u_n = \dfrac{7}{15}$

3. A sequence has the general term $u_n = an - 7$. Given that the fourth term of the sequence is 9, find the value of a.

4. The nth term of a sequence is defined by the formula: $u_n = a(2n - b)$. Given that the fourth term is 9 and the fifth term is 15, find the values of a and b.

5. The nth term of a sequence is defined by the formula: $u_n = \dfrac{n - 1}{an - b}$ where a and b are constants. Given $u_3 = \dfrac{2}{9}$ and $u_4 = \dfrac{3}{13}$, find the values of a and b.

6. The first three terms of a sequence are 6, 12 and 20. The sequence is defined by the formula: $u_n = an^2 + bn + c$. Given a, b and c are all positive constants, find their values.

Exercise 5B...

7. A sequence is defined by the formula: $u_n = n^2 - 4n + 8$. Show that all the terms of the sequence are positive.
   (Hint: complete the square.)

8. Find the smallest term in the sequence defined by the formula: $u_n = n^2 - 6n + 4$.
   (Hint: complete the square.)

9. (a) Show that all the terms of the sequence $u_n = 4n - 7$ are odd numbers.
   (b) Give a formula for a sequence in which all the terms are even numbers.

10. The first, second and third terms of a sequence are –1, 4 and 9. Find a formula for the nth term that would give these terms.

11. A sequence is defined by the formula: $u_n = k(k - 1)$ where $k = 3n - 2$. Show that all the terms in this sequence are multiples of 3.

5.4 Recurrence Relationships

Recurrence relationships for a sequence often take the form:

$$u_{n+1} = f(u_n)$$

or

$$u_n = f(u_{n-1})$$

That is, each term is some function of the previous term.

Recurrence relationships are also known as **recursion formulae**.

Worked Example

11. A sequence is defined by the recurrence formula: $u_n = u_{n-1} + 3$. Given $u_1 = 7$, find the first 4 terms.

    $u_1 = 7$
    $u_2 = u_1 + 3 = 10$
    $u_3 = u_2 + 3 = 13$
    $u_4 = u_3 + 3 = 16$

Sometimes you may be asked to find the formula for the recurrence relationship. Sometimes this may involve trial and improvement.

5: SEQUENCES AND SERIES

Worked Example

12. Find the recurrence formula for the following sequence: 1, 3, 7, 15, 31, …

Since the first two terms are 1 and 3, we try:
$u_{n+1} = 3u_n$

However this does not work, because the third term would be 9.

Try: $u_{n+1} = u_n + 2$

This does not work either, since the third term would be 5.

Try: $u_{n+1} = 2u_n + 1$

This gives the correct sequence: 1, 3, 7, 15, 31, …

Sometimes, finding the recurrence formula may involve solving simultaneous equations.

Worked Example

13. A recurrence relationship is defined by the formula: $u_{n+1} = au_n + b$. Given the first three terms are 3, 4 and 6, find the values of a and b.

$u_1 = 3$

Using the recurrence formula:
$u_2 = a(3) + b = 4$ (1)

Using the recurrence formula:
$u_3 = a(4) + b = 6$ (2)

Rewrite (1):
$3a + b = 4$

Rewrite (2):
$4a + b = 6$

Subtract (1) from (2):
$a = 2$

Using (1):
$3(2) + b = 4$
$b = -2$

The recurrence formula is:
$u_{n+1} = 2u_n - 2$

Exercise 5C

1. Write down the first 4 terms of each of these sequences.
 (a) $u_{n+1} = u_n - 4$, $u_1 = 1$
 (b) $u_{n+1} = (u_n)^2 - 2$, $u_1 = 1$
 (c) $u_{n+1} = (u_n - 1)^2$, $u_1 = 3$
 (d) $u_{n+1} = \frac{1}{4}u_n + 1$, $u_1 = 2$
 (e) $u_{n+1} = \frac{2u_n}{3}$, $u_1 = 27$
 (f) $u_{n+1} = u_n(u_n - 1) + 1$, $u_1 = 3$
 (g) $u_{n+1} = \frac{u_n}{1 + u_n}$, $u_1 = 3$
 (h) $u_{n+1} = 2u_n - 1$, $u_1 = \frac{1}{4}$
 (i) $u_{n+1} = -2u_n + \frac{1}{2}$, $u_1 = -\frac{3}{4}$
 (j) $u_{n+1} = (-1)^{u_n}$, $u_1 = 2$

2. Write a recurrence relationship linking u_{n+1} to u_n for each of the following sequences.
 (a) 2, 5, 8, 11, …
 (b) −5, −10, −15, −20, …
 (c) 37, 37, 37, 37, …
 (d) 2, −2, 2, −2, 2, …
 (e) 2, 4, 2, 4, 2, …
 (f) 2, 4, 8, 16, …
 (g) $1, \frac{1}{2}, \frac{1}{4}, \frac{1}{8}, \frac{1}{16}, …$
 (h) 256, 16, 4, 2, …
 (i) 2, 4, 16, 256, …
 (j) 1, 2, 6, 22, 86, …

3. Write down the first 5 terms of the sequence defined by the recurrence formula:
$u_{n+1} = \frac{1 + 2u_n}{3 + 4u_n}$ where $u_1 = 1$,
giving your answers to 2 decimal places.

4. The sequence of positive numbers $u_1, u_2, u_3, …$ is given by: $u_{n+1} = (u_n - 3)^2$, $u_1 = 4$
 (a) Find u_2, u_3 and u_4.
 (b) Write down the value of u_{50}.

5. A sequence is defined by the recurrence relationship: $u_{n+1} = ku_n - 2k$, where k is an integer. Given $u_1 = 1$ and $u_3 = -15$, find the two possible values of k.

6. A sequence is generated by the recurrence formula: $u_{n+1} = \frac{d}{u_n} + 1$, where d is a constant.
Given $u_1 = 2$ and $u_3 u_2 = \frac{11}{3}$, find the value of d.

Exercise 5C...

7. The recursion formula: $u_{n+1} = au_n + bu_n^2$
   is used to generate the sequence of numbers
   $u_1 = 1, u_2 = -2, u_3 = 16, \ldots$. Find the values
   of the constants a and b.

8. The sequence $u_1, u_2, u_3, \ldots u_n$ is defined by the
   recurrence relation: $u_{n+1} = pu_n + 9, u_1 = 5$,
   where p is a constant. Given that $u_3 = 11$, show
   that one possible value of p is 0.2 and find the
   other value of p.

9. A sequence is defined by the recurrence
   relation:
   $$u_{n+1} = \sqrt{\frac{u_n}{3} + \frac{a}{u_n}}, n = 1,2,3$$
   where a is a constant.
   (a) Given that $a = 19$ and $u_1 = 3$, find the
       values of u_2, u_3 and u_4 giving your answers
       to 2 decimal places.
   (b) Given instead that $u_1 = u_2 = 3$, calculate
       the value of a.
   (c) Given this value of a, write down the value
       of u_5.

10. A recursion formula is used to generate a
    sequence: $u_{n+1} = (-1)^n u_n + q$ where $u_1 = 1$.
    (a) Show that $u_4 = 1 - q$.
    (b) Given that $u_4 = -5u_5$, find the value of q.

5.5 Behaviour of Sequences

A sequence is said to **converge** if the terms get closer and closer to some value. This value is called the **limit** of the sequence.

If each term is a constant multiple of the next, there is a simple test for convergence:

> If a sequence is defined by the formula:
> $u_{n+1} = ku_n$
> then the sequence converges with a limit of zero if
> $-1 < k < 1$ (i.e. $|k| < 1$).
>
> These sequences are called **geometric sequences** and will be discussed further in a later section.

Worked Example

14. A sequence is defined by the recurrence relationship:
    $$u_{n+1} = \frac{u_n}{2}, u_1 = 1$$
    (a) Find the first 3 terms and u_{15}.
    (b) Does the sequence converge?

    (a) The terms of this sequence are:
        $$u_1 = 1, u_2 = \frac{1}{2}, u_3 = \frac{1}{4}, \ldots$$
        $$u_{15} = \left(\frac{1}{2}\right)^{14} = 6.1 \times 10^{-5}$$

    (b) This sequence is of the form
        $$u_{n+1} = ku_n \text{ where } k = \frac{1}{2}$$
        Since the sequence is of this form and $|k| < 1$, the sequence converges to a limit of zero.

        > **Note:** This sequence converges to a limit of 0. You could guess this, since the 15th term is very close to 0.

If we know a sequence converges, it is possible to use the recurrence formula to find the limit. If a sequence converges to a limit u, eventually each term will approach u. Using mathematical notation:

As $n \to \infty$,

$u_n \to u$ and $u_{n+1} \to u$

Hence, we can replace both u_{n+1} and u_n in the formula with u and solve the equation.

Worked Example

15. A sequence is defined by the recurrence relationship:
    $$u_{n+1} = 1 + \frac{1}{u_n}, u_1 = 1$$
    Given that the sequence does converge, find the limit of the sequence.

    To find the limit, replace both u_{n+1} and u_n in the formula with u:
    $$u = 1 + \frac{1}{u}$$
    Multiply both sides by u and re-arrange:
    $$u^2 - u - 1 = 0$$
    Using the quadratic formula:
    $$u = \frac{1 \pm \sqrt{5}}{2}$$

Since the initial value is 1, every term of the sequence is positive. Therefore, the convergent value must be greater than 1.

Hence the convergent value is $\frac{1+\sqrt{5}}{2}$.

If a sequence does not converge, it **diverges**.

Worked Example

16. A sequence is defined by the recurrence relationship:
$u_{n+1} = \frac{4u_n}{3}, \ u_1 = 1$

(a) Find the first 3 terms of the sequence.
(b) Does the sequence converge or diverge?

(a) The terms of this sequence are:
$u_1 = 1, u_2 = \frac{4}{3}, u_3 = \frac{16}{9}, \ldots$

(b) This sequence is of the form
$u_{n+1} = ku_n$ where $k = \frac{4}{3}$
Since $|k| > 1$, the sequence diverges.

It is possible for both convergent and divergent sequences to **oscillate**. An oscillating sequence is one in which successive terms are alternately higher then lower than the last.

Worked Example

17. By calculating the first 5 terms in each case, state whether the following sequences are convergent or divergent and whether or not they oscillate.

(a) $u_{n+1} = -\frac{7}{5}u_n + 1, u_1 = 0$

(b) $u_{n+1} = \frac{6}{1+u_n}, u_1 = 3$

(a) The terms are:
0, 1, −0.4, 1.56, −1.184
The sequence oscillates and diverges.

(b) The terms are:
3, 1.5, 2.4, 1.76, 2.17 (the last two to 2 d.p.)
The sequence oscillates and converges.

Exercise 5D

1. A sequence is defined recursively by the formula: $u_{n+1} = \frac{3}{4}u_n, \ u_1 = 1$
   (a) Find u_2, u_3 and u_4.
   (b) State whether this sequence converges or diverges.

2. A sequence is defined by the recurrence formula: $u_{n+1} = 3au_n, \ u_1 = 1$, where a is a constant.
   (a) Find the first four terms of the sequence in terms of a.
   (b) Find the range of values of a for which this is a convergent sequence.

3. By finding the first 4 terms, determine whether the sequence defined by the recurrence formula $u_{n+1} = 1 + u_n^2, \ u_1 = 1$ converges or diverges.

4. (a) Find the first 5 terms of the sequence defined by the recurrence formula:
   $u_{n+1} = \frac{3}{2+u_n}, u_1 = 3$
   (b) Hence state whether the sequence converges or diverges, and whether it oscillates.

5. A sequence is defined by the recurrence formula: $u_{n+1} = \frac{u_n}{5} + 2, u_1 = 1$.
   By forming and solving an equation, show that the sequence converges to a limit c and find the exact value of c.

6. The terms of a sequence are given by the recurrence relationship: $u_{n+1} = 1 + u_n, \ u_1 = 1$
   Does the sequence converge or diverge?

7. A sequence is generated using the recurrence formula: $u_{n+1} = 1 + \frac{u_n}{2}, u_1 = 3$
   Do the terms of the sequence converge to a limit or diverge? If the sequence converges, find the limit.

8. The terms of a sequence are generated using the formula: $u_{n+1} = -\frac{7}{10}u_n + 1, u_1 = 1$
   (a) Find the first 5 terms of the sequence, to two decimal places where necessary.
   (b) Is the sequence oscillating?
   (c) The sequence converges to a limit c. By forming and solving an equation, find c.

Exercise 5D...

9. Find the range of values of p for which the sequence: $u_{n+1} = (1-p)u_n$ is a convergent sequence.

10. A sequence has the recurrence formula:
$u_{n+1} = \dfrac{a-1}{a+1} u_n$ where a is a constant.
Find the range of values of a that ensures this is a convergent sequence.

5.6 Arithmetic Sequences and Series

An **arithmetic sequence** or **arithmetic progression** (often abbreviated to **AP**) is a special type of sequence. The difference between a term and the previous one remains constant.

An example of an arithmetic progression is:

5, 7, 9, 11, …

In this case, the **common difference** is 2.

An **arithmetic series** is a special kind of series. Just like the arithmetic progression, an arithmetic series is a series in which there is a common difference between successive terms.

An example of an arithmetic series is:

$1 + \dfrac{3}{2} + 2 + \dfrac{5}{2} + 3 + \cdots$

In this case, the common difference is $\dfrac{1}{2}$.

Recurrence formulae are sometimes used to give the terms of a sequence or series. A recurrence formula for the terms of an arithmetic series is:

$u_{n+1} = u_n + d$ where d is a constant.

The first term of an arithmetic series is denoted a. Hence, the first three terms are:
$u_1 = a$
$u_2 = a + d$
$u_3 = a + 2d$
…

From this we can see that:

> The general term of an arithmetic sequence or series is:
> $u_n = a + (n-1)d$

The formula for the general term is useful in solving many different types of problem.

Worked Example

18. Find the 50th term in the arithmetic series:
$4 + 6 + 8 + 10 + \cdots$

Find the first term and common difference:
$a = 4$ and $d = 2$

To find the 50th term, use:
$u_n = a + (n-1)d$
$u_{50} = 4 + (50-1)2$
$\phantom{u_{50}} = 102$

It is possible to find the number of terms in an arithmetic sequence or series.

Worked Example

19. Find the number of terms in the series:
$47 + 40 + 33 + 26 + \cdots - 58 - 65$.

$u_n = a + (n-1)d$
$-65 = 47 + (n-1)(-7)$
$n - 1 = \dfrac{-65 - 47}{-7}$
$n - 1 = 16$
$n = 17$

You can also find the first term of an arithmetic sequence or series.

Worked Example

20. The final term of an arithmetic series is 76. Given that the common difference is 5 and there are 22 terms, find the first term.

$u_n = a + (n-1)d$
$76 = a + (21)(5)$
$a = 76 - 105$
$a = -29$

You can find where in a sequence or series the terms become larger or smaller than a certain value.

Worked Example

21. An arithmetic series is given by the recursion formula: $u_{n+1} = 6 + u_n$, $u_1 = -30$. Which term is the first that is greater than or equal to 100?

$u_n > 100$
$\Rightarrow a + (n-1)d > 100$
$-30 + (n-1)6 > 100$

$$n - 1 > \frac{130}{6}$$
$$n > 22.67 \ (2 \text{ d.p.})$$

The 23rd term is greater than 100.

You can use the common difference to find an unknown in an arithmetic sequence or series.

Worked Example

22. Three terms of an arithmetic progression are:
$x - 1, 2x, 4x + 3$.
Find the value of x and evaluate the first three terms. Hence state the common difference.

Since this is an AP, the difference between the second and first terms is the same as the difference between the third and second.

$$2x - (x - 1) = (4x + 3) - 2x$$
$$x + 1 = 2x + 3$$
$$x + 2 = 0$$
$$x = -2$$

The first three terms are –3, –4 and –5.

The common difference is –1.

Exercise 5E

1. Which of the following are arithmetic series?
   (a) $1 + 2 + 3 + 4 + \cdots$
   (b) $30 + 28 + 26 + 24 + \ldots$
   (c) $10^1 + 10^2 + 10^3 + 10^4 + \ldots$
   (d) $\frac{1}{2} + \frac{1}{3} + \frac{1}{4} + \frac{1}{5} + \ldots$
   (e) $\frac{1}{3} + \frac{2}{3} + 1 + \frac{4}{3} + \frac{5}{3} + \cdots$
   (f) $(1 + \sqrt{2}) + (3 + 2\sqrt{2}) + (5 + 3\sqrt{2}) + (7 + 4\sqrt{2}) + \cdots$
   (g) $100 + -100 + -300 + -500 + \ldots$
   (h) $\frac{1}{3} + \frac{2}{4} + \frac{3}{5} + \frac{4}{6} + \frac{5}{7} + \cdots$
   (i) $(2z + 1) + (2.5z + 3) + (3z + 5) + (3.5z + 7) + (4z + 9) \ldots$
   (j) $16f + 8f + 4f + 2f + f + \ldots$

2. Find the number of terms in the sequence:
   $1, 7, 13, 19, \ldots, 49$

Exercise 5E...

3. For each of the following arithmetic series, find the 10th and 50th terms.
   (a) $5 + 11 + 17 + 23 + 29 + \ldots$
   (b) $-1 + 2 + 5 + 8 + 11 \ldots$
   (c) $4.7 + 2.7 + 0.7 + -1.3 + -3.3 \ldots$
   (d) $-2.2 + -1.45 + -0.7 + 0.05 + 0.8 \ldots$
   (e) $5p + 7p + 9p + 11p + 13p \ldots$
   (f) $\frac{11}{3} + \frac{13}{3} + \frac{15}{3} + \frac{17}{3} + \frac{19}{3} \ldots$
   (g) $(3y + 1) + (y + 3) + (-y + 5) + (-3y + 7) + (-5y + 9) \ldots$
   (h) $2 \times 10^4 + 2.5 \times 10^4 + 3 \times 10^4 + 3.5 \times 10^4 + 4 \times 10^4 \ldots$
   (i) $(7 - 7\sqrt{2}) + (6 - 6\sqrt{2}) + (5 - 5\sqrt{2}) + (4 - 4\sqrt{2}) + (3 - 3\sqrt{2}) \ldots$
   (j) $1001, 1002.5, 1004, 1005.5, 1007$

4. The first three terms of an arithmetic sequence are: $p, 6p - 8, 3p + 8$
   (a) Show that $p = 3$.
   (b) Find the value of the 50th term of this sequence.

5. Three consecutive terms of an arithmetic sequence are $(7x - 7), (x - 3)$ and $(3 - x)$. Find the next term.

6. The first three terms of an arithmetic sequence are: $k, 4k - 9, 3k + 6$
   (a) Show that $k = 6$.
   (b) Find the value of the 60th term of this sequence.

5.7 Sum of an Arithmetic Series

How would you add the terms in an arithmetic series to find the sum?

Notation

You will use the notation S_n a lot. For example, S_{100} is the sum of the first 100 terms, S_{19} the sum of the first 19 terms, etc.

In the real world...

There is a well-known story, which may or may not be true, about the mathematician Karl Friedrich Gauss when he was at primary school. His teacher asked the class to add the numbers 1 to 100, thinking this would keep them busy until the end of the lesson. About 30 seconds later Gauss gave him the correct answer. How did he do it?

Gauss rearranged the numbers to add them like this:

$(1 + 100) + (2 + 99) + (3 + 98) + \cdots + (50 + 51) = ?$

Notice that every pair of numbers adds up to 101. There are 50 pairs of numbers, so the answer is:

$50 \times 101 = 5050$.

You can see that Gauss's method would work for any number of integers. It leads us to a formula that can be used to find the sum of any arithmetic series.

Proof of the formula for the sum of an arithmetic series

Note: You should learn this proof and the formula.

Consider the series whose first term is a and common difference is d. Let the sum of the first n terms be S_n.

Then:
$S_n = a + [a + d] + [a + 2d] + \cdots + [a + (n-2)d]$
$\qquad + [a + (n-1)d]$ \hfill (1)

Simply reversing the order of the terms, we can also write:
$S_n = [a + (n-1)d] + [a + (n-2)d] + \cdots$
$\qquad + [a + 2d] + [a + d] + a$ \hfill (2)

Add equations (1) and (2):
$2S_n = [2a + (n-1)d] + [2a + (n-1)d] + \cdots$
$\qquad + [2a + (n-1)d] + [2a + (n-1)d]$

In this series, there are n terms, which are all the same. So:

$2S_n = n[2a + (n-1)d]$

$S_n = \dfrac{n}{2}[2a + (n-1)d]$

Proof of the sum of the first n natural numbers

Note: You should learn this proof and the formula.

Consider the series: $1 + 2 + 3 + \cdots + n$, the sum of the first n natural numbers.

The first term $a = 1$ and the common difference $d = 1$.

The general formula for the sum of an arithmetic series is:

$S_n = \dfrac{n}{2}[2a + (n-1)d]$

Substitute for a and d:

$S_n = \dfrac{n}{2}[2(1) + (n-1)(1)]$

$S_n = \dfrac{n}{2}[2 + (n-1)]$

$S_n = \dfrac{n}{2}(1 + n)$

Worked Examples

23. What is the sum of the first 31 terms of the arithmetic series: $5 + 8 + 11 + 14 + \cdots$?

Always begin by writing down what we know:
$a = 5, d = 3$ and $n = 31$. Then use the formula:

$S_n = \dfrac{n}{2}[2a + (n-1)d]$

$S_{31} = \dfrac{31}{2}[2(5) + (31-1)3]$

$S_{31} = 15.5 \times (10 + 90)$

$S_{31} = 1550$

24. Find the sum of the series: $20 + 18 + 16 + \cdots + -90$

We know: $a = 20$ and $d = -2$. We need to know how many terms there are. So we use:

$u_n = a + (n-1)d$

$-90 = 20 + (n-1)(-2)$

$(n-1) = \dfrac{-110}{-2}$

$n = 56$

Now apply the formula:

$S_n = \dfrac{n}{2}[2a + (n-1)d]$

$S_{56} = \dfrac{56}{2}[2(20) + 55(-2)]$

$S_{56} = 28(40 - 110)$

$S_{56} = -1960$

Exercise 5F

1. Find the sum of the following series to the specified number of terms.
   (a) $2 + 4 + 6 + 8 + 10 \ldots$ (10 terms)
   (b) $10 + 8 + 6 + 4 + 2 \ldots$ (11 terms)

Exercise 5F...

(c) $0.5 + 1.5 + 2.5 + 3.5 + 4.5 \ldots$ (12 terms)
(d) $-10 + -15 + -20 + -25 + -30 \ldots$ (10 terms)
(e) $\frac{17}{3} + \frac{18}{3} + \frac{19}{3} + \frac{20}{3} + \frac{21}{3} + \ldots$ (9 terms)
(f) $10^4 + (2 \times 10^4) + (3 \times 10^4) + (4 \times 10^4) + \ldots$ (10 terms)
(g) $-5 + 5i, -4 + 4i, -3 + 3i, -2 + 2i, -1 + 1i \ldots$ (11 terms)
(h) $3\sqrt{5} + 5\sqrt{5} + 7\sqrt{5} + 9\sqrt{5} + 11\sqrt{5} + \cdots$ (20 terms)
(i) $(1 + x) + 1 + (1 - x) + (1 - 2x) + (1 - 3x) \ldots$ (11 terms)
(j) $\frac{1}{4} + \frac{21}{4} + \frac{41}{4} + \frac{61}{4} + \frac{81}{4} \ldots$ (8 terms)

2. Sum the arithmetic series with first term 6, common difference 7 and 13 terms.

3. Find the sum of the integers from 1 to 2000 which are not divisible by 5.

4. Consider the arithmetic series: $3 + 5 + 7 + \cdots$
   (a) Using the general formula for the nth term, find and simplify a formula for the nth term of this series, leaving n in your answer.
   (b) Using the general formula for the sum to n terms, find and simplify a formula for the sum to n terms of this series, again in terms of n.

5. There is an alternative formula for the sum to terms of an arithmetic series:
$$S_n = \frac{n}{2}(a + l)$$
where l is the last term. Can you prove this formula?

6. On the first day of Christmas, my true love sent to me a partridge in a pear tree. On the second day of Christmas, my true love sent to me two turtle doves and a partridge in a pear tree… etc. How many presents do I receive on the 12th day of Christmas?

5.8 Sigma Notation

Sigma notation provides a more concise way to write series. Sigma (written Σ) is a Greek letter and in mathematics is always used to represent a sum.

For example:
$$\sum_{r=1}^{r=n} r = 1 + 2 + 3 + \cdots + n$$

The subscript and superscript $r = 1$ and $r = n$ mean that these are the first and last values. The r following the sigma sign will be replaced by every value in this range, and all the resulting values will be summed.

Sometimes the subscript and/or superscript will simply be a number. In this case, assume the variable r is being substituted.

Worked Example

25. Evaluate: $\displaystyle\sum_{r=1}^{4}(2r + 1)$

Substitute the values 1, 2, 3 and 4 into $(2r + 1)$ and sum:

$$\sum_{r=1}^{4}(2r + 1) = 3 + 5 + 7 + 9$$
$$= 24$$

Be aware that r may not start from 1.

Worked Example

26. Evaluate: $\displaystyle\sum_{r=2}^{5} r^2$

Substitute the values 2, 3, 4 and 5 into r^2 and sum:

$$\sum_{r=2}^{5} r^2 = 4 + 9 + 16 + 25$$
$$= 54$$

The upper or lower limit of the summation may be a general term.

Worked Example

27. Write down the series equivalent to: $\displaystyle\sum_{r=2}^{n} r^{-1}$

Substitute the values $2, 3, 4, \ldots, n$ into r^{-1} and sum:

$$\sum_{r=2}^{n} r^{-1} = \frac{1}{2} + \frac{1}{3} + \frac{1}{4} + \cdots + \frac{1}{n}$$

PURE MATHEMATICS FOR CCEA A2

You may be asked to write a series in sigma notation.

Worked Example
28. Use sigma notation to denote the following arithmetic series: $7 + 9 + 11 + \cdots + 23$

> **Note:** Revise how to make a formula for the general term of a sequence, discussed in section 5.1. Now apply this method to finding the general term of this arithmetic series.

We know that $a = 7$ and $d = 2$. This indicates that the general term is $2r + 5$. This will be our expression to be summed over.

Find the number of terms:
$$u_n = a + (n-1)d$$
$$23 = 7 + (n-1)(2)$$
$$(n-1) = \frac{16}{2}$$
$$n = 9$$

Therefore:
$$7 + 9 + 11 + \cdots + 23 = \sum_{1}^{9}(2r+5)$$

Check: If you use sigma notation to denote a series, always check your answer by evaluating some of the terms:
$$\sum_{1}^{9}(2r+5) = (2(1)+5) + (2(2)+5) + (2(3)+5)$$
$$+ \cdots + (2(9)+5)$$
$$= 7 + 9 + 11 + \cdots + 23$$

Our answer appears to be correct.

Exercise 5G

1. Write down the arithmetic series corresponding to each of the following.

   (a) $\sum_{1}^{4}(r+1)$ (b) $\sum_{3}^{7}\left(\frac{r}{2}\right)$

   (c) $\sum_{1}^{5}\left(\frac{r}{10}\right)$ (d) $\sum_{-3}^{3}(-r)$

   (e) $\sum_{0}^{4}(20-5r)$ (f) $\sum_{97}^{100}(100r)$

Exercise 5G...

   (g) $\sum_{0}^{3}\left(\frac{r}{4}\right)$ (h) $\sum_{3}^{4}(5r+1)$

   (i) $\sum_{5}^{8}\left(\frac{r}{2}-1\right)$ (j) $\sum_{1}^{5}(1)$

2. Find the formula for the general term of each series. Use this to write the series in sigma notation, beginning at $r = 1$.

   (a) $3 + 4 + 5 + 6$
   (b) $10 + 13 + 16 + \cdots + 28$
   (c) $-5 + -7 + -9 + \cdots$ (20 terms)
   (d) $1000 + 998 + 996 + \cdots$ (10 terms)
   (e) $15 + 8 + 1 + -6 + -13 + -20$
   (f) $21 + 41 + 61 + \cdots$ (10 terms)
   (g) $\frac{5}{2} + \frac{7}{2} + \frac{9}{2} + \frac{11}{2} + \frac{13}{2}$
   (h) $3a + 5a + 7a + \cdots$ (b terms)
   (i) $5\sqrt{3} + 7\sqrt{3} + 9\sqrt{3} + 11\sqrt{3} + \cdots$ (13 terms)
   (j) $t^2 + 2t^2 + 3t^2 + \cdots$ (6 terms)

3. Find the following sums as simply as possible.

   (a) $\sum_{1}^{5}(5r)$ (b) $\sum_{2}^{6}(3r+1)$

   (c) $\sum_{r=0}^{4}(3+rx)$ (d) $\sum_{1}^{8}\left(\frac{r}{3}+1\right)$

   (e) $\sum_{r=1}^{10}\left(\frac{3r-1}{2}\right)$ (f) $\sum_{1}^{20}(0.05r+1)$

   (g) $\sum_{r=-5}^{5}(2r+y)$ (h) $\sum_{1}^{15}\left(\frac{3r}{4}+2\right)$

   (i) $\sum_{1}^{100}(-2r-98)$ (j) $\sum_{-4}^{0}\left(\frac{r}{2}+2\right)$

4. Prove that $\sum_{1}^{n}(6r-1) = n(3n+2)$

5. For some value of n, $\sum_{1}^{n}(-2r-5) = -160$

   Form and solve a quadratic equation to find the value of n.

Exercise 5G...

6. Consider the arithmetic series: $\sum_{1}^{n}(8-2r)$

   (a) Write out the first 5 terms of the series.
   (b) Using the general formula for the sum to n terms, show that the sum to n terms of this series is given by: $S_n = 7n - n^2$
   (c) Using the general formula for the nth term, show that the nth term of this series is given by: $u_n = 8 - 2n$
   (d) By equating your answers to part (b) and part (c), form and solve a quadratic equation to find where in the series the sum is equal to the individual term.

5.9 Geometric Sequences and Series

Another special type of **sequence** is a geometric progression (abbreviated to **GP**). In a geometric progression, the ratio between successive terms is constant. For example:

2, 6, 18, 54, ...

In this geometric progression, the **common ratio** is 3.

Summing the terms of a geometric progression gives a geometric series. Like the geometric progression, a geometric series is a series in which there is a common ratio between successive terms.

An example of a geometric series is:

$1 + \frac{1}{2} + \frac{1}{4} + \frac{1}{8} + \cdots$

In this case, the common ratio is $\frac{1}{2}$.

A recurrence formula for the terms of a geometric series is:

$u_{n+1} = ru_n$

where r, the common ratio, is a constant.

The first term of a geometric series is denoted a.

Hence, the first three terms are:
$u_1 = a$
$u_2 = ar$
$u_3 = ar^2$
...

From this, we can see that:

> The general term of a geometric series is:
> $u_n = ar^{n-1}$

The formula for the general term is useful in solving many different types of problem.

Worked Example

29. Find the general term for the geometric series:
    $7 + 14 + 28 + 56 + \cdots$

    $a = 7$ and $r = 2$

    Hence the general term is:
    $u_n = ar^{n-1}$
    $= 7 \times 2^{n-1}$

If r is negative, the geometric series oscillates.

If $|r|$ is less than one, each term in the geometric series is smaller in magnitude than the last.

Worked Example

30. Find the general term for each of these geometric series:
    (a) $1 - 2 + 4 - 8 + 16 - \cdots$
    (b) $3 + 1 + \frac{1}{3} + \frac{1}{9} + \cdots$

    (a) $a = 1$ and $r = -2$

    General term:
    $u_n = ar^{n-1}$
    $= (1)(-2)^{n-1}$
    $= (-2)^{n-1}$

    (b) $a = 3$ and $r = \frac{1}{3}$
    $u_n = ar^{n-1}$
    $= 3\left(\frac{1}{3}\right)^{n-1}$

> **Note:** Remember that a sequence is simply a list of numbers, whereas a series is the sum of that list.

Sometimes a geometric progression will involve algebraic expressions.

Worked Example

31. The first three terms of a geometric progression are:
    $p - 2$, $2p$ and $3p + 20$.
    Find the two possible values of p.

    If this is a geometric progression, then the ratio between successive terms remains constant, i.e.

$$\frac{2p}{p-2} = \frac{3p+20}{2p}$$

Cross-multiply:
$$4p^2 = (3p+20)(p-2)$$

Expand brackets:
$$4p^2 = 3p^2 + 14p - 40$$

Re-arrange:
$$p^2 - 14p + 40 = 0$$

Factorise:
$$(p-4)(p-10) = 0$$
$$p = 4 \text{ or } p = 10$$

If you are asked to find the first term of a GP that is greater than or less than a certain value, logarithms can be used.

Worked Example

32. (a) In a geometric progression, the first term $a = 2$ and the common ratio $r = \sqrt{2}$. Find the first term of the sequence that is greater than 50.
(b) In a different geometric progression, the first term $a = 5$ and the common ratio $r = \frac{1}{5}$. Find the first term of the sequence that is smaller than 0.01.

(a) The general term is $ar^{n-1} = 2(\sqrt{2})^{n-1}$, which must be greater than 50.
$$2(\sqrt{2})^{n-1} > 50$$
$$(\sqrt{2})^{n-1} > 25$$

We are trying to find the smallest value of n that satisfies this inequality. Since the unknown is in the power, we take logs of both sides. We could use any base for the log function; here base 10 is used:

$$\log(\sqrt{2})^{n-1} > \log 25$$
$$\log(2)^{(n-1)/2} > \log 25$$
$$\left(\frac{n-1}{2}\right) \log 2 > \log 25$$
$$\left(\frac{n-1}{2}\right) > \frac{\log 25}{\log 2}$$
$$n > \frac{2 \log 25}{\log 2} + 1$$
$$n > 10.29$$

i.e. the 11th term of the sequence is greater than 50.

(b) The general term is $ar^{n-1} = 5\left(\frac{1}{5}\right)^{n-1}$, which must be less than 0.01.

$$5\left(\frac{1}{5}\right)^{n-1} < 0.01$$

$$\left(\frac{1}{5}\right)^{n-1} < 0.002$$

Again we take logs of both sides since the unknown is in the power.

$$\log\left(\frac{1}{5}\right)^{n-1} < \log 0.002$$

$$(n-1) \log\left(\frac{1}{5}\right) < \log 0.002$$

Now be careful. $\log\left(\frac{1}{5}\right)$ is a negative number. If we divide both sides of an inequality by a negative number the inequality sign must change, in this case to a greater-than sign. So:

$$n - 1 > \frac{\log 0.002}{\log(1/5)}$$

$$n > \frac{\log 0.002}{\log(1/5)} + 1$$

$$n > 4.86$$

i.e. the 5th term of the sequence is less than 0.01.

If you are given two non-adjacent terms of a GP, you can find the first term and the common ratio by solving simultaneous equations.

Worked Example

33. The third and fifth terms of a GP are 18 and 40.5. Find the first term and the two possible values for the common ratio.

$$ar^2 = 18 \qquad (1)$$
$$ar^4 = 40.5 \qquad (2)$$

Divide equation (2) by equation (1):
$$r^2 = \frac{9}{4}$$
$$\Rightarrow r = \pm\frac{3}{2}$$

Substitute into equation (1):
$$\Rightarrow a = 8$$

5: SEQUENCES AND SERIES

Exercise 5H

1. Which of the following are geometric progressions?
   (a) $1, 2, 3, 4, \ldots$
   (b) $-5, 10, -20, 40, \ldots$
   (c) $32, 30, 28, 26, \ldots$
   (d) $10^1, 10^2, 10^3, 10^4, \ldots$
   (e) $\dfrac{1}{2}, \dfrac{1}{3}, \dfrac{1}{4}, \dfrac{1}{5}, \ldots$
   (f) $1, \sqrt{2}, 3, 2\sqrt{2}, 5, 3\sqrt{2}, 7, 4\sqrt{2}, \ldots$
   (g) $1, \sqrt{2}, 2, 2\sqrt{2}, 4, \ldots$
   (h) $100, -100, -300, -500, \ldots$
   (i) $100, 1, 0.01, 0.0001, \ldots$
   (j) $\dfrac{1}{3}, \dfrac{2}{4}, \dfrac{3}{5}, \dfrac{4}{6}, \dfrac{5}{7}, \ldots$
   (k) $16f, 8f, 4f, 2f, f, \ldots$

2. Write down the first 5 terms of the following geometric progressions.
   (a) First term 1, common ratio 3
   (b) First term −4, common ratio 2
   (c) First term −2, common ratio −2
   (d) First term 64, common ratio ½
   (e) First term 10^3, common ratio 10
   (f) First term 32, common ratio 1.5
   (g) First term 2, common ratio $\sqrt{2}$
   (h) First term ½, common ratio ½
   (i) First term a, common ratio b
   (j) First term y, common ratio $\dfrac{1}{y}$

3. The second and fourth terms of a geometric series are 2 and 0.32 respectively. Given that all the terms in the series are positive, find the common ratio and the first term.

4. Find the 5th term of the sequence $1, 10, 100, \ldots$

5. Find the 6th term of the sequence $6, 36, 216, \ldots$

6. A sequence of positive integers, $u_1, u_2, u_3, \ldots$ is given by: $u_{n+1} = 5u_n$, $u_1 = 7$
   (a) Write down the first 4 terms of this sequence.
   (b) Give u_n in terms of n.

7. The terms of a geometric progression are $(x + 1)$, $(x + 2)$ and $(x + 5)$. Find the value of x and hence find the three terms.

Exercise 5H...

8. In a geometric progression, the first term $a = 5/2$ and the common ratio $r = 3/2$. Find the first term of the sequence that is greater than 100.

9. In a geometric progression, the first term $a = 27$ and the common ratio $r = 1/3$. Find the first term of the sequence that is smaller than $1/100$.

5.10 The Sum of a Finite Geometric Series

There are two formulae for the sum of a geometric series. In this section we look at a **finite geometric series**, for example:

$1 + 2 + 4 + 8 + 16$

Proof of the formula for the sum of a finite geometric series

> **Note:** You should learn this proof and the formula.

Consider the series whose first term is a and common ratio is r. The series has n terms and the sum is S_n. Then:

$$S_n = a + ar + ar^2 + \cdots + ar^{n-1} \quad (1)$$

Multiplying both sides by r, we can also write:

$$rS_n = ar + ar^2 + ar^3 + \cdots + ar^n \quad (2)$$

Now subtract equation (2) from equation (1). Most of the terms cancel out, leaving:

$$S_n - rS_n = a - ar^n$$

Factorise both sides:

$$S_n(1 - r) = a(1 - r^n)$$

$$\boxed{S_n = \dfrac{a(1 - r^n)}{1 - r}}$$

Sometimes you may see the formula in this form:

$$\boxed{S_n = \dfrac{a(r^n - 1)}{r - 1}}$$

This is easier to use when $r > 1$.

Worked Example

34. Find the sum of the first 5 powers of 2.

The series is: $2 + 4 + 8 + 16 + 32$

First term $a = 2$, common ratio $r = 2$ and number of terms $n = 5$.

$$S_n = \frac{a(r^n - 1)}{r - 1}$$

$$S_n = \frac{2(2^5 - 1)}{2 - 1}$$

$$= 62$$

Sigma notation can be used with geometric series, as with arithmetic series.

Worked Example

35. Expand, then evaluate: $\sum_{r=1}^{4} 3^r$

To expand the series, replace r with each value from 1 to 4:

$$\sum_{r=1}^{4} 3^r = 3^1 + 3^2 + 3^3 + 3^4$$

This is a geometric series, with first term $a = 3$, 4 terms and common ratio $r = 3$.

$$S_n = \frac{a(r^n - 1)}{r - 1}$$

$$S_4 = \frac{3(3^4 - 1)}{3 - 1}$$

$$= 120$$

Exercise 5I

1. Find the sum of each geometric series. Give your answers as fractions or surds where appropriate, otherwise to 3 significant figures.
   (a) $1 + 3 + 9 + 27 + \cdots$ (5 terms)
   (b) $\frac{1}{2} + \frac{1}{4} + \frac{1}{8} + \cdots$ (6 terms)
   (c) $1 + -2 + 4 + -8 + \cdots$ (5 terms)
   (d) $\frac{3}{4} + \frac{3}{16} + \frac{3}{64} + \cdots$ (5 terms)
   (e) $30 + 5 + \frac{5}{6} + \frac{5}{36} + \cdots$ (6 terms)
   (f) $100 + 150 + 225 + \cdots$ (10 terms)
   (g) $1 + 1.1 + 1.21 + 1.331 + \cdots$ (7 terms)

Exercise 5I...

   (h) $1 + (0.8) + (0.8)^2 + (0.8)^3 + \cdots$ (7 terms)
   (i) $10 + 1 + 0.1 + 0.01 + \cdots$ (6 terms)
   (j) $\sqrt{2} + (\sqrt{2})^2 + (\sqrt{2})^3 + (\sqrt{2})^4$
   (k) $1 + -1 + 1 + -1 + \cdots$ (9 terms)

2. Evaluate:
   (a) $\sum_{1}^{5} 3^r$
   (b) $\sum_{1}^{10} \left(\frac{1}{2}\right)^r$
   (c) $\sum_{0}^{4} (\sqrt{2})^r$ (as a surd)
   (d) $\sum_{1}^{6} \frac{1}{2}(2)^r$
   (e) $\sum_{-3}^{3} 3^r$
   (f) $\sum_{0}^{5} (-2)^r$
   (g) $\sum_{1}^{4} 4^{r-1}$
   (h) $\sum_{0}^{4} \left(\frac{1}{\sqrt{2}}\right)^r$ (as a surd)
   (i) $\sum_{0}^{3} 2^{2r}$
   (j) $\sum_{1}^{10} 2^{1-r}$

3. Find: $\sum_{1}^{8} 200(3)^r$

4. The first and second terms of a geometric series G are 18 and 9 respectively. Find, to 3 significant figures, the sum of the first 16 terms of G.

5. Find the sum of the first 5 terms of the geometric series: $1 + 6 + 36 + \cdots$

6. The sum of a geometric series with four terms is an integer. Given that the common ratio is ½, find one possible value for the first term.

7. The first term of a geometric series is a and the second term is b.
   (a) What are the third and fourth terms?
   (b) What is the 10th term?

8. The second term of a geometric series is 6 and the third term is $3(x + 1)$. Given the sum of the first 3 terms is 21:
   (a) Find the two possible values of x.
   (b) Find the two possibilities for the first three terms of the series.

5.11 The Sum of an Infinite Geometric Series

In this section, we will discuss summing an infinite number of terms of a geometric series (the **sum to infinity**).

We discussed **convergent sequences** in section 5.5. For a **sequence** to converge, its terms must get closer and closer to a particular value. If this is not the case, the sequence diverges.

Infinite geometric **series** can also be convergent or divergent. A convergent series is a series in which the **sum to infinity** exists. We use the notation S_∞ to denote the sum to infinity.

Consider the following geometric series:
$$1 + \frac{11}{10} + \frac{121}{100} + \frac{1331}{1000} \cdots$$
For this series, $a = 1$ and $r = \frac{11}{10}$.

The series could also be written with its terms as decimals:

$1 + 1.1 + 1.21 + 1.331 + \cdots$

It is clear that the terms are increasing in size. It is not possible to find a sum to infinity. The series is divergent.

Consider a second geometric series:
$$1 + \frac{9}{10} + \frac{81}{100} + \frac{729}{1000} + \cdots$$
For this series, $a = 1$ and $r = \frac{9}{10}$.

The terms in this series are getting smaller and smaller. The sum changes less and less with each added term. This series converges to a particular value, which is 10.

> A geometric series is convergent if and only if $|r| < 1$.

Proof of the formula for the sum of an infinite geometric series

> **Note:** At the time of publication, the CCEA specification does not require you to know this proof. However, you should remember the formula.

Consider the infinite geometric series whose first term is a and common ratio is r. The series has n terms and the sum is S_n. Then:

$S_n = a + ar + ar^2 + \cdots$

For all geometric series:
$$S_n = \frac{a(1 - r^n)}{1 - r}$$
If the series is convergent, $|r| < 1$. As $n \to \infty$, $r^n \to 0$.

Therefore for convergent geometric series:
$$S_\infty = \frac{a(1 - 0)}{1 - r}$$
$$S_\infty = \frac{a}{1 - r}$$

Worked Example

36. Find the sum to infinity of the geometric series:
$$\sum_{1}^{\infty} 2^{1-r}$$

The series is: $1 + \frac{1}{2} + \frac{1}{4} + \cdots$

So $a = 1$ and $r = \frac{1}{2}$.

$S_\infty = \frac{a}{1 - r}$

$= \frac{1}{½}$

$= 2$

You may be given the sum to infinity and asked to find other properties of the series.

Worked Example

37. A geometric series has its first term equal to its common ratio. The sum to infinity of this series is 11. Find the exact value of the common ratio of this series.

We have been told $a = r$ and $S_\infty = 11$.

$S_\infty = \frac{a}{1 - r}$

Substitute the information we know:

$11 = \frac{r}{1 - r}$

$11(1 - r) = r$

$12r = 11$

$r = \frac{11}{12}$

Exercise 5J

1. Find the sum to infinity of the following geometric series.
   (a) $\dfrac{1}{2} + \dfrac{1}{4} + \dfrac{1}{8} + \cdots$
   (b) $1 + (0.8) + (0.8)^2 + (0.8)^3 + \cdots$
   (c) $10 + 1 + 0.1 + 0.01 + \cdots$
   (d) $-4 + -2 + -1 + -0.5 + \cdots$
   (e) $100 + 50 + 25 + 12.5 + \cdots$
   (f) $1 + \dfrac{1}{\sqrt{2}} + \dfrac{1}{(\sqrt{2})^2} + \dfrac{1}{(\sqrt{2})^3} + \cdots$ (as a surd)
   (g) $6.4 + 1.6 + 0.4 + 0.1 + \cdots$
   (h) $8 + -4 + 2 + -1 + \ldots$
   (i) $1 + \dfrac{1}{\pi^2} + \dfrac{1}{\pi^4} + \dfrac{1}{\pi^6} + \cdots$
   (j) $6x + 1 + \dfrac{1}{6x} + \cdots$ (where $\left|\dfrac{1}{6x}\right| < 1$)

2. Evaluate:
   (a) $\displaystyle\sum_{1}^{\infty} 2^{3-2r}$
   (b) $\displaystyle\sum_{1}^{\infty} \left(\dfrac{1}{2}\right)^r$
   (c) $\displaystyle\sum_{1}^{\infty} \left(\dfrac{1}{\sqrt{3}}\right)^r$ (as a surd)
   (d) $\displaystyle\sum_{1}^{\infty} \left(\dfrac{1}{3}\right)^{r-1}$
   (e) $\displaystyle\sum_{1}^{\infty} a^r$ (where $|a| < 1$)
   (f) $\displaystyle\sum_{1}^{\infty} 2^{1-r}$
   (g) $\displaystyle\sum_{1}^{\infty} 2\left(\dfrac{7}{8}\right)^r$
   (h) $\displaystyle\sum_{1}^{\infty} \left(\dfrac{x}{x+1}\right)^r$ (where $x \neq -1$)
   (i) $\displaystyle\sum_{1}^{\infty} 9\left(\dfrac{1}{4}\right)^r$
   (j) $\displaystyle\sum_{1}^{\infty} 10(10)^{-r}$

3. Find the sum to infinity of the geometric series: $5, 0.5, 0.05, \ldots$

4. The sum to infinity of a geometric series is 6 times the first term. Find the common ratio.

5. The second and fourth terms of a geometric series are 4.5 and 3.645 respectively. Given that all the terms in the series are positive, find:
   (a) the common ratio and the first term.
   (b) the sum to infinity of the series.

Exercise 5J...

6. The first term of a geometric series is 140. The sum to infinity is 700.
   (a) Show that the common ratio r is 0.8.
   (b) Find, to 2 decimal places, the difference between the 6th and 7th terms.
   (c) Calculate the sum of the first 8 terms.

7. Find the sum to infinity of the geometric series:
   $\dfrac{5}{6} + \dfrac{5}{18} + \dfrac{5}{54} + \cdots$

8. A geometric series has first term a and common ratio r. The second term is -4 and the sum to infinity is -25.
   (a) Show that: $25r^2 - 25r + 4 = 0$
   (b) Find the two possible values of r.
   (c) Find the corresponding values of a.

9. The first and second terms of a geometric series G are 120 and 12 respectively.
   (a) Find, to 3 significant figures, the sum of the first 19 terms of G.
   (b) Find the sum to infinity of G.

10. A geometric series has first term 1400 and its sum to infinity is 800.
    (a) Show that the common ratio of the series is $-\tfrac{3}{4}$.
    (b) Find, to 3 decimal places, the difference between the 9th and 10th terms.
    (c) Write down an expression for the sum of the first n terms of the series.
    (d) Given that n is odd, prove that the sum of the first n terms of the series is $800(1 + 0.75^n)$.

5.12 Sequences and Series in Modelling

Sequences and series are used to model many situations in the real world. Examples include interest calculations on loans or savings and changes in animal populations.

Modelling involving sequences

Both arithmetic and geometric sequences can be used to model a problem. You may have to decide, as a part of the problem, whether an AP or a GP most closely fits the given situation.

Geometric sequences are particularly useful when calculating the interest payable on a loan or a savings account each year or month.

5: SEQUENCES AND SERIES

Worked Example

38. Oliver took out a loan of £2000 to buy his car. The interest added to the loan is 5% of the outstanding amount every year.
  (a) How much will he owe after 1 year?
  (b) How much will he owe after 5 years?
  (c) What assumption has been made?

Initially Oliver owes £2000. This is the first term in the sequence.

(a) After one year, the amount owing is:
£2000 × 1.05 = £2100 (2nd term)

(b) After 2 years: £2000 × $(1.05)^2$ = £2205 (3rd term).

This is a geometric sequence, since we are multiplying by the same number (the common ratio) to get from one term of the sequence to the next. In this case $r = 1.05$.

The general term of a GP is:
$u_n = ar^{n-1}$

We are interested in the 6th term of the sequence. (Careful: not the 5th term!) So:
$u_6 = 2000 \times (1.05)^5$
$= £2552.56$

(c) We assume Oliver does not pay back any of the loan during the first 5 years.

Exercise 5K

1. In the first year after opening, a car showroom sold 210 cars. A model for future trading assumes that sales will increase by x cars per month for the next 37 months, so that $(210 + x)$ will be sold in the second month, $(210 + 2x)$ in the third month, and so on. Using this model with $x = 6$, calculate the number of cars sold in the 38th month.

2. On Zoe's 11th birthday she started to receive an annual allowance. The first annual allowance was £500 and on each following birthday the allowance was increased by £200.
   (a) Show that, immediately after her 12th birthday, the total of the allowances that Zoe had received was £1200.
   (b) Find the amount of Zoe's annual allowance on her 18th birthday.

Exercise 5K...

3. A ball is dropped from a height of h metres. A model of the trajectory of the ball assumes that, every time the ball bounces, it reaches a certain constant fraction f of its previous height, where $f < 1$.
   (a) Show that the sequence of heights forms a geometric progression.
   (b) If the height reached after the second bounce (the third term in the progression) is 0.32 metres and the height after the fourth bounce (the fifth term) is 0.0512 m, find the value of f.
   (c) Find the initial height of the ball.
   (d) Name one factor that might make this model unreliable.

4. **Note:** This question illustrates the idea of **chaos** in populations. You may find it useful to set this task up as a spreadsheet.

In the natural world, the population of a group of animals can sometimes be modelled from year to year using a simple recurrence relationship: $p_{n+1} = r \dfrac{p_n}{p_m}(|p_m - p_n|)$

(rounding the answer to the nearest whole number, if necessary) where p_m is the maximum population the local environment can sustain and r is called a breeding factor. r takes low values, such as 1.2, for species that do not breed very quickly (for example giant pandas) and high values, such as 4, for species that breed very quickly (for example rabbits).

In a particular population of snakes, $r = 2.5$. Assume the initial population $p_0 = 300$, and the maximum population $p_m = 5000$. Next year's population is given by:

$p_1 = r \left(\dfrac{p_0}{p_m}\right)(|p_m - p_0|)$

$= 2.5 \left(\dfrac{300}{5000}\right)(|5000 - 300|)$

$= 705$

In the second year:

$p_2 = 2.5 \left(\dfrac{705}{5000}\right)(|5000 - 705|)$

$= 1514$ (to the nearest whole number)

   (a) By calculating the next 8 terms of the sequence, describe what happens to the population of snakes during the first 10 years.

Exercise 5K...

(b) The breeding factor for a population of owls is much lower, with $r = 0.8$. Assume again that the population starts at 300 and the maximum is 5000. Calculate the population for each of the first ten years and describe what happens to the owls.

(c) For a group of wild mice, $r = 3.7$. Work out the population for the first 10 years, assuming the initial population is 2000 and $p_m = 50000$.

Note: Your answers to this question should demonstrate some of the different types of behaviour we see within animal populations: stability, extinction and unpredictability or **chaos**.

Modelling involving series summations

Again, both arithmetic and geometric series can be used to model real-life problems and a part of a problem may be to decide which of these most closely fits the given situation.

Geometric series are often used when calculating the total in a savings account or the balance of a loan after a certain time period.

Worked Examples

39. A girl saves money over a period of 100 weeks. She saves 7p in Week 1, 12p in Week 2, 17p in Week 3, and so on until Week 100. Her weekly savings form an arithmetic series.
(a) Find the amount she saves in Week 100.
(b) Calculate her total savings over the complete 100 week period.

(a) $a = 7, d = 5, n = 100$
For week 100:
$u_n = a + (n-1)d$
$= 7 + 99(5)$
$= 502$ pence $= £5.02$

(b) $S_n = \dfrac{n}{2}[2a + (n-1)d]$
$S_{100} = 50[2(7) + (99)5]$
$= 25450$ pence $= £254.50$

40. Mr Wise puts £100 into his savings account every year on the first of January. The rate of interest paid is 4% per year.
(a) Show that the amount of money Mr Wise has in his account at the end of 3 years can be given by the geometric series:
$= 104 + (104)(1.04) + (104)(1.04)^2$
(b) Using the formula for the sum to n terms of a geometric series, calculate the amount Mr Wise has saved after 3 years.

(a) Balance at end of first year:
$1.04 \times 100 = 104$

At the start of the second year, Mr Wise deposits another £100.

Balance at start of second year:
$100 + 104$

Balance at end of second year:
$(1.04)(100 + 104)$
$= 104 + (104)(1.04)$

At the start of the third year, Mr Wise deposits another £100.

Balance at start of third year:
$100 + (104) + (104)(1.04)$

Balance at end of third year:
$1.04 \times (100 + (104) + (104)(1.04))$
$= 104 + (104)(1.04) + (104)(1.04)^2$

(b) We have a geometric series with first term $a = 104$ and common ratio $r = 1.04$. There are three terms, so $n = 3$.

To find the total:
$S_n = \dfrac{a(r^n - 1)}{r - 1}$

$S_3 = \dfrac{104(1.04^3 - 1)}{1.04 - 1}$

$= £324.65$ (to the nearest penny).

Exercise 5L

1. A company makes a profit of £49 000 in the year 2019. A model for future performance assumes that yearly profits will increase in an arithmetic sequence with common difference d. This model predicts total profits of £275 000 for the 5 years 2019 to 2023 inclusive.
   (a) Find the value of d.
   (b) Using your value of d find the predicted profit for the year 2026.
   (c) A different model for future performance assumes that yearly profits will increase in a geometric sequence with common ratio 1.1.

Exercise 5L...

Using this model find the predicted profit for the year 2026. Give your answer to 3 significant figures.

(d) If you were the company's financial director, which model would you recommend using and why?

2. Aideen repays a loan over a period of n months. Her monthly repayments are modelled as an arithmetic sequence. She repays £129 in the first month, £127 in the second month, £125 in the third month, and so on. She makes her final repayment in the nth month, where $n > 16$.
   (a) Find the amount Aideen repays in month number 16.
   (b) Over the n months, she repays a total of £4000. Form an equation in n, and show that your equation may be written as $n^2 - 130n + 4000 = 0$
   (c) Solve the equation in part (b) to find two solutions.
   (d) State, with a reason, which of these solutions to the equation is not a sensible solution to the repayment problem.

3. A marathon runner prepares for a race by completing a practice run on each of 9 consecutive days. On each day after the first run, she runs further than she did on the previous day. The lengths of her 9 practice runs form an arithmetic sequence with first term a km and common difference d km. She runs 16.4 km on the 9th day, and she runs a total of 118.8 km over the 9 day period. Find the value of a and the value of d.

4. A ball is dropped from a height of h metres, then bounces 4 times. A model of the trajectory of the ball assumes that, every time it bounces, the ball reaches some fraction r of its previous height, where $r < 1$. It is caught at the top of its trajectory after the fourth bounce.
   (a) Show that the total distance d travelled by the ball is given by:
   $d = h(1 + 2r + 2r^2 + 2r^3 + r^4)$
   (b) If $h = 2$ and $r = ¾$ use this formula to find how far the ball travels before being caught.
   (c) State one factor that might make this model unreliable.

Exercise 5L...

5. A banker received a Christmas bonus of £11 000 in the year 2011. The banker's contract promises a 4% increase in bonus every year. The first increase was given in 2012.
   (a) Find, to the nearest £100, the banker's bonus in the year 2014.

   The banker receives a bonus each year from 2011 until he retires at the end of 2027.
   (b) Find, to the nearest £1000, the total amount of bonus he will receive in the period from 2011 until he retires at the end of 2027.

5.13 Summary

A **sequence** is a list of numbers, generated by a rule.

The **general term** of a sequence is denoted u_n.

Sequences can be generated by a formula involving n, or by a **recurrence relation** involving the previous term.

An **arithmetic progression** is a sequence in which successive terms differ by a constant, called the **common difference**.

The recurrence relation for an arithmetic progression is:
$u_{n+1} = u_n + d$
where d is the common difference.

A **geometric progression** is a sequence in which the ratio of successive terms is constant.

The recurrence relation for a geometric progression is:
$u_{n+1} = u_n r$.

A **series** is the sum of the terms of a sequence.

An **arithmetic series** $a + (a + d) + (a + 2d) + \cdots$ has general term $u_n = a + (n-1)d$, where a is the first term, d is the common difference and n is the number of terms.

The sum to n terms of an arithmetic series is given by:
$S_n = \dfrac{n}{2}[2a + (n-1)d]$.

A **geometric series** $a + ar + ar^2 + \cdots$ has general term ar^{n-1}. The first term is a and the common ratio is r.

The sum to n terms of a geometric series is given by:
$S_n = \dfrac{a(1 - r^n)}{1 - r}$.

An infinite geometric series converges if $|r| < 1$.

The sum to infinity of a convergent geometric series is given by: $S_n = \dfrac{a}{1-r}$.

Sigma notation can be used to denote the sum of both arithmetic and geometric series.

You will be asked to model real-life situations involving sequences and series.

Chapter 6
Binomial Expansion

6.1 Introduction

In AS Mathematics, you were introduced to the **binomial expansion** to expand expressions of the form $(a + bx)^n$.

The binomial expansion is very useful. For example, it provides a method for expanding the brackets in expressions such as $(1 + 2x)^4$.

Until now, you have used the binomial expansion with integer powers. In these cases, the expansion had a finite number of terms.

In this chapter, you will learn that the binomial expansion can be used for any rational value of n, for example $5/3$. It can also be used for negative numbers. When used in these ways, the binomial expansion is an infinite series. We will usually look at an **approximation** to the expansion by taking the first few terms.

Key words
- **Binomial expansion**: The expansion of expressions of the type $(a + bx)^n$.
- **Rational number**: Any number that can be written as a fraction.

Before you start
You should know:
- How to use the binomial expansion for positive integer powers.
- How to manipulate expressions involving surds.
- How to multiply out brackets involving terms in various powers of x.
- How to use partial fractions.

Worked Examples

1. Using the binomial expansion, expand $(a - b)^4$

    Make the first term inside the brackets 1.
    $$(a - b)^4 = a^4 \left(1 - \frac{b}{a}\right)^4$$
    Be careful with the second term. It is $-\frac{b}{a}$.

    $$= a^4 \left[1 + 4\left(-\frac{b}{a}\right) + \frac{(4)(3)}{2!}\left(-\frac{b}{a}\right)^2 \right.$$
    $$\left. + \frac{(4)(3)(2)}{3!}\left(-\frac{b}{a}\right)^3 + \left(-\frac{b}{a}\right)^4\right]$$
    $$= a^4\left[1 - 4\left(\frac{b}{a}\right) + 6\left(\frac{b}{a}\right)^2 - 4\left(\frac{b}{a}\right)^3 + \left(\frac{b}{a}\right)^4\right]$$
    $$= a^4 - 4a^3b + 6a^2b^2 - 4ab^3 + b^4$$

2. Write $\sqrt{0.8}$ in terms of $\sqrt{5}$.

    $$\sqrt{0.8} = \sqrt{\frac{80}{100}}$$
    $$= \sqrt{\frac{16 \times 5}{100}}$$
    $$= \sqrt{\frac{16}{100}} \times \sqrt{5}$$
    $$= \frac{4}{10} \times \sqrt{5}$$
    $$= \frac{2}{5}\sqrt{5}$$

3. Write $\dfrac{1}{\left(\sqrt[3]{1 + \frac{5}{x}}\right)^2}$ in the form $\left(a + \frac{b}{x}\right)^n$.

    $$\frac{1}{\left(\sqrt[3]{1 + \frac{5}{x}}\right)^2} = \left(\sqrt[3]{1 + \frac{5}{x}}\right)^{-2}$$
    $$= \left(1 + \frac{5}{x}\right)^{-\frac{2}{3}}$$

What you will learn
In this chapter you will learn:
- How to use the binomial expansion for expressions with fractional or negative powers.
- When an expansion of this type is valid.

PURE MATHEMATICS FOR CCEA A2

- How to use partial fractions in conjunction with the binomial expansion.
- How to make approximations using the binomial expansion.

In the real world...

In October 1971, physicist Joseph Hafele and astronomer Richard Keating took four atomic clocks on board aeroplanes and flew twice around the world.

They compared the times measured by the atomic clocks with the United States Naval Observatory's clocks.

This was one of the most rigorous tests of Einstein's theories of Special and General Relativity, which state that time is distorted by velocity and also by gravitational fields.

For the distortion due to velocity, relativity predicts that the time T is given by:

$$T = T_0\left(1 - \frac{v^2}{c^2}\right)^{-\frac{1}{2}}$$

where T_0 is the 'proper time', v is the velocity and c is the speed of light.

A similar equation describes the distortion expected due to gravitational differences.

Using the binomial expansion, it is possible to expand the brackets in the equation above. In this way, the scientists approximated the time they expected to pass according to the atomic clocks. The predictions came very close to the actual times recorded.

Today, GPS (the Global Positioning System) can provide incredibly accurate data on your exact position on Earth. However, because the satellites used are travelling at high velocities and are subjected to weaker gravity, their onboard clocks have to be corrected for these strange effects.

Time may fly when you're having fun, but it slows down when you're travelling at high speeds!

Exercise 6A (Revision)

1. Expand the following using the binomial expansion.
   (a) $(1 + x)^4$ (b) $(x + 2)^3$

2. Find the first three terms of the binomial expansion for $(a + b)^{15}$.

3. Which term of the binomial expansion of $(1 + 3x)^5$ contains the coefficient 270?

Exercise 6A...

4. Write the following as $a\sqrt{b}$ where a is a fraction and b is a positive integer.

   (a) $\sqrt{\frac{3}{4}}$ (b) $\sqrt{\frac{12}{49}}$ (c) $\sqrt{\frac{125}{81}}$ (d) $\sqrt{0.96}$

5. Write the following in the form $(a + f(x))^n$ where a is a positive integer, $f(x)$ is some function of x and n is a rational number.

   (a) $\dfrac{1}{(1+x)^{-2}}$ (b) $\left(\dfrac{x}{x+2}\right)^{-7}$

   (c) $\sqrt[5]{\left(\dfrac{1}{2+x^3}\right)^2}$

6. By expanding the brackets, find the term in x^2 in each of the following.

   (a) $(1 + x)(x^2 + 2x + 1)$

   (b) $\left(1 + \dfrac{1}{x}\right)(x^3 + 3x^2 + 3x + 1)$

   (c) $\left(x + 2 + \dfrac{3}{x} + \dfrac{4}{x^2}\right)\left(\dfrac{6}{x} + 5 + 4x\right)$

7. Express the following in terms of their partial fractions.

   (a) $\dfrac{2}{(x+1)(2x+5)}$

   (b) $\dfrac{4x+3}{(x+1)(x+2)}$

   (c) $\dfrac{7x^2+19x+14}{(x+2)(x+1)^2}$

6.2 Binomial Series For Any Rational Value of n

In AS Mathematics you learnt how to use the binomial expansion to expand $(a + bx)^n$ into a finite series of powers of x. This can be extended so that n can be any rational number, including negative numbers. In these cases, the expansion is an infinite series. We usually take the first few terms of the series as an approximation.

$$(1+x)^n = 1 + nx + \frac{n(n-1)}{2!}x^2 + \frac{n(n-1)(n-2)}{3!}x^3 + \cdots$$

In A2 Mathematics, n will not be a positive integer, and it is important to note the following:

- In AS Mathematics you were able to find the coefficients using Pascal's triangle, or using the ^nC_r button on your calculator. Neither of these methods can be used.
- When expanding $(a + bx)^n$ you must re-arrange the expression to: $a^n \left(1 + \frac{bx}{a}\right)^n$. The binomial expansion formula is then used to expand $\left(1 + \frac{bx}{a}\right)^n$.
- In AS Mathematics you may have learnt an alternative formula for the expansion of $(a + bx)^n$. This cannot be applied in A2 Mathematics.
- Because the series is infinite, we must consider whether the series is convergent or divergent. When expanding $(a + bx)^n$, the criterion for convergence is $\left|\frac{bx}{a}\right| < 1$.

Worked Examples

4. Find the first three terms in the binomial expansion of $(1 + x)^{\frac{2}{3}}$. State the range of values for which this expansion is valid.

The formula for the infinite version of the binomial expansion is:

$$(1 + x)^n = 1 + nx + \frac{n(n-1)}{2!}x^2 + \frac{n(n-1)(n-2)}{3!}x^3 + \cdots$$

Therefore:

$$(1 + x)^{\frac{2}{3}} \approx 1 + \frac{2}{3}x + \frac{\frac{2}{3}\left(-\frac{1}{3}\right)}{2!}x^2 + \cdots$$

$$(1 + x)^{\frac{2}{3}} \approx 1 + \frac{2x}{3} - \frac{x^2}{9} + \cdots$$

This expansion is valid if $|x| < 1$.

5. Using the binomial expansion, expand $(4 - 3x)^{\frac{5}{2}}$ as far as the term in x^3. State for which values of x this is a convergent series.

$(4 - 3x)^{\frac{5}{2}}$

$= 4^{\frac{5}{2}}\left(1 - \frac{3x}{4}\right)^{\frac{5}{2}}$

$= 32\left[1 + \frac{5}{2}\left(-\frac{3x}{4}\right) + \frac{\left(\frac{5}{2}\right)\left(\frac{3}{2}\right)}{2!}\left(-\frac{3x}{4}\right)^2 \right.$

$\left. + \frac{\left(\frac{5}{2}\right)\left(\frac{3}{2}\right)\left(\frac{1}{2}\right)}{3!}\left(-\frac{3x}{4}\right)^3 + \cdots\right]$

$= 32\left[1 - \frac{15x}{8} + \frac{15}{8}\left(\frac{9x^2}{16}\right) - \frac{15}{48}\left(\frac{27x^3}{64}\right) + \cdots\right]$

$= 32 - 60x + \frac{135}{4}x^2 - \frac{135}{32}x^3 + \cdots$

The series converges if $\left|\frac{3x}{4}\right| < 1$, or $|x| < \frac{4}{3}$.

You may need to apply the binomial expansion twice.

Worked Example

6. Using the binomial expansion, find an approximation for $\frac{\sqrt{1-x}}{(3-x)^2}$ up to and including the term in x^2.

Find the range of values of x for which the expansion is valid.

$\frac{\sqrt{1-x}}{(3-x)^2}$

$= (1-x)^{\frac{1}{2}}(3-x)^{-2}$

$= 3^{-2}(1-x)^{\frac{1}{2}}\left(1 - \frac{x}{3}\right)^{-2}$

$= \frac{1}{9}\left[1 - \frac{1}{2}x + \frac{\left(\frac{1}{2}\right)\left(-\frac{1}{2}\right)}{2!}(-x)^2 + \cdots\right]\left[1 + (-2)\left(-\frac{x}{3}\right) + \frac{(-2)(-3)}{2!}\left(-\frac{x}{3}\right)^2 + \cdots\right]$

$= \frac{1}{9}\left[1 - \frac{x}{2} - \frac{x^2}{8} + \cdots\right]\left[1 + \frac{2x}{3} + \frac{x^2}{3} + \cdots\right]$

Expand brackets, but ignore all terms in x^3 or above:

$= \frac{1}{9}\left[1 + \frac{2x}{3} + \frac{x^2}{3} - \frac{x}{2} - \frac{x^2}{3} - \frac{x^2}{8} + \cdots\right]$

$= \frac{1}{9}\left[1 + \frac{x}{6} - \frac{x^2}{8}\right]$

$= \frac{1}{9} + \frac{x}{54} - \frac{x^2}{72}$

This sequence is only valid if $|x| < 1$ (from the first expansion) and $\left|\frac{x}{3}\right| < 1$ (from the second), i.e. if $|x| < 1$ and $|x| < 3$.

Since both conditions must be true, the expansion is valid if $|x| < 1$.

You may be given certain terms of the expansion and be asked to find the expression that generated it. In these cases, you will often have to solve simultaneous equations.

PURE MATHEMATICS FOR CCEA A2

Worked Example

7. When $(1 + ax)^n$ is expanded as a series in ascending powers of x, the coefficients of x and x^2 are $\frac{10}{3}$ and $\frac{125}{9}$ respectively.

(a) Find the value of a and the value of n.
(b) Find the coefficient of x^3.
(c) State the range of values of x for which the expansion is valid.

(a) $(1 + ax)^n$
$= 1 + nax + \dfrac{n(n-1)}{2!}(ax)^2$
$\quad + \dfrac{n(n-1)(n-2)}{3!}(ax)^3$
$= 1 + nax + \dfrac{n(n-1)}{2}a^2x^2 + \dfrac{n(n-1)(n-2)}{6}a^3x^3$

Coefficient of x is: $na = \dfrac{10}{3}$
$\Rightarrow a = \dfrac{10}{3n}$ (1)

Coefficient of x^2 is: $\dfrac{n(n-1)}{2}a^2 = \dfrac{125}{9}$

Substitute for a from (1):
$\dfrac{n(n-1)}{2}\left(\dfrac{10}{3n}\right)^2 = \dfrac{125}{9}$
$\Rightarrow \dfrac{50n(n-1)}{9n^2} = \dfrac{125}{9}$
$2n(n-1) = 5n^2$
$3n^2 = -2n$
$n = -\dfrac{2}{3}$
($n = 0$ is not a valid solution)

Substitute into (1):
$a = -5$

(b) Coefficient of x^3 is: $\dfrac{n(n-1)(n-2)a^3}{6}$
$= \dfrac{\left(-\frac{2}{3}\right)\left(-\frac{5}{3}\right)\left(-\frac{8}{3}\right)(-5)^3}{6}$
$= \dfrac{5000}{81}$

(c) The expansion is valid if $|ax| < 1$
$\Rightarrow |x| < \dfrac{1}{5}$

Exercise 6B

1. Find the first four terms in the binomial expansion for each of the following. State the range of values for which each expansion is valid.

(a) $(1 + x)^{\frac{1}{2}}$ (b) $\dfrac{1}{1+x}$ (c) $(1 + x^2)^{\frac{3}{2}}$

(d) $\sqrt{1 + 3x}$ (e) $\dfrac{1}{(1+x)^2}$ (f) $\left(1 - \dfrac{x}{2}\right)^{\frac{5}{2}}$

(g) $\dfrac{1}{\sqrt{1-2x}}$ (h) $\dfrac{1}{(1-2x)^3}$ (i) $\left(1 - \dfrac{x}{2}\right)^{\frac{1}{4}}$

(j) $\sqrt[3]{1 + x^2}$

2. Find the binomial expansion up to and including the term in x^3 for each of the following. State the range of values for which each expansion is valid.

(a) $(2 + 3x)^{-2}$ (b) $\sqrt{2 + x}$
(c) $(6 + 2x)^{-\frac{1}{2}}$ (d) $(4 + x)^{-\frac{1}{2}}$

3. $f(x) = (2 - 5x)^{-2}$, $|x| < \dfrac{2}{5}$

Find the binomial expansion of $f(x)$ in ascending powers of x, as far as the term in x^3, giving each coefficient in its simplest terms.

4. Given: $f(x) = (2 + 3x)^{-3}$, $|x| < \dfrac{2}{3}$

find the binomial expansion of $f(x)$, in ascending powers of x, as far as the term in x^3. Give each coefficient as a simplified fraction.

5. Use the binomial theorem to expand $\sqrt{9 - 4x}$, $|x| < \dfrac{9}{4}$, in ascending powers of x, up to and including the term in x^3, simplifying each term.

6. (a) Expand: $(1 - 3x)^{-\frac{2}{5}}$ in ascending powers of x up to and including the term in x^2.
(b) State the set of values of x for which the expansion is valid.

7. (a) Expand $(1 + 2x)^{-3}$, $|x| < \dfrac{1}{2}$, in ascending powers of x, up to and including the term in x^3, simplifying each term.
(b) Hence, or otherwise, find the first three terms in the expansion of $\dfrac{x+4}{(1+2x)^3}$ as a series in ascending powers of x.

Exercise 6B...

8. A geologist suspects a relationship exists between the size s of a sediment particle and the depth d at which it occurs, such that:
$$s = (1 + 4d)^{-\frac{2}{3}}$$
He wishes to approximate the relationship using an expansion in ascending powers of d.
   (a) Find the first three terms of the expansion.
   (b) State the range of values of d for which the approximation is valid.

9. By applying the binomial expansion twice, find approximations for the following. Include terms up to and including the term in x^2. Give the range of values of x for which the approximation is valid.
   (a) $\dfrac{(1+x)^2}{(1-x)^2}$ (b) $(2-x)^3\sqrt{1+4x}$
   (c) $\dfrac{1}{(1-x)^5(2-x)^4}$ (d) $\dfrac{(3+3x)^2}{2+x}$

10. When $(1 + px)^q$ is expanded as a series in ascending powers of x, the coefficients of x and x^2 are -8 and 31 respectively.
    (a) Find the value of p and the value of q.
    (b) Find the coefficient of x^3.
    (c) State the set of values for which the expansion is valid.

11. Given: $f(x) = \dfrac{1}{\sqrt{9 + 4x^2}}$
    find the first three non-zero terms of the binomial expansion of $f(x)$ in ascending powers of x. Give each coefficient as a simplified fraction.

12. Expand: $\dfrac{1}{(1+x+x^2)^2}$ up to and including the term in x^3.

6.3 Partial Fractions

You have already learnt how to separate a rational function into its partial fractions, for example:
$$\frac{2-x}{(1+2x)(3+x)} = \frac{1}{1+2x} - \frac{1}{3+x}$$

In this section you will use this technique in conjunction with the binomial expansion.

Worked Example

8. (a) Show that: $\dfrac{2-x}{(2x+1)(x+3)} = \dfrac{1}{1+2x} - \dfrac{1}{3+x}$
   (b) Hence, using the binomial expansion, obtain an approximation for $\dfrac{2-x}{(2x+1)(x+3)}$, up to and including a term in x^2. State the range of values of x for which this approximation is valid.

(a) $\dfrac{2-x}{(2x+1)(x+3)} \equiv \dfrac{A}{2x+1} + \dfrac{B}{x+3}$
$\Rightarrow 2 - x = A(x+3) + B(2x+1)$

Let $x = -3$:
$$5 = -5B \Rightarrow B = -1$$

Let $x = -\dfrac{1}{2}$:
$$\frac{5}{2} = \frac{5A}{2} \Rightarrow A = 1$$

(b) Hence:
$$\frac{2-x}{(2x+1)(x+3)} = (1+2x)^{-1} - (3+x)^{-1}$$

$(1+2x)^{-1} = 1 - 2x + \dfrac{(-1)(-2)(2x)^2}{2!} + \cdots$

$= 1 - 2x + 4x^2 + \cdots$

$(3+x)^{-1} = 3^{-1}\left(1 + \dfrac{x}{3}\right)^{-1}$

$= \dfrac{1}{3}\left(1 - \dfrac{x}{3} + \dfrac{(-1)(-2)\left(\frac{x}{3}\right)^2}{2!} + \cdots\right)$

$= \dfrac{1}{3}\left(1 - \dfrac{x}{3} + \dfrac{x^2}{9} + \cdots\right)$

$= \dfrac{1}{3} - \dfrac{x}{9} + \dfrac{x^2}{27} + \cdots$

Putting the two together:
$\dfrac{2-x}{(2x+1)(x+3)}$

$= (1 - 2x + 4x^2) - \left(\dfrac{1}{3} - \dfrac{x}{9} + \dfrac{x^2}{27}\right) + \cdots$

$= \dfrac{2}{3} - \dfrac{17x}{9} + \dfrac{107x^2}{27} + \cdots$

The first expansion is valid when:
$$|2x| < 1 \Rightarrow |x| < \frac{1}{2}$$

The second expansion is valid when:
$$\left|\frac{x}{3}\right| < 1 \Rightarrow |x| < 3$$

Both conditions must apply, so $|x| < \frac{1}{2}$.

In the case of improper fractions, you may need to use long division before you can find partial fractions. For further examples, see section 1.4.

Worked Example

9. (a) Using long division, show that
$$\frac{8x^2 - 2x - 9}{4x + 3} = 2x - 2 - \frac{3}{4x + 3}$$

(b) Expand $\frac{3}{4x + 3}$ in a series of ascending powers of x up to and including the term in x^3.

(c) Hence show that $\frac{8x^2 - 2x - 9}{4x + 3}$ can be approximated as:
$$-3 + \frac{10x}{3} - \frac{16x^2}{9} + \frac{64x^3}{27}$$

(d) Give the range of values of x for which this expansion is valid.

(a)
$$\begin{array}{r} 2x - 2 \\ 4x+3 \overline{\smash{)}8x^2 - 2x - 9} \\ \underline{8x^2 + 6x} \\ -8x - 9 \\ \underline{-8x - 6} \\ -3 \end{array}$$

Hence:
$$\frac{8x^2 - 2x - 9}{4x + 3} = 2x - 2 - \frac{3}{4x + 3}$$

(b) $\frac{3}{4x + 3} = 3(3 + 4x)^{-1}$

Taking the 3 outside brackets, it becomes 3^{-1}:

$$= \frac{3}{3}\left(1 + \frac{4x}{3}\right)^{-1}$$

$$= 1 - \frac{4x}{3} + \frac{(-1)(-2)\left(\frac{4x}{3}\right)^2}{2!}$$

$$+ \frac{(-1)(-2)(-3)\left(\frac{4x}{3}\right)^3}{3!} + \cdots$$

$$= 1 - \frac{4x}{3} + \frac{16x^2}{9} - \frac{64x^3}{27} + \cdots$$

(c) $\frac{8x^2 - 2x - 9}{4x + 3}$

$$= 2x - 2 - \frac{3}{4x + 3}$$

$$\approx 2x - 2 - \left(1 - \frac{4x}{3} + \frac{16x^2}{9} - \frac{64x^3}{27}\right)$$

$$= -3 + \frac{10x}{3} - \frac{16x^2}{9} + \frac{64x^3}{27}$$

(d) Expansion is valid for:
$$|4x| < 3$$
i.e. $|x| < \frac{3}{4}$

Exercise 6C

1. Express the following in terms of their partial fractions. Hence, using the binomial expansion, expand each expression in a series of ascending powers of x, as far as the term in x^3. In each case, state the range of values of x for which the expansion is valid.

   (a) $\dfrac{x + 3}{(-3x + 1)(2x + 1)}$

   (b) $\dfrac{5x - 3}{(-x + 1)(2x - 3)}$

   (c) $\dfrac{-x + 2}{(1 - x)(x + 1)}$

   (d) $\dfrac{-4x - 1}{(2x + 1)(-x + 1)}$

   (e) $\dfrac{-x - 2}{(5x + 1)(-x + 1)}$

   (f) $\dfrac{-x - 4}{(5x + 3)(-3x - 2)}$

   (g) $\dfrac{4x + 1}{(2 - x)(5 - 4x)}$

   (h) $\dfrac{-4x + 4}{(4 - 2x)(3x - 4)}$

   (i) $\dfrac{-5x}{(1 + 3x)(1 + x)}$

   (j) $\dfrac{3x + 3}{(2x - 5)(5x - 2)}$

2. By finding partial fractions for the following expressions, expand each in a series of ascending powers of x, as far as the term in x^3. In each case, state the range of values of x for which the expansion is valid.

   (a) $\dfrac{1}{x^2 - 1}$

   (b) $\dfrac{1 + 2x}{(1 - 3x)^2}$

   (c) $\dfrac{x}{(1 + 2x)^2}$

   (d) $\dfrac{2}{(x + 2)(x + 1)^2}$

Exercise 6C

(e) $\dfrac{4}{(x-3)(x+1)^2}$ (f) $\dfrac{9x+3}{(x-1)^2(x+2)}$

(g) $\dfrac{2(x^2+1)}{(x-1)^2(x+1)}$ (h) $\dfrac{2x^2-x+1}{(x+1)(x-1)^2}$

(i) $\dfrac{(3x+1)(2x-5)}{(1+4x)(1-x)^2}$

3. Using partial fractions, expand the following in a series of ascending powers of n, as far as the term in n^3: $\dfrac{n+1}{(3n-1)^2}$

4. (a) Using long division, show that:
$$\dfrac{-4x^2+5x+3}{8x+6} = -\dfrac{x}{2}+1-\dfrac{3}{8x+6}$$

   (b) Expand $\dfrac{3}{8x+6}$ in a series of ascending powers of x up to and including the term in x^3.

   (c) Hence show that $\dfrac{-4x^2+5x+3}{8x+6}$ can be approximated as:
$$\dfrac{1}{2}+\dfrac{1}{6}x-\dfrac{8}{9}x^2+\dfrac{32}{27}x^3$$

   (d) Give the range of values of x for which this expansion is valid.

5. (a) Using long division, show that:
$$\dfrac{2x^3+5x^2-1}{x^2+2x-3} = 2x+1+\dfrac{4x+2}{x^2+2x-3}$$

   (b) Using partial fractions, show that:
$$\dfrac{4x+2}{x^2+2x-3} = \dfrac{3}{2(x-1)}+\dfrac{5}{2(x+3)}$$

   (c) Expand $\dfrac{3}{2(x-1)}$ in a series of ascending powers of x up to and including the term in x^3.

   (d) Expand $\dfrac{5}{2(x+3)}$ in a series of ascending powers of x up to and including the term in x^3.

   (e) Hence show that $\dfrac{2x^3+5x^2-1}{x^2+2x-3}$ can be approximated as:
$$\dfrac{1}{3}+\dfrac{2}{9}x-\dfrac{38}{27}x^2-\dfrac{124}{81}x^3$$

   (f) Give the range of values of x for which this expansion is valid.

Exercise 6C...

6. (a) Use long division to rewrite the following fraction in the form $Ax+B+\dfrac{C}{Dx+E}$ where A, B, C, D and E are constants to be found: $\dfrac{9x^2+6x-8}{3x+1}$

   (b) Hence find a binomial expansion for $\dfrac{9x^2+6x-8}{3x+1}$, up to and including the term in x^3.

7. The function $f(x)$ is defined such that:
$$f(x) = \dfrac{3x^2+15}{(1-4x)(2+x)^2}$$

   (a) By expressing $f(x)$ in the form:
$$f(x) = \dfrac{A}{1-4x}+\dfrac{B}{2+x}+\dfrac{C}{(2+x)^2}, \quad |x|<\dfrac{1}{4}$$
   find the values of A and C and show that $B=0$.

   (b) Hence, or otherwise, find the series expansion of $f(x)$ in ascending powers of x, up to and including the term in x^3. Simplify each term.

6.4 Approximation Using the Binomial Expansion

You can use the binomial expansion to approximate numerical expressions.

Worked Examples

10. (a) Find the binomial expansion for $(1+x)^{-6}$ up to and including the term in x^4.

    (b) State the range of values of x for which your expansion is valid.

    (c) By letting $x=0.01$ in your binomial expansion, find the value of $\left(\dfrac{100}{101}\right)^6$ correct to 5 decimal places.

(a) $(1+x)^{-6}$
$$= 1-6x+\dfrac{(-6)(-7)x^2}{2!}$$
$$+\dfrac{(-6)(-7)(-8)x^3}{3!}$$
$$+\dfrac{(-6)(-7)(-8)(-9)x^4}{4!}+\cdots$$
$$= 1-6x+21x^2-56x^3+126x^4+\cdots$$

(b) The expansion is valid for $|x| < 1$

(c) Note that $\left(\dfrac{100}{101}\right)^6 = \left(\dfrac{101}{100}\right)^{-6} = (1.01)^{-6}$.

Hence we can use our expansion with $x = 0.01$.
$(1+x)^{-6} = 1 - 6x + 21x^2 - 56x^3 + 126x^4 + \cdots$

Letting $x = 0.01$:
$(1.01)^{-6}$
$= 1 - 6(0.01) + 21(0.01)^2 - 56(0.01)^3$
$\quad + 126(0.01)^4$
$= 1 - 0.06 + 0.0021 - 0.000056 + 0.00000126$
$= 0.94205 \text{ (5 decimal places)}$

---

11. (a) Find the binomial expansion for $(1 - 4x)^{\frac{1}{2}}$ up to and including the term in x^4.

(b) State the values of x for which this is a valid expansion.

(c) By using an appropriate value of x in your answer to part (a), find an approximation to $\sqrt{0.96}$ correct to 4 decimal places.

(d) Using your answer to part (c), approximate $\sqrt{6}$.

(a) $(1 - 4x)^{\frac{1}{2}}$
$= 1 - \left(\dfrac{1}{2}\right)(4x) + \dfrac{\left(\frac{1}{2}\right)\left(-\frac{1}{2}\right)(4x)^2}{2!}$
$\quad - \dfrac{\left(\frac{1}{2}\right)\left(-\frac{1}{2}\right)\left(-\frac{3}{2}\right)(4x)^3}{3!}$
$\quad + \dfrac{\left(\frac{1}{2}\right)\left(-\frac{1}{2}\right)\left(-\frac{3}{2}\right)\left(-\frac{5}{2}\right)(4x)^4}{4!} + \cdots$
$= 1 - 2x - 2x^2 - 4x^3 - 10x^4 + \cdots$

(b) The expansion is valid for $|4x| < 1 \Rightarrow |x| < \dfrac{1}{4}$.

(c) From (a):
$(1 - 4x)^{\frac{1}{2}} = 1 - 2x - 2x^2 - 4x^3 - 10x^4 + \cdots$

Let $x = 0.01$ in the expansion:
$\sqrt{0.96} = 1 - 2(0.01) - 2(0.01)^2 - 4(0.01)^3$
$\quad - 10(0.01)^4 + \cdots$
$= 1 - 0.02 - 0.0002 - 0.000004$
$\quad - 0.0000001 + \cdots$
$= 0.9798 \text{ (4 decimal places)}$

(d) $\sqrt{0.96} = \sqrt{\dfrac{96}{100}} = \sqrt{\dfrac{16 \times 6}{100}} = \sqrt{\dfrac{16}{100}}\sqrt{6} = \dfrac{4}{10}\sqrt{6}$
$= \dfrac{2}{5}\sqrt{6}$

$\therefore \sqrt{6} = \dfrac{5}{2}\sqrt{0.96}$
$= \dfrac{5}{2}(0.9798)$
$= 2.4495 \text{ (4 decimal places)}$

Exercise 6D

1. (a) Find an approximation for $(1 + x)^{\frac{1}{2}}$ up to and including the term in x^3.

(b) Substitute $x = -0.02$ into your answer to part (a) to obtain an approximation for $\sqrt{0.98}$ to 6 decimal places.

(c) Write $\sqrt{0.98}$ as a multiple of $\sqrt{2}$.

(d) Using your answers to parts (b) and (c), obtain an approximation to $\sqrt{2}$ to 6 decimal places.

2. (a) Expand $(1 - 4x)^{\frac{1}{3}}$, $|x| < \dfrac{1}{4}$ in ascending powers of x, up to and including the term in x^3.

(b) By substituting $x = 10^{-3}$ in your expansion, find, to 9 significant figures, the cube root of 996.

3. (a) Expand $(8 - 5x)^{\frac{1}{3}}$, $|x| < \dfrac{8}{5}$ in ascending powers of x up to and including the term in x^3, giving each term as a simplified fraction.

(b) Use your expansion with a suitable value of x to obtain an approximation to the cube root of 7.5 giving your answer to 7 significant figures.

4. (a) Expand $\left(2 + \dfrac{1}{4}x\right)^7$ in ascending powers of x as far as the term in x^3, simplifying each term.

(b) Hence find $(2.025)^7$ correct to 3 decimal places.

5. (a) Find the binomial expansion for $\left(1 + \dfrac{1}{x}\right)^{\frac{1}{2}}$ in descending powers of x, up to and including the term in x^{-3}.

(b) Using your answer to part (a) with $x = 100$, find an approximation to $\sqrt{101}$, correct to 2 decimal places.

6.5 Summary

The **formula for the binomial expansion** is:

$$(1+x)^n = 1 + nx + \frac{n(n-1)}{2!}x^2 + \frac{n(n-1)(n-2)}{3!}x^3 + \cdots$$

In AS Mathematics you applied this for positive integer values of n. In this chapter you learnt that it can also be applied for **any rational power** n.

When using the expansion in this way it becomes an **infinite series**. Approximations can be made by truncating after a finite number of terms.

When expanding $(a + bx)^n$ for **non-positive integer values** of n, you must re-arrange the expression to

$$a^n \left(1 + \frac{bx}{a}\right)^n$$

Since the expansion of $(a + bx)^n$ is an infinite series, we must consider whether the series is **convergent** or **divergent**. The criterion for convergence is $\left|\frac{bx}{a}\right| < 1$.

You may need to apply the binomial expansion more than once. For example, you may be required to find two expansions, then find the product.

A rational function may need to be written as a sum of its **partial fractions**, then the binomial expansion applied to both. Long division may be required for improper fractions.

A binomial expansion can be used to obtain **numerical approximations**, by using carefully chosen values of x.

Chapter 7
Trigonometric Functions

7.1 Introduction

Keywords
- **Trigonometric ratio**: Any of the trigonometry functions acting on an angle, for example sin 30°.
- **Cosec**: Reciprocal function of sin.
- **Sec**: Reciprocal function of cos.
- **Cot**: Reciprocal function of tan.
- **Arcsin**: Inverse function of sin.
- **Arccos**: Inverse function of cos.
- **Arctan**: Inverse function of tan.
- **Domain**: The set of x-values a function can take.
- **Range**: The set of y-values that can result from a function.
- **Restricted domain**: A part of the domain of a function. Used when finding an inverse to ensure the inverse is also a function.

Before you start
You should know:
- About radian measure.
- The values of certain 'special' trigonometric ratios, both in degrees and radians, for example sin 60° and $\cos\left(\frac{\pi}{3}\right)$.
- The shapes of the graphs of the sin, cos and tan functions.
- About transformations of graphs.
- How to find an inverse function algebraically.
- How to find the domain and range of a function and its inverse.

Worked Examples

1. Using the special triangles, find the exact values for the following:
   (a) sin 60°   (b) cos 45°

   (a) From the triangle shown:
   $$\sin 60° = \frac{\text{opp}}{\text{hyp}} = \frac{\sqrt{3}}{2}$$

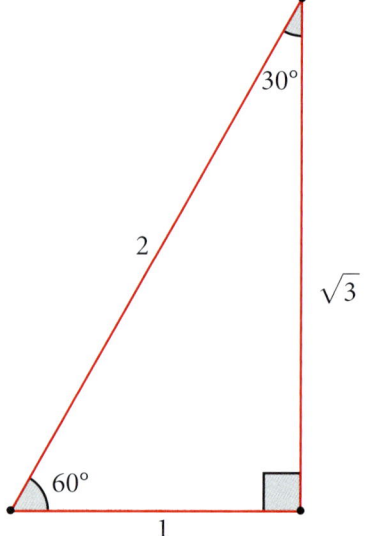

   (b) From the triangle shown:
   $$\cos 45° = \frac{\text{adj}}{\text{hyp}} = \frac{1}{\sqrt{2}} = \frac{\sqrt{2}}{2}$$

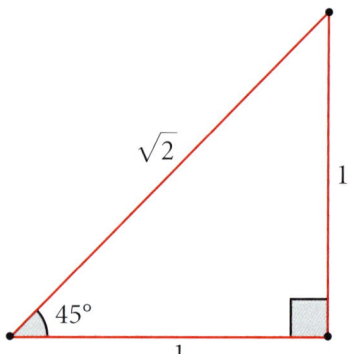

2. $g(x) = \sin(2x) + 1$
   (a) Sketch the graph of $y = g(x)$ for $0° \leq x \leq 360°$
   (b) State the domain and range of the function.

   (a) First consider the graph of $f(x) = \sin x$:

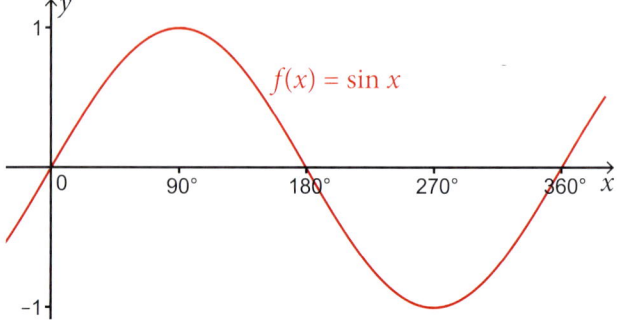

Two transformations take place:
1. Stretch, scale factor ½, in the x-direction.
2. Translation by 1 unit in the positive y-direction.

The graph of the transformed function is:

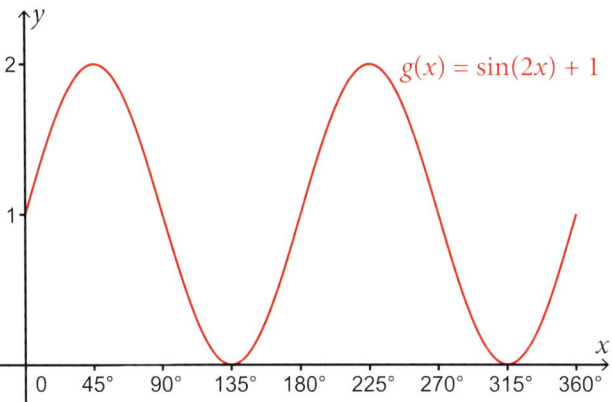

(b) The domain is: $0° \leq x \leq 360°$ (this was given in the question). The range is: $0 \leq g(x) \leq 2$.

3. Find the inverse of the following function and state its domain and range:
$f(x) = 6 - \dfrac{1}{x}, x \in \mathbb{R}, x \neq 0$

$y = 6 - \dfrac{1}{x}$

$\dfrac{1}{x} = 6 - y$

$x = \dfrac{1}{6 - y}$

So the inverse function is:
$f^{-1}(x) = \dfrac{1}{6 - x}$

Domain: $x \in \mathbb{R}, x \neq 6$ (since we can't divide by zero).

The range is the same as the domain of the original function. Remember to state the range using the name of the function:

Range: $f^{-1}(x) \in \mathbb{R}, f^{-1}(x) \neq 0$

What you will learn

In this chapter you will learn:

- About the **reciprocal trigonometric functions** sec, cosec and cot; how to use them and how to sketch their graphs.
- About the **inverse trigonometric functions** and how to sketch their graphs.
- About the domains and ranges of all these functions.

In the real world...

THE EARTH IS FLAT! And I will give £500 to anybody who can prove otherwise!

These were the words, in 1870, of John Hampden, a member of the Flat Earth Society.

Alfred Russel Wallace, intrigued by the challenge and short of money at the time (£500 was equivalent to about £35,000 in today's money), designed an experiment in which he set up two objects along a 10 km stretch of a canal. Both objects were at the same height above the water. He mounted a telescope on a bridge at the same height above the water.

When seen through the telescope, one object appeared higher than the other, showing the curvature of the Earth. Using trigonometry, it was even possible to estimate the circumference of the Earth.

The judge for the wager declared Wallace the winner, but Hampden refused to accept the result. He sued Wallace and over the next few years launched a campaign of writing letters to denounce Wallace as a con-man and a thief. Wallace won several libel suits against Hampden and Hampden was sent to prison for libel and threatening to kill Wallace. But the legal action had cost Wallace far more than the amount of the wager and cost him several years of his life.

Exercise 7A (Revision)

1. Using the graphs of the trigonometric functions or the special triangles, find the exact values of the following. Do not use your calculator for this question.
   (a) $\sin\left(\dfrac{\pi}{4}\right)$
   (b) $\cos 180°$
   (c) $\tan\left(\dfrac{\pi}{3}\right)$
   (d) $\sin 30° - \cos 60°$

2. Sketch the graph of $y = f(x)$ for each of the following. Use the domain $0° \leq x \leq 360°$.
   (a) $f(x) = |\sin x|$
   (b) $f(x) = \tan\left(\dfrac{x}{2}\right)$
   (c) $f(x) = \cos(3x) - 1$

Exercise 7A...

3. Find the inverse of the following functions and state the domain and range.

   (a) $f(x) = -1 - \dfrac{x}{5}, x \in \mathbb{R}$

   (b) $f(x) = 8x^3, x \in \mathbb{R}$

   (c) $f(x) = +\sqrt{2x}, x \in \mathbb{R}, x > 0$

7.2 Reciprocal Trigonometric Functions

The reciprocal trigonometric functions are **secant**, **cosecant** and **cotangent**. They are usually abbreviated to **sec**, **cosec** and **cot**. They are defined as follows:

$$\sec\theta = \frac{1}{\cos\theta} \qquad \operatorname{cosec}\theta = \frac{1}{\sin\theta} \qquad \cot\theta = \frac{1}{\tan\theta}$$

There are no buttons for sec, cosec and cot on most calculators, so you will use $\dfrac{1}{\cos\theta}$ when calculating $\sec\theta$, etc.

Worked Example

4. Find the exact values of:

   (a) $\operatorname{cosec} 60°$ (b) $\sec 45°$ (c) $\cot\left(\dfrac{\pi}{3}\right)$

   (a) $\operatorname{cosec} 60° = \dfrac{1}{\sin 60°} = \dfrac{1}{\sqrt{3}/2} = \dfrac{2\sqrt{3}}{3}$

   (b) $\sec 45° = \dfrac{1}{\cos 45°} = \dfrac{1}{1/\sqrt{2}} = \sqrt{2}$

   (c) $\cot\left(\dfrac{\pi}{3}\right) = \dfrac{1}{\tan\left(\frac{\pi}{3}\right)} = \dfrac{\sqrt{3}}{3}$

If you are asked for trigonometric ratios of an obtuse or reflex angle, first consider the related acute angle. The answer can be obtained using trigonometric graphs or the CAST diagram.

Worked Examples

5. Without using a calculator, find the exact value of $\operatorname{cosec} 300°$.

   In this example, we use the CAST diagram.

   First find the value of $\sin 300°$. The angle is in the fourth quadrant, where the sine function is always negative. The equivalent acute angle is $60°$.

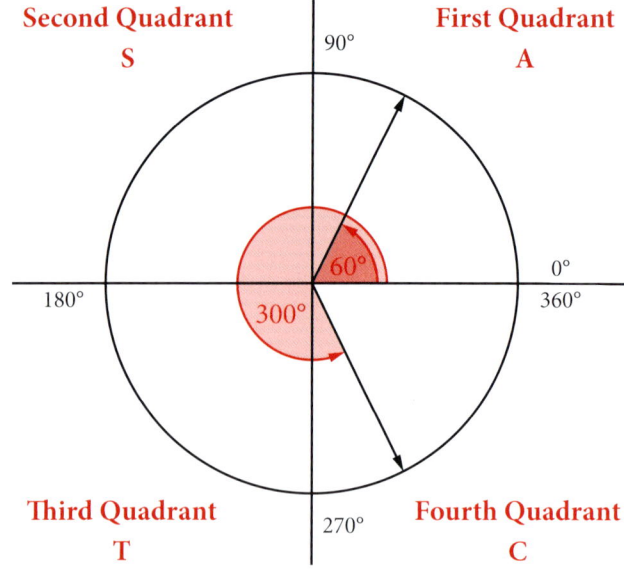

We know that:
$$\sin 60° = \frac{\sqrt{3}}{2}$$
Therefore:
$$\sin 300° = -\frac{\sqrt{3}}{2}$$
Hence:
$$\operatorname{cosec} 300° = \frac{1}{\sin 300°} = -\frac{2\sqrt{3}}{3}$$

6. $\cos\theta = -\dfrac{\sqrt{2}}{2}$

   Given that θ is a reflex angle, evaluate the following:
   (a) $\cot\theta$ (b) $\operatorname{cosec}\theta$

   (a) θ is reflex and $\cos\theta$ is negative, so the angle lies in the third quadrant:

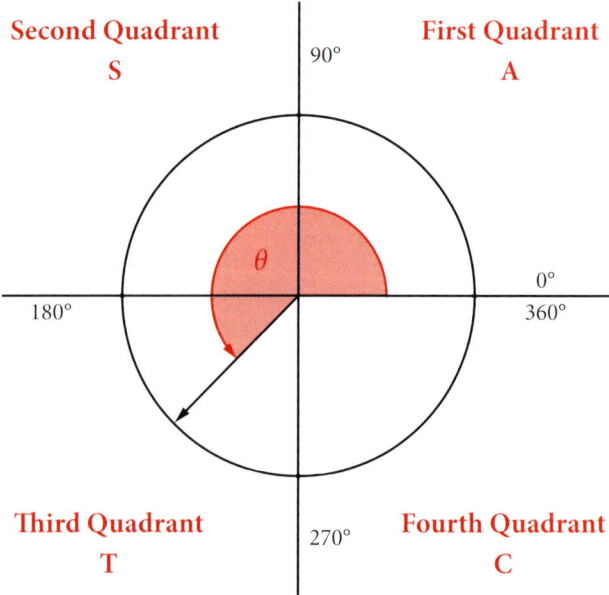

We have been given: $\cos\theta = -\dfrac{\sqrt{2}}{2}$

Recall from AS Mathematics the identity:

$$\sin^2\theta \equiv 1 - \cos^2\theta$$

$$\sin^2\theta = 1 - \left(-\dfrac{\sqrt{2}}{2}\right)^2 = \dfrac{1}{2}$$

$$\sin\theta = \sqrt{\dfrac{1}{2}} = \pm\dfrac{\sqrt{2}}{2}$$

But since θ lies in the third quadrant, $\sin\theta$ is negative, i.e.:

$$\sin\theta = -\dfrac{\sqrt{2}}{2}$$

$$\tan\theta = \dfrac{\sin\theta}{\cos\theta} = \dfrac{-\sqrt{2}/2}{-\sqrt{2}/2} = 1$$

$$\cot\theta = \dfrac{1}{\tan\theta} = 1$$

(b) $\operatorname{cosec}\theta = \dfrac{1}{\sin\theta} = \dfrac{1}{-\sqrt{2}/2} = -\sqrt{2}$

(The angle is 225° or $\dfrac{5\pi}{4}$ radians, but you are not asked to find this.)

Exercise 7B

1. Find the values of the following using your calculator, giving your answers to 3 significant figures.
   (a) $\sec 35°$
   (b) $\cot(-13°)$
   (c) $\operatorname{cosec} 107°$
   (d) $\cot 131°$
   (e) $\sec\left(\dfrac{13\pi}{9}\right)$
   (f) $\operatorname{cosec}\left(\dfrac{11\pi}{10}\right)$
   (g) $\cot\left(\dfrac{2\pi}{11}\right)$
   (h) $\sec\left(\dfrac{17\pi}{8}\right)$
   (i) $\operatorname{cosec}\left(\dfrac{\pi}{100}\right)$
   (j) $\sec\left(-\dfrac{\pi}{9}\right)$

2. Without using a calculator, find the exact values of the following.
   (a) $\operatorname{cosec} 60°$
   (b) $\cot 120°$
   (c) $\sec\left(\dfrac{\pi}{6}\right)$
   (d) $\operatorname{cosec}\left(\dfrac{2\pi}{3}\right)$
   (e) $\cot(-30°)$
   (f) $\sec\left(-\dfrac{\pi}{2}\right)$
   (g) $\operatorname{cosec}\left(\dfrac{5\pi}{4}\right)$
   (h) $\cot\left(\dfrac{7\pi}{6}\right)$
   (i) $\sec(-2\pi)$
   (j) $\operatorname{cosec}\left(\dfrac{\pi}{2}\right)$

Exercise 7B...

3. θ is an obtuse angle and $\sin\theta = \dfrac{\sqrt{3}}{2}$. Find the exact values of the following.
   (a) $\cos\theta$
   (b) $\tan\theta$
   (c) $\operatorname{cosec}\theta$
   (d) $\sec\theta$
   (e) $\cot\theta$

4. Given θ is a reflex angle and $\sec\theta = -3$, find the following, giving your answer to 2 decimal places where appropriate.
   (a) $\cos\theta$
   (b) $\sin\theta$
   (c) $\tan\theta$
   (d) $\operatorname{cosec}\theta$
   (e) $\cot\theta$

5. (a) Find $\tan\theta$ if $\operatorname{cosec}\theta = \dfrac{2}{\sqrt{3}}$, where θ is an acute angle.
   (b) Given $\cot x = -7$, find $\sin x$, where x is an obtuse angle.

7.3 The Graphs of the Reciprocal Trigonometric Functions

Using your knowledge of the graph of the sin function, you can build up the shape of the cosec graph.

$$\operatorname{cosec} x = \dfrac{1}{\sin x}$$

Whenever $\sin x = 1$, $\operatorname{cosec} x = 1$.

Likewise, when $\sin x = -1$, $\operatorname{cosec} x = -1$.

However, when $\sin x$ is between 0 and 1, $\operatorname{cosec} x > 1$.

And when $\sin x$ is between 0 and -1, $\operatorname{cosec} x < -1$.

The value of $\operatorname{cosec} x$ is undefined wherever $\sin x = 0$. The cosec function approaches infinity at these points ($x = 0, \pi, 2\pi$, etc), so we can mark asymptotes on the cosec graph:

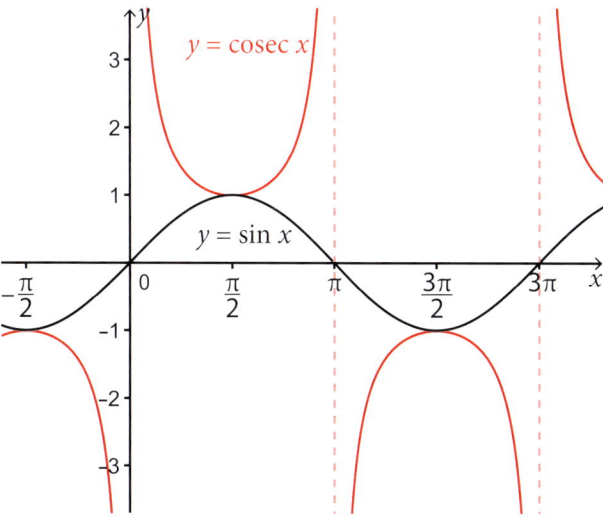

The cosec graph, like the sin graph, has a period of 2π or $360°$.

Drawing a sketch of the sec graph in a similar way produces the following:

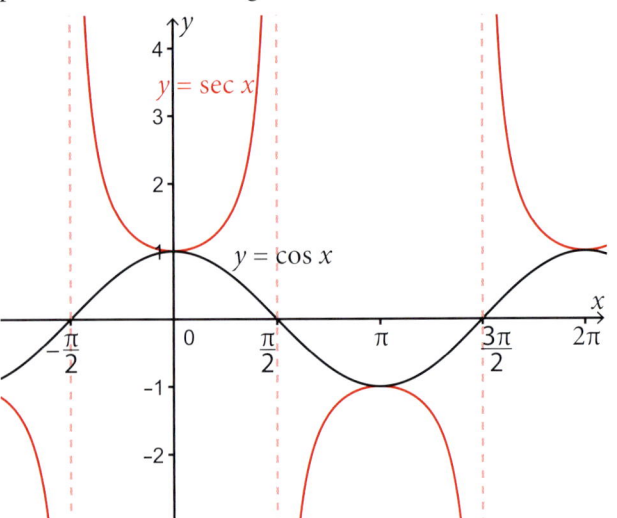

The sec graph, like the cos graph, has a period of 2π or $360°$.

Finally, the shape of the cot graph is as shown below. The curve cuts the x-axis where the tan curve has an asymptote, and vice versa.

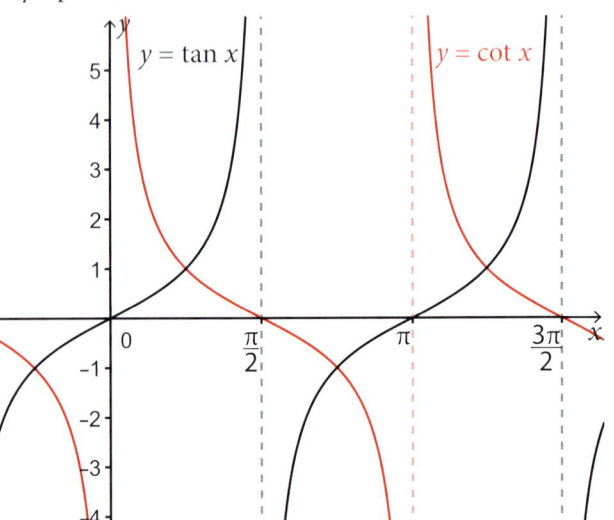

The tan and cot functions both take the value of 1 when $x = \frac{\pi}{4}$ (or $45°$) and both take the value -1 when $x = \frac{3\pi}{4}$ (or $135°$). Both the cot and tan graphs have a period of π or $180°$.

You should become familiar with the graphs of all three reciprocal trigonometric functions and be able to draw the sketches when required.

Domains and ranges

You may be asked about the domains and ranges of the reciprocal trigonometric functions, which can be found from the graphs of the three functions.

$f(x) =$	Domain (in radians, then degrees)	Range
cosec θ	$\theta \in \mathbb{R}, \theta \neq 0, \pm\pi, \pm 2\pi, \ldots$ $\theta \in \mathbb{R}, \theta \neq 0, \pm 180°, \pm 360°, \ldots$	$f(x) \in \mathbb{R}, f(x) \geq 1$ or $f(x) \leq -1$
sec θ	$\theta \in \mathbb{R}, \theta \neq \pm\frac{\pi}{2}, \pm\frac{3\pi}{2}, \ldots$ $\theta \in \mathbb{R}, \theta \neq \pm 90°, \pm 270°, \ldots$	$f(x) \in \mathbb{R}, f(x) \geq 1$ or $f(x) \leq -1$
cot θ	$\theta \in \mathbb{R}, \theta \neq 0, \pm\pi, \ldots$ $\theta \in \mathbb{R}, \theta \neq 0, \pm 180°, \ldots$	$f(x) \in \mathbb{R}$

You can use your knowledge of transformations to sketch the graphs of trigonometric functions.

Worked Example

7. Sketch the graph of $f(x) = \frac{1}{2} \operatorname{cosec}\left(\frac{x}{2}\right)$

   State the domain and range of $f(x)$.

   Beginning with the graph of $f(x) = \operatorname{cosec} x$ (shown earlier in this section), two transformations have taken place:
   1. Stretch factor 2 in the x-direction;
   2. Stretch factor ½ in the y-direction.

   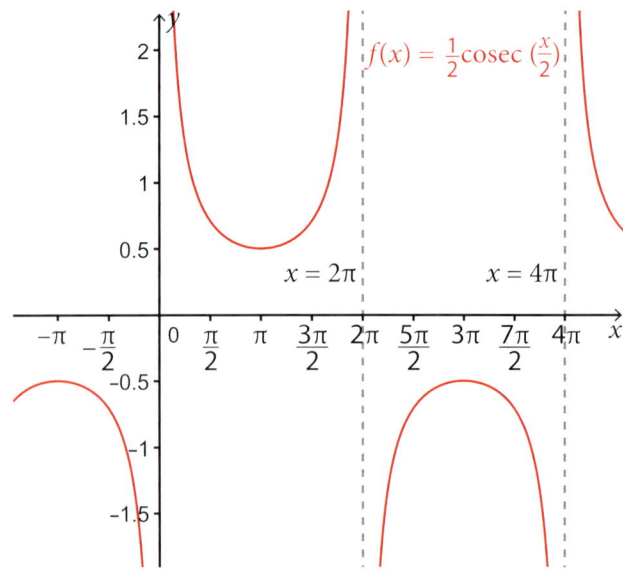

   By inspection of the graph, the domain and range of the function can be found:

   Domain: $x \in \mathbb{R}, x \neq 0, \pm 2\pi, \pm 4\pi, \ldots$

   Range: $f(x) \in \mathbb{R}, f(x) \geq 0.5$ or $f(x) \leq -0.5$.

Some important results

In AS Mathematics you learnt some of the key values from the sin, cos and tan functions. These are summarised in the table below, along with the equivalent results for the cosec, sec and cot functions.

	0° or 0 radians	30° or $\frac{\pi}{6}$	45° or $\frac{\pi}{4}$	60° or $\frac{\pi}{3}$	90° or $\frac{\pi}{2}$
$\sin\theta$	0	$\frac{1}{2}$	$\frac{\sqrt{2}}{2}$	$\frac{\sqrt{3}}{2}$	1
$\cos\theta$	1	$\frac{\sqrt{3}}{2}$	$\frac{\sqrt{2}}{2}$	$\frac{1}{2}$	0
$\tan\theta$	0	$\frac{\sqrt{3}}{3}$	1	$\sqrt{3}$	$\pm\infty$
$\text{cosec}\,\theta$	$\pm\infty$	2	$\sqrt{2}$	$\frac{2\sqrt{3}}{3}$	1
$\sec\theta$	1	$\frac{2\sqrt{3}}{3}$	$\sqrt{2}$	2	$\pm\infty$
$\cot\theta$	$\pm\infty$	$\sqrt{3}$	1	$\frac{\sqrt{3}}{3}$	0

These results can be found readily on the calculator. They can also be obtained from the **special triangles**. You first came across these two triangles in AS Mathematics:

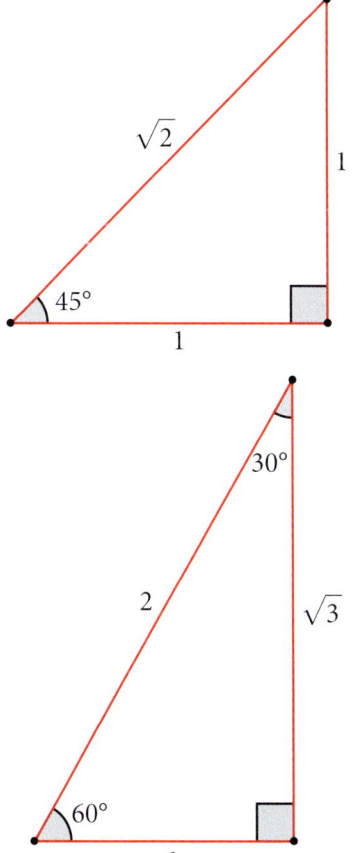

These results will help you to find the exact values of other trigonometric ratios. In some cases you can also use the symmetry of the trigonometric graphs.

Worked Example

8. By inspecting the graphs of the trigonometric functions, find the value of:

   (a) $\sec(-4\pi)$ (b) $\cot\left(\frac{7\pi}{2}\right)$

   (a) $\sec(-4\pi)$

   The sec function has period 2π, which means $\sec(-4\pi) = \sec(-2\pi) = \sec 0$.

   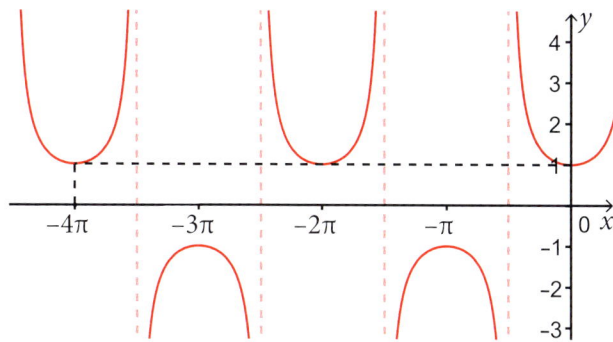

   Therefore: $\sec(-4\pi) = \sec 0 = \dfrac{1}{\cos 0} = \dfrac{1}{1} = 1$

   (b) $\cot\left(\frac{7\pi}{2}\right)$

   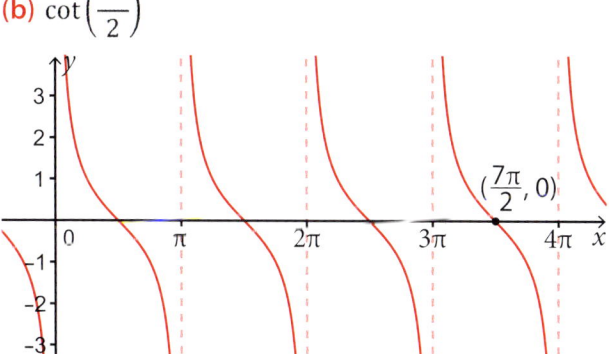

   The cot graph has period π. Therefore:

   $\cot\left(\dfrac{7\pi}{2}\right) = \cot\left(\dfrac{5\pi}{2}\right) = \cot\left(\dfrac{3\pi}{2}\right) = \cot\left(\dfrac{\pi}{2}\right)$

   Wherever the tan function has a vertical asymptote, such as at $\dfrac{\pi}{2}$, the cot function takes the value zero.

   $\therefore \cot\left(\dfrac{7\pi}{2}\right) = 0$

You will recall that, because of similarities between the sin and cos curves:

$$\cos\theta \equiv \sin\left(\frac{\pi}{2} - \theta\right)$$
$$\sin\theta \equiv \cos\left(\frac{\pi}{2} - \theta\right)$$

Note: We use the identity symbol because these relationships are always true.

By comparing the graphs of the tan and cot functions, above, you may be able to see that:

$$\tan\theta \equiv \cot\left(\frac{\pi}{2} - \theta\right)$$
$$\cot\theta \equiv \tan\left(\frac{\pi}{2} - \theta\right)$$

Likewise:

$$\sec\theta \equiv \csc\left(\frac{\pi}{2} - \theta\right)$$
$$\csc\theta \equiv \sec\left(\frac{\pi}{2} - \theta\right)$$

In degrees, the equivalent formulae are:

$$\cos\theta \equiv \sin(90° - \theta)$$
$$\sin\theta \equiv \cos(90° - \theta)$$
$$\tan\theta \equiv \cot(90° - \theta)$$
$$\cot\theta \equiv \tan(90° - \theta)$$
$$\sec\theta \equiv \csc(90° - \theta)$$
$$\csc\theta \equiv \sec(90° - \theta)$$

Worked Example

9. Given that $\tan\left(\frac{\pi}{6}\right) = \frac{\sqrt{3}}{3}$ and $\cos\left(\frac{\pi}{6}\right) = \frac{\sqrt{3}}{2}$ find, without a calculator, the value of $\cot\left(\frac{\pi}{3}\right) + \sin\left(\frac{\pi}{3}\right)$.

There are various ways to proceed, but we will use the identity:

$$\cot\theta \equiv \tan\left(\frac{\pi}{2} - \theta\right):$$

$$\cot\left(\frac{\pi}{3}\right) = \tan\left(\frac{\pi}{2} - \frac{\pi}{3}\right)$$
$$= \tan\left(\frac{\pi}{6}\right) = \frac{\sqrt{3}}{3}$$

And recall that $\sin\left(\frac{\pi}{3}\right) = \frac{\sqrt{3}}{2}$:

$$\therefore \cot\left(\frac{\pi}{3}\right) + \sin\left(\frac{\pi}{3}\right) = \frac{\sqrt{3}}{3} + \frac{\sqrt{3}}{2}$$
$$= \frac{5\sqrt{3}}{6}$$

Exercise 7C

1. Sketch the graph of $y = f(x)$ for the following functions. State the domain and range in each case.
   (a) $f(x) = \csc 2x$
   (b) $f(x) = \cot\left(\frac{x}{3}\right)$
   (c) $f(x) = 2\sec x$
   (d) $f(x) = 1 + \csc x$
   (e) $f(x) = \sec x - 1$
   (f) $f(x) = |\cot x|$
   (g) $f(x) = \csc\left(x + \frac{\pi}{4}\right)$
   (h) $f(x) = |\sec x|$
   (i) $f(x) = \cot(x - \pi)$
   (j) $f(x) = \cot|x|$

2. By inspecting the graphs of the trigonometric functions, evaluate each of the following.
   (a) $\sin\left(\frac{\pi}{3}\right)$
   (b) $\csc\left(\frac{\pi}{3}\right)$
   (c) $2\csc\left(\frac{\pi}{4}\right)$
   (d) $\cot\left(\frac{\pi}{4}\right)$
   (e) $\sec\left(-\frac{\pi}{3}\right)$
   (f) $\sec(-3\pi)$

3. Find a value of α that makes the following identities true. Give your answers in radians.
   (a) $\sin x \equiv \cos(x + \alpha)$
   (b) $\csc x \equiv \sec(x + \alpha)$

4. Without using a calculator, evaluate the following.
   (a) $\sin(2\pi) + \sin(\pi)$
   (b) $\sin\left(\frac{\pi}{4}\right)\cos\left(\frac{\pi}{4}\right)$
   (c) $\dfrac{\tan\left(\frac{\pi}{4}\right)}{\sin\left(\frac{\pi}{4}\right)}$
   (d) $\cot\left(-\frac{\pi}{2}\right)\csc\left(-\frac{\pi}{2}\right)$
   (e) $\dfrac{\tan\left(\frac{\pi}{3}\right)}{\tan\left(\frac{\pi}{6}\right)}$
   (f) $\csc\left(\frac{\pi}{2}\right) - \csc\left(-\frac{\pi}{2}\right)$

Exercise 7C...

(g) $\dfrac{1}{\sqrt{3}} \tan\left(\dfrac{4\pi}{3}\right)$

(h) $-\sec\left(-\dfrac{\pi}{4}\right) - \csc\left(-\dfrac{\pi}{4}\right) - \cot\left(-\dfrac{\pi}{4}\right)$

7.4 Inverse Trigonometric Functions

The definitions of arcsin, arccos and arctan

In chapter 2 you learnt about inverse functions. An inverse function does the opposite of the original function.

We use the notation $f^{-1}(x)$ for the inverse function.

For example, the positive square root function is the inverse of the square function:

If $f(x) = x^2$ then $f^{-1}(x) = +\sqrt{x}$.

The trigonometric functions also have inverses:

$f(x) = \sin x \Rightarrow f^{-1}(x) = \arcsin x$

$f(x) = \cos x \Rightarrow f^{-1}(x) = \arccos x$

$f(x) = \tan x \Rightarrow f^{-1}(x) = \arctan x$

You may also see this notation style for all the trigonometric inverses:

$\sin^{-1} x$

which means the same as arcsin x.

You have already used the inverse trigonometric functions in AS Mathematics for solving trigonometric equations.

> **Note:** Do not confuse the inverse trigonometric functions with the reciprocal functions.
>
> For example, $\sin^{-1} x$ is the **inverse** of the sin x function, whereas $(\sin x)^{-1}$ is the **reciprocal**, i.e. $\dfrac{1}{\sin x}$.

> **Note:** You can use your calculator to find inverse trigonometric values. The buttons are usually marked $\sin^{-1}$, $\cos^{-1}$ and $\tan^{-1}$ and are used by pressing SHIFT, then sin, cos or tan.

Worked Examples

10. Using a calculator, find the value of θ, in radians, if:
    $\sin \theta = \frac{1}{2}$

    Firstly, make sure your calculator is in radians mode.
    $\sin \theta = \frac{1}{2}$
    $\Rightarrow \theta = \arcsin(\frac{1}{2})$

    On the calculator type $\sin^{-1}(\frac{1}{2})$:
    $\theta = \dfrac{\pi}{6}$

11. Given $\sin 44.4° = 0.7$, find arcsin 0.7 as an angle in degrees.

    $\sin 44.4° = 0.7$
    $\Rightarrow 44.4° = \arcsin 0.7$

12. Using a calculator:
    (a) Find $\arcsin(0.73)$ in radians.
    (b) Given that $\arcsin x = \frac{3}{4}$, find x in radians.

    (a) From the calculator, $\sin^{-1}(0.73) = 0.818$ radians (3 s.f.)
    (b) $\arcsin x = \frac{3}{4}$
    $x = \sin(\frac{3}{4})$
    $x = 0.682$ radians (3 s.f.)

13. Using the special triangles, find the following angles. Give exact answers in radians.
    (a) $\arctan(\sqrt{3})$ (b) $\arccos\left(\dfrac{\sqrt{2}}{2}\right)$

    (a) From the triangle shown:
    $\tan\left(\dfrac{\pi}{3}\right) = \dfrac{\text{opp}}{\text{adj}} = \dfrac{\sqrt{3}}{1} = \sqrt{3}$
    $\therefore \dfrac{\pi}{3} = \arctan(\sqrt{3})$

    (b) From the triangle shown:
    $\cos\left(\dfrac{\pi}{4}\right) = \dfrac{\text{adj}}{\text{hyp}} = \dfrac{1}{\sqrt{2}} = \dfrac{\sqrt{2}}{2}$
    $\therefore \dfrac{\pi}{4} = \arccos\left(\dfrac{\sqrt{2}}{2}\right)$

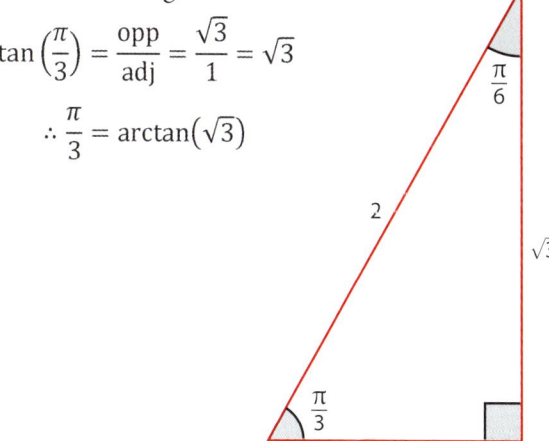

Sometimes angles are given in terms of the inverse trigonometric functions. For example, in mechanics, you may see a sentence like this:

The slope is inclined at an angle of $\tan^{-1}\left(\frac{1}{13}\right)$.

This means the angle whose tan is $\frac{1}{13}$, about 4.4°.

Often, you do not need to calculate the angle. The trigonometric ratios will be used in the question, not the angle itself.

If you have been given one of the trigonometric ratios, you can calculate the others.

Worked Examples

14. A slope is inclined at an angle θ, where $\theta = \tan^{-1}\left(\frac{1}{13}\right)$. Find $\cos\theta$ and $\sin\theta$, giving your answers as simplified surds.

$\theta = \tan^{-1}\left(\frac{1}{13}\right) \Rightarrow \tan\theta = \frac{1}{13}$

Sketch the angle in a right-angled triangle, marking the opposite side as 1 unit and the adjacent as 13:

Calculate the hypotenuse using Pythagoras' Theorem:
$\text{hyp}^2 = 1^2 + 13^2 \Rightarrow \text{hyp} = \sqrt{170}$

$\sin\theta = \frac{\text{opp}}{\text{hyp}} = \frac{1}{\sqrt{170}} = \frac{\sqrt{170}}{170}$

$\cos\theta = \frac{\text{adj}}{\text{hyp}} = \frac{13}{\sqrt{170}} = \frac{13\sqrt{170}}{170}$

> **Note:** Having found $\sin\theta$, an alternative method to find $\cos\theta$ would be to use the identity: $\sin^2\theta + \cos^2\theta = 1$

15. Without a calculator, find one possible value of
$\sin\left(\arccos\left(\frac{12}{13}\right)\right)$

> **Note:** Another way to word the question would be:
> Find one possible value of $\sin\theta$ where:
> $\theta = \arccos\left(\frac{12}{13}\right)$

Consider first $\theta = \arccos\left(\frac{12}{13}\right)$.

Method 1

Sketch the triangle and mark the angle θ whose cosine is $\frac{12}{13}$:

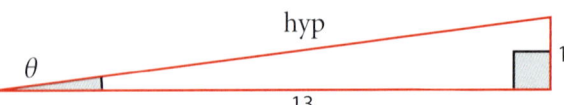

Calculate the missing side b:
$b = \sqrt{13^2 - 12^2}$
$= 5$

From the triangle, $\sin\theta = \frac{\text{opp}}{\text{hyp}} = \frac{5}{13}$

> **Note:** We did not need to find the angle itself.

> **Note:** Method 1 gives only one solution. By drawing a triangle, we are ensuring θ is an angle between 0 and $\frac{\pi}{2}$ radians.

Method 2

Use the identity $\sin^2\theta + \cos^2\theta = 1$

$\theta = \arccos\left(\frac{12}{13}\right) \Rightarrow \cos\theta = \frac{12}{13}$

$\sin^2\theta + \cos^2\theta = 1 \Rightarrow \sin^2\theta = 1 - \cos^2\theta$

$\sin^2\theta = 1 - \left(\frac{12}{13}\right)^2 = \frac{25}{169}$

$\sin\theta = \pm\frac{5}{13}$

> **Note:** Method 2 gives more than one answer because we are not restricting the value of $\arccos\left(\frac{12}{13}\right)$. In the next section you will learn that the value of the arccos function is usually restricted to angles between 0 and π radians.

16. By considering a right-angled triangle with two sides of length x and 1, show that:

$\arcsin x \equiv \frac{\pi}{2} - \arccos x$

Consider a right-angled triangle with hypotenuse length 1. Name one of the other sides x and the two acute angles α and β:

7: TRIGONOMETRIC FUNCTIONS

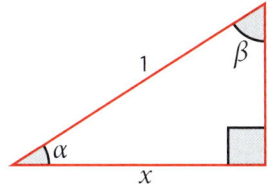

Then:
$$\cos \alpha = \frac{x}{1} = x \Rightarrow \alpha = \arccos x$$

And:
$$\sin \beta = \frac{x}{1} = x \Rightarrow \beta = \arcsin x$$

But $\alpha + \beta = \frac{\pi}{2}$

$\therefore \arccos x + \arcsin x = \frac{\pi}{2}$

$$\arcsin x \equiv \frac{\pi}{2} - \arccos x$$

Exercise 7D

1. Using a calculator, find exact values for the following.
   (a) $\arcsin\left(\frac{\sqrt{3}}{2}\right)$ (b) $\arctan(-1)$
   (c) $\arccos(1)$ (d) $\arcsin\left(-\frac{1}{2}\right)$
   (e) $\arctan(-\sqrt{3})$ (f) $\arccos 0$

2. Using the special triangles, find the following. Give exact answers in radians.
   (a) $\arcsin\left(\frac{1}{2}\right)$ (b) $\arccos\left(\frac{1}{2}\right)$
   (c) $\arctan\left(\frac{1}{\sqrt{3}}\right)$ (d) $\arctan 1$
   (e) $\arcsin\left(\frac{1}{\sqrt{2}}\right)$

3. Explain why $\arccos \sqrt{3}$ is undefined.

4. Using a calculator, find x to 3 significant figures, given the following.
   (a) $\arcsin x = 0.8$ (b) $\arccos x = -0.9$
   (c) $\arctan x = 1.5$ (d) $\arcsin x = -0.1$
   (e) $\arccos x = 0.4$ (f) $\arctan x = -5$

5. By sketching an appropriate triangle, find one possible value for each of the following, giving an exact answer.
   (a) $\sin(\arccos(0.5))$ (b) $\sin\left(\arctan\left(\frac{7}{24}\right)\right)$
   (c) $\cos(\arctan(1))$ (d) $\sin\left(\arccos\left(\frac{4}{5}\right)\right)$

Exercise 7D...

   (e) $\tan\left(\arccos\left(\frac{1}{4}\right)\right)$

6. Using a sketch of a triangle and/or the identity $\sin^2 \theta + \cos^2 \theta = 1$:
   (a) Find $\cos A$ if $A = \arcsin \frac{1}{2}$.
   (b) Find $\tan B$ if $B = \arccos\left(-\frac{2}{5}\right)$.

7. By considering a right-angled triangle with appropriate length sides, simplify the following.
   (a) $\sec\left(\arccos\left(\frac{1}{2}\right)\right)$
   (b) $\csc(\arcsin(y))$
   (c) $\cot\left(\arctan\left(\frac{2}{3}\right)\right)$
   (d) $\cot\left(\arctan\left(\frac{1}{x}\right)\right)$
   (e) $\csc\left(\arcsin\left(\frac{4}{5}\right)\right)$

8. Consider a right-angled triangle with hypotenuse 1 and another side of length x. Given $A = \arccos x$, find $\tan A - \sin A$ in terms of x.

9. Consider a right-angled triangle whose two shorter sides are of length x and 1. Show that:
   $$\cot\left(\frac{\pi}{2} - \arctan x\right) \equiv x$$

7.5 The Graphs of the Inverse Trigonometric Functions

In chapter 2 you learnt that the graph of an inverse function is always a reflection of the graph of the original function in the line $y = x$. To use this technique with the trigonometric functions the x values must be in radians.

Restricted domains

The graph of $f(x) = \sin x$ is shown in the following sketch, in black, and $f^{-1}(x) = \arcsin x$ is shown in red. Also shown is the mirror line $y = x$.

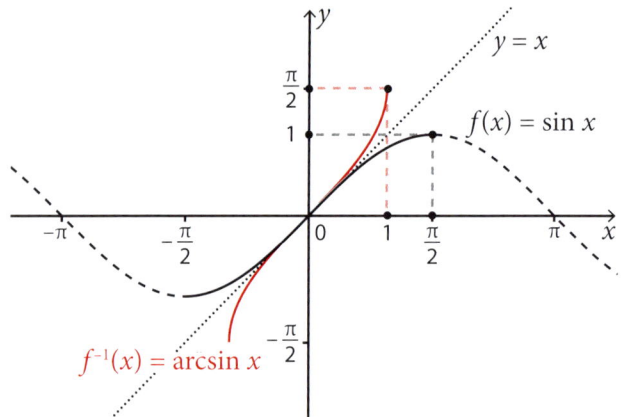

The graph of $f(x) = \sin x$ passes through $\left(\frac{\pi}{2}, 1\right)$.

The graph of the inverse function, $f^{-1}(x) = \arcsin x$, therefore passes through $\left(1, \frac{\pi}{2}\right)$.

Only a part of the curve $y = f(x)$, the part shown as a solid line, has been reflected in the line $y = x$ to obtain the inverse function.

We use this **restricted domain** for $f(x)$, $-\frac{\pi}{2} \leq x \leq \frac{\pi}{2}$, to ensure that the inverse function is one-to-one.

Consider $f(x) = \cos x$. We use a different restricted domain, $0 \leq x \leq \pi$, to obtain the graph of $f^{-1}(x) = \arccos x$. The graph of $y = f(x)$ using this restricted domain is shown as a solid black line in the following sketch.

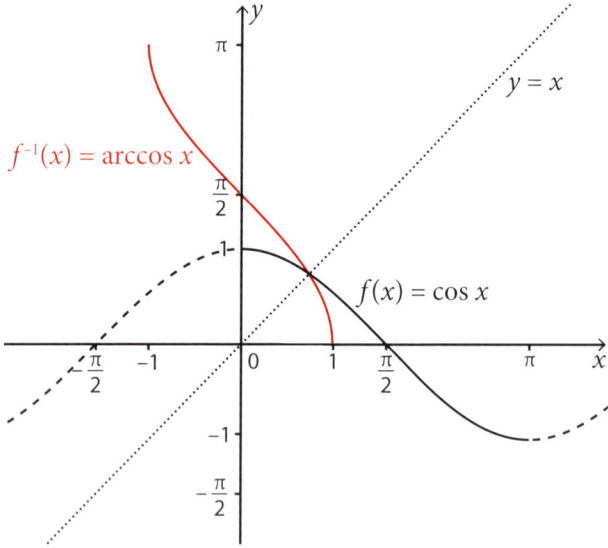

In the case of $f(x) = \tan x$, we use only the central branch of the curve; i.e. we use the restricted domain $-\frac{\pi}{2} < x < \frac{\pi}{2}$ as shown in the following sketch.

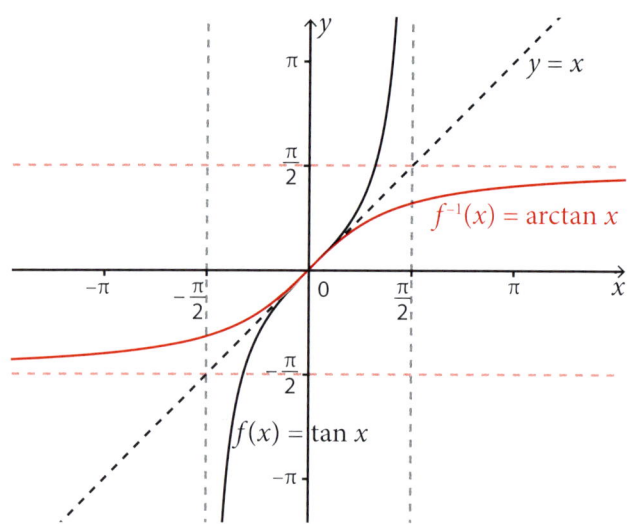

Note that, because the tan graph has vertical asymptotes, the arctan graph has two horizontal asymptotes.

Domains and ranges of the inverse functions

Hence, we can deduce the domains and ranges of the three inverse trigonometric functions:

$f(x) =$	Domain	Range
$\arcsin x$	$x \in \mathbb{R}, -1 \leq x \leq 1$	$f(x) \in \mathbb{R}, -\frac{\pi}{2} \leq f(x) \leq \frac{\pi}{2}$
$\arccos x$	$x \in \mathbb{R}, -1 \leq x \leq 1$	$f(x) \in \mathbb{R}, 0 \leq f(x) \leq \pi$
$\arctan x$	$x \in \mathbb{R}$	$f(x) \in \mathbb{R}, -\frac{\pi}{2} < f(x) < \frac{\pi}{2}$

Worked Example

17. (a) Given the function $f(x) = 2\sin(2x)$, find $f^{-1}(x)$, the inverse mapping.
(b) Sketch the graphs of $y = f(x)$ and $y = f^{-1}(x)$ on the same diagram.
(c) What restricted domain of $f(x)$ is required to ensure $f^{-1}(x)$ is a one-to-one function?
(d) State the domain and range of the inverse function.

(a)
$$f(x) = 2\sin(2x)$$
$$y = 2\sin(2x)$$
$$\frac{y}{2} = \sin(2x)$$
$$\arcsin\left(\frac{y}{2}\right) = 2x$$
$$x = \frac{1}{2}\arcsin\left(\frac{y}{2}\right)$$

Therefore, the inverse function is given by:
$$f^{-1}(x) = \frac{1}{2}\arcsin\left(\frac{x}{2}\right)$$

(b) To help draw the sketch of $y = f^{-1}(x)$, first draw $y = f(x)$, shown in black on the following diagram. The inverse function is obtained by reflecting the sketch of $y = f(x)$ in the line $y = x$. The inverse function is shown in red.

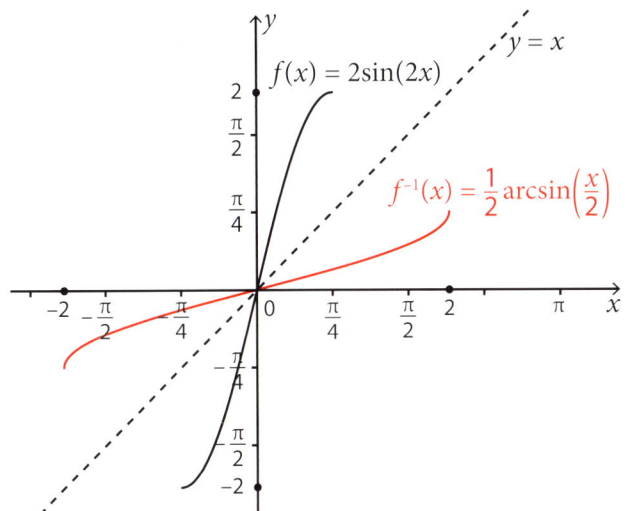

(c) The restricted domain used is: $-\frac{\pi}{4} \leq x \leq \frac{\pi}{4}$.

(d) Domain: $x \in \mathbb{R}, -2 \leq x \leq 2$
Range: $f^{-1}(x) \in \mathbb{R}, -\frac{\pi}{4} \leq f^{-1}(x) \leq \frac{\pi}{4}$

Exercise 7E

1. Find the inverse of the following functions.
   (a) $f(x) = \sin(2x) + 1$
   (b) $f(x) = 2\cos x - 2$
   (c) $f(x) = 2\tan\left(\frac{x}{2}\right)$
   (d) $f(x) = \sin\left(2x + \frac{\pi}{4}\right)$
   (e) $f(x) = \frac{1}{2}\cos\left(x - \frac{\pi}{6}\right)$

2. (a) Sketch the curve of $y = \sin^{-1} x$.
   (b) Sketch the curve of $y = (\sin x)^{-1}$. What is the other name for this curve?

3. The function $f(x)$ is defined such that $f(x) = 2\cos x$.
   (a) Find $f^{-1}(x)$, the inverse function.
   (b) Sketch the graph of $y = f^{-1}(x)$. (You may find it helpful to sketch the graph of $y = f(x)$, using a restricted domain, then find the inverse function by reflecting in the line $y = x$.)

Exercise 7E...

   (c) What restricted domain of $f(x)$ is required to ensure $f^{-1}(x)$ is a one-to-one function?
   (d) State the domain and range of the inverse function.

4. The function $f(x)$ is defined such that $f(x) = \pi \tan x$.
   (a) Find $f^{-1}(x)$, the inverse function.
   (b) Sketch the graphs of $y = f(x)$ and $y = f^{-1}(x)$ on the same diagram.
   (c) What restricted domain of $f(x)$ is required to ensure $f^{-1}(x)$ is a one-to-one function?
   (d) State the domain and range of the inverse function.

7.6 Problems in Context

You may be asked to solve problems involving the trigonometric functions in context. There may be little guidance in the wording of the question about which approach to take. You may need a combination of the techniques you have learnt in this chapter, as well as your knowledge of radian measure.

Exercise 7F

1. A car travels along a straight road that runs up a steep hill. The road has a warning sign displaying "10%", which means that for every 10 metres travelled horizontally, the car rises through 1 metre.
   (a) Write down the value of m, the gradient of the hill, giving your answer as a fraction.
   (b) If θ is the angle of inclination of the hill, show that $\theta = \arctan m$.
   (c) Find the angle of inclination θ, giving your answer in degrees.
   (d) Further up the hill the road gets steeper. The angle of inclination is now 10°. Find the gradient on this section of the road. Give your answer as a decimal to 3 significant figures.
   (e) The council puts up a warning sign on this section of the road, again with a percentage figure for the gradient, given to the nearest integer. What should it say?

Exercise 7F...

2. In mechanics, the **angle of repose** is the maximum angle at which an object can rest on an inclined plane without sliding down. The diagram below shows all the forces acting on such an object.

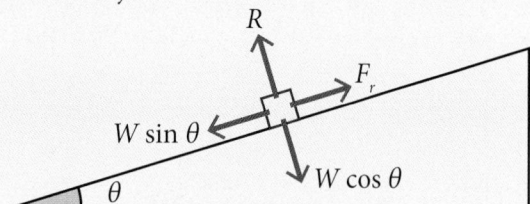

If the object is in equilibrium, then:

$F_r = W \sin \theta$ (1) and

$R = W \cos \theta$ (2),

where F_r is the size of the frictional force, W is the weight of the object and θ is the angle of repose. R is called the **normal reaction** force.

There is a further relationship:

$F_r = \mu R$ (3)

linking the size of the frictional force and the normal reaction force, where μ is a constant, called the **coefficient of friction**.

(a) Using equations (1) and (3), show that:
$$\sin \theta = \frac{\mu R}{W} \quad (4)$$
(b) Using equations (2) and (4), prove that:
$\theta = \arctan \mu$
(c) If the coefficient of friction is 1, show that the angle of repose is 45°.
(d) A different object has an angle of repose of 30°. Find the coefficient of friction, giving your answer as a simplified surd.

3. The atoms in a methane molecule can be modelled in the shape of a tetrahedron, as shown in the diagram. The molecule consists of a single carbon atom at O and four hydrogen atoms at the points A, B, C and D. The coordinates of all five points are shown.

Exercise 7F...

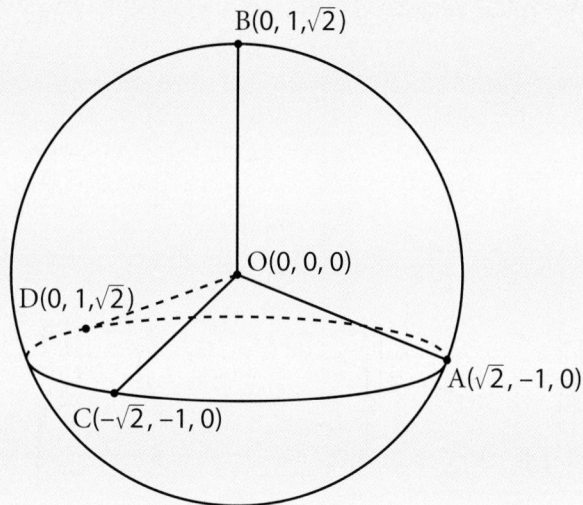

Note: It is not important to try to visualise the positions of the x, y and z axes on this diagram.

(a) A tetrahedron has 6 edges of equal length (not shown in the diagram). Verify that the edges AB and AC are equal in length.
(b) In a tetrahedron, all four vertices are equidistant from a central point. Verify that the hydrogen atoms at points A and B lie the same distance from the carbon atom at point O.
(c) The diagram below shows triangle OAC. The third coordinate of each point is zero and has been omitted. (The triangle lies in the $x - y$ plane.)

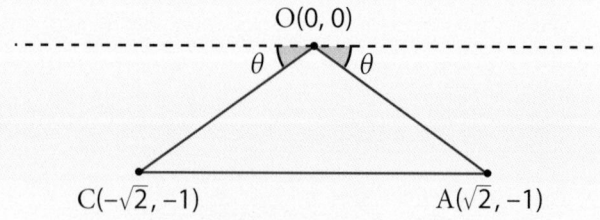

Using trigonometry, show that the two angles marked θ are given by:

$$\theta = \arctan\left(\frac{\sqrt{2}}{2}\right)$$

(d) Hence find the size of the **bond angle** AOC.

Exercise 7F...

4. A mountain railway carriage comprises five identical sections, as shown in the diagram. Each section has a cross-section in the shape of a trapezium. The greatest height of each section is h metres and the step between each section is 20 cm. The floor of each section is x metres long.

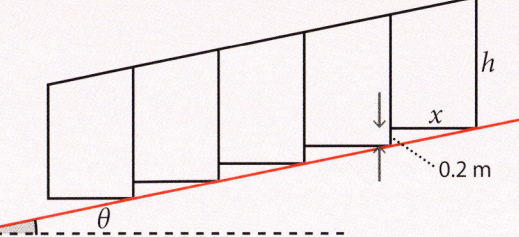

(a) Show that the cross-sectional area of each section of the carriage is given by:
$A = (h - 0.1)x$

You may use the formula $A = \frac{1}{2}(a + b)h$ for the area of a trapezium.

(b) When measured across the tracks, the width of each section is 2 metres. Show that the volume of **the entire carriage** is given by:
$V = 2(h - 0.1) \cot \theta$
where θ is the angle of the slope.
You may use the formula $V = Al$ for the volume of a prism.

(c) Find the exact volume of the carriage in terms of h if the angle of the slope is $\frac{\pi}{12}$ radians.

(d) If instead the volume of the carriage is 100 m³ and $h = 2.5$ m,
  (i) Show that the angle of the slope is given by: $\theta = \arctan\left[\frac{2}{V}(h - 0.1)\right]$
  (ii) Hence find the angle of the slope in radians to 3 decimal places.

7.7 Summary

The **reciprocal trigonometric functions** are defined as follows:

$$\sec\theta = \frac{1}{\cos\theta} \quad \csc\theta = \frac{1}{\sin\theta} \quad \cot\theta = \frac{1}{\tan\theta}$$

There are no buttons for sec, cosec and cot on most calculators, so you will use $\frac{1}{\cos\theta}$ when calculating $\sec\theta$, and so on.

You should be familiar with the shapes of the graphs of these three functions, as well as their domains and ranges.

You should also understand the three **inverse trigonometric functions** arcsin x, arccos x, and arctan x (sometimes written sin⁻¹ x, cos⁻¹ x and tan⁻¹ x) and the shapes of their graphs.

Restricted domains are used for the sin, cos and tan functions to ensure that the three inverses are one-to-one functions.

You may be asked questions involving the reciprocal and inverse trigonometric functions in a real-life context. In these questions you should give your answers in the context of the question.

Chapter 8
Trigonometric Identities and Equations

8.1 Introduction

Key words
- **Trigonometric ratio**: Any of the trigonometry functions acting on an angle, for example sin 30°.

Before you start
You should know:
- About radian measure.
- About the reciprocal trigonometric functions.
- The values of certain 'special' trigonometric ratios, for example $\sin 60°$, $\cos\left(\frac{\pi}{4}\right)$.
- The shapes of the graphs of the sin, cos and tan functions.
- How to solve trigonometric equations involving sin, cos and tan, giving answers in degrees.
- How to use the trigonometric graphs and/or the CAST diagram to obtain solutions in all four quadrants.
- How to prove trigonometric identities involving the sin, cos and tan functions.
- How to find one trigonometric ratio given another.

When solving a trigonometric equation, you should find the first solution on your calculator. This is called the **principal value**. Use the CAST diagram or the graph of the relevant trigonometric function to obtain the second solution. If further solutions are required:

- For equations involving cos or sin add or subtract multiples of 360°.
- For equations involving tan add or subtract multiples of 180°.

Worked Example

1. Find two solutions within the range $0° \leq x \leq 360°$ to the following equations.
   (a) $\sin x = 0.6$ (b) $\cos x = -\frac{1}{3}$ (c) $\sin x = \cos x$

(a) $\sin x = 0.6$
Get the principal value from the calculator:
$x = \sin^{-1}(0.6)$

Note: You could also write $x = \arcsin(0.6)$. These both mean 'inverse sin'.

$x = 36.9°$
The graph below shows that the second solution can be found by subtracting the first from 180°.

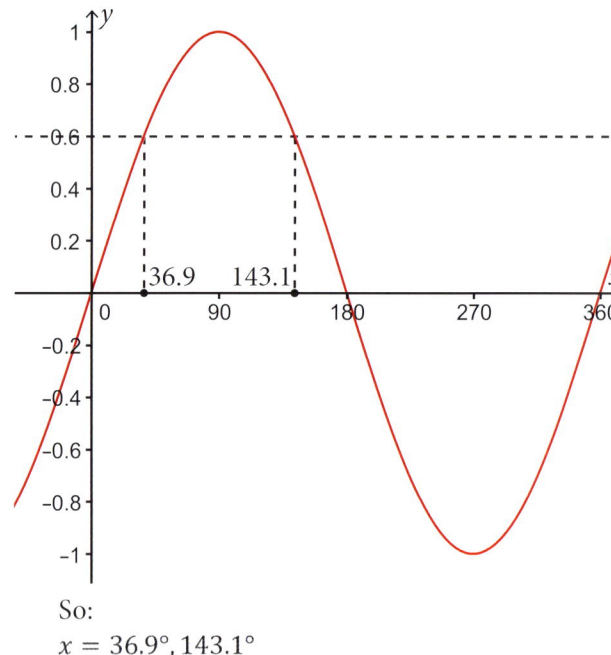

So:
$x = 36.9°, 143.1°$

(b) $\cos x = -\frac{1}{3}$
Get the principal value from the calculator:
$x = \cos^{-1}\left(-\frac{1}{3}\right)$

Note: You could also write $x = \arccos\left(-\frac{1}{3}\right)$. These both mean 'inverse cos'.

$x = 109.5°$

The following graph shows that the second solution can be found by subtracting the first from 360°.

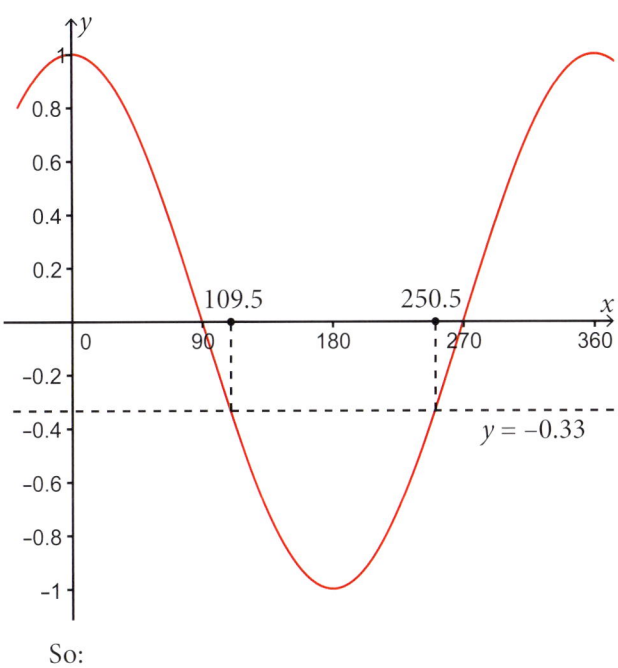

So:
$x = 109.5°, 250.5°$

(c) $\sin x = \cos x$

Divide both sides by $\cos x$:
$\tan x = 1$

Get the principal value from the calculator:
$x = \tan^{-1}(1)$

> **Note:** You could also write $x = \arctan(1)$.

$x = 45°$

The second solution to an equation involving $\tan x$ can be found by adding 180° to the first. This can be visualised by inspecting the tan graph:

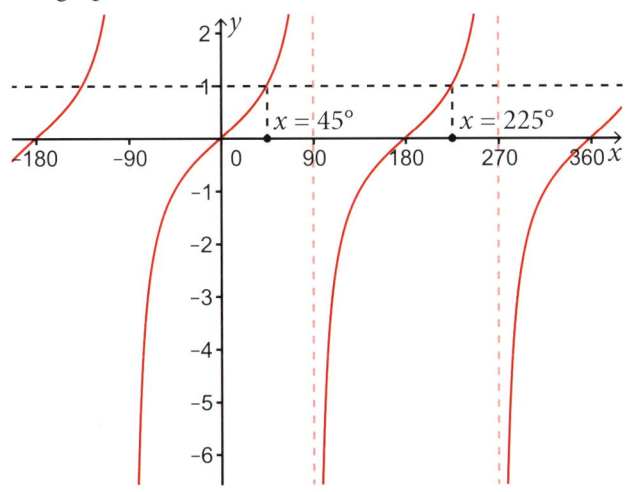

So:
$x = 45°, 225°$

Using the CAST diagram is always an alternative to inspection of the trigonometric graphs.

Worked Examples

2. Solve these equations, giving all solutions in the range $0° \leq x \leq 360°$, correct to 3 significant figures where appropriate.
   (a) $\cos 2x = 0.4$
   (b) $\tan^2 x + 2\tan x - 2 = 0$

(a) $\cos 2x = 0.4$

Use the substitution $y = 2x$. Then we must solve:
$\cos y = 0.4$

Adjust the range:
$0° \leq x \leq 360°$
$0° \leq y \leq 720°$ (since $y = 2x$)

Find the principal value from the calculator:
$y = \cos^{-1}(0.4)$
$y = 66.422°$
Work to 3 or 4 decimal places at this stage.

From the CAST diagram the second solution for y is in the fourth quadrant:

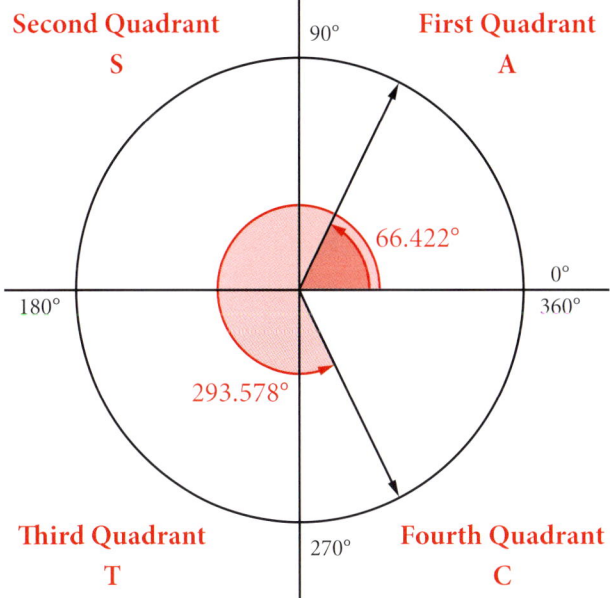

$y = 360 - 66.422° = 293.578°$

To find further solutions add multiples of 360° to each solution. Ignore solutions outside of the range $0° \leq y \leq 720°$.

Solutions are:
$y = 66.422°, 293.578°$
So further solutions are:
$426.422°, 653.578°, \ldots$

Divide by 2 to get x values, since $y = 2x$:
$x = 33.211°, 213.211°, 146.789°, 326.789°$

Round to the required accuracy in the final line:
$x = 33.2°, 147°, 213°, 327°$ (3 s.f.)

(b) $\tan^2 x + 2\tan x - 2 = 0$

This is a quadratic equation in $\tan x$. Use the substitution $y = \tan x$. Then we must solve:
$y^2 + 2y - 2 = 0$

The equation cannot be factorised, so we use the quadratic formula.
$$y = \frac{-2 \pm \sqrt{2^2 - 4(1)(-2)}}{2}$$

First set of solutions:
$y = -1 + \sqrt{3}$
$\tan x = -1 + \sqrt{3}$
$x = 36.206°, 216.206°$

Second set of solutions:
$y = -1 - \sqrt{3}$
$\tan x = -1 - \sqrt{3}$
$x = -69.896°, 110.104°, 290.104°$

Solutions within the range are:
$x = 36.2°, 110°, 216°, 290°$ (3 s.f.)

3. Simplify the following trigonometric expression:
$(1 + \cos\theta)^2 + \sin^2\theta$

$(1 + \cos\theta)^2 + \sin^2\theta$
$= 1 + 2\cos\theta + \cos^2\theta + \sin^2\theta$

Using the identity $\cos^2\theta + \sin^2\theta \equiv 1$:
$= 1 + 2\cos\theta + 1$
$= 2 + 2\cos\theta$

If one side of the identity involves more than one term, start with this side. Usually you will find a common denominator to combine the terms.

Worked Example

4. Prove the following trigonometric identity:
$1 + \tan^2 x \equiv \dfrac{1}{\cos^2 x}$

Start with the LHS, which has two terms:
$LHS = 1 + \tan^2 x$
$= 1 + \dfrac{\sin^2 x}{\cos^2 x}$

Find a common denominator:
$= \dfrac{\cos^2 x}{\cos^2 x} + \dfrac{\sin^2 x}{\cos^2 x}$
$= \dfrac{\cos^2 x + \sin^2 x}{\cos^2 x}$

Since $\cos^2 x + \sin^2 x \equiv 1$:
$= \dfrac{1}{\cos^2 x}$
$= RHS$

What you will learn

In this chapter you will learn:

- How to use and prove trigonometric identities involving the reciprocal trigonometric functions.
- About the compound angle and double angle formulae and how to apply them.
- More about solving trigonometric equations.
- How to simplify the sum of two trigonometric functions, such as $\sin x + 2\cos x$.

In the real world...

Flight engineers must consider the speed, distance, and direction of an aeroplane, along with the speed and direction of the wind. The wind plays an important role in how and when a plane will arrive.

Such problems are solved using trigonometry and a vector diagram of a triangle. For example, if a plane is travelling at 200 mph on a bearing of 050°, and there is a wind blowing due south at 20 mph, trigonometry will help to find the third side of the triangle, which will lead the plane in the right direction.

Exercise 8A (Revision)

1. By considering the CAST diagram or the trigonometric graphs, find solutions to the following trigonometric equations in the range $0° \leq x \leq 360°$.

   (a) $\sin x = \dfrac{1}{2}$ (b) $\cos x = -\dfrac{1}{\sqrt{2}}$

   (c) $\tan x = 0.1$ (d) $\sin\theta = -1$

2. Use the CAST diagram or the graphs of the trigonometric functions to solve the following equations within the intervals specified. Give your answers in degrees, exactly where possible, or to 1 decimal place.

   (a) $\sin\theta = 0.4$, $0° < \theta < 360°$
   (b) $\cos 2y = -0.7$, $-90° < y < 90°$
   (c) $\sin\left(\dfrac{x}{3}\right) = 1 - \sqrt{2}$, $0° < x < 180°$
   (d) $\cos(x - 180°) - 1 = -\dfrac{1}{4}$, $0° < x < 360°$

Exercise 8A...

3. Use the quadratic formula to solve the following equation: $2\tan^2 x + \tan x = 5$
   Give your answers in radians, to 3 significant figures where appropriate, between $-\pi$ and π.

4. Simplify the following trigonometric expression: $\tan^2 x \sin^2 x \cos^2 x$

5. Prove the following identity:
   $$1 + \tan\theta + \tan^2\theta \equiv \frac{(1 + \cos\theta \sin\theta)}{\cos^2\theta}$$

6. (a) Show that: $\sin A \tan A \equiv \dfrac{1 - \cos^2 A}{\cos A}$

   (b) Hence find all the values of θ in the range $0° \leq \theta \leq 360°$ satisfying: $3\sin\theta \tan\theta = 8$

8.2 Proving Trigonometric Identities

Proving trigonometric identities is a large part of the work in this chapter. In doing so, you will often use certain other identities, which you have already learnt, including

$$\tan\theta \equiv \frac{\sin\theta}{\cos\theta}$$

and

$$\sin^2\theta + \cos^2\theta \equiv 1$$

The technique is always to take the expression on one side of the identity and manipulate it until you obtain the expression on the other side. Begin with the expression that looks the most complicated.

Worked Example

5. Prove that: $\cos\theta \equiv \sec\theta - \tan\theta \sin\theta$

   In this case the right-hand side looks more complicated, so we begin with that.

   $RHS = \sec\theta - \tan\theta \sin\theta$

   Since $\sec\theta = \dfrac{1}{\cos\theta}$ and $\tan\theta = \dfrac{\sin\theta}{\cos\theta}$:

   $= \dfrac{1}{\cos\theta} - \dfrac{\sin^2\theta}{\cos\theta}$

   $= \dfrac{1 - \sin^2\theta}{\cos\theta}$

   Since $1 - \sin^2\theta \equiv \cos^2\theta$:

   $= \dfrac{\cos^2\theta}{\cos\theta}$

   $= \cos\theta$

   $= LHS$

The equivalent forms of $\sin^2\theta + \cos^2\theta \equiv 1$

Using

$$\sin^2\theta + \cos^2\theta \equiv 1$$

we can derive two other important results:

Dividing each term in the identity by $\sin^2\theta$ gives:

$$1 + \cot^2\theta \equiv \csc^2\theta$$

Dividing each term by $\cos^2\theta$ gives:

$$\tan^2\theta + 1 \equiv \sec^2\theta$$

All three identities are used widely in proofs in A2 Mathematics.

Worked Example

6. Prove the identity:
   $(\cos A + \sec A)^2 \equiv \tan^2 A + \cos^2 A + 3$

   $LHS = (\cos A + \sec A)^2$
   $= \cos^2 A + 2\cos A \sec A + \sec^2 A$

   Since $\cos A \sec A = \cos A \times \dfrac{1}{\cos A} = 1$:

   $= \cos^2 A + 2 + \sec^2 A$

   Since $\sec^2 A \equiv \tan^2 A + 1$:

   $= \cos^2 A + 2 + \tan^2 A + 1$
   $= \tan^2 A + \cos^2 A + 3$
   $= RHS$

Exercise 8B

1. Simplify: $\sec^2\theta - \tan^2\theta$

2. Simplify the following expression, giving your answer as one of the reciprocal trigonometric functions: $\dfrac{\tan x}{\sin x}$

3. Write each of the following expressions as a power of $\csc\theta$, $\sec\theta$ or $\cot\theta$.

   (a) $\dfrac{1}{\tan^3\theta}$ (b) $\dfrac{\sec\theta}{\cos^3\theta}$

Exercise 8B...

(c) $\dfrac{\sin\theta}{\csc^2\theta}$ (d) $\dfrac{1-\sin^2\theta}{\cos^3\theta}$

4. Show that:
   $\sec^2 y + \csc^2 y \equiv \sec^2 y \csc^2 y$

5. Using the identity:
   $1 + \cot^2\theta \equiv \csc^2\theta$
   show that:
   $\csc^4\theta - \cot^4\theta \equiv \csc^2\theta + \cot^2\theta$

6. Prove the following identities.
   (a) $\sec^2 x - \csc^2 x \equiv \tan^2 x - \cot^2 x$
   (b) $\dfrac{\sin\theta}{\cos\theta} + \dfrac{\cos\theta}{\sin\theta} \equiv \sec\theta\csc\theta$
   (c) $\sec^2 x - \sin^2 x \equiv \tan^2 x + \cos^2 x$
   (d) $\sec\theta\,(1 - \sin\theta) \equiv \dfrac{\cos\theta}{1+\sin\theta}$
   (e) $\cot^2\theta + \cos^2\theta \equiv (\csc\theta - \sin\theta)(\csc\theta + \sin\theta)$
   (f) $\csc^2 x\,(\tan^2 x - \sin^2 x) \equiv \tan^2 x$
   (g) $\dfrac{1+\cos\theta}{\sin\theta} \equiv \dfrac{\sin\theta}{1-\cos\theta}$
   (h) $\sqrt{1-\sin^2\theta}\,\csc\theta \equiv \cot\theta$
   (i) $\cos^2 x + 3\sin^2 x \equiv 3 - 2\cos^2 x$
   (j) $(2\sec x - 2\tan x)(2\sec x + 2\tan x) \equiv 4$
   (k) $\csc x - \sin x \equiv \cos x \cot x$
   (l) $\cos^4\theta - \sin^4\theta \equiv \cos^2\theta - \sin^2\theta$
   (m) $\sec^4\theta - \tan^4\theta \equiv \sec^2\theta + \tan^2\theta$

7. Show that: $\cot x + \tan x \equiv \sec x \csc x$

8. Prove the following identity:
   $\dfrac{\csc\theta}{\cot\theta + \tan\theta} \equiv \cos\theta$

9. Show that:
   $\sec^2\theta \equiv \sin^2\theta\csc^2\theta + \sin^2\theta\sec^2\theta$

10. Use the difference of two squares to show that:
    (a) $\sin^4 x - \cos^4 x \equiv 2\sin^2 x - 1$
    (b) $\sec^4\theta - \tan^4\theta \equiv 2\sec^2\theta - 1$

11. Show that:
    (a) $(1-\cos^2\theta)(1+\cos^2\theta) \equiv 2\sin^2\theta - \sin^4\theta$
    (b) $\tan^2 y - \cot^2 y \equiv \dfrac{(\tan^2 y - 1)(\tan^2 y + 1)}{\tan^2 y}$

8.3 Solving Trigonometric Equations

In AS Mathematics, you learnt how to solve trigonometric equations involving the functions sin, cos and tan.

In A2 Mathematics you will need to solve equations that feature the reciprocal trigonometric functions. You may be asked to give your answer in degrees or in radians.

Questions are usually one of the following types:

1. Simple equations with multiple solutions, e.g.
   $\csc x = -2$

2. Equations involving compound angles, e.g.
   $\sec(3x - 45°) = 2$

3. Quadratic equations involving just one trigonometric function, or an equation involving one of the functions and its reciprocal e.g.
   $\cot^2 x - 2\cot x + 1 = 0$ or $\sin x + \csc x = 2$

4. Equations requiring $\tan x = \dfrac{\sin x}{\cos x}$

5. Quadratics requiring the identity:
   $\sin^2 x + \cos^2 x \equiv 1$
   or one of its equivalent forms:
   $\csc^2 x \equiv 1 + \cot^2 x$
   $\sec^2 x \equiv \tan^2 x + 1$

6. Equations requiring a combination of the identities above. A trigonometric equation may need any of the skills you have used when proving trigonometric identities, to reduce the equation to one of the types 1, 2 or 3 above.

Whatever type of equation you are faced with, always attempt to form an equation in one of the trigonometric functions sin, cos or tan before finding a principal value.

....

Worked Example

7. (Type 1) Solve $\csc x = -2$ for values of x between 0 and 2π.

$\csc x = -2$

$\sin x = -\dfrac{1}{2}$

Obtain the principal value from the calculator:

$x = -\dfrac{\pi}{6}$

From the CAST diagram, the sine function is negative in the third and fourth quadrants. The second solution is a reflection of the first in the vertical.

8: TRIGONOMETRIC IDENTITIES AND EQUATIONS

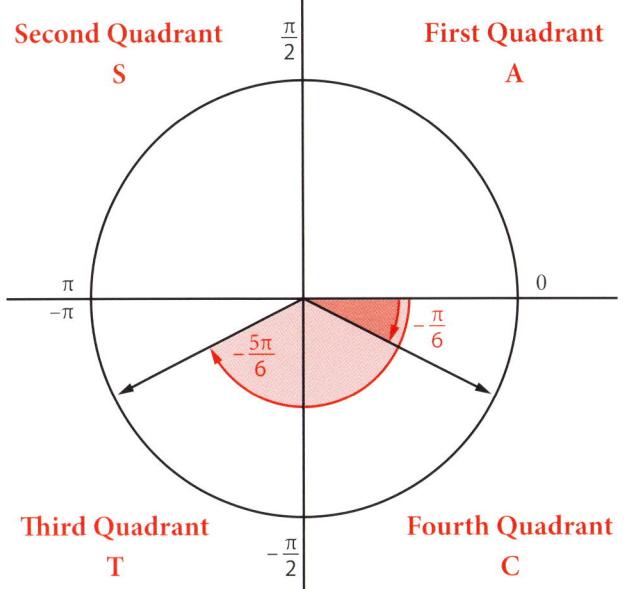

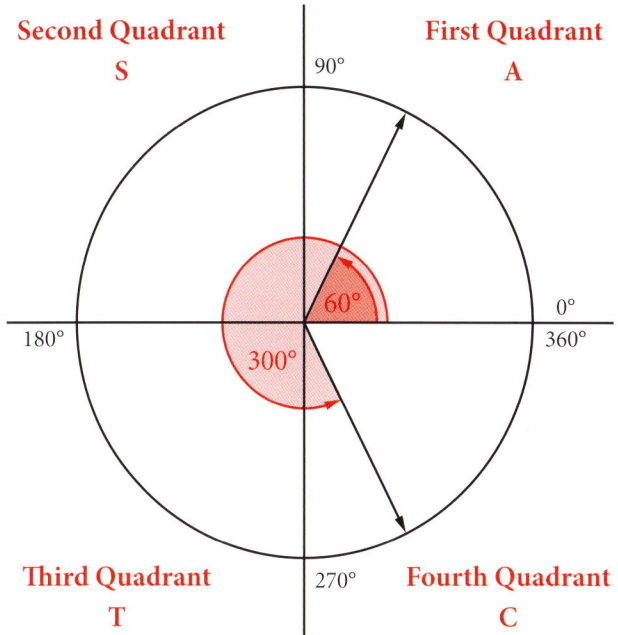

Neither of these solutions are within the required range. So add 2π to each one to obtain subsequent solutions between 0 and 2π:

$$x = \frac{7\pi}{6}, \frac{11\pi}{6}$$

In the next example we convert an equation involving sec into an equation involving cos and solve using a substitution.

Worked Example

8. (Type 2) Solve, for $0° \leq x \leq 360°$, $\sec(2x - 45°) = 2$

$\sec(2x - 45°) = 2$

$\cos(2x - 45°) = \frac{1}{2}$

$\cos\theta = \frac{1}{2}$, where $\theta = 2x - 45°$

Adjust the range:
$0° \leq x \leq 360°$
$\Rightarrow 0° \leq 2x \leq 720°$
$\Rightarrow -45° \leq 2x - 45° \leq 675°$
i.e. $-45° \leq \theta \leq 675°$

Find the principal value on the calculator:
$\theta = 60°$

Use the CAST diagram to obtain a second solution for θ. The second solution is 300°, since cosine is positive in the first and fourth quadrants.

Subsequent solutions are obtained by repeatedly adding 360° to the first two.

The solutions within the range $-45° \leq \theta \leq 675°$ are:

$\theta = 60°, 300°, 420°, 660°$

$\theta = 2x - 45° \Rightarrow x = \frac{\theta + 45°}{2}$

So: $x = 52.5°, 172.5°, 232.5°, 352.5°$

In the next example we convert an equation involving cosec into an equation involving sin and use a substitution.

Worked Example

9. (Type 2) Find all solutions to: $\csc\left(x + \frac{\pi}{3}\right) = 2$ for $-\pi \leq x \leq \pi$.

$\csc\left(x + \frac{\pi}{3}\right) = 2$

Taking the reciprocal of each side:

$\Rightarrow \sin\left(x + \frac{\pi}{3}\right) = \frac{1}{2}$

Note that here the angle x is measured in radians.

Use a substitution $\theta = x + \frac{\pi}{3}$
Now we must solve:

$\sin\theta = \frac{1}{2}$

111

The rest of this example is left as an exercise for the reader. The steps are:

- Find the range of values for θ using $-\pi \le x \le \pi$ and $\theta = x + \dfrac{\pi}{3}$
- Find the principal value for θ on the calculator.
- Find the second value for θ using the CAST diagram or a sketch of the sine function.
- Find any subsequent values for θ within the range.
- From your θ values, find solutions for x.

These steps will show that, within the specified range $-\pi \le x \le \pi$, there are two solutions:

$$x = -\dfrac{\pi}{6}, \dfrac{\pi}{2}$$

An equation involving $\cot^2 x$ can be rewritten as an equation involving $\tan^2 x$.

Worked Example

10. (Type 3) Solve, for $-\pi \le x \le \pi$, $\dfrac{\cot^2 x}{4} = 1$

$$\dfrac{\cot^2 x}{4} = 1$$

This is a quadratic equation in $\cot x$, but its simplicity means it is not necessary to factorise or use the quadratic formula. So:

$$\Rightarrow \cot^2 x = 4$$

Taking the reciprocal of each side:

$$\Rightarrow \tan^2 x = \dfrac{1}{4}$$

$$\Rightarrow \tan x = \pm \dfrac{1}{2}$$

Consider first $\tan x = \dfrac{1}{2}$. Since the tan function is positive, solutions will lie in the first and third quadrants.

The calculator gives a principal value $x = 0.464$ radians, in the first quadrant.

From the CAST diagram we obtain a second solution by adding π radians, giving $x = 3.605$ radians, but this is outside the specified range.

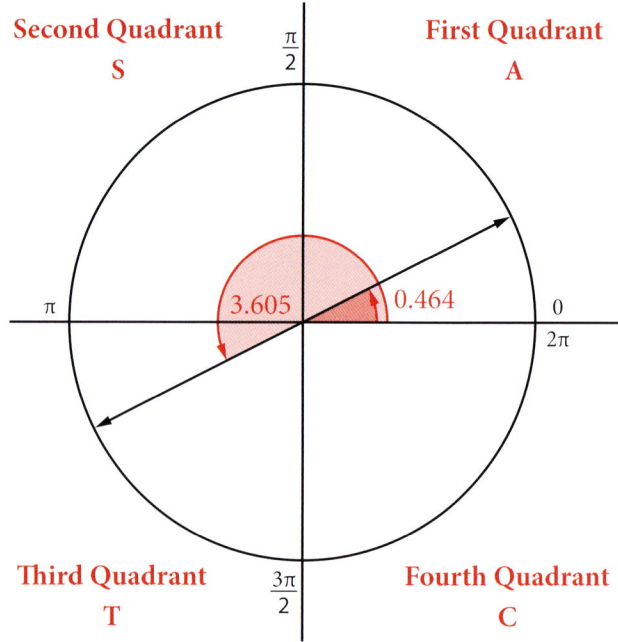

The tan function has period π radians, so we add and subtract π to find subsequent solutions:

$0.464 - \pi = -2.678$ radians. This is the only other solution within the specified range.

So the two solutions to $\tan x = \dfrac{1}{2}$ are $x = 0.464$ radians and $x = -2.678$ radians.

Now consider $\tan x = -\dfrac{1}{2}$.

The tan function is negative, so the two solutions lie in the second and fourth quadrants. The calculator gives a principal value $x = -0.464$ radians.

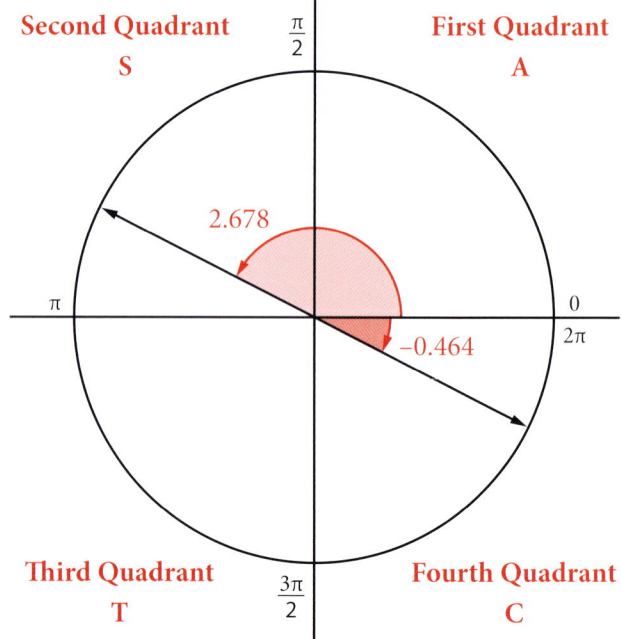

Add π radians to obtain the second solution

$x = 2.678$ radians. This is within the specified range.

Adding and subtracting π from these two solutions does not give us any additional solutions within the range.

Combining the solutions, we have:
$x = -2.68, -0.464, 0.464, 2.68$ radians

You may need to solve a quadratic equation involving one of the reciprocal trigonometric functions.

Worked Example

11. (Type 3) Find all solutions to:
$$\cot^2 x - \frac{4\sqrt{3}}{3} \cot x + 1 = 0$$
within the range $-\pi \leq x \leq \pi$, giving exact answers.

$$\cot^2 x - \frac{4\sqrt{3}}{3} \cot x + 1 = 0$$

Multiplying both sides by 3 to simplify:
$$3\cot^2 x - 4\sqrt{3} \cot x + 3 = 0$$

Using the quadratic formula:
$$\cot x = \frac{4\sqrt{3} \pm \sqrt{(4\sqrt{3})^2 - 4(3)(3)}}{2 \times 3}$$
$$\cot x = \frac{4\sqrt{3} \pm \sqrt{48 - 36}}{6}$$
$$= \frac{4\sqrt{3} \pm \sqrt{12}}{6}$$
$$= \frac{4\sqrt{3} \pm 2\sqrt{3}}{6}$$
$$\cot x = \sqrt{3} \text{ or } \cot x = \frac{\sqrt{3}}{3}$$

Therefore:
$$\tan x = \frac{1}{\sqrt{3}} \text{ or } \tan x = \sqrt{3}$$

The principal values are: $x = \frac{\pi}{6}$ or $x = \frac{\pi}{3}$

Use the CAST diagram, or recall that the tan function has period π radians.

Therefore, subtracting π from our two solutions gives $-\frac{5\pi}{6}$ and $-\frac{2\pi}{3}$, the only other solutions within the required interval.

Altogether, the solutions are:
$$x = -\frac{5\pi}{6}, -\frac{2\pi}{3}, \frac{\pi}{6}, \frac{\pi}{3}$$

There are many trigonometric equations that require the use of $\tan x = \frac{\sin x}{\cos x}$.

Worked Example

12. (Type 4) Solve for $-\pi < x < \pi$:
(a) $\operatorname{cosec} x + \sqrt{2} \sec x = 0$
(b) $\tan x + \sqrt{2} \sin x = 0$
(c) $3 \tan x + \cos x = 0$

(a) An equation involving just $\operatorname{cosec} x$ and $\sec x$ (or $\sin x$ and $\cos x$) can be reduced to a simple (Type 1) equation involving $\tan x$:
$$\operatorname{cosec} x + \sqrt{3} \sec x = 0$$
$$\frac{1}{\sin x} + \frac{\sqrt{3}}{\cos x} = 0$$
$$1 + \frac{\sqrt{3} \sin x}{\cos x} = 0$$
$$1 + \sqrt{3} \tan x = 0$$
$$\tan x = -\frac{1}{\sqrt{3}}$$
$$x = -\frac{\pi}{6}, \frac{5\pi}{6}$$

(b) In this example we replace $\tan x$ and factorise to form two equations:
$$\tan x + \sqrt{2} \sin x = 0$$
$$\Rightarrow \frac{\sin x}{\cos x} + \sqrt{2} \sin x = 0$$
$$\Rightarrow \sin x \left(\frac{1}{\cos x} + \sqrt{2}\right) = 0$$
$$\Rightarrow \sin x (\sec x + \sqrt{2}) = 0$$
$$\Rightarrow \sin x = 0 \text{ or } \sec x = -\sqrt{2}$$

Therefore:
$\sin x = 0 \quad (1)$
or:
$\cos x = -\frac{1}{\sqrt{2}} \quad (2)$

Considering (1):
$\Rightarrow x = 0$ (note that $x = -\pi$ and $x = \pi$ are not within the required range)

Considering (2):
$\Rightarrow x = \pm \frac{3\pi}{4}$

The three solutions are $x = -\frac{3\pi}{4}, 0, \frac{3\pi}{4}$

(c) $3\tan x + \cos x = 0$

Eliminate $\tan x$:
$$\frac{3\sin x}{\cos x} + \cos x = 0$$

Multiply through by $\cos x$:
$$3\sin x + \cos^2 x = 0$$
$$3\sin x + (1 - \sin^2 x) = 0$$

Then solve as a quadratic in $\sin x$ using the quadratic formula:
$$\sin x = \frac{3 \pm \sqrt{(-3)^2 - 4(1)(-1)}}{2 \times 1}$$

So:
$\sin x = -0.30278$
$x = -0.308, -2.83$

or
$\sin x = 3.30278$
giving no solutions

The next example demonstrates an equation that reduces to a quadratic equation in $\operatorname{cosec} x$. Use the identity $\operatorname{cosec}^2 x \equiv 1 + \cot^2 x$ to obtain an equation involving just one trigonometric function.

Worked Example

13. (Type 5) Solve $\operatorname{cosec} x + \cot^2 x = 5$, giving solutions in the range $0 \leq x \leq 2\pi$.

$$\operatorname{cosec} x + \cot^2 x = 5$$

Use the identity $\operatorname{cosec}^2 x \equiv 1 + \cot^2 x$ to eliminate $\cot^2 x$:
$$\operatorname{cosec} x + \operatorname{cosec}^2 x - 1 = 5$$
$$\operatorname{cosec}^2 x + \operatorname{cosec} x - 6 = 0$$

Factorise:
$$(\operatorname{cosec} x - 2)(\operatorname{cosec} x + 3) = 0$$

> **Note:** Alternatively you could use a substitution $y = \operatorname{cosec} x$ to obtain $y^2 + y - 6 = 0$ and hence $(y-2)(y+3) = 0$.

So either $\operatorname{cosec} x = 2$
$$\sin x = \frac{1}{2}$$
$$x = \frac{\pi}{6} \text{ (principal value)}$$
$$x = \frac{5\pi}{6} \text{ (from CAST diagram)}$$

or: $\operatorname{cosec} x = -3$
$$\sin x = -\frac{1}{3}$$
$x = -0.3398$ (principal value)
$x = -2.8018$ (from CAST diagram)

Both the negative solutions are outside the range. Adding 2π to each gives two solutions within the range, 3.4814 and 5.9433. Therefore:
$$x = \frac{\pi}{6}, \frac{5\pi}{6}, 3.48, 5.94$$

> **Note:** In this type of question, always eliminate the trigonometric function that is squared, i.e. $\cot^2 x$ in this example.

The next example reduces to an equation involving $\cos\theta$ and $\sin^2\theta$. Eliminate the squared trigonometric function, $\sin^2\theta$ in this case, to obtain a quadratic equation in $\cos\theta$.

Worked Example

14. (Type 6) Find all solutions to the equation $3\operatorname{cosec}^2\theta = 2\sec\theta$ in the interval $0 \leq \theta \leq 2\pi$.

$$3\operatorname{cosec}^2\theta = 2\sec\theta$$

Since $\operatorname{cosec}^2\theta = \dfrac{1}{\sin^2\theta}$ and $\sec\theta = \dfrac{1}{\cos\theta}$:
$$\frac{3}{\sin^2\theta} = \frac{2}{\cos\theta}$$

Cross-multiplying:
$$3\cos\theta = 2\sin^2\theta$$

Use the identity $\sin^2 x + \cos^2 x \equiv 1$ to eliminate $\sin^2 x$:
$$3\cos\theta = 2(1 - \cos^2\theta)$$
$$2\cos^2\theta + 3\cos\theta - 2 = 0$$
$$(\cos\theta + 2)(2\cos\theta - 1) = 0$$

Therefore:
$$\cos\theta + 2 = 0 \text{ or } 2\cos\theta - 1 = 0$$

Taking $\cos\theta + 2 = 0$ gives:
$$\cos\theta = -2$$
which gives no solutions.

Taking $2\cos\theta - 1 = 0$ gives:
$$\cos\theta = \frac{1}{2}$$

Giving the solutions:
$$\theta = \frac{\pi}{3}, \frac{5\pi}{3}$$

(The principal value $\frac{\pi}{3}$ comes from the calculator. The second solution is from the CAST diagram.)

In the final example the left-hand side can be factorised, leaving two equations to solve.

Worked Example

15. (Type 6) Find all solutions to the equation $2\cos^2\theta - 3\cot^2\theta + \cos\theta\cot\theta = 0$ in the interval $0 \leq \theta \leq 2\pi$.

$2\cos^2\theta - 3\cot^2\theta + \cos\theta\cot\theta = 0$

Factorise:
$(\cos\theta - \cot\theta)(2\cos\theta + 3\cot\theta) = 0$

> **Note:** Alternatively you could use substitutions $x = \cos\theta$ and $y = \cot\theta$ to give $2x^2 - 3y^2 + xy = 0$, and then factorise to give $(x - y)(2x + 3y) = 0$.

First consider:
$$\cos\theta - \cot\theta = 0$$
$$\cos\theta - \frac{\cos\theta}{\sin\theta} = 0$$

Factorise to give:
$$\cos\theta\left(1 - \frac{1}{\sin\theta}\right) = 0$$

So either:
$$\cos\theta = 0$$
giving:
$$\theta = \frac{\pi}{2}, \frac{3\pi}{2}$$
or:
$$1 - \frac{1}{\sin\theta} = 0$$
$$\sin\theta = 1$$
giving:
$$\theta = \frac{\pi}{2}$$

Then consider:
$2\cos\theta + 3\cot\theta = 0$
$2\cos\theta + \frac{3\cos\theta}{\sin\theta} = 0$

Factorise to give:
$$\cos\theta\left(2 - \frac{3}{\sin\theta}\right) = 0$$

So either:
$\cos\theta = 0$ (see solutions above)
or:

$$2 - \frac{3}{\sin\theta} = 0$$
$$\sin\theta = \frac{3}{2}$$

which gives no solutions.

So the complete list of solutions is: $\theta = \frac{\pi}{2}, \frac{3\pi}{2}$

Exercise 8C

1. Find solutions for the angle θ, giving all answers in the range specified.
   (a) $\sec\theta = 2$, $0 \leq \theta \leq 2\pi$
   (b) $\cot\theta = \frac{1}{3}$, $0° \leq \theta \leq 360°$
   (c) $\operatorname{cosec}\theta = \frac{3}{2}$, $-\pi \leq \theta \leq \pi$
   (d) $\cot\theta = -1.9$, $0° \leq \theta \leq 360°$
   (e) $\operatorname{cosec} 2x = -4$, $0 \leq x \leq \pi$
   (f) $\sec\theta = -1.1$, $0 \leq \theta \leq 4\pi$
   (g) $\cot x = -\sqrt{3}$, $-2\pi \leq x < 2\pi$

2. Solve these equations, giving all solutions between 0 and 2π.
   (a) $\tan\left(x + \frac{\pi}{3}\right) = 1$
   (b) $\cos\left(2x + \frac{\pi}{6}\right) = -\frac{1}{2}$
   (c) $\sec\left(x + \frac{5\pi}{6}\right) = \sqrt{3}$
   (d) $\cot\left(2\theta - \frac{\pi}{4}\right) = -1$

3. Solve the following equation, giving values of θ between 0° and 360°: $\operatorname{cosec}(\theta - 45°) = 2$

4. Solve $\cot\theta = \frac{1}{2}$ for the range $0 \leq \theta \leq 2\pi$.

5. Solve for $0 < \theta < \pi$: $\operatorname{cosec} 3\theta = \sqrt{2}$

6. Solve the following equation for 0° to 360°, giving your answers to 1 decimal place: $\operatorname{cosec} x = -4$

7. Solve the following equation, giving all solutions for x within the interval $0 \leq x \leq 2\pi$. $2\sin x + \operatorname{cosec} x = 3$

8. Solve for the range $0° \leq \theta \leq 360°$ the equation: $\tan^2\theta + 2\sec\theta = 2$
   Give your answers to 3 significant figures where appropriate.

9. Find all solutions to: $4\sin\theta + 1 = 3\operatorname{cosec}\theta$ for $0 \leq \theta \leq 360°$

Exercise 8C...

10. Solve the following for $0 \leq \theta \leq 2\pi$:
    $\csc^2 \theta = 3 \cot \theta - 1$

11. Solve for $0° \leq x \leq 360°$ the equation:
    $2 \tan x \csc x = 3$.

12. Solve for $0° \leq x \leq 360°$ the equation:
    $\tan^2 x = \sqrt{3} \tan x$.

13. Solve the following equation for x between $-\pi$ and π: $4 \cos x - 3 \sec x = 2 \tan x$

14. Solve for $0° \leq \theta \leq 360°$ the equation:
    $\sec^2 \theta = 1 - 6 \tan \theta$
    giving your answers to 1 decimal place where appropriate.

15. Solve for $0 \leq \theta \leq 2\pi$ the equation:
    $\csc^2 \theta - 3 = \dfrac{4}{\tan \theta}$

16. Solve the equation: $\sin x = \cos x$
    where $0 < x < 2\pi$.

17. (a) Show that $\dfrac{\sec^2 \theta}{\csc \theta} \equiv \sec \theta \tan \theta$

    (b) Hence, or otherwise, find all solutions in the range $0 \leq \theta \leq 2\pi$ to:
    $$\dfrac{\sec^2 \theta}{\csc \theta} = \tan \theta$$

18. (a) Show that $\sin x \cos x \tan x \equiv 1 - \cos^2 x$

    (b) Hence find all the solutions to the equation:
    $\sin x \cos x \tan x = \dfrac{3}{4}$
    in the range $0 \leq x \leq 2\pi$.

8.4 Compound and Double Angle Formulae

Compound angle formulae

You will often see equations involving the cosine or sine of a sum or difference, for example

$\cos(x + 60°)$

$\sin\left(x - \dfrac{\pi}{2}\right)$

$\cos(A + B)$

It is very important to remember that **expanding out brackets is not possible** with the trigonometric functions. For example:

$\cos(A + B) \neq \cos A + \cos B$

(Substitute some numbers in for A and B on both sides to convince yourself.)

Instead, we must use special formulae called the **compound angle formulae**.

> $\sin(A \pm B) = \sin A \cos B \pm \cos A \sin B$
>
> $\cos(A \pm B) = \cos A \cos B \mp \sin A \sin B$
>
> $\tan(A \pm B) = \dfrac{\tan A \pm \tan B}{1 \mp \tan A \tan B}$
>
> **Note:** For the cosine compound angle formula, use the plus sign on the left with the minus sign on the right, and vice versa. For the tan formula, use the plus sign on the left with a plus sign in the numerator and a minus sign in the denominator on the right.

Proof of the cosine compound angle formula
$\cos(A + B) = \cos A \cos B - \sin A \sin B$

> **Note:** At the time of publication, the CCEA specification does not require you to know this proof.

Consider the following diagram, which consists of two right-angled triangles.

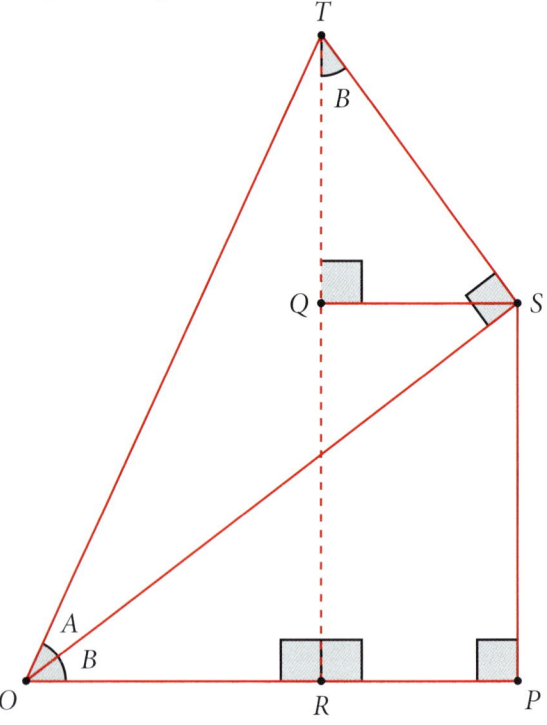

From $\triangle TOS$: $\cos A = \dfrac{OS}{OT}$ (1)

and: $\sin A = \dfrac{ST}{OT}$ (2)

From $\triangle POS$: $\cos B = \dfrac{OP}{OS}$ (3)

Note that ∠POS = ∠QTS. (Left as an exercise for the reader to prove.)

From ΔQTS: $\sin B = \dfrac{QS}{ST}$ (4)

From ΔTOR:
$$\cos(A+B) = \dfrac{OR}{OT} = \dfrac{OP - PR}{OT}$$

So: $\cos(A+B) = \dfrac{OP - SQ}{OT}$ (since $PR = SQ$)

$$\cos(A+B) = \dfrac{OP}{OT} - \dfrac{SQ}{OT}$$

Multiply the top and bottom of the fractions by OS and ST respectively, giving:

$$\cos(A+B) = \left(\dfrac{OP}{OS} \times \dfrac{OS}{OT}\right) - \left(\dfrac{QS}{ST} \times \dfrac{ST}{OT}\right)$$

Substitute from (1), (2), (3) and (4):

$$\cos(A+B) = \cos A \cos B - \sin A \sin B$$

Worked Example

16. Write the following as a single trigonometric ratio. Hence find its exact value.

$$\cos\left(\dfrac{8\pi}{9}\right)\cos\left(\dfrac{5\pi}{9}\right) + \sin\left(\dfrac{8\pi}{9}\right)\sin\left(\dfrac{5\pi}{9}\right)$$

Using the cosine compound angle formula:

$$\cos(A)\cos(B) + \sin(A)\sin(B) = \cos(A - B)$$

$$\therefore \cos\left(\dfrac{8\pi}{9}\right)\cos\left(\dfrac{5\pi}{9}\right) + \sin\left(\dfrac{8\pi}{9}\right)\sin\left(\dfrac{5\pi}{9}\right)$$

$$= \cos\left(\dfrac{8\pi}{9} - \dfrac{5\pi}{9}\right)$$

$$= \cos\left(\dfrac{\pi}{3}\right)$$

$$= \dfrac{1}{2}$$

The compound angle formulae, used with the results from the special triangles, can help you find trigonometric ratios of other angles.

Worked Example

17. Using the compound angle formulae, find the exact values of:
 (a) sin 15°   (b) cos 15°

(a) $\sin 15 = \sin(45 - 30)$

$= \sin 45 \cos 30 - \cos 45 \sin 30$

$= \left(\dfrac{\sqrt{2}}{2} \times \dfrac{\sqrt{3}}{2}\right) - \left(\dfrac{\sqrt{2}}{2} \times \dfrac{1}{2}\right)$

$= \dfrac{\sqrt{6} - \sqrt{2}}{4}$

(b) $\cos 15 = \cos(45 - 30)$

$= \cos 45 \cos 30 + \sin 45 \sin 30$

$= \left(\dfrac{\sqrt{2}}{2}\right)\left(\dfrac{\sqrt{3}}{2}\right) + \left(\dfrac{\sqrt{2}}{2}\right)\left(\dfrac{1}{2}\right)$

$= \left(\dfrac{\sqrt{6}}{4}\right) + \left(\dfrac{\sqrt{2}}{4}\right)$

$= \dfrac{\sqrt{6} + \sqrt{2}}{4}$

Given the cosine or sine of two angles, it is possible to combine them to find the cosine or sine of the sum or difference.

Worked Example

18. Find the exact value of $\cos(p + q)$ given:

$$\cos p = \dfrac{2}{5}, \sin q = \dfrac{5}{8}$$

where p is an acute angle and q is an obtuse angle.

$\cos(p + q) = \cos p \cos q - \sin p \sin q$

To find $\sin p$ and $\cos q$, use the identity $\sin^2 A + \cos^2 A \equiv 1$:

$$\sin^2 p = 1 - \cos^2 p$$

$$\sin^2 p = 1 - \left(\dfrac{2}{5}\right)^2 = \dfrac{21}{25}$$

$$\sin p = \pm\sqrt{\dfrac{21}{25}} = \pm\dfrac{\sqrt{21}}{5}$$

Since p is an acute angle, it lies in the first quadrant, where $\sin p$ is positive.

$$\therefore \sin p = \dfrac{\sqrt{21}}{5}$$

$$\cos^2 q = 1 - \sin^2 q$$

$$\cos^2 q = 1 - \left(\dfrac{5}{8}\right)^2 = \dfrac{39}{64}$$

$$\cos q = \pm\sqrt{\dfrac{39}{64}} = \pm\dfrac{\sqrt{39}}{8}$$

Since q is an obtuse angle, it lies in the second quadrant, where $\cos q$ is negative.

$$\therefore \cos q = -\frac{\sqrt{39}}{8}$$

$$\cos(p+q) = \cos p \cos q - \sin p \sin q$$
$$= \left(\frac{2}{5} \times -\frac{\sqrt{39}}{8}\right) - \left(\frac{\sqrt{21}}{5} \times \frac{5}{8}\right)$$
$$= \frac{-2\sqrt{39} - 5\sqrt{21}}{40}$$

Double angle formulae

Setting $B = A$ in the compound angle formulae allows us to derive three more important formulae: the **double angle formulae**.

$$\cos 2A = \cos^2 A - \sin^2 A$$
$$\sin 2A = 2 \sin A \cos A$$
$$\tan 2A = \frac{2 \tan A}{1 - \tan^2 A}$$

Proof of the cosine double angle formula in its three different forms

Begin with the compound angle formula:
$$\cos(A+B) = \cos A \cos B - \sin A \sin B$$

Let $B = A$. Then:
$$\cos(2A) = \cos A \cos A - \sin A \sin A$$
$$\cos 2A = \cos^2 A - \sin^2 A$$

We can derive two alternative forms for the cosine double angle formula:
$$\cos 2A = \cos^2 A - \sin^2 A$$
$$\Rightarrow \cos 2A = \cos^2 A - (1 - \cos^2 A)$$
$$\Rightarrow \cos 2A = 2\cos^2 A - 1$$

$$\cos 2A = \cos^2 A - \sin^2 A$$
$$\Rightarrow \cos 2A = (1 - \sin^2 A) - \sin^2 A$$
$$\Rightarrow \cos 2A = 1 - 2\sin^2 A$$

In summary:
$$\cos 2A = \cos^2 A - \sin^2 A$$
$$= 2\cos^2 A - 1$$
$$= 1 - 2\sin^2 A$$

Proof of the sine double angle formula

Begin with the compound angle formula:
$$\sin(A+B) = \sin A \cos B + \cos A \sin B$$

Let $B = A$. Then:
$$\sin(2A) = \sin A \cos A + \cos A \sin A$$
$$\sin 2A = 2 \sin A \cos A$$

Proof of the tan double angle formula

Begin with the compound angle formula:
$$\tan(A+B) = \frac{\tan A + \tan B}{1 - \tan A \tan B}$$

Let $B = A$. Then:
$$\tan(2A) = \frac{\tan A + \tan A}{1 - \tan A \tan A}$$

$$\tan 2A = \frac{2 \tan A}{1 - \tan^2 A}$$

Note: The compound angle formulae appear on your formula sheet under the heading *Trigonometric Identities*. The double angle formulae are **not given**. You will need to know how to derive them from the compound angle formulae.

Re-arranging the cosine double angle formulae gives two more important results:

$$\cos 2A = 2\cos^2 A - 1$$
$$\Rightarrow \cos^2 A = \frac{1}{2}(1 + \cos 2A)$$

$$\cos 2A = 1 - 2\sin^2 A$$
$$\Rightarrow \sin^2 A = \frac{1}{2}(1 - \cos 2A)$$

These two formulae are used in Chapter 10 for integrating expressions involving $\cos^2 A$ or $\sin^2 A$. They do not appear on the formula sheet.

Worked Examples

19. Given $p = \sin 37°$ and $q = \cos 37°$, find $\sin 74°$ in terms of p and q.

$$\sin 2A = 2 \sin A \cos A$$

If $A = 37$, then:
$$\sin 74 = 2 \sin 37 \cos 37$$
$$= 2pq$$

20. Given $\cos\left(\frac{\theta}{2}\right) = \frac{3}{7}$, find $\cos \theta$.

$$\cos 2A = 2\cos^2 A - 1$$

Letting $A = \frac{\theta}{2}$:

$$\cos \theta = 2 \cos^2\left(\frac{\theta}{2}\right) - 1$$

$$= 2\left(\frac{3}{7}\right)^2 - 1$$

$$= -\frac{31}{49}$$

21. Given $\cos\left(\frac{\theta}{2}\right) = \frac{15}{17}$:

   (a) Find $\sin\left(\frac{\theta}{2}\right)$
   (b) Using the appropriate double angle formula, find $\sin\theta$.
   (c) Find $\tan\left(\frac{\theta}{2}\right)$
   (d) Using the appropriate double angle formula, find $\tan\theta$.

(a) Use $\sin^2 A + \cos^2 A \equiv 1$ to find $\sin\left(\frac{\theta}{2}\right)$

$$\sin^2\left(\frac{\theta}{2}\right) = 1 - \cos^2\left(\frac{\theta}{2}\right)$$

$$\sin^2\left(\frac{\theta}{2}\right) = 1 - \left(\frac{15}{17}\right)^2 = \frac{64}{289}$$

$$\sin\left(\frac{\theta}{2}\right) = \sqrt{\frac{64}{289}} = \frac{8}{17}$$

(b) $\sin 2A = 2\sin A \cos A$

Letting $A = \frac{\theta}{2}$:

$$\sin\theta = 2\sin\left(\frac{\theta}{2}\right)\cos\left(\frac{\theta}{2}\right)$$

$$= 2\left(\frac{15}{17}\right)\left(\frac{8}{17}\right)$$

$$= \frac{240}{289}$$

(c) $\tan\left(\frac{\theta}{2}\right) = \dfrac{\sin\left(\frac{\theta}{2}\right)}{\cos\left(\frac{\theta}{2}\right)} = \dfrac{8/17}{15/17} = \dfrac{8}{15}$

(d) $\tan 2A = \dfrac{2\tan A}{1 - \tan^2 A}$

Letting $A = \frac{\theta}{2}$:

$$\tan\theta = \frac{2\tan\left(\frac{\theta}{2}\right)}{1 - \tan^2\left(\frac{\theta}{2}\right)}$$

$$= \frac{2\left(\frac{8}{15}\right)}{1 - \left(\frac{8}{15}\right)^2} = \frac{240}{161}$$

8: TRIGONOMETRIC IDENTITIES AND EQUATIONS

Exercise 8D

1. Using the appropriate compound angle formulae, find the exact values of the following.

   (a) $\sin 120°$
   (b) $\cos\left(\frac{7\pi}{12}\right)$
   (c) $\tan 75°$
   (d) $\sin\left(\frac{3\pi}{4}\right)$
   (e) $\tan 150°$
   (f) $\sin\left(-\frac{\pi}{12}\right)$

2. Write each of the following as a single trigonometric ratio. Hence find the exact value of each expression.

   (a) $\cos 20° \cos 25° - \sin 20° \sin 25°$
   (b) $\sin\left(\frac{\pi}{4}\right)\cos\left(\frac{\pi}{2}\right) - \cos\left(\frac{\pi}{4}\right)\sin\left(\frac{\pi}{2}\right)$
   (c) $\sin 125° \cos 55° + \cos 125° \sin 55°$
   (d) $\cos 95° \cos 5° + \sin 95° \sin 5°$
   (e) $\cos\frac{3\pi}{7}\cos\frac{\pi}{14} - \sin\frac{3\pi}{7}\sin\frac{\pi}{14}$
   (f) $\sin 21° \cos 39° + \cos 21° \sin 39°$
   (g) $\sin\left(\frac{15\pi}{16}\right)\cos\left(\frac{11\pi}{16}\right) - \cos\left(\frac{15\pi}{16}\right)\sin\left(\frac{11\pi}{16}\right)$
   (h) $\dfrac{\tan 50° - \tan 5°}{1 + \tan 50° \tan 5°}$
   (i) $\dfrac{\tan(-\pi/10) + \tan(13\pi/30)}{1 - \tan(-\pi/10)\tan(13\pi/30)}$

3. Given $m = \sin 16°$ and $n = \cos 16°$, find $\sin 32°$ in terms of m and n.

4. Using the appropriate compound angle formula, show that: $\tan\left(\frac{13\pi}{6}\right) = \frac{\sqrt{3}}{3}$

5. Find the exact value of $\cos(\alpha + \beta)$ given:
   $\cos\alpha = \frac{2}{3}$, $\sin\beta = \frac{1}{4}$
   where α and β are both acute angles.

6. Given that: $\cos A = -\frac{3}{7}$, $\sin B = \frac{1}{8}$ and given that A and B are both obtuse angles show that: $\sin(A - B) = \dfrac{3(1 - \sqrt{5}\sqrt{7}\sqrt{8})}{56}$

7. Without using a calculator, find the exact value of $\tan 2x$ given that $\tan x = \frac{1}{9}$ and that x is an acute angle.

Exercise 8D...

8. Two angles A and B have the following properties:
$$\sin(A+B) = -\frac{\sqrt{3}}{2}$$
$$\cos A = -\frac{\sqrt{2}}{2}$$
$$\sin B = \frac{(\sqrt{6}+\sqrt{2})}{4}$$
$$\cos B = \frac{(\sqrt{6}-\sqrt{2})}{4}$$
Find $\sin A$.

9. Giving exact answers, find the values of $\cos\theta$, $\sin\theta$ and $\tan\theta$ when:
   (a) $\cos\frac{\theta}{2} = \frac{7}{10}$ (b) $\sin\frac{\theta}{2} = \frac{2}{5}$ (c) $\tan\frac{\theta}{2} = \frac{9}{10}$

Identities and equations involving compound and double angles

The double angle formulae are frequently used in proving trigonometric identities.

When proving an identity, it is usually best to start with the side involving the double or compound angle. As with previous work proving trigonometric identities, if one method doesn't appear to work, try to think of another approach.

Worked Examples

22. Show that: $\dfrac{\cos 2\theta}{\cos^2\theta + \cos\theta \sin\theta} \equiv 1 - \tan\theta$

$$\text{LHS} = \frac{\cos 2\theta}{\cos^2\theta + \cos\theta \sin\theta}$$
$$= \frac{\cos^2\theta - \sin^2\theta}{\cos^2\theta + \cos\theta \sin\theta}$$

Factorise the numerator using difference of two squares. Factorise the denominator, taking out a common factor of $\cos\theta$:
$$= \frac{(\cos\theta - \sin\theta)(\cos\theta + \sin\theta)}{\cos\theta(\cos\theta + \sin\theta)}$$

Cancel the factor $(\cos\theta + \sin\theta)$:
$$= \frac{\cos\theta - \sin\theta}{\cos\theta}$$
$$= \frac{\cos\theta}{\cos\theta} - \frac{\sin\theta}{\cos\theta}$$
$$= 1 - \tan\theta$$
$$= \text{RHS}$$

23. Show that: $\dfrac{\cot 2\theta \tan\theta}{1+\tan\theta} \equiv \dfrac{1}{2}(1-\tan\theta)$

$$\text{LHS} = \cot 2\theta \left(\frac{\tan\theta}{1+\tan\theta}\right)$$

Since $\cot 2\theta = \dfrac{1}{\tan 2\theta}$:
$$= \left(\frac{1}{\tan 2\theta}\right)\left(\frac{\tan\theta}{1+\tan\theta}\right)$$

Since $\tan 2\theta = \dfrac{2\tan\theta}{1-\tan^2\theta}$, so $\dfrac{1}{\tan 2\theta} = \dfrac{1-\tan^2\theta}{2\tan\theta}$.

Therefore:
$$= \left(\frac{1-\tan^2\theta}{2\tan\theta}\right)\left(\frac{\tan\theta}{1+\tan\theta}\right)$$

Factorise $1 - \tan^2\theta$ using difference of two squares:
$$= \left(\frac{(1-\tan\theta)(1+\tan\theta)}{2\tan\theta}\right)\left(\frac{\tan\theta}{1+\tan\theta}\right)$$

Cancel factors $(1+\tan\theta)$ and $\tan\theta$:
$$= \frac{1-\tan\theta}{2}$$
$$= \frac{1}{2}(1-\tan\theta)$$
$$= \text{RHS}$$

24. Show that: $\tan 3\theta \equiv \dfrac{\tan\theta(3-\tan^2\theta)}{1-3\tan^2\theta}$

$$\text{LHS} = \tan(\theta + 2\theta)$$

Using the tan compound angle formula:
$$= \frac{\tan\theta + \tan 2\theta}{1 - \tan\theta \tan 2\theta}$$

Using the tan double angle formula to replace $\tan 2\theta$:
$$= \frac{\tan\theta + \left(\dfrac{2\tan\theta}{1-\tan^2\theta}\right)}{1 - \tan\theta\left(\dfrac{2\tan\theta}{1-\tan^2\theta}\right)}$$

Multiplying top and bottom by $(1-\tan^2\theta)$ gives:
$$= \frac{\tan\theta(1-\tan^2\theta) + 2\tan\theta}{(1-\tan^2\theta) - 2\tan^2\theta}$$
$$= \frac{3\tan\theta - \tan^3\theta}{1 - 3\tan^2\theta}$$
$$= \frac{\tan\theta(3-\tan^2\theta)}{1-3\tan^2\theta}$$
$$= \text{RHS}$$

8: TRIGONOMETRIC IDENTITIES AND EQUATIONS

The compound and double angle formulae can be used to solve trigonometric equations. Begin by expanding any trigonometric functions of compound or double angles using the appropriate formula.

Worked Examples

25. Solve the equation: $\cos(\theta - 45°) = 2\sin\theta$ in the interval $-180° < \theta \leq 180°$.

$$\cos(\theta - 45°) = 2\sin\theta$$
$$\cos\theta\cos 45 + \sin\theta\sin 45 = 2\sin\theta$$
$$\frac{1}{\sqrt{2}}\cos\theta + \frac{1}{\sqrt{2}}\sin\theta = 2\sin\theta$$
$$\frac{1}{\sqrt{2}}\cos\theta = \left(2 - \frac{1}{\sqrt{2}}\right)\sin\theta$$
$$\frac{1}{\sqrt{2}}\cos\theta = \left(\frac{2\sqrt{2}-1}{\sqrt{2}}\right)\sin\theta$$
$$\frac{1}{2\sqrt{2}-1} = \tan\theta$$
$$\theta = -151.3°, 28.7°$$

26. Solve the equation: $\tan 2x = 4\tan x$ in the interval $0 \leq x \leq 2\pi$.

$$\tan 2x = 4\tan x$$
$$\Rightarrow \frac{2\tan x}{1 - \tan^2 x} = 4\tan x$$
$$\Rightarrow 2\tan x = 4\tan x(1 - \tan^2 x)$$
$$\Rightarrow \tan x = 2\tan x(1 - \tan^2 x)$$
$$\Rightarrow 2\tan x(1 - \tan^2 x) - \tan x = 0$$
$$\Rightarrow \tan x[2(1 - \tan^2 x) - 1] = 0$$
$$\Rightarrow \tan x(1 - 2\tan^2 x) = 0$$
$$\Rightarrow \tan x = 0 \text{ or } (1 - 2\tan^2 x) = 0$$

So: $\tan x = 0$ or $\tan^2 x = \frac{1}{2}$

giving: $\tan x = 0$ or $\tan x = \pm\frac{1}{\sqrt{2}}$

Therefore:
$x = 0, 0.62, 2.53, 3.14, 3.76, 5.67, 6.28$ radians

Exercise 8E

1. Simplify: $\cos A\cos(A-B) + \sin A\sin(A-B)$

2. Prove the following identities.
   (a) $\csc 2\theta - \cot 2\theta \equiv \tan\theta$
   (b) $\tan\theta + \cot\theta \equiv \dfrac{2}{\sin 2\theta}$
   (c) $\cos 2\theta \equiv \dfrac{1 - \tan^2\theta}{1 + \tan^2\theta}$
   (d) $\cot(A + B) \equiv \dfrac{\cot A\cot B - 1}{\cot A + \cot B}$
   (e) $\tan 2\theta \sec\theta \equiv 2\sin\theta \sec 2\theta$
   (f) $\tan\theta + \cot 2\theta \equiv \csc 2\theta$
   (g) $\dfrac{\cos 2A}{\cos A - \sin A} \equiv \cos A + \sin A$
   (h) $\sin\theta \equiv \dfrac{2\tan\left(\frac{\theta}{2}\right)}{1 + \tan^2\left(\frac{\theta}{2}\right)}$
   (i) $\cot 2\theta \equiv \dfrac{1}{2}(\cot\theta - \tan\theta)$
   (j) $\cot\theta \equiv \cot 2\theta + \dfrac{1}{\sin 2\theta}$

3. Starting with the cosine compound angle formula: $\cos(A + B) = \cos A\cos B - \sin A\sin B$ replace B with $-B$ to prove the compound angle formula for $\cos(A - B)$.

4. (a) Show that, if $\cos(x - 60°) = \sin(x + 45°)$ then $\tan x = \sqrt{6} - \sqrt{3} - \sqrt{2} + 2$
   (b) Hence find the possible values of x where $0 \leq x \leq 360°$.

5. (a) Show that $\cos 3\theta = \cos^3\theta - 3\sin^2\theta\cos\theta$
   (b) Hence solve the equation:
   $2\cos^3\theta - 6\sin^2\theta\cos\theta = \sqrt{2}$
   giving answers in the range $0 \leq \theta \leq \dfrac{2\pi}{3}$.

6. Solve: $\cos^2\theta = \sin^2\theta + \sin 2\theta$ within the interval $0 \leq \theta \leq \pi$.

7. Solve for x within the interval $0 < x < 2\pi$, giving all answers to 3 significant figures:
$$\sin\left(x + \frac{\pi}{2}\right) = \tan x$$

8. (a) Show that if: $\tan\theta = \tan 2\theta$, then:
   $\tan\theta(1 + \tan^2\theta) = 0$
   (b) Hence show that there are two solutions to $\tan\theta = \tan 2\theta$ in the range $0 \leq \theta \leq \pi$ and find these solutions.

Exercise 8E...

9. Solve, giving answers in the range $0° \leq x \leq 360°$:
$$\frac{1}{2} \sin x \sin 2x = \cos x$$

10. Show that:
$$\sqrt{\frac{1 - \sin 2\theta}{1 - \cos 2\theta} \times \frac{1 + \sin 2\theta}{1 + \cos 2\theta}} = \frac{1 - \tan^2 \theta}{2 \tan \theta}$$

11. (a) Show that $\cos^4 \theta - \sin^4 \theta = \cos 2\theta$
    (b) Hence solve $\cos^4 \theta - \sin^4 \theta = \frac{1}{2}$, giving answers in the interval $0 \leq \theta \leq 2\pi$.

12. (a) Show that:
$$3 \sin^2 A + 2 \sec^2 A + 7 \tan A \equiv (3 \sin A + \sec A)(\sin A + 2 \sec A)$$
    (b) Hence show that solving the equation:
    $3 \sin^2 \theta + 2 \sec^2 \theta + 7 \tan \theta = 0$
    is equivalent to solving the equation
    $$\sin 2\theta = -\frac{2}{3}$$
    (c) Hence, or otherwise, find all solutions in the range $0 \leq \theta \leq 2\pi$ to:
    $3 \sin^2 \theta + 2 \sec^2 \theta + 7 \tan \theta = 0$

Note: At the time of publication, the proofs in questions 13 and 14 are not required by the CCEA specification. They are presented here for students who want to stretch themselves.

13. The diagram opposite has already been used to prove the cosine compound angle formulae.
    (a) Use the same diagram to prove the compound angle formula for sine:
    $\sin(A + B) = \sin A \cos B + \cos A \sin B$
    (b) Replace B with $-B$ to prove the compound angle formula for $\sin(A - B)$:
    $\sin(A - B) = \sin A \cos B - \cos A \sin B$

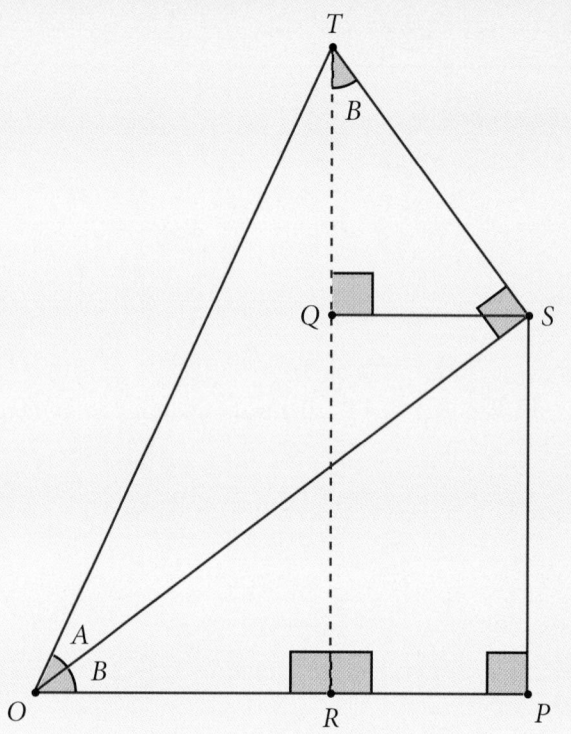

14. Use the compound angle formulae for $\sin(A + B)$ and $\cos(A + B)$ to prove the compound angle formula for $\tan(A + B)$.

8.5 Harmonic Form

Expressing $a \sin x \pm b \cos x$ in the equivalent forms $r \sin(x + \alpha)$ and $r \cos(x + \alpha)$

All expressions of the form $a \sin x \pm b \cos x$ can be written in the form $r \sin(x + \alpha)$ or $r \cos(x + \alpha)$, where r and α are constants. This is known as **harmonic form**.

Proof of harmonic form

Note: At the time of publication, the CCEA specification does not require you to know this proof.

Suppose:
$a \sin x + b \cos x \equiv r \sin(x + \alpha)$

Expand the right-hand side using the sine double angle formula:
$a \sin x + b \cos x \equiv r \sin x \cos \alpha + r \cos x \sin \alpha$

Equate coefficients of $\cos x$ and $\sin x$:
$$a = r \cos \alpha \quad (1)$$
$$b = r \sin \alpha \quad (2)$$

Square and add (1) and (2):

$$a^2 + b^2 = r^2(\cos^2 \alpha + \sin^2 \alpha)$$

Since $\cos^2 \alpha + \sin^2 \alpha \equiv 1$:
$$a^2 + b^2 = r^2$$
$$r = \sqrt{a^2 + b^2}$$

Divide (2) by (1):
$$\frac{r \sin \alpha}{r \cos \alpha} = \frac{b}{a}$$
$$\tan \alpha = \frac{b}{a}$$
$$\alpha = \tan^{-1}\left(\frac{b}{a}\right)$$

Hence $a \sin x \pm b \cos x$ can always be written in the form $r \sin(x + \alpha)$ where $r = \sqrt{a^2 + b^2}$ and $\alpha = \tan^{-1}\left(\frac{b}{a}\right)$.

Note: A similar proof shows that
$a \sin x + b \cos x \equiv r \cos(x + \alpha)$

In other words, adding any two sine or cosine functions together gives another function that can be written as a single sine or cosine. The graphs below demonstrate this for two particular functions $f(x)$ and $g(x)$ and their sum $h(x)$.

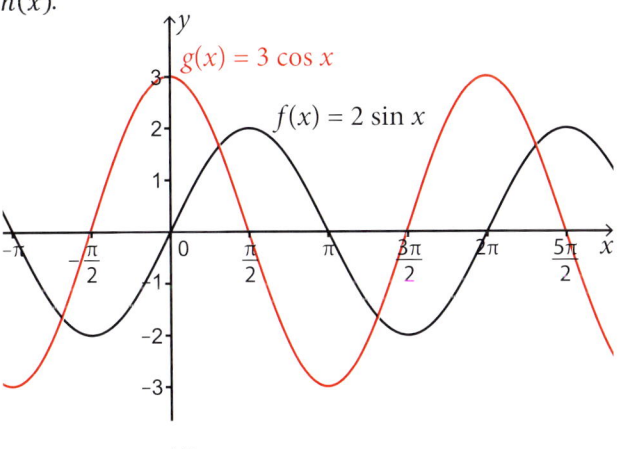

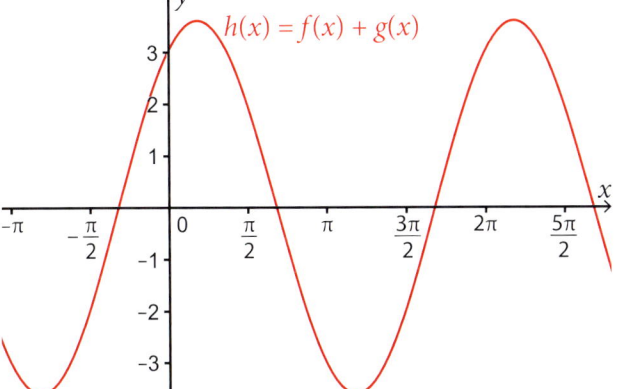

Worked Example

27. Given: $f(x) = 3 \cos \theta - 4 \sin \theta$, express $f(x)$ in the form $r \cos(\theta + \alpha)$ where α is an acute angle to be found and r is a positive constant.

$$f(x) = 3 \cos \theta - 4 \sin \theta$$
$$3 \cos \theta - 4 \sin \theta \equiv r \cos(\theta + \alpha)$$

Note: Use the equivalence sign $\equiv$ because this is always true, not just for certain values of θ.

$\Rightarrow 3 \cos \theta - 4 \sin \theta = r \cos \theta \cos \alpha - r \sin \theta \sin \alpha$

Equate coefficients of $\cos \theta$ and $\sin \theta$:
$$3 = r \cos \alpha \quad (1)$$
$$-4 = -r \sin \alpha$$
$$\Rightarrow 4 = r \sin \alpha \quad (2)$$

Square and add (1) and (2):
$$3^2 + 4^2 = r^2(\cos^2 \alpha + \sin^2 \alpha)$$
$$25 = r^2$$

We are told that r is a positive constant, so:
$$r = 5$$

Divide (2) ÷ (1):
$$\frac{r \sin \alpha}{r \cos \alpha} = \frac{4}{3}$$
$$\tan \alpha = \frac{4}{3}$$
$$\alpha = \tan^{-1}\left(\frac{4}{3}\right) = 53.1°$$

Hence:
$$f(x) = 5 \cos(\theta + 53.1°)$$

This technique can be used to help you to:
- find the maximum and minimum values of functions;
- sketch the curves of these functions;
- solve trigonometric equations.

Worked Example

28. A function is defined as: $f(x) = 6 \sin x + 5 \cos x$
(a) Express $f(x)$ in the form $R \sin(x + \alpha)$, where $R > 0$ and $0 < \alpha < \frac{\pi}{2}$.
(b) Hence find the maximum and minimum values of $f(x)$.
(c) Find the smallest positive values of x for which the maximum and minimum occur.
(d) Sketch the curve $y = f(x)$.
(e) Find the greatest value of $(6 \sin x + 5 \cos x)^4$.

(f) Solve, for $0 < x < 2\pi$, the equation:
$6 \sin x + 5 \cos x = 2$
giving your answers to 3 decimal places.

(a) $6 \sin x + 5 \cos x = R \sin(x + \alpha)$
$6 \sin x + 5 \cos x = R(\sin x \cos \alpha + \cos x \sin \alpha)$

Equate coefficients:
$6 = R \cos \alpha$; $5 = R \sin \alpha$
$R = \sqrt{36 + 25} = \sqrt{61}$
$\alpha = \tan^{-1}\left(\dfrac{5}{6}\right) = 0.695$

Hence:
$6 \sin x + 5 \cos x = \sqrt{61} \sin(x + 0.695)$

(b) $6 \sin x + 5 \cos x = \sqrt{61} \sin(x + 0.695)$

The maximum value of $\sqrt{61} \sin(x + 0.695)$ is $\sqrt{61}$. Hence the maximum value of $6 \sin x + 5 \cos x$ is $\sqrt{61}$ or 7.81 (3 s.f.).

The minimum value is $-\sqrt{61}$ or -7.81 (3 s.f.).

(c) The maximum occurs when $x + 0.695 = \dfrac{\pi}{2}$:
$x = 0.876$ (3 s.f.)

The minimum occurs when $x + 0.695 = \dfrac{3\pi}{2}$:
$x = 4.02$ (3 s.f.)

(d) $f(x) = \sqrt{61} \sin(x + 0.695)$
The curve $y = f(x)$ is a sine curve translated 0.695 units in the negative x-direction and stretched by a factor $\sqrt{61}$ in the y-direction:

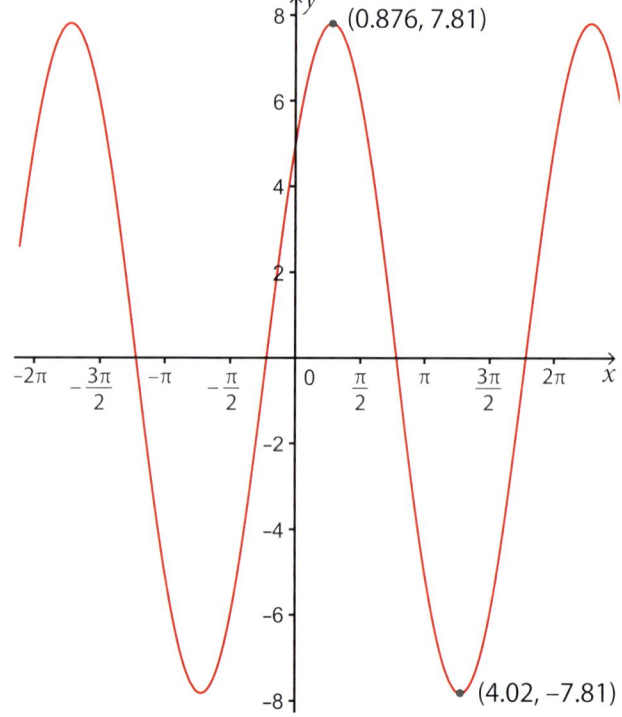

(e) From part (b), the maximum value of $6 \sin x + 5 \cos x$ is $\sqrt{61}$.
Hence the maximum value of $(6 \sin x + 5 \cos x)^4$ is $\left(\sqrt{61}\right)^4 = 61^2 = 3721$.

(f) $6 \sin x + 5 \cos x = 2$
$\Rightarrow \sqrt{61} \sin(x + 0.695) = 2$
$\Rightarrow \sin(x + 0.695) = \dfrac{2}{\sqrt{61}}$
$x + 0.695 = 0.259, 2.883, 6.542$
$x = 2.188, 5.847$ radians
(2 solutions within interval $0 < x < 2\pi$.)

Exercise 8F

1. Find an expression of the form $r \cos(\theta - \alpha)$ equivalent to each of the following, where r is a positive constant and α is an acute angle in degrees.
   (a) $2 \cos \theta + 6 \sin \theta$ (b) $7 \cos \theta + 8 \sin \theta$
   (c) $4 \cos \theta + 5 \sin \theta$ (d) $8 \cos \theta + 5 \sin \theta$

2. Find an expression of the form $r \cos(\theta + \alpha)$ equivalent to each of the following, where r is a positive constant and α is an acute angle in degrees.
   (a) $8 \cos \theta - 4 \sin \theta$ (b) $5 \cos \theta - 7 \sin \theta$
   (c) $3 \cos \theta - 6 \sin \theta$ (d) $6 \cos \theta - 9 \sin \theta$

3. Convert to the form $r \sin(\theta - \alpha)$ for each of the following, where r is a positive constant and α is an acute angle in degrees.
   (a) $6 \sin \theta - 3 \cos \theta$ (b) $4 \sin \theta - 6 \cos \theta$
   (c) $5 \sin \theta - 8 \cos \theta$ (d) $8 \sin \theta - 2 \cos \theta$

4. Find an expression of the form $r \sin(\theta + \alpha)$ equivalent to each of the following, where r is a positive constant and α is an acute angle in degrees.
   (a) $8 \sin \theta + 5 \cos \theta$ (b) $3 \sin \theta + 8 \cos \theta$
   (c) $5 \sin \theta + 7 \cos \theta$ (d) $4 \sin \theta + 9 \cos \theta$

5. For each of the following, convert to the form specified. R is a positive constant and α is an acute angle in radians. Give both R and α to 3 significant figures.
   (a) $6 \cos \theta - 3 \sin \theta = R \cos(\theta + \alpha)$
   (b) $3 \cos \theta + 9 \sin \theta = R \cos(\theta - \alpha)$
   (c) $6 \sin \theta - 9 \cos \theta = R \sin(\theta - \alpha)$
   (d) $4 \sin \theta + 7 \cos \theta = R \sin(\theta + \alpha)$

Exercise 8F...

6. (a) Express $3\sin x + 7\cos x$ in the form $R\sin(x + \alpha)$, where $R > 0$ and $0 < \alpha < \frac{\pi}{2}$.
   (b) Hence find the greatest value of $(3\sin x + 7\cos x)^2$.
   (c) Solve, for $0 \leq x < 2\pi$, the equation $3\sin x + 7\cos x = 2$ giving your answers to 3 significant figures.

7. The function f is defined such that $f(x) = 10\cos x - 5\sin x$. Given that $f(x) = R\cos(x + \alpha)$, where $R \geq 0$ and $0 \leq \alpha \leq 90°$:
   (a) Find the value of R and the value of α.
   (b) Hence solve the equation: $10\cos x - 5\sin x = 11$ for $0 \leq x < 360$, giving your answers to 1 decimal place.
   (c) Write down the minimum value of $10\cos x - 5\sin x$.
   (d) Find, to 3 significant figures, the smallest positive value of x for which this minimum value occurs.

8. (a) Show that:
   $2\sin 2\theta - 7\cos 2\theta - 7\sin\theta + 7$
   $\equiv \sin\theta(4\cos\theta + 14\sin\theta - 7)$
   (b) Express $4\cos\theta + 14\sin\theta$ in the form $R\sin(\theta + \alpha)$ where $R > 0$ and $0 < \alpha < \frac{\pi}{2}$.
   (c) Hence, for $0 < \theta < \pi$, solve:
   $2\sin 2\theta = 7(\cos 2\theta + \sin\theta - 1)$
   giving your answers in radians to 3 significant figures where appropriate.

9. (a) Express $3.5\sin 2x + 7\cos 2x$ in the form $R\sin(2x + \alpha)$, where $R > 0$ and $0 < \alpha < \frac{\pi}{2}$. Give the values of R and α to 3 significant figures.
   (b) Express $7\sin x \cos x + 14\cos^2 x$ in the form $a\cos 2x + b\sin 2x + c$, where a, b and c are constants to be found.
   (c) Using your answers to parts (a) and (b), deduce the maximum value of $7\sin x \cos x + 14\cos^2 x$.

10. (a) Express $2\sin x - 3\cos x$ in the form $R\sin(x - \alpha)$ where R is a positive constant, α is an acute angle. x and α are both measured in degrees.
    (b) State the maximum and minimum values of $2\sin x - 3\cos x$ and find the smallest positive values of x for which the maximum and minimum occur.
    (c) Hence sketch the graph of:
    $y = 2\sin x - 3\cos x$ for $-360° < x < 360°$.
    Mark the coordinates of every maximum and minimum within this interval. Show also where the curve intersects the y-axis.

11. The function f is defined such that:
    $f(x) = 7\sin x + 24\cos x$.
    (a) Show that the graph of $y = f(x)$ crosses the x-axis where $x = -1.29$ and $x = 1.85$ to 3 significant figures.
    (b) What is the maximum value of the function?
    (c) What is the minimum value of
    $g(x) = \dfrac{1}{7\sin x + 24\cos x}$
    within the interval $[-1.29, 1.85]$?

12. Find the minimum value of $\dfrac{1}{|f(x)|}$ where $f(x) = 8\cos x - 15\sin x$.

8.6 Problems in Context

You may be asked to solve problems involving the trigonometric functions in context. There may be little guidance in the wording of the question about which approach to take. You may need a combination of the techniques you have learnt in this chapter, as well as your knowledge of radian measure.

Exercise 8G

1. An electronics component provides a voltage that varies according to the function $I(t) = 5\sin t$ where t is the time, measured in seconds. A second component provides a voltage according to the function $J(t) = 12\cos t$ (measured in volts).
   (a) Find $K(t)$, the combined voltage from the two components, giving your answer in the form $R\cos(t - \alpha)$, where R is an integer and α is an acute angle in radians, given to 3 significant figures.
   (b) What is the maximum value of the combined voltage?

Exercise 8G...

2. A Cepheid Variable is a star whose magnitude (its apparent brightness) fluctuates. The magnitude $M(t)$ of one particular Cepheid Variable star varies according to the relationship $M(t) = 6 \sin t + 12$ where t is the time in seconds.
   (a) What is the maximum value for $M(t)$?
   (b) A second Cepheid Variable fluctuates according to the relationship $N(t) = 8\cos(t) + 10$. Through a telescope, the two stars appear very close to each other. If their combined magnitude is $P(t)$, show that $P(t)$ can be approximated using: $P(t) = 10\sin(t + \alpha) + k$, where α (in radians) and k are constants to be found.
   (c) Hence find the maximum value of the combined magnitude of the two stars.

3. (a) Using the compound angle formula for $\sin(A + B)$, show that:
   $$\sin 105° = \frac{\sqrt{6} + \sqrt{2}}{4}$$
   (b) A children's play area is in the shape of a quadrilateral, shown below. It is made of two triangles S and T. All lengths are measured in metres.

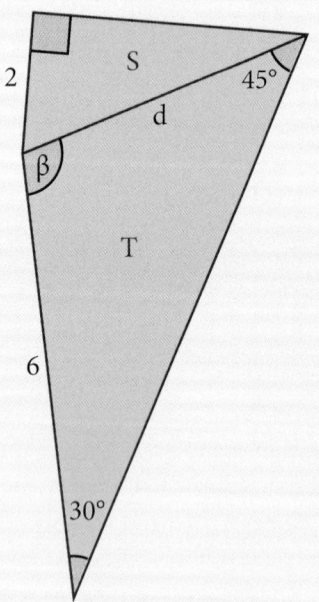

   (i) Find the size of angle β.
   (ii) Find the length d as a surd.
   (iii) Using your answer to part (a), show that
   $$\text{area T} = \frac{9}{2}(\sqrt{3} + 1)\,\text{m}^2.$$

Exercise 8G...

   (iv) Find the total area of the quadrilateral in square metres, giving your answer in surd form.

4. The number of hours of daylight per day on an island is given by the formula:
   $$L = 1.26\sin\theta - 4.32\cos\theta + \frac{49}{4}$$
   where θ is measured in radians and is defined as:
   $$\theta = \frac{2\pi d}{365}$$
   where d is the day number of the year (with $d = 1$ on 1st January and $d = 365$ on 31st December).
   (a) Show that: $L = \frac{9}{2}\sin(\theta - 1.287) + \frac{49}{4}$
   (b) Hence find which day numbers correspond to the minimum and maximum number of daylight hours. Find these dates and the amount of daylight in hours and minutes for each. You may assume this is not a leap year.

5. (a) Express: $3\cos\theta + 6\sin\theta$ in the form $R\cos(\theta - \alpha)$ where $R > 0$ and $0 < \alpha < \frac{\pi}{2}$. Give the values of R and α to 3 significant figures.
   (b) Find the maximum value of $3\cos\theta + 6\sin\theta$ and the smallest positive value of θ for which this maximum occurs.
   (c) The temperature, $T°C$, of a store room is modelled using the equation:
   $$T = 9 + 3\cos\left(\frac{\pi t}{12}\right) + 6\sin\left(\frac{\pi t}{12}\right), 0 \leq t < 24$$
   where t is the number of hours after 12:00 noon. Calculate the maximum temperature predicted by this model and the time at which this maximum occurs.

8.7 Summary

You will need to prove trigonometric identities involving the reciprocal trigonometric functions. Begin with the side that looks most complicated, then re-arrange until you reach the expression on the other side. You will often use one or more of the following when proving identities:

$$\tan\theta \equiv \frac{\sin\theta}{\cos\theta}$$

$$\sin^2\theta + \cos^2\theta \equiv 1$$

$$1 + \cot^2\theta \equiv \operatorname{cosec}^2\theta$$

$$\tan^2\theta + 1 \equiv \sec^2\theta$$

Trigonometric equations will often involve the reciprocal functions. To solve them, you will often use one or more of the identities above. You may need to solve a quadratic equation involving one of the reciprocal functions.

The **compound angle formulae** are:

$$\sin(A \pm B) = \sin A \cos B \pm \cos A \sin B$$

$$\cos(A \pm B) = \cos A \cos B \mp \sin A \sin B$$

$$\tan(A \pm B) = \frac{\tan A \pm \tan B}{1 \mp \tan A \tan B}$$

From these, the **double angle formulae** can be derived:

$$\sin 2A = 2\sin A \cos A$$

$$\cos 2A = \cos^2 A - \sin^2 A = 2\cos^2 A - 1 = 1 - 2\sin^2 A$$

$$\tan 2A = \frac{2\tan A}{1 - \tan^2 A}$$

You will use these formulae to solve trigonometric equations and to prove identities.

Any expression in the form $a\cos x \pm b\sin x$ can be expressed in the form $r\cos(x + \alpha)$ or $r\sin(x + \alpha)$, where r and α are constants. This is known as **harmonic form**. It can be used to find the maximum and minimum values of the function, sketch the curve and to solve trigonometric equations.

You may be asked to solve problems in context involving any of these techniques. You will be required to give answers in the context of the question.

Chapter 9
Differentiation

9.1 Introduction

Key words
- **Gradient**: The steepness of a curve at any point.
- **Differentiation**: A technique used to find the gradient function.
- **Derivative / gradient function:** A function that allows you to calculate the gradient at any point on a curve, often denoted $\frac{dy}{dx}$.
- **Quotient Rule**: A technique used to find the derivative of a quotient (fraction).
- **Product Rule**: A technique used to find the derivative of a product of two functions.
- **Chain Rule**: A technique used to find the derivative of composite functions.
- **Calculus**: The area of mathematics that includes differentiation and integration.

Before you start
You should know:

- How to find the first derivative (usually $\frac{dy}{dx}$) for expressions involving x^n.
- How to find the gradient of a curve at any point.
- How to solve problems involving rates of change.
- How to find second derivatives (usually $\frac{d^2y}{dx^2}$).
- How to find the equations of tangents and normals to a curve.
- How to find the maximum and minimum points (turning or stationary points) of curves.
- How to investigate whether functions are increasing or decreasing.

What you will learn
In this chapter you will learn how to:

- Differentiate expressions involving e^x and $\ln x$.
- Differentiate expressions involving the trigonometric functions.
- Differentiate products, quotients and composite functions.

Notation
You are used to seeing the notation $\frac{dy}{dx}$, which means 'differentiate y with respect to x'.

However you may also come across the notation $\frac{d}{dx}[f(x)]$, which means 'differentiate $f(x)$ with respect to x'.

For example, you may be asked:

Find $\frac{d}{dx}[3x^2]$

This is equivalent to asking:

$y = 3x^2$. Find $\frac{dy}{dx}$.

In this chapter you will learn several new techniques for finding a derivative.

In the real world...
Shipwrecks at sea were common while the mathematician Isaac Newton was alive in the 17th century. Although sailors had been using the stars to navigate for centuries, there was an insufficient understanding of how the Earth moved in relation to the other celestial bodies. It was Newton's work on calculus that revolutionised navigation at sea. Today, calculus forms the bedrock of much of the technological maritime navigation equipment in use.

Calculus, discovered by Isaac Newton and the German Gottfried Leibniz, is arguably the greatest mathematical innovation in all of human history.

Exercise 9A (Revision)

1. Find the first derivative $\frac{dy}{dx}$ for the curves defined by each of the following equations.
   - (a) $y = 3x^2$
   - (b) $y = 2x^3 - 3x^2$
   - (c) $y = \frac{1}{2x}$
   - (d) $y = 2\sqrt{x}$
   - (e) $y = 5x - 2x^{5/2}$

Exercise 9A...

2. Using your answers to question 1, find the gradient function $\frac{dy}{dx}$ in each case at the point where $x = 2$.

3. By setting $\frac{dy}{dx} = 0$ for each of your answers to question 1, find the coordinates of any stationary points (maximum and minimum points) for the curves defined.

4. Differentiate your answers to question 1 to obtain the second derivative $\frac{d^2y}{dx^2}$ in each case.

5. By substituting the appropriate value of x into your expressions for $\frac{d^2y}{dx^2}$ in question 4, determine the nature of each stationary point (i.e. maximum or minimum).

6. A farmer has 30 metres of fencing and a fixed brick wall. They want to create a rectangular enclosure using the wall and three sides made from fencing. What is the maximum possible area for the enclosure?

7. Find the equation of the tangent to the curve $y = 3x^2 - 4x + 1$ at the point $(1, 0)$.

8. Is the function $f(x) = -4x^3 - 5x + 1$ always increasing, always decreasing or neither?

9.2 Differentiation of e^x and $\ln x$

In AS Mathematics, you learnt about the differentiation of **sums and differences of powers of x**, or some other variable.

Worked Example (Revision)

1. Find the first derivative for each of the following.

   (a) $y = x^2 + 3x + 1$ (b) $y = x + 2 + \frac{3}{x}$
   (c) $y = z^{24} + z^{-24}$

   (a) $\frac{dy}{dx} = 2x + 3$

   (b) Re-write as:
   $y = x + 2 + 3x^{-1}$
   $\Rightarrow \frac{dy}{dx} = 1 - 3x^{-2}$

   (c) $\frac{dy}{dz} = 24z^{23} - 24z^{-25}$

In this section you will learn how to differentiate expressions involving exponentials and logarithms.

Exponentials

You may remember from AS Mathematics that the exponential function $y = e^x$ has a gradient that is equal to its y value at every point. In other words:

$$y = e^x \Rightarrow \frac{dy}{dx} = e^x$$

Worked Example

2. Differentiate to obtain $\frac{dy}{dx}$:

   (a) $y = e^x + 1$ (b) $y = 2e^x - x^2$

   Remember: with a sum of terms, you can differentiate each term in turn.

   (a) $y = e^x + 1$
   $\frac{dy}{dx} = e^x$ (differentiating 1 gives 0)

   (b) $y = 2e^x - x^2$
   $\frac{dy}{dx} = 2e^x - 2x$

Stationary points and second derivatives

Remember that you can find the coordinates of **stationary points** by setting $\frac{dy}{dx} = 0$.

Differentiating $\frac{dy}{dx}$ gives the second derivative, $\frac{d^2y}{dx^2}$.

By investigating the sign of the second derivative, you can usually determine the **nature** of a stationary point.

Worked Example

3. Find the coordinates of any stationary points on the curve $y = x - 3e^x$. Determine the nature of the stationary points.

   Differentiate:
   $y = x - 3e^x$
   $\frac{dy}{dx} = 1 - 3e^x$

Set $\dfrac{dy}{dx} = 0$:

$\dfrac{dy}{dx} = 0 \Rightarrow 1 - 3e^x = 0$

$3e^x = 1$

$e^x = \dfrac{1}{3}$

$x = \ln\left(\dfrac{1}{3}\right) = -1.10$

Substitute back to find y:

$y = -1.10 - 3e^{-1.10} = -2.10$

So the coordinates of the only stationary point are $(-1.10, -2.10)$ (3 significant figures).

Differentiate again to obtain $\dfrac{d^2 y}{dx^2}$:

$\dfrac{d^2 y}{dx^2} = -3e^x$

When $x = -1.10$, $\dfrac{d^2 y}{dx^2} < 0$

Hence, this stationary point is a maximum point.

Logarithms

To differentiate $\ln x$:

$$y = \ln x \Rightarrow \dfrac{dy}{dx} = \dfrac{1}{x}$$

A proof of this result is given in section 11.5.

You can often simplify expressions involving logs to make them easier to differentiate.

Worked Examples

4. Find the gradient function $\dfrac{dy}{dx}$ for each of the following:

   (a) $y = \ln(6x)$ (b) $y = \ln(4\sqrt{x})$

   (a) $y = \ln(6x)$
   $= \ln 6 + \ln x$

   $\ln 6$ is a constant, so differentiation gives 0.

   $\dfrac{dy}{dx} = \dfrac{1}{x}$

   (b) $y = \ln(4\sqrt{x})$
   $= \ln 4 + \ln \sqrt{x}$
   $= \ln 4 + \ln x^{1/2}$
   $= \ln 4 + \dfrac{1}{2}\ln x$

   $\ln 4$ is a constant, so differentiation gives 0.

   $\dfrac{dy}{dx} = \dfrac{1}{2} \times \dfrac{1}{x}$
   $= \dfrac{1}{2x}$

5. The curve C has equation $y = a + b \ln x$ where a and b are constants. The curve passes through the point $(1, 3)$. At the point on the curve where $x = 2$, $\dfrac{dy}{dx} = 1$.

   (a) Find the values of a and b.
   (b) Find the equation of the normal to the curve at the point $(1, 3)$. Write down the gradient and y-intercept of this normal.
   (c) Sketch the curve and the normal, marking the point where the curve intersects the x-axis.

   (a) $y = a + b \ln x$

   At point $(1, 3)$:
   $3 = a + b \ln 1$
   $\therefore a = 3$

   To find b:
   $\dfrac{dy}{dx} = \dfrac{b}{x}$

   When $x = 2$, $\dfrac{dy}{dx} = 1$

   $\therefore 1 = \dfrac{b}{2}$

   $b = 2$

   (b) The gradient function of curve C is $\dfrac{dy}{dx} = \dfrac{2}{x}$.

   At $(1, 3)$, gradient $= \dfrac{2}{1} = 2$.

   The gradient of the tangent is the same as the gradient of the curve, so the gradient of the tangent at this point is 2.

   The gradient of the normal is $-\tfrac{1}{2}$ (the negative reciprocal of the gradient of the tangent).

   The equation of the normal can be found using:

   $y - y_1 = m(x - x_1)$

   $y - 3 = -\dfrac{1}{2}(x - 1)$

   $y = -\dfrac{1}{2}x + \dfrac{7}{2}$

   The gradient is $-\tfrac{1}{2}$ and the y-intercept $\tfrac{7}{2}$ (or 3.5).

   (c) To find the intersection of the curve with the x-axis:

   $y = 0 \Rightarrow 3 + 2 \ln x = 0$

   $\ln x = -\dfrac{3}{2}$

$x = e^{-3/2}$
$= 0.22$ (2 d.p.)

So we can sketch:

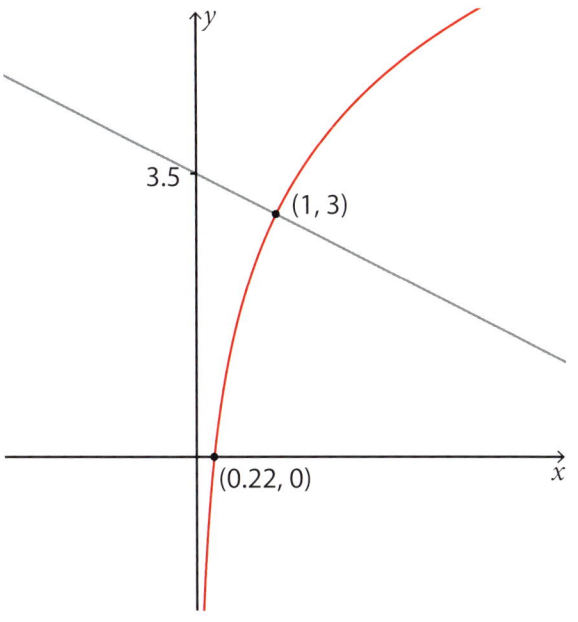

6. Find the coordinates of the stationary points on the curve: $y = e^{2\ln x} - 6e^{\ln x} + 8$. Determine the nature of the stationary points.

$y = e^{2\ln x} - 6e^{\ln x} + 8$
$= e^{\ln x^2} - 6e^{\ln x} + 8$
$= x^2 - 6x + 8$

$\dfrac{dy}{dx} = 2x - 6$

Stationary points occur when $2x - 6 = 0$:
$x = 3, y = -1$

$\dfrac{d^2y}{dx^2} = 2$, which is positive.

Therefore, the only stationary point is $(3, -1)$, a minimum point.

Exercise 9B

1. Differentiate the following with respect to x.
   (a) $y = 2e^x$
   (b) $y = x^2 - e^x$
   (c) $y = \dfrac{e^x}{2}$
   (d) $y = 3(e^x - x)$
   (e) $y = x^{-2} - 2e^x$
   (f) $y = e^x + 3x^4$
   (g) $y = \dfrac{3}{x} - e^x$
   (h) $y = 3(e^x + 1)$
   (i) $y = 5(1 - 2e^x)$

Exercise 9B...

   (j) $y = \left(e^{1/x}\right)^x + e^x + \left(e^{-1/x}\right)^x$
   (k) $y = e^x(2 - 3e^{-x})$
   (l) $y = e^{2x} - e^x(1 + e^x)$
   (m) $y = e^{-x}(e^{2x} - 5xe^x)$
   (n) $y = 5x\left(7 - \dfrac{3}{x}e^x\right)$
   (o) $y = \dfrac{1}{x}(7x^3 - 6x^2 + xe^x - x)$
   (p) $y = e^{x+1}$
   (q) $y = 3e^x + 5$
   (r) $y = \dfrac{10x^2 e^x + 6}{x^2}$

2. Differentiate the following with respect to x.
   (a) $y = 3\ln x$
   (b) $y = x + \ln x$
   (c) $y = x^3 - \ln x$
   (d) $y = \ln x^2$
   (e) $y = \ln 6x$
   (f) $y = \ln\left(\dfrac{x}{7}\right)$
   (g) $y = \ln(4x^2)$
   (h) $y = \ln\left(\dfrac{x^3}{4}\right)$
   (i) $y = \ln 6x - \ln 4x$
   (j) $y = \ln\left(\dfrac{1}{x^4}\right)$
   (k) $y = \ln\left(\dfrac{a^5\sqrt{b}}{x^3}\right)$
   (l) $y = 3(x + \ln x)$
   (m) $y = \left(\dfrac{\ln 6x}{x} + 1\right)x$
   (n) $y = \dfrac{1}{x}\left(x\ln\left(\dfrac{1}{x^4}\right) - x - 1\right)$

3. Differentiate the following with respect to x.
   (a) $y = 10e^x - \ln 7x$
   (b) $y = 6e^x + \ln 3x^2$
   (c) $y = e^{\ln x}$
   (d) $y = e^{2\ln x}$
   (e) $y = e^{2\ln x+1}$
   (f) $y = e^{2\ln x-1}$
   (g) $y = \ln(e^{3x})$
   (h) $y = \ln(3e^{3x})$
   (i) $y = \ln(3e^{3x^2})$
   (j) $y = \ln(4e^{3x^2+x+1})$

4. Find the equation of the tangent to each curve at the point given.
   (a) $y = 2e^x + x^2$; $(0, 2)$
   (b) $y = x^3 - \dfrac{e^x}{3}$; $(0, -\frac{1}{3})$
   (c) $y = \ln 2x$; $(\frac{1}{2}, 0)$
   (d) $y = \ln(x^2) - 2e^x - 2x$; $(1, -2(e+1))$

Exercise 9B...

5. Find the equation of the normal to each curve at the point given.
   (a) $y = e^x$; $(0, 1)$
   (b) $y = 2e^x - x + 1$; $(0, 3)$
   (c) $y = \ln x + x$; $(1, 1)$
   (d) $y = \ln 2x + x^2$; $(½, ¼)$

6. Find the coordinates of all the stationary points of the following curves, giving your answers in an exact form. By finding $\frac{d^2y}{dx^2}$, determine whether each stationary point is a maximum or a minimum.
   (a) $y = \ln x - x$
   (b) $y = e^x - x$
   (c) $y = e^{2\ln x} - 2e^{\ln x} + 1$
   (d) $y = 2x - \ln(4x^2 e^x)$

7. The curve with equation $y = \frac{1}{4}e^x$ meets the y-axis at the point A.
   (a) Prove that the tangent at A to the curve has equation $4y = x + 1$.
   (b) The point B has x-coordinate $\ln 16$ and lies on the curve. Find the y-coordinate of B.
   (c) Find the equation of the normal to the curve at B.
   (d) The normal at B intersects the tangent at A at the point C. Show that the x-coordinate of C is $\ln 4 + {}^{15}\!/_{\!2}$.
   (e) Find the y-coordinate of C.

8. The curve C has equation $y = p + qe^x$, where p and q are positive constants.
   (a) Find $\frac{dy}{dx}$.
   At the point $P(\ln 3, p + 3q)$ on C, the gradient is 3.
   (b) Find the value of q.
   (c) Given that C also passes through the point $(0, 4)$, find the value of p.
   (d) Show that the equation of the normal to C at point P is $3y + x = 18 + \ln 3$.
   This normal crosses the x-axis at point L and the y-axis at point M.
   (e) Find the coordinates of L and M.
   (f) Sketch the curve C and the normal.
   (g) Show that the area of triangle OLM, where O is the origin, is approximately 60.8.

Exercise 9B...

9. The curve with equation $y = \frac{1}{2}e^x$ meets the y-axis at the point A.
   (a) Show that the tangent T to the curve at point A has equation $2y = x + 1$.
   (b) The point B has x-coordinate $\ln 4$ and lies on the curve. Find the y-coordinate of point B.
   (c) Show that the normal N to the curve at point B has equation: $2y + x = 2(\ln 2 + 2)$
   (d) The lines T and N meet at the point C. Prove that the x-coordinate of C is $\ln 2 + \frac{3}{2}$ and find the y-coordinate of C.

9.3 Differentiation of Trigonometric Functions

The derivatives of sin, cos and tan

The derivatives of the trigonometric functions are summarised in the following table. All angles must be measured in radians.

y	$\frac{dy}{dx}$
$\sin x$	$\cos x$
$\cos x$	$-\sin x$
$\tan x$	$\sec^2 x$

Note: The proofs of the derivatives of $\sin x$ and $\cos x$ are beyond the scope of this book and, at the time of publication, are not required by the CCEA specification. The proof of the derivative of $\tan x$ is an exercise for the reader in Exercise 9H. You will need to memorise all three results.

Worked Examples

7. Differentiate: $y = 2\sin x - 3\cos x - 3x^2$

   $\frac{dy}{dx} = 2\cos x + 3\sin x - 6x$

8. Find the gradient of the curve: $y = 2\tan x + x$ at the point where $x = \dfrac{\pi}{4}$.

$y = 2\tan x + x$

$\dfrac{dy}{dx} = 2\sec^2 x + 1$

When $x = \dfrac{\pi}{4}$:

$\dfrac{dy}{dx} = 2\sec^2\left(\dfrac{\pi}{4}\right) + 1$

$= \dfrac{2}{\cos^2\left(\dfrac{\pi}{4}\right)} + 1$

$= \dfrac{2}{\left(\dfrac{\sqrt{2}}{2}\right)^2} + 1$

$= 5$

9. Find the equation of the tangent to the curve: $y = \sin x - x^2$ at the point where $x = \dfrac{\pi}{2}$.

$y = \sin x - x^2$

$\dfrac{dy}{dx} = \cos x - 2x$

When $x = \dfrac{\pi}{2}$:

$\dfrac{dy}{dx} = \cos\left(\dfrac{\pi}{2}\right) - 2\left(\dfrac{\pi}{2}\right)$

$= 0 - \pi$

$= -\pi$

To find y when $x = \dfrac{\pi}{2}$:

$y = \sin\left(\dfrac{\pi}{2}\right) - \left(\dfrac{\pi}{2}\right)^2$

$= 1 - \dfrac{\pi^2}{4}$

Equation of tangent:

$y - y_1 = m(x - x_1)$

$y - \left(1 - \dfrac{\pi^2}{4}\right) = -\pi\left(x - \dfrac{\pi}{2}\right)$

$y = -\pi x + \dfrac{\pi^2}{2} - \dfrac{\pi^2}{4} + 1$

$y = -\pi x + \dfrac{\pi^2}{4} + 1$

Exercise 9C

1. Differentiate the following.
   (a) $y = \sin x - \cos x$
   (b) $y = 5\sin x + 4\cos x$
   (c) $y = 3\tan x - x^2 - 1$
   (d) $y = -2\tan x - 7x^2 - x$
   (e) $y = x^3 - \sin x$
   (f) $y = 1 - x^3 + \dfrac{\sin x}{2}$
   (g) $y = 3\cos x - x^2 + 5\sin x$
   (h) $y = 1 - \tan x$
   (i) $y = 2\sqrt{1 - \cos^2 x}$
   (j) $y = \sqrt{16 - 16\sin^2 x}$
   (k) $y = \dfrac{\cos x}{2} - \dfrac{1}{x}$
   (l) $y = \dfrac{1}{2}\sin x - \dfrac{1}{3}\tan x$
   (m) $y = a\sin x + b\cos x$
   (n) $y = 3p\sin x - 4q\cos x$
   (o) $y = 2(\ln x - \cos x)$
   (p) $y = (\sec x - \tan x)(\sec x + \tan x)$
   (q) $y = \sin^2 x + \sin x - \cos x + \cos^2 x$
   (r) $y = e^x(2e^{-x}\sin x + e^{-x}\cos x)$
   (s) $y = \dfrac{1}{x}(3x\cos x - x\sin x)$
   (t) $y = \tan x \cos x$

2. Find the gradient of the curve at the point whose x-coordinate is specified.
   (a) $y = e^x - \sin x - \cos x$; when $x = 0$
   (b) $y = \tan x - 2x^2 + 1$; when $x = \dfrac{\pi}{4}$
   (c) $y = \tan x - \ln x$; when $x = \pi$
   (d) $y = 3\sqrt{2}\sin x + 4\sqrt{2}\cos x$; when $x = \dfrac{\pi}{4}$

3. Find the equation of the tangent to the curve at the point specified.
   (a) $y = 1 - \cos x$ at the point $\left(\dfrac{\pi}{2}, 1\right)$
   (b) $y = e^x + \sin x$ at the point $(0, 1)$
   (c) $y = \ln x - \cos x$ at the point $(\pi, \ln(\pi) + 1)$
   (d) $y = \cos x + 2\tan x$ at the point $(0, 1)$

Exercise 9C...

4. Find the equation of the normal to the curve at the point specified.
   (a) $y = \sin x + 1$ at the point $(0, 1)$
   (b) $y = 2\cos x + \sin x$ at the point $(0, 2)$
   (c) $y = 2e^x - \sin x$ at the point $(0, 2)$
   (d) $y = \tan x - \cos x$ at the point $(\pi, 1)$

5. Given that $y = \tan x + 5\cos x$, find the exact value of $\dfrac{dy}{dx}$ at $x = \dfrac{\pi}{4}$.

6. A curve C has the equation: $y = x - \tan x$
   Point P lies on the curve C and its x-coordinate is between 0 and $\dfrac{\pi}{2}$ radians.
   (a) Given that $\dfrac{dy}{dx} = -3$ at point P, find the coordinates of P.
   (b) Find the equation of the tangent to C at point P.

7. Differentiate the following to obtain $f'(x)$:
   $f(x) = \dfrac{1}{x^2} + \sin x$

9.4 The Product Rule

Consider two functions $u = f(x)$ and $v = g(x)$, which are multiplied together, so that $y = uv$.

For example, if $u = 2x$ and $v = \sin x$, then $y = 2x \sin x$.

Then, a technique called the **product rule** will allow you to find $\dfrac{dy}{dx}$.

The product rule

If: $y = uv$

then: $\dfrac{dy}{dx} = u\dfrac{dv}{dx} + v\dfrac{du}{dx}$

Or, using function notation we could write:

If: $f(x) = u(x)v(x)$

then: $f'(x) = u(x)v'(x) + u'(x)v(x)$

Worked Examples

10. $y = 2x \sin x$ Find $\dfrac{dy}{dx}$.

    $u = 2x$ and $v = \sin x$

    Differentiate both:
    $\dfrac{du}{dx} = 2$ and $\dfrac{dv}{dx} = \cos x$

    Use the product rule formula:
    $\dfrac{dy}{dx} = u\dfrac{dv}{dx} + v\dfrac{du}{dx}$

    $= 2x \cos x + 2\sin x$

11. Find the gradient function $\dfrac{dy}{dx}$ if $y = (x^2 - 2x + 3)e^x$

    $u = (x^2 - 2x + 3)$ and $v = e^x$

    $\dfrac{du}{dx} = 2x - 2$ and $\dfrac{dv}{dx} = e^x$

    $\dfrac{dy}{dx} = u\dfrac{dv}{dx} + v\dfrac{du}{dx}$

    $= (x^2 - 2x + 3)e^x + e^x(2x - 2)$

    $= e^x[(x^2 - 2x + 3) + (2x - 2)]$

    $= e^x(x^2 + 1)$

12. A curve is defined by the equation $y = x^3 \ln x$.
    (a) Find $\dfrac{dy}{dx}$.
    (b) Find the gradient of the curve at the point where $x = 1$.

    (a) $u = x^3$ and $v = \ln x$

    $\dfrac{du}{dx} = 3x^2$ and $\dfrac{dv}{dx} = \dfrac{1}{x}$

    $\dfrac{dy}{dx} = x^3\left(\dfrac{1}{x}\right) + \ln x\,(3x^2)$

    $= x^2 + 3x^2 \ln x$

    $= x^2(1 + 3\ln x)$

    (b) When $x = 1$:
    $\dfrac{dy}{dx} = 1^2(1 + 3\ln(1))$

    $= 1(1 + 3(0))$

    $= 1$

9: DIFFERENTIATION

Exercise 9D

1. Find $\frac{dy}{dx}$ for the following: $y = x^6(x + 5)$
   (a) By expanding the brackets;
   (b) Using the product rule

2. Find $\frac{dy}{dx}$ for the following.
   (a) $y = 2x\,e^x$ (b) $y = 6x \sin x$
   (c) $y = (x^6 + 6) \ln x$ (d) $y = x^7 \tan x$
   (e) $y = \ln x \sin x$

3. The curve C has equation: $y = x^{1/3} e^x$
   Find the x-coordinate of the minimum point of the curve.

4. The diagram shows part of the curve with equation: $y = (12x - 4) \tan x$, $0 \leq x < \frac{\pi}{4}$

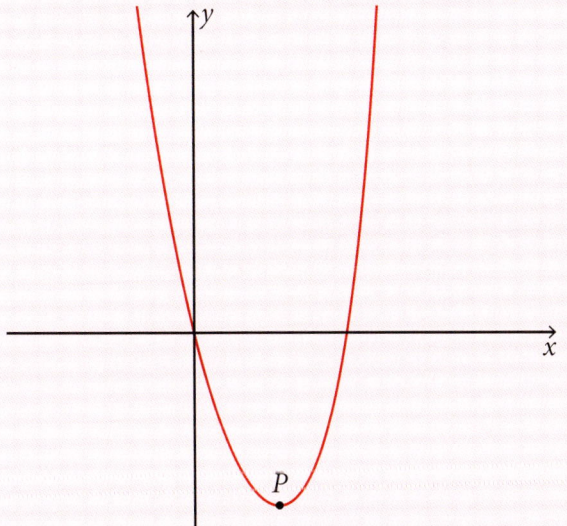

   The curve has a minimum at the point P. The x-coordinate of P is k. Show that k satisfies the equation: $3 \sin k \cos k = 1 - 3k$

5. The curve C has equation: $y = 2x^2 e^x$
   (a) Find $\frac{dy}{dx}$ using the product rule.
   (b) Hence find the coordinates of the turning points of C.
   (c) Find $\frac{d^2y}{dx^2}$.
   (d) Determine the nature of each turning point of the curve C.

9.5 The Quotient Rule

Again, we consider two functions $u = f(x)$ and $v = g(x)$, this time divided so that $y = \frac{u}{v}$.

For example, if $u = 2x$ and $v = \sin x$, then $y = \frac{2x}{\sin x}$.

Then, the **quotient rule** will allow you to find $\frac{dy}{dx}$.

The quotient rule

If: $y = \dfrac{u}{v}$

then: $\dfrac{dy}{dx} = \dfrac{v \frac{du}{dx} - u \frac{dv}{dx}}{v^2}$

Or, using function notation we could write:

If: $f(x) = \dfrac{u(x)}{v(x)}$

then: $f'(x) = \dfrac{u'(x)v(x) - u(x)v'(x)}{[v(x)]^2}$

Worked Examples

13. $y = \dfrac{2x}{\sin x}$ Find $\dfrac{dy}{dx}$.

    $u = 2x$ and $v = \sin x$

    Differentiate both:
    $\dfrac{du}{dx} = 2$ and $\dfrac{dv}{dx} = \cos x$

    Use the quotient rule formula:
    $\dfrac{dy}{dx} = \dfrac{v \frac{du}{dx} - u \frac{dv}{dx}}{v^2}$

    $= \dfrac{(\sin x)(2) - 2x(\cos x)}{\sin^2 x}$

    $= \dfrac{2 \sin x - 2x \cos x}{\sin^2 x}$

    $= \dfrac{2}{\sin x} - \dfrac{2x \cos x}{\sin^2 x}$

    $= 2 \csc x - 2x \cot x \csc x$

    $= 2 \csc x (1 - x \cot x)$

14. Find the gradient function $\dfrac{dy}{dx}$ if $y = \dfrac{(x^2 - 2x + 3)}{e^x}$

    $u = (x^2 - 2x + 3)$ and $v = e^x$

    $\dfrac{du}{dx} = 2x - 2$ and $\dfrac{dv}{dx} = e^x$

$$\frac{dy}{dx} = \frac{v\frac{du}{dx} - u\frac{dv}{dx}}{v^2}$$

$$= \frac{e^x(2x-2) - (x^2 - 2x + 3)e^x}{e^{2x}}$$

$$= \frac{e^x[(2x-2) - (x^2 - 2x + 3)]}{e^{2x}}$$

$$= e^{-x}(-x^2 + 4x - 5)$$

15. A curve is defined by the equation $y = \frac{\ln x}{x^2}$.

 (a) Find $\frac{dy}{dx}$.

 (b) Find the gradient of the curve at the point where $x = 1$.

(a) $u = \ln x$ and $v = x^2$

$$\frac{du}{dx} = \frac{1}{x} \text{ and } \frac{dv}{dx} = 2x$$

$$\frac{dy}{dx} = \frac{v\frac{du}{dx} - u\frac{dv}{dx}}{v^2}$$

$$\frac{dy}{dx} = \frac{x^2\left(\frac{1}{x}\right) - \ln x\,(2x)}{x^4}$$

$$= \frac{1 - 2\ln x}{x^3}$$

(b) When $x = 1$:

$$\frac{dy}{dx} = \frac{1 - 2\ln(1)}{1^3}$$

$$= \frac{1 - 2(0)}{1}$$

$$= 1$$

You may need to combine the quotient rule with the product rule.

Worked Example

16. Find $\frac{dy}{dx}$ given: $y = \frac{e^x \sin x}{x^3}$

$$y = \frac{e^x \sin x}{x^3}$$

Firstly consider $u = e^x \sin x$

Using the product rule:

$$\frac{du}{dx} = e^x \cos x + e^x \sin x$$

$$= e^x(\cos x + \sin x)$$

Now use the quotient rule:

$y = \frac{u}{v}$ where $u = e^x \sin x$ and $v = x^3$:

$$\frac{du}{dx} = e^x \cos x + e^x \sin x \text{ (from above) and } \frac{dv}{dx} = 3x^2$$

$$\frac{dy}{dx} = \frac{v\frac{du}{dx} - u\frac{dv}{dx}}{v^2}$$

$$\frac{dy}{dx} = \frac{x^3 e^x(\cos x + \sin x) - (e^x \sin x)(3x^2)}{(x^3)^2}$$

$$= \frac{x^3 e^x(\cos x + \sin x) - 3x^2 e^x \sin x}{x^6}$$

$$= \frac{x e^x(\cos x + \sin x) - 3e^x \sin x}{x^4}$$

$$= \frac{e^x(x \cos x + x \sin x - 3 \sin x)}{x^4}$$

Exercise 9E

1. Find $\frac{dy}{dx}$ when

 (a) $y = \frac{x+1}{x^2}$ (b) $y = \frac{5x}{(x-2)^2}$

 (c) $y = \frac{x^9}{x+3}$ (d) $y = \frac{x^3 + 2x^2}{x+1}$

 (e) $y = \frac{1+x}{2e^x}$ (f) $y = \frac{\ln x}{x}$

 (g) $y = \frac{4x}{e^x}$ (h) $y = \frac{\cos x}{x}$

 (i) $y = \frac{\tan x}{x^2}$ (j) $y = \frac{x^4}{\sin x}$

 (k) $y = \frac{\cos x}{\sqrt{x}}$ (l) $y = \frac{\sin x}{e^x}$

 (m) $y = \frac{\tan x}{1+x}$

2. Given that: $y = \frac{4x^2 - 24x + 5}{(x-3)^2}, x \neq 3$

 show that: $\frac{dy}{dx} = \frac{62}{(x-3)^3}$

3. The curve C has equation: $y = \frac{x}{36 + x^2}$

 Use calculus to find the coordinates of the turning points of C.

4. $f(x) = \frac{x^2 + 2x + 3}{x + 3}$

 Find $f'(x)$ and solve the equation: $f'(x) = \frac{19}{25}$

Exercise 9E...

5. Use a combination of the product rule and quotient rule to find $\dfrac{dy}{dx}$ for each of the following.

   (a) $y = \dfrac{(x+1)(x-2)}{x+3}$

   (b) $y = \dfrac{xe^x}{x+1}$

   (c) $y = \dfrac{e^x \cos x}{x}$

   (d) $y = \dfrac{x}{(x+1)\sin x}$

   (e) $y = e^{-x} \sin x \cos x$

   (f) $y = \dfrac{e^x \ln x}{x}$

9.6 The Chain Rule

The chain rule is used to differentiate a compound function $y = gf(x)$. You did some work on compound functions in chapter 2.

For example, $y = e^{3x}$ is a compound function, where $f(x) = 3x$ and $g(x) = e^x$.

It can be helpful to use the substitution $u = f(x)$. Then $y = g(u)$.

The derivative is found using the formula:

$$\dfrac{dy}{dx} = \dfrac{dy}{du} \times \dfrac{du}{dx}$$

Note: This formula is quite easy to remember. Think of the du cancelling out on the right-hand side.

Worked Example

17. Find $\dfrac{dy}{dx}$ for each of the following:

    (a) $y = e^{3x}$ (b) $y = \ln(x^2 + 2)$

    (a) $y = e^{3x}$
    Let $u = 3x$. Then $y = e^u$ where $u = 3x$.

    Differentiate y with respect to u:
    $$\dfrac{dy}{du} = e^u$$

    Differentiate u with respect to x:
    $$\dfrac{du}{dx} = 3$$

    Then:
    $$\dfrac{dy}{dx} = \dfrac{dy}{du} \times \dfrac{du}{dx}$$
    $$= e^u \times 3$$
    $$= 3e^u$$
    $$= 3e^{3x}$$

    (b) $y = \ln(x^2 + 2)$
    Let $u = x^2 + 2$. Then $y = \ln u$ where $u = x^2 + 2$.
    $$\dfrac{dy}{du} = \dfrac{1}{u} \text{ and } \dfrac{du}{dx} = 2x$$

    So:
    $$\dfrac{dy}{dx} = \dfrac{dy}{du} \times \dfrac{du}{dx}$$
    $$= \dfrac{1}{u} \times 2x$$
    $$= \dfrac{2x}{x^2 + 2}$$

Other examples of compound functions are $\sin 3x$ and $\tan 2x$.

With some practice using the chain rule, you will probably begin to perform the substitution mentally.

For example, if you were asked to differentiate $y = \sin(3x)$, you would obtain $\cos(3x)$, multiplied by the derivative of $3x$, which is 3. The answer is $\dfrac{dy}{dx} = 3\cos 3x$.

Differentiating $y = 2(\ln x + 1)^3$, gives $6(\ln x + 1)^2$ multiplied by the derivative of $(\ln x + 1)$, which is $\dfrac{1}{x}$.
The answer is $\dfrac{dy}{dx} = \dfrac{6}{x}(\ln x + 1)^2$.

Worked Example

18. Differentiate the following to find $\dfrac{dy}{dx}$.

    (a) $y = (x^4 - 8)^6$
    (b) $y = \sin^5 x$
    (c) $y = \tan 5x$
    (d) $y = e^{4x^2}$
    (e) $y = \ln(5x^5 + x^4 + 6x)$
    (f) $y = \ln(5 \cos x)$

    (a) $y = (x^4 - 8)^6$
    $$\dfrac{dy}{dx} = 6(x^4 - 8)^5 \times 4x^3$$
    $$= 24x^3(x^4 - 8)^5$$

(b) $y = \sin^5 x$

$\quad = (\sin x)^5$

$\quad \dfrac{dy}{dx} = 5(\sin x)^4 \times \cos x$

$\quad = 5 \sin^4 x \cos x$

(c) $y = \tan 5x$

$\quad \dfrac{dy}{dx} = \sec^2 5x \times 5$

$\quad = 5 \sec^2 5x$

(d) $y = e^{4x^2}$

$\quad \dfrac{dy}{dx} = e^{4x^2} \times 8x$

$\quad = 8x e^{4x^2}$

(e) $y = \ln(5x^5 + x^4 + 6x)$

$\quad \dfrac{dy}{dx} = \dfrac{25x^4 + 4x^3 + 6}{5x^5 + x^4 + 6x}$

(f) $y = \ln(5 \cos x)$

$\quad \dfrac{dy}{dx} = \dfrac{-5 \sin x}{5 \cos x}$

$\quad = -\tan x$

The next example demonstrates that you may need to use the chain rule twice in one question.

Worked Example

19. $y = \sin^3(3x^3)$ Find $\dfrac{dy}{dx}$.

$y = \sin^3(3x^3)$

$\quad = (\sin(3x^3))^3$

$\dfrac{dy}{dx} = 3(\sin(3x^3))^2 \times [\text{derivative of } \sin(3x^3)]$

$\dfrac{dy}{dx} = 3(\sin(3x^3))^2 \times [\cos(3x^3) \times 9x^2]$

$\quad = 27x^2 \sin^2(3x^3) \cos(3x^3)$

You may have to differentiate using any combination of the product, quotient and chain rules, or even all three.

Worked Example

20. $y = \dfrac{x \sin 3x}{e^x}$ Find $\dfrac{dy}{dx}$.

$\sin 3x$ requires the chain rule. The numerator $x \sin 3x$ is a product. The fraction means that, in the final step, we will require the quotient rule.

First consider $f(x) = \sin 3x$:

To differentiate $f(x)$ we need the chain rule.

$f'(x) = \cos 3x \times 3$

$\quad = 3 \cos 3x$

Now consider $g(x) = x \sin 3x$:

This is a product: $u = x$ and $v = \sin 3x$.

$\dfrac{du}{dx} = 1$ and $\dfrac{dv}{dx} = 3 \cos 3x$ (from above).

$g'(x) = u \dfrac{dv}{dx} + v \dfrac{du}{dx}$

$\quad = (x \times 3 \cos 3x) + (\sin 3x \times 1)$

$\quad = 3x \cos 3x + \sin 3x$

Finally consider the quotient:

$y = \dfrac{u}{v}$ where $u = x \sin 3x$ and $v = e^x$.

$\dfrac{du}{dx} = 3x \cos 3x + \sin 3x$ (from above) and $\dfrac{dv}{dx} = e^x$.

$\dfrac{dy}{dx} = \dfrac{v \dfrac{du}{dx} - u \dfrac{dv}{dx}}{v^2}$

$\dfrac{dy}{dx} = \dfrac{e^x(3x \cos 3x + \sin 3x) - (x \sin 3x)e^x}{e^{2x}}$

$\quad = \dfrac{(3x \cos 3x + \sin 3x) - (x \sin 3x)}{e^x}$

$\quad = e^{-x}(3x \cos 3x + \sin 3x - x \sin 3x)$

$\quad = e^{-x}(3x \cos 3x + (1 - x) \sin 3x)$

Exercise 9F

1. Find $\dfrac{dy}{dx}$ when:

(a) $y = e^{4x}$

(b) $y = e^{2x^2}$

(c) $y = (x^{11} - 8)^4$

(d) $y = \sin^3 x$

(e) $y = \tan 3x$

(f) $y = (x - 10)^6$

(g) $y = (11x^2 + 8x)^9$

(h) $y = \sin^{10} x$

(i) $y = e^{6x^5 + 8}$

(j) $y = e^{4 \sin x}$

(k) $y = e^{5x} + \ln 3x$

(l) $y = (x + \ln 3x)^7$

(m) $y = (10 + x^2)^{\frac{6}{5}}$

Exercise 9F...

2. Find $\dfrac{dy}{dx}$ when:
   (a) $y = \ln(x^{10} - 8)$
   (b) $y = \ln(4x^9 + x^8 + 8x)$
   (c) $y = \ln(8 \sin x)$
   (d) $y = \ln(9 \cos x)$

3. Given $y = \ln(5x^2)$, find $\dfrac{dy}{dx}$
   (a) by expanding y using the laws of logarithms;
   (b) using the chain rule.

4. Given that: $y = (1 + e^{2x})^{\frac{3}{2}}$ find the exact value of $\dfrac{dy}{dx}$ at the point $x = \ln 2$.

5. Given that: $y = (1 + e^{3x})^{\frac{4}{3}}$ find the exact value of $\dfrac{dy}{dx}$ at the point $x = \dfrac{1}{3} \ln 5$.

6. The function f is defined such that $f(x) = 16e^{6x}, x \in \mathbb{R}$. Find the value of x for which $f'(x) = 8$ giving an exact answer.

7. The diagram shows part of the curve with equation $y = f(x)$.

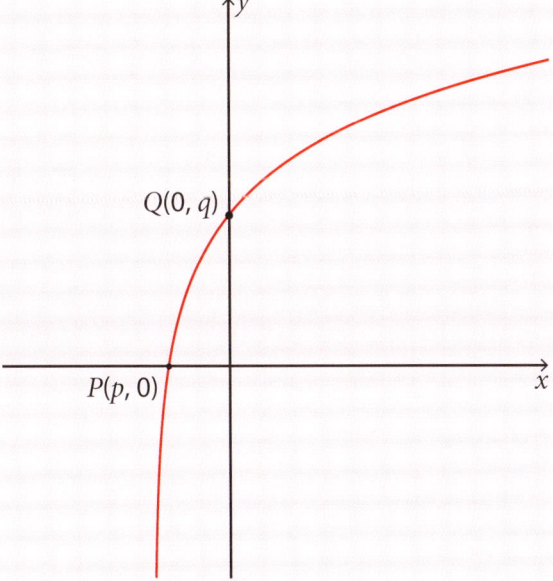

The curve meets the x-axis at $P(p, 0)$ and the y-axis at $Q(0, q)$. Given that $f(x) = 6 \ln(5x + 5)$
(a) state the exact value of q;
(b) find the value of p;
(c) find an equation for the tangent at P.

Exercise 9F...

Note: Questions 8 to 11 are presented for students who want to stretch themselves.

8. The function $f(x)$ is defined such that:
   $f(x) = e^{2x} - 2e^x + 1$
   (a) Considering the curve $y = f(x)$, use the substitution $u = e^x$ to find the point of intersection of the curve and the x-axis.
   (b) Find the coordinates of all stationary points on the curve.

9. The curve C is defined by the equation:
   $$y = \dfrac{4}{x^2} + \dfrac{1}{2(1-x)^2}.$$
   (a) Show that there is only one stationary point on the curve C and find the coordinates of this point.
   (b) By finding an expression for $\dfrac{d^2y}{dx^2}$, show that this stationary point is a minimum.

10. Find $\dfrac{dy}{dx}$ when:
    (a) $y = \dfrac{\cos(5x^5)}{5x}$
    (b) $y = x^6 e^{6x+4}$
    (c) $y = 6 \sin^2 x + \sec 5x$
    (d) $y = \cos(x^6 - 5)^7$

11. Find $\dfrac{dy}{dx}$ when:
    (a) $y = \sin^4(3x^2 + 7)$
    (b) $y = \sin(3x^2 + 7)^4$

9.7 Mixed Questions

The questions in the following exercise use the various techniques described in this chapter.

Exercise 9G

1. Differentiate the following using the product rule, the quotient rule, the chain rule, or a combination.
   (a) $y = \dfrac{1 + 2xe^x}{x}$
   (b) $f(x) = 3\ln(4x)$

Exercise 9G...

(c) $y = 4xe^x$

(d) $f(x) = \dfrac{1 + \sin x}{x^2}$

(e) $y = e^{\tan x}$

(f) $f(x) = 2x^6 \cos(3x^2)$

2. Find the equation of the normal to the curve $y = 5 \sin x + e^{x^2}$ at the point $(0, 1)$.

3. Given: $y = \dfrac{x^8 + 5}{\sqrt{x + 5}}$, find $\dfrac{dy}{dx}$ and simplify the expression.

4. Find the value of x for which $\dfrac{dy}{dx} = 0$, where $y = \dfrac{6x^2}{(x + 10)^{\frac{1}{2}}}$ and $x \geq -10$.

5. Find the gradient function $\dfrac{dy}{dx}$ given: $y = \dfrac{xe^{2x}}{1 + x}$

9.8 Differentiation of cosec x, sec x and cot x

The following three results are on the formula sheet, but the CCEA specification requires you to know the derivations of them. Derivation of the first result is given in Worked Example 21. Derivation of the other two results form part of Exercise 9H.

$$\dfrac{d}{dx}(\sec x) = \tan x \sec x$$

$$\dfrac{d}{dx}(\csc x) = -\cot x \csc x$$

$$\dfrac{d}{dx}(\cot x) = -\csc^2 x$$

Worked Examples

21. By writing $\sec x$ as $(\cos x)^{-1}$, use the chain rule to show that the derivative of $\sec x$ is $\tan x \sec x$.

$y = \sec x$

$= \dfrac{1}{\cos x} = (\cos x)^{-1}$

Using the chain rule:

$\dfrac{dy}{dx} = -1(\cos x)^{-2} \times (-\sin x)$

$= (\cos x)^{-2} (\sin x)$

$= \dfrac{\sin x}{\cos^2 x}$

$= \dfrac{\sin x}{\cos x} \times \dfrac{1}{\cos x}$

$= \tan x \sec x$

22. Use the result from Worked Example 21 and the chain rule to find:

(a) $\dfrac{d}{dx}(\sec 3x)$ (b) $\dfrac{d}{dx}\left(2 \sec\left(\dfrac{x}{2}\right)\right)$

(c) $\dfrac{d}{dx}(3 \sec x^2)$

(a) $y = \sec(3x)$

$\dfrac{dy}{dx} = \tan(3x) \sec(3x) \times 3$

$= 3 \tan(3x) \sec(3x)$

(b) $y = 2 \sec\left(\dfrac{x}{2}\right)$

$\dfrac{dy}{dx} = 2 \tan\left(\dfrac{x}{2}\right) \sec\left(\dfrac{x}{2}\right) \times \dfrac{1}{2}$

$= \tan\left(\dfrac{x}{2}\right) \sec\left(\dfrac{x}{2}\right)$

(c) $y = 3 \sec x^2$

$\dfrac{dy}{dx} = 3 \tan(x^2) \sec(x^2) \times 2x$

$= 6x \tan(x^2) \sec(x^2)$

Exercise 9H

1. (a) By writing $\csc x$ as $\dfrac{1}{\sin x}$, use the chain rule to show that the derivative of $\csc x$ is $-\cot x \csc x$.

   (b) By writing $\tan x$ as $\dfrac{\sin x}{\cos x}$, use the quotient rule to show that the derivative of $\tan x$ is $\sec^2 x$.

   (c) By writing $\cot x$ as $\dfrac{\cos x}{\sin x}$, use the quotient rule to show that the derivative of $\cot x$ is $-\csc^2 x$.

Exercise 9H...

2. Using the results above and the chain rule, find the first derivative of the following expressions.

   (a) $\sec(4x)$
   (b) $\frac{1}{4}\operatorname{cosec} 4x$
   (c) $\cot\left(\frac{x}{3}\right)$
   (d) $\sec(4x^2)$
   (e) $\operatorname{cosec}\left(\frac{1}{x}\right)$
   (f) $\cot\left(\frac{x^3}{3}\right)$
   (g) $\ln(\sec x)$
   (h) $\operatorname{cosec}(e^x)$
   (i) $-\cot(x^3 + x^2)$

To differentiate compound functions, use the **chain rule**:

If $y = f(u)$ where $u = g(x)$:
$$\frac{dy}{dx} = \frac{dy}{du} \times \frac{du}{dx}$$

Having found the **derivative**, or **gradient function** using one of these techniques, you can obtain the gradient at any point on the curve by substituting in the value of x.

9.9 Summary

In this chapter you learnt how to differentiate the **exponential function** e^x, the reciprocal function $\frac{1}{x}$ and the trigonometric functions:

$$\frac{d}{dx}(e^x) = e^x$$

$$\frac{d}{dx}(\ln x) = \frac{1}{x}$$

$$\frac{d}{dx}(\sin x) = \cos x$$

$$\frac{d}{dx}(\cos x) = -\sin x$$

$$\frac{d}{dx}(\tan x) = \sec^2 x$$

$$\frac{d}{dx}(\sec x) = \tan x \sec x$$

$$\frac{d}{dx}(\operatorname{cosec} x) = -\cot x \operatorname{cosec} x$$

$$\frac{d}{dx}(\cot x) = -\operatorname{cosec}^2 x$$

To differentiate a product of two functions, use the **product rule**:

$$y = uv \Rightarrow \frac{dy}{dx} = u\frac{dv}{dx} + v\frac{du}{dx}$$

To differentiate a quotient of two functions, use the **quotient rule**:

$$y = \frac{u}{v} \Rightarrow \frac{dy}{dx} = \frac{v\frac{du}{dx} - u\frac{dv}{dx}}{v^2}$$

Chapter 10
Further Differentiation

10.1 Introduction

Key words
- **Implicit equation**: A complicated equation involving both x and y that cannot be expressed in the form $y = f(x)$.
- **Implicit differentiation**: A technique to find $\frac{dy}{dx}$ from an implicit equation.
- **Parameter**: A third variable (after x and y) in a system of equations.
- **Parametric equations**: A system of (usually two) equations involving a parameter.
- **Parametric differentiation**: A technique to find $\frac{dy}{dx}$ from a set of parametric equations.

Before you start
You should know how to:
- Find the first derivative (usually $\frac{dy}{dx}$) for expressions involving x^n, the trigonometric functions, $\ln x$ and e^x.
- Find the gradient of a curve at any point.
- Find second derivatives (usually $\frac{d^2y}{dx^2}$).
- Solve two simultaneous equations with one a quadratic equation.
- Find the equations of tangents and normals to a curve.
- Find the coordinates of stationary points on curves.

What you will learn
In this chapter you will learn how to:
- Differentiate using implicit differentiation.
- Differentiate using parametric differentiation.

In the real world...
In the world of finance, a **derivative** is a financial product that is often based not on the value of something, but on the changes in that value. For example, a futures contract is the right to buy or sell something at a fixed price sometime in the future. These contracts can themselves be traded. If gold is trading at $900 per ounce and I hold a futures contract allowing me to buy gold at $800 per ounce next week, I could sell my futures contract at a very good price. However, if my contract said I could buy gold at $1000 per ounce next week, it would be almost worthless. I would have lost all the money I paid for it.

There are good things and bad things about financial derivatives. Futures contracts were invented to bring some certainty about the price you would pay for a particular commodity at some time in the future. However, because the potential gains and losses can become large if the price of the underlying commodity changes, derivative trading can be dangerous. There have been high-profile cases of city traders bringing bankruptcy to their companies because of a single derivative contract that went wrong.

Calculus is used widely in financial transactions, to model various aspects of the economy, for example predicting share prices and the future profitability of companies. If you can solve a **differential equation** (introduced in chapter 12), a career in the city could be an option for you, even in difficult economic times!

Exercise 10A (Revision)

1. Find the first derivative $\frac{dy}{dx}$ for the curves defined by each of the following equations.
   (a) $y = \sin(\pi x)$ for $0 \leq x \leq 2$
   (b) $y = 2x - \ln(2x)$

2. Using your answers to question 1, find the gradient function $\frac{dy}{dx}$ in each case at the point where $x = 1$.

3. By setting $\frac{dy}{dx} = 0$ for each of your answers to question 1, find the coordinates of any stationary points for the curves defined.

4. Differentiate your answers to question 1 to obtain the second derivative $\frac{d^2y}{dx^2}$ in each case.

10: FURTHER DIFFERENTIATION

Exercise 10A...

5. By substituting the appropriate value of x into your expressions for $\frac{d^2y}{dx^2}$, determine the nature of each stationary point.

6. Find the equation of the normal to the curve $y = \frac{1}{x} + 1$ at the point $(1, 2)$.

10.2 Implicit Differentiation

You have learnt how to find $\frac{dy}{dx}$ from equations of the form $y = \cdots$. You differentiate both sides of the equation with respect to x to obtain $\frac{dy}{dx} = \cdots$.

With some equations, however, it is difficult or impossible to make y the subject. These equations are known as **implicit equations**.

Consider the equation $y^3 - y = x^2 + 1$. The curve obtained when this equation is plotted is shown in the following diagram.

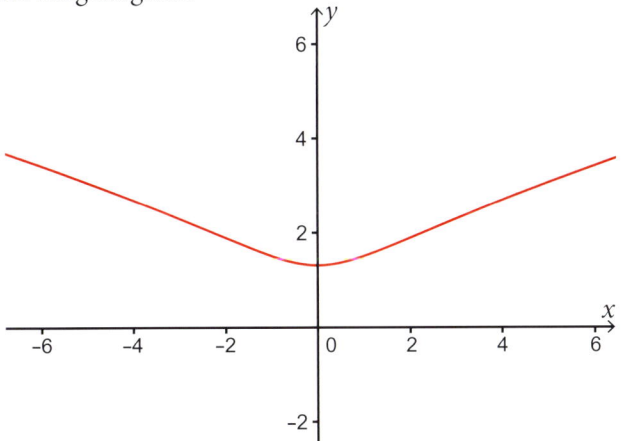

What is the gradient function $\frac{dy}{dx}$?

To find the gradient function with equations like this, we need to use **implicit differentiation**.

Implicit Differentiation

As before, differentiate both sides of the equation.

To differentiate a function of y with respect to x, follow these two steps:

1. Differentiate with respect to y.
2. Multiply by $\frac{dy}{dx}$.

Worked Example

1. Find $\frac{dy}{dx}$ given $y^3 - y = x^2 + 1$

$$y^3 - y = x^2 + 1$$

Differentiation of y^3 gives $3y^2 \frac{dy}{dx}$, and differentiation of y gives $1 \frac{dy}{dx}$:

$$3y^2 \frac{dy}{dx} - 1 \frac{dy}{dx} = 2x$$

Factorise the LHS:

$$\frac{dy}{dx}(3y^2 - 1) = 2x$$

$$\frac{dy}{dx} = \frac{2x}{(3y^2 - 1)}$$

Note: You will often end up with $\frac{dy}{dx}$ as a function of both x and y.

Why does this work?

You have already learnt that:

$\frac{dz}{dx} = \frac{dz}{dy} \times \frac{dy}{dx}$ (imagine the dy cancelling out)

Letting $z = f(y)$ then: $\frac{df(y)}{dx} = \frac{df(y)}{dy} \times \frac{dy}{dx}$

For example, $\frac{d(y^3)}{dx} = 3y^2 \times \frac{dy}{dx} = 3y^2 \frac{dy}{dx}$

The product rule is used to differentiate expressions like xy.

Worked Examples

2. $x^2 - 5xy + y^3 = 0$. Find $\frac{dy}{dx}$.

Differentiation of $5xy$ requires the product rule:

$$u = 5x \Rightarrow \frac{du}{dx} = 5$$

$$v = y \Rightarrow \frac{dv}{dx} = \frac{dy}{dx}$$

$$\therefore \frac{d}{dx}(5xy) = 5x\left(\frac{dy}{dx}\right) + 5y$$

So we differentiate the whole equation:
$$x^2 - 5xy + y^3 = 0$$
$$2x - \left(5x\frac{dy}{dx} + 5y\right) + 3y^2\frac{dy}{dx} = 0$$

Take all terms involving $\frac{dy}{dx}$ to one side of the equation and all the remaining terms to the other side:
$$3y^2\frac{dy}{dx} - 5x\frac{dy}{dx} = 5y - 2x$$

Factorise the LHS:
$$\frac{dy}{dx}(3y^2 - 5x) = 5y - 2x$$

Give the answer in terms of x and y:
$$\frac{dy}{dx} = \frac{5y - 2x}{3y^2 - 5x}$$

Note: When using the product rule, be careful with signs. In this example, the product rule work is kept inside brackets. The negative sign will then affect both terms.

3. Find $\frac{dy}{dx}$, given: $\sin(xy) = y$

Use the chain rule to differentiate $\sin(xy)$. Using the product rule, the derivative of xy is $x\frac{dy}{dx} + y$.

So we can differentiate the whole equation:
$$\sin(xy) = y$$
$$\left(x\frac{dy}{dx} + y\right)\cos(xy) = \frac{dy}{dx}$$

Group the terms involving $\frac{dy}{dx}$:
$$x\frac{dy}{dx}\cos(xy) - \frac{dy}{dx} = -y\cos(xy)$$

Factorise:
$$\frac{dy}{dx}(x\cos(xy) - 1) = -y\cos(xy)$$
$$\frac{dy}{dx} = \frac{y\cos(xy)}{1 - x\cos(xy)}$$

You can find the gradient of a curve at any point on the curve by substituting the x and y coordinates into your expression for $\frac{dy}{dx}$.

Worked Example

4. A curve C is described by the equation:
$$3x^2 + 3y^2 - 5x + 9xy - 10 = 0$$
Find an equation of the tangent to C at the point $(1, -4)$ giving your answer in the form $ax + by + c = 0$ where a, b and c are integers.

$$3x^2 + 3y^2 - 5x + 9xy - 10 = 0$$
$$6x + 6y\frac{dy}{dx} - 5 + 9x\frac{dy}{dx} + 9y = 0$$
$$6x - 5 + 9y + (6y + 9x)\frac{dy}{dx} = 0$$
$$\frac{dy}{dx} = \frac{5 - 6x - 9y}{6y + 9x}$$

At $(1, -4)$:
$$\frac{dy}{dx} = \frac{35}{-15} = -\frac{7}{3}$$

So the equation of the tangent is:
$$y - (-4) = -\frac{7}{3}(x - 1)$$
$$3y + 12 = -7x + 7$$
$$7x + 3y + 5 = 0$$

You may need to differentiate a second time to find $\frac{d^2y}{dx^2}$.

Worked Example

5. A curve C has the equation: $y^3 = x^2$

Show that: $\frac{d^2y}{dx^2} = \frac{ay^3 - bx^2}{cy^5}$

where a, b and c are constants to be found.

$$y^3 = x^2$$

Differentiate each side with respect to x:
$$3y^2\frac{dy}{dx} = 2x \quad (1)$$

Differentiate again, using the product rule for the LHS:
$$3y^2\frac{d^2y}{dx^2} + 6y\left(\frac{dy}{dx}\right)^2 = 2$$

But equation (1) gives $\frac{dy}{dx} = \frac{2x}{3y^2}$, so:
$$3y^2\frac{d^2y}{dx^2} + 6y\left(\frac{2x}{3y^2}\right)^2 = 2$$
$$3y^2\frac{d^2y}{dx^2} + \frac{24x^2}{9y^3} = 2$$

$$3y^2 \frac{d^2y}{dx^2} = 2 - \frac{24x^2}{9y^3}$$

$$3y^2 \frac{d^2y}{dx^2} = \frac{18y^3 - 24x^2}{9y^3}$$

$$\frac{d^2y}{dx^2} = \frac{6y^3 - 8x^2}{9y^5}$$

To find stationary points on a curve, set $\frac{dy}{dx}$ to zero.

Worked Example

6. (a) Find the coordinates of the stationary point on the curve: $x^3 - 3x^2y = 4$
(b) Determine the nature of this stationary point.

(a) $\qquad x^3 - 3x^2y = 4 \qquad (1)$

Differentiate each side with respect to x:

$$3x^2 - 3x^2 \frac{dy}{dx} - 6xy = 0$$

$$\frac{dy}{dx} = \frac{3x^2 - 6xy}{3x^2}$$

$$\frac{dy}{dx} = \frac{x - 2y}{x}$$

To find any stationary points set $\frac{dy}{dx}$ equal to zero:

$$0 = \frac{x - 2y}{x}$$

$$x - 2y = 0$$

$$x = 2y \qquad (2)$$

Instead of giving us the x-coordinate of the stationary point, the process has given an equation linking x and y. We need to treat this and the equation of the curve as two simultaneous equations.

Substitute for x from equation (2) into equation (1):

$$(2y)^3 - 3(2y)^2 y = 4$$
$$8y^3 - 12y^3 = 4$$
$$-4y^3 = 4$$
$$y^3 = -1$$
$$y = -1$$

Using (2):
$$x = -2$$

The coordinates of the stationary point are $(-2, -1)$.

(b) $\frac{dy}{dx} = \frac{x - 2y}{x}$

Differentiate using the quotient rule:

$$\frac{d^2y}{dx^2} = \frac{x\left(1 - 2\frac{dy}{dx}\right) - (x - 2y)}{x^2}$$

At the stationary point $(-2, -1)$, $\frac{dy}{dx} = 0$, so:

$$\frac{d^2y}{dx^2} = \frac{-2(1 - 2(0)) - ((-2) - 2(-1))}{(-2)^2}$$

$$\frac{d^2y}{dx^2} = -\frac{1}{2} < 0$$

∴ it is a maximum stationary point.

Exercise 10B

1. Use implicit differentiation to find $\frac{dy}{dx}$ in terms of x and y for each of the following.

(a) $y^4 + y = \frac{1}{x^3}$

(b) $y(1 - xy) = 3x^2$

(c) $\sin y = \frac{y}{x^2}$

(d) $\ln y - y = x^2$

(e) $\tan(x + y) = y$

(f) $y^2 - \cos y = x^2 - \cos x$

(g) $\cos y = x + e^{2y}$

2. For each of the following, use implicit differentiation to find the value of $\frac{dy}{dx}$ at the point given.

(a) $x^2 - y^2 = 5$ at $(-3, -2)$

(b) $x^3 - 8y^2 = 12xy$ at $(-4, 2)$

(c) $x^2y = 12$ at $(2, 3)$

(d) $x + xy - 12 = 0$ at $(2, 5)$

(e) $xe^y = 5$ at $(5, 0)$

(f) $x^3 - 3x^2y + 2y^2 = 3$ at $(1, 2)$

(g) $\frac{x}{1+x} - x^2 + \frac{y}{1+y} = 0$ at $(-2, -2)$

(h) $4y - x - xy = 0$ at $(5, -5)$

(i) $\cos x - \sin y - 1 = 0$ at $(0, 0)$

(j) $3x^2 + xy = 2y^2$ at $(-4, 4)$

Exercise 10B...

3. A curve C is described by the equation:
   $2x^2 + 3y^2 - 2x + 4xy - 4 = 0$
   (a) Find $\dfrac{dy}{dx}$.
   (b) Find an equation of the tangent to C at the point $(4, -2)$ giving your answer in the form $ax + by + c = 0$ where a, b and c are integers.

4. The curve C has equation:
   $9x^2 + 6xy - 7y^2 + 7 = 663$
   The point P on the curve C has coordinates $(8, 4)$.
   (a) Find the gradient of the curve at P.
   (b) Find the equation of the normal to the curve C at P, in the form $y = ax + b$, where a and b are constants.

5. A curve C is described by the equation:
   $3x^2 - 4y^2 + 2x - 8y + 55 = 0$
   Find an equation of the normal to C at the point $(1, 3)$ giving your answer in the form $ax + by + c = 0$ where a, b and c are integers.

6. The curve C is defined by the equation:
   $ye^{-4x} = 6x + y^2$
   (a) Find $\dfrac{dy}{dx}$ in terms of x and y.
   The point P lies on C and has coordinates $(0, 1)$.
   (b) Find the equation of the normal to C at P. Give your answer in the form $ax + by + c = 0$ where a, b and c are integers.

7. The curve C has equation:
   $10x^2 + 51xy - 4y^2 + 66 = 0$
   A and B are distinct points on the curve. At each of these points the gradient of the curve is equal to $\tfrac{1}{10}$.
   (a) Use implicit differentiation to show that $x = -2y$ at the points A and B.
   (b) Find the coordinates of the points A and B.

8. A leaflet for the Scouts demonstrates how to tie a knot from two ropes, as shown in the following diagram. The scout leader creates the diagram using the curves:
   $-x^2 + y^3 - y = -1$ (Curve 1)
   $-x^2 - y^3 + y = -1$ (Curve 2)

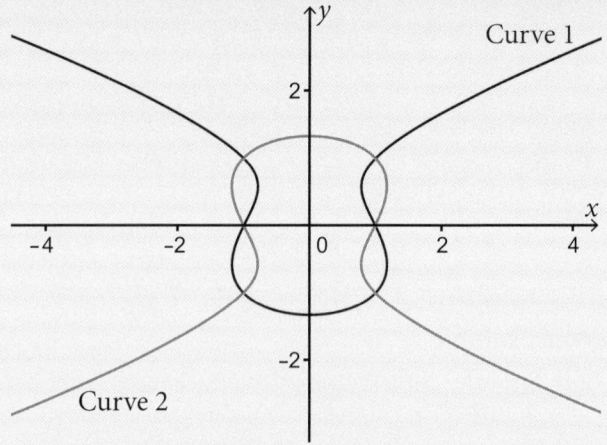

   (a) Solve the equations simultaneously to find the six intersection points of the two curves.
   (b) Find the gradient function $\dfrac{dy}{dx}$ for both curves.
   (c) Hence find the gradient $\dfrac{dy}{dx}$ of both curves at each of the six intersection points.
   (d) At which points are the two curves perpendicular?

9. The curve C has equation:
   $x^2 + 14xy - 3y^2 + 36 = 0$
   A and B are distinct points on the curve. At each of these points the gradient of the curve is equal to $\tfrac{1}{6}$.
   (a) Use implicit differentiation to show that $x = -3y$ at the points A and B.
   (b) Find the coordinates of the points A and B.

10. A set of curves is given by the equation:
    $\sin x + \cos y = 0.5$
    (a) Use implicit differentiation to find an expression for $\dfrac{dy}{dx}$.
    (b) Find the coordinates of the points where $\dfrac{dy}{dx} = 0$ for $-\pi < x < \pi$ and $-\pi < y < \pi$.

11. The curve C has the implicit equation:
    $y^2 + 1 = x^2 - 1$
    Show that: $y\dfrac{d^2y}{dx^2} + \left(\dfrac{dy}{dx}\right)^2 - 1 = 0$

12. A curve has the implicit equation:
    $5x^2 + 6y^2 - 2xy = 29$
    (a) Show that $\dfrac{dy}{dx} = \dfrac{y - 5x}{6y - x}$

Exercise 10B...

(b) The curve has two turning points. Find the coordinates of each one in surd form.

(c) Find $\dfrac{d^2y}{dx^2}$ in terms of x, y and $\dfrac{dy}{dx}$.

(d) Hence determine the nature of each turning point.

10.3 Parametric Differentiation

In chapter 3 you learnt about **parametric curves**. Parametric equations do not link x and y directly. Instead, there are two equations in which a parameter is involved, often t or θ.

You learnt how to sketch parametric curves and how, in some cases, you can eliminate the parameter to obtain a Cartesian equation of the curve (the equation linking x and y directly).

In this section, you will learn how to differentiate parametric curves to find the gradient function.

To find the gradient function, use:
$$\frac{dy}{dx} = \frac{dy}{dt} \times \frac{dt}{dx}$$
or
$$\frac{dy}{dx} = \frac{dy}{dt} \div \frac{dx}{dt}$$

You will often be asked to find $\dfrac{dy}{dx}$ in terms of the parameter.

Worked Example

7. The curve C is defined parametrically by the equations: $x = 2t$; $y = t^2$. Find $\dfrac{dy}{dx}$ in terms of t.

Differentiate x with respect to t:
$x = 2t$
$\dfrac{dx}{dt} = 2$

Differentiate y with respect to t:
$y = t^2$
$\dfrac{dy}{dt} = 2t$

$\dfrac{dy}{dx} = \dfrac{dy}{dt} \div \dfrac{dx}{dt}$

$\dfrac{dy}{dx} = \dfrac{2t}{2}$

$\dfrac{dy}{dx} = t$

You may be asked to find the second derivative $\dfrac{d^2y}{dx^2}$.

As with Cartesian equations, the second derivative can be used to determine the nature of stationary points. The second derivative is found using the formula:
$$\frac{d^2y}{dx^2} = \frac{d}{dt}\left(\frac{dy}{dx}\right) \times \frac{dt}{dx}$$

Worked Example

8. A curve C is defined by the parametric equations:
$$x = \sin\theta + 1; \quad y = 2 - \cos 2\theta; \quad -\frac{\pi}{2} \leq \theta \leq \frac{\pi}{2}$$

(a) Find $\dfrac{dy}{dx}$ in terms of θ.

(b) Show that the curve has a stationary point at $(1, 1)$.

(c) By finding the second derivative $\dfrac{d^2y}{dx^2}$, show that this stationary point is a minimum.

(a) $x = \sin\theta + 1 \Rightarrow \dfrac{dx}{d\theta} = \cos\theta$

$y = 2 - \cos 2\theta \Rightarrow \dfrac{dy}{d\theta} = 2\sin 2\theta$

$\dfrac{dy}{dx} = \dfrac{2\sin 2\theta}{\cos\theta} = \dfrac{4\sin\theta\cos\theta}{\cos\theta} = 4\sin\theta$

(b) Stationary points occur when
$\dfrac{dy}{dx} = 0 \Rightarrow 4\sin\theta = 0$

$\sin\theta = 0 \Rightarrow \theta = 0$ (only solution in range).

When $\theta = 0, x = \sin(0) + 1 = 1$. So:
$y = 2 - \cos(0) = 1$

Therefore, the coordinates of the stationary point are $(1, 1)$.

(c) $\dfrac{d^2y}{dx^2} = \dfrac{d}{d\theta}\left(\dfrac{dy}{dx}\right) \times \dfrac{d\theta}{dx}$

$= 4\cos\theta \times \dfrac{1}{\cos\theta}$

$= 4$

$\dfrac{d^2y}{dx^2} > 0$

Hence, the stationary point is a minimum.

You may be asked to find the equation of a tangent or a normal to a parametric curve.

Worked Example

9. The curve C has parametric equations:
$x = t^2$; $y = 4t$; $-5 \leq t \leq 5$
What is the equation of the tangent to the curve at the point $(1, -4)$?

$x = t^2 \Rightarrow \dfrac{dx}{dt} = 2t$

$y = 4t \Rightarrow \dfrac{dy}{dt} = 4$

$\dfrac{dy}{dx} = \dfrac{4}{2t} = \dfrac{2}{t}$

When $x = 1, t^2 = 1 \Rightarrow t = \pm 1$

When $t = +1, y = 4$

When $t = -1, y = -4$

Therefore, we are interested in the point on the curve where $t = -1$:

$\dfrac{dy}{dx} = \dfrac{2}{t} = \dfrac{2}{-1} = -2$

Equation of tangent:
$y - y_1 = m(x - x_1)$
$y + 4 = -2(x - 1)$
$y = -2x - 2$

Exercise 10C

1. Find $\dfrac{dy}{dx}$ in terms of the parameter for each pair of parametric equations.

   (a) $x = 1 + t$; $y = \dfrac{1}{t}$

   (b) $x = t^2 - 2$; $y = t^3 + 2$

   (c) $x = \dfrac{1}{t}$; $y = t^3$

   (d) $x = t^4 - 1$; $y = 4t + 1$

   (e) $x = \sin t$; $y = 1 - t$

   (f) $x = \sqrt{t}$; $y = 4t^2 + 1$

   (g) $x = e^t$; $y = \sin(2t)$

   (h) $x = \tan \theta$; $y = \sec^2 \theta$

   (i) $x = \ln t$; $y = \dfrac{1}{t}$

   (j) $x = \sec t$; $y = \sin(2t)$

Exercise 10C...

2. A curve has parametric equations:
   $x = 2t$; $y = t^3 - 3t$

   (a) Find $\dfrac{dy}{dx}$.

   (b) Hence show that there are two stationary points on the curve and find their coordinates.

   (c) By finding $\dfrac{d^2y}{dx^2}$ determine the nature of the two stationary points.

3. A curve is given by the parametric equations:
   $x = 3 \sin^3 \theta$, $y = 9 \cos 2\theta$, $0 \leq \theta \leq \dfrac{\pi}{4}$

   Show that $\dfrac{dx}{dy} = -\dfrac{1}{4} \sin \theta$

4. A picture of a raindrop is modelled using the parametric equations:
   $x = 3 \sin t$; $y = t^2$; $-\pi \leq t \leq \pi$

   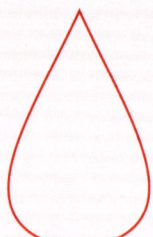

   (a) By considering $\dfrac{dy}{dx}$, find the coordinates of the base of the raindrop.

   (b) Find the coordinates of the top of the raindrop, giving an exact answer.

5. The diagram shows the logo of a company called *Sinusoid Sports*.

   It has been created using the parametric equations:
   $x = 2 \sin \theta$, $y = \theta \cos \theta$, $-\pi \leq \theta \leq \pi$
   Show that the two stationary points occur where $1 - \theta \tan \theta = 0$.

Exercise 10C...

6. A curve has parametric equations:

   $x = 5\cot t, y = 2\sin^2 t, \dfrac{\pi}{6} \leq t \leq \dfrac{5\pi}{6}$

   (a) Find an expression for $\dfrac{dy}{dx}$ in terms of the parameter t.

   (b) Find an equation of the tangent to the curve at the point where $t = \dfrac{\pi}{4}$.

   (c) Find the coordinates of the stationary point and determine its nature.

7. The diagram shows the curve with parametric equations:

   $x = 8\cos 2t, \quad y = 24\sin t, \quad 0 < t \leq \dfrac{\pi}{2}$

   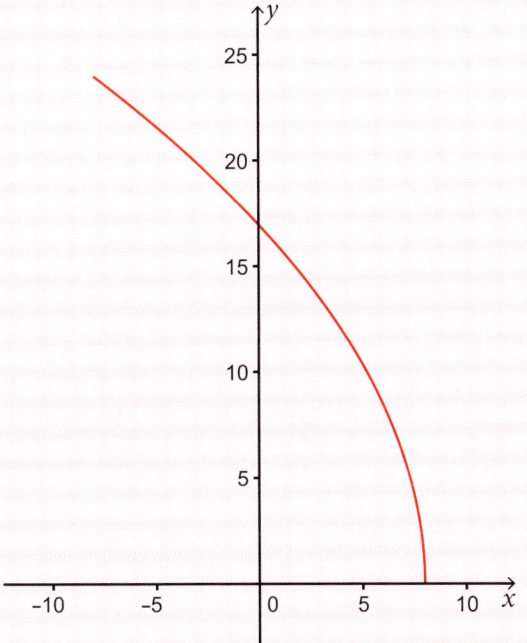

   Find the equation of the tangent to the curve at the point where $t = \dfrac{\pi}{3}$.

   Give your answer in the form $ay + \sqrt{b}x + c\sqrt{b} = 0$ where a, b and c are integers to be found.

8. The shape shown in the diagram is known as an astroid. It is created using the parametric equations:

   $x = \cos^3 \theta, \quad y = \sin^3 \theta, \quad -\pi \leq \theta \leq \pi$

Exercise 10C...

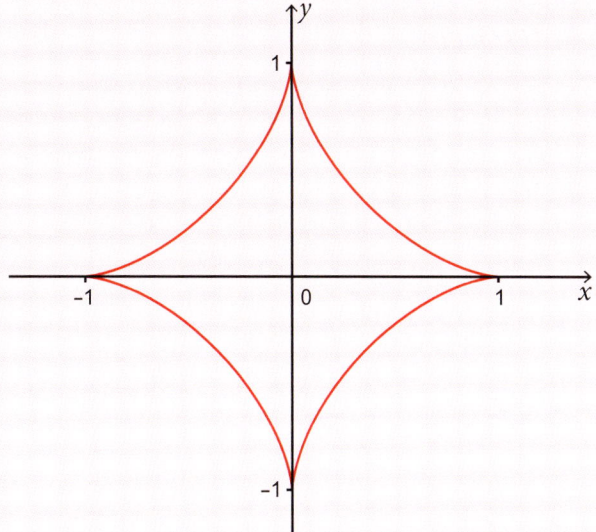

(a) Show that $\dfrac{dy}{dx} = -\tan \theta$

(b) Find the equations of the four tangents to the curve that have a gradient of ± 1.

(c) These four tangents intersect to form a square. Find the area of this square.

9. The diagram shows the parametric curve:

   $x = \sec \theta; \quad y = \sin 2\theta; \quad -\pi \leq \theta \leq \pi$

   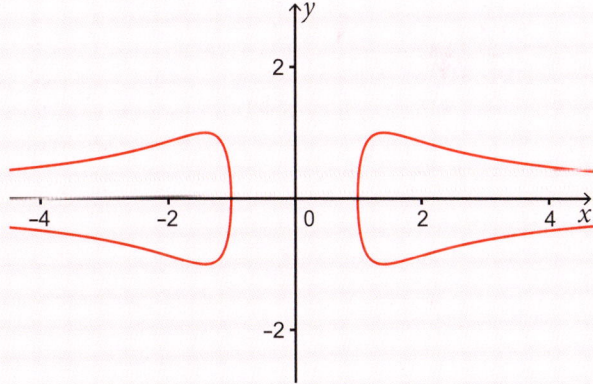

   Find exactly:

   (a) The coordinates of the points where the curve crosses the x-axis.

   (b) The coordinates of the four stationary points.

10. The shape of a bath is modelled on the parametric equations:

    $x = 4t; \quad y = t^4 - 1; \quad -1 \leq t \leq 1$

    (a) Find the points of intersection of the curve with both coordinate axes.

    (b) Find the coordinates of the stationary point.

    (c) Sketch the shape of the bath.

10.4 Summary

Sometimes an equation involving x and y cannot be re-arranged to make y the subject.

In these cases, use **implicit differentiation** to find $\dfrac{dy}{dx}$.

If you are given a pair of **parametric equations**, find $\dfrac{dx}{dt}$ and $\dfrac{dy}{dt}$. Then use:

$$\frac{dy}{dx} = \frac{dy}{dt} \times \frac{dt}{dx} = \frac{dy}{dt} \div \frac{dx}{dt}$$

With both implicit and parametric differentiation, you can:
- find the coordinates of stationary points by finding where $\dfrac{dy}{dx} = 0$;
- find the equations of tangents and normals to curves using: $y - y_1 = m(x - x_1)$.

With parametric differentiation, the second derivative is found using the formula:

$$\frac{d^2y}{dx^2} = \frac{d}{dt}\left(\frac{dy}{dx}\right) \times \frac{dt}{dx}$$

This can be used to determine the nature of stationary points.

Chapter 11
Integration

11.1 Introduction

In this chapter you will learn further techniques for integration.

Key words
- **Integration by recognition / integration on sight**: Using a known formula to integrate a function, usually without working.
- **Integration by parts**: A technique for the integration of a function that is a product of two other functions.
- **Integration by substitution**: A technique for integration involving substitution of one variable for another, to make the integral simpler.
- **Volume of revolution**: The volume generated when a curve rotates around one of the coordinate axes.

Before you start
You should know:
- How to perform integration of powers of x and related functions.
- How to perform definite integration.
- How to find partial fractions.

Worked Examples

1. Find: $\int_1^4 2\sqrt{x} - \dfrac{2}{\sqrt{x}} \, dx$

$$\int_1^4 2\sqrt{x} - \dfrac{2}{\sqrt{x}} \, dx$$
$$= \int_1^4 2x^{\frac{1}{2}} - 2x^{-\frac{1}{2}} \, dx$$
$$= \left[\dfrac{4}{3} x^{\frac{3}{2}} - 4x^{\frac{1}{2}}\right]_1^4$$
$$= \left(\dfrac{4}{3}(4)^{\frac{3}{2}} - 4(4)^{\frac{1}{2}}\right) - \left(\dfrac{4}{3}(1)^{\frac{3}{2}} - 4(1)^{\frac{1}{2}}\right)$$
$$= \left(\dfrac{4}{3}(8) - 4(2)\right) - \left(\dfrac{4}{3}(1) - 4(1)\right)$$
$$= \left(\dfrac{32}{3} - 8\right) - \left(\dfrac{4}{3} - 4\right)$$
$$= \dfrac{16}{3}$$

2. The curve C has a gradient function given by: $\dfrac{dy}{dx} = 3x$. Given that the curve passes through the point $(4, 6)$, find the equation of C.

Find the equation of the curve by integrating $\dfrac{dy}{dx}$:
$$y = \int 3x \, dx$$
$$y = \dfrac{3}{2} x^2 + c$$

When $x = 4, y = 6$. Hence:
$$6 = \dfrac{3}{2}(4)^2 + c$$
$$c = 6 - 24 = -18$$

Hence:
$$y = \dfrac{3}{2} x^2 - 18$$

3. Write the following rational function as a sum of its partial fractions:
$$\dfrac{1}{(x+1)(x-2)}$$

$$\dfrac{1}{(x+1)(x-2)} = \dfrac{A}{x+1} + \dfrac{B}{x-2}$$
$$1 = A(x-2) + B(x+1)$$

Equate coefficients of x:
$$0 = A + B \quad (1)$$

Equate number terms:
$$1 = -2A + B \quad (2)$$

(1) − (2):
$$-1 = 3A$$
$$A = -\dfrac{1}{3}$$

Using (1):
$$0 = -\dfrac{1}{3} + B$$
$$B = \dfrac{1}{3}$$

$$\therefore \dfrac{1}{(x+1)(x-2)} = -\dfrac{1}{3(x+1)} + \dfrac{1}{3(x-2)}$$

PURE MATHEMATICS FOR CCEA A2

What you will learn
In this chapter you will learn:
- How to integrate expressions involving e^x and $\frac{1}{x}$.
- How to integrate expressions involving the trigonometric functions.
- How to spot some types of integral that can be performed by **recognition** (sometimes known as **integration on sight**).
- Integration by parts.
- Integration by substitution.
- Integration using partial fractions.
- How to find a volume of revolution.

In the real world...
The world's atmosphere is turbulent and chaotic, and this is one reason weather forecasting is so difficult. Predicting the motion of the Earth's atmosphere is one example of a **fluid dynamics** problem.

Many fluid dynamics problems can be described by a set of equations called the Navier-Stokes equations. They can be used to model ocean currents, water flow in a pipe and the airflow around an aircraft wing.

The Navier-Stokes equations are **differential equations**, which means they link derivatives (e.g. $\frac{dv}{dt}$) to other quantities. To obtain solutions for velocity, they must be **integrated**. You will learn more about differential equations in Chapter 12.

However, despite their wide range of practical uses, mathematicians have not yet shown that exact solutions always exist to the Navier-Stokes equations. In weather forecasting, for example, the solutions must be approximated using a technique called **numerical integration**.

The Clay Mathematics Institute has declared the Navier-Stokes equations to be one of the seven most important open problems in mathematics and has offered a $1 million prize for a solution.

Any solution would not only revolutionise the modelling of the Earth's atmosphere; it would have huge consequences for many areas of physics, engineering and mathematics.

Exercise 11A (Revision)

1. Integrate the following.
   (a) $4x^3$
   (b) $6 - \frac{x}{2}$
   (c) $2x^3 - 3x^{-5}$
   (d) $2x - x^2 - 2x^{-2}$

2. Evaluate the following indefinite integrals, giving exact answers.
   (a) $\int_0^1 1 - \frac{x^2}{2}\,dx$
   (b) $\int_0^1 \pi - \frac{1}{\sqrt{x}}\,dx$

3. Find partial fractions for the following rational functions.
   (a) $\dfrac{2x}{(3x+1)(2x+3)}$
   (b) $\dfrac{-x+5}{(-x-3)(4x-4)}$
   (c) $\dfrac{1-2x}{(x^2-1)(x-2)}$
   (d) $\dfrac{(4x-3)(x+1)}{(x-1)(2x-1)}$

11.2 Integration of Trigonometric Functions, e^x and $\frac{1}{x}$

In AS Mathematics you learnt how to integrate functions that were powers of x, for example:

$$\int 2x^2\,dx = \frac{2}{3}x^3 + c$$

The standard result, which you must learn, is:

$$\int ax^n\,dx = \frac{a}{n+1}x^{n+1} + c$$

In this section, you will learn how to integrate functions that involve the trigonometric functions, the exponential function e^x and $\frac{1}{x}$.

Remember that indefinite integration can be thought of as the reverse of differentiation. Hence, some of these results are the reverse of the results we obtained using differentiation.

You will need to remember the following standard results.

11: INTEGRATION

Note: These results are **not** provided on the formula sheet. You must learn them.

$$\int \cos x \, dx = \sin x + c$$

$$\int \sin x \, dx = -\cos x + c$$

$$\int e^x \, dx = e^x + c$$

$$\int \frac{1}{x} \, dx = \ln|x| + c$$

Generalising these results, we get:

$$\int \cos(ax+b) \, dx = \frac{1}{a}\sin(ax+b) + c$$

$$\int \sin(ax+b) \, dx = -\frac{1}{a}\cos(ax+b) + c$$

$$\int e^{(ax+b)} \, dx = \frac{1}{a}e^{(ax+b)} + c$$

$$\int \frac{1}{ax+b} \, dx = \frac{1}{a}\ln|ax+b| + c$$

Note: Remember the modulus signs when performing a log-type integration. The reason for the modulus signs is explained in section 11.5.

Finally, the following results **are** provided on your formula sheet in the differentiation section.

$$\frac{d}{dx}(\tan x) = \sec^2 x$$

$$\frac{d}{dx}(\sec x) = \sec x \tan x$$

$$\frac{d}{dx}(\cot x) = -\csc^2 x$$

$$\frac{d}{dx}(\csc x) = -\csc x \cot x$$

Reversing these, we get:

$$\int \sec^2 x \, dx = \tan x + c$$

$$\int \sec x \tan x \, dx = \sec x + c$$

$$\int \csc^2 x \, dx = -\cot x + c$$

$$\int \csc x \cot x \, dx = -\csc x + c$$

These can all be generalised, for example:

$$\int \sec^2(ax+b) \, dx = \frac{1}{a}\tan(ax+b) + c$$

Note: Don't forget to include a constant of integration with indefinite integrals. In an exam, there is often a mark awarded for this!

Worked Example

4. Find: $\int \sec^2(3x-1) \, dx$

Using the standard result for $\int \sec^2(ax+b) \, dx$:

$$\int \sec^2(3x-1) \, dx = \frac{1}{3}\tan(3x-1) + c$$

In addition to the results above, the formula sheet provides several standard results under the headings Differentiation and Integration. You should be prepared to use these interchangeably.

Worked Examples

5. Find: $\int \frac{1}{2} \sec x \tan x \, dx$

From the formula sheet:

$$\int \sec x \tan x \, dx = \sec x + c$$

Hence:

$$\int \frac{1}{2} \sec x \tan x \, dx = \frac{1}{2} \sec x + c$$

6. Find:

(a) $\int \frac{5}{3x+1} \, dx$

(b) $\int e^{\frac{x}{4}} \, dx$

(a) $I = \int \frac{5}{3x+1} \, dx$

$$= 5 \int \frac{1}{3x+1} \, dx$$

Now use the standard result for log-type integrals:

$$\int \frac{1}{ax+b} \, dx = \frac{1}{a}\ln|ax+b| + c$$

Hence:
$$I = 5\left(\frac{1}{3}\ln|3x+1|\right) + c$$
$$= \frac{5}{3}\ln|3x+1| + c$$

(b) $I = \int e^{\frac{x}{4}}\,dx$

$$= \int e^{\frac{1}{4}x}\,dx$$

Using the formula:
$$\int e^{(ax+b)}\,dx = \frac{1}{a}e^{(ax+b)} + c$$

$$I = \frac{1}{\frac{1}{4}} e^{\frac{1}{4}x} + c$$

$$= 4e^{\frac{x}{4}} + c$$

Exercise 11B

1. Using the standard results, find the following integrals.
   (a) $\int \sin 3x\,dx$
   (b) $\int \cos\frac{x}{2}\,dx$
   (c) $\int \sec^2 4x\,dx$
   (d) $\int \frac{1}{2}\cos x\,dx$
   (e) $\int e^x\,dx$
   (f) $\int \frac{12}{x}\,dx$
   (g) $\int \cos(2x + \pi)\,dx$
   (h) $\int \sec^2(x - 1)\,dx$
   (i) $\int e^{(2x-2)}\,dx$
   (j) $\int \frac{1}{4x-1}\,dx$
   (k) $\int \sin(1 - 2x)\,dx$
   (l) $\int \sec^2\left(-\frac{x}{2} - 1\right)dx$
   (m) $\int 4\cos(-4x)\,dx$

2. Using the formulae provided on the formula sheet, find the following integrals.
   (a) $\int 2\sec x \tan x\,dx$
   (b) $\int \operatorname{cosec}^2 x\,dx$
   (c) $\int 3\operatorname{cosec} x \cot x\,dx$
   (d) $\int \sec 2x \tan 2x\,dx$
   (e) $\int -5\operatorname{cosec} 2x \cot 2x\,dx$

Exercise 11B...

3. Find the following indefinite integrals.
   (a) $\int \left(\frac{7}{x} - \cos 3x - \operatorname{cosec}^2 x - \frac{x}{2}\right)dx$
   (b) $\int \left(\frac{2}{x} - \frac{x}{10} + \sec 3x \tan 3x + 1\right)dx$
   (c) $\int \left(6 + e^{4x} + \frac{4}{x} + 2\sec^2 x\right)dx$
   (d) $\int \left(2x^2 + e^{-x} + 2\operatorname{cosec} x \cot x + \frac{4}{x}\right)dx$
   (e) $\int \left(\frac{4}{3x^2} - \frac{4}{3x} - \frac{4x}{3}\right)dx$
   (f) $\int (\sin 4x - \cos 4x - \sec 4x \tan 4x)\,dx$

11.3 Definite Integration

You will remember from AS Mathematics that you can use integration **between limits** to find the area between a curve and the x-axis. This type of integration is known as **definite integration**.

Having studied indefinite integration of the exponential and trigonometric functions above, you will be able to apply these results to definite integration.

Worked Examples

7. Find the exact area of the shaded region A shown in the diagram. It is enclosed by the curve $y = \cos 2x$, the x- and y-axes and the line $x = \frac{\pi}{6}$.

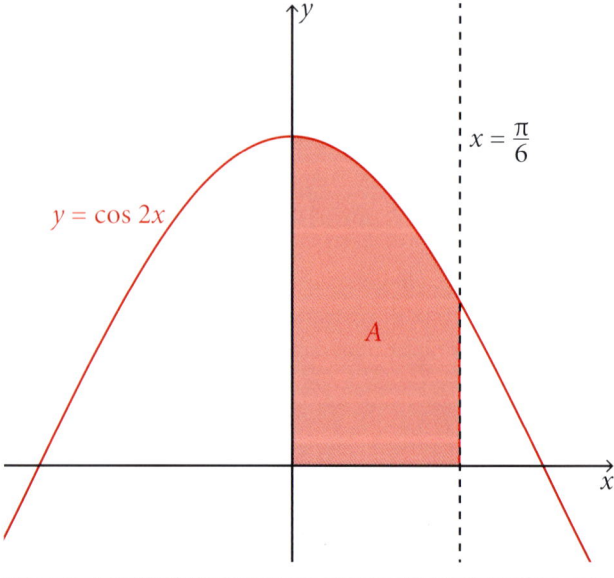

$$A = \int_0^{\frac{\pi}{6}} \cos 2x \, dx$$

$$= \left[\frac{1}{2} \sin 2x\right]_0^{\frac{\pi}{6}}$$

$$= \left(\frac{1}{2} \sin\left(\frac{\pi}{3}\right) - \frac{1}{2} \sin(0)\right)$$

$$= \frac{1}{2} \times \frac{\sqrt{3}}{2}$$

$$= \frac{\sqrt{3}}{4}$$

8. Find the area bounded by the curve $y = e^{2x}$, the lines $x = 1$ and $x = 2$ and the x-axis. Give your answer in terms of e.

Sketch the graph:

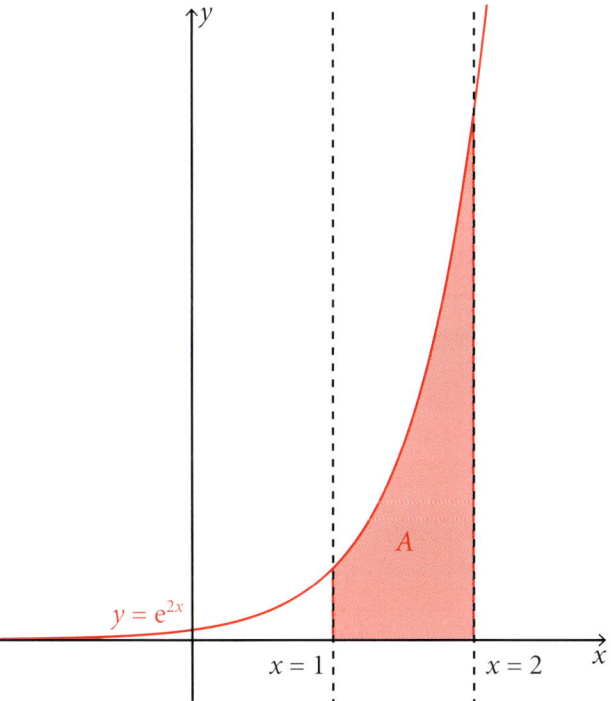

$$A = \int_1^2 e^{2x} \, dx$$

$$= \left[\frac{1}{2} e^{2x}\right]_1^2$$

$$= \frac{1}{2}(e^4 - e^2)$$

Note on using calculators: Many calculators can evaluate definite integrals, giving a decimal value, never an exact answer. This feature cannot be used to answer an exam question, since working will be required, but you can use the feature to check an answer.

Exercise 11C

1. Evaluate the following definite integrals, giving exact answers.

   (a) $\int_0^{\pi/4} \cos 2x \, dx$ (b) $\int_0^{\pi/3} \sec^2 x \, dx$

   (c) $\int_0^{\pi/6} \sin 3x \, dx$ (d) $\int_0^3 e^{3x} \, dx$

   (e) $\int_{\pi/4}^{3\pi/4} \cosec^2 x \, dx$ (f) $\int_0^{\pi/6} \sec 2x \tan 2x \, dx$

   (g) $\int_1^2 \frac{2}{x} \, dx$ (h) $\int_{\pi/4}^{\pi/2} \cosec x \cot x \, dx$

   (i) $\int_{3\pi/8}^{5\pi/8} (2 + \sec^2 2x) \, dx$

   (j) $\int_{-2}^{2} 2e^{x/2} \, dx$

   (k) $\int_1^e \frac{5}{2x} \, dx$

   (l) $\int_{\pi/8}^{3\pi/8} \cosec^2 2x + 2x \, dx$

   (m) $\int_0^1 1 + \frac{1}{2} e^{2x} \, dx$

   (n) $\int_{-\pi/2}^{\pi/2} \left(1 + \sec\left(\frac{x}{2}\right) \tan\left(\frac{x}{2}\right)\right) dx$

2. Find the area enclosed by the x-axis, the lines $x = 2$ and $x = 3$ and the curve $y = \frac{1}{x}$. Give your answer to 2 decimal places.

3. Find the area R shaded in the diagram below. It is enclosed by the curve $y = e^{\frac{x}{2}}$, the x-axis and the lines $x = 1$ and $x = 2$. Give your answer to 3 significant figures.

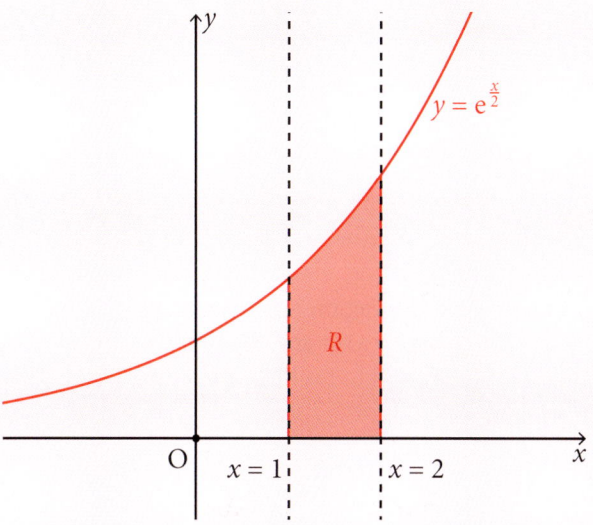

Exercise 11C...

4. A ski run is modelled using the equation: $y = 1 + 10e^{-\frac{x}{10}}$ between $x = 1$ and $x = 50$ metres, as shown in the diagram.

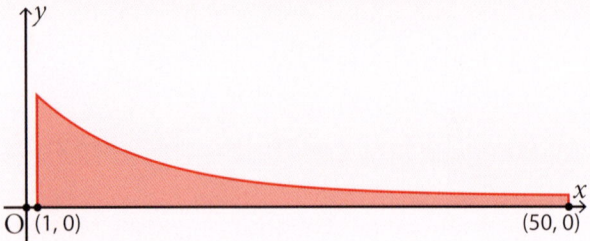

Find the area enclosed between the curve and the x-axis.

5. The curve C has equation $y = f(x)$. The diagram shows a part of C and the straight line with equation $x = 1$.

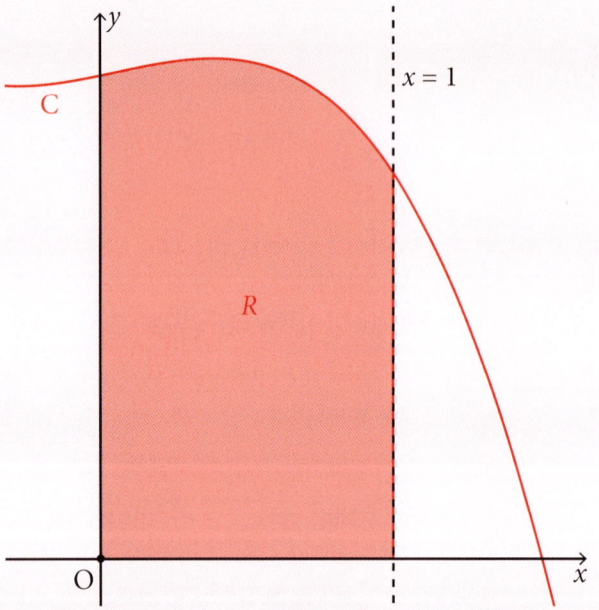

The curve C has a single maximum point at $x = k$. Given that $\frac{dy}{dx} = e^x - 10x^2$:

(a) By considering the value of $\frac{dy}{dx}$ at $x = 0.38$ and $x = 0.39$, show that $0.38 < k < 0.39$.

(b) Given also that the point $(0, 8)$ lies on C, find $f(x)$.

(c) The finite region R is bounded by C, the coordinate axes and the line $x = 1$. Use integration to find the exact area of R.

Exercise 11C...

6. A children's slide can be modelled using the equation of the curve: $y = \frac{6}{1+x} + 2e^{2x} - 5$ between $x = 0$ and $x = 1$ metres, as shown.

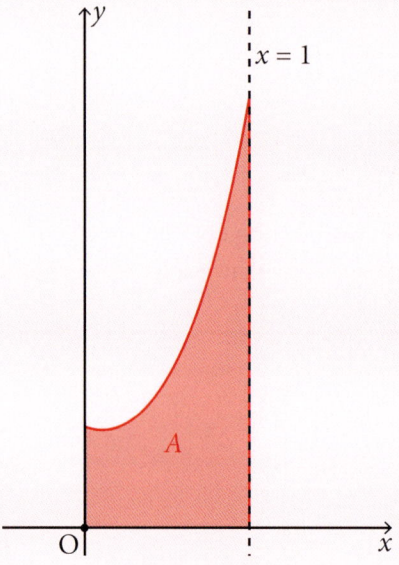

(a) Find the height of the slide in metres.
(b) Find the exact area A shaded.

7. A fairground ride called the tea cup, shown in the diagram, is modelled using a part of the curve $y = \sec^2 x$ between $x = -\frac{\pi}{3}$ and $x = \frac{\pi}{3}$.

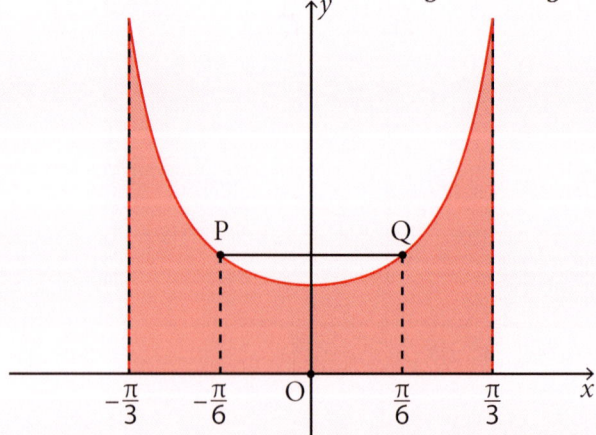

(a) Find the exact area shaded below the tea cup.
(b) A seat is attached at the points P and Q, as shown. Find the exact area enclosed between the seat and the tea cup.

11.4 Area Between Two Curves

It is also possible to find the area between a curve and a straight line, or between two curves. If a diagram is not given, a sketch is essential in these cases.

The area is found by integrating the **difference** between the two functions, i.e.:

$$A = \int_a^b \left(f(x) - g(x)\right) dx$$

Worked Example

9. Find the area enclosed between the curve $y = x^2$ and the straight line $y = x$.

No diagram is given, so we draw a sketch of the two functions and the area enclosed. To find out the intersection points, we must solve:

$$x^2 = x$$
$$x(x - 1) = 0$$
$$x = 0 \text{ or } x = 1$$

When $x = 0$, $y = 0$. When $x = 1$, $y = 1$. Therefore the intersection points are $(0, 0)$ and $(1, 1)$.

So we can sketch:

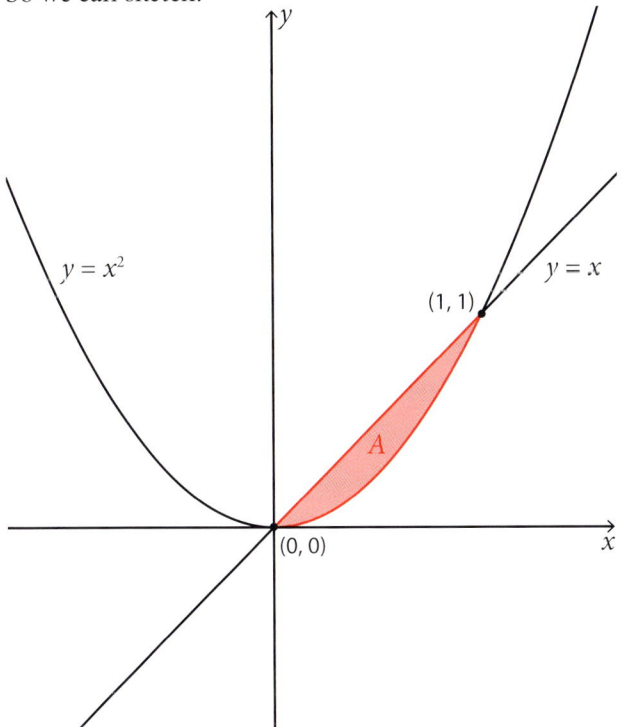

This example was given in chapter 11 of the AS Pure Mathematics book. The method used there was to find the difference between the area of a triangle and the area under the curve. However, here we will subtract the equations of the line and curve before integrating.

Note: It is important to subtract the function with the lower values in the range from the function with the higher values. If your subtraction is the wrong way around, your answer will be a negative number.

From the diagram we can see that the function $y = x^2$ is less than $y = x$ between $x = 0$ and $x = 1$. Therefore we must subtract x^2 from x and integrate.

$$A = \int_0^1 (x - x^2)\, dx$$

$$= \left[\frac{x^2}{2} - \frac{x^3}{3}\right]_0^1$$

$$= \left(\frac{1^2}{2} - \frac{1^3}{3}\right) - \left(\frac{0^2}{2} - \frac{0^3}{3}\right)$$

$$= \frac{1}{6}$$

Exercise 11D

1. The diagram shows the curves $y = x^2 - 3$ and $y = 4 - x^2$ and the area enclosed between them.

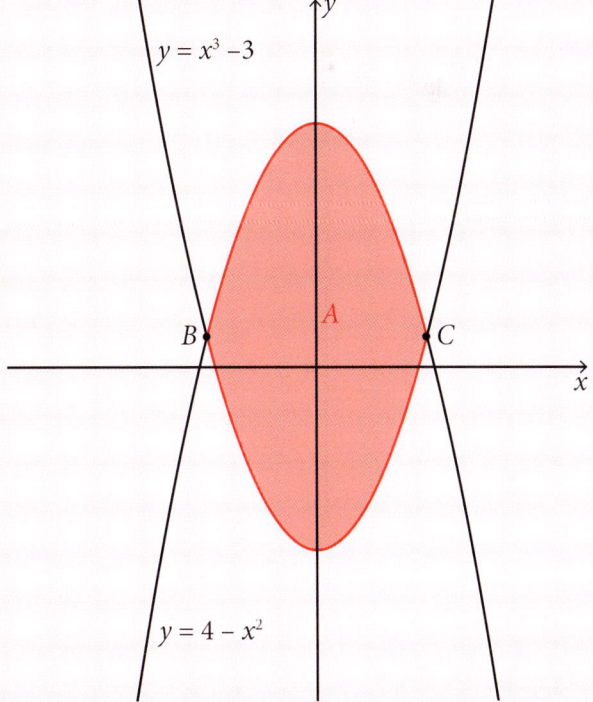

(a) Show that the x-coordinates of points B and C are $\pm\sqrt{\frac{7}{2}}$.

(b) Find the area A to 3 significant figures.

Exercise 11D...

2. The line with equation: $y = 5x + 17$ and the curve with equation $y = x^2 + 8x + 7$ intersect at the points A and B, as shown.

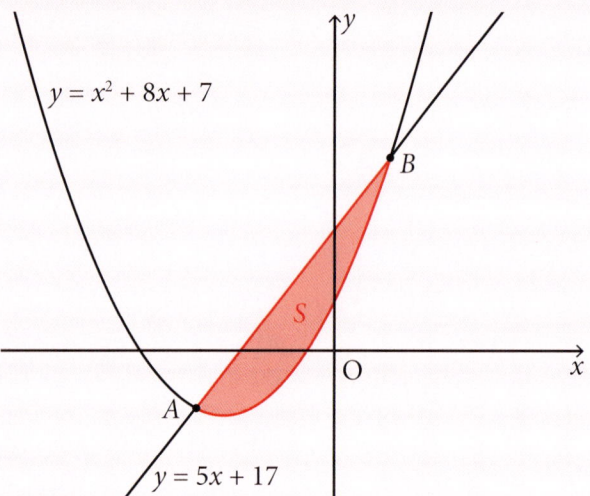

(a) Find the coordinates of the points A and B.

The shaded region S is bounded by the line and the curve.

(b) Use calculus to find the area of S.

3. The diagram shows the curves $f(x) = x^2$ and $g(x) = x^3$.

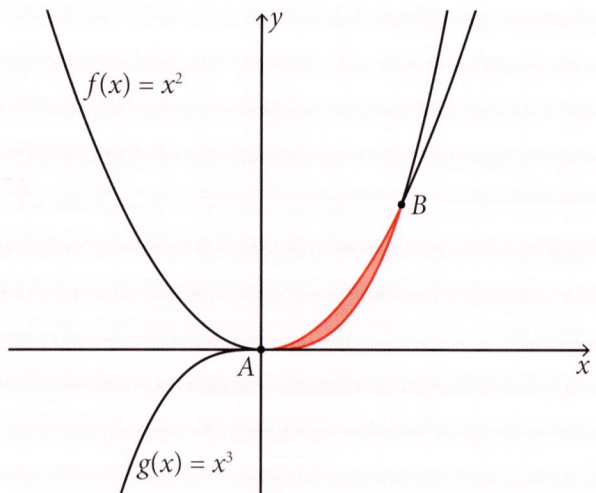

The two curves intersect at points $A(0, 0)$ and B.
(a) Find the coordinates of B.
(b) Using integration, find the shaded area between the curves.

Exercise 11D...

4. The diagram shows the line with equation $y = 10 - x$ and the curve $y = x^2 - 3x + 2$.

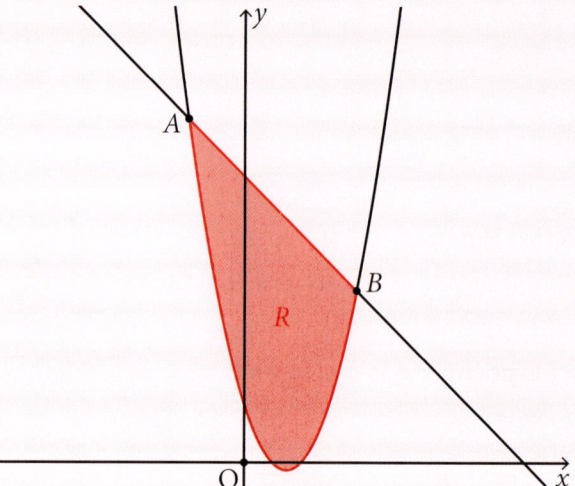

The line and the curve intersect at the points A and B, and O is the origin.
(a) Calculate the coordinates of A and B.

The shaded region R is bounded by the line and the curve.
(b) Calculate the area of R.

11.5 Integration by Substitution

Some integrals are easier to manipulate if the variable is changed. Most often, the variable u is used for the substitution, but this can be θ, or any other variable.

Every instance of x and the dx must be replaced. The integration is then performed with the new variable. After integration, the original variable is substituted back in, to give an answer in terms of x.

Integration by substitution is the reverse of the chain rule used for differentiation.

Worked Example

10. Using the substitution $u = 3x$, find $\int \cos 3x \, dx$

First find $\dfrac{du}{dx}$ and re-arrange to find dx:

$$u = 3x \Rightarrow \frac{du}{dx} = 3 \Rightarrow dx = \frac{du}{3}$$

Substitute for x and dx:

$$\int \cos 3x \, dx = \int \cos u \, \frac{du}{3}$$

$$= \frac{1}{3}\int \cos u \, du$$

$$= \frac{1}{3}\sin u + c$$

Substitute back to x:

$$= \frac{1}{3}\sin 3x + c$$

The previous example could be carried out using the formulae in section 11.2 above. In that section we briefly discussed **integration by recognition** or **integration on sight**. Many of the integrals below can be performed by recognition.

Log-type integrals

If you can differentiate the denominator to obtain the numerator, it is a log-type integral:

$$\int \frac{f'(x)}{f(x)} dx = \ln|f(x)| + c$$

If the integral is of this form, you can proceed using a substitution $u = f(x)$ or integrate by recognition.

Proof of $\int \frac{f'(x)}{f(x)} dx = \ln|f(x)| + c$

Note: At the time of publication, the CCEA specification does not require you to know this proof.

We will show that if $y = \ln|f(x)|$ then $\frac{dy}{dx} = \frac{f'(x)}{f(x)}$.

Consider two cases:

Case 1: $f(x) > 0$

$$y = \ln|f(x)| = \ln(f(x))$$

Let $u = f(x)$, so:

$$\frac{du}{dx} = f'(x)$$

Also $y = \ln u$, so:

$$\frac{dy}{du} = \frac{1}{u} = \frac{1}{f(x)}$$

Then:

$$\frac{dy}{dx} = \frac{dy}{du} \times \frac{du}{dx}$$

$$= \frac{1}{f(x)} \times f'(x)$$

$$= \frac{f'(x)}{f(x)}$$

Case 2: $f(x) < 0$

$$y = \ln|f(x)| = \ln(-f(x))$$

Let $u = -f(x)$, so:

$$\frac{du}{dx} = -f'(x)$$

Also $y = \ln u$, so:

$$\frac{dy}{du} = \frac{1}{u} = \frac{1}{-f(x)}$$

Then:

$$\frac{dy}{dx} = \frac{dy}{du} \times \frac{du}{dx}$$

$$= \frac{1}{-f(x)} \times -f'(x)$$

$$= \frac{f'(x)}{f(x)}$$

In both cases

$$\therefore \int \frac{f'(x)}{f(x)} dx = \ln(|f(x)|) + c$$

Worked Examples

11. Find $\int \frac{1}{x} dx$

This is an integral of the form $\int \frac{f'(x)}{f(x)} dx$, with $f(x) = x$, and $f'(x) = 1$.

$$\therefore \int \frac{1}{x} dx = \ln(|x|) + c$$

Note: This also shows that $\frac{d}{dx}(\ln|x|) = \frac{1}{x}$

If $x > 0$ then $\frac{d}{dx}(\ln x) = \frac{1}{x}$

This is a proof of the result discussed in section 9.2.

12. Find $\int \cot x \, dx$

$$\int \cot x \, dx = \int \frac{\cos x}{\sin x} dx$$

Again, notice this is an integral of the type $\int \frac{f'(x)}{f(x)} dx$

$$\therefore \int \cot x \, dx = \ln|\sin x| + c$$

Note: This could also be done using the substitution $u = \sin x$.

13. Find $\int \dfrac{3x+1}{3x^2+2x} \, dx$

No substitution is suggested, but assuming a log-type integral, we try $u = 3x^2 + 2x$. So:

$$\dfrac{du}{dx} = 6x + 2$$

$$\Rightarrow dx = \dfrac{du}{6x+2}$$

Then:

$$\int \dfrac{3x+1}{3x^2+2x} dx = \int \dfrac{(3x+1)}{u} \dfrac{du}{(6x+2)}$$

$$= \int \dfrac{(3x+1)}{2u(3x+1)} du$$

$$= \dfrac{1}{2} \int \dfrac{1}{u} du$$

$$= \dfrac{1}{2} \ln|u| + c$$

$$= \dfrac{1}{2} \ln|3x^2 + 2x| + c$$

Note: Bringing a factor of ½ outside the integral sign would make this integral one of the form $\int \dfrac{f'(x)}{f(x)} dx$.

Hence $\int \dfrac{3x+1}{3x^2+2x} dx = \dfrac{1}{2} \int \dfrac{6x+2}{3x^2+2x} dx$

In this way, integration by recognition could be used, but this is more difficult to spot.

When evaluating a definite integral, either
- change the upper and lower limits to the new variable, or
- after integration, substitute back to the original variable and use the original variable's limits.

Worked Example

14. Using the substitution $u = 2x - 1$, evaluate:

$$I = \int_1^2 \dfrac{x}{(2x-1)^4} dx$$

Find $\dfrac{du}{dx}$ and re-arrange to find dx:

$$u = 2x - 1 \Rightarrow \dfrac{du}{dx} = 2 \Rightarrow dx = \dfrac{du}{2}$$

Also:

$$u = 2x - 1 \Rightarrow x = \dfrac{1}{2}(u+1)$$

So when $x = 1$, $u = 1$
and when $x = 2$, $u = 3$

Replace all instances of x, dx and the limits:

$$I = \int_1^2 \dfrac{x}{(2x-1)^4} dx$$

$$= \int_1^3 \dfrac{\tfrac{1}{2}(u+1)}{u^4} \dfrac{du}{2}$$

$$= \dfrac{1}{4} \int_1^3 \dfrac{(u+1)}{u^4} du$$

$$= \dfrac{1}{4} \int_1^3 (u^{-3} + u^{-4}) du$$

$$= \dfrac{1}{4} \left[-\dfrac{1}{2} u^{-2} - \dfrac{1}{3} u^{-3} \right]_1^3$$

There are two methods for proceeding from here.

Method 1 – substitute for u and subtract.

$$I = \dfrac{1}{4}\left[\left(-\dfrac{1}{2}(3)^{-2} - \dfrac{1}{3}(3)^{-3}\right) - \left(-\dfrac{1}{2}(1)^{-2} - \dfrac{1}{3}(1)^{-3}\right)\right]$$

$$= 0.191 \text{ (3 s.f.)}$$

Method 2 – substitute back for the original variable, x and use its limits.

$$I = \dfrac{1}{4}\left[-\dfrac{1}{2}(2x-1)^{-2} - \dfrac{1}{3}(2x-1)^{-3}\right]_1^2$$

$$I = \dfrac{1}{4}\left[\left(-\dfrac{1}{2}(3)^{-2} - \dfrac{1}{3}(3)^{-3}\right) - \left(-\dfrac{1}{2}(1)^{-2} - \dfrac{1}{3}(1)^{-3}\right)\right]$$

$$= 0.191 \text{ (3 s.f.)}$$

Note: Using Method 2, we did not need to calculate the upper and lower limits for u.

Watch out for integrals of the type $\dfrac{ax+b}{cx+d}$.

If a substitution is not suggested, use $u = cx + d$.

Worked Example

15. Find $\int_1^3 \dfrac{3x+4}{6x-2} dx$ giving an exact answer.

Let $u = 6x - 2$.

Find $\dfrac{du}{dx}$ and re-arrange to find dx:

$\dfrac{du}{dx} = 6 \Rightarrow dx = \dfrac{du}{6}$

Find the numerator in terms of u:

$u = 6x - 2 \Rightarrow \dfrac{u}{2} = 3x - 1 \Rightarrow \dfrac{u}{2} + 5 = 3x + 4$

Substitute for x and dx. We are going to return to x before the substitution of values, so we don't need to calculate limits for u.

$\displaystyle\int_1^3 \dfrac{3x+4}{6x-2} dx = \int_{u_1}^{u_2} \dfrac{\frac{u}{2}+5}{u} \dfrac{du}{6}$

$= \dfrac{1}{6}\displaystyle\int_{u_1}^{u_2} \dfrac{1}{2} + \dfrac{5}{u} du$

$= \dfrac{1}{6}\left[\dfrac{u}{2} + 5\ln|u|\right]_{u_1}^{u_2}$

Substitute back to x:

$= \dfrac{1}{6}\left[(3x-1) + 5\ln|6x-2|\right]_1^3$

$= \dfrac{1}{6}\Big[\big((3(3)-1) + 5\ln|6(3)-2|\big)$
$\quad - \big((3(1)-1) + 5\ln|6(1)-2|\big)\Big]$

$= \dfrac{1}{6}[(8 + 5\ln(16)) - (2 + 5\ln(4))]$

$= \dfrac{1}{6}\left[\left(6 + 5\ln\left(\dfrac{16}{4}\right)\right)\right]$

$= 1 + \dfrac{5}{6}\ln 4$

$= 1 + \dfrac{5}{3}\ln 2$

It is possible to obtain more than one solution for an indefinite integral if you apply different methods. The answers will differ only by a constant.

Worked Example

16. (a) Show that $\dfrac{x-1}{x-2}$ can be written as $1 + \dfrac{1}{x-2}$.

(b) Hence find $\displaystyle\int \dfrac{x-1}{x-2} dx$.

(c) Find $\displaystyle\int \dfrac{x-1}{x-2} dx$ using the substitution $u = x - 2$.

(a) $\dfrac{x-1}{x-2} = \dfrac{x-2+1}{x-2}$

$= \dfrac{x-2}{x-2} + \dfrac{1}{x-2}$

$= 1 + \dfrac{1}{x-2}$

(b) Hence:

$\displaystyle\int \dfrac{x-1}{x-2} dx = \int 1 + \dfrac{1}{x-2} dx$

$= x + \ln(x-2) + c$

(c) Let $u = x - 2$. Then: $\dfrac{du}{dx} = 1 \Rightarrow du = dx$

So:

$\displaystyle\int \dfrac{x-1}{x-2} dx = \int \dfrac{u+1}{u} du$

$= \displaystyle\int 1 + \dfrac{1}{u} du$

$= u + \ln u + d$

$= x - 2 + \ln(x-2) + d$

The two answers obtained in parts (b) and (c) look different. This is because the two constants of integration differ. In this case $c = d - 2$.

Exercise 11E

1. Integrate the following, using the substitution given.

(a) $\displaystyle\int \dfrac{x}{x-1} dx;\ u = x - 1$

(b) $\displaystyle\int \dfrac{1}{\sqrt[3]{3x+4}} dx;\ u = 3x + 4$

(c) $\displaystyle\int (5x+2)^3 dx;\ u = 5x + 2$

(d) $\displaystyle\int \dfrac{e^x}{(e^x+3)^3} dx;\ u = e^x + 3$

(e) $\displaystyle\int \dfrac{(\ln x)^3}{x} dx;\ u = \ln x$

(f) $\displaystyle\int \sin 5x\, dx;\ u = 5x$

(g) $\displaystyle\int \sec^2 x\, \sqrt{1 + \tan x}\, dx;\ u = 1 + \tan x$

(h) $\displaystyle\int \dfrac{5x}{\sqrt{x-2}} dx;\ u = x - 2$

(i) $\displaystyle\int \dfrac{x}{1-5x^2} dx;\ u = 1 - 5x^2$

(j) $\displaystyle\int \sin\left(2x + \dfrac{\pi}{3}\right) dx;\ u = 2x + \dfrac{\pi}{3}$

2. Evaluate the following definite integrals using the substitution given. Give exact answers where appropriate.

(a) $\displaystyle\int_3^4 (x-2)(x-3)^4 dx;\ u = x - 3$

Exercise 11E...

(b) $\int_{-1}^{0} x\sqrt{x+1}\,dx;\ u = x+1$

(c) $\int_{4}^{\sqrt{24}} \sqrt{32-x^2}\,dx;\ x = 2\sqrt{8}\sin\theta$

(d) $\int_{0}^{1/2} \dfrac{3}{(1-x^2)^{3/2}}\,dx;\ x = \sin\theta$

(e) $\int_{5}^{13} \dfrac{6x}{\sqrt{2x-1}}\,dx;\ u^2 = 2x-1$

(f) $\int_{0}^{4} \dfrac{5^x}{5^x+1}\,dx;\ u = 5^x$

(g) $\int_{0}^{\pi/2} \dfrac{\cos x}{\sin x + 1}\,dx;\ u = \sin x + 1$

(h) $\int_{0}^{2} x\,e^{x^2+3}\,dx;\ u = x^2 + 3$

(i) $\int_{\pi^2/16}^{\pi^2/4} \dfrac{1}{\sqrt{x}}\sin(\sqrt{x})\,dx;\ u = \sqrt{x}$

(j) $\int_{-\pi/2}^{0} -2\sin x\,e^{2\cos x}\,dx;\ u = 2\cos x$

3. Find: $\int \dfrac{3x^2 + 6}{x^3 + 6x + 1}\,dx$

4. Find: $\int \dfrac{2x^3 + 2x^{-5}}{x^4 - 2 - x^{-4}}\,dx$

5. Find the exact value of: $\int_{2}^{4} \dfrac{3t^2 + 2t}{t^3 + t^2 + 1}\,dt$

6. Using the substitution: $u = 3(\cos x + 1)$, or otherwise, show that:

$$\int_{0}^{\frac{\pi}{2}} e^{3(\cos x + 1)} \sin x\,dx = \frac{1}{3}e^3(e^3 - 1)$$

7. Find, using the substitution $u = \ln|x|$:

$$\int \left(\frac{1}{x}\right)\cos(\ln|x|)\,dx$$

8. Using the substitution $u = 1 + \cos x$, or otherwise, show that:

$$\int \dfrac{\sin 2x}{1 + \cos x}\,dx = 2\ln|1 + \cos x| - 2\cos x + k$$

Exercise 11E...

9. Using the substitution $x = \sqrt{2}\sin\theta$, show that:

$$\int_{0}^{1} \sqrt{2 - x^2}\,dx = \dfrac{\pi + 2}{4}$$

10. Given that $I = \int_{4}^{7} e^{\sqrt{3x+4}}\,dx$, use the substitution $t = \sqrt{3x+4}$ to show that I may be expressed as $\int_{a}^{b} kt\,e^t\,dt$, giving the values of a, b and k.

11. Using the substitution $u = 5 + \sin x$, show that:

$$\int \sin x \cos x\,(5 + \sin x)^3\,dx = \dfrac{1}{20}(5 + \sin x)^4(4\sin x - 5) + c$$

12. The finite region R is bounded by the curve $f(x) = \dfrac{1}{x-1} - \dfrac{1}{x} - \dfrac{2}{(x-1)^2}$, the x-axis and the line $x = -0.5$, as shown in the diagram.

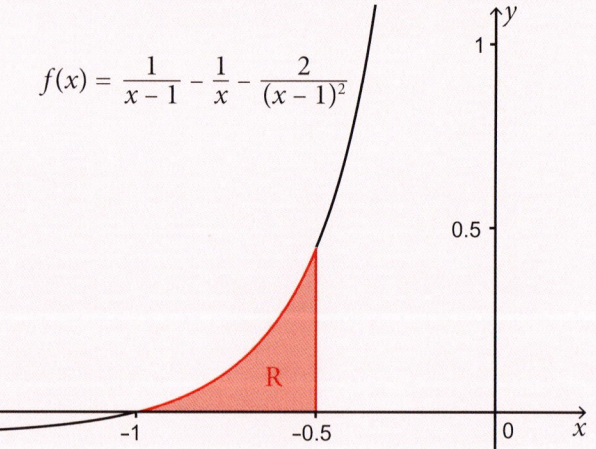

$f(x) = \dfrac{1}{x-1} - \dfrac{1}{x} - \dfrac{2}{(x-1)^2}$

Find the area of R, giving your answer in the form $\ln p - q$, where p and q are rational numbers to be found.

13. The number of vehicles using a motorway junction each hour can be modelled by the equation:

$$N = 60\left(\dfrac{t}{6} - 2\right)^2\left(1 - \left(\dfrac{t}{6} - 2\right)^2\right) + 720,$$

$$0 \le t \le 24$$

where t is the time in hours since midnight, as shown in the diagram.

Exercise 11E...

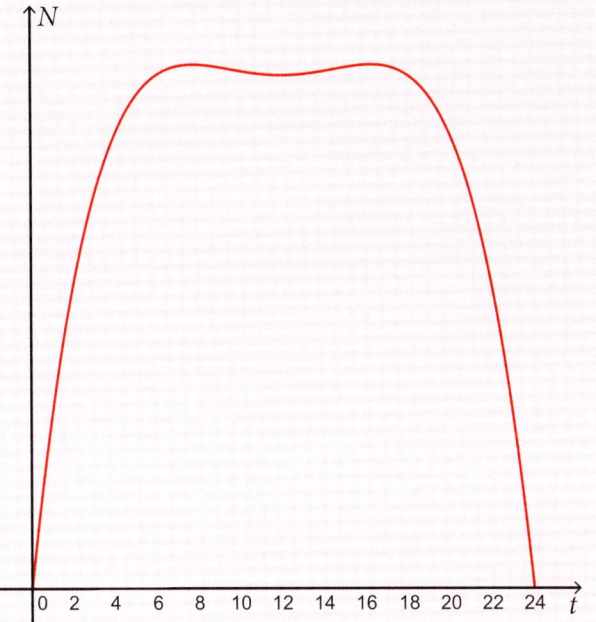

(a) Using the substitution $u = \dfrac{t}{6} - 2$, or otherwise, show that the rate of change of N is given by:
$$\dfrac{dN}{dt} = 20\left(\dfrac{t}{6} - 2\right)\left(1 - 2\left(\dfrac{t}{6} - 2\right)^2\right)$$

(b) Show that, according to this model, the peak times for traffic at this motorway junction are, to the nearest minute, 7:45 am and 4:15 pm.

(c) Find the traffic flow N expected at these peak times.

(d) Between these two rush hour peaks, the traffic is quieter. At what time between the two peaks, according to the model, does the traffic reach its minimum?

(e) Find the traffic flow N expected at this minimum.

(f) The total number of cars using the junction during one day can be found using
$$N_{total} = \int_0^{24} N \, dt$$
Using the substitution $u = \dfrac{t}{6} - 2$, or otherwise, find N_{total}.

11.6 Integration Using Trigonometric Identities

You may need to re-arrange a function before it can be integrated, especially using trigonometric identities.

You will need the following trigonometry identities, which were covered in chapters 7 and 8. They do not appear on the formula sheet.

$$\sin^2 x + \cos^2 x = 1$$
$$\tan^2 x + 1 = \sec^2 x$$
$$1 + \cot^2 x = \csc^2 x$$
$$\sin 2x = 2 \sin x \cos x$$
$$\cos 2x = \cos^2 x - \sin^2 x$$
$$\cos 2x = 2\cos^2 x - 1$$
$$\cos 2x = 1 - 2\sin^2 x$$

The last two formulae in this list are particularly useful for integrating $\cos^2 x$ and $\sin^2 x$.

Worked Examples

17. Find $\int \sin^2 x \, dx$

To integrate $\cos^2 x$ or $\sin^2 x$ use one of the cosine double angle formulae you learnt in chapter 8. There are three versions of this formula.

To integrate $\sin^2 x$ use:
$$\cos 2A = 1 - 2\sin^2 A$$

Re-arranging gives:
$$\sin^2 A = \dfrac{1}{2} - \dfrac{1}{2}\cos 2A$$
$$\therefore \int \sin^2 x \, dx = \int \dfrac{1}{2} - \dfrac{1}{2}\cos 2x \, dx$$
$$= \dfrac{1}{2}x - \dfrac{1}{4}\sin 2x + c$$

Note: To integrate $\cos^2 x$ use $\cos 2A = 2\cos^2 A - 1$
This is included as a question in Exercise 11F.

18. Find $\int (\cos x + \sec x)^2 \, dx$

$$I = \int (\cos x + \sec x)^2 \, dx$$
$$= \int (\cos^2 x + \sec^2 x + 2 \cos x \sec x) \, dx$$

Use $\cos^2 x = \frac{1}{2}(\cos 2x + 1)$:

$$I = \int \frac{1}{2}(\cos 2x + 1) + \sec^2 x + 2 \, dx$$

$$= \int \frac{1}{2}\cos 2x + \sec^2 x + \frac{5}{2} \, dx$$

$$= \frac{1}{4}\sin 2x + \tan x + \frac{5}{2}x + c$$

19. Find $\int \left(\frac{\sin 2x + \cos^3 2x}{\cos^2 2x}\right) dx$

$$\int \left(\frac{\sin 2x + \cos^3 2x}{\cos^2 2x}\right) dx$$

$$= \int \left(\frac{\sin 2x}{\cos^2 2x} + \frac{\cos^3 2x}{\cos^2 2x}\right) dx$$

$$= \int \left(\frac{\sin 2x}{\cos 2x} \times \frac{1}{\cos 2x} + \cos 2x\right) dx$$

$$= \int (\tan 2x \sec 2x + \cos 2x) \, dx$$

$$= \frac{1}{2}\sec 2x + \frac{1}{2}\sin 2x + c$$

20. Find $\int \tan^2 x \, dx$

Use the identity $\sec^2 A = 1 + \tan^2 A$.

$$\therefore \int \tan^2 x \, dx = \int \sec^2 x - 1 \, dx$$

$$= \tan x - x + c$$

You can find all integrals of the form $\sin^n x \cos x$ and $\cos^n x \sin x$. In general:

$$\int \sin^n x \cos x \, dx = \frac{1}{n+1}\sin^{n+1} x + c$$

$$\int \cos^n x \sin x \, dx = -\frac{1}{n+1}\cos^{n+1} x + c$$

Worked Example

21. Find $\int \sin^3 x \cos x \, dx$

Use the substitution $u = \sin x$.

Then $\frac{du}{dx} = \cos x \Rightarrow dx = \frac{du}{\cos x}$

$$\int \sin^3 x \cos x \, dx = \int \frac{u^3 \cos x \, du}{\cos x}$$

$$= \int u^3 \, du$$

$$= \frac{1}{4}u^4 + c$$

$$= \frac{1}{4}\sin^4 x + c$$

Note: This type of integration can be performed by recognition, using the formulae above.

Note: You can check your answer by differentiating:

$$y = \frac{1}{4}\sin^4 x = \frac{1}{4}(\sin x)^4$$

$$\frac{dy}{dx} = \frac{4}{4}(\sin x)^3(\cos x)$$

$$= \sin^3 x \cos x$$

These results also come in useful when integrating higher odd powers of trigonometric functions, e.g. $\cos^3 x$.

Worked Example

22. Find $\int \cos^3 x \, dx$

$$\int \cos^3 x \, dx = \int \cos x \cos^2 x \, dx$$

$$= \int \cos x \, (1 - \sin^2 x) \, dx$$

$$= \int \cos x - \cos x \sin^2 x \, dx$$

$$= \sin x - \frac{1}{3}\sin^3 x + c$$

Note: $\int \sin^3 x \, dx$ is included as a question in Exercise 11F.

Exercise 11F

1. Find $\int \cos^2 x \, dx$

2. Find $\int \sin^3 x \, dx$

3. Using the substitution $u = \sin x$, or otherwise, find $\int \sin^4 x \cos x \, dx$

Exercise 11F...

4. Evaluate $\int_0^{\pi/2} \cos^3 x \sin x \, dx$, giving an exact answer.

5. Find an exact value for $\int_0^{\pi/8} \tan^2 2x \, dx$.

6. By using the substitution $u = \sin x$ or otherwise, find $\int (7 \sin^7 x \sin 2x) \, dx$ giving your answer in terms of x.

7. (a) Using the substitution $u = \tan \theta$, find $\int \sec^2 \theta \tan^3 \theta \, d\theta$.

   (b) Find $\int \sec^2 \theta \tan^5 \theta \, d\theta$ without using a substitution (i.e. by recognition).

8. Find the following integrals.

   (a) $\int \dfrac{\cos x}{\sin^2 x} \, dx$ (b) $\int \dfrac{\sin x}{\cos^2 x} \, dx$

   (c) $\int \dfrac{\sin x + 1}{\cos^2 x} \, dx$ (d) $\int \dfrac{1 + \cos \theta}{\sin^2 \theta} \, d\theta$

   (e) $\int (\sin x + \operatorname{cosec} x)^2 \, dx$

   (f) $\int (\sec \theta - \tan \theta \sin \theta) \, d\theta$

   (g) $\int (\sec^2 x - \tan^2 x) \, dx$

   (h) $\int \left(\dfrac{\tan 2x}{\sin 2x}\right)^2 dx$

   (i) $\int (\tan^2 \theta - \cot^2 \theta) \, d\theta$

9. Evaluate the following definite integrals, giving exact answers where possible.

   (a) $\int_0^{\pi} \tan\left(\dfrac{x}{2}\right) \cos^2\left(\dfrac{x}{2}\right) dx$

   (b) $\int_0^{\pi/4} \sin(2x) \cot(2x) \, dx$

   (c) $\int_{\pi/4}^{\pi/2} \sin^2 x \, dx$

   (d) $\int_{\pi/4}^{\pi/3} \dfrac{\tan(3x)}{\cos(3x)} dx$

   (e) $\int_0^{\pi/4} \sin 2x \cos 2x \, dx$

   (f) $\int_0^{\pi/16} (\sin 2x + \cos 2x)^2 \, dx$

Exercise 11F...

   (g) $\int_0^{\pi} \sin 2x \cos x \, dx$

   (h) $\int_0^{\pi/4} \sin 3x \sin 4x \, dx$

   (i) $\int_{\pi/6}^{5\pi/6} \cot^2 x \, dx$

10. Find $\int \left(\dfrac{\cos 3x + \sin^3 3x}{\sin^2 3x}\right) dx$

11. Integrate the following expression with respect to θ, giving your answer as a trigonometric function of 8θ:
    $\sec^2 4\theta \, \operatorname{cosec}^2 4\theta$

12. Find $\int \operatorname{cosec}^2 x \, (\tan^2 x - \sin^2 x) \, dx$

13. In a model railway, a tunnel through a hill is created using the two curves shown in the diagram. The hill has the equation $y = 2\cos^2\left(\dfrac{x}{2}\right), -\pi \leq x \leq \pi$ and the tunnel has the equation $y = \cos 2x, -\dfrac{\pi}{4} \leq x \leq \dfrac{\pi}{4}$.

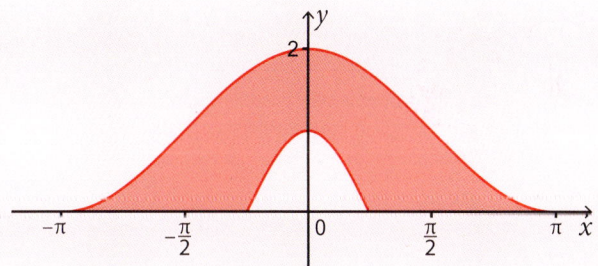

Find the exact area of the cross section of the hill, shaded in the diagram.

11.7 Integration By Parts

When integrating a product of terms, such as $x \cos x$, it is not always possible to use a substitution to simplify the problem. In such cases, it is often necessary to integrate by parts. The formula is:

$$\int u \dfrac{dv}{dx} dx = uv - \int v \dfrac{du}{dx} dx$$

This process is the reverse of the product rule for differentiation.

Proof of the integration by parts formula

Note: At the time of publication, the CCEA specification does not require you to know this proof.

Consider $y = uv$ where u and v are both functions of x.

Then, using the product rule:

$$\frac{dy}{dx} = u\frac{dv}{dx} + v\frac{du}{dx}$$

Hence:

$$\int u\frac{dv}{dx} + v\frac{du}{dx} \, dx = uv$$

Remember that when integrating a sum or difference, each term can be integrated separately. So:

$$\int u\frac{dv}{dx} \, dx + \int v\frac{du}{dx} \, dx = uv$$

$$\Rightarrow \int u\frac{dv}{dx} \, dx = uv - \int v\frac{du}{dx} \, dx$$

From the product of two terms:

- Choose one term that will be u. We will differentiate this to obtain $\frac{du}{dx}$.
- Choose the other term to be $\frac{dv}{dx}$. We will integrate this to find v.

Worked Example

23. Find $\int xe^{2x} \, dx$

Let $u = x$, $\frac{dv}{dx} = e^{2x}$

Then:

$$u = x \Rightarrow \frac{du}{dx} = 1$$

$$\frac{dv}{dx} = e^{2x} \Rightarrow v = \frac{1}{2}e^{2x}$$

Using:

$$\int u\frac{dv}{dx} \, dx = uv - \int v\frac{du}{dx} \, dx$$

$$= \frac{1}{2}xe^{2x} - \int \frac{1}{2}e^{2x}(1) \, dx$$

$$= \frac{1}{2}xe^{2x} - \frac{1}{4}e^{2x} + c$$

$$= \frac{1}{4}e^{2x}(2x - 1) + c$$

How do we decide which term should be u and which $\frac{dv}{dx}$?

In general, any term that can be differentiated to give a constant should be chosen as u. This, of course, means any multiple of x.

However, if the integral involves a logarithmic term (e.g. $\ln x$, $\log_2 x$, etc.) then this term should be u.

The following list gives, in order of priority, the term that should be chosen as , if it appears in the integral. You may find it helpful to remember the mnemonic LATE.

1. Logarithmic terms.
2. Algebraic terms, i.e. terms involving x, x^2, etc.
3. Trigonometric terms: $\sin x$, $\tan x$, etc.
4. Exponential terms: e^x, 2^x, etc.

The integral of $\ln x$ is a special case that requires integration by parts, although it is not obviously a product.

Worked Example

24. Find $\int \ln x \, dx$

Make it a product of two terms:

$$\int \ln x \, dx = \int 1 . \ln x \, dx$$

Logarithmic terms have highest priority when deciding on u, so:

Let $u = \ln x \Rightarrow \frac{du}{dx} = \frac{1}{x}$

and $\frac{dv}{dx} = 1 \Rightarrow v = x$

Then:

$$\int u\frac{dv}{dx} \, dx = uv - \int v\frac{du}{dx} \, dx$$

$$= (\ln x)(x) - \int x\left(\frac{1}{x}\right) dx$$

$$= x \ln x - \int 1 \, dx$$

$$= x \ln x - x + c$$

Note: In questions involving integration by parts, you will not be required to use the process more than once.

In other words, when you find $\int v\frac{du}{dx} \, dx$, it should always be integrable without using parts again.

Exercise 11G

1. Integrate the following by parts.

   (a) $\int (x-1)(x-2)\,dx$

   (b) $\int x \cos x\,dx$ (c) $\int 2x \cos 2x\,dx$

   (d) $\int xe^x\,dx$ (e) $\int \ln 5x\,dx$

   (f) $\int xe^{3x}\,dx$ (g) $\int (6x+4)e^{5x}\,dx$

   (h) $\int x^2 \ln x\,dx$

2. Evaluate the following definite integrals by parts.

   (a) $\int_1^2 x(x-1)\,dx$ (b) $\int_0^1 xe^{-x}\,dx$

   (c) $\int_1^2 x^3 \ln x\,dx$ (d) $\int_1^5 (x-1)\ln x\,dx$

   (e) $\int_{\pi/4}^{3\pi/4} x \csc^2 x\,dx$

   (f) $\int_0^{\pi/4} 6x \cos 2x\,dx$ (g) $\int_0^{\pi/4} x \sec^2 x\,dx$

   (h) $\int_0^1 (x+e^x)^2\,dx$

3. Find $\int 3x \ln 2x\,dx$

4. (a) Find $\int \sqrt{5-x}\,dx$

   The diagram shows the curve defined by:
   $f(x) = (x-1)\sqrt{5-x}$, $1 \le x \le 5$

   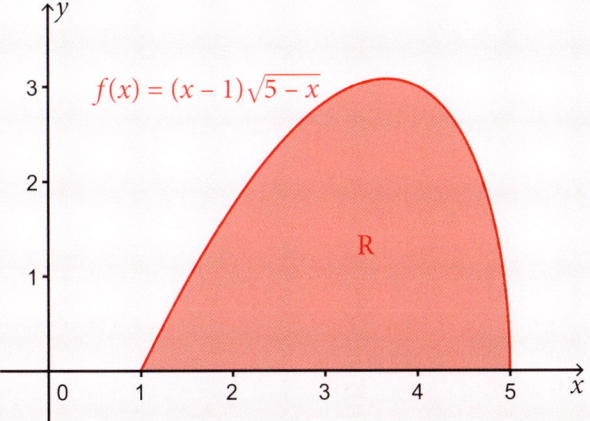

Exercise 11G...

   (b) Using integration by parts, or otherwise, find: $\int (x-1)\sqrt{5-x}\,dx$

   (c) Hence, find the area R shown in the diagram.

5. (a) Find $\int \sin^2\left(\dfrac{x}{2}\right) dx$

   (b) Using your answer to part (a), or otherwise, find $\int_0^\pi x \sin^2\left(\dfrac{x}{2}\right) dx$, giving an exact answer.

6. (a) Show that:
   $\int 4x \cos 2x\,dx = 2x \sin 2x + \cos 2x + c$

   (b) Hence, using the identity
   $\cos 2x = 2\cos^2 x - 1$, find $\int x \cos^2 x\,dx$.

7. (a) Find $\int x \ln x\,dx$

   Use your answer to part (a) to find:

   (b) $\int x \ln x^4\,dx$ (c) $\int x \ln 4x\,dx$

8. Find the following integral:
   $\int (x^2 - 3x)(2x^3 + 5)\,dx$

   (a) by parts;
   (b) by expanding the brackets.

> **Note:** Questions 9 and 10 are presented for students who want to stretch themselves.

9. (a) Show that $\int_0^3 xe^{-x}\,dx = 1 - 4e^{-3}$

   (b) Show that
   $\int x^2 e^{-x}\,dx = -x^2 e^{-x} + 2\int xe^{-x}\,dx$

   (c) Using your answers to parts (a) and (b), show that $\int_0^3 x^2 e^{-x}\,dx = 2 - 17e^{-3}$

10. My grandfather smokes a pipe. The upper surface is modelled on the curve $y = f(x)$ where $f(x) = \dfrac{1}{2} xe^{\frac{x}{2}}$. The lower surface of the pipe is modelled on the curve $y = \int f(x)\,dx$ as shown in the diagram on the next page.

    x and y are both measured in centimetres.

Exercise 11G...

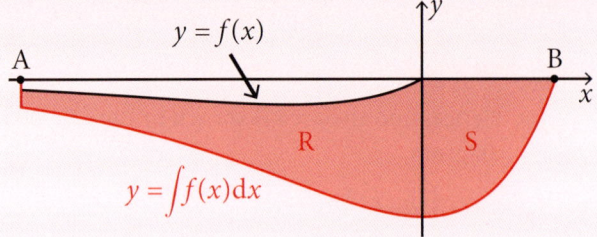

(a) Show that the lower surface of the pipe has the equation $y = e^{\frac{x}{2}}(x - 2)$.
(b) Find the x-coordinate of the point B, where the lower surface meets the x-axis.
(c) The total length of the pipe is 8 cm. Find the x-coordinate of the point A shown.

My grandfather wants to know the cross-sectional area of the pipe.

(d) Using integration to find the area between the two curves, show that the area R is $6(1 - 2e^{-3})$.
(e) Using integration to find the area between the lower surface and the x-axis, show that the area S is $4e - 8$. (Remember that using definite integration for a curve below the x-axis will give a negative answer.)
(f) Hence find the total cross-sectional area of the pipe, correct to 3 significant figures.

11.8 Integration Using Partial Fractions

In chapter 1 you learnt about **partial fractions**. Expressing a function in partial fractions can often be useful in integration.

Worked Example

25. (a) Express $\dfrac{-x + 4}{(x + 1)(4x - 1)}$ in terms of its partial fractions.
    (b) Hence find $\displaystyle\int \dfrac{-x + 4}{(x + 1)(4x - 1)} dx$

(a) Let:
$$\dfrac{-x + 4}{(x + 1)(4x - 1)} = \dfrac{A}{x + 1} + \dfrac{B}{4x - 1}$$
$$-x + 4 = A(4x - 1) + B(x + 1)$$

Let $x = -1$:
$$5 = A(-5) + B(0) \Rightarrow A = -1$$

Let $x = \dfrac{1}{4}$:
$$\dfrac{15}{4} = A(0) + B\left(\dfrac{5}{4}\right) \Rightarrow B = 3$$

Hence:
$$\dfrac{-x + 4}{(x + 1)(4x - 1)} \equiv \dfrac{-1}{x + 1} + \dfrac{3}{4x - 1}$$

(b) Hence:
$$\int \dfrac{-x + 4}{(x + 1)(4x - 1)} dx$$
$$= \int \dfrac{-1}{x + 1} + \dfrac{3}{4x - 1} dx$$
$$= -\ln|x + 1| + \dfrac{3}{4}\ln|4x - 1| + c$$

You will find that integration using partial fractions often gives answers involving logarithms.

Worked Example

26. Using partial fractions, evaluate $\displaystyle\int_2^3 \dfrac{1}{4x^2 - 9} dx$

Give your answer in the form $p \ln q$ where p and q are rational numbers.

$$\dfrac{1}{4x^2 - 9} = \dfrac{1}{(2x + 3)(2x - 3)}$$

Let:
$$\dfrac{1}{(2x + 3)(2x - 3)} = \dfrac{A}{2x + 3} + \dfrac{B}{2x - 3}$$
$$1 = A(2x - 3) + B(2x + 3)$$

Equate units:
$$1 = -3A + 3B \Rightarrow 2 = -6A + 6B \quad (1)$$

Equate coefficients of x:
$$0 = 2A + 2B \Rightarrow 0 = 6A + 6B \quad (2)$$

$(1) + (2) \Rightarrow 12B = 2 \Rightarrow B = \dfrac{1}{6}$

$(1) - (2) \Rightarrow -12A = 2 \Rightarrow A = -\dfrac{1}{6}$

$$\therefore \dfrac{1}{(2x + 3)(2x - 3)} = -\dfrac{1}{6}\left(\dfrac{1}{2x + 3}\right) + \dfrac{1}{6}\left(\dfrac{1}{2x - 3}\right)$$

So:
$$\int_2^3 \dfrac{1}{(2x + 3)(2x - 3)} dx$$
$$= \int_2^3 -\dfrac{1}{6}\left(\dfrac{1}{2x + 3}\right) + \dfrac{1}{6}\left(\dfrac{1}{2x - 3}\right) dx$$

$$= \left[-\frac{1}{12}\ln|2x+3| + \frac{1}{12}\ln|2x-3|\right]_2^3$$

$$= \frac{1}{12}\left[\ln\left|\frac{2x-3}{2x+3}\right|\right]_2^3$$

$$= \frac{1}{12}\left[\ln\left(\frac{3}{9}\right) - \ln\left(\frac{1}{7}\right)\right]$$

$$= \frac{1}{12}\ln\left(\frac{7}{3}\right)$$

The following example demonstrates writing an improper fraction as a sum of its partial fractions. It also involves a repeated factor in the denominator.

Worked Example

27. Find $\int \dfrac{x^3 + 6x^2 + 20x + 9}{(x-3)(x+2)^2}\,dx$

The integrand is an improper fraction, so we need to perform long division. First expand the brackets in the denominator:

$$\frac{x^3 + 6x^2 + 20x + 9}{(x-3)(x+2)^2} = \frac{x^3 + 6x^2 + 20x + 9}{x^3 + x^2 - 8x - 12}$$

This leads, by long division, to:

$$\frac{x^3 + 6x^2 + 20x + 9}{(x-3)(x+2)^2} = 1 + \frac{5x^2 + 28x + 21}{x^3 + x^2 - 8x - 12}$$

$$= 1 + \frac{5x^2 + 28x + 21}{(x-3)(x+2)^2} \quad (1)$$

Therefore:

$$\int \frac{x^3 + 6x^2 + 20x + 9}{(x-3)(x+2)^2}\,dx$$

$$= \int\left(1 + \frac{5x^2 + 28x + 21}{(x-3)(x+2)^2}\right)dx$$

Next consider the algebraic fraction alone. Write this in terms of its partial fractions:

$$\frac{5x^2 + 28x + 21}{(x-3)(x+2)^2} = \frac{A}{x-3} + \frac{B}{x+2} + \frac{C}{(x+2)^2}$$

So:
$$5x^2 + 28x + 21 = A(x+2)^2 + B(x+2)(x-3) + C(x-3)$$

Let $x = -2$:
$$5(-2)^2 + 28(-2) + 21 = A(0) + B(0) + C(-5)$$
$$\Rightarrow -15 = -5C$$
$$\Rightarrow C = 3$$

Let $x = 3$:
$$5(3)^2 + 28(3) + 21 = A(5)^2 + B(0) + C(0)$$
$$\Rightarrow 150 = 25A$$
$$\Rightarrow A = 6$$

Let $x = 0$:
$$5(0)^2 + 28(0) + 21 = A(2)^2 + B(2)(-3) + C(-3)$$
$$\Rightarrow 21 = 4A - 6B - 3C$$
$$\Rightarrow 21 = 24 - 6B - 9$$
$$6B = -6$$
$$B = -1$$

Therefore:
$$\frac{5x^2 + 28x + 21}{(x-3)(x+2)^2} = \frac{6}{x-3} - \frac{1}{x+2} + \frac{3}{(x+2)^2}$$

Using (1):
$$\frac{x^3 + 6x^2 + 20x + 9}{(x-3)(x+2)^2} = 1 + \frac{5x^2 + 28x + 21}{(x-3)(x+2)^2}$$

$$= 1 + \frac{6}{x-3} - \frac{1}{x+2} + \frac{3}{(x+2)^2}$$

Therefore:
$$\int \frac{x^3 + 6x^2 + 20x + 9}{(x-3)(x+2)^2}\,dx$$

$$= \int\left(1 + \frac{6}{x-3} - \frac{1}{x+2} + \frac{3}{(x+2)^2}\right)dx$$

$$= \int\left(1 + \frac{6}{x-3} - \frac{1}{x+2} + 3(x+2)^{-2}\right)dx$$

$$= x + 6\ln|x-3| - \ln|x+2| - 3(x+2)^{-1} + c$$

Exercise 11H

1. Integrate the following, by first expressing each in partial fractions.

   (a) $\dfrac{1}{x^2 - 4}$ (b) $\dfrac{x-1}{x^2 + x}$

   (c) $\dfrac{1}{(x+4)(x-1)}$ (d) $\dfrac{x}{(x+4)(x-1)}$

   (e) $\dfrac{6}{x^2 - 1}$ (f) $\dfrac{2x+3}{x^2 - 9}$

   (g) $\dfrac{2-x}{x^2 + 5x}$ (h) $\dfrac{x^2 + x - 1}{x(x^2 - 1)}$

   (i) $\dfrac{x+7}{x^2(x+2)}$

Exercise 11H...

2. Evaluate the following definite integrals, giving exact answers.

   (a) $\displaystyle\int_2^3 \frac{2x+1}{(x-1)(x+2)}\,dx$

   (b) $\displaystyle\int_2^3 \frac{x}{(x+3)(x+2)}\,dx$

   (c) $\displaystyle\int_0^1 \frac{3x+6}{x^2+5x+4}\,dx$

   (d) $\displaystyle\int_3^4 \frac{x}{(x-2)^2}\,dx$

   (e) $\displaystyle\int_1^2 \frac{x-3}{x^3+x^2}\,dx$

   (f) $\displaystyle\int_3^4 \frac{3x^2+7x-1}{(x-1)(x+2)^2}\,dx$

   (g) $\displaystyle\int_{-3}^3 \frac{14}{16-x^2}\,dx$

3. (a) Write $\dfrac{x+9}{x^2+2x-3}$ in terms of its partial fractions.

   (b) Find $\displaystyle\int \frac{x+9}{x^2+2x-3}\,dx$

4. (a) Using partial fractions, show that
   $$\frac{1}{u^2-1} \equiv \frac{1}{2}\left(\frac{1}{u-1}-\frac{1}{u+1}\right)$$

   (b) Using your answer to part a) and the substitution $u = e^x$, show that
   $$\int \frac{1}{e^x - e^{-x}}\,dx = \frac{1}{2}\ln\left|\frac{e^x-1}{e^x+1}\right| + c$$

5. The function $f(x)$ is defined as
   $$f(x) = \frac{5-4x}{(2x+1)(x+1)(x+4)}$$

   (a) Write this in the form
   $$f(x) = \frac{A}{2x+1} + \frac{B}{x+1} + \frac{C}{x+4}$$

   (b) Hence find $\displaystyle\int f(x)\,dx$

   (c) Find $\displaystyle\int_0^2 f(x)\,dx$, giving your answer as a single logarithm in its simplest form.

6. $f(x) = \dfrac{-5x-1}{(x+5)(2x+4)} = \dfrac{A}{x+5} + \dfrac{B}{2x+4}$

   (a) Find the values of the constants A and B.

   (b) Hence find $\displaystyle\int f(x)\,dx$.

Exercise 11H...

   (c) Find $\displaystyle\int_2^7 f(x)\,dx$, giving your answer in the form $\ln p^3 + \ln q^4$ where p and q are rational numbers.

7. $f(x) = \dfrac{4x^3 - 3x + 5}{x^2 - 2x}$

   (a) Show that $f(x)$ can be written as
   $$f(x) = 4x + 8 + \frac{13x+5}{x^2-2x}$$

   (b) Use partial fractions to write $\dfrac{13x+5}{x^2-2x}$ in the form $\dfrac{1}{2}\left(\dfrac{A}{x} + \dfrac{B}{x-2}\right)$ where A and B are integer constants.

   (c) Hence integrate $f(x)$ with respect to x.

8. Find $\displaystyle\int \frac{x^2-1}{x^2-16}\,dx$

9. (a) Using long division, or otherwise, express $\dfrac{x^3+3x^2+1}{(x-1)^2}$ in the form $Ax + B + \dfrac{Cx+D}{(x-1)^2}$

   (b) Hence find $\displaystyle\int_2^6 \frac{x^3+3x^2+1}{(x-1)^2}\,dx$

10. Find $\displaystyle\int \frac{x^4+x^3+x^2+1}{x^2+x-2}\,dx$

11.9 Integration As The Limit Of A Sum

The figure below shows an area bounded by the curve $y = f(x)$, the x-axis and the lines $x = a$ and $x = b$.

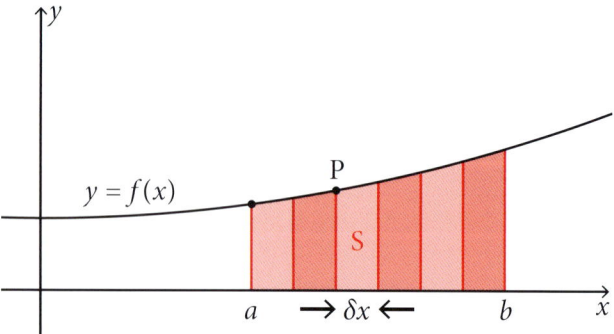

To estimate the area, we can split it into thin vertical strips, as shown, and treat each strip as being approximately rectangular. The sum of the areas of the rectangular strips then gives an approximate value for the area under the curve. The thinner the strips, the better will be the approximation. The width of each strip is δx.

(The symbol δ is used to indicate a small increase in the variable being considered, in this case x.)

Consider the strip labelled S. The height of the strip is equal to the y-value of the function at point P, i.e. $f(x)$. So the area of the strip S is approximately $f(x)\delta x$. Suppose we let the area of this small strip be δA (using the delta notation again, because this strip makes a small contribution, δA, to the total area, A, under the curve.) Then:

$\delta A \approx f(x)\delta x$

So the total area A under the curve from a to b is given by the sum of the areas of all the strips:

$$A = \sum_{x=a}^{b} \delta A \approx \sum_{x=a}^{b} f(x)\delta x$$

The approximation improves if we use a greater number of thinner strips. To make this approximation very accurate we must let the thickness of each strip become very small indeed, that is, we let $\delta x \to 0$. Then, we obtain:

$$A = \lim_{\delta x \to 0} \sum_{x=a}^{b} f(x)\delta x$$

The notation $\lim \delta x \to 0$ means that we consider what happens to the expression as the width of a strip δx approaches zero. This is known as the limit of a sum. If this limit exists we write it formally as:

$$\int_{a}^{b} f(x)\,dx$$

In other words, a definite integral is defined as the limit of a sum.

$$\int_{a}^{b} f(x)\,dx = \lim_{\delta x \to 0} \sum_{x=a}^{b} f(x)\delta x$$

Integration can therefore be regarded as a summation of infinitely many small pieces. Whenever we wish to find areas under curves, volumes etc, we can do this by finding the area or volume of a small portion, and then summing over the whole region of interest. The calculation can then be performed using the technique of definite integration.

Worked Example

28. Write down, but do not calculate, the integral defined by the limit as $\delta x \to 0$, of the following sums.

(a) $\displaystyle\sum_{x=-2}^{x=2} 3x^5 \delta x$

(b) $\displaystyle\sum_{x=2}^{x=8} \frac{1}{x^2} \delta x$

(a) $\displaystyle\int_{-2}^{2} 3x^5\,dx$

(b) $\displaystyle\int_{2}^{8} \frac{1}{x^2}\,dx$

You can use this approach to prove the formulae for many areas and volumes.

Worked Example

29. The cone shown has a base radius r and height h. The apex of the cone lies at the origin and the x-axis lies along the axis of the cone

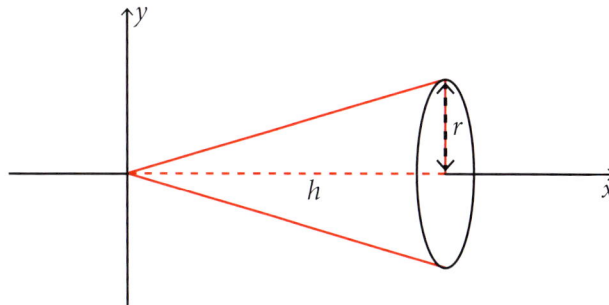

Consider the cone as comprising flat circular discs of thickness δx. One such disc is shown below.

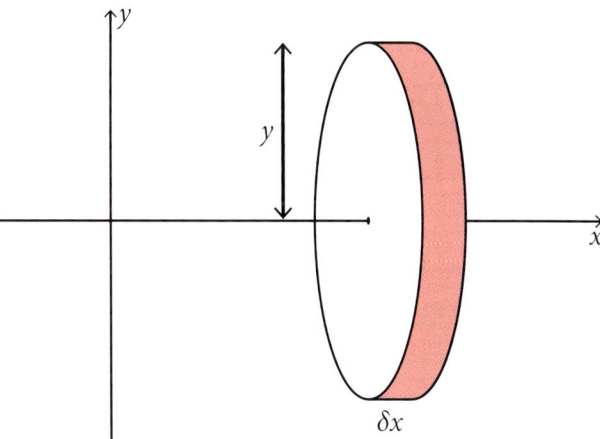

The radius y of a disc depends on its horizontal position x according to the linear equation:

$$y = \frac{r}{h}x$$

Show that the formula for the volume V of the cone is given by:

$$V = \frac{1}{3}\pi r^2 h$$

Each disc is a cylinder with volume $\pi y^2 \delta x$. The total volume of the cone could be approximated using a summation of all these discs:

$$V = \sum_{x=0}^{h} \pi y^2 \delta x$$

As $\delta x \to 0$: $V = \int_0^h \pi y^2 \, dx$

But: $y = \dfrac{r}{h} x$

So: $V = \int_0^h \pi \left(\dfrac{r}{h} x\right)^2 dx$

$= \pi \dfrac{r^2}{h^2} \int_0^h x^2 \, dx$

$= \pi \dfrac{r^2}{h^2} \left[\dfrac{x^3}{3}\right]_0^h$

$= \pi \dfrac{r^2}{h^2} \left(\dfrac{h^3}{3} - 0\right)$

$= \dfrac{1}{3} \pi r^2 h$

Exercise 11I

1. Write down, but do not calculate, the integral which is defined by the limit as $\delta x \to 0$, of the following sums.

   (a) $\sum_{x=1}^{x=4} 2x^3 \delta x$

   (b) $\sum_{x=2}^{x=6} 4\pi x^2 \delta x$

2. The circle shown in the next column has centre $(0, 0)$ and radius r. A quarter of the circle is divided into several strips, each of width δx.

Exercise 11I...

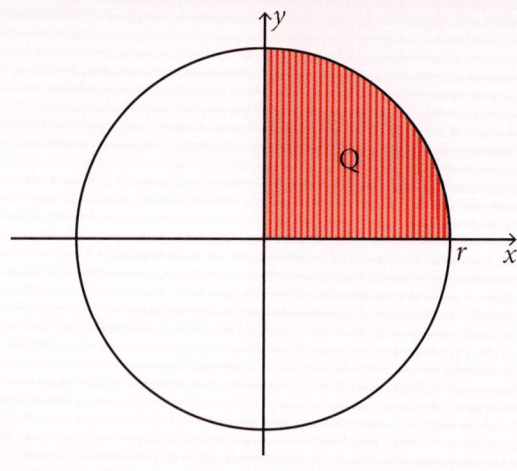

(a) Write down the equation of the circle.
(b) Re-arrange the equation to make y the subject.
(c) Find the area of one strip in terms of x and δx.
(d) Use summation notation to obtain an expression for the area Q of the quarter circle shown.
(e) By allowing the width of a strip to approach zero ($\delta x \to 0$), show that the area Q is given by the definite integral: $Q = \int_0^r \sqrt{r^2 - x^2} \, dx$
(f) Use the substitution $x = r \cos \theta$ to show that $Q = r^2 \int_0^{\pi/2} \cos^2 \theta \, d\theta$
(g) Hence find Q in terms of r.
(h) Hence show that the area of the full circle is given by the formula $A = \pi r^2$

3. The diagram shows a hemisphere of radius r.

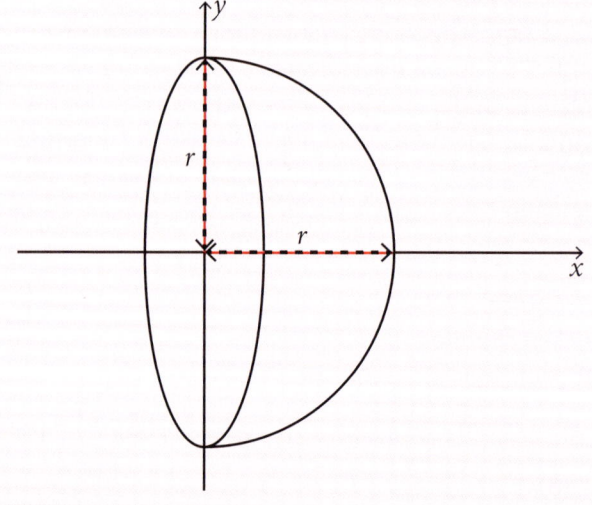

Exercise 11I...

(a) Consider the hemisphere as a series of circular discs, each one with its centre on the x-axis. Hence find a summation formula to approximate the volume of the hemisphere.

(b) Hence show that the volume is given by:
$$V = \int_0^r \pi(r^2 - x^2)\,dx$$

(c) Hence derive the formula for the volume of the hemisphere, $V = \frac{2}{3}\pi r^3$.

4. Use the techniques in this section to prove the formula for the volume of a cylinder: $V = \pi r^2 h$

11.10 Volume Of Revolution

You will be asked to find **volumes of revolution**. A volume of revolution is the volume generated by the rotation of an area through a complete 360° (or 2π radians) around the x-axis. Usually, this area is the area under a curve.

The formula for the volume is:
$$V = \pi \int_a^b y^2\,dx$$

where a and b are the lower and upper x-values of the area being rotated.

> **Note:** This formula is not provided on your formula sheet.

Derivation of the volume of revolution formula

> **Note:** At the time of publication, the CCEA specification does not require you to know this derivation.

Consider a curve $y = f(x)$. We wish to know the volume generated when the area between two limits $x = a, b$ is rotated about the x-axis.

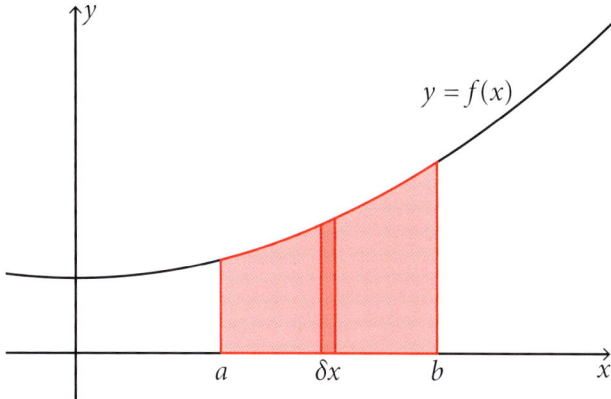

Consider the strip of width δx, shown above. When it is rotated about the x-axis, a disc is generated, as shown below.

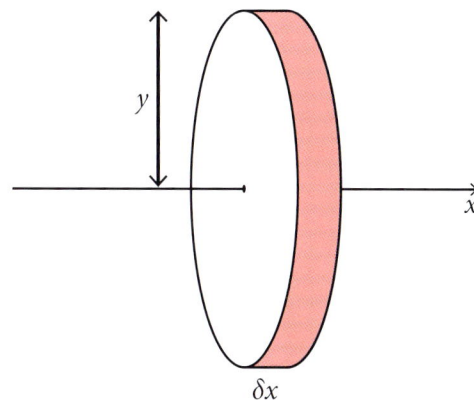

The volume of this disc is $\pi y^2 \delta x$. To find the total volume between a and b, we must sum all such discs:
$$V = \sum_{x=a}^{b} \pi y^2 \delta x$$

We are interested in the value of this summation as δx approaches zero, i.e. as the number of discs approaches infinity. The limiting value of a summation was discussed in section 11.9. The summation becomes an integral with respect to x:

$$V = \lim_{\delta x \to 0} \sum_a^b \pi y^2 \delta x = \int_a^b \pi y^2\,dx$$

$$V = \pi \int_a^b y^2\,dx$$

PURE MATHEMATICS FOR CCEA A2

Worked Example

30. The diagram shows the curve $y = 3x - x^2$
The finite region bounded by the curve and the x-axis is also shown.

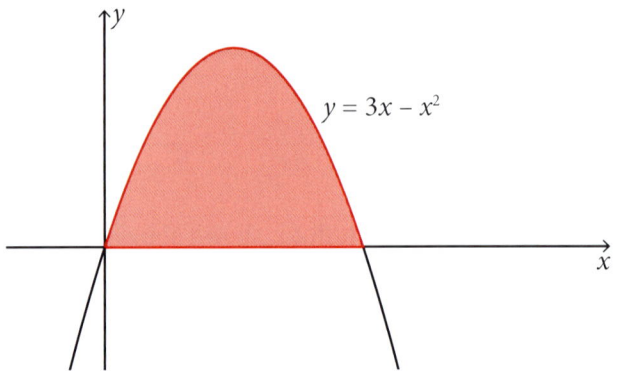

(a) Find the x-coordinates of the two points of intersection of the curve and the x-axis.
(b) The area is rotated through 360° about the x-axis. Using integration find, in terms of π, the volume of the solid generated.

(a) At the points of intersection:
$$3x - x^2 = 0$$
$$x(3 - x) = 0$$
$$x = 0 \text{ or } x = 3$$

(b) $V = \pi \int_a^b y^2 \, dx$

$= \pi \int_0^3 (3x - x^2)^2 \, dx$

$= \pi \int_0^3 (9x^2 - 6x^3 + x^4) \, dx$

$= \pi \left[\dfrac{9}{3}x^3 - \dfrac{6}{4}x^4 + \dfrac{1}{5}x^5 \right]_0^3$

$= \pi \left[\left(3(3)^3 - \dfrac{3}{2}(3)^4 + \dfrac{1}{5}(3)^5 \right) - 0 \right]$

$= \pi \left(81 - \dfrac{243}{2} + \dfrac{243}{5} \right)$

$= \dfrac{81\pi}{10}$

Exercise 11J

1. A bowl is formed by rotating the arc of the curve $y = \sqrt{2x}$ through 2π radians about the x-axis, between $x = 0$ and $x = h$, where h is a positive constant. The bowl is full of water. Find, in terms of h the volume of water in the bowl.

2. Find the volume of revolution when the curve $y = e^{\frac{x}{4}}$ is rotated 2π radians about the x-axis between $x = 0$ and $x = 2$. Give your answer to 3 significant figures.

3. A paperweight is made by rotating the curve $y = \sqrt{64 - x^2}$ through 2π radians about the x-axis between $x = -8$ and $x = 2$. Calculate the volume of the paperweight, giving an exact answer.

4. The curve with equation $y = 2 + 4\sqrt{x}$ is shown in the diagram.

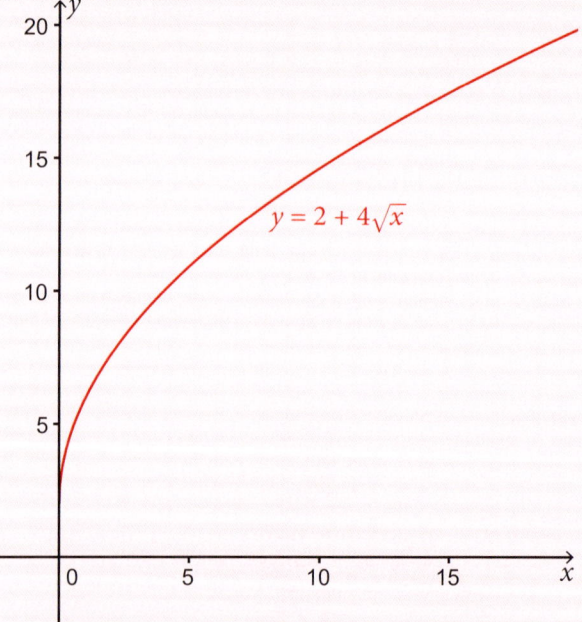

The shape for a coffee pot is formed when the area between this curve and the lines $x = 0$ and $x = 10$ is rotated through 360° about the x-axis. Find the volume of the coffee pot to 3 significant figures.

5. The design for a Christmas decoration is made by rotating a part of the curve $y = \sin x$ by 2π radians around the x-axis. The curve is shown in the diagram.

Exercise 11J...

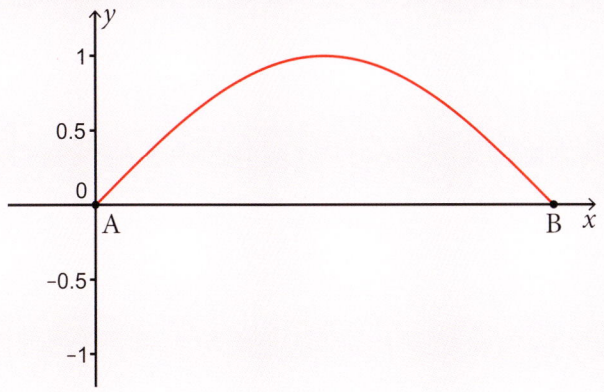

(a) Write down the x-coordinates of points A and B.
(b) Calculate the volume of the Christmas decoration.

6. Consider the semicircle with equation $x^2 + y^2 = r^2$, where $y > 0$. The semicircle is rotated through 2π radians about the x-axis. Find the volume of revolution and hence show that the volume of a sphere is given by:
$$V = \frac{4}{3}\pi r^3$$

7. The diagram shows the curve with equation $y = 5\sin\left(\frac{x}{3}\right)$, $0 \leq x \leq 3\pi$.
The finite region enclosed by the curve and the x-axis is shaded.

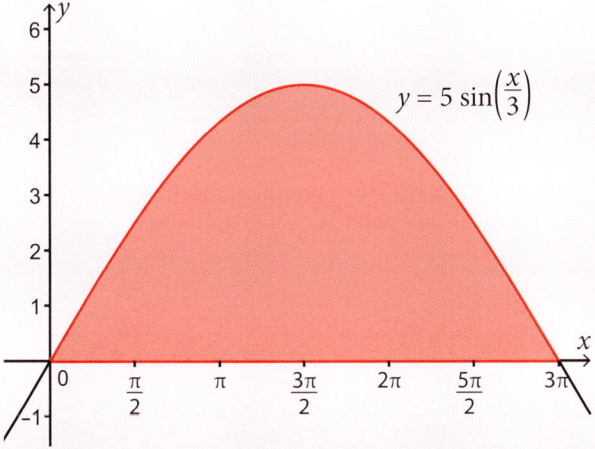

(a) Find, by integration, the area of the shaded region.

This region is rotated through 2π radians about the x-axis.
(b) Find the volume of the solid generated.

Exercise 11J...

8. The curve shown has equation $y = \sqrt{x}\,e^{-3x}$

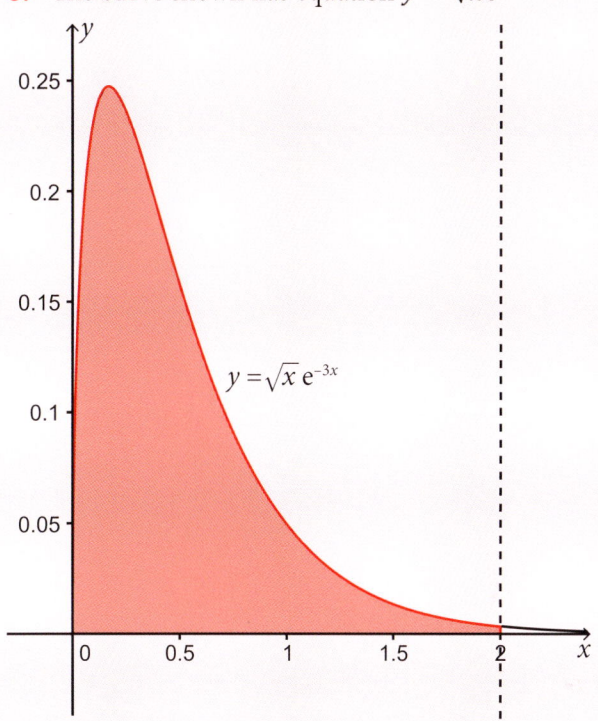

The finite region enclosed by the curve, the x-axis and the line $x = 2$ is rotated through 2π radians about the x-axis. Find, in terms of π and e, the volume of the solid generated.

9. (a) Find, using the substitution $u = 2x - 1$,
$$\int \frac{x}{\sqrt{2x-1}}\,dx$$
(b) Find the volume of revolution generated by rotation of the curve $y = 3x^{\frac{1}{2}}(2x-1)^{-\frac{1}{4}}$ through 360° around the x-axis, between $x = 1$ and $x = 5$.

11.11 Mixed Questions

You will not always be told which technique to use when integrating a function. To decide which approach to take, consider these techniques in turn:

- Integration by recognition;
- Integrals that result in a logarithm;
- Reverse chain rule;
- Substitution;
- Using trigonometric identities;
- Partial fractions;
- Integration by parts.

Worked Example

31. Find $\int \dfrac{75x^4 - 12x^3 + 18}{-5x^5 + x^4 - 6x}\,dx$

Assuming this is a log-type integral, use the substitution $u = -5x^5 + x^4 - 6x$. So:

$$\dfrac{du}{dx} = -25x^4 + 4x^3 - 6 \Rightarrow dx = \dfrac{du}{-25x^4 + 4x^3 - 6}$$

Therefore:

$$\int \dfrac{75x^4 - 12x^3 + 18}{-5x^5 + x^4 - 6x}\,dx$$

$$= \int \left(\dfrac{75x^4 - 12x^3 + 18}{u}\right) \dfrac{du}{-25x^4 + 4x^3 - 6}$$

$$= \int \dfrac{-3(-25x^4 + 4x^3 - 6)}{u(-25x^4 + 4x^3 - 6)}\,du$$

$$= -3\int \dfrac{1}{u}\,du$$

$$= -3\ln(|u|) + c$$

$$= -3\ln\left|-5x^5 + x^4 - 6x\right| + c$$

> **Note:** Taking a factor of −3 out would turn this integral into one of the form $\int \dfrac{f'(x)}{f(x)}\,dx$ which can then be done by recognition:
>
> $\int \dfrac{75x^4 - 12x^3 + 18}{-5x^5 + x^4 - 6x}\,dx = -3\int \dfrac{-25x^4 + 4x^3 - 6}{-5x^5 + x^4 - 6x}\,dx$
>
> $= -3\ln\left|-5x^5 + x^4 - 6x\right| + c$

The questions in the following exercise use the various techniques described in this chapter.

Exercise 11K

1. Find the following indefinite integrals.

   (a) $\int 3x^5\,dx$ (b) $\int \dfrac{1}{x+1}\,dx$

   (c) $\int (3x+5)^6\,dx$ (d) $\int \dfrac{4}{5x-3}\,dx$

   (e) $\int (\cos^2 x + \sec^2 x + \sin^2 x - \tan^2 x)\,dx$

   (f) $\int (4x+1)^7\,dx$

   (g) $\int e^{-3x}\,dx$ (h) $\int \dfrac{1}{(x-5)(x+1)}\,dx$

Exercise 11K...

   (i) $\int \dfrac{2x+1}{3x-4}\,dx$ (j) $\int \cos 5x\,dx$

   (k) $\int 3\sec^2 2x\,dx$ (l) $\int \dfrac{2x}{x^2+8}\,dx$

   (m) $\int \sin^3 x \cos x\,dx$

   (n) $\int -\cot\left(\dfrac{x}{2}\right)\operatorname{cosec}\left(\dfrac{x}{2}\right)\,dx$

   (o) $\int x^2 \sin(x^3+1)\,dx\,;\ u = x^3+1$

   (p) $\int \dfrac{3x^2+1}{x^3+x-4}\,dx$ (q) $\int \dfrac{13x-4}{6x^2-x-2}\,dx$

   (r) $\int \sec 6x \tan 6x\,dx$ (s) $\int -\operatorname{cosec}^2(bx)\,dx$

   (t) $\int \sin^5 x\,dx$ (u) $\int \tan^4 x + \tan^2 x\,dx$

   (v) $\int x + x\cot^2 x\,dx$ (w) $\int \dfrac{xe^x + xe^{-x}}{e^{-x}}\,dx$

   (x) $\int \sin^2 3x\,dx$ (y) $\int 4\tan^4 x \sec^2 x\,dx$

   (z) $\int \sqrt{1 - \sin^2 \theta}\,\operatorname{cosec}\theta\,d\theta$

2. Evaluate the following definite integrals, giving exact answers.

   (a) $\displaystyle\int_0^1 3x^2 e^{x^3}\,dx$

   (b) $\displaystyle\int_0^2 \dfrac{11x+5}{(2x+1)(3x+1)}\,dx$

3. Evaluate the following definite integrals. Give your answers to 3 significant figures.

   (a) $\displaystyle\int_2^3 x\sin(x^2+1)\,dx$ using the substitution $u = x^2+1$

   (b) $\displaystyle\int_1^2 (2x+3)^7\,dx$

> **Note:** Question 4 is presented for students who want to stretch themselves.

4. Find the following integrals.

   (a) $\int \sin^2 2x\,dx$ (b) $\int \sin^3 4x\,dx$

   (c) $\int \cos^5 x\,dx$ (d) $\int \cos^2(2x-1)\,dx$

   (e) $\int \tan^3 x\,dx$

11.12 Summary

You need to learn and know how to apply these results:

$$\int \cos x \, dx = \sin x + c$$

$$\int \sin x \, dx = -\cos x + c$$

$$\int e^x \, dx = e^x + c$$

$$\int \frac{1}{x} \, dx = \ln|x| + c$$

In addition, you should be familiar with these results, which are on your formula sheet:

$$\int \sec^2 x \, dx = \tan x + c$$

$$\int \sec x \tan x \, dx = \sec x + c$$

$$\int \csc^2 x \, dx = -\cot x + c$$

$$\int \csc x \cot x \, dx = -\csc x + c$$

All these results can be generalised: replacing x with $ax + b$ and dividing by a, for example:

$$\int \frac{1}{ax+b} \, dx = \frac{1}{a} \ln|ax+b| + c$$

In addition, you should be able to use **integration by recognition** with:

- Log-type integrals.
- Reverse chain rule.

Several other techniques were introduced in this chapter:

- Integration by **substitution**. The substitution will usually be given.
- Using **trigonometric identities**.
- **Partial fractions**.
- **Integration by parts** using the formula

$$\int u \frac{dv}{dx} \, dx = uv - \int v \frac{du}{dx} \, dx$$

You should be able to find **volumes of revolution** using the formula $V = \pi \int_a^b y^2 \, dx$

You should also understand that a definite integral is the limit of a summation and that you can use this approach to prove formulae for areas and volumes.

The 'Cheat Sheet' below and overleaf summarises the various types of integral you will encounter.

Integration – 'Cheat Sheet'

Integral	Solution	Example (without constant)
$\int x^n \, dx$	$\dfrac{x^{n+1}}{n+1}$	$\int x^3 \, dx = \dfrac{x^4}{4}$
$\int (ax+b)^n \, dx$	$\dfrac{(ax+b)^{n+1}}{a(n+1)}$	$\int (3x+4)^5 \, dx = \dfrac{1}{18}(3x+4)^6$
$\int e^{(ax+b)} \, dx$	$\dfrac{1}{a} e^{(ax+b)}$	$\int e^{3x} \, dx = \dfrac{1}{3} e^{3x}$
$\int \dfrac{k}{(ax+b)} \, dx$	$\dfrac{k}{a} \ln(ax+b)$	$\int \dfrac{5}{x} \, dx = 5 \ln x$
$\int \cos(ax+b) \, dx$	$\dfrac{1}{a} \sin(ax+b)$	$\int \cos \dfrac{x}{3} \, dx = 3 \sin \dfrac{x}{3}$
$\int \sin(ax+b) \, dx$	$-\dfrac{1}{a} \cos(ax+b)$	$\int \sin 4x \, dx = -\dfrac{1}{4} \cos 4x$

Integral	Solution	Example (without constant)
$\int \sec^2(ax+b)\,dx$	$\dfrac{1}{a}\tan(ax+b)$	$\int \sec^2 2x\,dx = \dfrac{1}{2}\tan 2x$
$\int \csc^2(ax+b)\,dx$	$-\dfrac{1}{a}\cot(ax+b)$	$\int \csc^2 4x\,dx = -\dfrac{1}{4}\cot 4x$
$\int \sec(ax+b)\tan(ax+b)\,dx$	$\dfrac{1}{a}\sec(ax+b)$	$\int \sec\dfrac{x}{2}\tan\dfrac{x}{2}\,dx = 2\sec\dfrac{x}{2}$
$\int \csc(ax+b)\cot(ax+b)\,dx$	$-\dfrac{1}{a}\csc(ax+b)$	$\int \csc 7x \cot 7x\,dx = -\dfrac{1}{7}\csc 7x$
$\int \cos^2 x\,dx$	$\dfrac{1}{4}\sin 2x + \dfrac{x}{2}$	
$\int \sin^2 x\,dx$	$\dfrac{x}{2} - \dfrac{1}{4}\sin 2x$	
$\int \tan^2 x\,dx$	$\tan x - x$	
$\int f'(x)g'(f(x))\,dx$ Recognition or substitution.	$g(f(x))$ Note: The substitution will usually be given.	$\int \dfrac{1}{x}\cos(\ln x)\,dx = \sin(\ln x)$ or use substitution $u = \ln x$ $\int \cos x \sin^3 x\,dx = \dfrac{1}{4}\sin^4 x$ or use substitution $u = \sin x$
$\int \dfrac{ax+b}{cx+d}\,dx$ Use substitution $u = cx+d$		$\int \dfrac{2x+3}{4x+5}\,dx = \dfrac{1}{8}(4x+5+\ln(4x+5))$ Use substitution $u = 4x+5$
Recognition: log-type $\int \dfrac{f'(x)}{f(x)}\,dx$	$\ln\lvert f(x) \rvert$	$\int \dfrac{6x+1}{(3x^2+x)}\,dx = \ln\lvert 3x^2+x \rvert$ $\int \cot x\,dx = \int \dfrac{\cos x}{\sin x}\,dx = \ln\lvert \sin x \rvert$
Partial fractions: $\int \dfrac{ax+b}{f(x)g(x)}\,dx$	Note: partial fractions will be found first.	$\int \dfrac{4x+1}{(x+1)(2x-1)}\,dx = \int \dfrac{1}{x+1} + \dfrac{2}{2x-1}\,dx$ $= \ln(x+1)(2x-1)$
Trigonometric identities		$\int \cos^3 x\,dx = \int \cos x\,(1 - \sin^2 x)\,dx$ $= \int \cos x - \cos x \sin^2 x\,dx$ $= \sin x - \dfrac{1}{3}\sin^3 x$
Integration by parts	$\int u\dfrac{dv}{dx}\,dx = uv - \int v\dfrac{du}{dx}\,dx$	$I = \int x\cos x\,dx$ $u = x \Rightarrow \dfrac{du}{dx} = 1$ $\dfrac{dv}{dx} = \cos x \Rightarrow v = \sin x$ $I = x\sin x - \int 1\sin x\,dx = x\sin x + \cos x$

Chapter 12
Differential Equations

12.1 Introduction

A **differential equation** is an equation that involves a derivative, for example $\frac{dy}{dx} = 3x^2 + y$.

You will be asked to form and solve simple differential equations. Often these problems will be set in a real-life context.

This chapter will only deal with **first order differential equations**. These differential equations involve only $\frac{dy}{dx}$, not $\frac{d^2y}{dx^2}$, or any higher derivatives.

Key words
- **Differential equation**: An equation involving a derivative.

Before you start
You should know:
- How to perform integration of powers of x and related functions.
- How to perform integration of trigonometric functions, the exponential function e^x and $\frac{1}{x}$.
- How to integrate using partial fractions.
- How to integrate using a substitution.
- How to perform integration by parts for a product of two terms.

Worked Example
1. Find $\int e^x \sec^2(e^x)\, dx$ using the substitution $u = e^x$.

$u = e^x \Rightarrow \frac{du}{dx} = e^x \Rightarrow dx = \frac{du}{e^x}$

So:

$\int e^x \sec^2(e^x)\, dx = \int e^x \sec^2(u) \frac{du}{e^x}$

$= \int \sec^2 u\, du$

$= \tan u + c$

$= \tan(e^x) + c$

What you will learn
In this chapter you will learn how to:
- Form a differential equation.
- Solve some types of differential equation.

In the real world...
In 2013 a one-year old boy, Emile Ouamouno, living in Guinea in West Africa, became seriously ill with a mysterious disease. He died in December of that year.

Unfortunately, before he died, his virus was transmitted to his sister, his mother and his grandmother. They also passed the virus on to others and died themselves.

The members of Emile's family were the first victims of an outbreak of the Ebola virus, which spread and eventually killed around 11 000 people in Guinea, Sierra Leone and Liberia.

When it was clear how fast the virus was spreading, the authorities found themselves unable to cope and many international agencies were called in to help. These were mainly medical organisations, but mathematicians also had a role to play.

The situation was modelled using a system of differential equations called the Lotka–Volterra equations, sometimes known as a Predator-Prey Model.

Initial predictions gave an enormous estimate for the number of deaths. But with the right intervention the outbreak was contained, both geographically and in its scale.

Eleven thousand deaths is a tragic loss, but the situation could have been far worse without accurate modelling working together with the correct medical intervention.

PURE MATHEMATICS FOR CCEA A2

Exercise 12A (Revision)

Find the following integrals.

1. $\int \left(3x^4 + \dfrac{1}{2x^3}\right) dx$

2. $\int \operatorname{cosec}^2 \left(\dfrac{x}{2}\right) dx$

3. $\int \dfrac{1}{(x+1)(x-1)} dx$

4. $\int x^4 \sqrt{1+x^5}\, dx$
   using the substitution $u^2 = 1 + x^5$

5. $\int \dfrac{1}{x^2} \ln x\, dx$

In section 12.2 you will learn how to **form** differential equations. In section 12.3, you will learn how to **solve** some differential equations.

12.2 Forming Differential Equations

You may be given information about the rate of change of a quantity. From this you can form a differential equation.

Worked Example

2. A particle moves such that its velocity decreases with the distance s in metres from its starting point at a rate that is proportional to the distance. Model this using a differential equation involving a positive constant.

   The rate of change of velocity with distance is proportional to distance.

   As an equation, this becomes: $\dfrac{dv}{ds} = -ks$

   Note: Since velocity falls with distance, we know $\dfrac{dv}{ds}$ is negative. Hence, if we use a positive constant k, we must also introduce a minus sign.

You may have to derive an equation which can be differentiated to obtain a differential equation.

Worked Example

3. The diagram shows a cylindrical metal rod which is expanding as it is heated. The radius of the rod is x cm and the length of the rod is $3x$ cm.

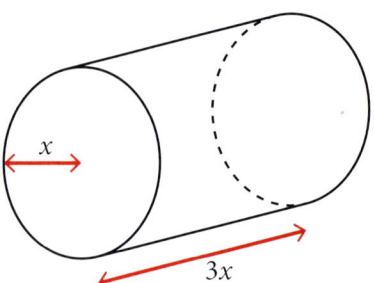

(a) Find an expression for the volume V in terms of the radius x.

(b) Show that $\dfrac{dV}{dx} = 9\pi x^2$

(c) Find $\dfrac{dV}{dx}$ when $x = 3$.

(a) Volume of prism = area of cross-section × length
$V = \pi x^2 \times 3x$
$V = 3\pi x^3$

(b) $V = 3\pi x^3$
Differentiate with respect to x:
$\dfrac{dV}{dx} = 9\pi x^2$

(c) When $x = 3$:
$\dfrac{dV}{dx} = 9\pi(3)^2 = 81\pi$ cm³ s⁻¹

You may be given an equation which can be differentiated to obtain a differential equation.

Worked Example

4. The population N of wombats in a region varies according to the equation $N = N_0 e^{rt}$ where t is the number of years after the beginning of 2010, $N_0 = 2100$ and $r = 0.005$.

   (a) Find the population of wombats at the beginning of 2010 (i.e. when $t = 0$).
   (b) Find the predicted population in 2020.
   (c) If the population continued to grow at this rate, find how long it will take for the population of wombats to double.
   (d) Form a differential equation in $\dfrac{dN}{dt}$.
   (e) Hence find the rate at which the wombat population is growing in the year 2015.

(a) When $t = 0$, $N = N_0 e^{r(0)} = N_0 = 2100$
Hence, the number of wombats in the region in 2010 was 2100.

(b) When $t = 10$, $N = 2100 e^{0.005 \times 10}$
$= 2207.67$
$= 2210$ (3 s.f.)

(c) Wombat population doubles when $N = 2N_0$. So:
$2N_0 = N_0 e^{rt}$
$2 = e^{rt}$
$\ln 2 = rt$
$t = \dfrac{\ln 2}{0.005}$
$= 138.63$
$= 139$ years (3 s.f.)

(d) $N = N_0 e^{rt}$
$\dfrac{dN}{dt} = N_0 r e^{rt}$

(e) The rate of change of N is given by $\dfrac{dN}{dt}$.
In the year 2015, $t = 5$. So:
$\dfrac{dN}{dt} = N_0 r e^{rt}$
$= 2100 \times 0.005 \times e^{0.005 \times 5}$
$= 10.77$
$= 11$ (nearest integer).

The population is growing at approximately 11 wombats per year.

Exercise 12B

1. Water is draining from a storage tank. The rate of change of the depth D of water is proportional to the square of the depth at time t. Model this by a differential equation.

2. Atmospheric air pressure P, measured in Pascals, decreases with the height h in km above sea level at a rate that is proportional to the pressure. Model this using a differential equation involving a positive constant.

3. A planet is moving so that the rate of change of its distance from a fixed star is inversely proportional to its distance s from the star at any time t. Show that this can be modelled using the differential equation $\dfrac{ds}{dt} = \dfrac{k}{s}$ where k is a constant.

Exercise 12B...

4. Liquid is flowing into a container at a constant rate of 30 cm³ s⁻¹. The liquid is also leaking from the container at a rate of $\dfrac{3}{10}V$ cm³ s⁻¹, where V cm³ is the volume of liquid in the container at time t seconds.
Show that: $-10\dfrac{dV}{dt} = 3V - 300$.

5. A walker pours a cup of hot tea from her flask. The temperature of the surroundings is a constant 15°C and the rate of change of the temperature T °C of the tea after time t minutes is proportional to the difference in temperature between the tea and the surroundings. Form a differential equation to express $\dfrac{dT}{dt}$ as a function of T, using a positive constant k.

6. The voltage V of the battery in a radio is modelled using the differential equation $\dfrac{dV}{dt} = -\dfrac{kV}{V_0}$ where t is the number of days after installation, V_0 is the initial voltage and k is a positive constant.
   (a) Find k if the voltage is falling at a rate of 0.1 volts per day when the voltage is $\dfrac{V_0}{2}$.
   (b) Find the rate of change of the voltage when $V = 0.1 V_0$.

7. A hemispherical bowl is shown in the diagram. Water is flowing into the bowl.

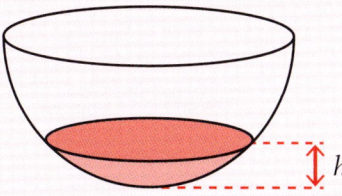

When the depth of the water is h cm, the volume V cm³ is given by:
$V = \pi h^2 \left(2 - \dfrac{h}{3}\right), 0 \leq h \leq 2$
Find $\dfrac{dV}{dh}$ in terms of π.

Exercise 12B...

8. The speed of an electric chainsaw R, measured in thousands of revolutions per minute, at time t seconds, is given by the equation:
   $R = 1.5 - 1.5(0.5)^t \quad t \geq 0$
   (a) Find $\dfrac{dR}{dt}$ in terms of t.
   (b) Find the value of $\dfrac{dR}{dt}$ when $t = 3$.
   Give your answer in the form $\ln a$, where a is a constant.

9. Fuel is flowing into the tank shown at a constant rate of 0.36π m³ min⁻¹. At time t minutes, the volume of fuel in the tank is V cubic metres.

   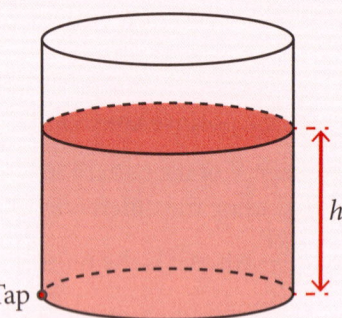

   There is a tap at the bottom of the tank at the point marked on the diagram. When the tap is open, fuel leaves the tank at a rate of $0.48\pi h$ m³ min⁻¹, where h is the depth of fuel. Show that, t minutes after the tap has been opened, $25\dfrac{dV}{dt} = 3\pi(3 - 4h)$

10. The container shown in the diagram is made in the shape of an inverted circular cone. The height of the container is 12 cm and the radius is 9 cm. Water is flowing into the container. When the height of water is h cm, the surface of the water has radius r cm and the volume of water is V cm³.

    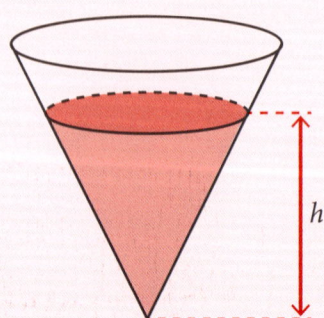

    (a) Show that $V = \dfrac{3\pi h^3}{16}$
    You may use the formula for the volume of a cone: $V = \dfrac{1}{3}\pi r^2 h$.
    (b) Find $\dfrac{dV}{dh}$ in terms of h and π.
    (c) Show that, when $h = 2$ cm, $\dfrac{dV}{dh} = \dfrac{9\pi}{4}$ cm².

11. After a nuclear disaster in the year 3050, the radioactive contamination in a particular region is slowly decreasing because of radioactive decay. However, there is additional fallout each year coming from the atmosphere. Overall, scientists record that the radiation levels Q are falling at a rate that is inversely proportional to the square of the time t, measured in years, since the accident, but are being increased at a rate that is twice the existing level of contamination. Model this situation using a differential equation, involving a positive constant.

12. The rate of change in the population of bacteria in a Petri dish is proportional to the existing number of bacteria, but inversely proportional to the time t. Model this population N using a differential equation.

13. The population P in the land of Calconia varies according to the equation: $P = P_0 e^{kt}$, where t is the number of years after the beginning of 2050, $P_0 = 5$ million and $k = 0.015$.
    (a) Find the population of Calconia at the beginning of 2050 (i.e. when $t = 0$).
    (b) Find the predicted population in 2075.
    (c) If the population continues to grow at this rate, find how long it will take for the population of Calconia to treble, giving your answer to the nearest whole number of years.
    (d) Form a differential equation in $\dfrac{dP}{dt}$.
    (e) Hence find the rate at which the population is growing in the year 2080.

12.3 Solving Differential Equations

In the last section, you learnt how to form a differential equation. These equations involve a rate of change, such as $\frac{dy}{dx}$.

In this section you will learn how to solve certain types of differential equation. The CCEA A2 Mathematics specification also requires that solutions are interpreted in the context of the problem.

> **Note:** The solution of a differential equation is also an equation. For example, the solution of a differential equation involving $\frac{dy}{dx}$ is usually an equation linking y and x. The solution of a differential equation is not a numerical value.

This section will only deal with the solution to some **first order differential equations**, i.e. differential equations involving only $\frac{dy}{dx}$. If you study A-Level Further Mathematics you will learn about solutions to a wider range of first order differential equations and some second order differential equations, which involve $\frac{d^2y}{dx^2}$.

Separation of variables

For those first order differential equations dealt with in this chapter, the key to the solution is a technique called **separation of variables**. $\frac{dy}{dx}$ is treated as a fraction and the equation is re-arranged with dx taken to the other side of the equation. All the terms involving y must stay on the same side as dy; all the terms involving x must be taken to the other side with dx. The equation is then integrated.

> **Note:** The solution of differential equations involves integration, so there will be a constant of integration to find.

Worked Example

5. Find the solution of the differential equation $\frac{dy}{dx} = xy$ given that when $x = 0$, $y = 1$.

   Use separation of variables. Put integral signs in at the same time:

   $$\frac{dy}{dx} = xy$$

   $$\Rightarrow \int \frac{1}{y} dy = \int x \, dx$$

   Integrate both sides, remembering to add the constant on one side:

   $$\ln y = \frac{1}{2}x^2 + c$$

   Calculate the constant.
   When $x = 0$, $y = 1$:

   $$\ln(1) = \frac{1}{2}(0)^2 + c$$

   $$c = 0$$

   $$\therefore \ln y = \frac{1}{2}x^2$$

   So the solution is:

   $$y = e^{\frac{x^2}{2}}$$

Instead of using a constant of integration, the solution of a differential equation can be treated as a definite integral with upper and lower limits. In Exercise 12C, which follows the next worked example, you may choose which method to use for each question.

Worked Example

6. A circular stain has area S cm² at time t seconds. The stain's area is increasing in size according to the differential equation: $\frac{dS}{dt} = \frac{3e^{3t}}{\sqrt{S}}$

   Given that $S = 81$ at time $t = 0$, solve the differential equation to find the time at which $S = 100$. Give your answer to 3 significant figures.

   $$\frac{dS}{dt} = \frac{3e^{3t}}{\sqrt{S}}$$

   Use separation of variables. Put integral signs in at the same time.
   - When $S = 81$, $t = 0$. These are the lower limits.
   - When $S = 100$, $t = T$ (the unknown). These are the upper limits.

   $$\int_{81}^{100} \sqrt{S} \, dS = \int_0^T 3e^{3t} \, dt$$

   Instead of finding a solution involving a constant of integration, we use definite integration:

   $$\Rightarrow \left[\frac{2}{3}S^{\frac{3}{2}}\right]_{81}^{100} = \left[e^{3t}\right]_0^T$$

   $$\frac{2}{3}(1000 - 729) = (e^{3T} - 1)$$

   $$\frac{542}{3} = (e^{3T} - 1)$$

$$\Rightarrow 181.667 = e^{3T}$$
$$\Rightarrow T = \frac{1}{3}\ln 181.667$$
$$T = 1.73 \text{ seconds (3 s.f.)}$$

Exercise 12C

1. Solve the differential equation:
$$\frac{dy}{dx} = xy\cos x, \quad y > 0$$
given that $y = 1$ at $x = 0$.

2. The quantity of a chemical x can be modelled using the differential equation:
$$\frac{dx}{dt} = q(x-3)(2-x)$$
where t is the time, q is a constant and $x = 0$ when $t = 0$. Find the value of q, given that $x = 4$ when $t = 10$.

3. Solve the differential equation:
$$\frac{dy}{dx} = \frac{2x(1+y)}{(1+x^2)}$$
to find y in terms of x, given that $x = 0$ when $y = 0$.

4. Given that when $x = 0$, $\theta = \frac{\pi}{4}$, solve the differential equation:
$$x^2 \frac{dx}{d\theta} = \frac{3}{2\sin^2 \theta}$$

5. (a) Solve the differential equation:
$$\frac{dy}{d\theta} = ky\cos^2\theta$$
given that $\theta = 0$ when $y = 1$. Give your answer in terms of k.
   (b) Given also that $\theta = \frac{\pi}{4}$ when $y = 2$, find the exact value of k.

6. When a snowflake grows inside a cloud, its area A can be modelled by the differential equation:
$$\frac{dA}{dt} = \frac{A^{3/2}}{t^2}, \quad t > 0$$
where t is the time in seconds. Given that the area of the flake is 1 mm^2 at $t = 1$ s:

Exercise 12C...

   (a) Find an expression for A in terms of t for this model.
   (b) Show that, according to this model, the value of A cannot exceed 4 mm^2.

7. On a particular planet, the air pressure P (measured in Pascals) in the atmosphere falls with height h (measured in metres). It can be modelled using the differential equation:
$$\frac{dP}{dh} = -kP$$
where k is a positive constant.
   (a) Solve the differential equation to give an equation linking P and h, involving k and another constant.
   (b) At the planet's surface $P = 70\,000$ Pa. At a height of 500 m, the pressure has fallen to 25 750 Pa. Find the value of both constants.
   (c) Find the pressure at a height of 1 km.

8. At time t seconds the volume of a cube is $V\text{ cm}^3$. The volume is increasing such that:
$$\frac{dV}{dt} = 4V^{\frac{1}{3}}$$
Given that $V = 8$ when $t = 0$, solve the differential equation and find the value of t when $V = 16$.

9. Liquid is flowing into a container at a constant rate of $30\text{ cm}^3/\text{s}$. At time t seconds liquid is leaking from the container at a rate of $\frac{1}{10}V\text{ cm}^3/\text{s}$, where $V\text{ cm}^3$ is the volume of liquid in the container at that time.
   (a) Show that $-10\frac{dV}{dt} = V - 300$
   (b) Given that $V = 1000$ when $t = 0$, find the solution of the differential equation in the form $V = f(t)$.
   (c) Find the limiting value of V as $t \to \infty$. Interpret this answer.

10. (a) Express $\frac{3x-2}{(2x-5)(x-2)}$ in partial fractions.
    (b) Given that $x \geq 3$ find the solution of the differential equation:
$$(2x-5)(x-2)\frac{dy}{dx} = (3x-2)y$$

Exercise 12C...

(c) Given that $y = 11$ at $x = 3$, find the constant of integration and express your solution in the form $y = f(x)$.

11. Water is pouring into a bucket at a constant rate of 30 cm³ s⁻¹ and is leaking out at a rate proportional to the volume of water already in the bucket.
    (a) Explain why, at time t seconds, the volume V cm³ of water in the bucket satisfies the differential equation:
    $$\frac{dV}{dt} = 30 - kV$$
    where k is a positive constant.

    The bucket is initially empty.
    (b) By solving the differential equation, show that $V = A + Be^{-kt}$ giving the values of A and B in terms of k.
    (c) Interpret your result by describing how the volume of water changes over time.

12. A bicycle tyre is being inflated. The rate of increase of the volume V of air in the tyre is inversely proportional to the square root of the volume. Initially, the volume of the air in the tyre is 81 cm³. Twenty seconds later, the volume is 225 cm³.
    (a) Model this situation using a differential equation, and then solve it to express V in terms of the time t.
    (b) State one limitation with this model.

13. A shower pumps water at a rate of 10 cm³ per second. The plughole is partially blocked and water begins to collect in the base tray. The water collecting in the tray drains through the plughole at a rate that is proportional to the volume of water already in the tray. The amount of water V in the tray can therefore be modelled by the differential equation:
    $$\frac{dV}{dt} = 10 - kV$$
    (a) Given that the shower tray is initially empty, show that $V = \frac{10}{k}(1 - e^{-kt})$
    (b) Giving your answer in terms of k, what value does V never exceed?

Exercise 12C...

(c) The dimensions of the shower tray are 50 cm by 50 cm by 10 cm. What value of k would allow the shower tray to completely fill, but not overflow?
(d) State one modelling assumption or simplification you have made.

12.4 Summary

A **differential equation** is an equation that involves a derivative.

You may be given information about the rate of change of a quantity. From this you can form a differential equation. Alternatively, you may have to form a differential equation from a standard equation.

You should also understand how to solve a first order differential equation by separating variables and integrating.

Be prepared to interpret your solution in the context of the problem.

Chapter 13
Numerical Methods

13.1 Introduction

Many real-life equations cannot be solved algebraically. In these cases, a numerical method can be used to approximate the solution. Using some methods, the approximation can be improved by **iteration**.

Key words
- **Root**: A solution to an equation of the form $f(x) = 0$.
- **Interval**: A range of values within which a solution (or root) lies.
- **Iteration**: The process of repeatedly improving an approximation to a solution.
- **Continuous**: A function whose graph is a single line without breaks from left to right

Before you start
You should know:
- How to re-arrange an algebraic equation.
- How to solve equations and simultaneous equations using graphical methods.

Worked Examples

1. Re-arrange the following equation to obtain $f(x) = 0$:
   $x - 1 = (x + 2)^2$

   This can be done in more than one way.

   The simplest way is to subtract $(x - 1)$ from both sides of the equation:
   $(x + 2)^2 - x + 1 = 0$

   Alternatively, take the square root of both sides:
   $\sqrt{x - 1} = (x + 2)$
   Then:
   $(x + 2) - \sqrt{x - 1} = 0$

2. (a) Plot the two curves
   $y = -x^2 + 3$ and $y = \dfrac{1}{x^2}$
   using values of x between -3 and 3.

   (b) Using your graph, state how many solutions there are to the equation $x^4 - 3x^2 + 1 = 0$

(a) Graph:

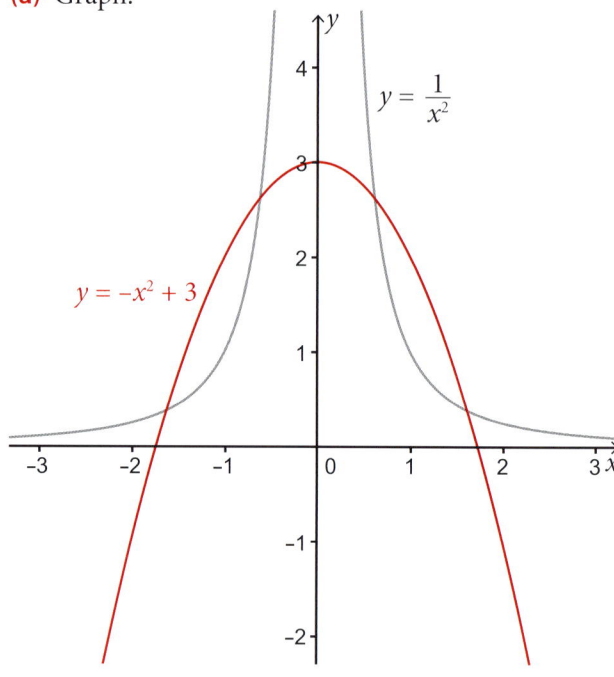

(b) The two curves intersect in 4 places, so there are 4 values of x that satisfy $\dfrac{1}{x^2} = -x^2 + 3$

Beginning with:
$\dfrac{1}{x^2} = -x^2 + 3$

Multiply both sides by x^2:
$1 = -x^4 + 3x^2$

Bring all terms to LHS:
$x^4 - 3x^2 + 1 = 0$

Hence, all intersection points of the above curves provide solutions to this equation. There are four solutions.

What you will learn
In this chapter you will learn how to:

- Use graphical methods to solve equations.
- Find roots to the equation $f(x) = 0$.
- Use iterative methods to solve equations.
- Determine whether an iterative method converges or diverges.

- Use the trapezium rule to find an approximation to a definite integral.

In the real world...

If anybody knows about numerical solutions, it is the Chudnovsky Brothers.

In 1987, the Chudnovsky brothers developed an algorithm for computing π.

They used this algorithm several times to calculate π to the largest number of decimal places. In the early 1990s they calculated π to two billion digits on a supercomputer called M-Zero, which they built themselves in their flat in New York.

Today, the Chudnovsky Brothers' algorithm is used by the software package Mathematica to calculate π, and by many others who have achieved world records in π calculation.

Exercise 13A (Revision)

1. Re-arrange the following equations to obtain $f(x) = 0$. There may be more than one solution.
   (a) $x^2 = x + 1$
   (b) $x = \sqrt{2x - 3}$
   (c) $x = \sqrt[3]{1 - \dfrac{x}{2}}$

2. Plot the graph of $y = x^2 + 2x - 2$, using x values between -4 and 2. Use your graph to find approximate solutions to $y = x^2 + 2x - 2$.

3. (a) Sketch these two curves on the same graph, using values of x between -2 and 2.
   $$y = x^2 + 2 \qquad y = \dfrac{1}{x}$$
   (b) Hence state how many solutions exist to the equation $x^3 + 2x - 1 = 0$.

13.2 Location of Roots

In some cases where an equation cannot be solved algebraically a graphical method can be used to find the solution or solutions. The solutions are obtained by finding the x-coordinates of the intersection points of two curves.

You will often see the notation $[a, b]$ to denote the **interval** between a and b.

Worked Examples

3. State the equations of two curves that could be sketched to find the number of solutions to $e^x - x - 5 = 0$

   $e^x - x - 5 = 0$
   $\Rightarrow e^x = x + 5$

   The number of solutions could be found by sketching the curves $y = e^x$ and the straight line $y = x + 5$.

4. (a) Sketch the curves $y = e^x$ and $y = -x$ on the same diagram.
   (b) Hence state the number of solutions to the equation $f(x) = 0$ where $f(x) = e^x + x$
   (c) By finding the value of $f(x)$ for suitable values of x, verify that the solution to this equation is $x = -0.57$ correct to 2 decimal places.

   (a) Sketch:

   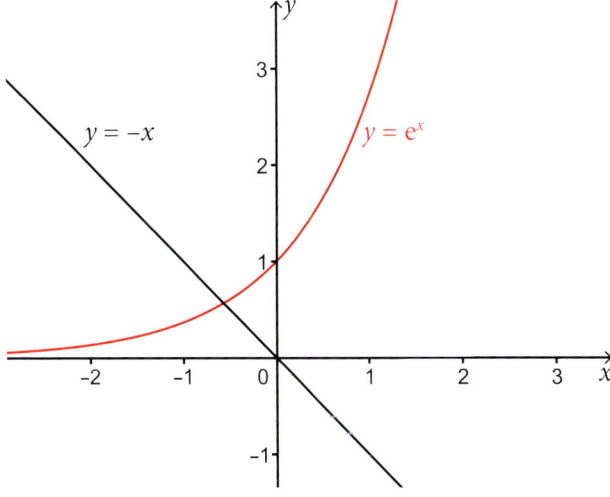

   (b) From the sketch, we can see there is only one solution to $e^x = -x$

   Therefore, there is also one solution to $e^x + x = 0$

   (c) When $x = -0.575$, $f(x) = -0.0123$ (3 s.f.)
   When $x = -0.565$, $f(x) = 0.00336$ (3 s.f.)

   There is a change of sign and $f(x)$ is a **continuous function**. (See the note on continuous functions below.)

   Hence the solution lies in the interval $[-0.575, -0.565]$.

   To 2 decimal places $x = -0.57$.

   Note: The following graphs may be helpful, but you would not be expected to draw them.

The first graph shows the function $y = f(x)$, where $f(x) = e^x + x$.

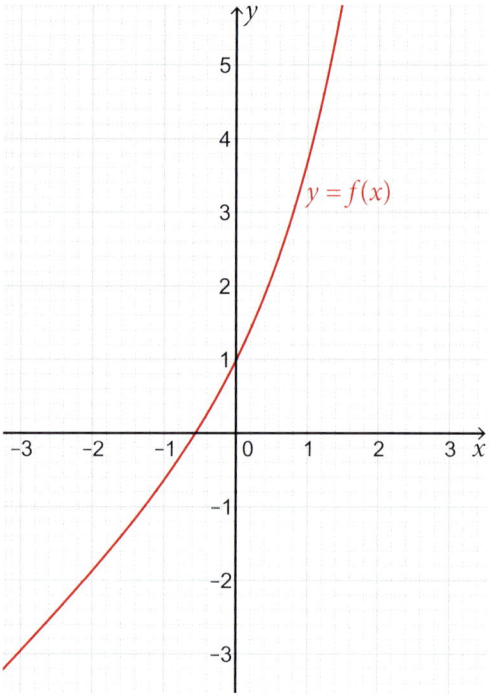

The next diagram shows the curve as we zoom in to the region where it crosses the x-axis. It shows that $f(-0.575) < 0$ and $f(-0.565) > 0$. This implies that the curve must cross the x-axis in the interval $[-0.575, -0.565]$. In turn, this implies that the equation $f(x) = 0$ has a root $x = -0.57$ to 2 d.p.

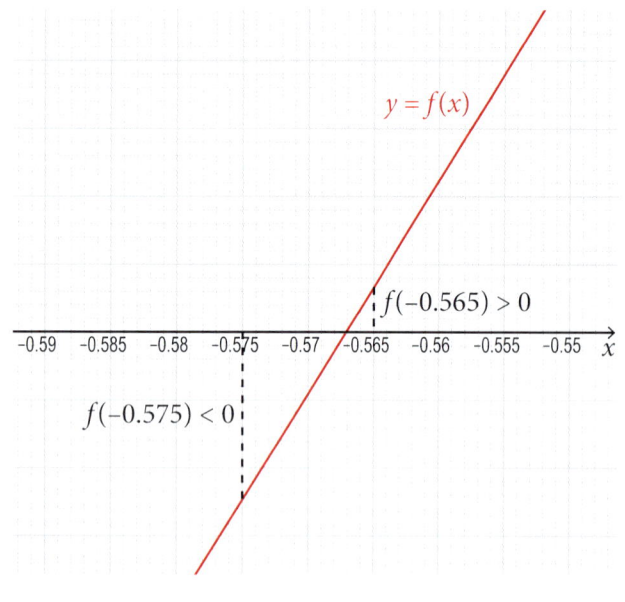

Note: You must state that the function is continuous, but you do not need to prove this is true. If the function $f(x)$ in Worked Example 3 were not a continuous function, it could approach an asymptote in the interval $[0.575, 0.565]$ and avoid passing through the x-axis. The diagrams below demonstrate this concept.

- A **continuous** function.

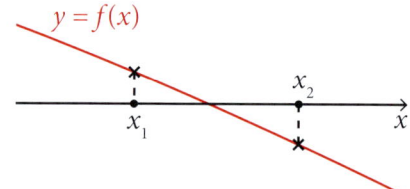

$f(x_1) > 0$ and $f(x_2) < 0$. There is a sign change. A root must exist in the interval $[x_1, x_2]$.

- A **discontinuous** function.

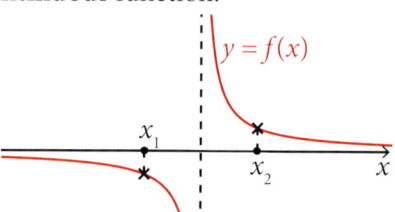

$f(x_1) < 0$ and $f(x_2) > 0$. There is a sign change, but there is no root in the interval $[x_1, x_2]$.

The diagrams show that we must consider **continuity**. A sign change in the value of a function **and** the function being continuous implies the existence of a root. Without a consideration of continuity, the argument is not complete.

Worked Examples

5. **(a)** By sketching two suitable functions on the same diagram, determine the number of solutions to the equation $\cos x - 2x = 0$ (with x measured in radians).
   (b) Verify that the solution α to this equation lies in the interval $[0.445, 0.455]$.
   (c) Hence state the value of α correct to 2 decimal places.

(a) $\cos x - 2x = 0$
$\Rightarrow \cos x = 2x$

Hence sketch the curves $y = 2x$ and $y = \cos x$ (with x measured in radians).

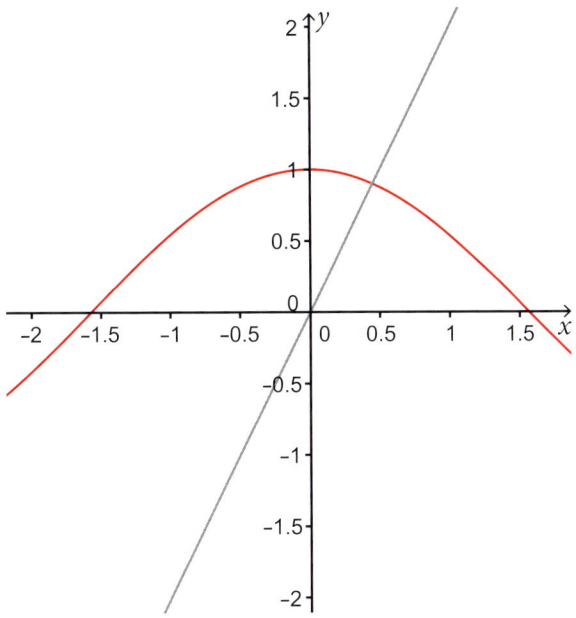

The sketch shows that there is only one solution to $\cos x = 2x$ and hence one solution to $\cos x - 2x = 0$.

(b) Consider $f(x) = \cos x - 2x$.

We are interested in the solution to $f(x) = 0$.

$f(0.445) = 0.0126$ (3 s.f.)

$f(0.455) = -0.0117$ (3 s.f.)

There is a change of sign and $f(x)$ is a continuous function. Therefore, the solution α lies within the interval $[0.445, 0.455]$.

(c) To two decimal places, $\alpha = 0.45$.

6. Show that there is a solution α to the equation
$x + 1 = 3\sqrt{x}$ \quad (1)
within the interval $[6.5, 7]$.

Consider $f(x) = x + 1 - 3\sqrt{x}$.

Solving equation (1) is equivalent to finding a root to $f(x) = 0$.

We must show that the value of $f(x)$ changes its sign between $x = 6.5$ and $x = 7$.

$f(6.5) = 6.5 + 1 - 3\sqrt{6.5} = -0.15$ (2 d.p.)

$f(7) = 7 + 1 - 3\sqrt{7} = 0.06$ (2 d.p.)

$f(x)$ changes its sign between $x = 6.5$ and $x = 7$. The function is continuous.

Hence a solution α exists within the interval $[6.5, 7]$.

Exercise 13B

1. Sketch the following pairs of curves on the same diagram. Hence determine how many intersection points there are.

   (a) $y = x$; $y = \dfrac{1}{x}$

   (b) $y = e^x$; $y = 1 - x$

   (c) $y = e^{-x}$; $y = 2 + x$

   (d) $y = \cos x$; $y = x$

   (e) $y = \ln x$; $y = -x$

   (f) $y = x^2 - 1$; $y = x$

   (g) $y = \sin x$; $y = -x$

   (h) $y = x^2$; $y = x^3$

   (i) $y = -x^2$; $y = x$

   (j) $y = x^3 + 1$; $y = x$

   (k) $y = (x-1)^2$; $y = 2$

   (l) $y = e^x + 2$; $y = x$

   (m) $y = \dfrac{1}{x}$; $y = x^2$

   (n) $y = \dfrac{1}{x^2}$; $y = -x^2$

2. By drawing two suitable sketches on the same diagram, determine how many solutions exist to the following equations.

   (a) $x^3 + x - 1 = 0$

   (b) $e^x + 7x + 1 = 0$

   (c) $\cos x - \sin x = 0$ for $-\pi \leq x \leq \pi$

   (d) $-x^3 - \dfrac{1}{x} - 1 = 0$

   (e) $\cos x + 1 - x^3 = 0$

   (f) $\dfrac{1}{x^2} - \dfrac{1}{x} - 1 = 0$ for $x < 0$

   (g) $1 + x^2 + e^{-x} = 0$

   (h) $\cos x - 1 - 2x = 0$

   (i) $e^{-x} - 2 + x^2 = 0$

   (j) $\ln x - \sin x + 1 = 0$

3. (a) Sketch the graphs of $y = e^x$ and $y = 2 - 2x$ on the same diagram.

   (b) Hence find the number of solutions of the equation $e^x + 2x - 2 = 0$.

   (c) Verify that the solution to $e^x + 2x - 2 = 0$ lies in the interval $[0.25, 0.35]$.

   (d) Hence find the solution correct to 1 decimal place.

Exercise 13B...

4. (a) Sketch the graphs of $y = x^3 + 1$ and $y = -2 - \dfrac{x}{2}$ on the same diagram.
   (b) Show that the solution to $x^3 + \dfrac{x}{2} + 3 = 0$ lies in the interval $[-1.35, -1.25]$.
   (c) Find the solution to $x^3 + \dfrac{x}{2} + 3 = 0$ to 2 decimal places.

5. (a) Sketch the graphs of $y = x^2 + 1$ and $y = \dfrac{1}{x}$ on the same diagram.
   (b) Using your sketch, determine how many roots exist to the equation $f(x) = 0$, where $f(x) = x^2 - \dfrac{1}{x} + 1$.
   (c) Show that a root to $f(x) = 0$ lies in the interval $[0.5, 1]$.
   (d) By evaluating $f(x)$ for two suitable values of x, find the root correct to 1 decimal place.

6. The function f is defined such that $f(x) = x^4 - 32x - 128$.
   By calculating the value of $f(x)$ at appropriate values of x, show that there is a root of $f(x) = 0$ in the interval $[-3, -2]$.

7. Show that the equation $\sin x = x^2 - 2$ has two solutions, one in the interval $[-1.5, -1]$, the other in the interval $[1.5, 2]$.

8. The equation $e^{-x} - \ln x + 1 = 0$ has a solution within the interval $[p, q]$ where p and q are consecutive integers. Find the value of p.

9. The equation:
   $e^x - 10 \sin x = 10$ (1)
   has an infinite number of solutions. Only one of these solutions, α, is a positive value.
   (a) Sketch two graphs that will give you a first estimate of α.
   (b) Re-arrange equation (1) to the form $f(x) = 0$.
   (c) By evaluating $f(x)$ for the appropriate values of x, show that α lies within the interval $[2.5, 3]$.
   (d) By evaluating $f(x)$ for two suitable values of x, find the value of α correct to 1 decimal place.

Exercise 13B...

10. Consider the function $f(x) = x^3 - 2x^2 + 2x + 1$. There is one root, α, of the equation $f(x) = 0$.
    (a) Verify that α lies in the interval $[-1, 0]$.
    (b) By evaluating $f(x)$ for suitable values of x, find α correct to one decimal place.

11. The function f is given by $f(x) = e^{x-9} - 9$. Show that the equation $f(x) = x$ has a solution in the interval $[12, 13]$.

13.3 Iterative Methods

There is a family of numerical methods for solving equations known as **iterative methods**. These use a first approximation to a solution, then improve this approximation by repeatedly applying some formula.

Recurrence relations of the form $x_{n+1} = f(x_n)$

In this method, the first step in the process is to re-arrange our equation to obtain:

$x = f(x)$

An initial approximation x_0 is taken for the solution of the equation.

Each successive approximation is then obtained using the iterative formula:

$x_{n+1} = f(x_n)$

> **Note:** There may be more than one possible iterative formula.

We denote our first approximation x_0, the second x_1 and so on.

Worked Example

7. Find the solution α of the equation $\sin x = \dfrac{x}{2}$ which lies between 1.5 and 2. Use $x_0 = 1.6$ as a first approximation. Give α correct to 1 decimal place.

Re-arrange the equation to give:
$x = 2 \sin x$
$x_0 = 1.6$
$x_1 = 2 \sin(1.6) = 1.99915$

This is our second approximation. We use this value in the formula to obtain a third approximation.

$x_2 = 2\sin(1.99915) = 1.81930$
$x_3 = 2\sin(1.81930) = 1.93856$
$x_4 = 2\sin(1.93856) = 1.86627$
$x_5 = 2\sin(1.86627) = 1.91333$

The approximations are converging to 1.9 (1 decimal place). Therefore:
$\alpha = 1.9$ (1 decimal place)

Why does this work? Here is a graphical representation.

The diagram shows the solution α, which is the x-coordinate of the intersection point between the graphs $y = x$ and $y = 2\sin x$.

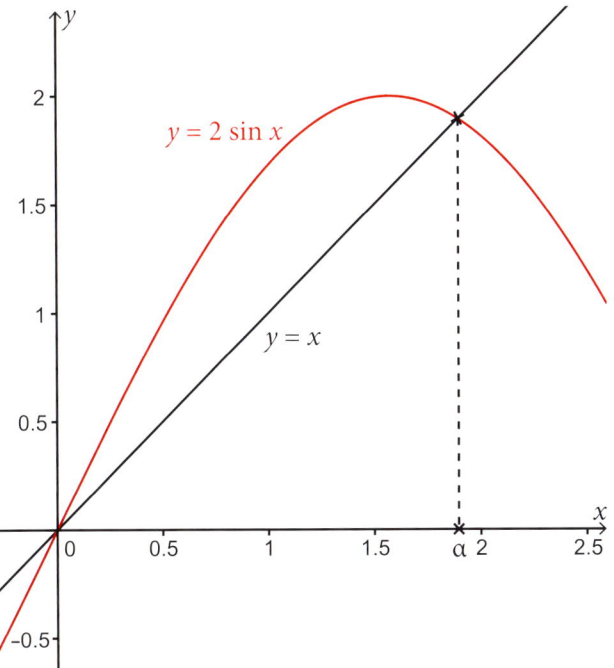

Now let us zoom in on the solution.

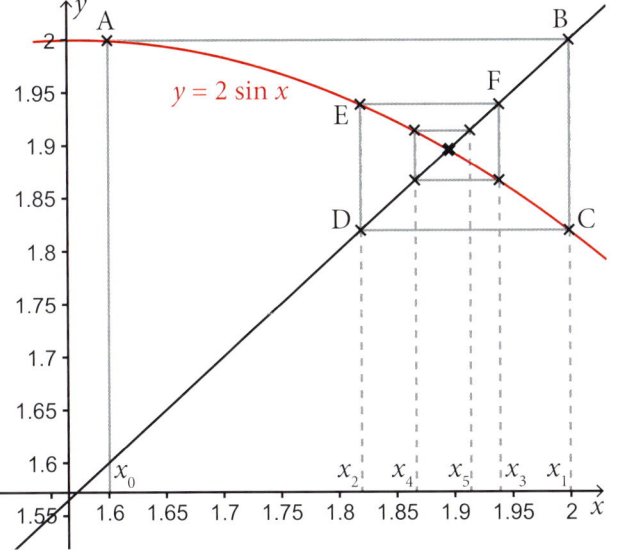

- Beginning with x_0, we find $f(x_0)$ (point A).
- We use $f(x_0)$ as our x_1. Graphically, this is the equivalent of following the horizontal AB to the line $y = x$.
- Then we find $f(x_1)$ (point C).
- Again, follow the horizontal to the line $y = x$ (point D) to obtain x_2.
- Find $f(x_2)$ (point E).
- Follow the horizontal to point F, which gives x_3.

This process continues until we have reached the desired degree of accuracy.

Note: Work to more decimal places than you need. In Worked Example 7, we worked to 5 decimal places, although the required degree of accuracy was only 1 decimal place.

Calculator tip

Make use of the ANS key on your calculator to perform iterations quickly.

1. Enter the value of x_0 and press the = key.
2. Enter the formula using ANS in place of x. In Worked Example 7 above, enter 2 sin(ANS). Press the = key. This gives your next approximation, x_1. Write it down to the required accuracy.
3. Press = again. The calculator evaluates the same formula, but with the new value of ANS. This gives x_2. Write it down.
4. Press = as many times as required to find x_3, x_4, etc.

In this way, you can ensure you only enter the formula once and only need to type the first approximation, x_0.

As mentioned above, there is often more than one way to re-arrange the original equation as $x = f(x)$. You may find that some formulae do not converge to a solution.

Worked Example

8. By using a formula of the form $x = f(x)$, find the only root α of the equation $x^3 - 2x - 1 = 0$. Use a first approximation to α of 1.7. Give your answer to 2 decimal places.

There are several ways to obtain $x = f(x)$. We will investigate two of them.

Method 1

$$x^3 - 2x - 1 = 0$$
$$\Rightarrow x^3 = 1 + 2x$$
$$\Rightarrow x = \sqrt[3]{1 + 2x}$$

$x_0 = 1.7$

$x_1 = \sqrt[3]{1 + 2(1.7)} = 1.63864$

$x_2 = \sqrt[3]{1 + 2(1.63864)} = 1.62326$

$x_3 = \sqrt[3]{1 + 2(1.62326)} = 1.61936$

$x_4 = \sqrt[3]{1 + 2(1.61936)} = 1.61837$

$x_5 = \sqrt[3]{1 + 2(1.61837)} = 1.61812$

$\alpha = 1.62$ (2 d.p.)

This method is **convergent**.

Method 2

$x^3 - 2x - 1 = 0$

$\Rightarrow x = \dfrac{x^3 - 1}{2}$

$x_0 = 1.7$

$x_1 = \dfrac{1.7^3 - 1}{2} = 1.95650$

$x_2 = \dfrac{(1.95650)^3 - 1}{2} = 3.24464$

$x_3 = \dfrac{(3.24464)^3 - 1}{2} = 16.57921$

$x_4 = \dfrac{(16.57921)^3 - 1}{2} = 2278.06558$

This method is **divergent**. The root cannot be found.

As you have seen, different iterative formulae can give different results. Some formulae are convergent upon a solution. Others diverge, and it is not possible to locate a solution using them.

Remember that many equations, including quadratic and cubic equations, have more than one solution. You may have to use different iterative formulae to find the different solutions to an equation.

Also, the process is dependent on the first approximation. Some first approximations will yield a divergent iteration; using other values may allow the same formula to converge upon a solution.

Newton-Raphson method

The Newton-Raphson method is an iterative method for finding roots of an equation $f(x) = 0$. It uses the formula:

$$x_{n+1} = x_n - \dfrac{f(x_n)}{f'(x_n)}$$

Note: This formula is provided in the formula booklet.

It is necessary to differentiate the function to obtain $f'(x)$.

It is important to remember you are finding a root, so if necessary you must first re-arrange to give an equation of the form $f(x) = 0$.

As with other iterative methods, there are cases in which the Newton-Raphson method does not converge upon a root.

Worked Examples

9. α is the positive root of the equation: $x^2 - 2 = 0$
   Using $x_0 = 1$ as a first approximation, use two iterations of the Newton-Raphson method to improve this approximation.

   $f(x) = x^2 - 2$

   $f'(x) = 2x$

   $x_0 = 1$

   $f(x_0) = 1^2 - 2 = -1$

   $f'(x_0) = 2(1) = 2$

   $x_1 = x_0 - \dfrac{f(x_0)}{f'(x_0)}$

   $= 1 - \dfrac{-1}{2} = 1.5$

   $f(x_1) = 1.5^2 - 2 = 0.25$

   $f'(x_1) = 2(1.5) = 3$

   $x_2 = x_1 - \dfrac{f(x_1)}{f'(x_1)}$

   $= 1.5 - \dfrac{0.25}{3}$

   $= 1.41667$

   Note: The Newton-Raphson method often provides very rapid convergence. In this example, it has taken only two iterations to obtain a value that is within 0.2% of the true value.

10. The equation $f(x) = 2\cos x - x^2$ has a root α.
    (a) Show that α lies between 1 and 1.1.
    (b) Using 1 as a first approximation, find α correct to 2 decimal places.

    Note: Because the question asks us to find a root, we are finding a solution to the equation $f(x) = 0$.

    (a) $f(x) = 2\cos x - x^2$

    $f(1) = 2\cos(1) - (1)^2 = 0.0806$

    $f(1.1) = 2\cos(1.1) - (1.1)^2 = -0.3028$

Sign change and function continuous. Hence α lies between 1 and 1.1.

(b) $f'(x) = -2\sin x - 2x$

$x_0 = 1$

$x_1 = x_0 - \dfrac{f(x_0)}{f'(x_0)}$

$= 1 - \dfrac{2\cos(1) - (1)^2}{-2\sin(1) - 2(1)}$

$= 1.02189$

$x_2 = x_1 - \dfrac{f(x_1)}{f'(x_1)}$

$= 1.02189 - \dfrac{2\cos(1.02189) - (1.02189)^2}{-2\sin(1.02189) - 2(1.02189)}$

$= 1.02169$

$\alpha = 1.02$ (2 d.p.)

Calculator tip

Using the Newton-Raphson method, as with the previous iterative method, it is possible to reduce your calculator work significantly using the ANS key.

First enter the first approximation and press the = key.

Then enter the formula. In Worked Example 10 it would be:

$\text{ANS} - \dfrac{2\cos(\text{ANS}) - (\text{ANS})^2}{-2\sin(\text{ANS}) - 2(\text{ANS})}$

Pressing = the required number of times will perform each successive iteration.

Exercise 13C

1. Re-arrange the following equations to obtain two different formulae of the form $x = f(x)$. In some cases there may be more than two answers.

   (a) $x^2 - x - 1 = 0$ (b) $2x^2 + 5x - 1 = 0$
   (c) $\cos x + \sin x = 0$ (d) $e^x - 2x = 0$
   (e) $\ln x + \dfrac{1}{x} + 2 = 0$ (f) $5x^3 + x^2 - 1 = 0$
   (g) $\dfrac{1}{x} = \dfrac{1}{x^2}$ (h) $\cos 2x + e^{2x} = 1$
   (i) $\sin^2 x = 1 - 2x^2$ (j) $\sqrt{x+1} = \sin^2 x$

2. The diagram shows the curve $y = f(x)$, where $f(x) = \cos x + x^2 - 2$. It shows that there are two roots to the equation $f(x) = 0$.

Exercise 13C...

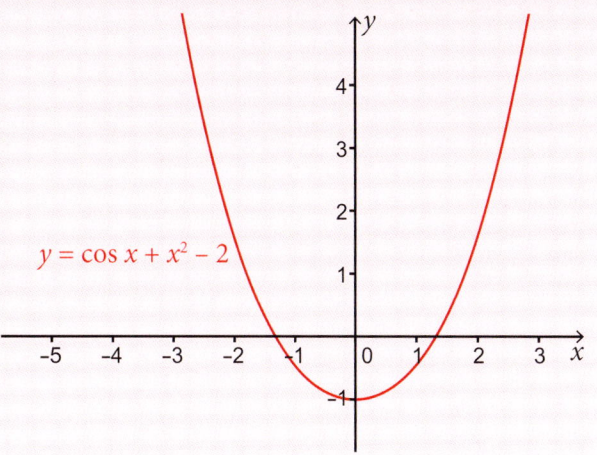

   (a) Verify that the positive root α of the equation $f(x) = 0$ lies in the interval $[1, 2]$.
   (b) Show that an iterative formula:

   $x_{n+1} = \sqrt{2 - \cos x_n}$

   can be used to investigate the roots of $f(x)$.
   (c) Using a first approximation of 1, use three iterations of this formula to find α to 1 decimal place.

3. The diagram shows a part of the curve $y = g(x)$, where $g(x) = e^{-x} - 2x + 1$.

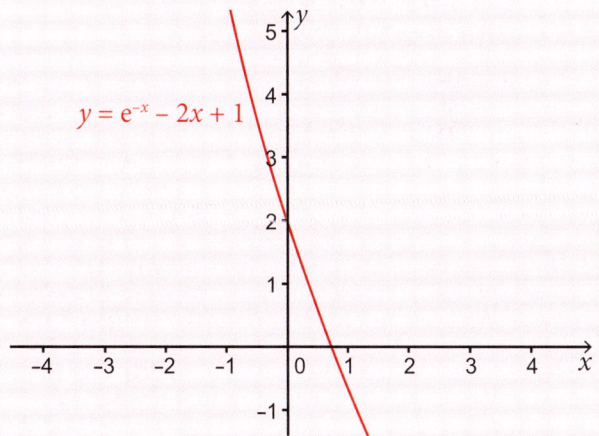

   (a) Verify that the root α of the equation $g(x) = 0$ lies in the interval $[0, 1]$.
   (b) Show that an iterative formula:

   $x_{n+1} = \dfrac{e^{-x_n} + 1}{2}$

   can be used to investigate the root of $g(x)$.
   (c) Using three iterations of this formula, find α to 2 decimal places. Use a first approximation of 1.

Exercise 13C...

4. (a) Sketch the graphs of $y = \cos x$ and $y = -3x - 1$ on the same diagram, showing that there is just one point of intersection. Label the x-coordinate of this point α.
   (b) By considering the function $f(x) = \cos x + 3x + 1$, show that α lies in the interval $[-1, 0]$.
   (c) Show also that α is a solution to the equation $x = -\dfrac{1}{3}(1 + \cos x)$.
   (d) Using the result from part (c) as an iterative formula, perform three iterations to show that $\alpha \approx -0.61$. Use $x_0 = -0.5$ as a first approximation.
   (e) By calculating the value of $f(x)$ for two appropriate values of x, show that $\alpha = -0.61$ correct to 2 decimal places.

5. Consider the function $f(x) = x^3 + 2x + 1$.
   (a) By investigating the value of $f(x)$ where $x = -0.5$ and $x = -0.4$ verify that there is a root to the equation $f(x) = 0$ within the interval $[-0.5, -0.4]$.
   (b) Use two iterations of the Newton-Raphson method to find this root correct to 2 decimal places, using -0.5 as a first approximation.

6. The diagram shows the two curves $y = e^{\frac{x}{2}}$ and $y = (x + 1)^2$ with two points of intersection A and B (0, 1).

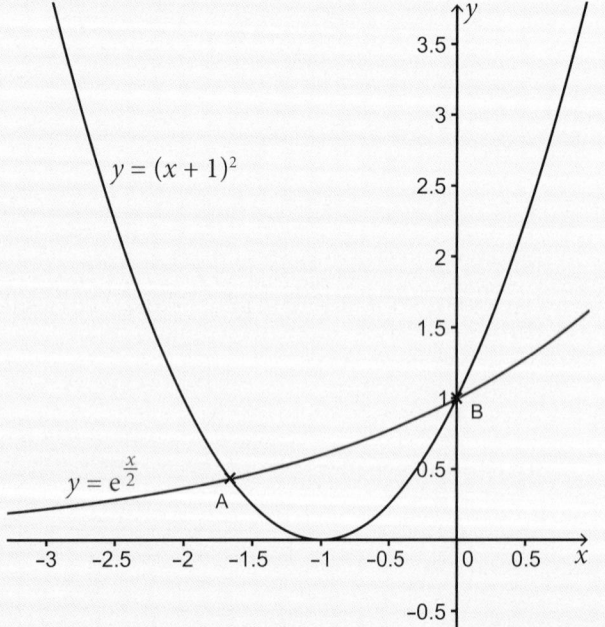

Exercise 13C...

(a) Show that the x-coordinates of the intersection points of these two curves are the solutions of the equation $f(x) = 0$ where $f(x) = e^{\frac{x}{2}} - (x + 1)^2$.
(b) Verify that the x-coordinate of point A lies in the interval $[-2, -1.5]$.
(c) Hence find the x-coordinate of point A using two iterations of the Newton-Raphson method, with a first approximation $x_0 = -1.5$. Give your answer to 2 decimal places.

7. (a) Sketch the two curves $y = \ln x$ and $y = 9 - x^2$ on the same diagram.
   (b) Show that there is a solution to the equation $\ln x = 9 - x^2$ within the interval $[2.5, 3]$.
   (c) Using $x = 3$ as a first approximation, use two iterations of the Newton-Raphson method to obtain an approximation to the solution of the equation $\ln x - 9 + x^2 = 0$, giving your answer to 3 decimal places.

8. The diagram shows a sketch of the two curves $y = \sin x$ and $y = 1 - x^3$.

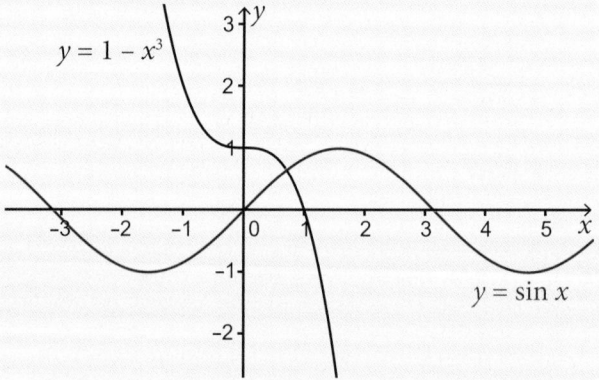

(a) Show that the point of intersection can be found by solving the equation:
$$\sin x + x^3 - 1 = 0$$
(b) Verify that the root α of this equation lies in the interval $[0.5, 1]$.
(c) With $x_0 = 0.5$ as a first approximation to α, use two iterations of the Newton-Raphson method to find approximations x_1 and x_2. Give your answers to 2 significant figures.

Exercise 13C...

9. The function f is defined such that:
$f(x) = 0.24x - 2 + 3\sin\sqrt{x}$
The equation $f(x) = 0$ has a root α between $x = 11.2$ and $x = 11.7$. Taking 11 as a first approximation to α, use the Newton-Raphson method on $f(x)$ once to obtain a second approximation to α. Give your answer to 2 decimal places.

10. Given: $f(x) = \ln x - 2 - \dfrac{2}{x}$
    (a) Show that the root α of the equation $f(x) = 0$ lies in the interval $[9, 10]$.
    (b) Taking 9.2 as your starting value, apply the Newton-Raphson procedure once to $f(x)$ to find a second approximation to α, giving your answer to 4 decimal places.

11. The function $f(x)$ is defined such that:
$f(x) = x^3 + x - 5$
The equation $f(x) = 0$ has a root α between 1 and 2.
    (a) Show that the gradient of the curve $y = f(x)$ is always positive.
    (b) Hence state the number of roots of the equation $f(x) = 0$.
    (c) By taking 1.6 as your first approximation to α, apply the Newton-Raphson procedure once to $f(x)$ to obtain a second approximation to α. Give your answer to 3 significant figures.
    (d) Show that your answer to part (c) gives the value of α correct to 3 significant figures.

12. The function f is defined such that:
$f(x) = e^{2x} - 12x - 4$
The equation $f(x) = 0$ has exactly one root α between 1.5 and 1.7.
    (a) Taking 1.6 as a first approximation to α apply the Newton-Raphson procedure once to $f(x) = 0$ to find a second approximation, giving your answer to 3 significant figures.
    (b) Show that your answer is the value of α correct to 3 significant figures.

13. The function f is defined such that:
$f(x) = \ln x + x - 7$
    (a) Find $f(5)$ and $f(5.5)$, each to 4 decimal places, and show that the root α of the equation $f(x) = 0$ satisfies $5 < \alpha < 5.5$.

Exercise 13C...

   (b) Taking 5.25 as your starting value, apply the Newton-Raphson procedure once to $f(x)$ to find a second approximation to α, giving your answer to 3 decimal places.
   (c) Show that your answer in part (b) gives α correct to 3 decimal places.

13.4 The Trapezium Rule

Sometimes you may need to find the area under a curve, but it is not possible to integrate the function.

There are various techniques to find an approximation of the area under a curve. In this section we introduce the **trapezium rule**. The area is divided into **strips** or **intervals**, with each strip the shape of a trapezium, as shown in the following diagram. The combined area of the trapezia is approximately equal to the area under the curve.

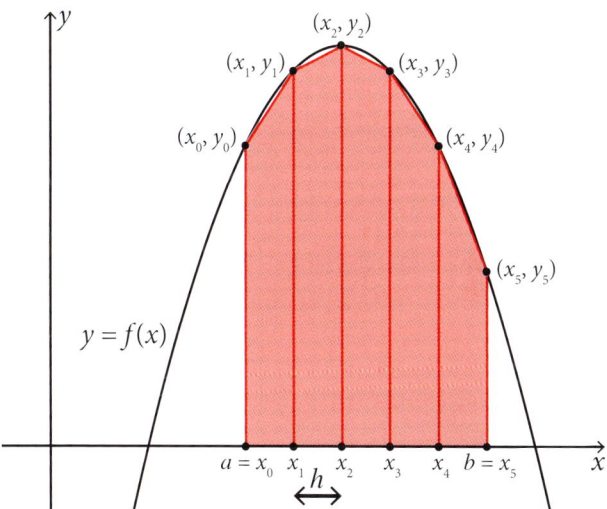

This diagram shows how we would approximate the integral:

$$\int_a^b f(x)\,dx$$

using 5 strips.

The trapezium rule

$$\int_a^b f(x)\,dx \approx \tfrac{1}{2}h[y_0 + 2(y_1 + \cdots + y_{n-1}) + y_n]$$

where $y_0, \ldots, y_n$ are the **ordinates** (y-values) and h is the width of each strip.

$h = \dfrac{b-a}{n}$ where n is the number of strips.

Notice that, in the example above, there are 5 strips (or intervals), but 6 ordinates. A question may specify the number of strips or the number of ordinates. The number of ordinates is always one more than the number of strips.

Proof of the trapezium rule

> **Note:** At the time of publication, the CCEA specification does not require you to know this proof.

The area of a trapezium is $\frac{1}{2}(a+b)h$ where a and b are the lengths of the parallel sides and h is the distance between them.

The area of the first trapezium is $\frac{1}{2}(y_1 + y_0)h$.

The area of the second trapezium is $\frac{1}{2}(y_2 + y_1)h$.

...

The area of the last trapezium is $\frac{1}{2}(y_n + y_{n-1})h$.

Adding all the trapezia to approximate the area, we get:

$$A \approx \frac{1}{2}(y_0 + y_1)h + \frac{1}{2}(y_1 + y_2)h + \cdots$$
$$+ \frac{1}{2}(y_{n-2} + y_{n-1})h + \frac{1}{2}(y_{n-1} + y_n)h$$

Factorising, by taking $\frac{1}{2}h$ outside brackets:

$$A \approx \frac{1}{2}h[(y_0 + y_1) + (y_1 + y_2) + \cdots + (y_{n-2} + y_{n-1})$$
$$+ (y_{n-1} + y_n)]$$

Notice that y_0 and y_n only appear once in the summation. All other y-values appear twice. Therefore:

$$A \approx \frac{1}{2}h[y_0 + 2(y_1 + \cdots + y_{n-1}) + y_n]$$

Worked Example

11. Use the trapezium rule with 5 strips to estimate:

$$\int_1^6 \frac{x}{1+x^2} \, dx$$

Use 5 decimal places where appropriate in your working and give your answer to 3 significant figures.

$a = 1$ and $b = 6$.

The width of each strip h is found using:

$$h = \frac{b-a}{n}$$
$$= \frac{6-1}{5} = 1$$

Five strips means 6 ordinates. The x values to use are 1, 2, 3, 4, 5 and 6. We calculate the ordinates:

x	1	2	3	4	5	6
$y = \frac{x}{1+x^2}$	0.5	0.4	0.3	0.23529	0.19231	0.16216

$$A \approx \frac{1}{2}h[y_0 + 2(y_1 + \cdots + y_{n-1}) + y_n]$$

$$A \approx \frac{1}{2}(1)[0.5 + 2(0.4 + 0.3 + 0.23529 + 0.19231) + 0.16216]$$

$A \approx 1.458683$

$A \approx 1.46$ (3 s.f.)

(The true area is 1.45889 to 6 s.f.)

Generally, the greater the number of strips, the better the approximation.

Exercise 13D

1. **(a)** Using the trapezium rule, find an approximation to the area bounded by the x-axis, the curve $y = 3x^2$ and the straight lines $x = 4$ and $x = 7$. Use 3 intervals (i.e. 4 ordinates).
   (b) Find the exact area using integration.

2. The diagram shows a part of the curve:
$$y = \frac{x}{(1+x)^2}$$

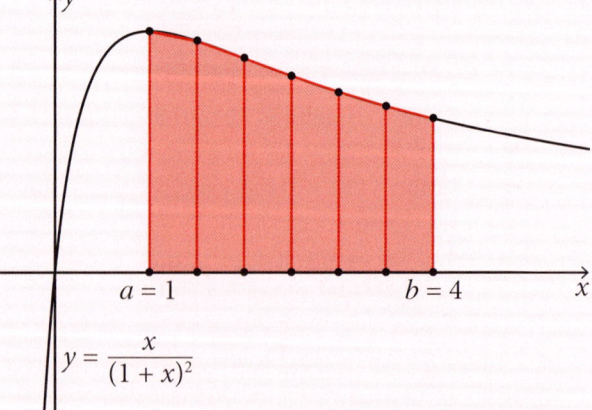

(a) Copy and complete the table below, to find the y-values associated with the x-values given. Give your answers to 5 decimal places where appropriate.

x	1	1.5	2	2.5	3	3.5	4
$y = \frac{x}{(1+x)^2}$							

Exercise 13D...

(b) Using the trapezium rule with 6 strips, find an approximation to: $\int_1^4 \dfrac{x}{(1+x)^2}\,dx$

3. Using the trapezium rule with 4 strips, find an approximation for the area under the curve $y = \dfrac{1}{1+x}$ between $x = 1$ and $x = 5$.

4. Find an approximation for $\int_0^3 2^x\,dx$
   Use the trapezium rule with 7 ordinates.

5. The diagram shows a part of the curve $y = \sqrt{5x + 25}$.

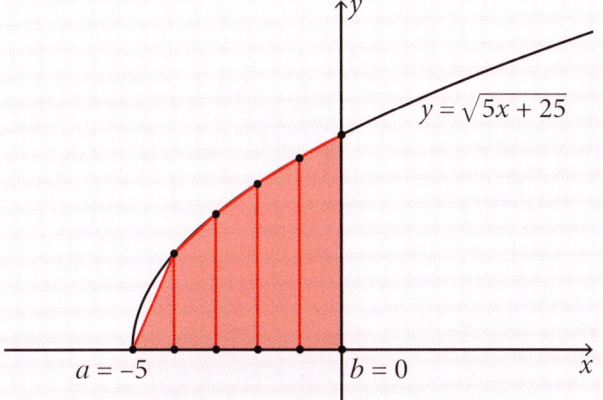

(a) Use the trapezium rule with 6 ordinates to approximate the following integral, giving your answer to 3 significant figures:
$$\int_{-5}^{0} \sqrt{5x + 25}\,dx$$

(b) Re-arrange $y = \sqrt{5x + 25}$ to make x the subject of the equation.

(c) Integrate to find the exact area between the curve and the axes.

6. (a) Copy and complete the following table of values for $y = x(2 - x)$.

x	0	0.5	1	1.5	2
$y = x(2-x)$	0		1		

(b) Using your table of values, or otherwise, sketch the curve $y = x(2 - x)$ for $0 \le x \le 2$.

(c) Use the trapezium rule with 4 strips to approximate: $\int_0^2 x(2-x)\,dx$

(d) Draw a new table using nine x values: 0, 0.25, 0.5, ..., 1.75 and 2. Calculate the y values and complete the table.

Exercise 13D...

(e) Use the trapezium rule with 8 strips to approximate: $\int_0^2 x(2-x)\,dx$

(f) By expanding the brackets and integrating, find the exact value of $\int_0^2 x(2-x)\,dx$

(g) Calculate the percentage errors:
   (i) When using 4 strips, using your answers to parts (c) and (f).
   (ii) When using 8 strips, using your answers to parts (e) and (f).

7. The trapezium rule is used to estimate the area between the curve $y = \sqrt{x^3 + 2}$, the lines $x = 3$ and $x = 7$ and the x-axis.

x	3	4	5	6	7
y	5.385	8.124	11.269		

(a) Copy and complete the table above. Calculate the values of y when $x = 6$ and $x = 7$, giving your answers to 3 decimal places.

(b) Use the values from the table and your answers to part (a) to find an estimate, to 2 decimal places, for this area.

8. The diagram shows a part of a circle of radius 1.

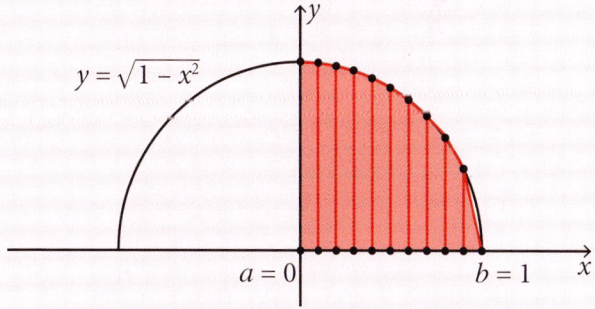

The circle has the equation: $y = \sqrt{1 - x^2}$

(a) Use the trapezium rule with 10 strips (shown) to approximate $\int_0^1 \sqrt{1 - x^2}\,dx$
Give your answer to 4 significant figures.

(b) Use your answer to part (a) to approximate the area of the whole circle to 4 significant figures.

(c) Find the exact area of the circle.

Exercise 13D...

Note: Question 9 is presented for students who want to stretch themselves.

9. (a) The diagrams show a **concave** curve and a **convex** curve. If you used the trapezium rule to find an approximation of the area beneath each curve, which approximation would be greater than the true value, which one less than it?

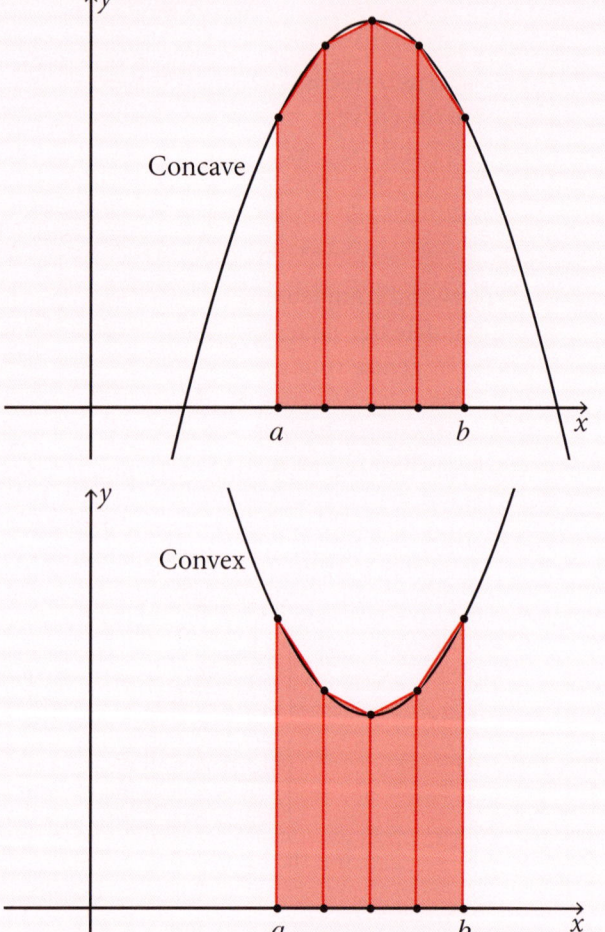

(b) The curve $y = -x^2 + 6x - 5$ is a concave curve. Find $\int_2^4 (-x^2 + 6x - 5)\,dx$

(c) Use the trapezium rule with 4 strips between $x = 2$ and $x = 4$ to approximate the same integral. Compare your answers to parts (b) and (c).

(d) The curve $y = x^2 - 6x + 11$ is a convex curve. Find $\int_2^4 (x^2 - 6x + 11)\,dx$

Exercise 13D...

(e) Use the trapezium rule with 4 strips between $x = 2$ and $x = 4$ to approximate the same integral. Compare your answers to parts (d) and (e).

13.5 Numerical Methods to Solve Problems in Context

You will be asked to solve real-life problems using numerical methods. Such problems may involve approximating an area using the trapezium rule, or finding a root of an equation using an iterative method.

Worked Example

12. The arched entrance to a hall is shown in the diagram. Its curved top is modelled using the equation $y = 2\cos\left(\dfrac{x}{2}\right) + 1$.

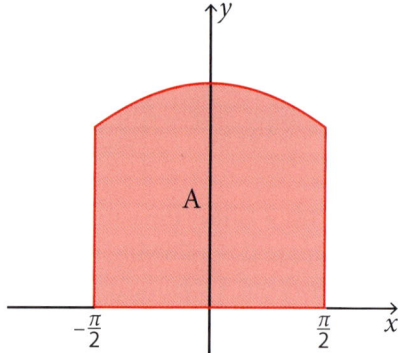

Assume that the left and right-hand edges of the arch are positioned at $x = -\dfrac{\pi}{2}$ and $x = \dfrac{\pi}{2}$ respectively.

Using the trapezium rule with 6 strips, find an approximation for the cross-sectional area A of the entrance.

$h = \dfrac{b-a}{n}$

$= \dfrac{\dfrac{\pi}{2} - -\dfrac{\pi}{2}}{6}$

$= \dfrac{\pi}{6}$

So the x values increase in steps of $\dfrac{\pi}{6}$.

When calculating the y-values work to 4 decimal places. This will ensure no accuracy is lost when the final answer is rounded to 3 significant figures:

13: NUMERICAL METHODS

x	$-\dfrac{\pi}{2}$	$-\dfrac{\pi}{3}$	$-\dfrac{\pi}{6}$	0
$y = 2\cos\left(\dfrac{x}{2}\right) + 1$	2.4142	2.7321	2.9319	3

x	$\dfrac{\pi}{6}$	$\dfrac{\pi}{3}$	$\dfrac{\pi}{2}$
$y = 2\cos\left(\dfrac{x}{2}\right) + 1$	2.9319	2.7321	2.4142

$$\int_a^b f(x)\,dx \approx \frac{1}{2}h[y_0 + 2(y_1 + \cdots + y_{n-1}) + y_n]$$

$$= \frac{1}{2} \times \frac{\pi}{6}\,[2.4142 + 2(2.7321 + 2.9319 + 3 + 2.9319 + 2.7321 + 2.4142)]$$

$$= 8.77 \text{ m}^2$$

Exercise 13E

1. A company logo is made from a triangle and a segment of a circle, as shown. The angle α, measured in radians, lies at the centre of this circle.

   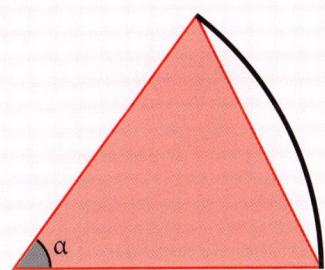

   The area of the triangle is ⅚ of the area of the entire sector (triangle plus segment).
   (a) Show that $6\sin\alpha - 5\alpha = 0$.
   (b) Using this equation, verify that α lies within the interval $[1.025, 1.035]$.
   (c) Hence write down the value of α correct to 2 decimal places.

2. The speed, v ms^{-1}, of a rocket at time t seconds is given by $v = \sqrt{1.7^t - 1}$, $0 \leq t \leq 24$. The following table shows the speed of the rocket at 4 second intervals.

t	0	4	8	12	16	20	24
v	0	2.71	8.29		69.75		

   (a) Copy and complete the table, giving the values of v to 2 decimal places.

Exercise 13E...

(b) The distance, s metres, travelled by the rocket in 24 seconds is given by:
$$s = \int_0^{24} \sqrt{1.7^t - 1}\,dt$$
Use the trapezium rule, with all the values from your table, to estimate the value of s.

3. The wall shown in the diagram is to be painted.

   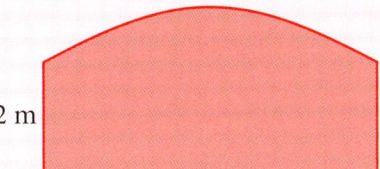

   The curve at the top of the wall is modelled by the equation: $y = \sin\left(\dfrac{x}{4}\right) + 2$
   The left- and right-hand sides are vertical. All lengths are measured in metres.
   (a) Given that the wall is symmetrical, find its **exact** width.
   (b) Approximate the area to be painted using the trapezium rule with 8 strips. Give your answer to 2 decimal places.
   (c) Find the wall's **exact** area using integration.
   (d) What is the percentage error when estimating the area using the trapezium rule? Give your answer to 2 significant figures.

4. The diagram shows the cross-section of a large marquee being used for a wedding party, with both axes measured in metres.

   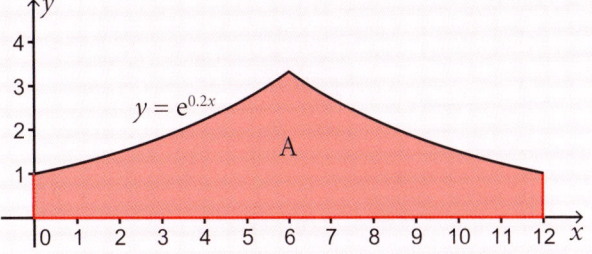

   Between $x = 0$ and $x = 6$ the roof of the marquee is described by the equation $y = e^{0.2x}$. The cross-section is symmetrical about the line $x = 6$.
   (a) At the entrance to the marquee, where $x = 0$, the height is 1 metre. Copy and complete the following table for the heights at 1 metre intervals, up to the centre of the

Exercise 13E...

marquee. Give your answers to 5 decimal places.

x	0	1	2	3	4	5	6
y	1						3.32012

(b) Use the trapezium rule with 6 strips to find the area of the cross-section between the entrance and the centre of the marquee. Give your answer to 2 decimal places.
(c) Hence estimate the total area of cross-section.
(d) Using integration, find the exact area beneath the curve $y = e^{0.2x}$ between $x = 0$ and $x = 6$. Again give your answer to 2 decimal places.
(e) What is the percentage error given by estimating the area using the trapezium rule?

5. A sports hall is being built. The roof is described by the equation: $y = 10 - \dfrac{x^2}{200}$, with x and y both measured in metres, as shown in the diagram.

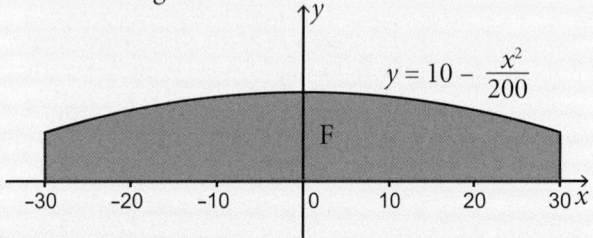

(a) Calculate the greatest height of the building.
(b) Find the height of the walls where $x = -30$ and $x = 30$.
(c) Copy and complete the following table with the values of y for the given values of x.

x	−30	−20	−10	0	10	20	30
$y = 10 - \dfrac{x^2}{200}$							

(d) Using the trapezium rule with these 7 ordinates, find the area of the front of the sports hall.
(e) Find the exact area F using integration.

6. A company logo is shown in the diagram. It is based on the curve $y = \dfrac{x}{\ln x}$ between $x = 1.5$ and $x = 9.5$.

Exercise 13E...

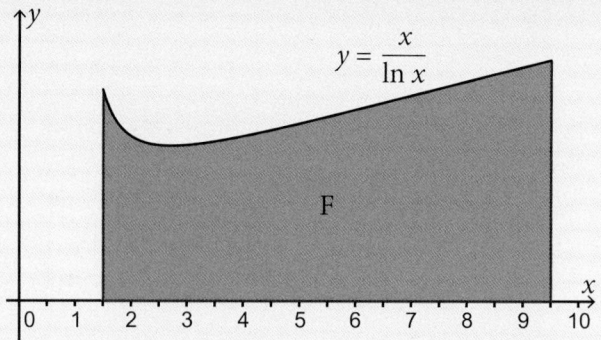

Using the trapezium rule with 4 strips, estimate the area F under the curve.

7. The diagram shows the cross-section of a model of a river between two hills in a geography department. The model uses the equation $y = \cos x + \sin x$ to describe the hills and the river bed.

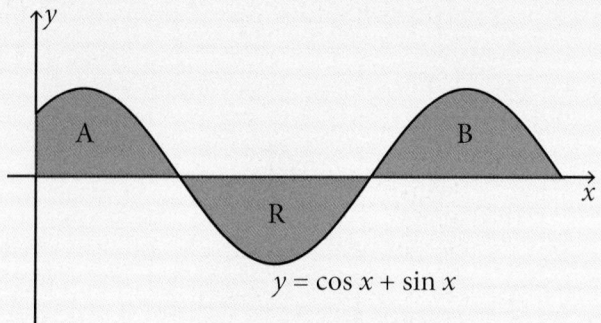

(a) In the model, the height of the terrain is zero where the curve crosses the x-axis. Show that the x-coordinates of these three points are $x = \dfrac{3\pi}{4}, \dfrac{7\pi}{4}, \dfrac{11\pi}{4}$.
(b) Copy and complete the following table for the height of hill A at the given points.

x	0	$\dfrac{3\pi}{16}$	$\dfrac{3\pi}{8}$	$\dfrac{9\pi}{16}$	$\dfrac{3\pi}{4}$
$\dfrac{3\pi}{4}$	1.00000				0.00000

(c) Hence, using the trapezium rule with 4 strips, estimate the cross-sectional area of hill A.
(d) Use integration to show that the exact area of hill A is $1 + \sqrt{2}$.
(e) Calculate the percentage error given by the trapezium rule for the area of hill A.
(f) Using the trapezium rule with 4 strips, estimate the cross-sectional area of hill B.

Exercise 13E...

(g) Use integration to find the exact area of hill B.

(h) Because of the symmetry of the curve $y = \cos x + \sin x$, the river has the same cross-sectional area as hill B. The geography department decide to paint the cross-sections of the hills green and the cross-section of the river blue. Using your answers to parts (d) and (g), calculate the ratio of green:blue paint needed. Give your answer in the form $\dfrac{a + b\sqrt{2}}{c}$, where a, b and c are integers to be found.

8. A landscape gardener is building a patio, shown in the diagram. The patio must be modelled on the equation $y = 3\cos x + 3$ and its area must be 9 m².

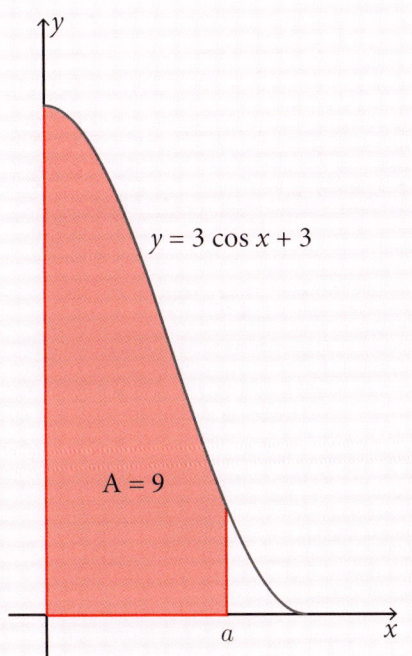

(a) If the patio is a metres wide, show that a is the solution to the equation: $f(x) = 0$, where $f(x) = \sin x + x - 3$

(b) Use two iterations of the Newton-Raphson method, with a first approximation of $\dfrac{3\pi}{4}$, to estimate the value of a. Give your answer to 3 significant figures.

(c) By evaluating $f(x)$ for two suitable values of x, show that the value of a you obtained in part (b) is correct to 3 significant figures.

Exercise 13E...

9. The diagram shows a plume of smoke rising from a factory chimney. An air pollution scientist models the trajectory of the plume using the function: $f(x) = \cos x + \ln x + 20$

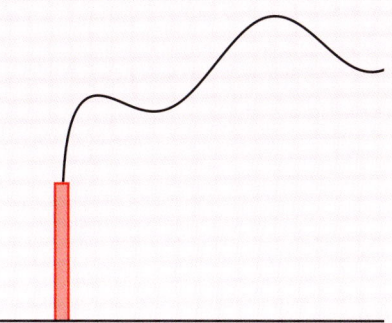

(a) Show that the turning points on the curve are given by solutions to the equation: $\sin x = \dfrac{1}{x}$.

(b) Hence show that an iterative formula to find the x-coordinate of a turning point is: $x_{n+1} = \operatorname{cosec} x_n$

(c) The scientist wishes to find the height of the plume at its first turning point. To do this she must first obtain the x-coordinate of that point on the curve. Using a first approximation $x_0 = 1$, use the iterative formula to find x_1, x_2 and x_3 to 2 significant figures.

(d) Show that the x-coordinate of the first turning point is 1.1 correct to 2 significant figures.

(e) Find the height of the plume at this turning point.

10. The wings of a glider are being designed on a computer, as shown in the diagram. The engineer models the wings using the implicit equation: $y^3 + y = x^2 + 1$

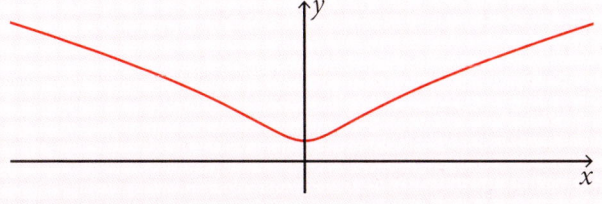

The curve has a single stationary point with coordinates (a, b).

(a) Use implicit differentiation to show that the stationary point lies on the y-axis.

Exercise 13E...

(b) Hence show that b satisfies the equation:
$f(b) = 0$, where $f(b) = b^3 + b - 1$

(c) Use two iterations of the Newton-Raphson method with $b_0 = 0.5$ to find an approximation to b, giving your answer to 2 decimal places.

(d) By evaluating $f(b)$ for two suitable values of b, show that your answer to part (c) is correct to 2 decimal places.

13.6 Summary

When an equation cannot be solved algebraically, a numerical method can often be used to find the solutions. Three numerical methods for solving equations have been studied in this chapter:

- **Considering sign changes**. Rewriting the equation as $f(x) = 0$, we can investigate whether $f(x) > 0$ or $f(x) < 0$ for values of x close to the solution. By narrowing the interval, we can pinpoint x to the required degree of accuracy.
- **Iterative methods**. These require writing the equation in the form $x = f(x)$. This can then be used as an iterative formula $x_{n+1} = f(x_n)$. Sometimes iterative formulae converge to a solution, other times they may diverge.
- **The Newton-Raphson method** is used to find roots to an equation of the form $f(x) = 0$. This method usually converges very quickly to a root. It uses the formula: $x_{n+1} = x_n - \dfrac{f(x_n)}{f'(x_n)}$.

Numerical methods can also be used to find approximations for definite integration. In this chapter you learnt about the **trapezium rule**, which can give very good approximations to definite integrals. The formula is:

$$\int_a^b y \, dx \approx \frac{h}{2}[y_0 + 2(y_1 + y_2 + \cdots + y_{n-1}) + y_n]$$

This method divides the area into strips, and each strip's area is approximated as a trapezium.

The number of y-values (ordinates) used is one more than the number of strips.

Chapter 14
Problem Solving

14.1 Introduction

The CCEA A2 Mathematics specification now has an emphasis on problem solving.

This chapter contains examples and a collection of exam-style questions. The questions may require techniques from any of the preceding chapters, and often more than one. They may also require understanding of the mathematics you learnt at GCSE.

What does a problem-solving task look like?
A question involving problem solving typically involves several of the following features, but not necessarily all of them:

- Many steps may be required to reach the correct solution.
- The task may have little or no 'scaffolding'. It will often contain minimal wording.
- The information given may not be in mathematical form or in mathematical language.
- It is not always clear from the wording of the question which way the problem should be tackled. The mathematical processes required are often not given. The task may require more than one process, or it may require different parts of mathematics to be brought together to reach a solution. There may be a choice of valid approaches.
- The task may require 'multiple representations', i.e. a sketch or diagram may be required, as well as calculations.
- The task may relate to a real-world situation. Results should be interpreted in the context of the question.
- Understanding of the processes involved is required, rather than just the application of techniques.

In the real world...
You have gained a lot of expertise in solving mathematical problems. These skills can be put to good use in many different careers, for example science, engineering, astronomy and finance.

Another way to apply your skills is to become a mathematician. There is exciting research in university departments in many different areas of mathematics.

Did you know that every even integer greater than 2 is the sum of two prime numbers? For example:

4 = 2 + 2, 6 = 3 + 3, 8 = 3 + 5, etc.

This is called *Goldbach's Conjecture* and, although it has been tested for the first 400 trillion integers, it remains unproved.

Despite the simplicity of the problem, some mathematicians believe that we will need to invent a whole new field of mathematics to prove this result.

Proving a long-standing conjecture like this often sheds light on other areas of mathematics, some of which seem unconnected. The benefits of the research can be applied in tackling surprising real-world problems. For example, who would have expected the multiplication of two prime numbers to play such an important role in Internet security?

There are very few areas of mathematical research that have not been applied to real-world problems in some way.

14.2 Examples and Problems

The following examples and problems demonstrate the types of question that could be asked. Each question can be answered using the mathematical techniques and skills you have learnt at GCSE and A-Level.

Worked Examples

1. A roll of sticky tape is made by wrapping the tape tightly around an inner cardboard cylinder. The cardboard cylinder has radius r mm. The circle of tape in contact with the cardboard has a radius $r + 1$ mm. Each successive circle has a radius 1 mm greater than the last. If the tape is wrapped around the central cylinder n times, show that the total length T of tape on the roll is given (in millimetres) by:
$T = \pi n(2r + n + 1)$

The innermost circle of tape has circumference $2\pi(r + 1)$. The second circle has circumference $2\pi(r + 2)$; the third $2\pi(r + 3)$, etc.

The nth has circumference $2\pi(r + n)$.

The total length of the sticky tape is given by:
$$T = 2\pi(r + 1) + 2\pi(r + 2) + \cdots + 2\pi(r + n)$$
$$= 2\pi[(r + 1) + (r + 2) + \cdots + (r + n)]$$
$$= 2\pi[nr + (1 + 2 + \cdots + n)]$$

The sum of the first n natural numbers is given by the formula:
$$S_n = \frac{n}{2}(n + 1)$$

So:
$$T = 2\pi\left[nr + \frac{n}{2}(n + 1)\right]$$
$$T = 2\pi\left[nr + \frac{n^2}{2} + \frac{n}{2}\right]$$
$$T = 2\pi nr + \pi n^2 + \pi n$$
$$T = \pi n(2r + n + 1)$$

2. Two balls rest on a flat table. The larger ball's radius R is 3 times the radius of the smaller ball. At the highest point on each ball, a red dot is marked, as shown in the following diagram. The balls start to roll towards each other.

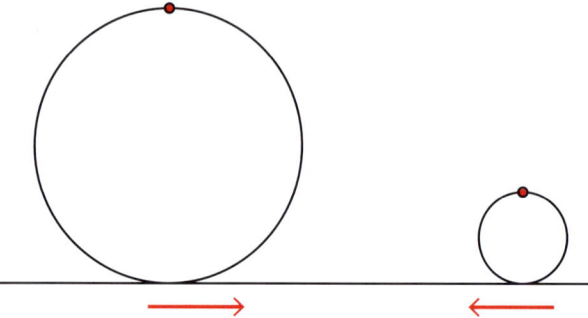

The balls meet with the red dots touching, as shown in the next diagram. Both balls have rotated less than one whole turn.

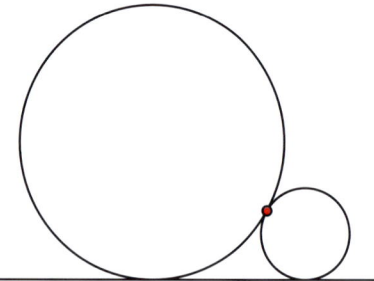

(a) Show that the angle through which the small ball has rotated is $\frac{\pi}{3}$ radians.

(b) Hence find the angle through which the larger ball has rotated.

(c) Show that the distances travelled horizontally by the large and small balls respectively are $\frac{2\pi R}{3}$ and $\frac{\pi R}{9}$ metres.

(d) Find the horizontal distance between the centres of the two balls when they meet.

(e) Hence show that, initially, the horizontal distance between the two centres was $\frac{(7\pi + 6\sqrt{3})R}{9}$.

(a) The following diagram shows the balls when they are touching.

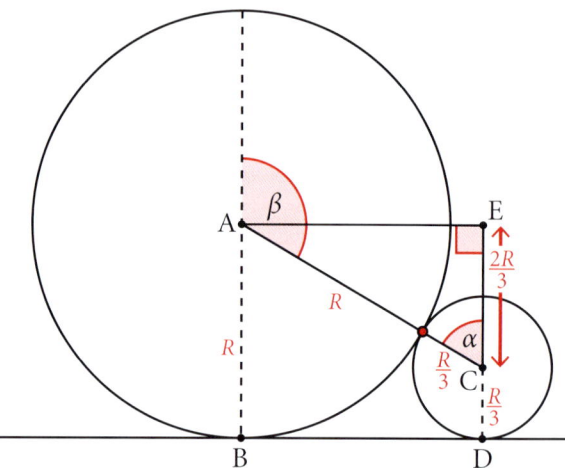

The large ball has centre A and the small ball centre C. Two vertical lines have been added from the centres to the table (AB and CD). These have lengths R and $\frac{R}{3}$. A right-angled triangle has been formed by drawing a horizontal line AE and a vertical line EC. The angle α marked is the angle through which the small ball has rotated.

In triangle AEC, the length of the hypotenuse AC is: $R + \frac{R}{3} = \frac{4R}{3}$

The length of EC is $\frac{2R}{3}$ (since it is the difference between the lengths AB and CD).

Hence: $\cos\alpha = \frac{2R/3}{4R/3} = \frac{1}{2}$

$$\alpha = \frac{\pi}{3}$$

(b) The angle β is the angle through which the large ball has rotated. Since α and β are supplementary angles between parallel lines, they add up to π radians.

$$\therefore \beta = \frac{2\pi}{3}$$

(c) We must find the arc length subtended by angle β to find the distance d_1 that the large ball has rolled. Recall that the formula for arc length is $s = r\theta$. So:
$$d_1 = R\beta = \frac{2\pi R}{3}$$

Similarly, if the distance the small ball has rolled is d_2, then:
$$d_2 = \frac{R}{3} \times \alpha = \frac{R}{3} \times \frac{\pi}{3} = \frac{\pi R}{9}$$

(d) The horizontal distance between the two centres is AE. Using Pythagoras' Theorem in triangle AEC:
$$AE^2 = \left(\frac{4R}{3}\right)^2 - \left(\frac{2R}{3}\right)^2 = \frac{4R^2}{3}$$
$$\therefore AE = \frac{2\sqrt{3}}{3}R$$

(e) If the large ball has rolled $\frac{2\pi R}{3}$ metres, the small ball has rolled $\frac{\pi R}{9}$ metres and the centres are still $\frac{2\sqrt{3}}{3}R$ metres apart, the distance D between the two centres at the start is given by:
$$D = \frac{2\pi R}{3} + \frac{\pi R}{9} + \frac{2\sqrt{3}}{3}R$$
$$= \frac{7\pi R}{9} + \frac{2\sqrt{3}}{3}R$$
$$= \frac{(7\pi + 6\sqrt{3})R}{9}$$

Exercise 14A

1. Each of the three small circles below has a radius of 1 cm. What is the exact radius of the large circle?

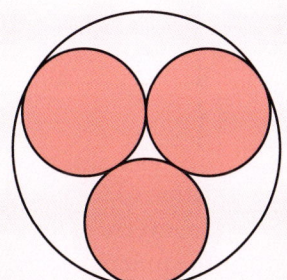

Exercise 14A...

2. A part of the graph of $x^3 + y^5 - 2y = 0$ is shown.

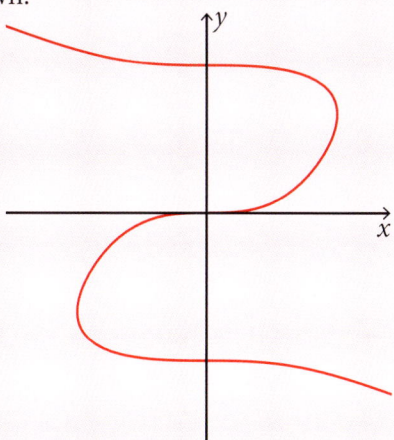

   (a) Verify that the point P(1, 1) lies on the curve.
   (b) Find the gradient of the curve at P.
   (c) Show that all stationary points on the curve lie on the y-axis.

3. The curve C is defined by the parametric equations:
$$x = 3 - t$$
$$y = 2 - \frac{1}{t}$$

   C passes through the point P(2, 1).

   Find the coordinates of the point at which the normal to the curve C at the point P intersects the curve again.

4. The quadrilateral shown in the diagram has four sides of equal length d. One of its angles is $\theta°$.

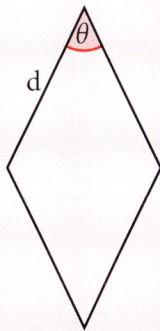

   Show that the area of the quadrilateral is given by the formula: $A = d^2 \sin\theta$

   Hence, using differentiation, show that the quadrilateral will have its maximum area when it is a square.

Exercise 14A...

5. The triangle shown in the diagram is right-angled. The two shorter sides have lengths 3 cm and 4 cm. The circle shown touches each of the three sides of the triangle.
   (a) Find the radius of the circle.
   (b) Find the area marked A.

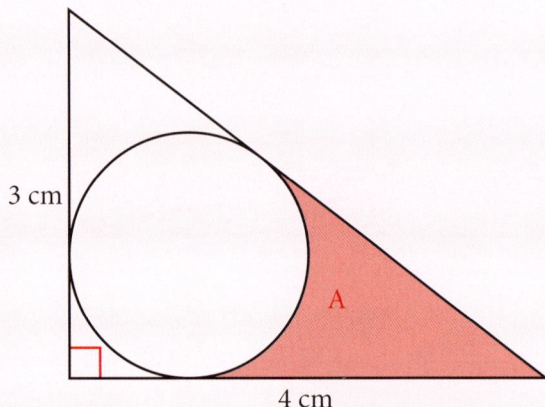

6. In the diagram, ODC is a sector of a small circle. OAB is a sector of a larger circle. The two sectors both have the angle θ at their centres. The two regions R_1 and R_2 have equal areas. They also have equal perimeters. Find the angle θ in radians, giving an exact answer.

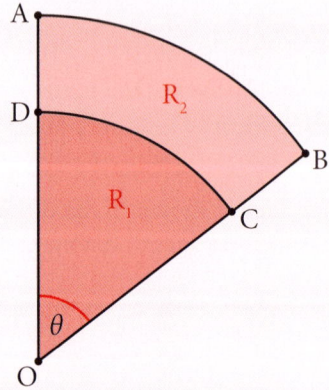

7. The diagram shows a sector of a large circle of radius R.

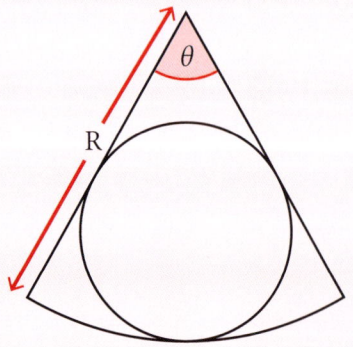

Exercise 14A...

The angle at the centre of the sector is θ. A smaller circle lies inside the sector. It touches the two straight edges and the arc. Show that the radius r of the small circle is given by the formula:

$$r = \frac{R \sin\left(\frac{\theta}{2}\right)}{1 + \sin\left(\frac{\theta}{2}\right)}$$

8. (a) On the same diagram, sketch the graphs of $f(x) = |x - 1|$ and $f(x) = |x + 1|$.
   (b) Use your results from part (a) to sketch the graph of $f(x) = |x - 1| + |x + 1|$.

9. An arithmetic progression has a first term of a and a common difference of d. Its nth term is u_n. The second, third and sixth terms of the arithmetic progression form a geometric progression.
   Another geometric progression can be formed using $u_2 + 1$, u_3 and $u_4 + 2$.
   Find the two possible values of a and the corresponding values of d.

10. The sketch of an inverse trigonometric function $h^{-1}(x)$ is shown.

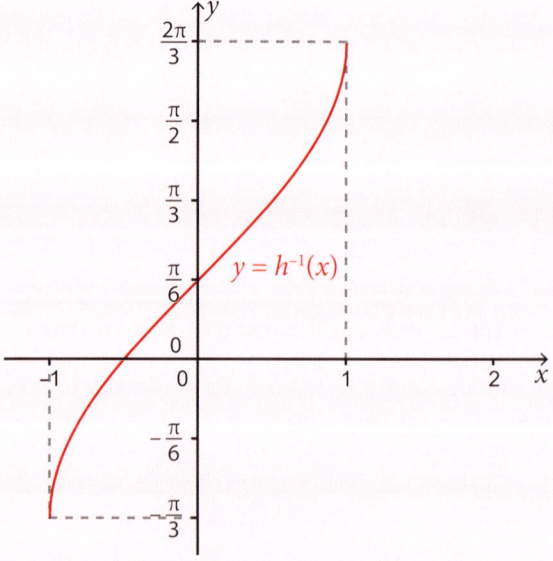

   (a) Find the equation of the curve.
   (b) By finding the inverse of $h^{-1}(x)$, find the equation of the function $h(x)$.

Exercise 14A...

11. A wigwam is in the shape of a right triangular pyramid, as shown. The three wooden struts AB, AC and AD are each of fixed length l. These struts meet at the apex of the wigwam, point A. Point A is positioned directly above the point O, which lies at the centre of the base, which is an equilateral triangle.

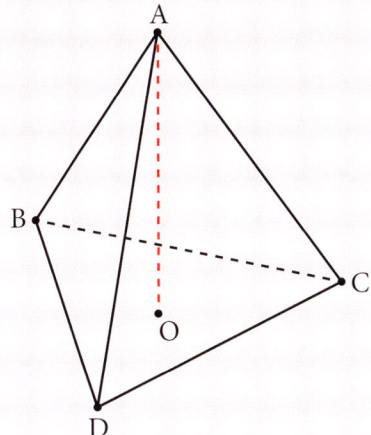

(a) The angle between each strut and the horizontal ground is θ radians. Show that for the wigwam to have a maximum or minimum volume, the value of θ must satisfy: $2\cot\theta = \tan 2\theta$.

You may use the formula for the volume of a triangular pyramid: $V = \dfrac{1}{3}Ah$, where A is the area of the base and h is the perpendicular height.

(b) One solution to the above equation is $\theta = \alpha$ radians, where $\alpha \approx 0.6$. Show that $\alpha = 0.6$ is correct to one decimal place.

(c) Show that the volume is a maximum when $\theta = \alpha$.

12. In the diagram in the next column, OBD is a quarter of a circle with radius r. OACE is a rectangle with point C on the circumference of the quarter circle. The width and height of the rectangle are w and h respectively.

(a) Show that the perimeter of the shaded region is given by $P = \dfrac{\pi r}{2} + 3r - w - h$.

(b) (Note: This is a more challenging question.) Show that the perimeter of the shaded region is at a minimum when $w = h$.

Exercise 14A...

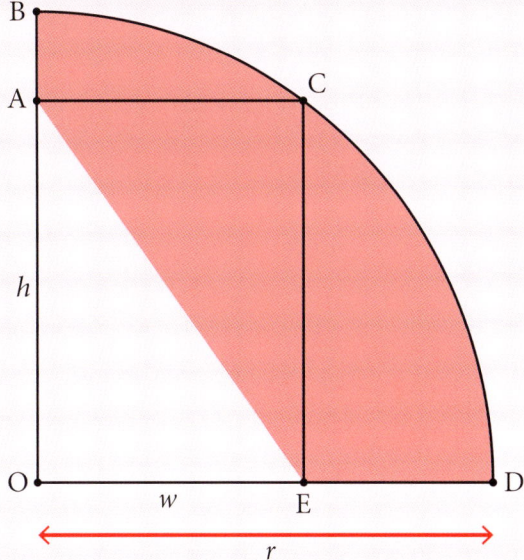

13. The diagram shows a circle with AC as a diameter of length d.

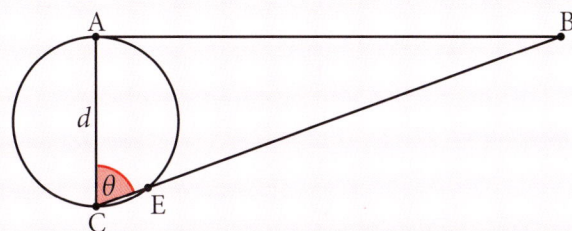

B is a point outside the circle and AB is a tangent to the circle. Angle ACB = θ, as shown.

(a) Show that BE = $d(\sec\theta - \cos\theta)$.

(b) Given that BE = $\dfrac{8d}{3}$, show that $\cos\theta = \dfrac{1}{3}$.

(c) Hence find CE in terms of d.

Answers

Exercise 1A
1. (a) $^{45}/_{16}$ (b) $^{9}/_{2}$ (c) $^{97}/_{56}$ (d) $^{3}/_{4}$
2. (a) $(x+1)(x+4)$
   (b) $(x-1)^2$ (c) $(2x+1)(x+2)$
   (d) $(4x-1)(x+1)$
   (e) $(x-1)(7x+3)$
3. (a)

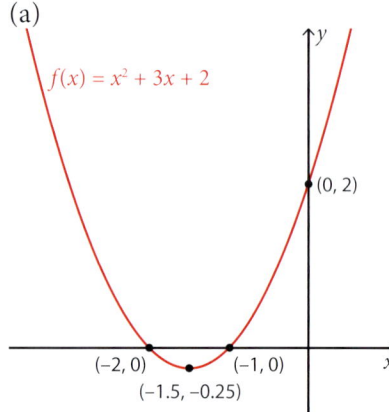

   (b)

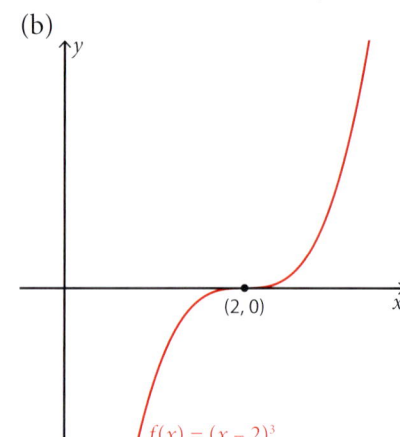

   (c)

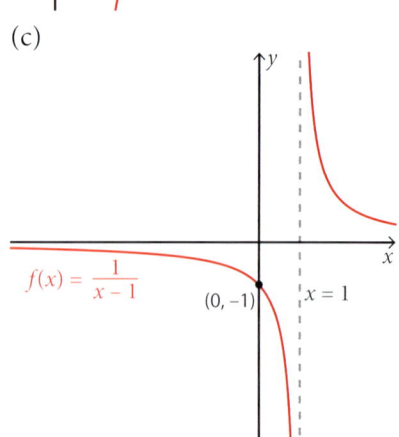

4. (a) $f(x) = x^2 + 3$
   (b) $f(x) = (x+2)^3$
   (c) $f(x) = -\dfrac{1}{2x}$

   (d) $f(x) = 2 - x$
   (e) $f(x) = 2x^2 + 4x + 2$

Exercise 1B
1. (a) $\dfrac{1}{ab}$ (b) 18 m^2 (c) $\dfrac{a^2b^2d}{c^3}$
   (d) $\dfrac{c}{d}$ (e) $2c^9d^8$ (f) $\dfrac{5}{p}$ (g) $x+12$
   (h) $\dfrac{x+15}{x+10}$

2. (a) $\dfrac{-x^2+14x+66}{6(x-8)}$
   (b) $\dfrac{x^2+16x-24}{(x-8)(x+13)}$
   (c) $\dfrac{x^2+14x-24}{(x-6)(x+10)}$
   (d) $\dfrac{-x^2+10x+48}{4(x-6)}$
   (e) $\dfrac{27-8x}{(x-3)(x+3)}$
   (f) $\dfrac{60-4x}{(x-12)(x+12)}$

3. (a) 2 (b) $\dfrac{5}{x+10}$ (c) 1 (d) $\dfrac{4}{x+9}$

4. $\dfrac{2(x+2)}{x+4}$

5. (a) $\dfrac{ac+b^2}{bc}$ (b) $\dfrac{p^2-q^2}{pq}$ (c) $\dfrac{x}{x+1}$
   (d) $\dfrac{2g^3-2}{g^2}$ (e) $\dfrac{2}{(b-1)(b+1)}$
   (f) $\dfrac{x+3}{(x+2)(x+1)}$ (g) $\dfrac{p+4}{p(p+2)}$
   (h) $-\dfrac{2}{(x+3)(x+4)(x+5)}$
   (i) $\dfrac{4(l+5)}{5l}$ (j) $\dfrac{6-x+6y-xy^2}{xy}$
   (k) $\dfrac{5s-8}{s(s+4)(s-4)}$

6. (a) $\dfrac{a^2}{4}$ (b) $\dfrac{2(b+1)}{b(2c+1)}$ (c) $\dfrac{3(d^2-1)}{d^3}$
   (d) $e^2(e+2)$

Exercise 1C
1. (a) $x-1$ (b) $-3x+1$
   (c) $-7x-1$ (d) $-\dfrac{2x}{3} - \dfrac{3}{2}$
   (e) $2x - \dfrac{9}{4}$ (f) $-2x-6$

   (g) $x^2 + \dfrac{x}{2}$ (h) $\dfrac{x^2}{2} - 1$
   (i) $7x^2 - 3x + 5$ (j) $-3x^2 - x$
   (k) $x^2 + x + 1$

2. (a) $2x + 4 + \dfrac{17}{2x-2}$
   (b) $7x + 29 - \dfrac{143}{-x+5}$
   (c) $9x + 25 - \dfrac{66}{-x+3}$
   (d) $-x - 1 + \dfrac{10}{6x+2}$
   (e) $-2x - 7 + \dfrac{34}{-x+4}$
   (f) $x - 2 + \dfrac{11}{-2x+1}$
   (g) $-\dfrac{4x^2}{3} + 2x - 4 + \dfrac{30}{6x+9}$
   (h) $-x^2 + x - 6 + \dfrac{14}{3-x}$
   (i) $-2x^2 - x - 5 + \dfrac{11}{2-x}$
   (j) $x^2 - x + 1 - \dfrac{3}{2x+9}$

3. (a) $x-2$ (b) $x-1$ (c) $x-1$
   (d) $3x-2$ (e) $x+1$ (f) $2x-2$
   (g) $x-1$
   (h) $2x - 4 + \dfrac{5x+8}{x^2+2x+3}$
   (i) (x^2+1) (j) (x^2+2x)
   (k) $x^2 - 2x + 1$

4. (a) $(x+3)(x-1)$
   (b) $(x+2)(x+1)$
   (c) $(x-1)(x-2)^2$
   (d) $x(3x+1)(x-1)$
   (e) $(-9x^2-2x-1)(x-1)$
   (f) $(x^2-x-1)(7x-1)$
   (g) $-(3x^2+2x+2)(x+2)$
   (h) $(2x^2+5x+7)(-x+1)$
   (i) $(x-4)(x^2+4x+16)$
   (j) $(x^2-4)(x^2+x+2)$

5. (a) $x - 1 + \dfrac{2x}{x^2+2x+1}$
   (b) $x - 7 + \dfrac{17x+21}{x^2+3x+3}$
   (c) $x + 1 + \dfrac{-8x-4}{x^2+x+3}$
   (d) $x + \dfrac{-5x+1}{2x^2+2x+3}$
   (e) $3x - 6 + \dfrac{17x+9}{x^2+3x+1}$

ANSWERS – 1F

6. (a) $4x^3 - x^2 - 3x + 3 - \dfrac{4}{-x-1}$
   (b) $-x^2 + 3x - 2 + \dfrac{12}{2x+3}$
   (c) $2x^3 - 9x^2 + 24x - 43 + \dfrac{80}{x+2}$
   (d) $-9x^3 + 3x^2 - 8x + 1$
   (e) $x^3 + x^2 - 3x + 2$
   (f) $-4x^3 - 4x^2 - x + 7$
   (g) $-x^2 + 4 + \dfrac{x+10}{-2x^2 + 2x - 4}$
   (h) $6x^2 + 11x + 15 - \dfrac{45x + 24}{-x^2 + x + 2}$
   (i) $-3x^2 - x - \dfrac{2x+8}{x^2-3}$
   (j) $-2x^2 + 3x - 1 + \dfrac{x-9}{x^2+2x-1}$

Exercise 1D

1. (a) $\dfrac{2}{2x-2} + \dfrac{1}{x+2}$
   (b) $\dfrac{1}{x+1} - \dfrac{1}{x+2}$
   (c) $\dfrac{5}{2x-5} + \dfrac{1}{x+2}$
   (d) $\dfrac{1}{x+1} + \dfrac{4}{x+6}$
   (e) $\dfrac{1}{1+2x} - \dfrac{1}{3+x}$
   (f) $\dfrac{3}{x+1} - \dfrac{3}{x+2}$
   (g) $\dfrac{-5}{x-1} + \dfrac{7}{x-2}$
   (h) $-\dfrac{10}{x} + \dfrac{16}{x+3}$
   (i) $-\dfrac{3}{x-3} + \dfrac{4}{x-4}$
   (j) $\dfrac{2}{x-3} - \dfrac{1}{2x+1}$

2. (a) $\dfrac{1}{x-1} + \dfrac{2}{x+2}$
   (b) $\dfrac{1}{x+2} + \dfrac{1}{x-3}$
   (c) $\dfrac{3}{x-2} - \dfrac{1}{x+1}$
   (d) $\dfrac{3}{x-1} - \dfrac{6}{2x-1}$
   (e) $\dfrac{1}{6(x-2)} - \dfrac{1}{6(x+4)}$
   (f) $\dfrac{2}{x+1} + \dfrac{3}{x-2}$
   (g) $\dfrac{3}{x+4} + \dfrac{4}{x+3}$
   (h) $\dfrac{3}{7(x-3)} - \dfrac{6}{7(2x+1)}$
   (i) $-\dfrac{1}{2x} + \dfrac{7}{2(x-2)}$
   (j) $\dfrac{1}{4}\left(-\dfrac{1}{x+3} + \dfrac{1}{x-1}\right)$

3. (a) $-\dfrac{4}{3x} + \dfrac{1}{x-1} + \dfrac{1}{3(x-3)}$
   (b) $\dfrac{5}{21(2x+1)} - \dfrac{1}{3(x-1)} + \dfrac{5}{7(x-3)}$
   (c) $-\dfrac{1}{12(x+1)} - \dfrac{5}{3(x-2)} + \dfrac{7}{4(x-3)}$

Exercise 1E

1. (a) $\dfrac{1}{x+1} + \dfrac{1}{(x+1)^2}$
   (b) $\dfrac{2}{x} + \dfrac{3}{x^2}$
   (c) $\dfrac{2}{x-3} + \dfrac{1}{(x-3)^2}$
   (d) $\dfrac{3}{2(2x-1)} - \dfrac{1}{2(2x-1)^2}$
   (e) $\dfrac{8}{(x-1)^2} - \dfrac{7}{x-1}$
   (f) $-\dfrac{1}{x-1} + \dfrac{2}{(x-1)^2}$
   (g) $\dfrac{3}{x+4} + \dfrac{2}{(x+4)^2}$
   (h) $\dfrac{5}{x+4} - \dfrac{2}{(x+4)^2}$

2. (a) $\dfrac{1}{x+2} - \dfrac{1}{x+1} + \dfrac{1}{(x+1)^2}$
   (b) $\dfrac{1}{16(x-3)} - \dfrac{1}{16(x+1)} - \dfrac{1}{4(x+1)^2}$
   (c) $-\dfrac{3}{4(x+1)} + \dfrac{3}{4(x-1)} - \dfrac{1}{2(x-1)^2}$
   (d) $\dfrac{5}{9(x-1)} + \dfrac{4}{3(x-1)^2} - \dfrac{5}{9(x+2)}$
   (e) $\dfrac{1}{2(x-1)} + \dfrac{1}{(x-1)^2} + \dfrac{1}{2(x+1)}$
   (f) $\dfrac{1}{x+1} + \dfrac{1}{x-1} + \dfrac{1}{(x-1)^2}$
   (g) $\dfrac{1}{x+2} + \dfrac{2}{(x+2)^2} + \dfrac{3}{2x+3}$
   (h) $\dfrac{1}{x+7} - \dfrac{1}{3x-2} + \dfrac{1}{(3x-2)^2}$

3. (a) $2 + \dfrac{7}{2x} + \dfrac{1}{2(x-2)}$
   (b) $x + \dfrac{9}{4(x-2)} + \dfrac{7}{4(x+2)}$
   (c) $2x^2 - 6x + 17 + \dfrac{6}{x+1} - \dfrac{45}{x+2}$
   (d) $3x + 1 + \dfrac{1}{5(x+2)} - \dfrac{1}{5(x-3)}$
   (e) $x + 1 + \dfrac{4}{3(x-1)} - \dfrac{1}{3(x+2)}$

Exercise 1F

1. (a) Type: $y = |f(x)|$

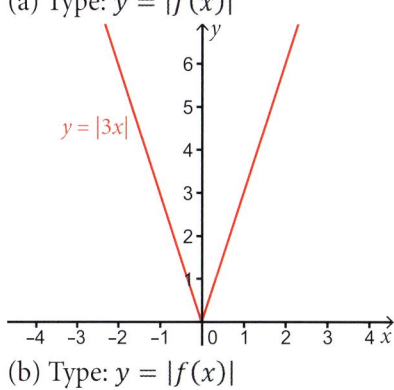

   (b) Type: $y = |f(x)|$

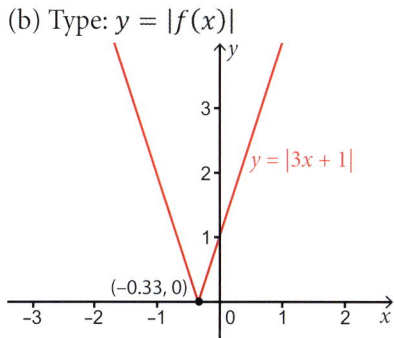

   (c) Type: $y = f(|x|)$

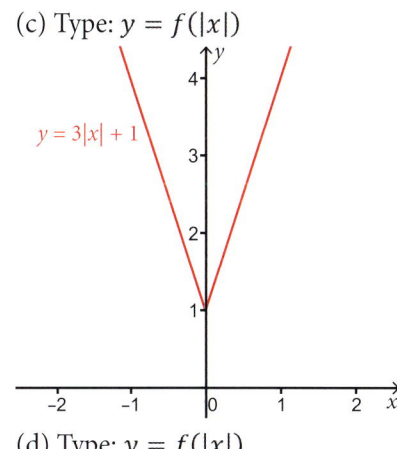

   (d) Type: $y = f(|x|)$

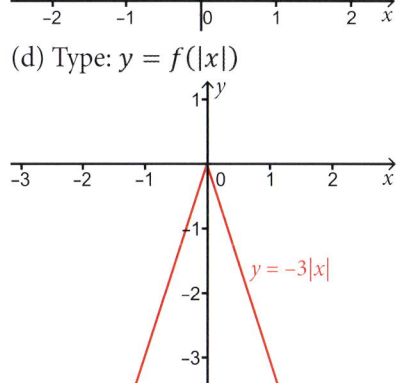

(e) Type: $y = |f(x)|$
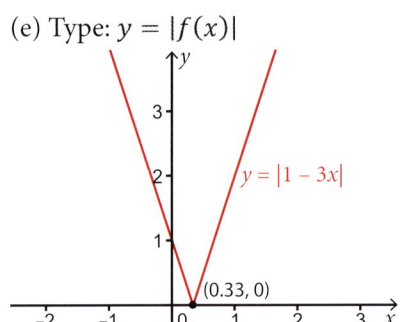

(f) Type: $y = |f(x)|$
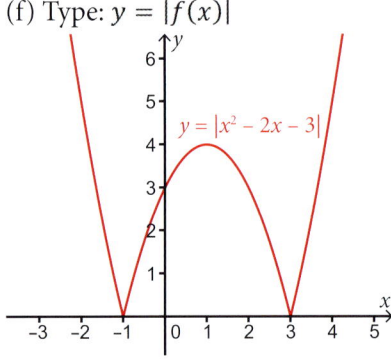

(g) Type: $y = f(|x|)$
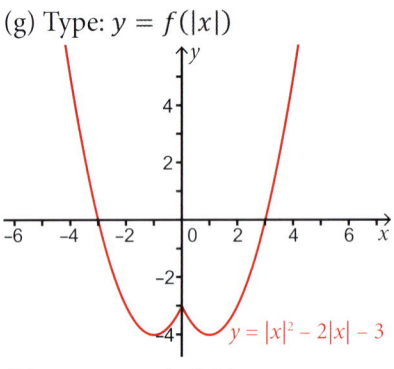

(h) Type: $y = |f(x)|$
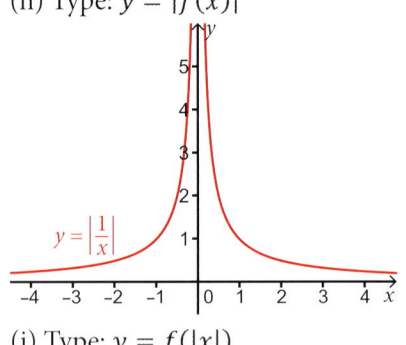

(i) Type: $y = f(|x|)$
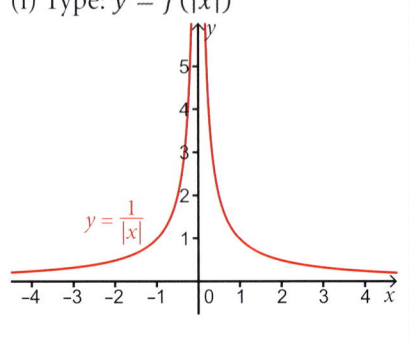

(j) Type: $y = f(|x|)$
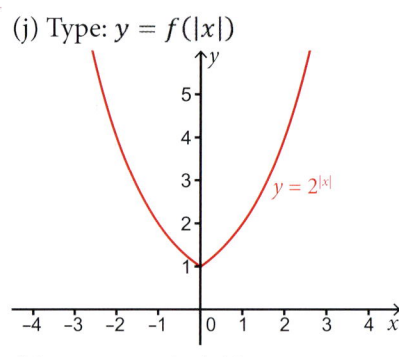

(k) Type: $y = |f(x)|$
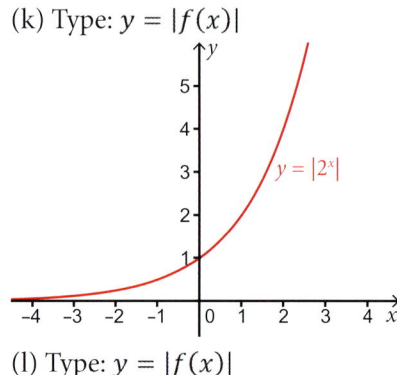

(l) Type: $y = |f(x)|$
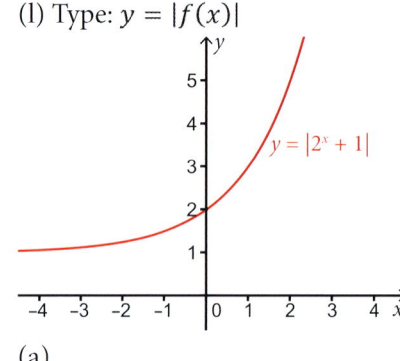

2. (a)
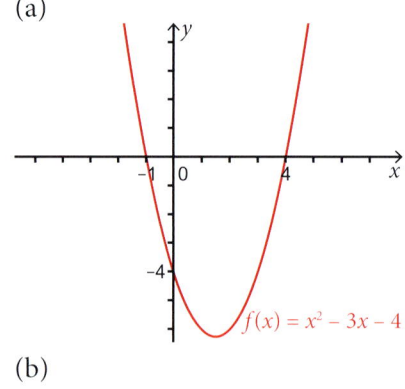

(b)
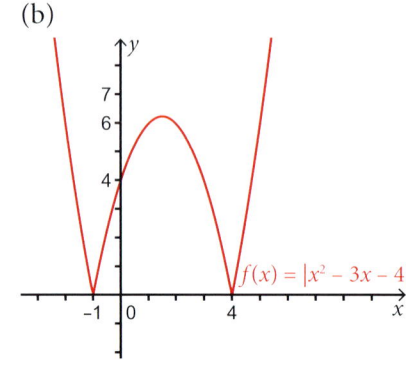

(c)
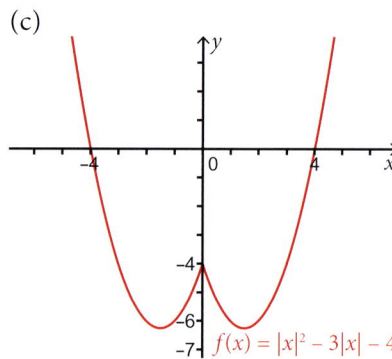

3. (a)
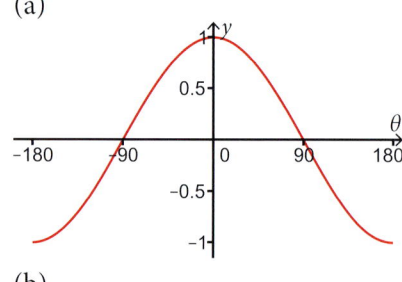

(b)
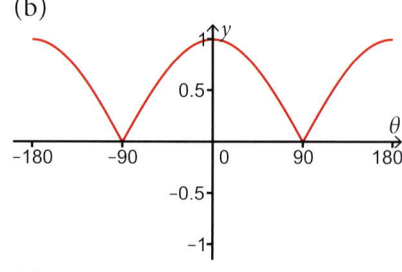

(c)
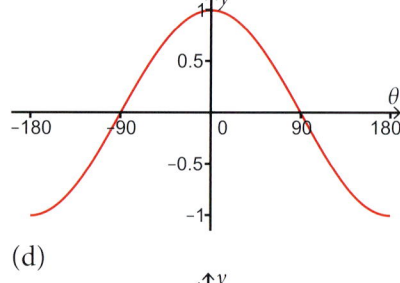

(d)
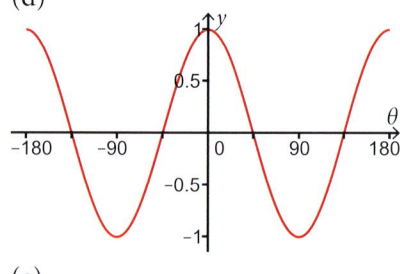

(e)
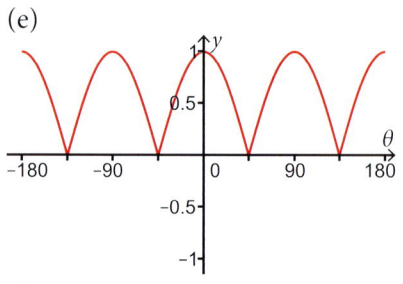

(f)

ANSWERS – 1F

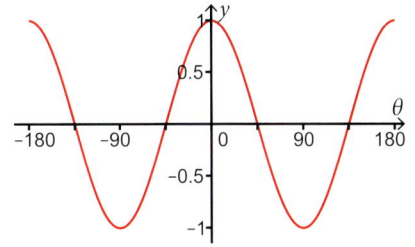

4. (a)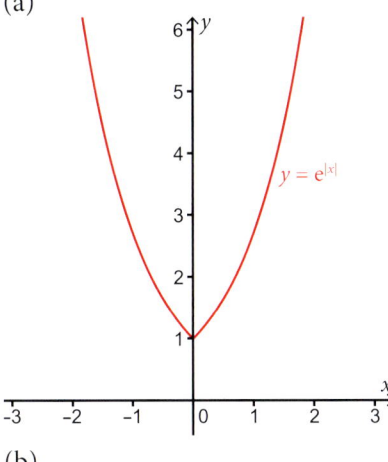

(b)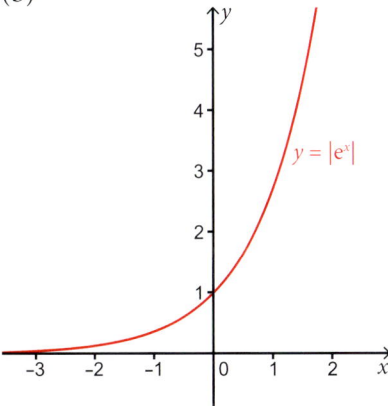

(c)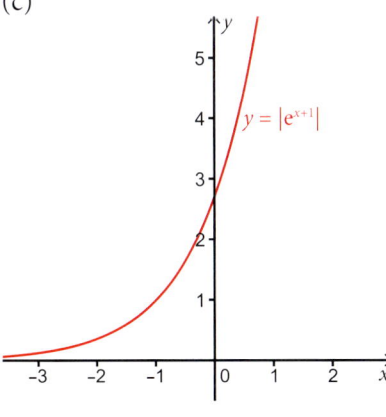

(d)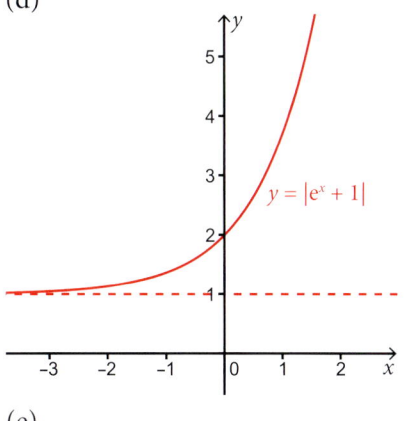

(e)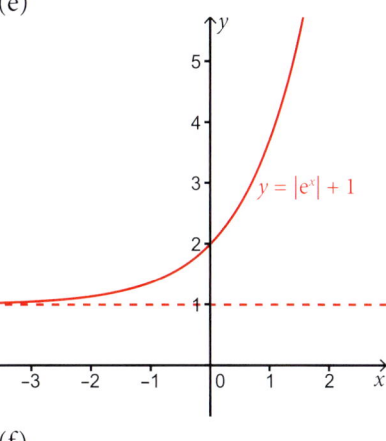

(f)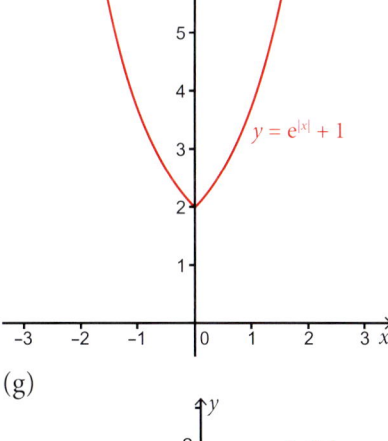

(g)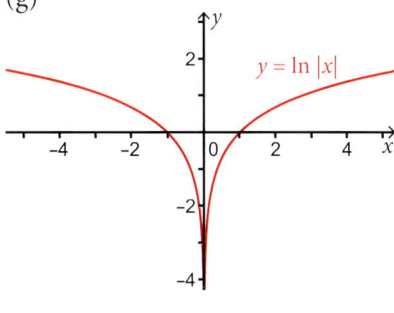

(h)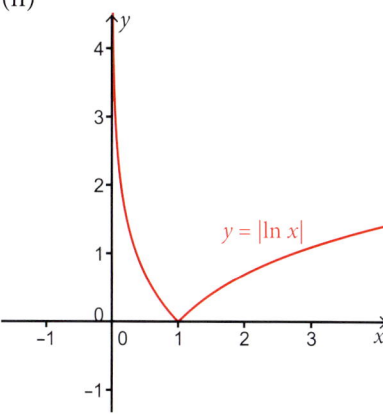

(i)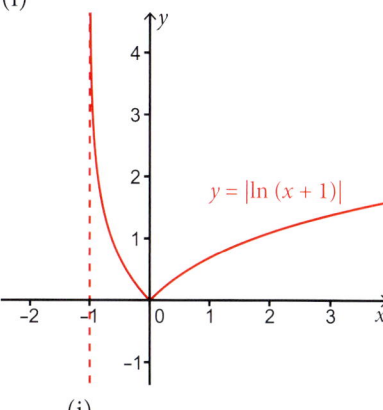

(j)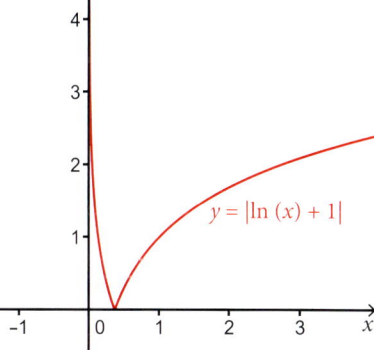

(k)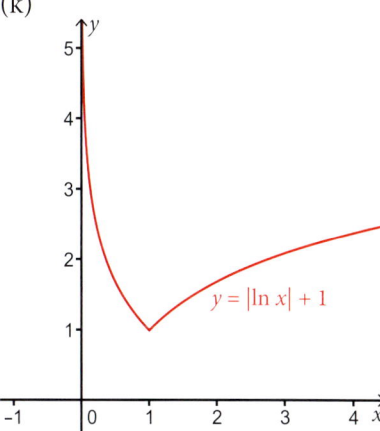

ANSWERS – 1F

(l)
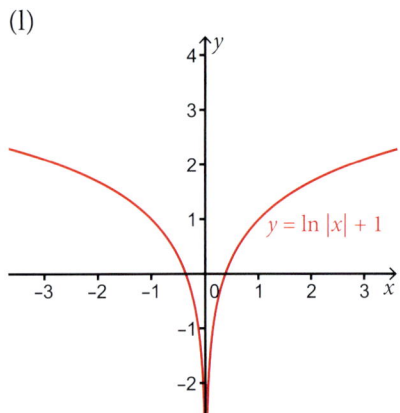

Exercise 1G

1. (a) $x = -1, 2$ (b) $-1 < x < 2$
2. (a) $x = 1, 6$ (b) No solutions
   (c) $x = -\dfrac{12}{5}, \dfrac{4}{5}$ (d) $x = -3, -1$
   (e) No solutions (f) $x = -\dfrac{13}{4}, \dfrac{3}{4}$
   (g) $x = 0, 2$
3. (a) $-\dfrac{1}{5} < x < 1$ (b) No solutions
   (c) $-\dfrac{3}{4} < x < \dfrac{9}{4}$ (d) $-13 < x < 1$
   (e) $-6 < x < 1$
4. (a)
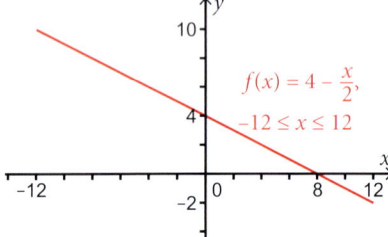

(b)
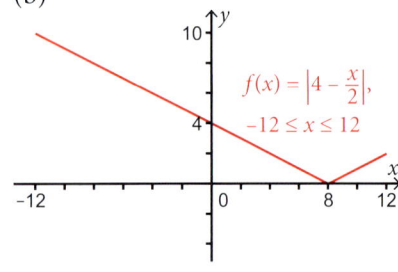

(c)
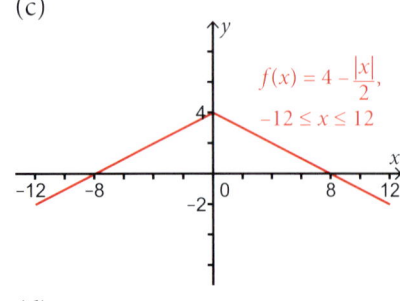

(d) $x = 4, 12$

Exercise 1H

1. (a) $y = |x| - 2$
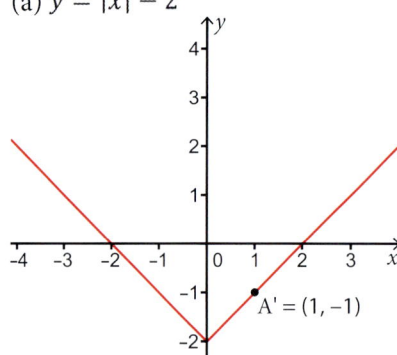

(b) $y = 2|x|$
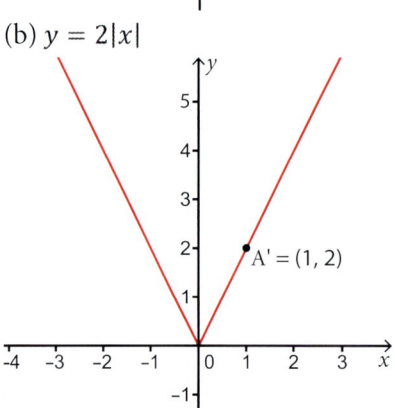

(c) $y = 2|x| - 2$
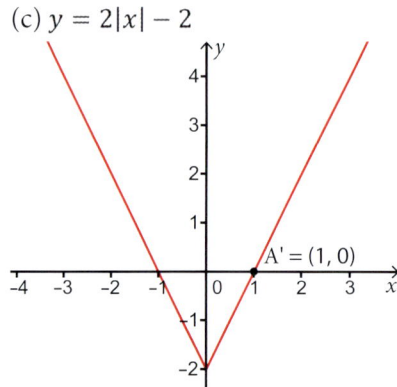

(d) $y = |2x|$
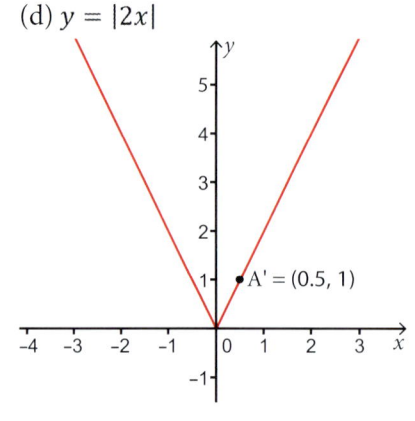

(e) $y = |2x| - 2$
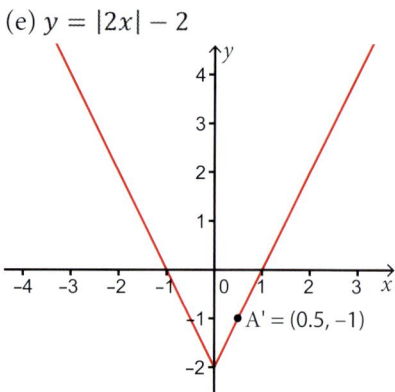

(f) $y = 2|2x|$
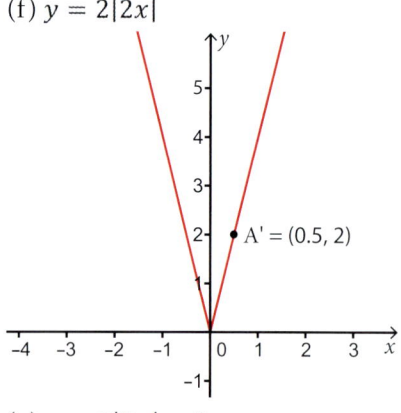

(g) $y = 2|2x| - 2$
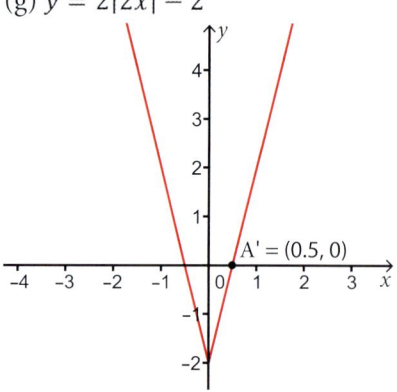

2. (a) $f(x) = -x^2$
   (b) $f(x) = 8x^2$
   (c) $f(x) = 4x^2$
   (d) $f(x) = (x-3)^2 + 1$
   (e) $f(x) = -(x-1)^2$
   (f) $f(x) = -x^2 + 2x - 2$
   (g) $f(x) = x^2$
   (h) $f(x) = -x^2$
3. (a) Stretch factor 2 in y-direction
   (b) Translation by $\begin{pmatrix} 0 \\ -2 \end{pmatrix}$ or translation by $\begin{pmatrix} 2 \\ 0 \end{pmatrix}$
   (c) Translation by $\begin{pmatrix} -3 \\ -3 \end{pmatrix}$
   (d) Stretch factor ½ in x-direction
   (e) Translation by $\begin{pmatrix} -45° \\ 0 \end{pmatrix}$

(f) Stretch factor ½ in x-direction
(g) Stretch factor ⅖ in y-direction or stretch factor 5/2 in x-direction
(h) Translation by $\binom{0}{1}$ (i) Stretch factor $\frac{1}{b}$ in y-direction
(j) Stretch factor $\frac{q}{p}$ in y-direction
(k) Reflection in y-axis

4. (a) Stretch factor 2 in y-direction; translation by $\binom{0}{1}$ (b) Stretch factor 2 in y-direction; reflection in x-axis (c) Translation by $\binom{-3}{-3}$; reflection in x-axis (d) Stretch factor 2 in y-direction; reflection in x-axis (e) Reflection in x-axis; translation by $\binom{0}{1}$ (f) Translation by $\binom{-1}{0}$; translation by $\binom{0}{1}$
(g) Reflection in x-axis; reflection in y-axis (h) Translation by $\binom{0}{9}$; stretch factor ½ in y-direction
(i) Stretch factor $\frac{a}{b}$ in y-direction; translation by $\binom{0}{b-a}$
(j) Translation by $\binom{-1}{0}$; Stretch factor $\frac{1}{p}$ in y-direction (k) Stretch factor ⅔ in x-direction; reflection in x-axis

5. (a) $g(x) = 2\sqrt{x}$
(b) $g(x) = -\sqrt{2x}$
(c) $g(x) = \frac{1}{3}x^{-\frac{1}{2}}$
(d) $g(x) = -2x^{-\frac{1}{2}}$
(e) $g(x) = 2 + \sin(x - 60°)$
(f) $g(x) = \cos x$
(g) $g(x) = \frac{1}{3}\tan(-3x)$ (h) $g(x) = 2\cos(x - 45°)\sin(x - 45°) - 2$
(i) $g(x) = |x - 6| - 1$
(j) $g(x) = |2x + 2|$

6. (a) Stretch factor ½ in x-direction

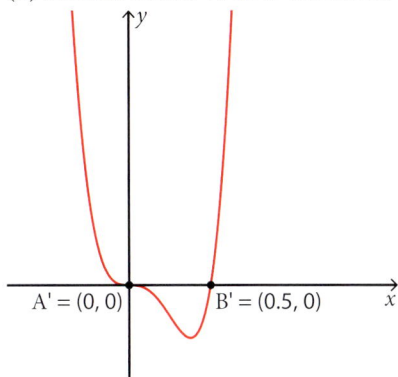

(b) Stretch factor 2 in y-direction.

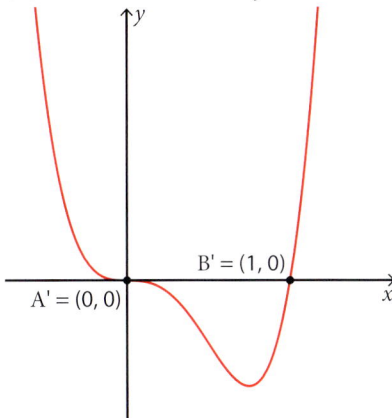

(c) Translation by $\binom{0}{1}$

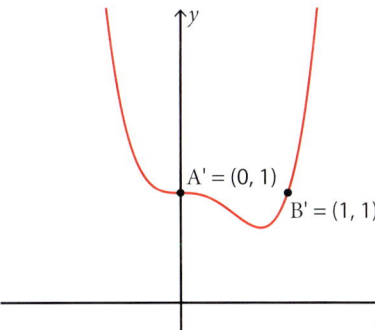

(d) Translation by $\binom{1}{0}$

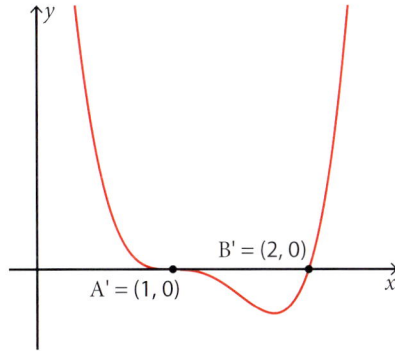

(e) Translation by $\binom{1}{-1}$

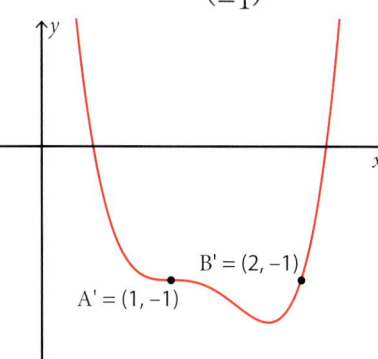

(f) Reflection in x-axis

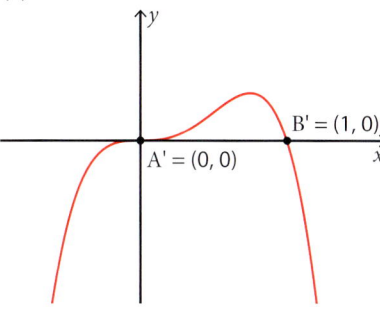

(g) Reflection in x-axis; translation by $\binom{0}{1}$

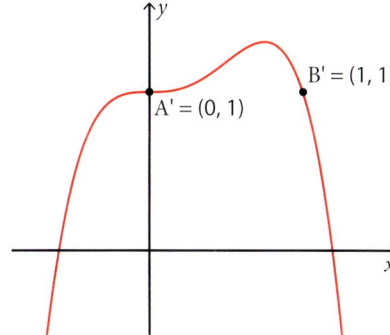

7. (a)

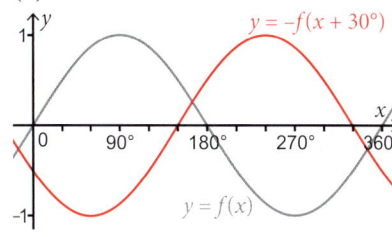

(b)
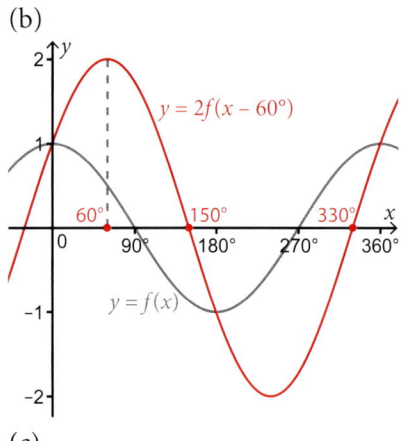

(c)
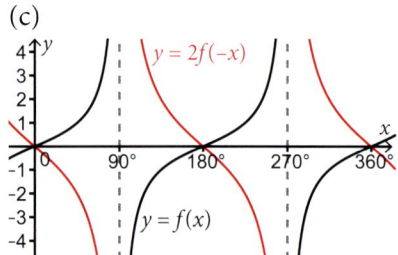

8.
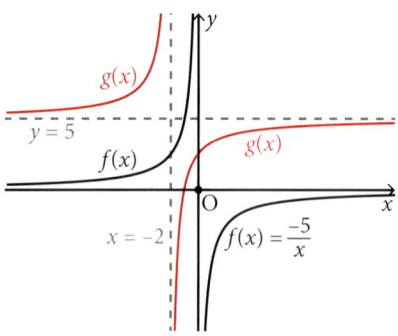

9. Translation by 1 unit in the negative x-direction, 3 units in the negative y-direction.

10. (a) $g(x) = -x^2$ (b) Translation by 1 unit in the negative x-direction, 1 unit in the negative y-direction.

Exercise 2A

1. (a) $m = \dfrac{3n-1}{2}$

(b) $q = \sqrt{p^2 - 1}$

(c) $t = \sqrt[3]{1+s}$

(d) $x = \dfrac{y}{1+y}$

2. (a)
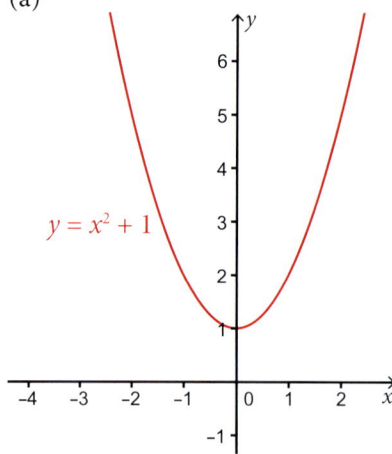

(b)
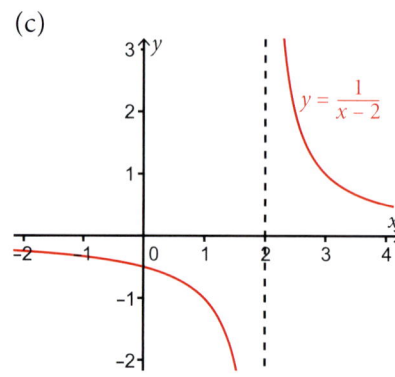

(c)
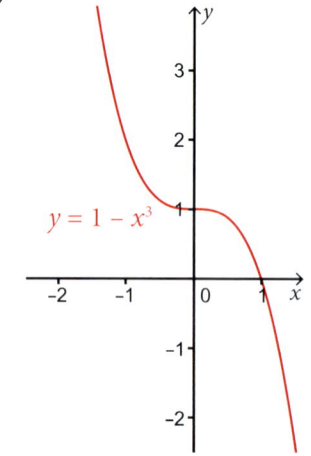

(d)

3. (a) $f(x) - 2 = x^2 - 2$
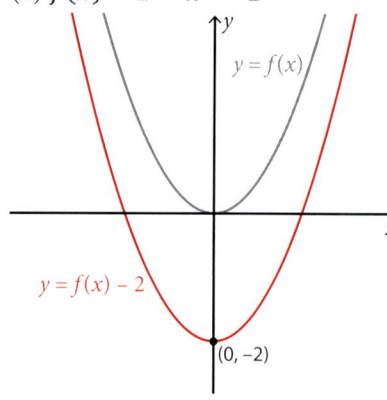

(b) $f(x - 90°) = \cos(x - 90°)$
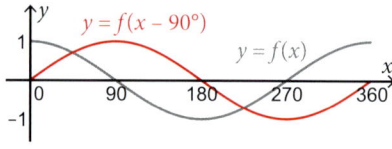

(c) $-f(x) = -\dfrac{1}{x}$
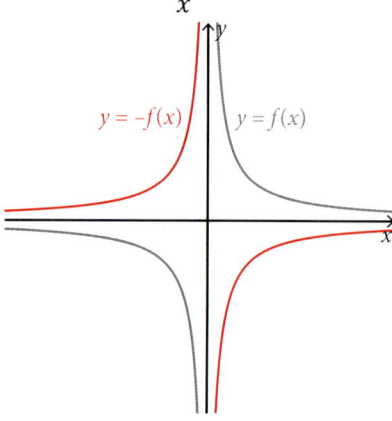

(d) $2f(x) = 2x^3$
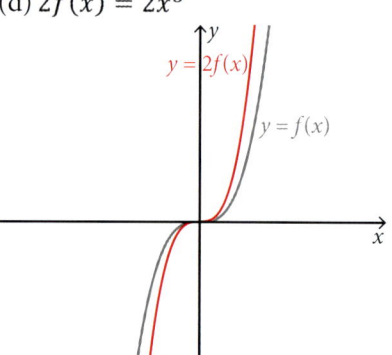

ANSWERS – 2B

Exercise 2B

1. (a)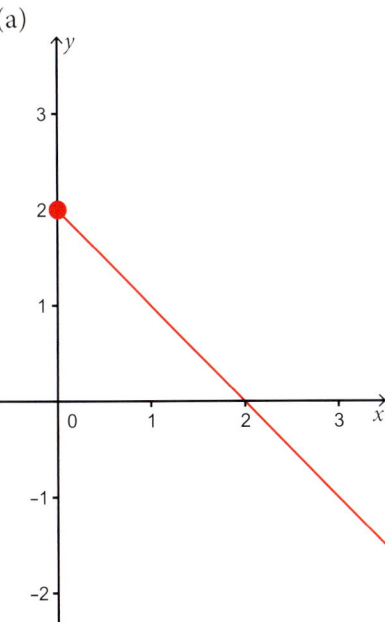

(b)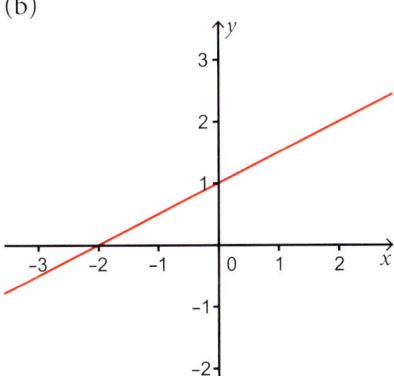

(c)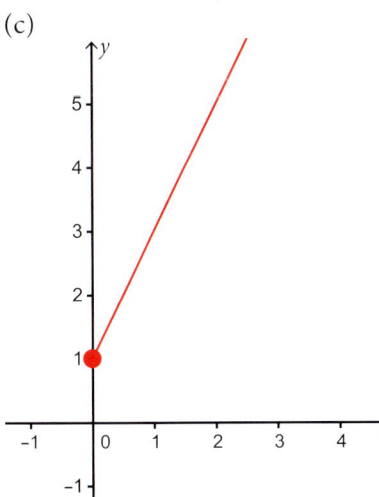

(d)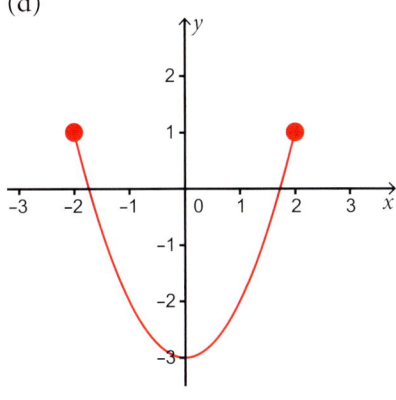

(e)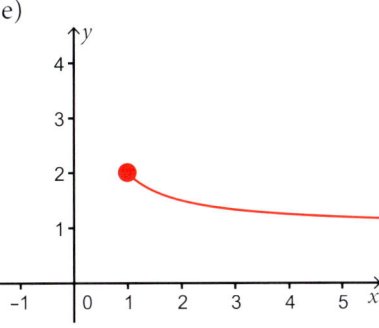

(f)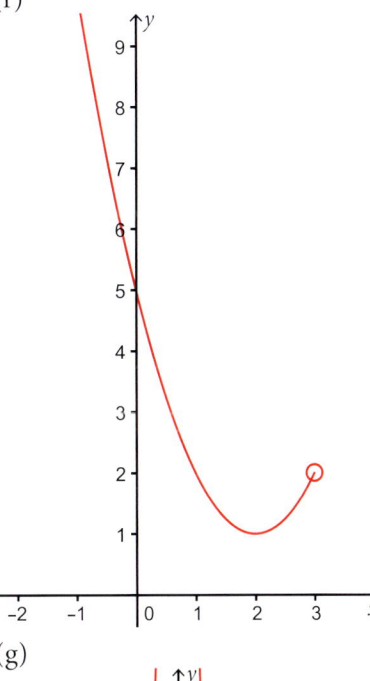

(g)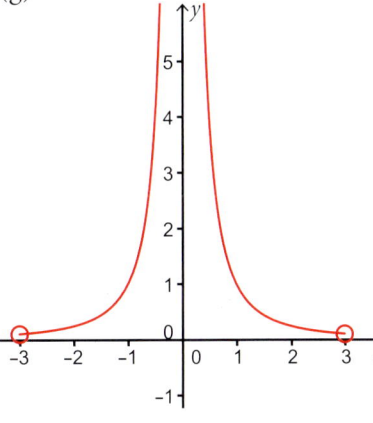

(h)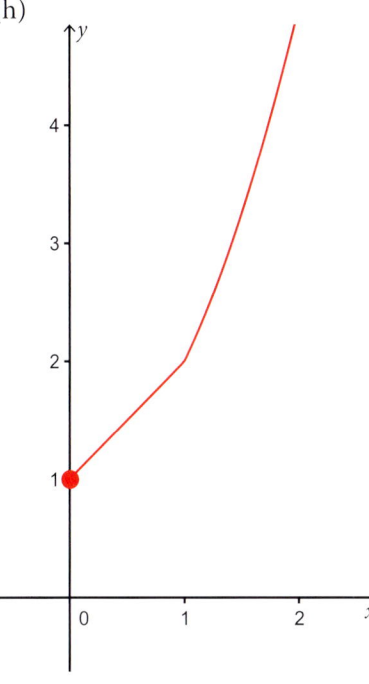

2. (a) One-to-one; function
(b) One-to-many; not a function
(c) Many-to-many; not a function
(d) One-to-one; function
(e) One-to-one; function
(f) Many-to-one; function
(g) One-to-one; function
(h) Many-to-one; function
(i) One-to-many; not a function
(j) One-to-one; function

3. (a) $f(x) \in \{-5, -2, 1, 4\}$; one-to-one (b) $f(x) \in \mathbb{R}, f(x) \leq 2$; many-to-one (c) $f(x) \in \mathbb{R}, f(x) < 2$; many-to-one
(d) $f(x) \in \mathbb{R}, f(x) \geq 1$; many-to-one (e) $f(x) \in \mathbb{R}, 0 < f(x) < 4$; many-to-one
(f) $f(x) \in \mathbb{R}, -7 \leq f(x) < 1$; one-to-one
(g) $f(x) \in \mathbb{R}, -1 \leq f(x) \leq 1$; one-to-one (h) $f(x) \in \{1, 2, 3, 4, 5\}$; one-to-one (i) $f(x) \in \mathbb{R}, f(x) > 0$; one-to-one

4. (a) $x \in \mathbb{R}, x > -1$ (b) $x \in \mathbb{R}$
(c) $x \in \mathbb{R}, x \geq 2$
(d) $x \in \mathbb{R}, -1 \leq x \leq 3$
(e) $x \in \mathbb{R}, x \geq 0$
(f) $x \in \mathbb{R}, -2 < x \leq 0$

5. $k = 2$
6. $p = 1, p = -3$
7. $m = 4, c = 2$
8. $a = 2, b = -1, c = 4$

ANSWERS – 2B

9. (a)

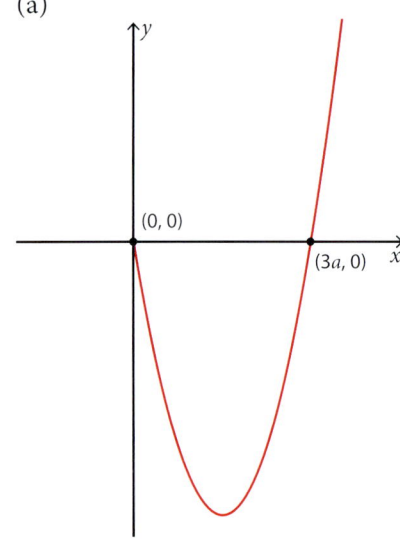

(b) $10a^2$ (c) $x = 12$

10. -3

Exercise 2C

1. (a) 9 (b) 69 (c) 1733 (d) -6
   (e) $h(5) = 0$. This cannot be used as input to $h(x)$ because the domain is $x > 0$.
2. (a) 69 (b) -52 (c) 4 (d) 22
3. (a) 27 (b) 0.538 or $7/13$
   (c) 78 (d) 4.118 or $70/17$
4. $gf(x) = \ln(2e^x) = \ln 2 + x$
   $fg(x) = e^{\ln(2x)} = 2x$
   $2x = \ln 2 + x \Rightarrow x = \ln 2$
5. (b) $gf(x) \geq 0$
6. (a) $fg(x) = \dfrac{k}{k+x}, x \in \mathbb{R}, x \neq -k$,
   $gf(x) = k + \dfrac{k}{x}, x \in \mathbb{R}, x \neq 0$
   (b) $\dfrac{k}{k+x} = k + \dfrac{k}{x} \Rightarrow$
   $\dfrac{k}{k+x} = \dfrac{kx+k}{x} \Rightarrow$
   $kx = (kx+k)(x+k) \Rightarrow$
   $kx^2 + k^2x + k^2 = 0$
   $\Rightarrow x^2 + kx + k = 0$
   (c) $x = -2$
   (d) $x = \dfrac{-5 \pm \sqrt{5}}{2}$
7. (a) $4 \leq f \leq 13$ (b) 1
8. $x = 10$
9. (a) $f(x) = -1 + \dfrac{12}{6-x}$
   (b) $p(x) = -1 + x, q(x) = \dfrac{12}{6-x}$

Exercise 2D

1. (a) $f^{-1}(x) = \dfrac{2}{x-1}$ (b) $x = -1, 2$
2. (a) $f^{-1}(x) = \sqrt{x+2}, x \in \mathbb{R}, x \geq -2$
   (b) $g^{-1}(x) = \dfrac{28-x^2}{7}, x \in \mathbb{R}, x \geq 0$
   (c) $h^{-1}(x) = \dfrac{x-8}{2}, x \in \mathbb{R}$
3. (a) $f^{-1}(y) = \sqrt{y-4}$
   (b) $g^{-1}(y) = \dfrac{5-y}{7}$
   (c) $h^{-1}(y) = -\dfrac{y+9}{2}$
4. $f^{-1}(x) = \ln(x+9) + 10$, $x \in \mathbb{R}, x > -9$
5. (a) $\dfrac{7x+63}{x+8}$ (b) $f^{-1}(x) = \dfrac{63-8x}{x-7}$
   (c) $x \in \mathbb{R}, x \neq 7$
6. (a) $f^{-1}(x) = \dfrac{3x+4}{x}$ (b) $x = \pm 4$
7. (a) $\ln 19$
   (b) $f^{-1}(x) = \dfrac{1}{6}(e^x + 5), x \in \mathbb{R}$
8. (a) $\dfrac{42}{x+5} + 6, x \in \mathbb{R}, x \neq -5$
   (b) $\dfrac{6}{7x+11}, x \in \mathbb{R}, x \neq -\dfrac{11}{7}$
   (c) $\dfrac{x-6}{7}, x \in \mathbb{R}$
   (d) $\dfrac{6}{x} - 5, x \in \mathbb{R}, x \neq 0$
   (e) $\dfrac{42}{x-6} - 5, x \in \mathbb{R}, x \neq 0$
   (f) $\dfrac{6}{7x} - \dfrac{11}{7}, x \in \mathbb{R}, x \neq 0$
9. (a) $f^{-1}(x) = 3 - \dfrac{x}{x-2}, x \in \mathbb{R}, x \neq 2$
   (b)

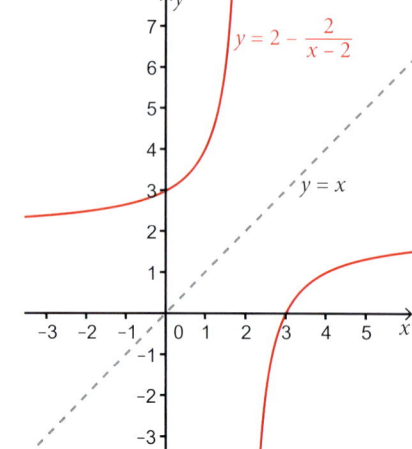

10. (a) $fg(x) = x$ (b) $gf(x) = x$
    (c) The two functions are inverses of each other:
    $f(x) = g^{-1}(x); g(x) = f^{-1}(x)$
11. (a) $f^{-1}(x) = \dfrac{1}{2}e^x$
    (b) $f^{-1}(x) = e^{\frac{x}{6}}$
    (c) $f^{-1}(x) = \dfrac{1}{2}e^{x/3}$
    (d) $f^{-1}(x) = \ln(2x)$
    (e) $f^{-1}(x) = \dfrac{1}{2}\ln x$
    (f) $f^{-1}(x) = \ln(x-1) - 1$
    (g) $f^{-1}(x) = e^{1-x}$
    (h) $f^{-1}(x) = \dfrac{1}{2}\ln x$
    (i) $f^{-1}(x) = \dfrac{1}{b}\ln\left(\dfrac{x}{a}\right)$
    (j) $f^{-1}(x) = \dfrac{1}{3}(e^{x+2} - 1)$

Exercise 2E

1. (a) 117 cm (b) 10 years 7 months
   (c) There is no differentiation for boys and girls. (d) No. The model predicts continued growth. In reality people stop growing, or even shrink in later years.
2. (a) In models B and D the waiting time falls when $s > 500$ and then reaches zero when $s = 1000$. This is unrealistic. In practice, the waiting time will continue to rise, but more slowly when $s > 500$ because some sick people will be put off by the long wait.
   (b) In model C the waiting time increases more slowly as s increases. This is realistic. In model A the waiting time continues to increase at a constant rate. In model E, the waiting time increases more rapidly as s increases. Both are unrealistic.
   (d) 28.8 days
   (e) For $s > 1250$ model C predicts that $w(s)$ begins to fall.
   (f) 100
3. (a) 15 000
   (b) $cn(r) = 1000 \ln(20r^{-3} + 1)$

ANSWERS – 4A

(c) (i) £9 620 (3 s.f.)
(ii) £13 100 (3 s.f.)
4. (a) 17.5 cm (b) 178 days after 1st March, i.e. 25th August.
(c) Whether the crop was ready; the weather. (d) The model doesn't work for $t = 0$; it could be refined as $h(t) = 10\log(t + 1)$
5. (a)

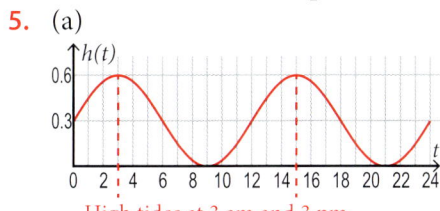

High tides at 3 am and 3 pm

(b)

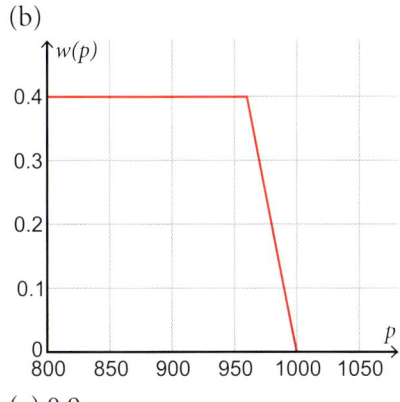

(c) 0.9
(d) There are many other factors that might cause flooding, e.g. heavy rainfall. The model predicts high tides at fixed times of 3 a.m. and 3 p.m. In reality, the times of the two high tides change daily.
6. (a) $t(x) = 1.2x$
(b) $f(x) = x + 15$
(c) $ft(x) = 1.2x + 15$
$tf(x) = 1.2(x + 15) = 1.2x + 18$
Roisin would pay £3 more using $tf(x)$, because she would be paying taxes on the delivery fee. It would be cheaper for her if the delivery fee were added after the taxes.
(d) If taxes are not paid on delivery fees, then the total charged should be calculated using $ft(x)$.
7. (a) $r(t) = 3t$
(b) $A(t) = 9\pi t^2$

Exercise 3A
1. $a = 7.73$ mm, $B = 19.5°, C = 11.5°$
2. 43.3 cm²
3. (a)

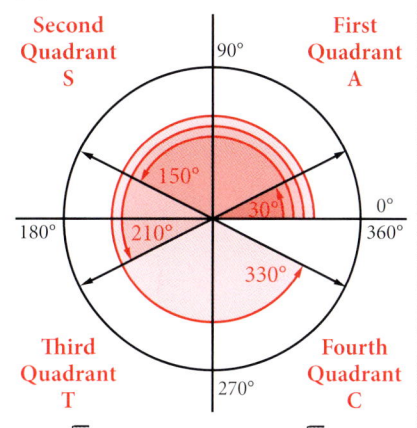

(b) $\frac{\sqrt{3}}{2}$ (c) $\cos 150° = -\frac{\sqrt{3}}{2}$, $\cos 210° = -\frac{\sqrt{3}}{2}$, $\cos 330° = \frac{\sqrt{3}}{2}$

Exercise 3B
1. (a) 0 (b) $-\frac{\sqrt{2}}{2}$ (c) –1
2. (a) $\frac{\pi}{6}$ (b) $\frac{\pi}{4}$ (c) $\frac{\pi}{3}$ (d) $-\frac{\pi}{3}$ (e) $-\frac{\pi}{2}$
(f) -2π (g) 3π (h) 20π
3. (a) 120° (b) 240° (c) 10° (d) 1°
(e) –6° (f) 450° (g) 27° (h) 0°
(i) 80°
4. (a) 0.576 (b) 0.489 (c) 3.18
(d) 5.74 (e) 3.12 (f) 1.19 (g) 10.4
(h) –1.55 (i) –4.10
5. (a) 720° (b) 1620° (c) 810°
(d) 30° (e) 150° (f) –45°
(g) $\frac{180}{\pi}$ (h) $-\frac{450}{\pi}$

Exercise 3C
1. 3.93 cm
2. 0.294 radians
3. 13.9 m
4. 1.03 radians
5. $B = 0.122$ radians; $C = 1.02$ radians; $c = 14.1$ cm
6. 42.0 cm²
7. 6.39 cm
8. 0.619 radians

Exercise 3D
1.

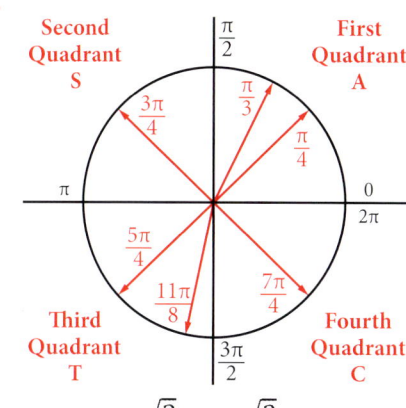

2. (a) 60° (b) $\frac{\sqrt{3}}{2}$ (c) $-\frac{\sqrt{3}}{2}$
3.

θ	$-\frac{\pi}{12}$	$\frac{\pi}{12}$	$\frac{11\pi}{12}$
$\sin\theta$	$\frac{\sqrt{2}-\sqrt{6}}{4}$	$\frac{\sqrt{6}-\sqrt{2}}{4}$	$\frac{\sqrt{6}-\sqrt{2}}{4}$
$\cos\theta$	$\frac{\sqrt{6}+\sqrt{2}}{4}$	$\frac{\sqrt{6}+\sqrt{2}}{4}$	$-\frac{\sqrt{6}+\sqrt{2}}{4}$
$\tan\theta$	$\sqrt{3}-2$	$2-\sqrt{3}$	$\sqrt{3}-2$

θ	$\frac{13\pi}{12}$	$\frac{23\pi}{12}$
$\sin\theta$	$\frac{\sqrt{2}-\sqrt{6}}{4}$	$\frac{\sqrt{2}-\sqrt{6}}{4}$
$\cos\theta$	$-\frac{\sqrt{6}+\sqrt{2}}{4}$	$\frac{\sqrt{6}+\sqrt{2}}{4}$
$\tan\theta$	$2-\sqrt{3}$	$\sqrt{3}-2$

Exercise 3E
1. (a) 3.14 cm (b) 9.42 m (c) 4.19 cm
(d) 209 m (e) 7.85 mm
2. (a) 8.38 cm² (b) 78.5 cm²
(c) 0.393 cm² (d) 0.00838 cm²
(e) 21.2 cm²
3. (a) ⅜
4. 5.53 m
5. 47.0 m

Exercise 3F
1. (a) 22.5 mm (b) 18.6 mm²
2. (b) 0.680 (c) 12.2 m² (d) 0.920 m²
3. (a) $2\sqrt{3}$ cm (b) 2π cm²
4. 22.9 cm²
5. (a) 24π cm² (b) 4 cm (c) 8π cm²

Exercise 4A
1. (a) $2^{5/2}$ (b) 24 (c) 8

ANSWERS – 4A

2. (a) $y = \dfrac{x+1}{x}$ (b) $y = \dfrac{1}{x+1}$
   (c) $y = \dfrac{3}{2}$
3. (a) $x = 8$; $y = -2$
   (b) $a = 0$; $b = 4$
   (c) $x = 10$; $y = 5$ or $x = -\dfrac{25}{2}$; $y = -\dfrac{5}{2}$

Exercise 4B

1. (a) $(0, 1)$
   (b) $(1, 0), (0, -1)$
   (c) $(0, -2), (8, 0)$
   (d) $(-1.25, 0), (0, 5)$
   (e) $(0, 0)$
   (f) $(0, 0), (0, 2\pi^2)$
   (g) $(0, 2), \left(\pm\dfrac{\pi}{2}, 0\right)$
   (h) $(1, 0), (0, 0), (-1, 0)$
   (i) $(1, 0), (-1, 0), (0, 1), (0, -1), (0.5, 0), (-0.5, 0)$
   (j) $(0, 0), (\sqrt{\pi}, 0)$
   (k) $(-1, 0), (0, 2)$
   (l) $\left(\dfrac{\sqrt{3}}{2}, 0\right), (0, 3), \left(-\dfrac{\sqrt{3}}{2}, 0\right), (0, -1)$

2.

	A	B	C	D	E	F	G	H
θ	0	$\dfrac{\pi}{4}$	$\dfrac{\pi}{2}$	$\dfrac{3\pi}{4}$	π	$\dfrac{5\pi}{4}$	$\dfrac{3\pi}{2}$	$\dfrac{7\pi}{4}$
x	1	$\dfrac{\sqrt{2}}{2}$	0	$-\dfrac{\sqrt{2}}{2}$	-1	$-\dfrac{\sqrt{2}}{2}$	0	$\dfrac{\sqrt{2}}{2}$
y	0	$\dfrac{\sqrt{2}}{2}$	1	$\dfrac{\sqrt{2}}{2}$	0	$-\dfrac{\sqrt{2}}{2}$	-1	$-\dfrac{\sqrt{2}}{2}$

3. (a) $(0, -1)$ (b) $\left(\dfrac{\sqrt{3}}{3}, 0\right), \left(-\dfrac{\sqrt{3}}{3}, 0\right)$
   (c) $y = 1$
4. (a) $\dfrac{\pi}{3}$ (b) $3\sqrt{3}$
5. (a) 2 (b) 1 (c) 1
6. (a) $t = 1$ (b) $a = -5$ (c) $(-3, 0)$
7. $a = -4, b = 2$ or $a = -\dfrac{9}{2}, b = -\dfrac{9}{4}$
8. (a)

	P1	P2	P3	P4	P5	P6	P7	P8	P9	P10
θ	0	$\dfrac{\pi}{4}$	$\dfrac{\pi}{2}$	$\dfrac{3\pi}{4}$	π	$\dfrac{5\pi}{4}$	$\dfrac{3\pi}{2}$	$\dfrac{7\pi}{4}$	2π	$\dfrac{9\pi}{4}$
x	0.00	0.56	1.57	1.67	0.00	-2.78	-4.71	-3.89	0.00	5.00
y	0.00	0.56	0.00	-1.67	-3.14	-2.78	0.00	3.89	6.28	5.00

(b)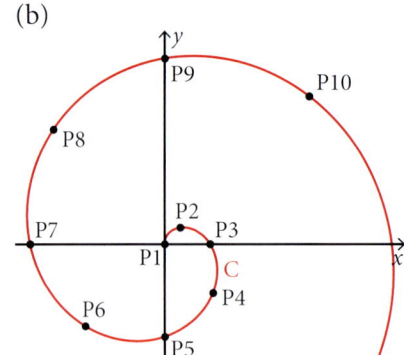

Exercise 4C

1. (a) $y = 8 - 2x$
   (b) $y = \dfrac{4}{x^2}$
   (c) $y = 4x^2 - 8x + 2$
   (d) $y = \dfrac{1}{2}\left(\dfrac{x}{2}\right)^{\frac{3}{2}}$
   (e) $y = \dfrac{3}{\sqrt{2x}}$
   (f) $y = 3\left(\dfrac{x+1}{x-1}\right)^2$
   (g) $x^2 + (y-1)^2 = 1$
   (h) $x^2 + y^4 = 16$
   (i) $y = \pm 3\sqrt{1-x^2}$
2. $y = \dfrac{3}{16}x^2$
3. (a) $(x+4)^2 + (y-3)^2 = 25$
   (b) Centre $(-4, 3)$, radius 5
4. (a) $(2x-4)^2 + (y-4)^2 = 16$
   (b) $(2, 0)$ (c) $(0, 4)$
5. $x = 5 - 2\sin\theta$, $y = \sqrt{1 + \sin\theta}$
6. $a = \pm 2$
7. (a) $y = \sqrt{1-x}$ (b) Parametric: $x = \sin^2 t$. Max and min values of x are 1 and 0. Cartesian: $y = \sqrt{1-x}$. Max value of x is 1, since you cannot take the square root of a negative number.
8. (a) $x^3 = \dfrac{1}{(t^3-1)^3}$, $x^2 = \dfrac{1}{(t^3-1)^2}$
   (b) $y = \dfrac{t^3}{(t^3-1)^3}$
   (c) $x^3 + x^2 = \dfrac{1}{(t^3-1)^3} + \dfrac{1}{(t^3-1)^2}$
   $= \dfrac{1}{(t^3-1)^3} + \dfrac{(t^3-1)}{(t^3-1)^3}$
   $= \dfrac{1 + (t^3-1)}{(t^3-1)^3} = \dfrac{t^3}{(t^3-1)^3} = y^3$
9. (a) $x = \dfrac{3}{\sin t} - 3$ (b) $t = \dfrac{\pi}{2}, \dfrac{3\pi}{2}$
   (c) $(-6, 0)$ (d) Max 3, min -3. L1: $y = 3$; L2: $y = -3$.
10. (a) $y = 2\cos^2\theta$ (b) $x = \dfrac{t-1}{t+1}$
11. $x = \dfrac{1-t}{2t}$, $y = \dfrac{1-t}{2}$

Exercise 4D

1. (a) 2.98 s (b) Yes, the ball clears the fence. When $x = 120$ m, $y = 31.1$ m
2. (a) $(1, 0), (-1, 0), (0, 2)$
   (b)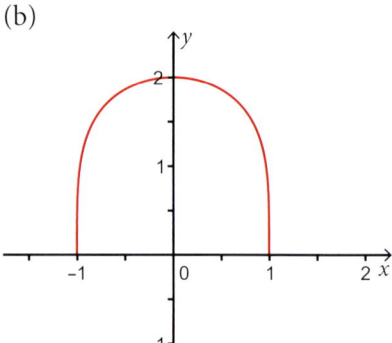
3. (a) $\sqrt{10}$ or 3.16 s (b) $10 + 5\sqrt{10}$ or 25.8 m
   (c) $y = -\dfrac{1}{5}x^2 + 4x + 30$
   (d) Wind may affect the trajectory of the car as it falls; air resistance; the equation for the vertical position of the car assumes $g = 10$ ms^{-2}.

Exercise 5A

1. (a) $x = 2$ (b) $w = -4$ (c) $z = -\dfrac{12}{7}$
   (d) $y = -\dfrac{5}{4}$ (e) $v = 1$
2. (a) $x = 1, -7$ (b) $x = 8, -10$
   (c) $x = 2, 4$ (d) $x = 1$ (e) $x = 0, 5$
3. (a) $x = 10, y = 5$
   (b) $x = 10, y = -1$
   (c) $x = -9, y = -8$
   (d) $x = -2, y = -1$
   (e) $x = -5, y = -7$
   (f) $x = 2, y = -3, z = -2$
4. (a) $3n - 2$ (b) $2n + 3$ (c) $4n - 7$
   (d) $-10n + 5$ (e) $-20n + 37$

Exercise 5B

1. (a) $-1, 1, 3, 5$ (b) $7, -2, -17, -38$
   (c) $1, 0, 1, 4$ (d) $-2, 4, 12, 22$

ANSWERS – 5H

(e) –6, –4, 0, 6 (f) 2, 9, 28, 65
(g) 0, 3, 16, 45 (h) 7, 22, 45, 76
(i) –2, 3, –4, 5 (j) $1, \frac{8}{7}, \frac{11}{9}, \frac{14}{11}$

2. (a) $n = 11$ (b) $n = 4$ (c) $n = 3$
   (d) $n = 5$ (e) $n = 6$ (f) $n = 2$
   (g) $n = 3$ (h) $n = 2$ (i) $n = 10$
   (j) $n = 3$
3. 4
4. $a = 3, b = 5$
5. $a = 4, b = 3$
6. $a = 1, b = 3, c = 2$
7. $u_n = (n - 2)^2 + 4 \geq 4$ for all values of n
8. –5
9. (a) $4n$ is always even, therefore $4n − 7$ is always odd (b) Examples $u_n = 2n, u_n = 2n + 4, u_n = 4n − 2$
10. $u_n = 5n − 6$
11. $u_n = k(k − 1)$
    $= (3n − 2)(3n − 3)$
    $= 3(3n − 2)(n − 1)$. Hence each term is a multiple of 3.

Exercise 5C

1. (a) 1, –3, –7, –11 (b) 1, –1, –1, –1
   (c) 3, 4, 9, 64 (d) 2, ³⁄₂, ¹¹⁄₈, ⁴³⁄₃₂
   (e) 27, 18, 12, 8 (f) 3, 7, 43, 1807
   (g) 3, ¾, ³⁄₇, ³⁄₁₀ (h) ¼, –½, –2, –5
   (i) –¾, 2, –⁷⁄₂, ¹⁵⁄₂ (j) 2, 1, –1, –1
2. (a) $u_{n+1} = u_n + 3, u_1 = 2$
   (b) $u_{n+1} = u_n − 5, u_1 = −5$
   (c) $u_{n+1} = u_n, u_1 = 37$
   (d) $u_{n+1} = −u_n, u_1 = 2$
   (e) $u_{n+1} = 6 − u_n, u_1 = 2$
   (f) $u_{n+1} = 2u_n, u_1 = 2$
   (g) $u_{n+1} = \frac{u_n}{2}, u_1 = 1$
   (h) $u_{n+1} = \sqrt{u_n}, u_1 = 256$
   (i) $u_{n+1} = (u_n)^2, u_1 = 2$
   (j) $u_{n+1} = 4u_n − 2, u_1 = 1$
3. 1, 0.43, 0.39, 0.39, 0.39
4. (a) 1, 4, 1 (b) 1
5. 3, –5
6. $d = \frac{16}{9}$
7. –4, 2
8. –2
9. (a) 2.70, 2.81, 2.77 (b) 24 (c) 3
10. (b) $q = 6$

Exercise 5D

1. (a) ¾, ⁹⁄₁₆, ²⁷⁄₆₄ (b) Converges
2. (a) $1, 3a, 9a^2, 27a^3$
   (b) $-\frac{1}{3} < a < \frac{1}{3}$
3. 1, 2, 5, 26; diverges
4. (a) 3, ³⁄₅, ¹⁵⁄₁₃, ³⁹⁄₄₁, ¹²³⁄₁₂₁
   (b) Converges and oscillates
5. 2.5
6. Diverges
7. Converges to 2.
8. (a) 1, 0.3, 0.79, 0.45, 0.69 (b) yes
   (c) $c = {}^{10}\!/_{17}$
9. $0 < p < 2$
10. $a > 0$

Exercise 5E

1. (a) yes (b) yes (c) no (d) no
   (e) yes (f) yes (g) yes (h) no
   (i) yes (j) no
2. 9
3. (a) 59, 299 (b) 26, 146
   (c) –13.3, –93.3 (d) 4.55, 34.55
   (e) $23p, 103p$ (f) ²⁹⁄₃, ¹⁰⁹⁄₃
   (g) $(−15y + 19), (−95y + 99)$
   (h) $6.5 \times 10^4, 2.65 \times 10^5$
   (i) $(-2 + 2\sqrt{2}), (-42 + 42\sqrt{2})$
   (j) 1014.5, 1074.5
4. (b) 346
5. 10.5
6. (b) 537

Exercise 5F

1. (a) 110 (b) 0 (c) 72 (d) –325
   (e) 63 (f) 5.5×10^5 (g) 0
   (h) $440\sqrt{5}$ (i) $11 − 44x$ (j) 142
2. 624
3. 1 600 000
4. (a) $u_n = 2n + 1$ (b) $S_n = n(n + 2)$
5. $S_n = \frac{n}{2}[2a + (n − 1)d]$
   $= \frac{n}{2}[a + (a + (n − 1)d)]$ (1)
   $u_n = a + (n − 1)d$
   $\Rightarrow l = a + (n − 1)d$ (2)
   Sub (2) in (1) $\Rightarrow S_n = \frac{n}{2}(a + l)$
6. 78

Exercise 5G

1. (a) $2 + 3 + 4 + 5$
   (b) $\frac{3}{2} + 2 + \frac{5}{2} + 3 + \frac{7}{2}$
   (c) $\frac{1}{10} + \frac{2}{10} + \frac{3}{10} + \frac{4}{10} + \frac{5}{10}$
   (d) $3 + 2 + 1 + 0 + -1 + -2 + -3$
   (e) $20 + 15 + 10 + 5 + 0$
   (f) $9700 + 9800 + 9900 + 10\,000$
   (g) $0 + \frac{1}{4} + \frac{1}{2} + \frac{3}{4}$
   (h) $16 + 21$
   (i) $\frac{3}{2} + 2 + \frac{5}{2} + 3$
   (j) $1 + 1 + 1 + 1 + 1$
2. (a) $\sum_{1}^{4}(r + 2)$ (b) $\sum_{1}^{7}(3r + 7)$
   (c) $\sum_{1}^{20}(-2r - 3)$
   (d) $\sum_{1}^{10}(1002 - 2r)$
   (e) $\sum_{1}^{6}(22 - 7r)$ (f) $\sum_{1}^{10}(20r + 1)$
   (g) $\sum_{1}^{5}\left(\frac{2r + 3}{2}\right)$ (h) $\sum_{r=1}^{b}(2r + 1)a$
   (i) $\sum_{1}^{13}(2r + 3)\sqrt{3}$ (j) $\sum_{r=1}^{6}(rt^2)$
3. (a) 75 (b) 65 (c) $15 + 10x$
   (d) 20 (e) 77.5 (f) 30.5 (g) $11y$
   (h) 120 (i) –19 900 (j) 5
4. $S_n = 5 + 11 + 17 + \cdots + (6n − 1)$
   $S_n = \frac{n}{2}[2a + (n − 1)d]$
   $= \frac{n}{2}[10 + 6(n − 1)]$
   $= 5n + 3n(n − 1)$
   $= 5n + 3n^2 − 3n$
   $= 3n^2 + 2n = n(3n + 2)$
5. $n^2 + 6n − 160 = 0; n = 10$
   (–16 is not possible)
6. (a) 6, 4, 2, 0, –2 (b) $n = 8$ or $n = 1$

Exercise 5H

1. (a) no (b) yes (c) no (d) yes (e) no
   (f) no (g) yes (h) no (i) yes (j) no
   (k) yes
2. (a) 1, 3, 9, 27, 81
   (b) –4, –8, –16, –32, –64
   (c) –2, 4, –8, 16, –32
   (d) 64, 32, 16, 8, 4
   (e) $10^3, 10^4, 10^5, 10^6, 10^7$
   (f) 32, 48, 72, 108, 162
   (g) $2, 2\sqrt{2}, 4, 4\sqrt{2}, 8$

ANSWERS – 5H

(h) $\dfrac{1}{2}, \dfrac{1}{4}, \dfrac{1}{8}, \dfrac{1}{16}, \dfrac{1}{32}$

(i) a, ab, ab^2, ab^3, ab^4

(j) $y, 1, \dfrac{1}{y}, \dfrac{1}{y^2}, \dfrac{1}{y^3}$

3. $r = 0.4, a = 5$
4. 10 000
5. 46 656
6. (a) 7, 35, 175, 875
   (b) $u_n = 7 \times 5^{n-1}$
7. $x = -\dfrac{1}{2}$, Terms: $\dfrac{1}{2}, \dfrac{3}{2}, \dfrac{9}{2}$.
8. 11th term
9. 9th term

Exercise 5I

1. (a) 121 (b) ⁶³⁄₆₄ (c) 11 (d) ¹⁰²³⁄₁₀₂₄
   (e) 36.0 (3 s.f.) (f) 11 333 (5 s.f.)
   (g) 9.49 (3 s.f.) (h) 3.95 (3 s.f.)
   (i) 11.1 (3 s.f.) (j) $6 + 3\sqrt{2}$ (k) 1
2. (a) 363 (b) 0.999 (3 s.f.)
   (c) $7 + 3\sqrt{2}$ (d) 63 (e) 40.5 (3 s.f.)
   (f) –21 (g) 85 (h) $\dfrac{6 + 3\sqrt{2}}{4}$ (i) 85
   (j) 4.00 (3 s.f.)
3. 1 968 000
4. 36.0
5. 1555
6. Any multiple of 8.
7. (a) $\dfrac{b^2}{a}, \dfrac{b^3}{a^2}$ (b) $\dfrac{b^9}{a^8}$
8. (a) $x = 0$ or $x = 3$.
   (b) 3, 6, 12 or 12, 6, 3.

Exercise 5J

1. (a) 1 (b) 5 (c) ¹⁰⁰⁄₉ (d) –8 (e) 200
   (f) $2 + \sqrt{2}$ (g) 8.53 (3 s.f.) (h) ¹⁶⁄₃
   (i) $\dfrac{\pi^2}{\pi^2 - 1}$ (j) $\dfrac{36x^2}{6x - 1}$
2. (a) ⁸⁄₃ (b) 1 (c) $\dfrac{(1 + \sqrt{3})}{2}$ (d) ³⁄₂
   (e) $\dfrac{a}{1 - a}$ (f) 2 (g) 14 (h) x
   (i) 3 (j) ¹⁰⁄₉
3. ⁵⁰⁄₉
4. ⅚
5. (a) $r = 0.9, a = 5$ (b) 50
6. (a) $S_\infty = \dfrac{a}{1 - r} \Rightarrow 700 = \dfrac{140}{1 - r}$
   $\Rightarrow 1 - r = \dfrac{140}{700} \Rightarrow r = 0.8$
   (b) 9.18 (c) 582.56
7. ⁵⁄₄

8. (b) ⅕, ⅘ (c) –20, –5
9. (a) 133 (b) ⁴⁰⁰⁄₃
10. (b) 245.277
    (c) $S_n = \dfrac{1400\left(1 - \left(-\dfrac{3}{4}\right)^n\right)}{1.75}$

Exercise 5K

1. 432
2. £1900
3. (a) $h, fh, f^2h, f^3h, \ldots$ GP common ratio f (b) ⅖ (c) 2 metres (d) Air resistance
4.

	Snakes $r = 2.5$ $p_m = 5000$	Owls $r = 0.8$ $p_m = 5000$	Mice $r = 3.7$ $p_m = 50000$
0	300	300	2000
1	705	226	7104
2	1514	173	22 550
3	2639	134	45 806
4	3115	104	14 216
5	2936	81	37 644
6	3030	64	34 420
7	2985	51	39 684
8	3007	40	30 294
9	2996	32	44 176
10	3002	25	19 039

(a) After the first 10 years the population of snakes is stable at a level of roughly 3000. (b) After 10 years the population of owls is rapidly becoming extinct. (c) The population of mice fluctuates wildly from one year to the next. It is also heavily dependent on the initial population. This is **chaotic** behaviour.

Exercise 5L

1. (a) £3000 (b) £70 000
   (c) £95 500
   (d) It may be better to use the AP, increasing profits by £3000 per year. The model using a GP predicts profits almost to double between 2019 and 2026. This could be difficult to achieve. It would also give increasingly difficult targets further ahead.
2. (a) £99 (c) 50 or 80 months
   (d) Cannot be 80. The repayments would be negative after 50 months.
3. $a = 10, d = 0.8$
4. (b) 9.57 m (c) Air resistance
5. (a) £12 400 (b) £261 000

Exercise 6A

1. (a) $1 + 4x + 6x^2 + 4x^3 + x^4$
   (b) $x^3 + 6x^2 + 12x + 8$
2. $a^{15} + 15a^{14}b + 105a^{13}b^2$
3. $270x^3$
4. (a) $\dfrac{1}{2}\sqrt{3}$ (b) $\dfrac{2}{7}\sqrt{3}$ (c) $\dfrac{5}{9}\sqrt{5}$ (d) $\dfrac{2}{5}\sqrt{6}$
5. (a) $(1 + x)^2$ (b) $\left(1 + \dfrac{2}{x}\right)^7$
   (c) $(2 + x^3)^{-\frac{2}{5}}$
6. (a) $3x^2$ (b) $4x^2$ (c) $4x^2$
7. (a) $\dfrac{2}{3(x + 1)} - \dfrac{4}{3(2x + 5)}$
   (b) $-\dfrac{1}{x + 1} + \dfrac{5}{x + 2}$
   (c) $\dfrac{4}{x + 2} + \dfrac{3}{x + 1} + \dfrac{2}{(x + 1)^2}$

Exercise 6B

1. (a) $1 + \dfrac{1}{2}x - \dfrac{1}{8}x^2 + \dfrac{1}{16}x^3 + \cdots$
   for $|x| < 1$
   (b) $1 - x + x^2 - x^3 + \cdots$
   for $|x| < 1$
   (c) $1 + \dfrac{3}{2}x^2 + \dfrac{3}{8}x^4 - \dfrac{1}{16}x^6 + \cdots$
   for $|x| < 1$
   (d) $1 + \dfrac{3}{2}x - \dfrac{9}{8}x^2 + \dfrac{27}{16}x^3 + \cdots$
   for $|x| < \dfrac{1}{3}$
   (e) $1 - 2x + 3x^2 - 4x^3 + \cdots$
   for $|x| < 1$
   (f) $1 - \dfrac{5}{4}x + \dfrac{15}{32}x^2 - \dfrac{5}{128}x^3 + \cdots$
   for $|x| < 2$
   (g) $1 + x + \dfrac{3}{2}x^2 + \dfrac{5}{2}x^3 + \cdots$
   for $|x| < \dfrac{1}{2}$
   (h) $1 + 6x + 24x^2 + 80x^3 + \cdots$
   for $|x| < \dfrac{1}{2}$

ANSWERS – 6C

(i) $1 - \frac{1}{8}x - \frac{3}{128}x^2 - \frac{7}{1024}x^3 + \cdots$
  for $|x| < 2$

(j) $1 + \frac{1}{3}x^2 - \frac{1}{9}x^4 + \frac{5}{81}x^6 + \cdots$
  for $|x| < 1$

2. (a) $\frac{1}{4} - \frac{3}{4}x + \frac{27}{16}x^2 - \frac{27}{8}x^3 + \cdots$

   (b) $\sqrt{2} + \frac{\sqrt{2}}{4}x - \frac{\sqrt{2}}{32}x^2 + \frac{\sqrt{2}}{128}x^3 + \cdots$

   (c) $\frac{\sqrt{6}}{6} - \frac{\sqrt{6}}{36}x + \frac{\sqrt{6}}{144}x^2 - \frac{5\sqrt{6}}{2592}x^3 + \cdots$

   (d) $\frac{1}{2} - \frac{1}{16}x + \frac{3}{256}x^2 - \frac{5}{2048}x^3 + \cdots$

3. $\frac{1}{1} + \frac{5}{9}x + \frac{75}{27}x^2 + \frac{125}{135}x^3 + \cdots$

4. $\frac{1}{8} - \frac{1}{16}x + \frac{1}{16}x^2 - \frac{1}{32}x^3 + \cdots$

5. $3 - \frac{2}{3}x - \frac{2}{27}x^2 - \frac{4}{243}x^3$

6. (a) $1 + \frac{6x}{5} + \frac{63x^2}{25}$

   (b) $-\frac{1}{3} < x < \frac{1}{3}$

7. (a) $1 - 6x + 24x^2 - 80x^3 + \cdots$

   (b) $4 - 23x + 90x^2$

8. (a) $1 - \frac{8}{3}d + \frac{80}{9}d^2 + \cdots$

   (b) $|d| < \frac{1}{4}$

9. (a) $1 + 4x + 8x^2 + \cdots$ for $|x| < 1$

   (b) $8 + 4x - 34x^2 + \cdots$ for $|x| < \frac{1}{4}$

   (c) $\frac{1}{16} + \frac{7}{16}x + \frac{55}{32}x^2 + \cdots$
   for $|x| < 1$

   (d) $\frac{9}{2} + \frac{27x}{4} + \frac{9x^2}{8} + \cdots$ for $|x| < 2$

10. (a) $p = -\frac{1}{4}, q = 32$

    (b) -77.5

    (c) $|x| < 4$

11. $\frac{1}{3} - \frac{2}{27}x^2 + \frac{2}{81}x^4$

12. $1 - 2x + x^2 + 2x^3$

Exercise 6C

1. (a) $\frac{2}{1-3x} + \frac{1}{2x+1}$;

   $3 + 4x + 22x^2 + 46x^3$
   for $|x| < \frac{1}{3}$

   (b) $\frac{2}{x-1} - \frac{9}{2x-3}$;
   $1 - \frac{2}{3}x^2 - \frac{10}{9}x^3$ for $|x| < 1$

   (c) $\frac{3}{2(x+1)} - \frac{1}{2(x-1)}$;
   $2 - x + 2x^2 - x^3$ for $|x| < 1$

   (d) $\frac{2}{3(2x+1)} + \frac{5}{3(x-1)}$;
   $-1 - 3x + x^2 - 7x^3$ for $|x| < \frac{1}{2}$

   (e) $\frac{1}{2(x-1)} - \frac{3}{2(5x+1)}$;
   $-2 + 7x - 38x^2 + 187x^3$
   for $|x| < \frac{1}{5}$

   (f) $\frac{17}{5x+3} - \frac{10}{3x+2}$;
   $\frac{2}{3} - \frac{35}{18}x + \frac{485}{108}x^2 - \frac{6065}{648}x^3$
   for $|x| < \frac{3}{5}$

   (g) $\frac{3}{x-2} - \frac{8}{4x-5}$;
   $\frac{1}{10} + \frac{53}{100}x + \frac{649}{1000}x^2 + \frac{6317}{10000}x^3$
   for $|x| < \frac{5}{4}$

   (h) $\frac{1}{x-2} - \frac{1}{3x-4}$;
   $-\frac{1}{4} - \frac{1}{16}x + \frac{1}{64}x^2 + \frac{11}{256}x^3$
   for $|x| < \frac{4}{3}$

   (i) $\frac{5}{2(3x+1)} - \frac{5}{2(x+1)}$;
   $-5x + 20x^2 - 65x^3 + 200x^4$
   for $|x| < \frac{1}{3}$

   (j) $\frac{1}{2x-5} - \frac{1}{5x-2}$;
   $\frac{3}{10} + \frac{117}{100}x + \frac{3093}{1000}x^2 + \frac{77997}{10000}x^3$
   for $|x| < \frac{2}{5}$

2. (a) $\frac{1}{2(x-1)} - \frac{1}{2(x+1)}$; $-1 - x^2$
   for $|x| < 1$

   (b) $\frac{2}{3(3x-1)} + \frac{5}{3(3x-1)^2}$;
   $1 + 8x + 39x^2 + 162x^3$
   for $|x| < \frac{1}{3}$

   (c) $\frac{1}{2(2x+1)} - \frac{1}{2(2x+1)^2}$;
   $x - 4x^2 + 12x^3$ for $|x| < \frac{1}{2}$

   (d) $\frac{2}{x+2} - \frac{2}{x+1} + \frac{2}{(x+1)^2}$;
   $1 - \frac{5}{2}x + \frac{17}{4}x^2 - \frac{49}{8}x^3$
   for $|x| < \frac{1}{2}$

   (e) $-\frac{1}{4(x+1)} - \frac{1}{(x+1)^2} + \frac{1}{4(x-3)}$;
   $-\frac{4}{3} + \frac{20}{9}x - \frac{88}{27}x^2 + \frac{344}{81}x^3$
   for $|x| < \frac{1}{3}$

   (f) $-\frac{5}{3(x+2)} + \frac{5}{3(x-1)} + \frac{4}{(x-1)^2}$;
   $\frac{3}{2} + \frac{27}{4}x + \frac{81}{8}x^2 + \frac{231}{16}x^3$
   for $|x| < \frac{1}{2}$

   (g) $\frac{1}{x+1} + \frac{1}{x-1} + \frac{2}{(x-1)^2}$;
   $2 + 2x + 6x^2 + 6x^3$ for $|x| < 1$

   (h) $\frac{1}{x+1} + \frac{1}{x-1} + \frac{1}{(x-1)^2}$;
   $1 + 3x^2 + 2x^3$ for $|x| < 1$

   (i) $-\frac{22}{25(4x+1)} + \frac{43}{25(x-1)} - \frac{12}{5(x-1)^2}$;
   $-5 - 3x - 23x^2 + 45x^3$
   for $|x| < \frac{1}{4}$

3. $1 + 7n + 33n^2 + 135n^3$ for $|n| < \frac{1}{3}$

ANSWERS – 6C

4. (b) $\dfrac{1}{2} - \dfrac{2}{3}x + \dfrac{8}{9}x^2 - \dfrac{32}{27}x^3$

   (d) $|x| < \dfrac{3}{4}$

5. (c) $-\dfrac{3}{2} - \dfrac{3}{2}x - \dfrac{3}{2}x^2 - \dfrac{3}{2}x^3$

   (d) $\dfrac{5}{6} - \dfrac{5}{18}x + \dfrac{5}{54}x^2 - \dfrac{5}{162}x^3$

   (f) $|x| < \dfrac{1}{3}$

6. (a) $3x + 1 - \dfrac{9}{3x+1}$

   (b) $-8 + 30x - 81x^2 + 243x^3$

7. (a) $A = 3$, $C = 3$

   (b) $\dfrac{15}{4} + \dfrac{45}{4}x + \dfrac{777}{16}x^2 + \dfrac{1533}{8}x^3$

Exercise 6D

1. (a) $1 + \dfrac{x}{2} - \dfrac{x^2}{8} + \dfrac{x^3}{16} - \dots$

   (b) $\sqrt{0.98} \approx 0.989950$ (6 decimal places) (c) $\sqrt{0.98} = \dfrac{7}{10}\sqrt{2}$

   (d) 1.414214

2. (a) $1 - \dfrac{4}{3}x - \dfrac{16}{9}x^2 - \dfrac{320}{81}x^3$

   (b) 9.98664885

3. (a) $2 - \dfrac{5}{12}x - \dfrac{25}{288}x^2 - \dfrac{625}{20736}x^3$

   (b) 1.957435

4. (a) $128 + 112x + 42x^2 + \dfrac{35}{4}x^3$

   (b) 139.629

5. (a) $1 + \dfrac{1}{2}x^{-1} - \dfrac{1}{8}x^{-2} + \dfrac{1}{16}x^{-3}$

   (b) 10.05

Exercise 7A

1. (a) $\dfrac{\sqrt{2}}{2}$ (b) -1 (c) $\sqrt{3}$ (d) 0

2. (a)

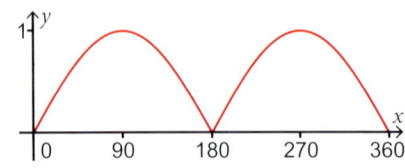

(b)

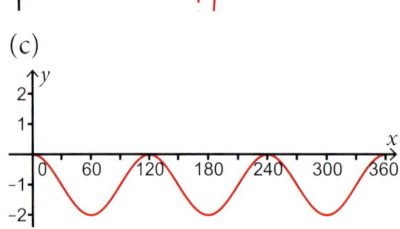

(c)

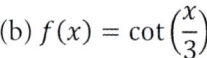

3. (a) $f^{-1}(x) = -5(x+1)$, $x \in \mathbb{R}$

   Range: $f^{-1}(x) \in \mathbb{R}$

   (b) $f^{-1}(x) = \dfrac{1}{2}\sqrt[3]{x}$, $x \in \mathbb{R}$

   Range: $f^{-1}(x) \in \mathbb{R}$

   (c) $f^{-1}(x) = \dfrac{x^2}{2}$, $x \in \mathbb{R}$

   Range: $f^{-1}(x) > 0$

Exercise 7B

1. (a) 1.22 (b) –4.33 (c) 1.05
   (d) –0.869 (e) –5.76 (f) –3.24
   (g) 1.56 (h) 1.08 (i) 31.8 (j) 1.06

2. (a) $\dfrac{2\sqrt{3}}{3}$ (b) $-\dfrac{\sqrt{3}}{3}$ (c) $\dfrac{2\sqrt{3}}{3}$ (d) $\dfrac{2\sqrt{3}}{3}$
   (e) $-\sqrt{3}$ (f) undefined (g) $-\sqrt{2}$
   (h) $-\sqrt{3}$ (i) 1 (j) 1

3. (a) $-\dfrac{1}{2}$ (b) $-\sqrt{3}$ (c) $\dfrac{2\sqrt{3}}{3}$ (d) -2
   (e) $-\dfrac{\sqrt{3}}{3}$

4. (a) $-\dfrac{1}{3}$ (b) $-\dfrac{2\sqrt{2}}{3}$ (c) $2\sqrt{2}$
   (d) $-\dfrac{3\sqrt{2}}{4}$ (e) $\dfrac{\sqrt{2}}{4}$

5. (a) $\sqrt{3}$ (b) $\dfrac{\sqrt{2}}{10}$

Exercise 7C

1. (a) $f(x) = \operatorname{cosec} 2x$

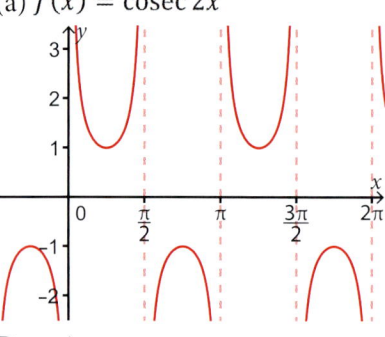

Domain:
$x \in \mathbb{R}, x \neq 0, \pm\dfrac{\pi}{2}, \pm\pi, \pm\dfrac{3\pi}{2}, \dots$

Range:
$f(x) \in \mathbb{R}, f(x) \geq 1$ or $f(x) \leq -1$

(b) $f(x) = \cot\left(\dfrac{x}{3}\right)$

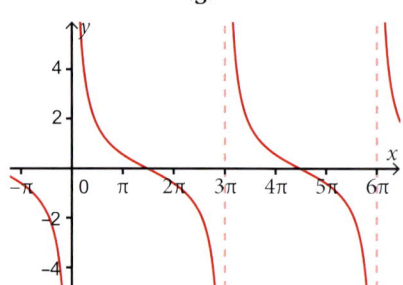

Domain:
$x \in \mathbb{R}, x \neq 0, \pm 3\pi, \pm 6\pi, \dots$
Range: $f(x) \in \mathbb{R}$

(c) $f(x) = 2\sec x$

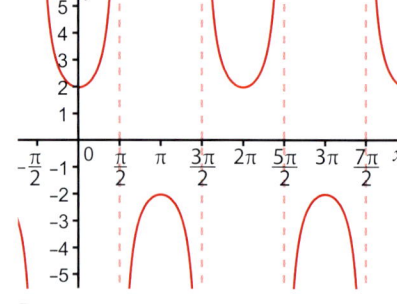

Domain:
$x \in \mathbb{R}, x \neq \pm\dfrac{\pi}{2}, \pm\dfrac{3\pi}{2}, \pm\dfrac{5\pi}{2}, \dots$

Range:
$f(x) \in \mathbb{R}, f(x) \geq 2$ or $f(x) \leq -2$

(d) $f(x) = 1 + \operatorname{cosec} x$

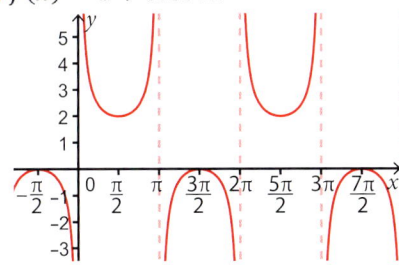

Domain: $x \in \mathbb{R}, x \neq 0, \pm\pi, \pm 2\pi, \pm 3\pi, \ldots$
Range: $f(x) \in \mathbb{R}, f(x) \geq 2$ or $f(x) \leq 0$

(e) $f(x) = \sec x - 1$

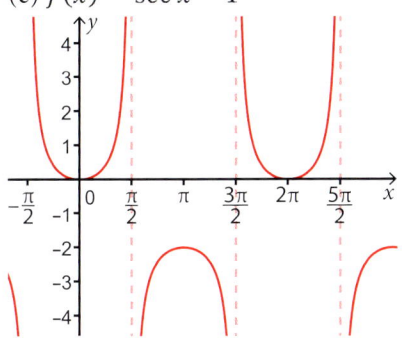

Domain: $x \in \mathbb{R}, x \neq \pm\frac{\pi}{2}, \pm\frac{3\pi}{2}, \pm\frac{5\pi}{2}, \ldots$
Range: $f(x) \in \mathbb{R}, f(x) \geq 0$ or $f(x) \leq -2$

(f) $f(x) = |\cot x|$

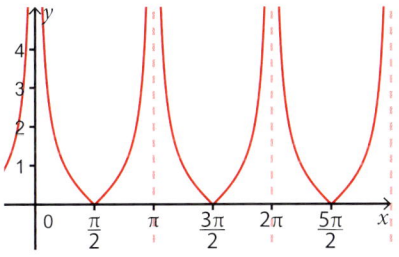

Domain: $x \in \mathbb{R}, x \neq 0, \pm\pi, \pm 2\pi, \pm 3\pi, \ldots$
Range: $f(x) \in \mathbb{R}, f(x) \geq 0$

(g) $f(x) = \operatorname{cosec}\left(x + \frac{\pi}{4}\right)$

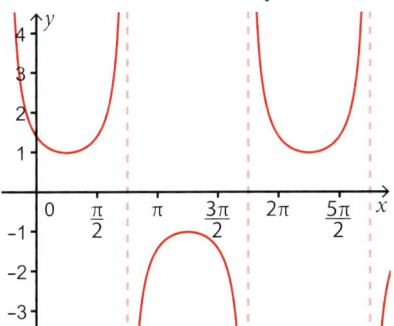

Domain:

$x \in \mathbb{R}, x \neq -\frac{\pi}{4}, \frac{3\pi}{4}, \frac{7\pi}{4}, \ldots$

Range:
$f(x) \in \mathbb{R}, f(x) \geq 1$ or $f(x) \leq -1$

(h) $f(x) = \left|\sec\left(\frac{x}{2}\right)\right|$

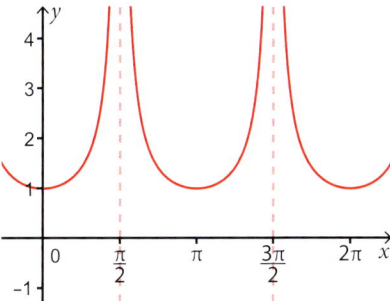

Domain: $x \in \mathbb{R}, x \neq \frac{\pi}{2}, \frac{3\pi}{2}, \frac{5\pi}{2}, \ldots$
Range: $f(x) \in \mathbb{R}, f(x) \geq 1$

(i) $f(x) = \cot(x - \pi)$

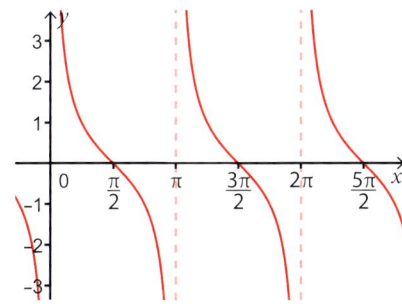

Domain:
$x \in \mathbb{R}, x \neq 0, \pm\pi, \pm 2\pi, \pm 3\pi, \ldots$
Range: $f(x) \in \mathbb{R}$

(j) $f(x) = \cot|x|$

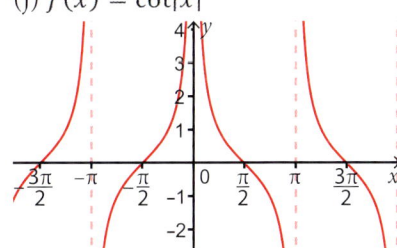

Domain:
$x \in \mathbb{R}, x \neq 0, \pm\pi, \pm 2\pi, \pm 3\pi, \ldots$
Range: $f(x) \in \mathbb{R}$

2. (a) $\frac{\sqrt{3}}{2}$ (b) $\frac{2\sqrt{3}}{3}$ (c) $2\sqrt{2}$
(d) 1 (e) 2 (f) –1

3. (a) $-\frac{\pi}{2}$ (b) $-\frac{\pi}{2}$

4. (a) 0 (b) ½ (c) $\sqrt{2}$ (d) 0 (e) 3
(f) 2 (g) 1 (h) 1

Exercise 7D

1. (a) $\frac{\pi}{3}$ (b) $-\frac{\pi}{4}$ (c) 0 (d) $-\frac{\pi}{6}$

(e) $-\frac{\pi}{3}$ (f) $\frac{\pi}{2}$

2. (a) $\frac{\pi}{6}$ (b) $\frac{\pi}{3}$ (c) $\frac{\pi}{6}$ (d) $\frac{\pi}{4}$ (e) $\frac{\pi}{4}$

3. There is no angle whose cosine is $\sqrt{3}$. The cosine of an angle is always between –1 and 1.

4. (a) 0.717 (b) 0.622 (c) 14.1
(d) –0.0998 (e) 0.921 (f) 3.38

5. (a) $\frac{\sqrt{3}}{2}$ (b) $\frac{7}{25}$ (c) $\frac{\sqrt{2}}{2}$ (d) $\frac{3}{5}$ (e) $\sqrt{15}$

6. (a) $\pm\frac{\sqrt{3}}{2}$ (b) $\pm\frac{\sqrt{21}}{2}$

7. (a) 2 (b) $\frac{1}{y}$ (c) $\frac{3}{2}$ (d) x (e) $\frac{5}{4}$

8. $\sqrt{(1 - x^2)}\left(\frac{1}{x} - 1\right)$

Exercise 7E

1. (a) $f^{-1}(x) = \frac{1}{2}\arcsin(x - 1)$

(b) $f^{-1}(x) = \arccos\left(\frac{x + 2}{2}\right)$

(c) $f^{-1}(x) = 2\arctan\left(\frac{x}{2}\right)$

(d) $f^{-1}(x) = \frac{1}{2}\left(\arcsin x - \frac{\pi}{4}\right)$

(e) $f^{-1}(x) = \arccos(2x) + \frac{\pi}{6}$

2. (a)

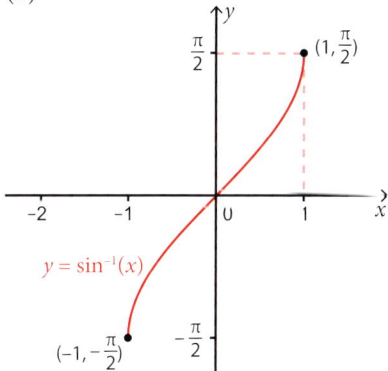

(b)

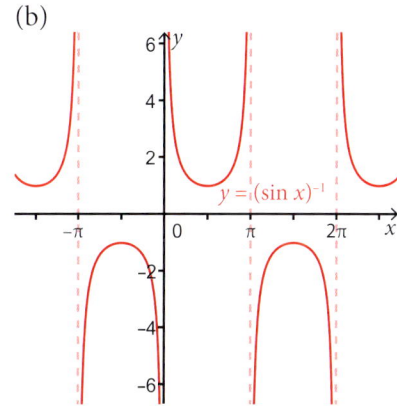

Other name: $y = \operatorname{cosec} x$

ANSWERS – 7E

3. (a) $f^{-1}(x) = \arccos\left(\frac{x}{2}\right)$
   (b)
   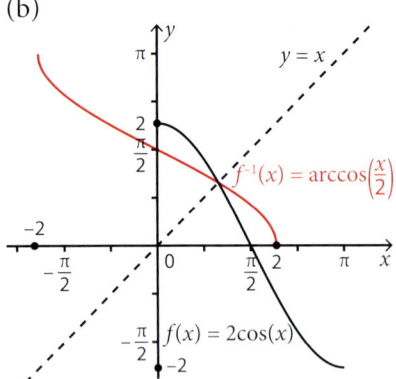
   (c) Restricted domain: $0 \leq x \leq \pi$
   (d) Domain: $-2 \leq x \leq 2$
   Range: $0 \leq f^{-1}(x) \leq \pi$

4. (a) $f^{-1}(x) = \arctan\left(\frac{x}{\pi}\right)$
   (b)
   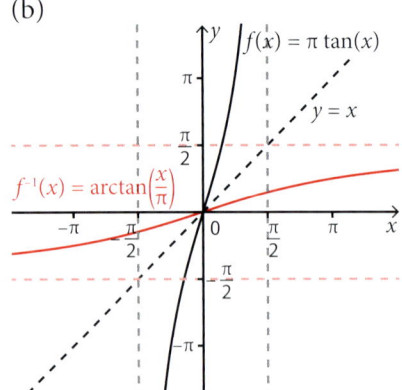
   (c) Restricted domain:
   $-\frac{\pi}{2} < x < \frac{\pi}{2}$
   (d) Domain: $x \in \mathbb{R}$
   Range: $-\frac{\pi}{2} < f^{-1}(x) < \frac{\pi}{2}$

Exercise 7F

1. (a) ¹⁄₁₀ (c) 5.71° (d) 0.176 (e) 18%
2. (d) $\frac{\sqrt{3}}{3}$
3. (d) 109.47°
4. (c) $2(h - 0.1)(2 + \sqrt{3})$
   (d) (ii) 0.048

Exercise 8A

1. (a) $x = 30°, 150°$
   (b) $x = 135°, 225°$
   (c) $x = 5.71°, 186°$
   (d) $\theta = 270°$
2. (a) $\theta = 23.6°, 156.4°$
   (b) $y = 67.2°, -67.2°$
   (c) No solutions
   (d) $x = 138.6°, 221.4°$
3. $-2.21, -1.08, 0.934, 2.07$
4. $\sin^4 x$
6. (b) $\theta = 70.5°, 289°$

Exercise 8B

1. 1
2. $\sec x$
3. (a) $\cot^3 \theta$ (b) $\sec^4 \theta$
   (c) $(\csc \theta)^{-3}$ (d) $\sec \theta$

Exercise 8C

1. (a) $\frac{\pi}{3}, \frac{5\pi}{3}$ (b) 71.6°, 251.6°
   (c) 0.730, 2.41 (d) 152.2°, 332.2°
   (e) 1.70, 3.02
   (f) 2.71, 3.57, 9.00, 9.85
   (g) $-\frac{7\pi}{6}, -\frac{\pi}{6}, \frac{5\pi}{6}, \frac{11\pi}{6}$
2. (a) $\frac{11\pi}{12}, \frac{23\pi}{12}$ (b) $\frac{\pi}{4}, \frac{7\pi}{12}, \frac{5\pi}{4}, \frac{19\pi}{12}$
   (c) 2.71, 4.62
   (d) $0, \frac{\pi}{2}, \pi, \frac{3\pi}{2}, 2\pi$
3. 75°, 195°
4. 1.11, 4.25
5. 0.262, 0.785, 2.36, 2.88
6. 194°, 346°
7. $\frac{\pi}{6}, \frac{\pi}{2}, \frac{5\pi}{6}$
8. 0°, 109°, 251°, 360°
9. 48.6°, 131°, 270°
10. 0.464, $\frac{\pi}{4}$, 3.61, $\frac{5\pi}{4}$
11. 48.2°, 312°
12. 0°, 60°, 180°, 240°, 360°
13. $-\frac{7\pi}{10}, -\frac{3\pi}{10}, \frac{\pi}{10}, \frac{9\pi}{10}$
14. 0°, 99.5°, 180°, 279.5°, 360°
15. 0.221, 1.99, 3.36, 5.13
16. $\frac{\pi}{4}, \frac{5\pi}{4}$
17. $0, \pi, 2\pi$
18. (b) $\frac{\pi}{3}, \frac{2\pi}{3}, \frac{4\pi}{3}, \frac{5\pi}{3}$

Exercise 8D

1. (a) $\frac{\sqrt{3}}{2}$ (b) $\frac{\sqrt{2} - \sqrt{6}}{4}$ (c) $2 + \sqrt{3}$
   (d) $\frac{\sqrt{2}}{2}$ (e) $-\frac{\sqrt{3}}{3}$ (f) $\frac{\sqrt{2} - \sqrt{6}}{4}$
2. (a) $\cos 45° = \frac{\sqrt{2}}{2}$
   (b) $\sin\left(-\frac{\pi}{4}\right) = -\frac{\sqrt{2}}{2}$
   (c) $\sin 180° = 0$ (d) $\cos 90° = 0$
   (e) $\cos \frac{\pi}{2} = 0$ (f) $\sin 60° = \frac{\sqrt{3}}{2}$
   (g) $\sin\left(\frac{\pi}{4}\right) = \frac{\sqrt{2}}{2}$ (h) $\tan 45° = 1$
   (i) $\tan\left(\frac{\pi}{3}\right) = \sqrt{3}$
3. $2mn$
5. $\frac{\sqrt{5}(2\sqrt{3} - 1)}{12}$
7. ⁹⁄₄₀
8. $-\frac{\sqrt{2}}{2}$
9. (a) $\cos \theta = -\frac{1}{50}, \sin \theta = \frac{7\sqrt{51}}{50}$,
   $\tan \theta = -7\sqrt{51}$
   (b) $\cos \theta = \frac{17}{25}, \sin \theta = \frac{4\sqrt{21}}{25}$,
   $\tan \theta = \frac{4\sqrt{21}}{17}$
   (c) $\cos \theta = \frac{19}{181}, \sin \theta = \frac{180}{181}$,
   $\tan \theta = \frac{180}{19}$

Exercise 8E

1. $\cos B$
4. (b) 52.5°, 232.5°
5. (b) $\frac{\pi}{12}, \frac{7\pi}{12}$
6. $\frac{\pi}{8}, \frac{5\pi}{8}$
7. 0.666, 2.48
8. (b) $0, \pi$
9. 90°, 270°
11. (b) $\frac{\pi}{6}, \frac{5\pi}{6}, \frac{7\pi}{6}, \frac{11\pi}{6}$
12. (c) 1.94, 2.78, 5.08, 5.92

Exercise 8F

1. (a) $6.32 \cos(\theta - 71.6°)$
   (b) $10.63 \cos(\theta - 48.8°)$
   (c) $6.40 \cos(\theta - 51.3°)$
   (d) $9.43 \cos(\theta - 32.0°)$
2. (a) $8.94 \cos(\theta + 26.6°)$
   (b) $8.60 \cos(\theta + 54.5°)$
   (c) $6.71 \cos(\theta + 63.4°)$
   (d) $10.82 \cos(\theta + 56.3°)$
3. (a) $6.71 \sin(\theta - 26.6°)$

ANSWERS – 9C

(b) $7.21 \sin(\theta - 56.3°)$
(c) $9.43 \sin(\theta - 58.0°)$
(d) $8.25 \sin(\theta - 14.0°)$

4. (a) $9.43 \sin(\theta + 32.0°)$
   (b) $8.54 \sin(\theta + 69.4°)$
   (c) $8.60 \sin(\theta + 54.5°)$
   (d) $9.85 \sin(\theta + 66.0°)$

5. (a) $6.71 \cos(\theta + 0.464)$
   (b) $9.49 \cos(\theta - 1.25)$
   (c) $10.82 \sin(\theta - 0.983)$
   (d) $8.06 \sin(\theta + 1.05)$

6. (a) $\sqrt{58} \sin(x + 1.166)$
   (b) 58 (c) 2.19, 5.85 radians

7. (a) $R = \sqrt{125}$; $\alpha = 26.6°$
   (b) $x = 323.1°, 343.7°$
   (c) $-\sqrt{125}$ (d) $153.4°$

8. (b) $\sqrt{212} \sin(\theta + 0.278)$
   (c) 0.224, 2.362

9. (a) $7.83 \sin(2x + 1.11)$
   (b) $3.5 \sin 2x + 7 \cos 2x + 7$
   (c) 14.83

10. (a) $3.61 \sin(x - 56.3°)$
    (b) Max: 3.61 when $x = 146.3°$;
    Min: –3.61 when $x = 326.3°$ (c)

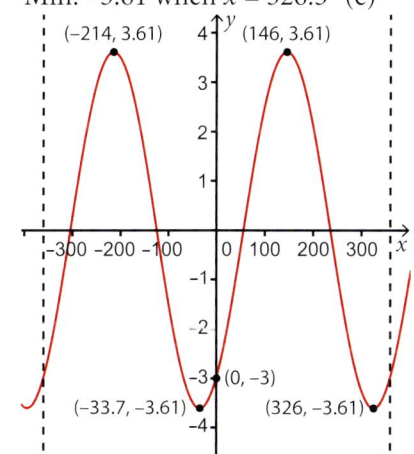

11. (b) 25 (c) ¹⁄₂₅
12. ¹⁄₁₇

Exercise 8G

1. (a) $13 \cos(t - 0.395)$ (b) 13 volts
2. (a) 18 (b) $\alpha = 0.927, k = 22$
   (c) 32
3. (b) (i) $105°$ (ii) $3\sqrt{2}$
   (iv) $\frac{9}{2}(1 + \sqrt{3}) + \sqrt{14}$
4. (b) Day 349 = December 15
   (7 hours, 45 mins); Day 166
   = June 15 (16 hours, 45 mins)
5. (a) $3 \cos \theta + 6 \sin \theta$
   $= 6.71 \cos(\theta - 1.11)$

(b) Max: 6.71 at $\theta = 1.11$.
(c) Max temp = 15.71°C at 1614
(to the nearest minute).

Exercise 9A

1. (a) $6x$ (b) $-\dfrac{1}{2x^2}$ (c) $6x^2 - 6x$
   (d) $\dfrac{1}{\sqrt{x}}$ (e) $5 - 5x^{3/2}$

2. (a) 12 (b) $-\dfrac{1}{8}$ (c) 12 (d) $\dfrac{1}{\sqrt{2}}$
   (e) $5 - 10\sqrt{2}$

3. (a) (0, 0) (b) No stationary
   points (c) (0, 0), (1, –1) (d) No
   stationary points (e) (1, 3)

4. (a) 6 (b) x^{-3} (c) $12x - 6$
   (d) $-\dfrac{1}{2}x^{-\frac{3}{2}}$ (e) $-\dfrac{15}{2}\sqrt{x}$

5. (a) Minimum (c) Maximum,
   Minimum (f) Maximum

6. 112.5 m²
7. $y = 2x - 2$
8. Always decreasing

Exercise 9B

1. (a) $2e^x$ (b) $2x - e^x$ (c) $\dfrac{e^x}{2}$
   (d) $3e^x - 3$ (e) $-2x^{-3} - 2e^x$
   (f) $e^x + 12x^3$ (g) $-3x^{-2} - e^x$
   (h) $3e^x$ (i) $-10e^x$ (j) e^x (k) $2e^x$
   (l) $-e^x$ (m) $e^x - 5$ (n) $35 - 15e^x$
   (o) $14x - 6 + e^x$ (p) e^{x+1} (q) $3e^x$
   (r) $10e^x - 12x^{-3}$

2. (a) $\dfrac{3}{x}$ (b) $1 + \dfrac{1}{x}$ (c) $3x^2 - \dfrac{1}{x}$ (d) $\dfrac{2}{x}$
   (e) $\dfrac{1}{x}$ (f) $\dfrac{1}{x}$ (g) $\dfrac{2}{x}$ (h) $\dfrac{3}{x}$ (i) 0 (j) $-\dfrac{4}{x}$
   (k) $-\dfrac{3}{x}$ (l) $3 + \dfrac{3}{x}$ (m) $\dfrac{1}{x} + 1$
   (n) $\dfrac{1}{x^2} - \dfrac{4}{x}$

3. (a) $10e^x - \dfrac{1}{x}$ (b) $6e^x + \dfrac{2}{x}$ (c) 1
   (d) $2x$ (e) $2ex$ (f) $\dfrac{2x}{e}$ (g) 3
   (h) 3 (i) $6x$ (j) $6x + 1$

4. (a) $y = 2x + 2$ (b) $y = -\dfrac{x}{3} - \dfrac{1}{3}$
   (c) $y = 2x - 1$
   (d) $y = -2(ex + 1)$

5. (a) $y = 1 - x$ (b) $y = 3 - x$
   (c) $y = \dfrac{3}{2} - \dfrac{x}{2}$ (d) $y = -\dfrac{x}{3} + \dfrac{5}{12}$

6. (a) (1, –1), maximum
   (b) (0, 1), minimum

(c) (1, 0), minimum
(d) (2, 2 – 4 ln 2), minimum

7. (b) 4 (c) $y = -\dfrac{x}{4} + 4 + \ln 2$
   (e) $\dfrac{1}{2}\ln 2 + \dfrac{17}{8}$

8. (a) $\dfrac{dy}{dx} = qe^x$ (b) $q = 1$ (c) $p = 3$
   (e) L (19.1, 0); M(0, 6.37) (3 s.f.)
   (f)

9. (b) 2 (d) $y = \dfrac{1}{2}\ln 2 + \dfrac{5}{4}$

Exercise 9C

1. (a) $\cos x + \sin x$
   (b) $5 \cos x - 4 \sin x$
   (c) $3 \sec^2 x - 2x$
   (d) $-2 \sec^2 x - 14x - 1$
   (e) $3x^2 - \cos x$
   (f) $-3x^2 + \dfrac{1}{2}\cos x$
   (g) $-3 \sin x - 2x + 5 \cos x$
   (h) $-\sec^2 x$ (i) $2 \cos x$
   (j) $-4 \sin x$ (k) $-\dfrac{1}{2}\sin x + x^{-2}$
   (l) $\dfrac{1}{2}\cos x - \dfrac{1}{3}\sec^2 x$
   (m) $a \cos x - b \sin x$
   (n) $3p \cos x + 4q \sin x$
   (o) $\dfrac{2}{x} + 2 \sin x$
   (p) 0
   (q) $\cos x + \sin x$
   (r) $2 \cos x - \sin x$
   (s) $-3 \sin x - \cos x$
   (t) $\cos x$

2. (a) 0 (b) $2 - \pi$ (c) $1 - \dfrac{1}{\pi}$ (d) -1

3. (a) $y = x - \dfrac{\pi}{2} + 1$ (b) $y = 2x + 1$
   (c) $y = \dfrac{x}{\pi} + \pi - 2$ (d) $y = 2x + 1$

4. (a) $y = -x + 1$ (b) $y = -x + 2$
   (c) $y = -x + 2$
   (d) $y = -x + \pi + 1$

ANSWERS – 9C

5. $2 - \dfrac{5\sqrt{2}}{2}$

6. (a) $\left(\dfrac{\pi}{3}, \dfrac{\pi}{3} - \sqrt{3}\right)$

   (b) $y = -3x + \dfrac{4\pi}{3} - \sqrt{3}$

7. $f'(x) = -2x^{-3} + \cos x$

Exercise 9D

1. $7x^6 + 30x^5$
2. (a) $2e^x(x+1)$
   (b) $6x\cos x + 6\sin x$
   (c) $x^5 + \dfrac{6}{x} + 6x^5 \ln x$
   (d) $x^7 \sec^2 x + 7x^6 \tan x$
   (e) $y = \dfrac{1}{x}\sin x + \ln x \cos x$
3. $-\frac{1}{3}$
5. (a) $2x^2 e^x + 4xe^x$
   (b) $(0,0), \left(-2, \dfrac{8}{e^2}\right)$
   (c) $2x^2 e^x + 8xe^x + 4e^x$
   (d) Minimum at $(0,0)$, maximum at $\left(-2, \dfrac{8}{e^2}\right)$

Exercise 9E

1. (a) $\dfrac{-x-2}{x^3}$ (b) $\dfrac{-5x-10}{(x-2)^3}$
   (c) $\dfrac{8x^9 + 27x^8}{(x+3)^2}$
   (d) $\dfrac{2x^3 + 5x^2 + 4x}{(x+1)^2}$
   (e) $-\dfrac{x}{2e^x}$ (f) $\dfrac{1 - \ln x}{x^2}$
   (g) $\dfrac{4(1-x)}{e^x}$
   (h) $\dfrac{-x\sin x - \cos x}{x^2}$
   (i) $\dfrac{x\sec^2 x - 2\tan x}{x^3}$
   (j) $\dfrac{x^3(4\sin x - x\cos x)}{\sin^2 x}$
   (k) $\dfrac{-\cos x - 2x\sin x}{2x^{3/2}}$
   (l) $\dfrac{\cos x - \sin x}{e^x}$
   (m) $\dfrac{(x+1)\sec^2 x - \tan x}{(x+1)^2}$
3. $\left(-6, -\dfrac{1}{12}\right), \left(6, \dfrac{1}{12}\right)$

4. $\dfrac{dy}{dx} = \dfrac{x^2 + 6x + 3}{(x+3)^2}$; $x = 2, -8$

5. (a) $\dfrac{x^2 + 6x - 1}{x^2 + 6x + 9}$
   (b) $\dfrac{e^x(x^2 + x + 1)}{(x+1)^2}$
   (c) $\dfrac{e^x(x-1)\cos x - xe^x \sin x}{x^2}$
   (d) $\dfrac{\sin x - x(x+1)\cos x}{(x+1)^2 \sin^2 x}$
   (e) $\dfrac{\cos^2 x - \sin^2 x - \cos x \sin x}{e^x}$
   (f) $\dfrac{e^x(\ln x (x-1) + 1)}{x^2}$

Exercise 9F

1. (a) $4e^{4x}$
   (b) $4xe^{2x^2}$
   (c) $44x^{10}(x^{11} - 8)^3$
   (d) $3\sin^2 x \cos x$
   (e) $3\sec^2 3x$
   (f) $6(x-10)^5$
   (g) $9(22x + 8)(11x^2 + 8x)^8$
   (h) $10\sin^9 x \cos x$
   (i) $30x^4 e^{6x^5 + 8}$
   (j) $4\cos x \, e^{4\sin x}$
   (k) $5e^{5x} + \dfrac{1}{x}$
   (l) $7\left(1 + \dfrac{1}{x}\right)(x + \ln 3x)^6$
   (m) $\dfrac{12}{5}x(10 + x^2)^{\frac{1}{5}}$

2. (a) $\dfrac{10x^9}{x^{10} - 8}$
   (b) $\dfrac{36x^8 + 8x^7 + 8}{4x^9 + x^8 + 8x}$
   (c) $\cot x$ (d) $-\tan x$

3. $\dfrac{2}{x}$

4. $12\sqrt{5}$

5. $20(\sqrt[3]{6})$

6. $-\dfrac{\ln 12}{6}$

7. (a) $q = 6\ln 5$ (b) $p = -\dfrac{4}{5}$
   (c) $y = 30x + 24$

8. (a) $(0,0)$ (b) $(0,0)$

9. (a) $\left(\dfrac{2}{3}, \dfrac{27}{2}\right)$
   (b) $\dfrac{d^2 y}{dx^2} = 24x^{-4} + 3(1-x)^{-4}$

10. (a) $\dfrac{-(25x^5 \sin(5x^5) + \cos(5x^5))}{5x^2}$
    (b) $6(x+1)x^5 e^{6x+4}$
    (c) $12\sin x \cos x + 5\sec 5x \tan 5x$
    (d) $-42x^5(x^6 - 5)^6 \sin(x^6 - 5)^7$

11. (a) $24x \sin^3(3x^2 + 7)\cos(3x^2 + 7)$
    (b) $24x(3x^2 + 7)^3 \cos(3x^2 + 7)^4$

Exercise 9G

1. (a) $\dfrac{dy}{dx} = -x^{-2} + 2e^x$
   (b) $f'(x) = \dfrac{3}{x}$
   (c) $\dfrac{dy}{dx} = 4e^x(x+1)$
   (d) $f'(x) = \dfrac{x\cos x - 2(1 + \sin x)}{x^3}$
   (e) $\dfrac{dy}{dx} = e^{\tan x}\sec^2 x$
   (f) $f'(x) = 12x^5(\cos(3x^2) - x^2 \sin(3x^2))$

2. $y = -\dfrac{1}{5}x + 1$

3. $\dfrac{dy}{dx} = \dfrac{5(3x^8 + 16x^7 + 1)}{2(x+5)^{\frac{3}{2}}}$

4. $(0,0)$

5. $\dfrac{dy}{dx} = \dfrac{e^{2x}(2x^2 + 2x + 1)}{(x+1)^2}$

Exercise 9H

2. (a) $4\sec(4x)\tan(4x)$
   (b) $-\cosec 4x \cot 4x$
   (c) $-\dfrac{1}{3}\cosec^2\left(\dfrac{x}{3}\right)$
   (d) $8x\sec(4x^2)\tan(4x^2)$
   (e) $\dfrac{1}{x^2}\cosec\left(\dfrac{1}{x}\right)\cot\left(\dfrac{1}{x}\right)$
   (f) $-x^2 \cosec^2\left(\dfrac{x^3}{3}\right)$
   (g) $\tan x$
   (h) $-e^x \cosec(e^x) \cot(e^x)$
   (i) $(3x^2 + 2x)\cosec^2(x^3 + x^2)$

Exercise 10A

1. (a) $\dfrac{dy}{dx} = \pi \cos(\pi x)$
   (b) $\dfrac{dy}{dx} = 2 - \dfrac{1}{x}$

2. (a) $-\pi$ (b) 1

3. (a) $(\frac{1}{2}, 1)$ and $(\frac{3}{2}, -1)$ (b) $(\frac{1}{2}, 1)$

4. (a) $-\pi^2 \sin(\pi x)$ (b) x^{-2}

ANSWERS – 11B

5. (a) Maximum at (½, 1); minimum at (³⁄₂, –1) (b) Minimum
6. $y = x + 1$

Exercise 10B

1. (a) $-\dfrac{3}{x^4(4y^3 + 1)}$ (b) $\dfrac{6x + y^2}{1 - 2yx}$
   (c) $\dfrac{2y}{x(1 - x^2 \cos y)}$ (d) $\dfrac{2xy}{1 - y}$
   (e) $-\operatorname{cosec}^2(x + y)$ (f) $\dfrac{2x + \sin x}{2y + \sin y}$
   (g) $-\dfrac{1}{2e^{2y} + \sin y}$

2. (a) ³⁄₂ (b) –³⁄₂ (c) –3 (d) –3 (e) –⅕
   (f) ⁹⁄₅ (g) –5 (h) 4 (i) 0 (j) –1

3. (a) $\dfrac{1 - 2x - 2y}{3y + 2x}$
   (b) $-3x - 2y + 8 = 0$

4. (a) 21 (b) $y = -\dfrac{1}{21}x + \dfrac{92}{21}$

5. $4x + y - 7 = 0$

6. (a) $\dfrac{6 + 4y\, e^{-4x}}{e^{-4x} - 2y}$
   (b) $x - 10y + 10 = 0$

7. (b) $A(-2, 1), B(2, -1)$

8. (a) $(-1, -1), (-1, 0), (-1, 1), (1, -1), (1, 0), (1, 1)$
   (b) Curve 1: $\dfrac{dy}{dx} = \dfrac{2x}{3y^2 - 1}$;
   Curve 2: $\dfrac{dy}{dx} = \dfrac{2x}{1 - 3y^2}$
   (c)

Point	Gradient of curve 1	Gradient of curve 2
(–1, –1)	–1	1
(–1, 0)	2	–2
(–1, 1)	–1	1
(1, –1)	1	–1
(1, 0)	–2	2
(1, 1)	1	–1

   (d) $(-1, -1), (-1, 1), (1, -1), (1, 1)$

9. (b) Find the coordinates of the points A and B. $(-3, 1), (3, -1)$

10. (a) $\dfrac{dy}{dx} = \dfrac{\cos x}{\sin y}$
    (b) $\left(\dfrac{\pi}{2}, \dfrac{2\pi}{3}\right), \left(\dfrac{\pi}{2}, -\dfrac{2\pi}{3}\right)$

12. (b) $\left(\dfrac{\sqrt{5}}{5}, \sqrt{5}\right), \left(-\dfrac{\sqrt{5}}{5}, -\sqrt{5}\right)$
    (c) $\dfrac{d^2y}{dx^2} = \dfrac{(6y - x)\left(\dfrac{dy}{dx} - 5\right) - (y - 5x)\left(6\dfrac{dy}{dx} - 1\right)}{(6y - x)^2}$
    (d) $\left(\dfrac{\sqrt{5}}{5}, \sqrt{5}\right)$ maximum; $\left(-\dfrac{\sqrt{5}}{5}, -\sqrt{5}\right)$ minimum

Exercise 10C

1. (a) $-t^{-2}$ (b) ³⁄₂t (c) $-3t^4$ (d) t^{-3}
   (e) $-\sec t$ (f) $16\, t^{\frac{3}{2}}$
   (g) $2e^{-t}\cos(2t)$ (h) $2\tan\theta$
   (i) $-\dfrac{1}{t}$ (j) $\dfrac{2\cos^2 t\,(2\cos^2 t - 1)}{\sin t}$

2. (a) $\dfrac{dy}{dx} = \dfrac{1}{2}(3t^2 - 3)$
   (b) $(2, -2), (-2, 2)$.
   (c) Min at $(2, -2)$; max at $(-2, 2)$.

4. (a) $(0, 0)$ (b) $(0, \pi^2)$

6. (a) $\dfrac{dy}{dx} = -\dfrac{4}{5}\sin^3 t \cos t$
   (b) $y = -\dfrac{x}{5} + 2$
   (c) $(0, 2)$, maximum

7. $2y + \sqrt{3}x - 20\sqrt{3} = 0$

8. (b) $y = \pm x \pm \dfrac{\sqrt{2}}{2}$ (c) 1

9. (a) $(1, 0), (-1, 0)$
   (b) $(\sqrt{2}, 1), (\sqrt{2}, -1), (-\sqrt{2}, 1), (-\sqrt{2}, -1)$

10. (a) $(-4, 0), (4, 0), (0, -1)$
    (b) $(0, -1)$
    (c)

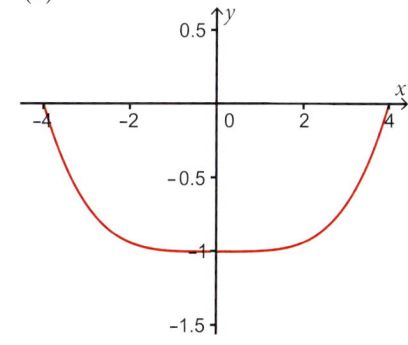

Exercise 11A

1. (a) $x^4 + c$ (b) $6x - \dfrac{x^2}{4} + c$
   (c) $\dfrac{x^4}{2} + \dfrac{3}{4}x^{-4} + c$
   (d) $x^2 - \dfrac{x^3}{3} + 2x^{-1} + c$

2. (a) ⅚ (b) $\pi - 2$

3. (a) $-\dfrac{2}{7(3x + 1)} + \dfrac{6}{7(2x + 3)}$
   (b) $\dfrac{1}{2(x + 3)} - \dfrac{1}{4x - 4}$
   (c) $\dfrac{1}{2(x + 1)} + \dfrac{1}{2(x - 1)} - \dfrac{1}{x - 2}$
   (d) $2 + \dfrac{2}{x - 1} + \dfrac{3}{2x - 1}$

Exercise 11B

1. (a) $-\dfrac{1}{3}\cos 3x + c$ (b) $2\sin\dfrac{x}{2} + c$
   (c) $\dfrac{1}{4}\tan 4x + c$ (d) $\dfrac{1}{2}\sin x + c$
   (e) $e^x + c$ (f) $12\ln x + c$
   (g) $\dfrac{1}{2}\sin(2x + \pi) + c$
   (h) $\tan(x - 1) + c$
   (i) $\dfrac{1}{2}e^{(2x-2)} + c$
   (j) $\dfrac{1}{4}\ln|4x - 1| + c$
   (k) $\dfrac{1}{2}\cos(1 - 2x) + c$
   (l) $-2\tan\left(-\dfrac{x}{2} - 1\right) + c$
   (m) $-\sin(-4x) + c$

2. (a) $2\sec x + c$ (b) $-\cot x + c$
   (c) $-3\operatorname{cosec} x + c$ (d) $\dfrac{1}{2}\sec 2x + c$
   (e) $\dfrac{5}{2}\operatorname{cosec} 2x + c$

3. (a) $7\ln x - \dfrac{1}{3}\sin 3x + \cot x - \dfrac{x^2}{4} + c$
   (b) $2\ln x - \dfrac{x^2}{20} + \dfrac{1}{3}\sec 3x + x + c$
   (c) $6x + \dfrac{1}{4}e^{4x} + 4\ln x + 2\tan x + c$
   (d) $\dfrac{2}{3}x^3 - e^{-x} - 2\operatorname{cosec} x + 4\ln x + c$
   (e) $-\dfrac{4}{3x} - \dfrac{4}{3}\ln x - \dfrac{2}{3}x^2 + c$
   (f) $-\dfrac{1}{4}(\cos 4x + \sin 4x + \sec 4x) + c$

ANSWERS – 11C

Exercise 11C

1. (a) ½ (b) $\sqrt{3}$ (c) ⅓ (d) $\frac{1}{3}(e^9 - 1)$
   (e) 2 (f) 1 (g) 2 ln 2 (h) $\sqrt{2} - 1$
   (i) $1 + \frac{\pi}{2}$ (j) $4\left(e - \frac{1}{e}\right)$ (k) 5/2
   (l) $1 + \frac{\pi^2}{8}$ (m) $\frac{1}{4}(3 + e^2)$ (n) π

2. 0.41
3. 2.14
4. 139 m² (3 s.f.)
5. (a) $x = 0.38$: $\frac{dy}{dx} = 0.018$;
   $x = 0.39$: $\frac{dy}{dx} = -0.04$
   Change of sign implies stationary point between these x-values.
   (b) $f(x) = e^x - \frac{10}{3}x^3 + 7$
   (c) $e + \frac{31}{6}$
6. (a) 12.8 metres (3 s.f.)
   (b) $6(\ln 2 - 1) + e^2$
7. (a) $2\sqrt{3}$ (b) $\frac{2}{3}\left(\frac{2\pi}{3} - \sqrt{3}\right)$

Exercise 11D

1. (b) 17.5
2. (a) $A(-5, -8), B(2, 27)$
   (b) 57.2 (3 s.f.)
3. (a) (1, 1) (b) 1/12
4. (a) $A(-2, 12); B(4, 6)$ (b) 36

Exercise 11E

1. (a) $x - 1 + \ln|x - 1| + c$
   (b) $\frac{1}{2}(3x + 4)^{\frac{2}{3}} + c$
   (c) $\frac{1}{20}(5x + 2)^4 + c$
   (d) $-\frac{1}{2}(e^x + 3)^{-2} + c$
   (e) $\frac{1}{4}(\ln x)^4 + c$
   (f) $-\frac{1}{5}\cos 5x + c$
   (g) $\frac{2}{3}(1 + \tan x)^{3/2} + c$
   (h) $\frac{10}{3}\sqrt{x - 2}(x + 4) + c$
   (i) $-\frac{1}{10}\ln|1 - 5x^2| + c$
   (j) $-\frac{1}{2}\cos\left(2x + \frac{\pi}{3}\right) + c$

2. (a) 11/30 (b) –4/15
   (c) $4\left(\sqrt{3} - 2 + \frac{\pi}{3}\right)$ (d) $\sqrt{3}$
   (e) 104 (f) $\frac{\ln(313)}{\ln(5)}$ (g) ln 2
   (h) $\frac{1}{2}(e^7 - e^3)$ (i) $\sqrt{2}$ (j) $e^2 - 1$

3. $\ln|x^3 + 6x + 1| + c$
4. $\frac{1}{2}\ln|x^4 - 2 - x^{-4}| + c$
5. $\ln\left(\frac{81}{13}\right)$
7. $\sin(\ln|x|) + c$
10. $a = 4, b = 5, k = ⅔$
12. $\ln\frac{3}{2} - \frac{1}{3}$
13. (c) 735 vehicles per hour
    (d) 12 noon (e) 720 vehicles per hour (f) 14 592

Exercise 11F

1. $\frac{1}{2}x + \frac{1}{4}\sin 2x + c$
2. $-\cos x + \frac{1}{3}\cos^3 x + c$
3. $\frac{1}{5}\sin^5 x + c$
4. ¼
5. $\frac{4 - \pi}{8}$
6. $\frac{14}{9}\sin^9 x + c$
7. (a) $\frac{1}{4}\tan^4 \theta + c$ (b) $\frac{1}{6}\tan^6 \theta + c$
8. (a) $-\csc x + c$
   (b) $\sec x + c$
   (c) $\sec x + \tan x + c$
   (d) $-\cot\theta - \csc\theta + c$
   (e) $\frac{5x}{2} - \frac{1}{4}\sin 2x - \cot x + c$
   (f) $\sin\theta + c$
   (g) $x + c$
   (h) $\frac{1}{2}\tan 2x + c$
   (i) $\csc\theta \sec\theta + c$
   or $\cot\theta + \tan\theta + c$
9. (a) 1 (b) 0.5 (c) $\frac{\pi}{8} + \frac{1}{4}$
   (d) $\frac{1}{3}(\sqrt{2} - 1)$ (e) ¼
   (f) $\frac{1}{16}(\pi - 2\sqrt{2} + 4)$ (g) 4/3
   (h) $\frac{2\sqrt{2}}{7}$ (i) $2\sqrt{3} - \frac{2\pi}{3}$

10. $-\frac{1}{3}(\csc 3x + \cos 3x) + c$
11. $-\frac{1}{2}\cot 8\theta + c$
12. $\tan x - x + c$
13. $2\pi - 1$

Exercise 11G

1. (a) $\frac{1}{3}x^3 - \frac{3}{2}x^2 + 2x + c$
   (b) $x\sin x + \cos x + c$
   (c) $x\sin 2x + \frac{1}{2}\cos 2x + c$
   (d) $e^x(x - 1) + c$
   (e) $x\ln x + x\ln 5 - x + c$
   (f) $\frac{1}{9}e^{3x}(3x - 1) + c$
   (g) $\frac{2}{25}e^{5x}(15x + 7) + c$
   (h) $\frac{x^3}{9}(3\ln x - 1) + c$

2. (a) 5/6 (b) $1 - \frac{2}{e}$ (c) $4\ln 2 - \frac{15}{16}$
   (d) $\frac{15}{2}\ln 5 - 2$ (e) π (f) $\frac{3}{4}(\pi - 2)$
   (g) $\frac{\pi}{4} - \frac{1}{2}\ln 2$ (h) $\frac{e^2}{2} + \frac{11}{6}$

3. $\frac{3}{2}x^2 \ln 2x - \frac{3x^2}{4} + c$

4. (a) $-\frac{2}{3}(5 - x)^{\frac{3}{2}} + c$
   (b) $-\frac{2}{15}(5 - x)^{\frac{3}{2}}(3x + 5) + c$
   (c) $\frac{128}{15}$

5. (a) $\frac{1}{2}(x - \sin x)$ (b) $\frac{\pi^2}{4} + 1$

6. (b) $\frac{1}{4}x\sin 2x + \frac{1}{8}\cos 2x + \frac{x^2}{2} + c$

7. (a) $\frac{x^2}{2}\ln x - \frac{x^2}{4} + c$
   (b) $2x^2 \ln x - x^2 + c$
   (c) $\frac{x^2}{2}\ln 4x - \frac{x^2}{4} + c$

8. $\frac{1}{30}x^2(10x^4 - 36x^3 + 50x - 225) + c$

10. (b) 2 (c) –6 (f) 8.28 cm²

Exercise 11H

1. (a) $\frac{1}{4}\ln\left|\frac{x - 2}{x + 2}\right| + c$
   (b) $2\ln|x + 1| - \ln|x| + c$
   (c) $\frac{1}{5}\ln\left|\frac{x - 1}{x + 4}\right| + c$

ANSWERS – 12B

(d) $\frac{4}{5}\ln|x+4| - \frac{1}{5}\ln|x-1| + c$

(e) $3\ln\left|\frac{x-1}{x+1}\right| + c$

(f) $\frac{1}{2}\ln|x+3| + \frac{3}{2}\ln|x-3| + c$

(g) $\frac{2}{5}\ln|x| - \frac{7}{5}\ln|x+5| + c$

(h) $\ln|x| + \frac{1}{2}\ln\left|\frac{x-1}{x+1}\right| + c$

(i) $-\frac{5}{4}\ln|x| - \frac{7}{2x} + \frac{5}{4}\ln|x+2| + c$

2. (a) $\ln\left(\frac{5}{2}\right)$ (b) $3\ln 6 + 2\ln 4 - 5\ln 5$
(c) $\ln\left(\frac{25}{8}\right)$ (d) $\ln 2 + 1$
(e) $4\ln\left(\frac{4}{3}\right) - \frac{3}{2}$ (f) $\ln\left(\frac{54}{25}\right) + \frac{1}{30}$
(g) $\frac{7}{2}\ln 7$

3. (a) $-\frac{3}{2(x+3)} + \frac{5}{2(x-1)}$
(b) $-\frac{3}{2}\ln|x+3| + \frac{5}{2}\ln|x-1| + c$

5. (a) $f(x) = \frac{4}{2x+1} - \frac{3}{x+1} + \frac{1}{x+4}$
(b) $2\ln|2x+1| - 3\ln|x+1| + \ln|x+4| + c$
(c) $\ln\left(\frac{25}{18}\right)$

6. (a) $A = -4; B = 3$
(b) $-4\ln|x+5| + \frac{3}{2}\ln|x+2| + c$
(c) $\ln\left(\frac{3}{2}\right)^3 + \ln\left(\frac{7}{12}\right)^4$

7. (b) $\frac{1}{2}\left(\frac{-5}{x} + \frac{31}{x-2}\right)$
(c) $2x^2 + 8x + \frac{1}{2}(31\ln|x-2| - 5\ln|x|) + c$

8. $x + \frac{15}{8}\ln\left|\frac{x-4}{x+4}\right| + c$

9. (a) $x + 5 + \frac{9x-4}{(x-1)^2}$
(b) $9\ln 5 + 40$

10. $\frac{x^3}{3} + 3x - \frac{13}{3}\ln|x+2| + \frac{4}{3}\ln|x-1| + c$

Exercise 11I

1. (a) $\int_1^4 2x^3 \, dx$ (b) $\int_2^6 4\pi x^2 \, dx$
2. (a) $x^2 + y^2 = r^2$
(b) $y = \sqrt{r^2 - x^2}$
(c) $\sqrt{r^2 - x^2}\delta x$
(d) $Q = \sum_0^r \sqrt{r^2 - x^2}\delta x$
(g) $Q = \frac{\pi r^2}{4}$

3. (a) $V \approx \sum_0^r \pi(r^2 - x^2)\,\delta x$

Exercise 11J

1. πh^2
2. 10.8
3. $\frac{1400\pi}{3}$
4. 3700
5. (a) $0, \pi$ (b) $\frac{\pi^2}{2}$
7. (a) 30 (b) $\frac{75}{2}\pi^2$
8. $\frac{\pi}{36}(1 - 13e^{-12})$
9. (a) $\frac{1}{6}(2x-1)^{\frac{3}{2}} + \frac{1}{2}(2x-1)^{\frac{1}{2}} + c$
(b) 48π

Exercise 11K

1. (a) $\frac{1}{2}x^6 + c$ (b) $\ln|x+1| + c$
(c) $\frac{1}{21}(3x+5)^7 + c$
(d) $\frac{4}{5}\ln|5x-3| + c$
(e) $2x + c$ (f) $\frac{1}{32}(4x+1)^8 + c$
(g) $-\frac{1}{3}e^{-3x} + c$
(h) $\frac{1}{6}\ln\left|\frac{x-5}{x+1}\right| + c$
(i) $\frac{1}{9}(6x-8) + \frac{11}{9}\ln(3x-4) + c$
(j) $\frac{1}{5}\sin 5x + c$ (k) $\frac{3}{2}\tan 2x + c$
(l) $\ln|x^2 + 8| + c$ (m) $\frac{1}{4}\sin^4 x + c$
(n) $2\csc\left(\frac{x}{2}\right) + c$
(o) $-\frac{1}{3}\cos(x^3 + 1) + c$

(p) $\ln|x^3 + x - 4| + c$
(q) $\frac{3}{2}\ln|2x+1| + \frac{2}{3}\ln|3x-2| + c$
(r) $\frac{1}{6}\sec 6x + c$ (s) $\frac{1}{b}\cot(bx) + c$
(t) $-\cos x + \frac{2}{3}\cos^3 x - \frac{1}{5}\cos^5 x + c$
(u) $\frac{1}{3}\tan^3 x + c$
(v) $\ln|\sin x| - x\cot x + c$
(w) $\frac{1}{4}\left(2x^2 + e^{2x}(2x-1)\right) + c$
(x) $\frac{x}{2} - \frac{1}{12}\sin 6x + c$
(y) $\frac{4}{5}\tan^5 x + c$ (z) $\ln|\sin\theta| + c$

2. (a) $e - 1$ (b) $\frac{1}{2}\ln 5 + \frac{4}{3}\ln 7$
3. (a) 0.561 (b) 3.36×10^5
4. (a) $\frac{1}{2}x - \frac{1}{8}\sin 4x + c$
(b) $-\frac{1}{4}\cos 4x + \frac{1}{12}\cos^3 4x + c$
(c) $\sin x - \frac{2}{3}\sin^3 x + \frac{1}{5}\sin^5 x + c$
(d) $\frac{1}{2}x + \frac{1}{8}\sin(4x - 2) + c$
(e) $\frac{1}{2}\tan^2 x + \ln|\cos x| + c$

Exercise 12A

1. $\frac{3}{5}x^5 - \frac{1}{4}x^{-2} + c$
2. $-2\cot\left(\frac{x}{2}\right) + c$
3. $\frac{1}{2}\ln\left|\frac{x-1}{x+1}\right| + c$
4. $\frac{2}{15}(1 + x^5)^{3/2} + c$
5. $-\frac{1}{x}(\ln x + 1) + c$

Exercise 12B

1. $\frac{dD}{dt} = kD^2$
2. $\frac{dP}{dh} = -kP$
5. $\frac{dT}{dt} = k(T - 15)$
6. (a) $k = 0.2$ (b) $\frac{dV}{dt} = -0.02$
7. $\frac{dV}{dh} = 4\pi h - \pi h^2$
8. (a) $\frac{dR}{dt} = \frac{3}{2}\ln 2\,(0.5)^t$

ANSWERS – 12B

(b) $\dfrac{3}{16}\ln 2$

10. (b) $\dfrac{dV}{dh} = \dfrac{9\pi h^2}{4}$

11. $\dfrac{dQ}{dt} = 2Q - \dfrac{k}{t^2}$

12. $\dfrac{dN}{dt} = \dfrac{kN}{t}$

13. (a) 5 million
    (b) 7.27 million (3 s.f.)
    (c) 73 years
    (d) $\dfrac{dP}{dt} = P_0 k e^{kt}$
    (e) 0.118 million per year (3 s.f.)

Exercise 12C

1. $\ln y = x\sin x + \cos x - 1$
2. $\dfrac{1}{10}\ln 3$
3. $y = x^2$
4. $x^3 = \dfrac{9}{2}(1 - \cot\theta)$
5. (a) $\ln y = \dfrac{k}{2}\left(\theta + \dfrac{1}{2}\sin 2\theta\right)$
   (b) $k = \dfrac{8\ln 2}{\pi + 2}$
6. (a) $A = \dfrac{4}{(t^{-1} + 1)^2}$
7. (a) $\ln P = -kh + c$
   (b) $c = \ln(70\,000)$, $k = 0.002$
   (c) 8250 Pa (3 s.f.)
8. $\dfrac{3}{2} V^{\frac{2}{3}} = 4t + 6$; $t = 0.88\text{s}$
9. (b) $V = 700e^{-t/10} + 300$
   (c) 300 cm³. After some time the volume of liquid settles at 300 cm³. The inflow and outflow must become equal.
10. (a) $\dfrac{11}{(2x - 5)} - \dfrac{4}{(x - 2)}$
    (b) $\ln y = \dfrac{11}{2}\ln(2x - 5) - 4\ln(x - 2) + c$
    (c) $c = \ln 11$; $y = \dfrac{11(2x - 5)^{\frac{11}{2}}}{(x - 2)^4}$
11. (a) Constant rate of increase
    $\dfrac{dV}{dt} = 30$; Leaking out rate
    $\dfrac{dV}{dt} = -kV$ (b) $V = \dfrac{30}{k} - \dfrac{30}{k}e^{-kt}$

(c) The volume of water starts at zero and increases. It approaches a limit of $\dfrac{30}{k}$ as $t \to \infty$.

12. (a) $V = (132.3t + 729)^{2/3}$
    (b) The relationship between V and t would not hold for large values of t.

13. (b) $\dfrac{10}{k}$ (c) 4×10^{-4} (d) Ignoring splashing, which could make the water overflow earlier. Ignoring the volume of person's feet.

Exercise 13A

1. (a) $x^2 - x - 1 = 0$
   (b) $x - \sqrt{2x - 3} = 0$ or $x^2 - 2x + 3 = 0$
   (c) $x - \sqrt[3]{1 - \dfrac{x}{2}} = 0$ or $x^3 + \dfrac{x}{2} - 1 = 0$

2. 0.7 and –2.7 (1 d.p.)

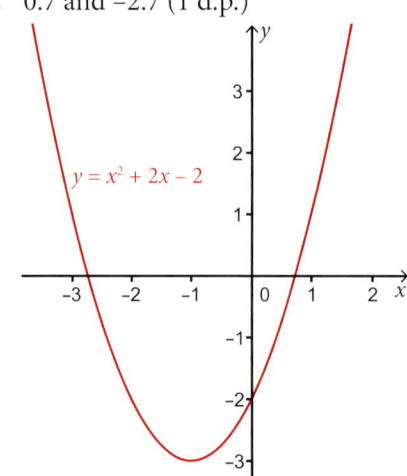

3. (a)

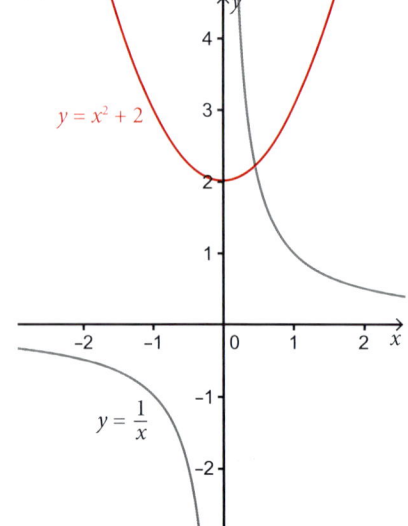

(b) The graph shows there is one solution to $x^2 + 2 = \dfrac{1}{x}$.
Re-arranging gives $x^3 + 2x - 1 = 0$, so there is one solution.

Exercise 13B

1. (a)

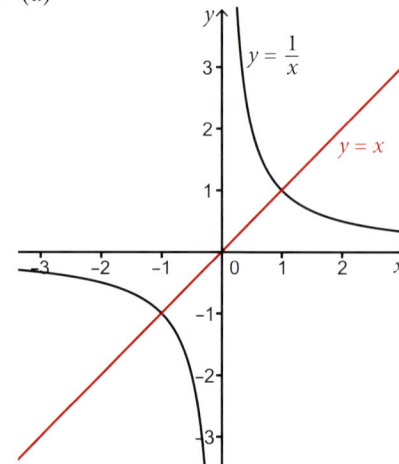

2 points

(b)

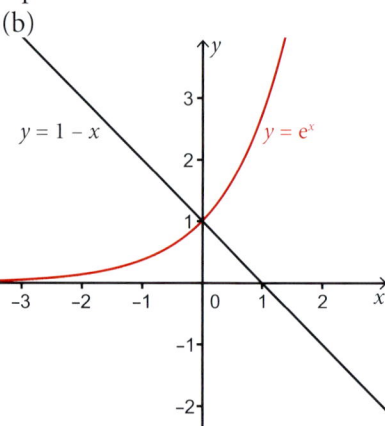

1 point

(c)

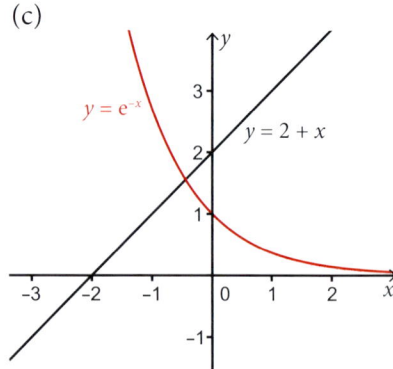

1 point

(d)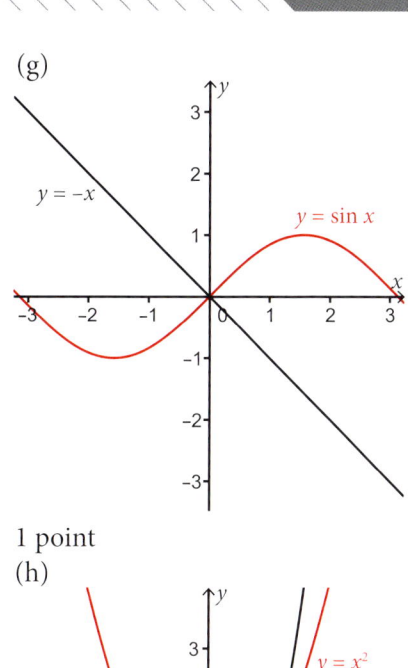
1 point

(e)
1 point

(f)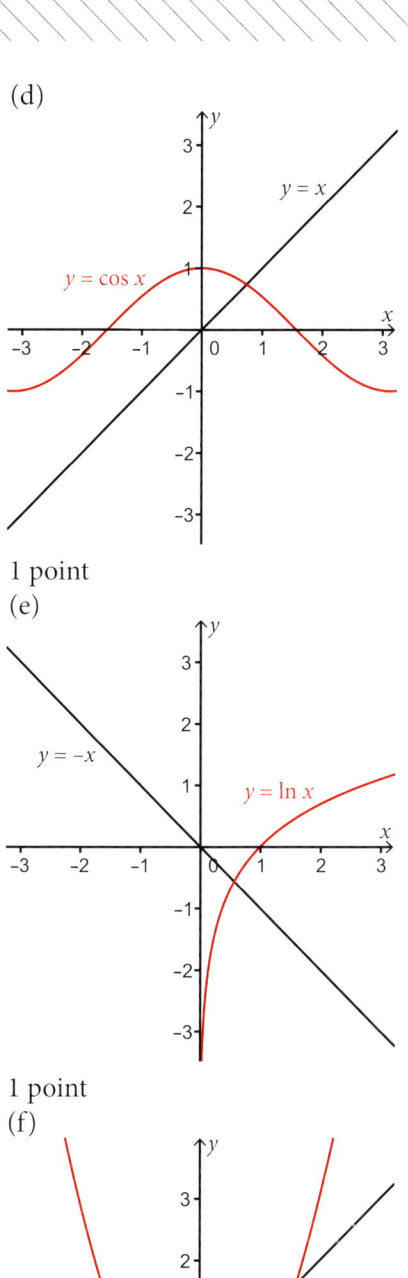
2 points

(g)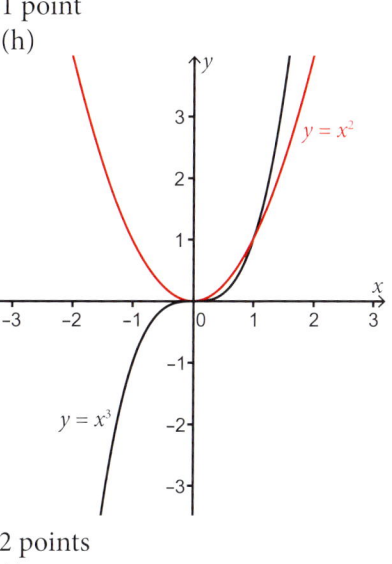
1 point

(h)
2 points

(i)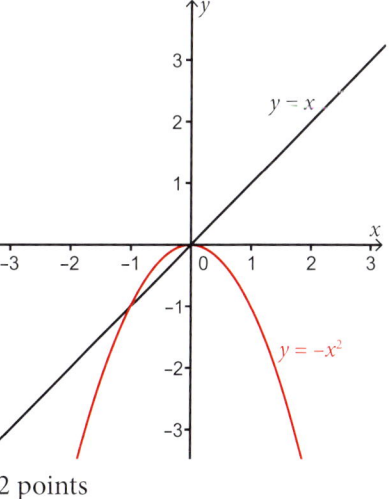
2 points

(j)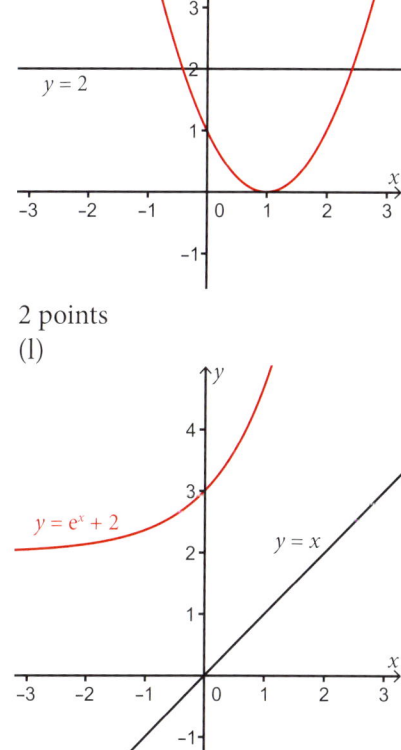
1 point

(k)
2 points

(l)
No points

ANSWERS – 13B

(m)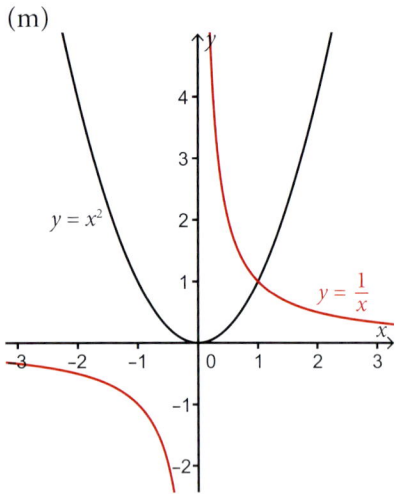
1 point

(n)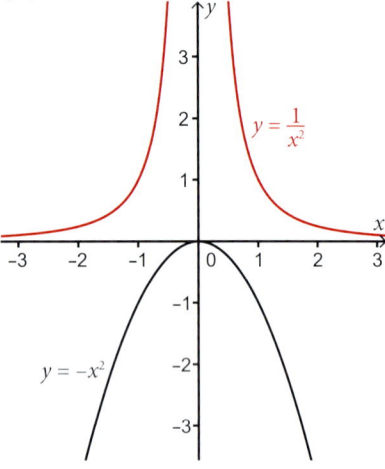
No points

2. (a)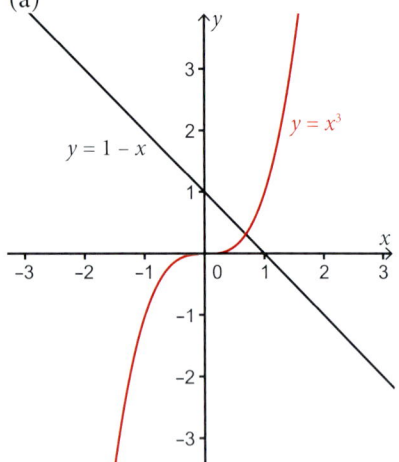
1 solution

(b)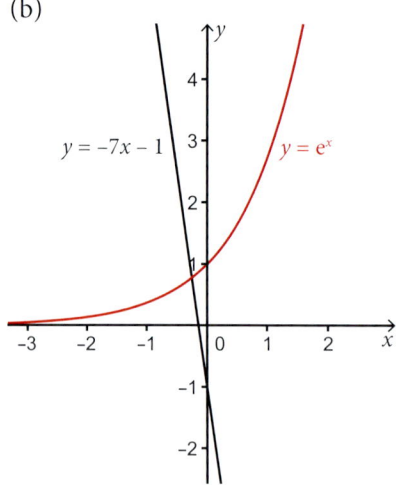
1 solution

(c)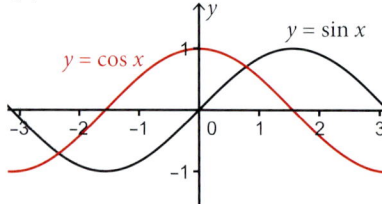
2 solutions

(d)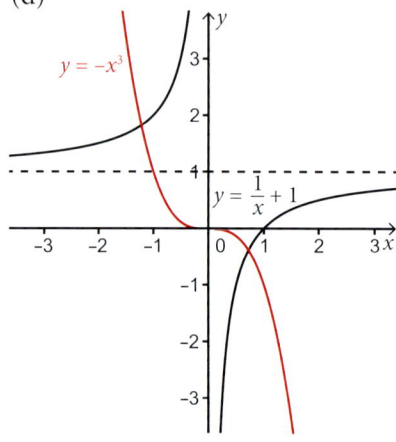
2 solutions

(e)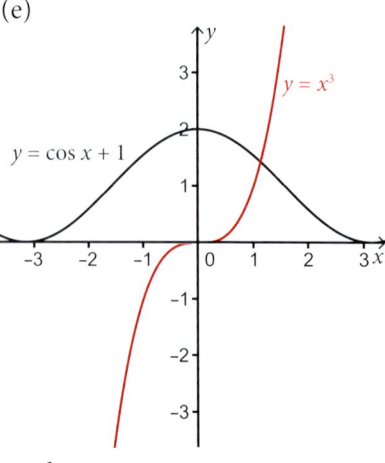
1 solution

(f)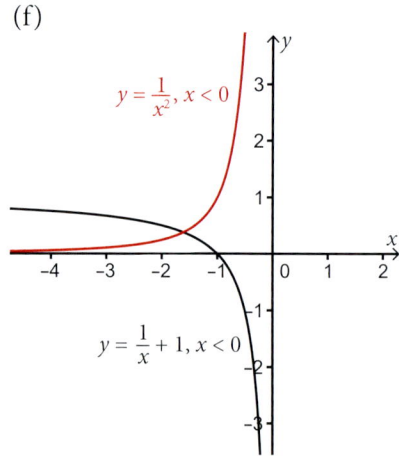
1 solution

(g)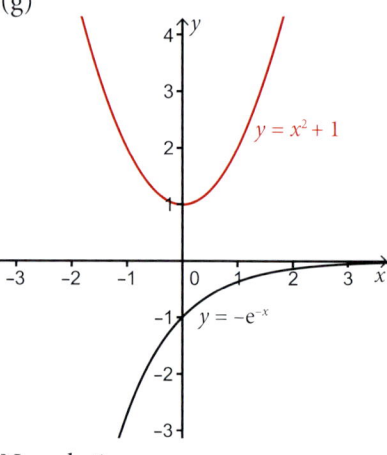
No solutions

(h)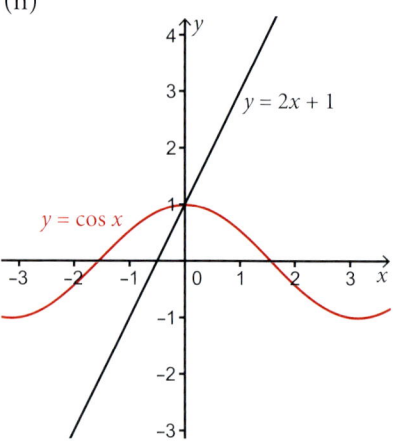
1 solution

(i)

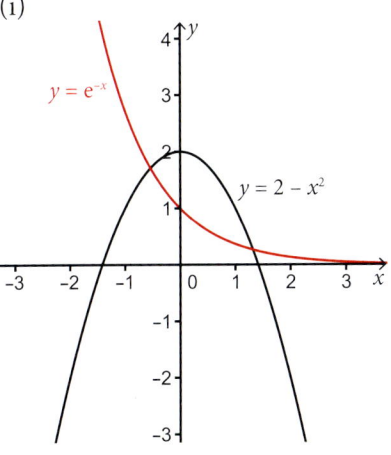

2 solutions

(j)

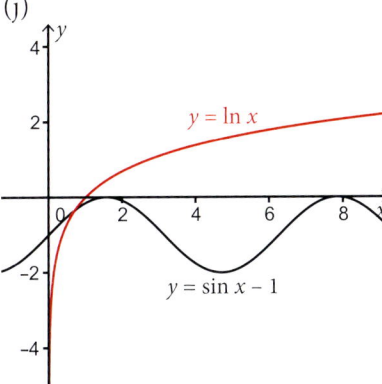

1 solution

3. (a)

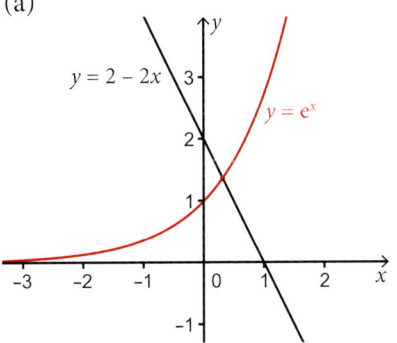

(b) The solution to $e^x + 2x - 2 = 0$ is found from the intersection of $y = e^x$ and $y = 2 - 2x$. There is one solution.
(c) $f(0.25) = -0.216$; $f(0.35) = 0.119$. Sign change and continuous function implies solution in interval $[0.25, 0.35]$.
(d) 0.3

4. (a)

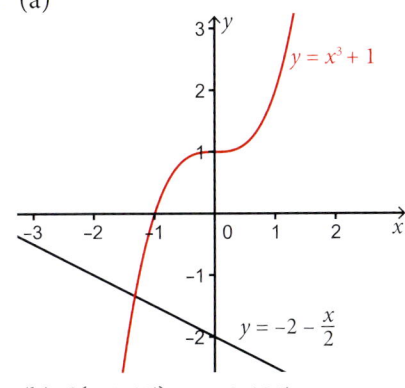

(b) $f(-1.35) = -0.135$; $f(-1.25) = 0.422$. Sign change and continuous function implies solution in interval $[-1.35, -1.25]$.
(c) -1.3

5. (a)

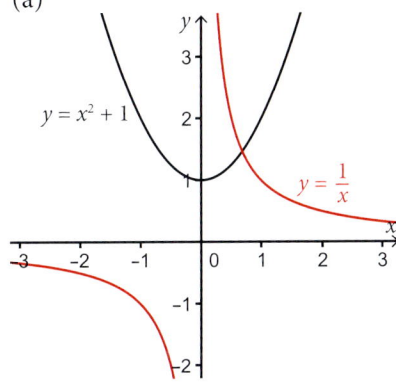

(b) 1
(c) $f(0.5) = -0.75$; $f(1) = 1$. Sign change and continuous function implies solution in interval $[0.5, 1]$.
(d) $f(0.65) = -0.116$; $f(0.75) = 0.229$. Sign change and continuous function implies solution in interval $[0.65, 0.75]$. Hence $x = 0.7$ to 1 d.p.

6. $f(-3) = 49$; $f(-2) = -48$. Change of sign; function is continuous. Implies root within interval $[-3, -2]$.

7. $f(x) = \sin x - x^2 + 2$; $f(-1.5) = -1.25$; $f(-1) = 0.16$; $f(1.5) = 0.75$; $f(2) = -1.09$. Sign changes across both intervals; function continuous. Hence solutions in $[-1.5, -1]$ and $[1.5, 2]$.

8. 2

9. (a)

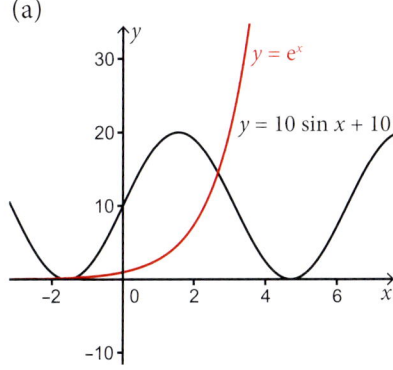

(b) $f(x) = e^x - 10\sin x - 10$
(c) $f(2.5) = -3.80$; $f(3) = 8.67$. Sign change and continuous function implies solution in interval $[2.5, 3]$.
(d) $f(2.65) = -0.566$; $f(2.75) = 1.83$. Hence $\alpha = 2.7$.

10. (a) $f(-1) = -4$; $f(0) = 1$. Change of sign and function continuous. Hence root within interval $[-1, 0]$.
(b) $f(-0.35) = 0.0121$; $f(-0.45) = -0.396$. Hence $\alpha = -0.4$ to 1 d.p.

11. $g(x) = e^{x-9} - 9 - x$; $g(12) = -0.914$; $g(13) = 32.598$. Change of sign; function is continuous. Implies root within interval $[12, 13]$.

Exercise 13C

1. (a) $x = x^2 - 1$; $x = \sqrt{1 + x}$
(b) $x = \dfrac{1}{5}(1 - 2x^2)$;
$x = \sqrt{\dfrac{1}{2}(1 - 5x)}$
(c) $x = \cos^{-1}(-\sin x)$; $x = \sin^{-1}(-\cos x)$
(d) $x = \dfrac{e^x}{2}$; $x = \ln(2x)$
(e) $x = e^{-2 - \frac{1}{x}}$; $x = -\dfrac{1}{2 + \ln x}$
(f) $x = \sqrt[3]{\dfrac{1 - x^2}{5}}$; $x = \sqrt{1 - 5x^3}$
(g) $x = x^2$; $x = \sqrt{x}$
(h) $x = \dfrac{1}{2}(\cos^{-1}(1 - e^{2x}))$; $x = \dfrac{1}{2}(\ln(1 - \cos 2x))$

ANSWERS – 13C

(i) $x = \sin^{-1}\left(\sqrt{1-2x^2}\right)$;

$x = \dfrac{1}{\sqrt{2}}\cos x$

(j) $x = \sin^4 x - 1$;

$x = \sin^{-1}(\sqrt[4]{x+1})$

2. (a) $f(1) = -0.46$; $f(2) = 1.58$. Change of sign and function continuous. Hence root within interval $[1, 2]$. (c) 1.3

3. (a) $f(0) = 2$; $f(1) = -0.63$. Change of sign and function continuous. Hence root within interval $[0, 1]$. (c) 0.74

4. (a)

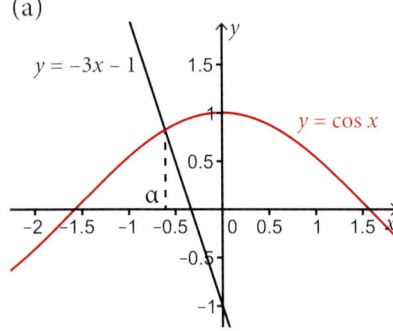

(b) $f(-1) = -1.45$; $f(0) = 2$. Sign change and continuous function implies root in interval $[-1, 0]$.
(d) $x_1 = -0.62586$; $x_2 = -0.60349$; $x_3 = -0.60779$
(e) $f(-0.615) = -0.028$; $f(-0.605) = 0.008$. Sign change and continuous function implies root in interval $[-0.615, -0.605]$. Hence $\alpha = -0.61$ to 2 dp.

5. (a) $f(-0.5) = -0.125$; $f(-0.4) = 0.136$. Sign change and function continuous implies root within interval $[-0.5, -0.4]$. (b) $x = -0.45$

6. (b) $f(-2) = -0.63$; $f(-1.5) = 0.22$. Sign change and function continuous implies root in interval $[-2, -1.5]$. (c) -1.66

7. (a)

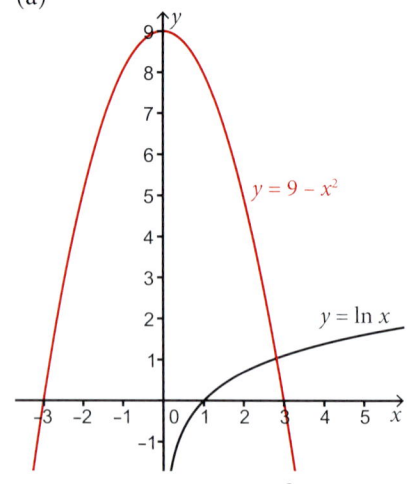

(b) $f(x) = \ln x - 9 + x^2$; $f(2.5) = -1.83$; $f(3) = 1.10$. Change of sign and function continuous implies solution to $f(x) = 0$ in interval $[2.5, 3]$. Hence solution also to $\ln x = 9 - x^2$ in this interval.
(c) 2.822

8. (b) $f(x) = \sin x + x^3 - 1$; $f(0.5) = -0.40$; $f(1) = 0.84$. Change of sign and function continuous implies root within interval $[0.5, 1]$.
(c) $x_1 = 0.74$; $x_2 = 0.71$

9. 11.57

10. (a) $f(9) = -0.02$; $f(10) = 0.1$. Sign change and function continuous implies root within interval $[9, 10]$. (b) 9.1863

11. (a) $f'(x) = 3x^2 + 1$. Since $x^2 > 0$, $f'(x) > 0$ for all values of x.
(b) Since $f(x)$ is always increasing it only crosses the x-axis once. α is the only real root of $f(x) = 0$.
(c) 1.52 (d) $f(1.515) = -0.01$; $f(1.525) = 0.07$; Change of sign implies root in interval $[1.515, 1.525]$. Hence $\alpha = 1.52$ to 3 s.f.

12. (a) 1.56 (b) $f(1.555) = -0.24$; $f(1.565) = 0.09$. Change in sign and function continuous implies root within interval $[1.555, 1.565]$. Hence $\alpha = 1.56$ to 3 significant figures.

13. (a) $f(5) = -0.3906$; $f(5.5) = 0.2047$. Change in sign and function continuous implies $5 < \alpha < 5.5$. (b) 5.327

(c) $f(5.3265) = -0.00081$; $f(5.3275) = 0.00038$. Change in sign and function continuous implies $5.3265 < \alpha < 5.3275$. Hence $\alpha = 5.327$ to 3 dp.

Exercise 13D

1. (a) 280.5 (b) 279

2. (a)

x	1	1.5	2	2.5
$y = \dfrac{x}{1+x^2}$	0.25	0.24	0.22222	0.20408

x	3	3.5	4
$y = \dfrac{x}{1+x^2}$	0.18750	0.17284	0.16

(b) 0.616 (3 s.f.)

3. 1.12 (3 s.f.)

4. 10.2 (3 s.f.)

5. (a) 16.2 (b) $x = \dfrac{y^2}{5} - 5$ (c) $\dfrac{50}{3}$

6. (a)

x	0	0.5	1	1.5	2
$y = x(2-x)$	0	0.75	1	0.75	0

(b)

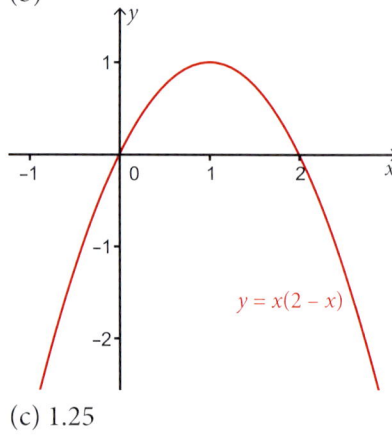

(c) 1.25
(d)

x	0	0.25	0.5	0.75	1
$y = x(x-2)$	0	0.4375	0.75	0.9375	1

x	1.25	1.5	1.75	2
$y = x(x-2)$	0.9375	0.75	0.4375	0

(e) 1.31 (3 s.f.) (f) $\tfrac{4}{3}$
(g) (i) 6.25% (ii) 1.56% (3 s.f.)

7. (a)

x	3	4	5	6	7
y	5.385	8.124	11.269	**14.765**	**18.574**

(b) 46.14

8. (a) 0.7761 (b) Multiply answer a) by 4. Gives 3.105. (c) π

ANSWERS – 14A

9. The approximation for the concave curve would be smaller than the true answer. The approximation for the convex curve would be greater than the true answer.

Exercise 13E

1. (b) $f(1.025) = 0.00329$; $f(1.035) = -0.0158$. Change of sign and function continuous implies solution within interval $[1.025, 1.035]$.
   (c) $\alpha = 1.03$ radians.

2. (a)

t	0	4	8	12	16	20	24
v	0	2.71	8.29	24.12	69.75	201.60	582.62

   (b) 2390 m (3 s.f.)

3. (a) 4π (b) 33.03 m²
   (c) $8(1+\pi)$ m² (d) 0.31%

4. (a)

x	0	1	2	3
y	1	1.22140	1.49182	1.82212

x	4	5	6
y	2.22554	2.71828	3.32012

   (b) 11.64 m² (c) 23.2 m²
   (d) 11.60 m² (e) 8.85×10^{-4} %

5. (a) 10 m (b) 5.5 m (c)

x	−30	−20	−10	0
$y = 10 - \dfrac{x^2}{200}$	5.5	8	9.5	10

x	10	20	30
$y = 10 - \dfrac{x^2}{200}$	9.5	8	5.5

   (d) 505 m² (e) 510 m²

6. 27.4

7. (b)

x	0	$\dfrac{3\pi}{16}$
$y = \cos x + \sin x$	1.00000	1.38704

x	$\dfrac{3\pi}{8}$	$\dfrac{9\pi}{16}$
$y = \cos x + \sin x$	1.30656	0.78569

x	$\dfrac{3\pi}{4}$
$y = \cos x + \sin x$	0.00000

   (c) 2.34 (e) 2.91% (f) 2.68 (g) $2\sqrt{2}$
   (h) $\dfrac{6 + \sqrt{2}}{4}$

8. (b) $a = 2.18$.
   (c) $f(2.175) = -0.002$; $f(2.185) = 0.002$. Change of sign and function continuous. Hence a solution to $f(a) = 0$ lies within interval $[2.175, 2.185]$. Hence $a = 2.18$ to 3 s.f.

9. (c) 1.2, 1.1, 1.1 (e) 20.5 m

10. (a) $\dfrac{dy}{dx} = \dfrac{2x}{2y+1} = 0 \Rightarrow x = 0$
    (b) $b_2 = 0.683$
    (c) $f(0.675) = -0.0175$; $f(0.685) = 0.00642$. Change of sign and continuous function implies that a root exists in interval $[0.675, 0.685]$. Hence $b = 0.68$ to 2 d.p.

Exercise 14A

1. $1 + \dfrac{2\sqrt{3}}{3}$

2. (b) −1

3. (4, 3)

5. (a) 1 cm (b) 1.75 cm²

6. $2\sqrt{2} - 2$

8.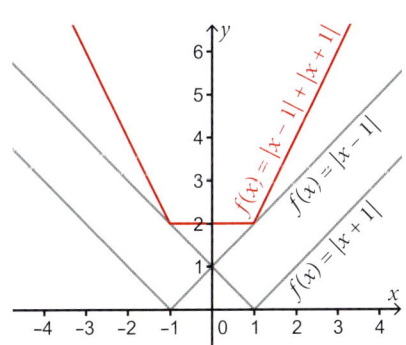

9. $a = -2, d = 4$ or $a = \dfrac{1}{4}, d = -\dfrac{1}{2}$

10. (a) $h^{-1}(x) = \sin^{-1}(x) + \dfrac{\pi}{6}$
    (b) $h(x) = \sin\left(x - \dfrac{\pi}{6}\right)$

11. (a) Vertical triangle ABO:

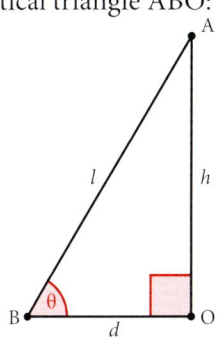

From triangle ABO:
$d = l\cos\theta$ and $h = l\sin\theta$

Triangle BCD (the base):

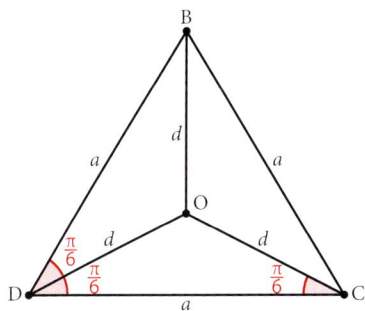

From triangle OCD:
$a = 2d\cos\left(\dfrac{\pi}{6}\right) = d\sqrt{3} = l\sqrt{3}\cos\theta$

Total area of base:
$A = \dfrac{1}{2}a^2 \sin\left(\dfrac{\pi}{3}\right)$
$= \dfrac{1}{2}\left(l\sqrt{3}\cos\theta\right)^2 \times \dfrac{\sqrt{3}}{2}$
$= \dfrac{3l^2\sqrt{3}}{4}\cos^2\theta$

$V = \dfrac{1}{3}Ah = \dfrac{1}{3}\left(\dfrac{3l^2\sqrt{3}}{4}\cos^2\theta\right)l\sin\theta$
$= \dfrac{l^3\sqrt{3}}{4}\cos^2\theta \sin\theta$
$= \dfrac{l^3\sqrt{3}}{8}\cos\theta \sin 2\theta$

$\dfrac{dV}{d\theta} = \dfrac{l^3\sqrt{3}}{8}(2\cos\theta\cos 2\theta - \sin\theta\sin 2\theta)$

$\dfrac{dV}{d\theta} = 0$ at max or min points

$\therefore 2\cos\theta\cos 2\theta = \sin\theta\sin 2\theta$
$\Rightarrow 2\cot\theta = \tan 2\theta$

(b) Consider
$f(x) = 2\cot\theta - \tan 2\theta = 0$:
$f(0.55) = 1.297$
$f(0.65) = -0.971$
Change of sign and $f(x)$ is

ANSWERS – 14A

continuous, therefore root lies between $\theta = 0.55$ and $\theta = 0.65$.
$\therefore \alpha = 0.6$ to 1 d.p.

(c) $\dfrac{d^2V}{d\theta^2} = \dfrac{l^3\sqrt{3}}{8}(-4\cos\theta\sin 2\theta$
$- 2\sin\theta\cos 2\theta - 2\sin\theta\cos 2\theta$
$- \cos\theta\sin 2\theta)$

When $\theta = 0.6$, $\dfrac{d^2V}{d\theta^2} < 0$
$\therefore$ a maximum volume.

12. (a) Arc BCD is a quarter of a circle, so: $BCD = \dfrac{1}{4}(2\pi r) = \dfrac{\pi r}{2}$
$DE = r - w$
$AB = r - h$
Note that $OC = r$ and that the two diagonals of the rectangle are equal. So $AE = r$. Therefore:
$P = \dfrac{\pi r}{2} + (r - w) + (r - h) + r$
$P = \dfrac{\pi r}{2} + 3r - w - h$

(b) $h = (r^2 - w^2)^{½}$
$\therefore P = \dfrac{\pi r}{2} + 3r - w - (r^2 - w^2)^{½}$
$\dfrac{dP}{dw} = w(r^2 - w^2)^{-½} - 1$
For maximum or minimum P,
$\dfrac{dP}{dw} = 0$, leading to: $w = \dfrac{r}{\sqrt{2}}$
$h = (r^2 - w^2)^{½}$, giving $h = \dfrac{r}{\sqrt{2}}$
So $w = h$
$\dfrac{d^2P}{dw^2} = \dfrac{(r^2 - w^2)^{½} + w^2(r^2 - w^2)^{-½}}{(r^2 - w^2)}$
When $w = \dfrac{r}{\sqrt{2}}$, $\dfrac{d^2P}{dw^2} = \dfrac{2\sqrt{2}}{r}$
which is > 0, hence P is at a minimum.

13. (c) $\dfrac{d}{3}$